BUSINESS ENGLISH AND COMMUNICATION

EIGHTH EDITION

BUSINESS ENGLISH AND COMMUNICATION

EIGHTH EDITION

LYN R. CLARK, ED.D.

Professor of Business
Los Angeles Pierce College
Woodland Hills, California

KENNETH ZIMMER, ED.D.

Professor Emeritus of Business Education
and Office Administration
California State University
Los Angeles, California

JOSEPH TINERVIA, B.A.

Adjunct Professor
Saddleback College
Mission Viejo, California

GLENCOE

Macmillan/McGraw–Hill

New York, New York   Columbus, Ohio   Mission Hills, California   Peoria, Illinois

Send all inquiries to:
GLENCOE DIVISION
Macmillan/McGraw-Hill
936 Eastwind Drive
Westerville, OH 43081

ISBN 0-02-800990-8 (Student Edition)

Printed in the United States of America.

2 3 4 5 6 7 8 9   RRC/MC   01 00 99 98 97 96 95 94

CONTENTS

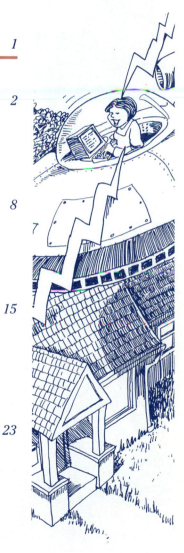

v

CHAPTER 4

LANGUAGE SKILLS

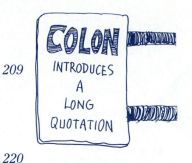

CHAPTER 7

July 13, 1993

Walter R. Frump
Acme Widget Company
1122 East Elm Street
Midtown, WA 98121

Dear Mr. Frump:

Thank you for your letter d
duction department has calc
proximately 300 more widg
to purchase from your comp
vised purchase order reflect

Your prompt attention to

Sincere

John

Enc.

CHAPTER 8

MEMORANDUMS   *385*

CHAPTER 11

EMPLOYMENT COMMUNICATION 483

Think about all the time you spend communicating. You may not even realize how much of your day is spent reading, writing, listening, and speaking. Whether you are an administrative assistant, a word processing operator, a marketing representative, an information systems manager, a customer service representative, or a corporate executive, much of your work involves communication. Even though technology helps you function more efficiently, you must still have polished communication skills to meet your responsibilities. In fact, your value as an employee and your very promotability may depend, in large part, on your ability to communicate.

Business English and Communication, Eighth Edition, has been designed to provide you with the broad, thorough training necessary to develop competence on the job in each of the communication skills: reading, writing, speaking, and listening.

THE EIGHTH EDITION

The Eighth Edition introduces you to the fundamentals of business communication skills and describes the impact on communication psychology, human relations, and technology on these skills. Then, you will start to improve your general word skills and study how mastery of grammar, punctuation, and style can make the difference between effective and ineffective communication. Next, you will start to develop your written and your oral communication skills. Finally, you will learn how to apply *all* your communication skills and talents toward getting a job. In addition to having developed your communication skills, you will also have an introduction to the language of business.

Business Communication, Human Relations, Technology, and International Issues
The Eighth Edition addresses some of the most interesting aspects of business communication: human relations and office technology. In Chapter 1, the communication skills of reading, writing, speaking, and listening are identified and illustrated through practical examples. Then you are shown what motivates us all to act. You will see how applying the principles of communication psychology and human relations will help you communicate more effectively. You will learn that technology makes communicating faster and easier but does not eliminate the need for mastering fundamental language and human relation skills.

Reading   The focus of Chapter 2 is reading skill. What are your purposes for reading, and how must you adjust your reading to suit your purpose? Applying principles from Chapter 2 can help you not only in employment situations but also in your schoolwork and your personal reading.

Editing and Word Skills   Chapter 3 offers a broad overview for developing word skills. You learn how to expand your vocabulary and how to use a dictionary and other word references. Of special interest in Chapter 3 is a section on spelling, which offers a three-step approach for mastering a basic business vocabulary. In addition, you learn to distinguish differences in meaning of many of the most commonly confused words.

Grammar and Punctuation   A solid foundation in English grammar is essential for successful communication, and Chapters 4 and 5 offer you all the grammar and punctuation know-how you will need to succeed on the job. Developed over several editions, these chapters stress the practical principles of grammar and punctuation—the ones that you *must* know. Much of the confusing, complex terminology has been eliminated. Moreover, Quick Trick features are frequently offered with those rules that are most confusing. These Quick Tricks take difficult principles and change them into easy-to-remember rules. Many practice exercises are provided throughout each unit in the grammar and punctuation chapters—after every Quick Trick section, for example—to help you understand each principle and to reinforce your understanding.

Writing—The Building-Block Approach   Expert writers do more than write correct messages. They create messages that are explicit and polished, and their ability to do so is what distinguishes their messages from everyday, routine messages. Chapter 6 uses a unique building-block approach to the writing process, beginning with word selection and moving onto sentence and paragraph writing.

Letters   Chapter 7 offers you a thorough training program on business letters, from the general to the specific. It begins with general business letter formats and proceeds to cover specific types of letters. You learn to write not only routine letters such as transmittals and requests, which would be assigned to beginning employees, but also more specialized letters such as sales and persuasive letters.

Memos   Memos are the primary means of written communication *within* an organization. Therefore, Chapter 8 gives expanded coverage on how memos are used in business. Because memos are used in so many ways, techniques for tailoring memos for special purposes—including the use of graphics and readability devices—are included.

Reports   Chapter 9 includes a thorough treatment of report writing. It also covers the use of commonplace form messages, minutes, and news releases.

Listening and Speaking Skills   In Chapter 10, the important skills of becoming a good listener and a good speaker are discussed. You will learn techniques that will help you master these crucial skills. In addition, ways that listening may bear on your job are discussed. Chapter 10 also prepares you to speak effectively by offering practical guidance on planning and giving a talk, meeting the public in person and by telephone, and participating in group discussions.

Résumés and Job Applications   The effectiveness with which you can prepare résumés and employment letters will have an immediate, direct impact on your success in seeking employment. Chapter 11 prepares you for all the employment messages you may write—application letters, résumés, reference letters, acceptance letters, and so on. In addition, it offers helpful suggestions—many of them provided by professional recruiters—that will prepare you for employment interviews.

COMMUNICATION LABORATORY

At the end of every text section is a Communication Laboratory, a set of exercises that will help you apply the principles learned in the section. Each Communication Laboratory offers a series of two different sets of exercises.

Application Exercises   These exercises test your understanding of the principles presented in the current section and review those presented in previous sections.

Vocabulary and Spelling Studies   This section of each Communication Laboratory emphasizes the development of spelling and vocabulary skills.

SUPPORTING MATERIALS

In addition to this text, *Business English and Communication*, Eighth Edition, includes a workbook of projects and activities for students; both computerized and printed test bank; teacher's editions of both the textbook and the workbook; a booklet of case studies; a set of blackline masters; and a series of English skills projects for the microcomputer.

The Workbook   A complete teaching-learning aid, *Student Projects and Activities for Business English and Communication* provides exercises closely correlated with the principles covered in each of the corresponding units of the textbook. These worksheets offer enrichment, reinforcement, and review exercises covering spelling and vocabulary development, reading comprehension, listening comprehension, proofreading, editing, rewriting, note-taking, and composition of letters and other types of business communications. All the exercises offered in this workbook differ from those given in the text.

Teacher's Edition of the Textbook   *Business English and Communication,* Eighth Edition, offers a page-for-page teacher's edition of the textbook. Short teaching suggestions, short exercise solutions, and special margin features (suggestion, tech prep, critical thinking, and global note) appear, in a second color, right on the page of the text to which they refer. In addition, grouped at the back of the teacher's edition are explanations of how to use the program; additional detailed unit-by-unit teaching suggestions; schedules and grading guidelines; and longer solutions to exercises in the text, carefully cross-referenced to the actual exercises.

Teacher's Edition of the Workbook   Another teaching aid is the teacher's edition of the workbook, a page-for-page facsimile key of all the workbook exercises.

Test Materials   Test materials for *Business English and Communication,* Eighth Edition, are available in two forms—a set of printed tests and a microcomputer test bank. The printed tests provide teachers with preprinted tests that can be used for quizzes, tests, and examinations. The microcomputer test bank (for IBM and compatibles) allows teachers to print preprogrammed tests, assemble unique tests from preprogrammed questions, and add questions of their own. Teachers may wish to use materials from other program components (case studies booklet or student projects workbook) or from other sources to establish alternate kinds of assessment situations.

Case Studies Booklet   *Case Studies for Critical Thinking* augments the text by simulating 70 business situations in which the student assumes the role of a typical business worker. Most of the case studies deal with common but awkward human relations situations that all business employees encounter; for example, dealing with a supervisor's grammatical errors, being asked for confidential information, working for more than one supervisor, and so on.

Blackline Masters   The blackline masters for *Business English and Communication,* Eighth Edition, have been designed to reinforce or supplement key principles and concepts presented in the text. By visually highlighting and reinforcing important communication precepts, the blackline masters are yet one more aid to student learning. Teachers may wish to use the master to create transparencies for use with the overhead projector or to photocopy them as class handouts.

English Skills Practice for the Microcomputer   A set of 25 language skills exercises for use on the computer offers a variety of practice exercises. In addition to practicing grammar and usage skills, the student experiences significant practice in proofreading and editing on the computer screen, a very different skill from working on hard copy. Each three-part project includes a set of sentences and two or three paragraphs that are section-specific. The third part is a document (memo, letter, report, and so on) drawing on the student's cumulative skills.

Strategies for Implementing Tech Prep Into Communication A new component for *Business English and Communication,* Eighth Edition, this booklet describes the tech prep concept; draws relationships between secondary programs, postsecondary programs, and employability; and then relates tech prep to the subject area of communication. This component can assist the teacher in relating *Business English and Communication* to specific state and local tech prep plans and competencies.

CHAPTER 1

The
Communication
Network

Think about the time you spend sending and receiving messages. When you read a report, listen to instructions, fill out an application form, or speak about your interests, you are communicating.

You may be communicating with one person or more than one. You may be communicating with people nearby, on the other side of the world, or even in space. When you send a message, you want the receiver to understand exactly what you mean. When you receive a message, you want to understand what the sender means.

To be an effective communicator, you need to know the importance of communication skills, both in your personal life and in your career. You also need to know how communication psychology and evolving technologies can affect your communication skill. You need to be aware that perceptions of communication may be different in different parts of the world.

OBJECTIVES

Given a situation requiring speaking, listening, reading, and writing skills, you will be able to do the following when you master the sections in this chapter:

1. Identify the kinds and levels of communication needed for success in your personal life, your personal-business activities, and your chosen career.

2. Select and use verbal and nonverbal communication to make your message effective.

3. Demonstrate your understanding of how the levels of human needs and how human relations affect the communication process.

4. Describe the impact that communication technology has made and will further make on all your roles as a communicator.

5. List ways that technology affects the communication process.

6. List ways that communication skills should be adjusted for communicating internationally.

COMMUNICATING IN YOUR PERSONAL AND WORK WORLDS

The ring of the telephone—someone wishes to speak with you. A knock at the door—the person on the other side is asking you to open it. The utterance of your name—the person speaking wants your attention. All these sounds are signals that someone wishes to communicate with you. That person has a message to convey.

THE COMMUNICATION PROCESS

The exchange of messages between and among human beings is known as communication. We send and receive messages in a variety of ways, both verbally and nonverbally. The examples given above rely on sounds to send messages; other methods of message transmission include speaking, writing, gestures, and facial expressions. Listening, reading, and observing are the means we use to receive messages. The most difficult task in the communication process is ensuring that the receiver interprets the message as the sender meant it to be interpreted.

This communication process is not so simple as it seems. Take, for example, the following case. Scott, a seventeen-year-old high school junior, received a telephone call from his friend Bob. "I can't go swimming with you tomorrow because I have to look for another job," said Bob. "OK," responded Scott, "give me a call when you can go." So ended the conversation! When Scott hung up, he told his parents that Bob had lost his job at Hathaway's Grocery Store and had to look for another one. It was not until a few days later that the true circumstances were uncovered. Bob had not lost his job at the grocery store; he was just looking for *another* part-time job to supplement the too-few hours he was working at Hathaway's.

Why did this breakdown in communication occur? Both the sender and the receiver were at fault. The sender, Bob, gave too little information; he was not specific or concrete in conveying his message. Too many details were left to the imagination of the receiver. Scott, the receiver, was also at fault because he reached an unwarranted conclusion based on the information given. Just because Bob was looking for another job, Scott should not have assumed that Bob had lost his current one.

Miscommunication can occur easily in any situation—especially in our electronic age, where even the pressing of a button can send an incorrect message. That is why it is important for you to study the entire communication process and sharpen your verbal skills. To communicate effectively, you need to develop your abilities in speaking, writing, listening, reading, and observing. Remember that both the sender and the receiver have responsibility in the communication process. You also need to understand the principles of communication psychology. This unit begins your study of the communication concepts necessary for success in your personal and business life.

YOUR PERSONAL COMMUNICATION

Communication begins early in life. The baby's cry *provokes* the parents' response. Is the baby hungry? Does he or she need to have a diaper changed? Is the cry for attention? The fact that the baby has a need is communicated by a simple cry. As children grow older, however, they use a more complex communication process. Words replace the cry as the means of communication.

As a person's vocabulary grows, that person's ability to communicate also grows. To a considerable degree the extent of a person's vocabulary governs his or her ability to send and receive messages. Besides communicating with family members and friends, the child must learn to communicate effectively in school in order to prepare properly for later life.

Verbal Skills for Everyday Life   Communication skills are important not only for functioning among family members and friends and in school but also for functioning in everyday life. Reading, writing, speaking, and listening all play an integral part in our contemporary lifestyle. Take, for example, the communication involved in obtaining a driver's license.

Reading plays a prominent role. You must read the directions to fill in the application form. You must also read the driving manual issued by the motor vehicle department, since a knowledge of the rules and regulations of the road is essential to pass the written test. Reading skills are also necessary for taking the written test. Complicated questions, sometimes with tricky choices for answers, require critical reading skills. Road signs, too, not only require interpretive skills but also may require reading skills.

Writing skills are needed to fill out the license application form. Correct information must be supplied clearly. Speaking skills come into play in asking questions, providing answers, and following through in the application process. Listening plays an especially important role in the practical test. If the examiner instructed you to turn left at an intersection and you instead turned into the first driveway, you would decrease your likelihood of passing the examination. If you did not hear the instruction and continued to drive straight ahead, points would be deducted from your score. Equally serious results would occur if you misinterpreted the instruction to turn left and instead turned right. Careful listening and appropriate interpreting govern your success in this and many other situations.

Skills for Avoiding Misunderstanding   As you can see, the entire communication process plays a vital role in acquiring a driver's license.

LIVING LANGUAGE

To be complete and effective, communication requires both a sender and a receiver. If a language barrier exists, the sender must be aware that the receiver may not understand the message whether it be written or oral.

WORLD VIEW

Only 7 percent of the world's people speak English as a primary language, but nine out of ten Americans cannot speak, read, or understand any language but English.
—Gallup polls and UNESCO studies

Communication skills are essential in many other aspects of the young adult's world. As an additional example, note the difficulties that can result from a communication breakdown in applying for a social security card.

Cindy Brooks, a sixteen-year-old high school sophomore, went to her local social security office to apply for a card. She already had obtained her first part-time job but needed the card to begin work. As instructed, Cindy brought with her a copy of her birth certificate. She carefully filled out the application, using the name shown on her birth certificate, Cynthia Jean Brooks. Satisfied that she had completed all the requirements, Cindy signed her application and went home.

A week later Cindy's application was returned to her by mail with a request to resubmit it. You see, Cindy had signed her application "Cindy Brooks" instead of "Cynthia Jean Brooks." Yet the instruction had clearly stated, "Sign name as shown on application." If Cindy had signed her name correctly, she could have started her job a week earlier. Not reading the instructions carefully had cost Cindy the money she would have earned if she had signed the application correctly and begun work the prior week.

YOUR PERSONAL BUSINESS COMMUNICATION

Even though you may never work in a business, you cannot escape communicating with business and government in conducting your personal business. Routine purchases of food, clothing, gas, and household supplies require reading, listening, and speaking skills. Reading labels and instructions carefully enables you to make proper and economical selections. Asking questions, making requests, giving instructions, and describing your needs all require precise and distinct speaking skills. Listening, too, is required to follow directions in meeting your personal purchasing needs.

Satisfying Your Needs as a Consumer
Purchasing a car, a home, life insurance, medical insurance, or a major home appliance requires communication skills. So do contractual agreements for home improvements, installment buying, or investment. Solving problems generated by faulty merchandise, insurance claims, legal matters, and medical concerns requires even more advanced communication skills. Not only must you rely on speaking, listening, and reading, but also you must draw on your writing skills for such tasks.

Notice how Dave Friedman, a twenty-eight-year-old bank clerk, solved the following problem. The Mitsubi electronic game he had purchased nearly two years ago was no longer working; one of the circuit boards was broken. Mitsubi had no authorized repair stores in the city where he lived, so Dave had to write a business letter to seek a solution to his problem. This meant writing to Mitsubi, explaining the nature of the problem, requesting shipment of the appropriate replacement part, and making arrangements for payments. Dave needed to state the information simply, exactly, and clearly in his letter. To plan and write his letter, Dave used his knowledge of spelling, grammar, writing style, message organization, and business-letter format—all areas you will be studying in this textbook.

Communicating With Government

Writing skills are essential for solving problems that may arise with government. Isabel Granadino, a twenty-six-year-old nurse's aide, was shocked when she opened a letter that stated, "If the enclosed parking ticket is not paid within 30 days, a warrant will be issued for your arrest." On examining the enclosed parking ticket, Isabel saw that it had been issued in a city more than 90 miles from her home on a day that she had been working. After a closer reading she noticed that the cited vehicle had the license plate number 1DSE438. Isabel's license number was 1DSE439! Evidently someone had made an error in entering the license number into the computer to locate the owner's name and address—a perfect example of miscommunication in our electronic age.

Nevertheless, Isabel was still faced with the problem of having to correct the situation. She could take a day off from work and drive 90 miles to the courthouse to correct the miscommunication, but why waste so much time and money when a well-written letter could achieve the same results? Isabel chose to write the letter. Again, the writer needed skillful and clear expression to ensure that the reader understood the circumstances and took the action requested.

COMMUNICATION IN THE WORLD OF WORK

No matter what occupation you select—accountant, electronic technician, office worker, business executive, nurse, construction worker, mail carrier, flight attendant, or computer programmer—you will need to deal with communication in the world of work.

Interactions in the Work Environment

In your work environment you will interact with coworkers, superiors, subordinates, customers, suppliers, and machines. You will be involved with face-to-face dialogues, telephone conversations, conferences, and committee meetings. All these activities will require you to exercise your speaking and listening *expertise*.

Media such as forms, letters, memorandums, reports, bulletins, news releases, meeting minutes, newsletters, and employee handbooks require reading and writing skills. At this point you may view yourself only as a reader of these documents, but your job may also involve your writing some of them or parts of them. You may be asked to *generate* letters to customers and suppliers, memos to coworkers or *subordinates*, reports to *superiors*, or any of the other written documents that an organization produces.

Responsibilities for Written Communications

Take for example, the *array* of written *communiqués* originating at the desk of an administrative assistant. Simple phone messages may not seem too important; but

> ### LIVING LANGUAGE
> The most immutable barrier in nature is between one man's thoughts and another's.
> —William James

think of the communication breakdowns that could occur if the assistant forgot to ask the name of the caller, jotted down the phone number incorrectly, misinterpreted the message, or even neglected to place the message on the *recipient's* desk.

Persons in other occupations, too, are faced with *originating* a variety of written documents. Salespeople draft letters to customers and suppliers, accountants prepare reports for clients, nurses chart patients' progress, insurance agents complete claims, and engineers write specifications. Almost all occupations require some kind of writing skill, and virtually all occupations require oral communication skills. Because your success as a communicator may well measure your success in a chosen field, you should strive consistently to improve your personal communication skills.

COMMUNICATION LABORATORY

APPLICATION EXERCISES

A. Select a person you know whom you would classify as an expert communicator. In your opinion what skills does this person possess that make him or her successful?

B. Select a well-known local, national, or international personality. Describe why you feel this individual is a good or poor communicator. Give concrete examples to substantiate your judgment.

C. Select a friend, a family member, or coworker whom you have the opportunity to observe frequently. Evaluate that person's ability to communicate effectively. Give specific incidents to justify your opinion.

D. Describe a situation, humorous or otherwise, in which you were involved and miscommunication occurred. What were the consequences? How could you have prevented the misunderstanding?

E. Search your local newspaper for an article that cites a language barrier or misinterpretation as the cause of a problem (or at least a contributory cause). Summarize and report the circumstances to your class.

F. Keep a log of your significant communication activities for a day, two days, or a week. Prepare your log in tabular format, using headings such as the following: "Date," "Time," "Persons Involved," "Summary of Content," "Communication Processes," and "Evaluation." Under "Evaluation" rate the effectiveness of the communication in the incident by using terms such as *Excellent, Good, Fair,* and *Poor.* The log can best be kept on 8½- by 11-inch paper, writing across the 11-inch side as the width. Note the details of any important conversations, telephone calls, business transactions, written materials, social encounters, or instructional programs in which you were involved. For each activity determine which communication skills (listening, speaking, reading, writing) were used, and evaluate your success in completing the communication process.

CONTINUED

G. Choose two activities in which you are presently involved—one that usually attracts your interest and one that rarely holds your attention. Analyze the factors that contribute to making one activity interesting and the other less so. Which of these factors can be related to the presence or absence of effective communication?

H. Interview a member of your family or a member of a family close to you. Discuss the kinds of personal-business correspondence written by this family and the circumstances that prompted each type of correspondence. Inquire specifically about claim letters, inquiry letters, order letters, and letters to correct problems. Describe in detail at least two situations that resulted in specific letters or that could be resolved through letters.

I. Communication skills are essential for job success. Choose one of the following occupations and discuss the various kinds of written communications needed to carry out the duties and responsibilities of this job.

1. salesperson	**5.** accountant
2. manager	**6.** administrative assistant
3. nurse	**7.** flight attendant
4. electrician	**8.** mechanic

J. Select an occupation in which you are interested. Discuss the oral and written communication skills necessary for success in that job.

VOCABULARY AND SPELLING STUDIES

A. The following words were used in the text in this unit. Locate them in the dictionary and write the definition of each word as it was used in the unit. Then construct a sentence using each word to show that you understand its meaning and use.

1. transmission	**6.** array
2. expertise	**7.** communiqués
3. generate	**8.** recipient
4. subordinates	**9.** originating
5. superiors	**10.** provokes

B. Words are not always spelled as they sound. For example, the sound of *f* in our language may be spelled *f, ff, ph,* or *gh.* The sound of *s* is prefaced with a silent *p* in *psychology.* Likewise, a number of other sounds use different letters in the formation of words. Complete the spelling of the following words. Use the correct letter or combination of letters to complete the sound shown in parentheses.

1. al (*f*) abet	**6.** (*f*) armacy
2. (*n*) eumonia	**7.** bu (*j*) et
3. le (*j*) er	**8.** h (*i*) giene
4. (*f*) enomenon	**9.** (*s*) issors
5. (*a*) rial	**10.** s (*i*) ndicate

USING COMMUNICATION TECHNOLOGY

Modern technology makes it possible to send oral and written messages around the world in a matter of seconds. Computers and electronic transmission systems have enabled business and government to speed up and improve the communication process. As a result, communicators today use communication technology to develop and transmit their oral and written messages.

Data, voice, and graphic networks supply the technology for rapid communication and decision making. These networks are composed of computer-based systems that "talk" to each other so that voices, images, and written data can be transmitted electronically and instantaneously.

Within the last three decades, this emerging new technology has caused a revolution in human communications. Think about the pace of human progress during past centuries and compare it with the developments that have taken place during the last thirty years—even the last ten years.

THE NEW TECHNOLOGY

Human beings have communicated from the beginning of time. Communication probably began with grunts, gestures, and expressions. The origins of speaking and writing are unknown, but signs and symbols were added very early in the time line of human development.

Even in the early times people kept records. The Egyptians developed a picture language called *hieroglyphics*; at the same time the Sumarians were writing on clay tablets with a system that used wedge-shaped signs. The Semites were the first to devise an alphabet, around 1500 B.C., and the Assyrians and Babylonians established libraries around 600 B.C .

In early societies writing was taught only to scribes and priests. It was such a laborious and time-consuming process that only a privileged few were allowed to learn to write. Even after the development of the pen and quill, writing was such a chore that few people ever saw a book, let alone owned one. Just imagine how long it would take you to copy by hand the pages of this textbook!

Not until the invention of the printing press in the fifteenth century was knowledge opened to everyone. Printing provided a more rapid and easy way to communicate. Although type was set by hand, multiple copies could be run once the type had been set. Then, in the middle of the nineteenth century, a machine appeared that would speed up the printing process. Little did Christopher Scholes realize that his invention—the typewriter—would be the forerunner of the sophisticated computers used in publishing and modern offices today.

Civilization has progressed from tediously chiseling signs and symbols into rock to communicating messages instantaneously by machine. Human beings, however, must still generate the messages processed by these machines. People are responsible for the content, organization, wording, and format of the information processed. Therefore, users of modern technology must still be skilled in the communication process. Your study of the principles and concepts in this textbook will prepare you to make effective use of the communication technology found in modern business settings today.

Advanced technologies have emerged during the last three decades in word processing, information processing, telecommunications, and networks. Each is defined and briefly described for you in the following sections.

WORD AND INFORMATION PROCESSING

People have been processing words since the Semites developed the first known alphabet, but the concept of word processing as we know it today was introduced by the IBM Corporation in the early 1960s. Modern-day *word processing* now involves the use of a standardized set of procedures (known as *software*) combined with computerized equipment to produce written documents. Popular software programs used for word processing include WordPerfect, Microsoft Word, WordStar, MultiMate, DisplayWrite, and Appleworks, to name just a few.

What Word Processing Can Do   To obtain a better understanding of word processing, let us first generally look at how it works. Computers have a typewriter keyboard. As data is entered into the computer through the keyboard and a word processing program, each keystroke is recorded for storage on a magnetic disk. If you wish to make a change on the disk, you may do so by "recording over" the present material. Similarly, if you make a keyboarding error, all you need do is backspace to erase the error and then retype the correct stroke in its spot.

With word processing you can also easily add and delete complete sentences and paragraphs. Once you have made any corrections and revisions in a letter, memorandum, report, or other document, you are ready to prepare the finished copy. Printers read the disk and print out your final copy error-free at speeds ranging from hundreds of words a minute to over a thousand words a minute.

In many situations the same originally typed document must be sent to a number of different people or the same paragraph must be repeated in different documents. By using word processing to record these materials, you may print as many original copies as needed without rekeying the contents.

Reports provide information that is often the basis for important decisions. The person who writes a report may rewrite it several times before the report is ready for distribution. Before word processing, the report had to be retyped with each rewrite, thereby requiring the tedious process of keyboarding and proofreading the entire document with each revision. By using word processing to prepare a report, you keyboard and proofread only the changes; the remainder of the report remains unaltered, waiting to be printed with the changes or additions to form a revised final copy.

Word Processing at Work Who uses word processing? For what purposes is it used? Frequent users include law firms, where many documents that require precise wording are produced. In addition, many legal documents contain large sections of wording that do not need to be changed for each new client. These standardized paragraphs are recorded on disks and recalled for the preparation of contracts, wills, trusts, agreements, dissolutions, testimonies, and many other legal documents.

Banks and other financial institutions use word processing to communicate with their current and prospective customers. Standardized form letters are entered into and stored by the word processing equipment. When a single letter needs to be sent to a list of customers, the standardized form can be retrieved and merged with the list of names to produce an originally typed letter for each name on the list.

Hospitals and other health care facilities use word processing to prepare patients' files and to compile reports of diagnoses and examinations. Standardized examination reports are stored for each specialty, so doctors can immediately cite any abnormal conditions that may exist. Word processing is also used for preparing government and insurance reports, professional papers presented by staff members, public service bulletins, applications for special projects, and a variety of other documents.

Insurance companies use word processing to communicate with their large number of clients. Specialized types of communication are sent to those clients who carry certain kinds of insurance. Personalized letters prepared on word processors are also used to solicit additional business.

All types of businesses use word processing equipment to prepare proposals. Volumes of paperwork describing specifications, costs, procedures, and schedules need to be prepared before a contract can be awarded. Thousands of hours of editing and revision may be required to prepare a proposal for submission. Word processing eases the keyboarding and proofreading burden and fosters accuracy.

Within the last few years, declining prices for computer hardware and software have made computers more affordable to both organizations and individuals. Because word processing simplifies and streamlines the document preparation process, its use has spread rapidly to small businesses, self-employed individuals, home office users, and students. Yesterday's electric typewriter has become virtually obsolete as computers and word processing software dominate in small businesses and households throughout the country.

Information Processing While *word processing* refers to the process of creating, editing, formatting, storing, retrieving, revising, and printing text materials electronically, *information processing* is the manipulation of data by electronic means to collect, organize, record, and store information for decision-making purposes. Information processing retains the text-editing and revision function but also has the capability to use the data in a wider range of applications.

Information Processing at Work   The hospital that uses word processing to prepare and maintain patients' records can use information processing technology many ways. For example, it can compile a list of patients by any one of many different categories—by specific disease or disorder, by admitting doctor, by admission date, or by age. Expanded applications (uses) and capabilities can be achieved by *interfacing* (connecting) word processing programs with other types of computer programs.

Picture the checkout stand of a modern supermarket. Notice how the clerk skims each product over a certain section of the countertop. Listen for the high-pitched beep as the name of the item and its price are recorded on the cash register tape. As a customer you may like this procedure because it provides you with an itemized tape listing the specific product purchased and its price. To the grocery store, however, the new system provides valuable inventory information that was not readily available before information processing technology. For example, the store buyers know how many frozen turkeys they should purchase for Friday. They know how many cases of a certain brand of canned peas are needed to restock the shelves. They may even be able to determine what products sell too slowly and should therefore be discontinued. Information processing technology is thus an important tool to help businesses cut costs and increase profit.

A Revolution in Technology   Since the early 1980s the flood of microcomputers entering business and industry has revolutionized business's ability to use information processing for management decision making. No longer must a company invest in expensive mainframe computer time or acquire costly minicomputers to take advantage of this tool. Reasonably priced microcomputers coupled with spreadsheet, data base, and graphics programs provide information processing capabilities to large and small companies alike—even home offices.

Business writers charged with preparing reports for management decision making may organize, enter, and store information in computerized data files. From this data base they may easily transfer information into a spreadsheet for either preparing analyses or making projections. Spreadsheet data can then be converted into graphic form for ease of understanding and interpretation through any one of a number of graphics software programs.

Integrated software programs allow the modern business communicator to combine word processing technology with information processing technology so that charts and tables derived from data bases and spreadsheets may be entered directly into reports prepared through word processing programs. The popularity of microcomputers and these kinds of programs is growing rapidly

WORLD VIEW

"Out of sight, out of mind," when translated into Russian (by computer), then back again into English, became "invisible maniac."
—Arthur Calder-Marshall

because of their relatively inexpensive cost in comparison with minicomputers and mainframes. Now even the small company or business can afford to use computer technology to increase its profit.

THE WORLD OF TELECOMMUNICATIONS

The documents produced by word and information processing equipment discussed so far have been printed on paper and carried to their destinations by intracompany mail systems, the U.S. Postal Service, and private mail carriers. Since paper is associated with slow delivery and high costs, more companies are turning to electronic methods for transmitting information. Distributing information electronically over telephone lines is called *telecommunication*.

You already know that information can be sent electronically through voice communications. Every time you make a telephone call, you are using a form of telecommunication. Perhaps you did not know, though, that printed words can also be sent electronically through telephone lines. You can type a document on a terminal at one location, transmit it over telephone lines to another location miles away, and have it play back on a terminal at the destination. In just seconds data can be communicated from city to city, from coast to coast, and from country to country.

Printed data may also be sent electronically. Copies of text, charts, graphs, maps, and diagrams may be sent from one location to another. An electronic device called a *facsimile* (fax) scans the copy to be sent, sends it over telephone wires, and produces a replica at the destination.

Teleconferencing is a type of video communication that involves sending pictures of people as well as voice and print communications. Once a teleconferencing room with the proper electronic equipment is rented, people in various locations can exchange ideas with gestures and facial expressions as well as through speaking, listening, and writing.

Presently the major carriers of telecommunication in business are telephone lines. However, scientists are continually experimenting with new technologies to move information more rapidly. Lasers, fiber optics, and satellites are all being explored further to speed up such business applications as teleconferencing and facsimile transmission.

NETWORKING IN THE BUSINESS ENVIRONMENT

Computer communications is and will continue to be a key factor in information exchange. You have already learned that written messages can be transmitted electronically over telephone lines from one computer terminal to another. Almost all kinds of computer-based equipment—microcomputers, minicomputers, mainframes, and mainframe terminals—are capable of exchanging messages. Those computers that are linked together and are able to communicate with one another are components of a network.

Local Area Networks   *Networking* is a way of connecting various kinds of computerized equipment so that data may be transferred from one location to another or from one piece of equipment to another without having to reenter the data. *Local area networks* link machines that are close, that is, machines that are within a building, several adjacent buildings, or the same geographical area.

Local area networks, often referred to as LANs, may use telephone wires, radio waves, coaxial cables, or fiber optics to connect the stations within the network. Dissimilar machines can work together as a team using one of these means and a series of interfaces that connect the machines to the data transportation medium used. In this way information can be transmitted from one machine to another in a matter of seconds or minutes.

Wide Area Networks   Local networks can be linked to larger networks that enable individuals and companies to send and receive information throughout the United States and other countries in the world. Networks that connect distant machines are known as *wide area networks* or *global networks* and use combinations of telephone wires, satellites, and microwave radio links to send information.

Electronic Mail   Electronic mail services provide faster delivery than the U.S. Postal Service, private mail carriers, and intracompany mail delivery services. This machine-to-machine method of communication is accomplished through networks and permits immediate or same-day delivery.

Large computer systems are evolving as the directors of electronic mail traffic. A microcomputer or computer terminal serves the user as a keyboard device for outgoing messages and a receptacle for incoming messages. Messages can be sent immediately or stored and forwarded at a time when transmission rates are less expensive.

To participate in an electronic mail system, each user must have communicating equipment, a number (known as an *electronic mail address*), a computer file to contain incoming and outgoing messages (known as an *electronic mailbox*), and a directory of user names and addresses.

Implications for the Business Communicator   Networking is the newest dimension in communication technology. It opens up to the business communicator avenues never before explored. With such expanded access to information, however, the communicator of the future must develop keen skills of analysis, organization, and verbalization to sort through the resources being made available by technology. Your study of the communication skills and knowledge in this textbook will better prepare you to deal with the communication technology of today and tomorrow.

COMMUNICATION LABORATORY

APPLICATION EXERCISES

A. Visit your local public library or school library. In a business periodical locate an article on any phase of word processing or information processing. Summarize in writing the important points made by the author of this article. Be prepared to share this article orally with the rest of the class.

B. Visit a local business or industry that uses microcomputers. Prepare a short written summary of your visit that describes briefly the equipment in use and the purposes for which it is used. Analyze whether the equipment is performing only word processing functions or whether it has been expanded to include information processing functions.

C. Visit a local business that provides public facsimile (fax) services. Briefly describe the fax services offered and their costs.

D. Collect mail samples that were prepared on computers. Analyze their effectiveness as communication devices. Which samples were effective in accomplishing their purposes?

E. Visit your local public or school library. Locate at least one magazine article that discusses microcomputers. Summarize the contents of this article. What impact do you foresee these computers having on your personal life?

VOCABULARY AND SPELLING STUDIES

A. Many computer terms are fast becoming everyday words. Because a knowledge of certain terms will be necessary for successful communication, you should incorporate them into your vocabulary. Locate the definitions of the following terms; copy each term and its definition on a separate sheet of paper.

1. communicating computer   **5.** program
2. microcomputer   **6.** software
3. minicomputer   **7.** compatibility
4. interface   **8.** mainframe

B. What letter should appear in the blank space in each of these words?

1. perc__late   **4.** controver__y
2. attend__nce   **5.** p__rsuade
3. sep__rate   **6.** vet__ran

C. The following words are spelled as they are often incorrectly enunciated. A letter or syllable has been added or dropped. Respell all words correctly.

1. Wenesday   **6.** sophmore
2. canidate   **7.** probly
3. filum   **8.** libary
4. labratory   **9.** naturly
5. strenth

SECTION 1.3

APPLYING PRINCIPLES OF COMMUNICATION PSYCHOLOGY

Communication is involved in every part of our lives, from the time we wake up until the time we go back to sleep. Talking with family, friends, other students or employees, teachers, or supervisors; listening to the radio or watching TV; buying or selling products or services; speaking, writing, listening, or "sizing up" a situation—when we do any of these things, we are involved in communication. Since communication has such a major effect on our lives and since everyone is a communicator, we need to understand what happens when people communicate. If we look at people who are successful communicators, we find that they apply effectively the principles of human behavior.

WHAT DO WE KNOW ABOUT HUMAN BEHAVIOR?

Many problems from communication mishaps are caused by a lack of understanding of human behavior. If we compare what we know about computer technology, space travel, and medicine, we can easily see that we are far ahead in these last areas. The inner workings of a giant mainframe computer are more easily explained than the inner workings of the human brain and mind!

Continued research in psychology, sociology, and anthropology contributes to our understanding of human behavior and helps us to apply its principles to communication psychology. Studies provide us with theories that are useful in understanding human behavior. However, we must remember that theories are useful only to understand how and why *most* people behave as they do—there are always exceptions. Throughout history, for instance, we find examples of people who have overcome almost insurmountable obstacles in reaching their goals. So while you are studying behavior theory in an attempt to improve your communication skills, remember that we are talking about the general behavior of most people and that there are exceptions.

HUMAN NEEDS AND BEHAVIOR

As a communicator, you must recognize that all human beings have certain needs at certain times. These needs determine our behavior and the goals we set for ourselves. A successful communicator has the ability to understand the needs of those who will receive his or her message. A successful communicator speaks and writes with the receiver's needs in mind at all times.

LIVING LANGUAGE

"Human action can be modified to some extent, but human nature cannot be changed."
—Abraham Lincoln

According to Abraham Maslow, a famous psychologist, most people will respond positively to messages that will meet their particular needs at particular times. Maslow theorizes that human needs are based on a system of priorities, similar to the rungs of a ladder. Once a person's foot is securely balanced on the first rung—that is, once that person's first-rung needs are met—he or she may be willing and ready to ascend to the second rung. And once that person's second-rung needs are met, he or she may be willing and ready to ascend to the third rung, and so on. The point is that until the primary needs (those associated with the first rung) have been reasonably well satisfied, most of us will reject messages that focus on fulfilling higher-level needs.

Maslow uses five "rungs," or classifications, to describe the hierarchy of human needs. These rungs are illustrated on page 17. Keep them in mind as you attempt to send messages to potential receivers.

Rung 1—Basic Physical Needs
What basic things do we need before we can turn our attention to other things? We need food, shelter, and clothing—physical needs. Until these needs are reasonably well met, we think of little else.

Rung 2—Safety and Security Needs
Next we think about keeping ourselves free from physical harm or mental abuse. Most of us try to avoid situations that could cause us physical harm or people that threaten our peace of mind.

The first two rungs represent lower-level needs. Once we have met these needs, we can turn our attention to our upper-level needs.

Rung 3—The Need to Belong
Most of us want to feel that we are part of a group. During our teen years, we place great importance on being "one of the gang." Our families also provide us with a sense of belonging. When we finally go to work full time, we will want to have friends and enjoy being with our coworkers.

Rung 4—The Need to Be "Somebody"
Once we have met the needs of Rung 3, feeling comfortable in the society in which we live, most of us want to feel that we are good at doing something. If we are good at swimming or bowling or some of our school subjects, we feel very pleased with the recognition we receive. We feel that we are "somebody." We have met the needs of our ego.

Rung 5—The Need to Help Others and to Be Creative
If we are reasonably able to meet all the previous needs, we seem to lose our anxieties and fears. Two things then happen: (1) We are more willing to help people who are still struggling on the lower rungs of the ladder, those still striving to meet their physical, safety, and security needs; and (2) we become more creative, and creative people improve the quality of life for us all.

Rung 5—The Need to Help Others and to Be Creative

Rung 4—The Need to Be "Somebody"

Rung 3—The Need to Belong

Rung 2—Safety and Security Needs

Rung 1—Basic Physical Needs

According to Maslow, human needs are based on a system of priorities, similar to the rungs of a ladder.

OUR NEEDS DETERMINE OUR REACTION

To be a successful communicator, you must try to determine the needs of the people to whom you are writing or speaking. You can do this by noticing which goals seem to motivate them. But remember that goals may change rapidly. For example, when you arrive at school in the morning, you have had a good breakfast, so you are not hungry (Rung 1). You feel safe and comfortable in your surroundings (Rung 2), and you have enjoyed visiting with friends before class (Rung 3). You have just finished a class that you enjoy and do well in, so you have satisfied the need to be "somebody" (Rung 4). However, 11:30 a.m. comes and you get hungry. The lunch hour doesn't begin till 12 noon. You shift in your chair and keep looking at your watch. You find concentrating very difficult because you now have a basic physical need, the need for food (Rung 1). Until that need is satisfied, the only really meaningful messages you will receive concern food.

An example of sending a positive message directed toward our needs is our government's appeal to us to use car pools. Although the main reason for car pools would be to conserve energy and to control traffic congestion, we are also told that riding to work with a group is more fun (Rung 3). Our reaction is favorable because the message also appeals to our personal needs.

Thus we can learn to identify these levels of needs and relate them to all our communications. Whether we are looking for a job, buying or selling products or services, ordering supplies, or asking for information, we must always put ourselves in the place of our receiver, decide what our receiver's needs are, and then phrase our message to meet those needs. In this way we go a long way toward getting the reaction we want.

OUR LANGUAGE AFFECTS OUR BEHAVIOR

The words we use can make us behave in different ways. To communicate successfully, we must remember that words are only symbols; meaning is added by people. Two people may interpret the same word differently. At the same time, words also have different kinds of meanings. The *denotative* meaning, the one that appears in the dictionary, is one kind; the feelings and impressions the words invokes, the *connotative* meaning, is another. The total meaning you get from a word is a combination of its denotation and connotation.

Consider these words: *slender, slim, thin, skinny,* and *scrawny.* These words mean essentially the same denotatively. If one of these words were being used to describe you, however, would you react the same to *scrawny* as you would to *slender?*

If a supervisor wished to describe an employee who did not give up easily, that supervisor could use terms such as *persistent, tenacious, persevering, obstinate, subborn,* or *unyielding.* All these words have essentially the same denotation—*following through regardless of the obstacles.* These words, however, are not interchangeable because they differ substantially in connotation.

A noted semanticist coined the terms *purr words* and *snarl words* to refer to words that affect people's emotions either positively or adversely. Purr words are ones such as *beautiful, kindness, freedom, successful, persevering,* and *slender.* People usually respond warmly to words such as these because of their positive or favorable connotation. Snarl words such as *cheap, negligent, fraud, delinquent, obstinate,* and *scrawny* stimulate distasteful images. Effective business communicators generally rely on purr words and avoid snarl words to convey their messages. They are also aware that the same words can convey different meanings to different people.

NONVERBAL COMMUNICATION

When we speak or write, we send our receivers two types of messages; those expressed in words and those not expressed in words. For example, if your teacher says to you, "Don't be late for class tomorrow," you could surmise that the message asks you to be on time. The sentence does not state in words but may, through your teacher's stern facial expression, imply such additional messages as "You are frequently late" or "I am upset that you may not be on time." These messages *not* expressed in words are called *nonverbal communication.*

Nonverbal communication—facial expression, gestures, posture, body movements, attire, grooming—contribute greatly to the meaning of a message. Keep in mind that cultural and environmental differences often determine how these nonverbal messages will be interpreted. On the one hand, people from most cultures seem to turn up the corners of their mouths to show amusement. On the other hand, people from some cultures require less "personal space" than people from other cultures.

Learning to use nonverbal communication can help us make the meanings of our oral messages clear. The following information on personal space, gestures and posture, and facial expressions can help us become better communicators.

Personal Space   All of us, as human beings, maintain our own environment. This means that we all need a certain amount of "space" in which to operate. Ths amount of space that we require depends on our particular culture, our circumstances, and the specific actions expected of us at the time.

The next time you sit with your friends at a table in the cafeteria, notice how each of you generally seems to use the same amount of space in which to eat. You have all unconsciously occupied approximately the same amount of space at the table.

In the United States people usually stand about two feet apart when they talk to each other. If someone moves too close to us and invades our personal space, we begin to exhibit uncomfortable and unnatural kinds of behavior. We may give signals of tension (uneasy movements) to get the intruder to move, or we may start to back up in an attempt to maintain the distance needed between the person speaking and ourselves.

Space violations occur not only in conversations. Picture yourself stepping into a crowded elevator on your way up to the twenty-third floor. As the elevator rises, everyone peers up at the floor indicator. Why? Because each person's personal space has been invaded, he or she feels uncomfortable and is unable to carry on a conversation. The abnormal or uncomfortable behavior exhibited at this point is looking up at the floor indicator.

Notice, however, how comfortable we feel when we step into an elevator with only one or two other persons in it. We might even exchange a casual "Hello," "Good morning," or some other kind of greeting. If the ride is lengthy, the discussion might even continue with some additional small talk, provided that a comfortable spatial distance can be maintained for everyone in the elevator.

An understanding of personal space can certainly help you communicate more successfully. If you back away from people because they have invaded your personal space, they may perceive this behavior as a sign that you don't like them. On the other hand, if you invade others' personal space, how much information can be assimilated when they are backing up, feeling uneasiness, or displaying discomfort? Ask yourself, "How much information has been lost during this stage of discomfort and uneasiness?" Obviously, a communicator who relies on oral communication must be conscious of proper spatial relationships under varying circumstances.

Gestures and Posture   People can communicate many moods through gestures and posture. Keeping your head down and hunching your shoulders may be your way of telling people to leave you alone. Crossing your arms may indicate that you do not accept what someone is saying. Sliding down in your chair may convey that you are bored. Shrugging your shoulders

WORLD VIEW

Even the amount of physical space people need to feel comfortable differs from culture to culture. In Latin America and the Middle East, for example, people engaged in business conversations may stand very close together. In the United States, the typical distance for business conversation is 3 to 5 feet apart.

may mean that you no longer have any interest in a situation. If you do not wish to convey these kinds of negative ideas, you need to monitor your body language in communicating with others.

As a receiver of messages in the communication process, you should keep in mind that nonverbal communication does not always tell the whole story. Interpret gestures, posture, and body movements in conjunction with what is being said and the whole context of the situation.

Facial Expressions

Looking *away* from a person can convey as much meaning as looking *at* a person. Looking away may tell people that we would not invade their privacy. Or it may mean that we are not comfortable with what they are saying. Or it may mean that we are trying to hide something. We know that facial expressions can convey a whole range of meanings—joy, hate, love, sorrow—but as with gestures and posture, we need to consider the entire situation and evaluate both the verbal and nonverbal signals in interpreting messages.

PROMOTING GOODWILL

Goodwill is difficult to define because it is a feeling, an emotion. Perhaps the nearest we can come to a definition is to say that *goodwill* results form satisfying people's needs. Whenever we do or say anything that causes people to like *themselves* better, they like *us* better. Keep in mind the workings of the needs ladder as you learn how to promote goodwill in the categories being discussed.

Be Courteous

To most people *courtesy* means saying "Please" and "Thank you," but "Please" and "Thank you" merely scratch the surface of the courtesy needed to promote goodwill.

The basis of true courtesy is consideration for the other person. Some of us seem to develop this quality easily; others must develop it by constantly saying to themselves, "How would I feel if this were said or done to me?" For example, if you were talking to a person and your telephone rang, would you excuse yourself before lifting the receiver? Would you keep taking calls while you had someone in your office? If people are behind you when you reach a closed door, do you hold the door for them or even let them precede you? These instances are but a few of the courtesies that mark a person whose good manners come from sincere consideration for others.

Be Pleasant and Cordial

Feeling welcome and wanted builds morale and satisfies our need to belong. We can give a person that satisfaction by being pleasant and cordial not only in the words we say but also in our facial expressions and our tone of voice. No matter how warm and gracious our words may be, they fall flat when they come from the lips of a deadpan or indifferent face.

Use the Person's Name Everyone considers his or her name very important; therefore, a person is pleased when recognized and called by name. One of the ways in which you can promote goodwill is to make a determined effort to learn and use people's names. Be sure to check spelling, and if it is an unusual name, like *Tarnowski,* be sure to check pronunciation.

Listen Attentively An attentive listener boosts the speaker's ego; an inattentive listener deflates it. Therefore, since ego satisfaction helps build goodwill, we must be concerned with how to listen, as well as with how to talk. Attentive listening will also help you to identify and correct any problem the person may be attempting to convey.

When listening to people, regardless of the importance or the triviality of what is said, look directly at them. Show that you are following their every word; don't interrupt or try to change the subject. Even if they are talking about an uninteresting subject, your listening techniques will make them feel warm and important.

Control Your Temper Expressing anger is a luxury that effective communicators cannot afford because it interferes with good human relations. Whether you receive an insulting, rude letter or are faced with direct verbal abuse, always try to get a grip on yourself *before* responding. Remember that although a sharp answer may relieve your feelings, it definitely will not foster goodwill with others.

Be Patient Patience in answering questions can be one of your most valuable assets. Each time a question is asked, you should answer as though it were the first time.

WORLD VIEW

In Chinese the last name appears first— *Yen Cheng* results in *Mr. Yen,* not *Mr. Cheng.* Be careful, though, because many Chinese have reversed their names for Americans. Ask politely before you blunder.

COMMUNICATION LABORATORY

APPLICATION EXERCISES

A. Visit a department store and note five ways that appeals are made to your physical and safety needs (Rung 1 and Rung 2) through advertising, displays, and pricing.

B. Tell which need levels the following items would appeal to (1) a gold necklace, (2) a school sweatshirt, (3) taking class notes for a fellow student whose hearing is impaired, (4) exercising daily, and (5) a home smoke-detector alarm.

C. Prepare an oral account of a newspaper or magazine advertisement or of a television or radio commercial that made a direct appeal to your need to be "somebody."

CONTINUED

D. Analyze the following advertisement, using your knowledge of the various levels of needs: "When you drive up on a Faunta XT80, the car itself says everything that can be said. From the bold hood ornament to the gold-plated rear bumper, the car proclaims success. All you need do is to quietly acknowledge the knowing glances."

E. Analyze the impact of body language on your own communication experiences. Summarize in writing on a single sheet one incident where personal space, gestures, facial expressions, or posture may have interfered with message transmission or caused miscommunication.

F. Suppose you wished to describe another person's personality. Words such as *aggressive, dynamic, forceful, assertive,* and *pushy* come to mind. Basically, these words have similar denotative meanings. Based on their connotative meanings, however, which words would you classify as "purr words" and which ones would you consider "snarl words"?

G. Calling people by name and pronouncing their names correctly are always of promoting goodwill. Gain skill here by canvassing your school, community, and social groups for names with unusual spellings or pronunciations. Bring these names to class and share them with your fellow students. Be sure that you can pronounce these names correctly so that you share only correct pronunciations.

VOCABULARY AND SPELLING STUDIES

A. Among the following words are several common misspellings. Find and correct any words that are misspelled.

1. preparation		**7.** dispair	
2. corespondence		**8.** disatisfied	
3. exagerated		**9.** technical	
4. seperately		**10.** commiting	
5. accidentally		**11.** briliant	
6. beneficial		**12.** chosing	

B. The following words were used in the text of this unit. Locate each word in the unit to determine how it was used in the sentence; then use your dictionary to find and write the appropriate definition. Write your own sentence using the word as it was used in the unit.

1. mishaps		**7.** assimilated	
2. insurmountable		**8.** denotation	
3. obstacles		**9.** connotation	
4. ascend		**10.** tenacious	
5. hierarchy		**11.** semanticist	
6. surmise		**12.** adversely	

COMMUNICATING INTERNATIONALLY

Within the last quarter century, rapid advancements in transportation systems and communication technology have enabled people from different parts of the world to develop closer relationships. Jet travel, improved telephone services, worldwide television broadcasting, electronic messaging, and fax transmissions are examples of developments that have broken down time and distance barriers among people in different parts of the world. In terms of time and distance, the world has grown smaller with each advancement in transportation and communication technology.

THE GLOBAL MARKETPLACE

In early cultures time and distance barriers restricted social and commercial activities to within the tribal community. As nations developed and methods of transportation improved, however, people exchanged ideas, traded goods and services, and even immigrated to other countries. Today travelers can fly halfway around the world in 26 hours, and nations from all over the world are brought into television viewers' living rooms. These are not just American travelers and American television viewers—they are also people in most other parts of the world.

This new age of global mobility and awareness has increased people's desire to exchange products and services. Cars, cameras, televisions, tennis shoes, designer clothes, tools, and computers are among the thousands of products regularly exchanged and sold internationally. Examples of services marketed internationally are banking, insurance, legal, medical, and consulting services.

Even foods play a dominant role in our global view. Tacos, burritos, lasagna, sushi, stir fry, egg rolls, spumoni, Wiener schnitzel, and French onion soup—to name just a few foreign foods—are as popular among Americans as McDonald's is among people in Paris, Frankfurt, Beijing, Rome, and Mexico City. As various foreign foods have become "regulars" in the American diet, so have hamburgers, Coke, and french fries won their way into foreign appetites.

Commercial enterprises worldwide no longer view just a domestic marketplace. Television penetration, newspaper coverage, expanded tourism, immigration, and advanced communication systems have created markets that cross national boundaries. Countries throughout the world have rapidly evolved from operating only in a domestic marketplace to buying and selling in the global marketplace.

The former major barriers to international trade—time and distance—have diminished. Their decline, however, has emphasized the presence of two others—cultural and language differences. These differences cause communication barriers that hamper exchange in the global marketplace.

UNDERSTANDING CUSTOMS AND TRADITIONS

One of the major problems in conducting business in foreign countries is a lack of understanding of those countries' customs, traditions, and laws. A common fault of many individuals is the misconception that all other people think and behave as they do. Such is not the case. People from different cultures approach social and business situations differently, and laws differ substantially among countries.

Before you can understand other cultures, you need to have a basic understanding of your own. Although the United States is a "melting pot" of different cultures and we are all members of our own subcultures, Americans tend to exhibit certain basic characteristics. These characteristics are only generalizations, though, and so we must keep in mind that not all Americans exhibit these traits.

The American Business Culture

Americans are viewed globally as people "on the go." They are in a hurry to reach an agreement, sign a contract, or meet a deadline. Time is viewed as money; to waste time is to waste money. Therefore, business meetings are conducted straightforwardly and to the point.

Punctuality is a must. A person is to be on time whether the occasion is a job interview, a sales call, or any other kind of business meeting. In America, visitors are kept waiting only briefly; otherwise, they become impatient.

Because of Americans' Puritan work ethic and basic belief in cause and effect (the harder we work, the greater our rewards will be), we take pride in our work. Americans are known to be hard workers and are often referred to by foreigners as "workaholics." Conducting business at social functions and even taking work home are common occurrences in the life of the American businessman or businesswoman.

Foreign Business Cultures

People in a number of other countries—such as Australia, Israel, Germany, Switzerland, and the Scandinavian countries—approach business similarly to people in the United States. Their regard for promptness and schedules as well as "getting down to business" corresponds with the American outlook toward conducting business. Just because the approach of some foreign businesspeople is similar to their own, though, Americans cannot assume that other cultural aspects are the same. Differences in language, customs, and laws are still potential barriers to communication and international trade.

In other parts of the world, time is flexible and people often arrive late for appointments—or don't even show up at all. This is typical in Arab, South American, and some Asian countries. People in these countries view time differently; they are not tied to schedules, agendas, calendars, and decision making based on a timeline.

Likewise, people in Arab, South American, and some Asian countries are not direct in accomplishing business objectives. First meetings are customarily devoted to drinking coffee or tea and carrying on idle conversation. People in these cultures use this time period to become acquainted with and to evaluate their prospective business associates. Oftentimes many such casual meetings will occur before any discussion of business becomes part of the conversation. An American businessperson who attempts to hurry the process will only set back any possible business agreement.

Yes and *No* in Different Cultures

The saying "Honesty is the best policy" is very American. Americans believe in telling the truth and stating situations as they are. They are not afraid to give advice and criticism, especially when someone asks for it.

These qualities of directness are not valued so highly in other cultures. Other cultures are no less honest or dishonest; they just have their own methods of conveying meaning and communicating. Social harmony takes priority in Asian cultures, and directness is not appropriate in requesting a simple "yes" or "no" answer.

Asians rarely say "no." In Thailand, in fact, there is no word for it. To save face for you and themselves, Asians will answer "yes." Keep in mind, though, that *yes* can mean "Yes, I heard you" or "Yes, I understand"—not "Yes, I agree with you." In Japan there are about sixteen ways to avoid saying "no." A banker in Tokyo was asked by one of his employees, "What does *maybe* mean in English? I know what it means in Japanese; it means "no," but what does it mean in English?"

At the other extreme, Europeans are inclined to say "no" quite readily, although they may later relent to "maybe" or "yes." They are not always quite as definite as they first appear.

Almost everywhere, except in Australia and Europe, people will tell you what they think you want to hear. If you ask for directions to a place, you will be obliged—even if the person doesn't know how to get there. Just ask how far some place is, and you will surely get the answer "Not far." The best advice for the American traveler is not to ask direct questions. Engage in conversations that will allow the information you need to emerge, if the person is able to supply it.

Gestures

Gestures, as well as words, communicate ideas and feelings. In the United States a raised hand in a restaurant beckons a waiter; the forefinger-thumb circle means *OK,* as does the thumbs-up sign. Beckoning a waiter with hand signals is rude in most other cultures, and the American *OK* signal is a vulgar sign in some other cultures. Since hand signals and other gestures convey different meanings in different cultures, they are best avoided in the communication process.

Symbols   Symbols differ among cultures. For instance, a lemon scent in the United States suggests freshness, but in the Philippines a lemon scent is associated with illness.

The number 4 in Japan is considered unlucky—like our 13. Our lucky 7 is viewed as unlucky in Ghana, Kenya, and Singapore. The owl in India is not perceived as wise; it is bad luck like our black cat. In Japan a fox is associated with witches.

The stork symbolizes maternal death in Singapore, certainly not the kind of message you would want to send to a new mother. In Arab countries sunsets are associated with death and sickness. Unintentional use of or reference to symbols that have negative meanings abroad can destroy a message.

LANGUAGE DIFFERENCES

Generally, Americans living in the United States are uniquely only English-speaking, whereas people living in foreign countries are more often multilingual. Modern-day Europeans speak at least two languages; some, three. Africans grow up with the language of the nation that once colonized theirs in addition to a number of different tribal dialects. Japan's three distinct languages are understood by virtually all its population, and Middle Eastern businesspeople converse easily in not only their own native languages but also English and French.

English-Speaking Foreign Countries   Even though English may be the primary language of a country, Americans cannot assume they will have no difficulties in English-speaking foreign countries. Accents, dialects, and vocabulary differences contribute to misunderstandings. Imagine the embarrassment you will feel asking people from England, Ireland, or Australia to repeat statements because you did not understand what they said. You might be able to do so once—or twice—but definitely not again without feeling embarrassment. After all, they speak the same language—or do they?

The keen ear can understand English spoken with almost any accent. Differences in word meanings among English-speaking nations, however, can cause confusion. How many Americans would know that a bonnet is the hood of a car? a counter jumper is a salesman? a panda is a police car? a chemist is a pharmacist? or a holiday is a vacation? These and other such word differences serve as barriers to communication.

Many spellings, too, differ in English-speaking countries. Notice just a few spelling differences between the United States and England.

UNITED STATES	ENGLAND	UNITED STATES	ENGLAND
honor	honour	defense	defence
color	colour	license	licence
center	centre	check	cheque
criticize	criticise	pajamas	pyjamas
jeweler	jeweller	aluminum	aluminium
inflection	inflexion	maneuver	manoeuvre

Non-English-Speaking Countries   Although English is recognized as the universal language of business, you cannot expect that every businessperson in non-English-speaking countries understands and speaks English. In many cases people's knowledge of English may be quite limited. To avoid embarrassment, however, they may nod in apparent agreement or respond "yes," even if they do not understand fully what you are saying. Just because a person says he or she speaks English, do not readily assume that person is fluent.

Before arriving in a non-English-speaking country, learn about the history, customs, food, and dress of that country so you do not mistakenly offend the citizens. Even learn some common phrases in the native language to show you are interested in the people and their country. Be careful, though, not to mislead anyone into thinking you understand more than you do.

Americans who wish to conduct business in a non-English-speaking country would be wise to engage the services of an interpreter if they themselves are not fluent in the native language. Interpreters can simplify the exchange of information and ideas and ensure understanding. Businesspeople should not, however, rely on the services of an interpreter provided by their foreign host. Instead, they should secure the services of an interpreter with whom they had an opportunity to discuss their objectives, define any technical terms, and develop a feeling of mutual understanding.

TAILORING YOUR COMMUNICATION

Whether you are speaking or writing, you need to adjust your communication style to accommodate your foreign counterpart. The most important rule, though, is to use and pronounce names correctly. If in doubt about using or pronouncing a person's name, just ask, "What would you like me to call you?"

Confusions can occur easily. For instance, in South American countries, last names are hyphenated. One is the surname of the father, and the other is the surname of the mother. *José Garcia-Flores* would be called *Señor (Mr.) Garcia* in most South American countries, since the father's name appears first. In Brazil, however, the mother's name appears first. Here *José Garcia-Flores* would be called *Señor (Mr.) Flores*.

In China a person's surname appears first. Therefore, *Yen Cheng* would be called *Mr. Yen*. Many Chinese who deal with American businesspeople reverse the order of their names to accommodate their American counterparts. Therefore, "What would you like me to call you?" is good advice for anyone entering the foreign "name game."

Follow these general guidelines in speaking to or corresponding with persons from non-English-speaking countries.

Develop a Conversational Strategy   Speak slowly—use a steady, slow speaking pace. Enunciate your words clearly, and avoid contractions such as *you'll, I'm,* and *we'll* and fillers such as *you know, right?,* and *ah . . . .*

> ## WORLD
> ### VIEW
> I am referred to in that splendid language [Urdu] as "Fella belong Mrs. Queen."
>
> —Prince Philip, Duke of Edinburgh

Use Easy-to-Understand Words

Avoid idioms that cannot be translated literally. Expressions such as *straight from the horse's mouth*, *play it by ear*, and *shoot the breeze* can only cause confusion. Picture what foreigners might perceive if you used any of these expressions: *we're over a barrel*, *we'll have to pay through the nose*, *you're pulling my leg*, or *they don't have a leg to stand on*.

Repeat, Paraphrase, and Summarize

To ensure understanding, repeat your ideas using different words or a different approach. Watch a person's eyes. If they wander or look glazed, you are probably not communicating effectively, especially if the person is not fluent in English. Do not be afraid to summarize what you have said previously, ask a person what has been said or agreed on, or pose a question that requires an informed response. Above all, learn to be a good listener. Keep in mind that effective communication is a two-way process.

Use Positive Body Language

Your words acquire meaning through your body language. Facial expressions and gestures often transmit more than words. Remember that the genuine smile conveys friendliness, happiness, and approval.

Adapt Your Written Communications

When writing letters to people in foreign countries, especially to those whose English may be limited, use short, simple sentences. Above all, don't use idioms, clichés, or slang.

Since the written word doesn't smile, avoid any attempt at humor. Cultural and language differences may cause your attempt at humor to be misinterpreted. Instead, keep your letter simple and related to your main purpose in writing. Do not hesitate to repeat an important idea in a different way.

Be polite—words such as *please*, *thank you*, *appreciate*, and *grateful* should be used readily. Do not be surprised, however, to receive flowery letters from overseas correspondents, especially where such letters are a custom of the land. They are merely translating that protocol into English. If appropriate, you may wish to follow suit.

Always proofread your letter for typographical errors, and read the letter objectively to see if there are any statements that could be misinterpreted.

COMMUNICATION LABORATORY

APPLICATION EXERCISES

A. Visit a local department store. Examine some of the goods on display to note their country of origin; this information is usually contained on the packaging or stamped on the bottom of the item. Locate ten items made in foreign countries. Describe each item and specify its country of origin—for example, *Women's leather boots made in Uruguay*.

CONTINUED

B. Locate the following countries on a world globe: Australia, Austria, Canada, China, Ecuador, France, Lebanon, Nigeria, Panama, and Portugal. List the country and then identify the continent in which the country is located. Visit your school library or your local public library if you do not have access to a world globe.

C. Find an article in your local newspaper that relates to a foreign country. Briefly summarize the contents of the article, and specify in which continent the country is located. If the country is an island or a group of islands, identify the continent it borders.

D. Select a foreign country. List and describe three cultural differences between this country and the United States. Visit your school library or public library to gather information on the country of your choice.

E. Consult an up-to-date encyclopedia to identify the national language of the following countries: Argentina, Australia, Austria, Brazil, Canada, Iran, Philippines, Saudi Arabia, Switzerland, and Thailand.

VOCABULARY AND SPELLING STUDIES

A. These words are often confused: *receipt, recipe; vein, vain, vane.* Explain the differences.

B. Each of the following sentences contains slang or an incorrect expression. Substitute a more formal word or expression for each.

1. I could of told you that this customer would complain.
2. We will really have to hustle to meet their competition.
3. I sort of think that we can improve our advertising.
4. Our salespeople should of featured the less expensive model.
5. I can't get a handle on the shipping problem.

C. Should *ei* or *ie* appear in the blank spaces in these sentences?

1. We bel__ve you will find this to be a conven__nt way to rec__ve the magazines you want each month.
2. It is a real ach__vement to become ch__f of police in a large city in such a br__f period of time
3. Th__r fr__ght was misdelivered to a n__ghboring warehouse.

CHAPTER 2

READING

Reading many kinds of written material will be a major part of your business experience, whatever your job may be. As a reader you will be judged by how quickly you understand written messages. Your understanding will be determined by your ability to accurately carry out the wishes expressed in the communication.

You can easily see, then, why improving all aspects of your reading skill will improve your total job effectiveness. Given a situation that requires reading, you will be able to do the following after you master the units in this chapter.

OBJECTIVES

1. Judge and explain which reading technique most benefits the purpose for which you are reading.

2. Increase your reading speed through timed practices.

3. Improve your reading comprehension.

4. Develop techniques to remember better what you have read.

READING FOR PERSONAL AND PROFESSIONAL GROWTH

Y ou are already aware of the necessity of reading in your personal life. Reflect for a moment how your life might be if you were not able to read. You would not be able to drive your car, read your favorite magazine, find your favorite CD, or even follow the instructions to play the latest video games. The pleasure of reading books, newspapers, and magazines would not be available to you. You wouldn't be able to make repairs in your home or to your car, follow a new recipe, or even select a menu item at your favorite restaurant.

As a student you are aware that your school success is closely linked with your ability to read well—but have you taken the time to consider that your reading ability may be even more important to you *after* you have completed your formal education? Whether you continue your education by attending college or decide to work after high school, reading will still contribute significantly to your life. Successful business and professional people spend much of their time reading all types of material—books, magazines, notices, bulletins, reports, memorandums, and letters, as well as other written materials that provide them with information that is essential to performing their jobs. Therefore, the greater your reading skill, the better equipped you will be to succeed in your chosen career.

PURPOSE DETERMINES READING TECHNIQUE

Why are you reading this book? Are you reading for pleasure? Probably not. Are you looking for a specific piece of information? Not necessarily. You are probably reading to absorb a great deal of information about business English and communication. Once you determine why you are reading (the purpose) you can better determine how you should read (the technique). There are several purposes to reading.

Reading for Pleasure   When reading for pleasure, you need not absorb every detail, remember every fact, or read critically. Therefore, you may read novels, biographies, and magazine articles at a rapid rate. You should try to target your pleasure reading at four hundred words a minute.

Reading for Specific Information   When searching for a particular piece of information such as a specific date or name, you should skip and skim material to make the best use of your time. When you *skip,* you visually jump over large portions of material not relevant to your needs. When you *skim,* you move your eyes rapidly down a page and stop to read only the significant facts and phrases. Most people read newspapers using this technique.

Reading to Absorb Information   As a student, you will be required to absorb information. When you study, you will actively participate in your reading. You must read for meaning and you must remember what you read. Thus you will read most words on a page and take the time to absorb and digest the information.

Reading for Accuracy   Most people will need to do this type of reading on the job. Every prepared document or typing job, every invoice, letter, and memo requires careful reading. This reading requires concentration and attention. This type of reading is so important that we will discuss it more fully in Section 6.5.

SETTING THE STAGE

Research has shown that the average executive spends approximately half the business day reading, and reading experts say that two hours could be cut from this load by learning to read faster and with greater understanding. What about you? Does it take you longer than it should to read your assigned work? Do you dread reading because you feel you are plodding through? Do you have to spend so much time reading for some courses that you do not have enough time for others? If you said "yes" to any of these questions, then you *can* and *should* do something to improve your reading skills. The suggestions in the remaining part of this chapter will help you to get off to the right start.

Your Eyes   The first step in your reading improvement program is to make certain that your eyes are in good condition. If you must hold ordinary written material either very close to your eyes or at arm's length to read it, if the material you are reading seems blurred, or if your eyes tire easily, then you should consult an eye doctor. You may need to wear glasses, perhaps only for reading. If you already wear glasses, you may need to have the lenses changed.

Whether or not you wear glasses, you should protect your eyes. Here are a few suggestions:

1. Rest your eyes every half hour or so by looking into the distance or by closing your eyes for a few minutes.
2. Exercise your eyes from time to time, particularly after doing close work. One good eye exercise is to rotate the eyes slowly, without moving your head. Move your eyes far to the right; then to the left; then up; and finally, down. These exercises will help to strengthen your eye muscles.

3. Avoid reading in bright sunlight or while riding in a car, train, or other moving vehicle.
4. Have eye injuries or infections attended to at once by a doctor.

Reading Conditions   Poor lighting contributes to eye fatigue and blurry vision. Of course, nonglaring daylight provides the best light for reading, and light-colored walls help reflect daylight. Indirect lighting, rather than semidirect or direct lighting, is the best artificial lighting. Therefore, make certain that there are no glaring light bulbs visible to your eyes or any other glaring spots anywhere near where you are reading.

For the best reading conditions, sit comfortably in a well-ventilated (not overheated) room that is free from distracting sights and sounds. Above all, do not attempt to do serious reading with the radio, television, or stereo turned on.

INCREASING YOUR SPEED

STUDY TIP

The purpose for reading should determine the speed.

As discussed earlier, how rapidly you should read depends on (a) the type of material you are reading and (b) the purpose for reading. Most "light" reading should be at a rate of at least 400 words a minute. Most studying and other serious reading should be at a rate of at least 200 to 250 words a minute.

You can do a number of things on your own to improve your reading speed. If you follow these six suggestions, you should soon note an increase in your reading speed. (If you already are a fast reader, these suggestions will help you to read even faster.)

Read in "Thought Units"   When you read in phrases, or thought units, rather than word by word, your eyes take in more information before each pause. Since you make fewer pauses on each line, you automatically read faster. To illustrate, read these short lines and notice the difference in your reading time for each line:

1. C R T N L B
2. WALKING but COUNTRY
3. read for meaning

You probably read each line with ease, but reading the first line took longer than reading the second line, and the second line took longer than the third. Why? Because in the first line you read *six* individual letters; in the second you read *three* individual words; but in the third you read *one* entire phrase.

You should be able to read a newspaper column line with one or two eye pauses and a book-width line with not more than four or five pauses. Now read the following sentence, and notice the difference in speed when you read word by word compared to when you read in phrases.

You / are / more / likely / to / understand / and / remember / what / you / read / if / you / actively / participate / in / what / you / read.

You are more likely / to understand and remember / what you read / if you actively participate / in what you read.

Reading in phrases means reading in *units of thought.* Reading this way enables you to understand better what you read, because sentences—complete thoughts—are made up of these smaller thought units.

Because slow readers usually *think* much faster than they can read, their thoughts often wander. On the other hand, phrase readers receive ideas from the printed page more rapidly and thus keep their minds so busy that they do not have time to let their thoughts wander. Therefore, the fast reader—the phrase reader—usually gets better results from reading.

STUDY TIP

Comprehension (understanding) and retention (remembering) are more important than reading speed.

Keep Eyes Moving From Left to Right   Once you have read a phrase, do not allow yourself to go back and read it a second time. Such backward movements of the eyes are called *regressions,* and they slow the reader considerably. For the untrained reader these regressions become a habit. Force yourself to get the meaning of a phrase the first time; force yourself to concentrate. This focus calls for practice and discipline, as well as for eliminating all distractions that might interfere with your reading.

Keep Lips and Tongue Motionless   Don't spell or pronounce the words you are reading, not even inwardly. Such vocalization slows down your reading; it makes you read silently only as fast as you can read aloud.

Read Word Beginnings   You can identify the following word endings without seeing the entire word: *undoub_____, remem_____, partici_____.* (You can tell from the meaning of the sentence whether the last word should be *participate, participating,* or *participation.*)

Keep Building Vocabulary   Try to increase your vocabulary. The more words you have at your command, the fewer pauses you will have to make to check the meanings of words and the faster you will read. Also, when your mind instantly recognizes words, you will better understand what you are reading.

Constantly Practice   Continual increase in reading speed means exercising your willpower and continually practicing rapid reading. If you force yourself always to read a little faster than is comfortable, rapid reading soon will become a habit.

INCREASING YOUR UNDERSTANDING

Reading speed is very important. More important, however, is understanding (comprehension) and remembering (retention). Some of the suggestions made for increasing your reading speed will also contribute to your greater understanding. Developing a wide vocabulary is one example. Reading in thought units is another. The following suggestions will further help improve your reading comprehension as well as your ability to remember what you read.

Scan or Preview the Material   Skim the material and note the main headings and subheadings; look at the illustrations and read the captions. This preview will help you to identify the main ideas before you begin your reading.

Think as You Read   If you try to relate what you are reading to what you already know, you will improve your reading comprehension. If you remain an active participant in your reading, you will also improve your reading comprehension. How can you do this? Ask yourself some of these questions.

1. What is the main message?
2. Who is the target audience?
3. Is the information accurate and up to date?
4. How is the message organized?
5. What do the visual aids illustrate?
6. Do the examples help in understanding the writer's message?

Make Brief Notes   If you own the material you are reading, it is often helpful to highlight or underline important words, phrases, or passages. Another helpful technique is to make notes in the margins. If you wish to refer to your notes in the future, it is best to write in a notebook. One clue: never take word-for-word (verbatim) notes; you'll miss the main idea in attempting to cover everything; simply summarize in your own words the main idea of the material.

So how do you select the essential material? How do you determine what is important? Often, the main idea is conveyed in the first sentence of each paragraph. Sometimes the writer conveys the main idea in the last sentence. Rarely will you find more than one idea in each paragraph; but if you do, you may need to read the paragraph carefully two or three times.

Reread and Review   How often you reread or review the material will depend on its difficulty and the use you plan to make of the material. Often a quick skimming of the material or a reading of your notes will be adequate for review if the first readings were done carefully.

If you immediately practice the suggestions made in this chapter, you will reap dividends not only in terms of improved schoolwork, but also in professional growth.

COMMUNICATION LABORATORY

APPLICATION EXERCISES

A. On a sheet of paper, write a short essay (about 350 words) telling how you used reading in your summer job or how you now use reading in your current, after-school job.

B. To get an idea of your reading speed, have someone time you with a stopwatch as you read the following excerpt:

When Larson was growing up in Tacoma, Washington, he didn't expect to become a cartoonist. He loved to draw animals, to read about animals, and to collect animals from a swamp near his home. He planned to study biology. "But I didn't know what to do with a biology degree so I switched to communications," he says. "After college I played music and worked in a music store, then tried drawing a few cartoons."

Where does he get all those strange ideas? Larson isn't really sure. "You can't go looking for ideas. They have to come to you. When I sit down at my drawing board and start to think, I usually don't have anything special in mind. I just let my mind free-flow. If nothing happens, and it usually doesn't, I start to draw things to get the juices going."

What advice would Larson give [young people] who want to try cartooning?

- Practice. The more you practice, the better you'll get.
- Draw things from different perspectives and angles.
- Don't overdraw or complicate the story line.
- Remember every cartoon has one thing that makes it funny, one make-or-break point. It may be a facial expression, the caption, or some other element.
- In a single-panel cartoon the strength of the humor is usually visual—one moment frozen in time.
- Try to learn many things. There's no point in being a good artist if you can't construct a sentence.

"The most important thing is to love doing it," he adds. "And know that this is a competitive field. It will be difficult. It might not work out. So have other options. If you are an imaginative person, you take in things and experiences and—in unexpected ways—they find their way into your work."

(Reprinted with permission by *National Geographic World*)

Note the time it took you to read the previous selection. Then locate this time on the chart on page 38. Your reading speed is the corresponding number in the second column. For example, if you read the paragraphs in 50 seconds, your reading speed is 300 words per minute (wpm); if it took you 1 minute, your speed is 250 words a minute. Most material such as this should be read at a rate no slower than 300 words a minute. How does your speed compare?

READING TIME	READING RATE
30 seconds	500 wpm
40 seconds	375 wpm
50 seconds	300 wpm
1 minute	250 wpm
1 minute 10 seconds	215 wpm
1 minute 20 seconds	190 wpm
1 minute 30 seconds	165 wpm
1 minute 40 seconds	150 wpm
1 minute 50 seconds	135 wpm
2 minutes	125 wpm

C. Without rereading the paragraphs in Exercise B, write a brief summary of them. Use your own words. Then compare your version with the selection. Were you accurate? Complete?

D. One good reading habit that will help you gain speed is to look only at the beginnings of familiar words rather than at the entire word. Test your ability to do so by reading as rapidly as possible the following paragraph in which the endings of some familiar words have been omitted.

The abil_____ to read caref_____ appli_____ not only to the writ_____ of others but also to your own writ_____. When you have finish_____ an applica_____ letter, for examp_____ , do you proofr_____ it caref_____? Do you look for spell_____ err_____ , or err_____ in punctua_____? If you do not read your work caref_____ bef_____ send_____ it, you should not ex_____ any_____ else to read it serious_____ or thought_____ .

Our most success_____ engine_____ have been assig_____ to the Hong Kong proj_____. They will spend approxi_____ six mont_____ on site dur_____ the plan_____ stag_____ for the new devel_____. Then they will retu_____ to our corpor_____ head-qua_____ to have quick access to our full resour_____. One or both of the engin_____ , along with additi_____ staff as neces_____ , will trav_____ to Hong Kong dur_____ site devel_____. Once con-struc_____ beg_____ , they will oper_____ from Hong Kong unt_____ the proj_____ is comple_____.

VOCABULARY AND SPELLING STUDIES

A. A skillful reader should have a well-developed vocabulary. Indicate whether the italicized word has been used correctly in each of the following sentences. If not, what is the correct word?

1. *Its* a touchdown!
2. Everyone *accept* Maria should be at the meeting.
3. What *percent* of students voted in the election?
4. I was *effected* by the movie.
5. The Board of Directors *past* the veto today.
6. Who *beside* me wants to visit the site?
7. If the new briefcase is not John's, it must be *her's.*
8. Ms. Perez *choose* the new logo yesterday.
9. I *herd* the answer, but I don't believe it.
10. Did you *except* delivery of the new delivery van?

B. Should *ance* or *ence* be added to the following?

1. refer_____
2. correspond_____
3. assist_____
4. appear_____
5. perform_____
6. preval_____
7. compli_____
8. signific_____
9. confid_____
10. import_____

C. Should *er, or, or ar* be added to the following?

1. gramm_____
2. supervis_____
3. calend_____
4. manag_____
5. lab_____
6. mediat_____
7. orat_____
8. present_____
9. direct_____
10. edit_____

CHAPTER 3

WORD USAGE

boy

buoy

a pair of pears

stal

steak

flower   flour

cursor

curser

Expressing yourself clearly is the key to communicating effectively with others. Think about how a situation can cause confusion and hostility because someone does not understand your messages. In business, misunderstandings can be costly.

The words you select help determine whether you can communicate your ideas exactly as you intended. The use of a dictionary and other kinds of word references can help you find words to say exactly what you mean. As you use the words you find, your vocabulary will grow. An expanded vocabulary will provide you with accurate and precise words, which can only help promote the understanding that is critical to effective communication.

OBJECTIVES

Given a situation that requires you to express yourself, you will be able to do the following when you master the sections in this chapter.

1. Use reference books such as a dictionary, a thesaurus, and a word division manual to increase your knowledge of words.

2. Use commonly confused words in sentences to show that you understand their different meanings and spellings.

3. List, with their correct spelling, many of the words frequently used in business writing.

USING THE DICTIONARY AND OTHER WORD REFERENCES

Is the noun *advice* or *advise*? Is the plural of *radio* formed by adding *s* or by adding *es*? When word division is necessary at the end of a line, should *describe* be divided into *des-cribe* or *de-scribe*? What does *moratorium* mean? Is it correct to pronounce *adult* either *'ad-ult* (with emphasis on *ad*) or *a-'dult* (with the emphasis on *dult*)? If you end a sentence with *in*, is *in* a preposition or an adverb? These are the kinds of questions that often confront even the most accomplished speakers and writers. The answers to such questions about words are to be found in the dictionary and other word references. You will find out more about these references in this section.

Today many authoritative references are available in both hardback and paperback. Because our language is constantly growing and changing, our references should be up to date. You can depend on your library to have the large, expensive, up-to-date references.

Occasionally, references may differ as to the spellings, pronunciations, or syllabications for some words. Regardless of the reasons for such differences, you should remember that language is constantly changing in all respects and that differences among references do not make one reference wrong and another one right. Any established, up-to-date reference can properly be cited as the authority for acceptable word usage.

DICTIONARIES

Many of the differences among dictionaries are of little consequence to the ordinary user. For example, one dictionary may show abbreviations, biographical names, and geographic names in separate sections at the end of the book; another dictionary may arrange this information alphabetically with the words in the main vocabulary list. Also, different dictionaries use different systems for indicating pronunciation and for showing definitions, word origins, and other information about words. See pages 44–45 for the system used in one popular dictionary.

Many extremely fine dictionaries are available and most—if not all—are arranged in alphabetical order. Although we all "know" the alphabet, we must all develop the ability to find words *quickly* using the alphabet. To be even more efficient, we need to use the guide words (the first and last words on each page) appearing at the top of the page.

LIVING LANGUAGE

I find that a great part of the information I have was acquired by looking up something and finding something else on the way.

—Franklin P. Adams

LIVING LANGUAGE

Words fascinate me. They always have. For me, browsing in a dictionary is like being turned loose in a bank.

—Eddie Cantor

The most nearly complete dictionaries are unabridged, such as *Webster's Third New International Dictionary* and *Funk & Wagnalls New Standard Dictionary of the English Language*. These comprehensive works contain approximately 450,000 words in the main vocabulary list.

For personal use at home, at school, or on the job, a good standard desk dictionary is the best choice. Among these are *Webster's Ninth New Collegiate Dictionary; The American Heritage Dictionary of the English Language; The American Heritage Dictionary, Second College Edition; Webster's New World Dictionary of American English; Random House Webster's College Dictionary; Funk & Wagnalls Standard College Dictionary;* and *The Thorndike/Barnhardt Advanced Dictionary. Webster's Ninth New Collegiate Dictionary* (Merriam-Webster Inc., Springfield, Massachusetts, 1991) is the source for spelling and syllabication for all words in this book as well as for the definitions and pronunciations given.

Every dictionary, no matter how small or how large, whether paperback or hardback, shows the spelling, word division, pronunciation, and meaning or meanings of each word listed. A good standard desk dictionary also gives the part of speech of a word, its origin, the ways in which it is used, any synonyms, and certain irregular forms; for example, the principal parts of the verb *(did, done, do, doing),* the plural of the noun *(alumna, alumnae),* and the comparative and superlative forms of the adjective *(heavy, heavier, heaviest).* In addition, the dictionary helps you determine whether a word should be capitalized.

A dictionary is the most frequently used reference for most writers. From the compact pocket-size versions to the most extensive unabridged editions, a writer's dictionary is always available to help the writer with spelling, word choice, and word use.

Determining Capitalization and Noun Plurals

The dictionary is an important source for capitalization and noun plurals. Suppose you are writing advertising copy for a sale of women's bathing suits—one-piece, skirted, and bikini types. You happen to know that Bikini is an *atoll* (a coral reef surrounding a lagoon) of the Marshall Islands, so you think you should capitalize the word. You check to make sure.

As you open the dictionary, you recall that each word entry is printed in small letters unless the word almost always, or more often than not, begins with a capital letter. Therefore, when you see *bikini* and read the definition, you know that the word, as you are using it, does *not* begin with a capital letter. The main part of your dictionary will help you with capitalization. You may also get further help from the rules for capitalization in the dictionary reference section.

The dictionary supplies any out-of-the-ordinary plural forms. It does not show most regular plurals—those formed by adding *s* or *es.* If you need to know the plural of *stadium,* for example, you would look in the dictionary and see this information after that word: "*n, pl* **-dia** or **-di•ums.**" And if it is the plural of *brother-in-law* that bothers you, you would find after that word: "*n, pl* **broth•ers-in-law.**"

Parts of speech (in abbreviated form) label each main entry.

re·peat·er \ri-'pēt-ər\ n (1598) : one that repeats: as **a** : one who relates or recites **b** : a watch or clock with a striking mechanism that upon pressure of a spring will indicate the time in hours or quarters and sometimes minutes **c** : a firearm having a magazine that holds a number of cartridges loaded into the chamber by the action of the piece **d** : an habitual violator of the laws **e** : one who votes illegally by casting more than one ballot in an election **f** : a student enrolled in a class or course for a second or subsequent time **g** : a device for receiving electronic communication signals and delivering corresponding amplified ones
re·peat·ing adj, of a firearm (1824) : designed to load cartridges from a magazine
repeating decimal n (1773) : a decimal in which after a certain point a particular digit or sequence of digits repeats itself indefinitely — compare TERMINATING DECIMAL
re·pe·chage \,rep-ə-'shäzh, rə-,pesh-'äzh\ n [F repêchage second chance, reexamination for a candidate who has failed, fr. repêcher to fish out, rescue, fr. re- + pêcher to fish, fr. L piscari — more at PISCATORY] (ca. 1928) : a trial heat (as in rowing) in which first-round losers are given another chance to qualify for the semifinals

Principal parts of verbs are often listed, especially when the verb ending changes or when the verb is irregular.

re·pel \ri-'pel\ vb re·pelled; re·pel·ling [ME repellen, fr. L repellere, fr. re- + pellere to drive — more at FELT] vt (15c) **1 a** : to drive back : REPULSE **b** : to fight against : RESIST **2** : TURN AWAY, REJECT ⟨repelled the insinuation⟩ **3 a** : to drive away : DISCOURAGE ⟨foul words and frowns must not ~ a lover —Shak.⟩ **b** : to be incapable of adhering to, mixing with, taking up, or holding **c** : to force away or apart or tend to keep apart by mutual action at a distance **4** : to cause aversion in : DISGUST ~ vi : to cause aversion — **re·pel·ler** n
re·pel·len·cy \ri-'pel-ən-sē\ n (1747) : the quality or capacity of repelling
1re·pel·lent also **re·pel·lant** \ri-'pel-ənt\ adj [L repellent-, repellens, prp. of repellere] (1643) **1** : serving or tending to drive away or ward off — often used in combination ⟨a mosquito-repellent spray⟩ **2** : arousing aversion or disgust : REPULSIVE **syn** see REPUGNANT — **re·pel·lent·ly** adv
2repellent also **repellant** n (1661) : something that repels; esp : a substance used to prevent insect attacks

Variant spellings are preceded by the word also.

1re·pent \ri-'pent\ vb [ME repenten, fr. OF repentir, fr. re- + pentir to be sorry, fr. L paenitēre — more at PENITENT] vi (13c) **1** : to turn from sin and dedicate oneself to the amendment of one's life **2 a** : to feel regret or contrition **b** : to change one's mind ~ vt **1** : to cause to feel regret or contrition **2** : to feel sorrow, regret, or contrition for — **pent·er** n
2re·pent \'rē-pənt\ adj [L repent-, repens, prp. of repere to creep — more at REPTILE] (1669) : CREEPING, PROSTRATE ⟨~ stems⟩
re·pen·tance \ri-'pent-²n(t)s\ n (14c) : the action or process of repenting esp. for misdeeds or moral shortcomings **syn** see PENITENCE
re·pen·tant \-²nt\ adj (13c) **1** : experiencing repentance : PENITENT **2** : expressive of repentance — **re·pen·tant·ly** adv
re·per·cus·sion \,rē-pər-'kəsh-ən, ,rep-ər-\ n [L repercussion-, repercussio, fr. repercussus, pp. of repercutere to drive back, fr. re- + percutere to beat — more at PERCUSSION] (1536) **1** : REFLECTION, REVERBERATION **2 a** : an action or effect given or exerted in return : a reciprocal action or effect **b** : a widespread, indirect, or unforeseen effect of an act, action, or event — usu. used in pl. — **re·per·cus·sive** \-'kəs-iv\ adj
rep·er·toire \'rep-ə(r)-,twär\ n [F répertoire, fr. LL repertorium] (1847) **1 a** : a list or supply of dramas, operas, pieces, or parts that a company or person is prepared to perform **b** : a supply of skills, devices, expedients ⟨part of the ~ of a quarterback⟩; broadly : AMOUNT, SUPPLY ⟨an endless ~ of summer clothes⟩ **c** : a list or supply of capabilities ⟨the instruction ~ of a computer⟩ **2 a** : the complete list or supply of dramas, operas, or musical works available for performance ⟨our modern orchestral ~⟩ **b** : the complete list or supply of skills, devices, or ingredients used in a particular field, occupation, or practice ⟨the ~ of literary criticism⟩

Pronunciations—even of foreign terms—are listed for each main entry.

rep·er·to·ry \'rep-ə(r)-,tōr-ē, -,tòr-\ n, pl **-ries** [LL repertorium list, fr. L repertus, pp. of reperire to find, fr. re- + parere to produce — more at PARE] (1593) **1** : a place where something may be found : REPOSITORY **2 a** : REPERTOIRE **b** : a company that presents several different plays, operas, or pieces usu. alternately in the course of a season at one theater **c** : a theater housing such a company **3** : the production and presentation of plays by a repertory company ⟨acting in ~⟩
rep·e·tend \'rep-ə-,tend\ n [L repetendus to be repeated, gerundive of repetere to repeat] (1904) : a repeated sound, word, or phrase; specif : REFRAIN
rep·e·ti·tion \,rep-ə-'tish-ən\ n [L repetition-, repetitio, fr. repetitus, pp. of repetere to repeat] (1526) **1** : the act or an instance of repeating or being repeated **2** : MENTION, RECITAL — **rep·e·ti·tion·al** \-'tish-nəl, -ən-²l\ adj

Syllable breaks for word division are shown for main entries.

rep·e·ti·tious \-'tish-əs\ adj (1675) : characterized or marked by repetition; esp : tediously repeating — **rep·e·ti·tious·ly** adv — **rep·e·ti·tious·ness** n
re·pet·i·tive \ri-'pet-ət-iv\ adj (1839) **1** : containing repetition : REPEATING **2** : REPETITIOUS — **re·pet·i·tive·ly** adv — **re·pet·i·tive·ness** n
re·pine \ri-'pin\ vi (1530) **1** : to feel or express dejection or discontent **2** : to long for something — **re·pin·er** n
re·place \ri-'plās\ vt (1595) **1** : to restore to a former place or position ⟨~ cards in a file⟩ **2** : to take the place of esp. as a substitute or successor **3** : to put something new in the place of ⟨~ a worn carpet⟩ — **re·place·able** \-'plā-sə-bəl\ adj — **re·plac·er** n

Synonyms offer words that are similar in meaning to the main entry. **Antonyms** (words that mean the opposite) are sometimes listed as well.

syn REPLACE, DISPLACE, SUPPLANT, SUPERSEDE mean to put out of a usual or proper place or into the place of another. REPLACE implies a filling of a place once occupied by something lost, destroyed, or no longer usable or adequate; DISPLACE implies an ousting or dislodging preceding a replacing; SUPPLANT implies either a dispossessing or usurping of another's place, possessions, or privileges or an uprooting of something and its replacement with something else; SUPERSEDE implies replacing a person or thing that has become superannuated, obsolete, or otherwise inferior.
re·place·ment \ri-'plā-smənt\ n (1790) **1** : the action or process of replacing : the state of being replaced : SUBSTITUTION **2** : something that replaces; esp : an individual assigned to a military unit to replace a loss or complete a quota
re·plant \(')rē-'plant\ vt (1575) **1** : to plant again or anew **2** : to provide with new plants **3** : to subject to replantation

Every dictionary shows the spelling, word division, and meaning or meanings of each word listed. A good standard desk dictionary also gives the part of speech of the word, its origins, the ways in which it is used, and certain of

Word origins help with understanding the meaning of a main entry.

Run-on entries list words that are derived from the main entry.

Different entries that are spelled the same way are indicated by numbers.

Plurals of nouns are given when the main entry's plural is formed irregularly.

Example phrases show how the main entry is commonly used.

Pronunciation guides are handy charts that explain pronunciation symbols.

re·plan·ta·tion \ˌrē-(ˌ)plan-ˈtā-shən\ n (1870) : reattachment or reinsertion of a bodily part (as a limb or tooth) after separation from the body

¹re·play \(ˈ)rē-ˈplā\ vt (1884) : to play again or over

²re·play \ˈrē-ˌplā\ n (1895) **1 a** : an act or instance of replaying **b** : the playing of a tape (as a videotape) **2** : REPETITION, REENACTMENT ⟨don't . . . ~ . . . of our old mistakes⟩

re·plead·er \(ˈ)rē-ˈplēd-ər\ n [replead (to plead again) + -er (as in misnomer)] (1607) **1** : a second legal pleading **2** : the right of pleading again granted usu. when the issue raised is immaterial or insufficient

re·plen·ish \ri-ˈplen-ish\ vb [ME replenisshen, fr. MF repleniss-, stem of replenir to fill, fr. OF, fr. re- + plein full, fr. L plenus — more at FULL] vt (14c) **1 a** : to fill with persons or animals : STOCK **b** archaic : to supply fully : PERFECT **c** : to fill with inspiration or power : NOURISH **2 a** : to fill or build up again ⟨~ed his glass⟩ **b** : to make good : REPLACE ~ vi : to become full : fill up again — re·plen·ish·able \-ə-bəl\ adj — re·plen·ish·er n — re·plen·ish·ment \-ish-mənt\ n

re·plete \ri-ˈplēt\ adj [ME, fr. MF & L: MF replet, fr. L repletus, pp. of replēre to fill up, fr. re- + plēre to fill — more at FULL] (14c) **1** : fully or abundantly provided or filled ⟨a book ~ with . . . delicious details —William Safire⟩ **2 a** : abundantly fed **b** : FAT, STOUT **3** : COMPLETE syn see FULL — re·plete·ness n

re·ple·tion \ri-ˈplē-shən\ n (14c) **1** : the act of eating to excess : the state of being fed to excess : SURFEIT **2** : the condition of being filled up or overcrowded **3** : fulfillment of a need or desire : SATISFACTION

¹re·plev·in \ri-ˈplev-ən\ n [ME, fr. AF replevine, fr. replevir to give security, fr. OF, fr. re- + plevir to pledge, fr. (assumed) LL plebere] (15c) **1** : the recovery by a person of goods or chattels claimed to be wrongfully taken or detained upon the person's giving security to try the matter in court and return the goods if defeated in the action **2** : the writ or the common-law action whereby goods and chattels are replevied

²replevin vt (1678) : REPLEVY

¹re·plevy \ri-ˈplev-ē\ n, pl re·plev·ies [ME, fr. AF replevir, v.] (15c) : REPLEVIN

²replevy vt re·plev·ied; re·plev·ing (1596) : to take or get back by a writ for replevin — re·plevi·able \-ē-ə-bəl\ adj

rep·li·ca \ˈrep-li-kə\ n [It. repetition, fr. replicare to repeat, fr. LL, fr. L, to fold back — more at REPLY] (1852) **1** : a close reproduction or facsimile esp. by the maker of the original **2** : COPY, DUPLICATE syn see REPRODUCTION

rep·li·case \ˈrep-li-ˌkās, -ˌkāz\ n [replication + -ase] (1963) : a polymerase that promotes synthesis of a particular RNA in the presence of a template of RNA

¹rep·li·cate \ˈrep-lə-ˌkāt\ vb -cat·ed; -cat·ing [LL replicatus, pp. of replicare] vt (1607) : DUPLICATE, REPEAT ⟨~ a statistical experiment⟩ ~ vi : to undergo replication : produce a replica of itself ⟨virus particles replicating in cells⟩

²replicate \-li-kət\ adj (1922) : MANIFOLD, REPEATED

³rep·li·cate \-li-kət\ n (1929) : one of several identical experiments, procedures, or samples

rep·li·ca·tion \ˌrep-lə-ˈkā-shən\ n (14c) **1 a** : ANSWER, REPLY **b** (1) : an answer to a reply : REJOINDER (2) : a plaintiff's reply to a defendant's plea, answer, or counterclaim **2** : ECHO, REVERBERATION **3 a** : COPY, REPRODUCTION **b** : the action or process of reproducing **4** : performance of an experiment or procedure more than once; esp : systematic or random repetition of agricultural test rows or plats to reduce error

rep·li·ca·tive \ˈrep-li-ˌkāt-iv\ adj (ca. 1890) : of, relating to, involved in, or characterized by replication ⟨the ~ form of tobacco mosaic virus⟩

rep·li·con \ˈrep-li-ˌkän\ n [replicate + ²-on] (1963) : a linear or circular section of DNA or RNA which replicates sequentially as a unit

¹re·ply \ri-ˈplī\ vb re·plied; re·ply·ing [ME replien, fr. MF replier to fold again, fr. L replicare to fold back, fr. re- + plicare to fold — more at PLY] vi (14c) **1 a** : to respond in words or writing **b** : ECHO, RESOUND **c** : to make a legal replication **2** : to do something in response; specif : to return gunfire or an attack ~ vt : to give as an answer syn see ANSWER — re·pli·er \-ˈplī(-ə)r\ n

²reply n, pl replies (1560) **1** : something said, written, or done in answer or response **2** : REPLICATION 1b(2)

re·po \ˈrē-ˌpō\ n, pl repos [by shortening & alter.] (1963) : REPURCHASE AGREEMENT

re·po·lar·iza·tion \ˌrē-ˌpō-lə-rə-ˈzā-shən\ n (1958) : polarization of a muscle fiber, cell, or membrane following depolarization — re·po·lar·ize \(ˈ)rē-ˈpō-lə-ˌrīz\ vb

¹re·port \ri-ˈpōrt, -ˈpȯrt\ n [ME, fr. MF, fr. OF, fr. reporter to report, fr. L reportare, fr. re- + portare to carry — more at FARE] (14c) **1 a** : common talk or an account spread by common talk : RUMOR **b** : quality of reputation ⟨a witness of good ~⟩ **2 a** : a usu. detailed . . . or statement ⟨a news ~⟩ **b** : an account or summary of a judicial opinion or decision **c** : a usu. formal record of the proceedings of a meeting or session **3** : an explosive noise — on report : subject to disciplinary action

²report vt (14c) **1 a** : to give an account of : RELATE **b** : to describe as being in a specified state ⟨~ed him much improved⟩ **2 a** : to serve as carrier of (a message) **b** : to relate the words or sense of (something said) **c** : to make a written record or summary of **d** (1) : to watch for and write about the newsworthy aspects or developments of : COVER (2) : to prepare or present an account of for broadcast **3 a** (1) : to give a formal or official account or statement of ⟨the treasurer ~ed a balance of ten dollars⟩ (2) : to return or present (a matter referred for consideration) with conclusions or recommendations **b** : to announce or relate as the result of investigation ⟨~ed no sign of disease⟩ **c** : to announce the presence, arrival, or sighting of **d** : to make known to the proper authorities ⟨~ a fire⟩ **e** : to make a charge of misconduct against ~ vi **1 a** : to give an account : TELL **b** : to present oneself **c** : to account for oneself ⟨~ed sick on Friday⟩ **2** : to

\ə\ abut \ˌ, ˌ\ kitten, F table \ər\ further \a\ ash \ā\ ace \ä\ cot, cart \au̇\ out \ch\ chin \e\ bet \ē\ easy \g\ go \i\ hit \ī\ ice \j\ job \ŋ\ sing \ō\ go \ȯ\ law \ȯi\ boy \th\ thin \t̶h\ the \ü\ loot \u̇\ foot \y\ yet \zh\ vision \à, ᵏ, ⁿ, œ, œ̄, ᵫ, ᵫ̄, ᵜ\ see Guide to Pronunciation

the irregular forms. (By permission. From *Webster's Ninth New Collegiate Dictionary,* © 1991 by Merriam-Webster Inc., publisher of the Merriam-Webster ® dictionaries.)

Following the Pronunciation Guide   As we have said, not all dictionaries agree on preferred pronunciations. Since the standard of English pronunciation is based on the usage that prevails among educated people, this collective usage is hard to measure. When a word has more than one pronunciation, the "preferred" pronunciation is generally the first one listed. In one dictionary you may find two pronunciations for *lever:* 'lev- ər, 'lē-vər. In another you may find the opposite arrangement. Thus it is essential that you know how your dictionary denotes pronunciation.

Each dictionary offers a pronunciation guide that explains the use of stress marks (') (,) for accented syllables and the meaning of the vowel and consonant symbols that stand for all the sounds in our language. This pronunciation guide usually appears at the front of the dictionary. To help users quickly find the meanings of these symbols, most dictionaries offer a short list of the most frequently used symbols at the bottom of every two-page spread:

> \ə\ **a**b**u**t \ᵊ \ kitt**e**n, F table \ər\ f**ur**th**er** \a\ **a**sh \ā\ **a**ce \ä\ c**o**t, c**a**rt \au̇\ **ou**t
> \ch\ **ch**in \e\ b**e**t \ē\ **ea**sy \g\ **g**o \i\ h**i**t \ī\ **i**ce \j\ **j**ob \n\ si**ng** \ō\ g**o** \ȯ\ l**aw**
> \ȯi\ b**oy** \th\ **th**in \t̲h̲\ **th**e \ü\ l**oo**t \u̇\ f**oo**t \y\ **y**et \zh\ vi**s**ion \ə, k̲, ", œ, œ̄,
> ue, ūe, ʸ\ *see* Guide to Pronunciation

Assume that you want to know how to pronounce the noun *datum.* Is the *a* long (as in *ace, ape, cape*), or is it short (as in *cap, at, happy*)? By referring to the mark above the vowel and then checking the handy guide at the bottom of the page, you would find that the *a* has the sound of the long *a,* as in *ace.*

Understanding the Explanatory Notes   To save you time and to promote accuracy, study the explanatory notes before you use your dictionary. These notes explain the different typefaces and labels, the significant symbols and punctuation, and the other means by which a dictionary can achieve compactness. Take just one example, that of word division.

Suppose you want to know if the noun *goodwill* is one word, two words, or a hyphenated word. When you look it up, you see *good·will.* The explanatory notes tell you that a centered period denotes a syllable break only; therefore, *goodwill* is one word. If you looked up the adjective *self-addressed,* you would find *self-ad·dressed.* This word, then, is hyphenated after *self* and syllabicated after the hyphen and after *ad.*

Knowing the Abbreviations and Symbols   So much information must be packed into a dictionary that abbreviations and symbols frequently are necessary. To get full use of your dictionary, you should read and know where to find the explanations of these abbreviations and symbols. For example, you need to know that *obs* stands for *obsolete,* which means that the word or the meaning listed is no longer in current usage. Knowing the abbreviations for the parts of speech—*n., v., adj., adv.,* and so on—may save you from making embarrassing errors when you speak and write.

Although you need not memorize all the abbreviations, you should learn those most commonly used. You should also know where to find the meanings of those used less often.

Finding Synonyms   Your writing will be more interesting if you use a variety of words. Using synonyms can make your writing more varied.

A synonym is a word that has the same or nearly the same meaning as another word. Although a dictionary is not primarily a book of synonyms (like a synonym dictionary or a thesaurus), it does offer synonyms for some words. Therefore, when you have a synonym problem, you ordinarily reach first for that good old reliable reference, the dictionary. Suppose you are writing a memo recommending a "new plan." Since you have already used the word *new* twice, you don't want to use it a third time. Looking in a dictionary, you might find these four substitutes listed: *novel, modern, original, fresh.* For a more detailed list of synonyms, see a thesaurus or a synonym dictionary.

THE THESAURUS

A thesaurus is a collection of words and phrases arranged according to ideas. The function that it serves is different from that of a dictionary. A dictionary gives the meaning of the word that one has in mind. A thesaurus enables one to find the best word with which to express an idea one has in mind.

In other words, a thesaurus goes one step further than a dictionary. In using the dictionary or a book of synonyms, you must have at least one word in mind; in using a thesaurus, you can start with a general idea from which comes one word that will start you on the hunt for the exact word you need.

Suppose, for example, that you want to change your job and job location. You know very little about the area to which you want to move. To find out what businesses are there, you decide to write to the local chamber of commerce. When writing the letter, you find that you are using the word *employment* so often that your language sounds repetitious. So you turn to a thesaurus for help.

A thesaurus usually gives three types of information about a word: its part of speech, its definition(s), and its synonyms. Sometimes it will even give you an example of how the word is used in a phrase or sentence. When you look up the noun *employment* in a thesaurus, you will find something like this:

---

employment   *noun*
1. The act of employing for wages: *investigated the company's methods of employment.*
2. The act of putting into play.
3. The condition of being put to use.
4. A specific use.
5. The state of being employed: *No person in our employment will betray trade secrets.*
6. Activity pursued as a livelihood.

1. *Syns:* engagement, engaging, hire, hiring.
2. EXERCISE *noun.*
3. DUTY.
4. APPLICATION.
5. *Syns:* employ, hire.
6. BUSINESS.

You can readily see that definition 1 and its synonyms are helpful. Using *engaging* or *hiring* at times instead of *employment* in your letter is an improvement in style. However, you would like to have even more words to use than *employment* and its synonyms, and you would like to use the word in a slightly different context. Therefore, you look up the word *job* in a thesaurus, and you find something like this:

---

job   *noun*
1. Activity pursued as a livelihood.
2. A post of employment.
3. The proper activity of a person or thing.
4. A piece of work that has been assigned.
5. A difficult or tedious undertaking.

1. BUSINESS.
2. POSITION *noun.*
3. FUNCTION *noun.*
4. TASK *noun.*
5. TASK *noun.*

Now you have several more words that you can use to help your letter sound less repetitive and boring. You can use *business*, *position*, *function*, and/or *task* as well as *job*.

(Thesaurus entries on pages 47 and 48 by permission. From *Roget's II: The Thesaurus,* © 1988 by Houghton Mifflin Company, Boston, Massachusetts.)

OTHER REFERENCES

Biographical and Geographical Names   Suppose you need some information about a famous person. For example, perhaps you heard the name Thomas Edison and want to know more about him. For fast identification you might check the Biographical Names section of your dictionary. Here you might find the following under *Edison:* "**Edison** \'ed-ə-sən \ Thomas Alva 1847–1931 Am. inventor." You would be able to find more information under *Edison* in an encyclopedia or by consulting a source such as *Webster's Biographical Dictionary* (Merriam-Webster Inc., Springfield, Massachusetts).

Have you ever been confused about the pronunciation of a foreign location? Suppose you wish to make travel arrangements to Montreal and Beauport, Canada, and you do not know how to pronounce *Beauport*. Checking the Geographical Names section of your dictionary or a source such as *Webster's New Geographical Dictionary* (Merriam-Webster Inc., Springfield, Massachusetts), you would learn that Beauport, pronounced 'bō-pərt, is a city in southern Quebec; it has a population of 60,447.

Abbreviations and Acronyms   Commonly used abbreviations such as *COD* (cash on delivery) and *CPU* (central processing unit) are usually listed in standard desk dictionaries. To find the meaning of abbreviations that are not listed in your dictionary, refer to a reference such as *Abbreviations Dictionary* (American Elsevier Publishing Co., Inc., New York).

LIVING LANGUAGE

Knowledge is of two kinds. We know a subject ourselves, or we know where we can find information upon it.

—Samuel Johnson
(1709–1784)

An *acronym* is a word formed from the initial letter (or letters) of other words. *Radar* is an acronym derived from the words "*ra*dio *de*tecting *a*nd *rang*ing"; *sitcom* is formed from "*sit*uation *com*edy." To find the meaning of an acronym, see a reference such as *Acronyms, Initialisms, and Abbreviations Dictionary* (Gale Research Company, Detroit, Michigan).

Foreign Words and Phrases

Foreign terms often become popular in our language. For example, we may see the words *par avion* on some international mail. To understand what these words signify, we need to know that *par avion* means "by airplane"—that is, *airmail.* To find the meaning of a foreign term that is not listed in your dictionary, you should use a reference such as *The Dictionary of Foreign Phrases and Abbreviations* (Wilson Publishing Co., New York).

Style Manuals

Everyone who writes or prepares written documents will periodically require a style manual to answer the common (and uncommon) questions that arise in ordinary written communications. Should you use a period at the end of a polite request, or should you use a question mark? When do you express numbers in word form? in figures? Where do you place the return address in a personal business letter? The answers to these and many more questions can be found in a good style manual.

Among the style manuals available today are *The Gregg Reference Manual* (Glencoe, Macmillan/McGraw-Hill, Columbus, Ohio), *HOW: A Handbook for Office Workers* (Wadsworth Publishing Company, Belmont, California), and *Reference Manual for the Office* (South-Western Publishing Company, Cincinnati).

Word Division Manuals

Everyone who writes or prepares written documents will also find useful a word division manual. To pinpoint quickly the spelling of a word or its proper syllabication for line-ending division, simply locate the word among the alphabetical listing of words in this manual. Include among the references you use a good word division manual such as *20,000+ Words Spelled and Divided for Quick Reference* (Glencoe, Macmillan/McGraw-Hill, Columbus, Ohio) or *Webster's Instant Word Guide* (Merriam-Webster Inc., Springfield, Massachusetts).

COMMUNICATION LABORATORY

APPLICATION EXERCISES

A. Do you really know the exact order of the letters of the alphabet? Locate the 15 words, in your dictionary, listed at the top of page 50, taking each one in the sequence shown. Note the exact time you start your search for the words and the exact time you finish.

CONTINUED

1. computation	**6.** fiscal	**11.** consolidate
2. expenditure	**7.** executive	**12.** submission
3. envelope	**8.** writ	**13.** insurance
4. amendment	**9.** clause	**14.** courteous
5. truly	**10.** computer	**15.** monitor

How many minutes did you take? If you took more than five minutes, you should practice the alphabetic sequence.

B. Now write the words listed in Exercise A in alphabetic order, without consulting a dictionary.

C. Words 1 through 18 are found on consecutive pages of a dictionary. Without using a dictionary, write them in alphabetic order. Note your starting and finishing times. How long did it take?

1. manufacture	**7.** marmalade	**13.** margarine
2. maple	**8.** marigold	**14.** mantel
3. market	**9.** marriage	**15.** marrow
4. manual	**10.** mankind	**16.** maroon
5. manor	**11.** mariner	**17.** marry
6. masonry	**12.** manner	**18.** maritime

D. Several of the following words are misspelled, and a few are spelled correctly. Rewrite the misspelled words as they should be spelled.

1. accamadate	**5.** servise	**8.** prefered
2. receive	**6.** message	**9.** cieling
3. ninety	**7.** libary	**10.** communication
4. truely		

E. The following words were used in this unit. If you are not already familiar with them, try to guess their meaning from the context of the sentences in which they are used. Then check your guesses in the dictionary.

1. accomplished	**3.** superlative	**5.** function
2. standard	**4.** significant	**6.** repetitious

F. Here are ten common words. You should know how to break them into syllables. Without consulting your dictionary, show all syllable divisions for each word. In words of more than one syllable, place a primary stress mark (') *before* the accented syllable. Check your decisions in the dictionary.

1. reference	**5.** primary	**8.** desirable
2. impossible	**6.** insurance	**9.** table
3. service	**7.** contract	**10.** frequent
4. opportune		

SECTION 3.2

LEARNING THE CORRECT SPELLING AND CHOOSING THE RIGHT WORD

One of the keys to successful communication is correct spelling. In writing, a misspelled word can detract the reader from the content of the message and cause misunderstanding. Incorrect spelling may also cause embarrassment because it lowers the writer's image in the reader's mind. Proper spelling, therefore, is basic to effective communication.

To become a good speller, you should be able to spell automatically those words used frequently by persons in the work world. You should also know the basic spelling rules commonly used in our language as well as the common spellings of word beginnings and commonly used secondary sounds. You can then use your dictionary effectively to locate the spellings of words that you do not know or that you doubt.

Finally, you should be able to distinguish between those words that are commonly confused because they sound alike or look alike but have different spellings and different meanings. Words such as *principal* and *principle, personal* and *personnel,* and *affect* and *effect* are examples of easily confused word pairs that should be distinguished by the effective communicator.

In this unit you will learn techniques for improving your spelling and using commonly confused words properly. Improvement in these two areas can make you a more effective, more efficient writer both in your school work now and in your work performance as you build your career.

MASTERY OF A "BASIC 200"

Even if most commonly used words do not cause you any spelling difficulties, a few tricky ones may. Many of the words in the following list are so frequently used in everyday writing that you should learn their spelling for your minimum spelling vocabulary. This list provides a starting point for your mastery of commonly used and misspelled words.

WORDS COMMONLY MISSPELLED

absence	acquaintance	analysis	assessment
abundant	acquisition	analyze	assistance
accessible	administrative	apologize	attendance
accidentally	advantageous	applicable	attorney
accommodate	advertise	appropriate	average
achievement	advisable	approximate	bankruptcy
acknowledgment	aggressive	argument	beginner

WORDS COMMONLY MISSPELLED (continued)

believe	equipment	neighbor	résumé
beneficiary	equipped	neither	schedule
benefited	especially	nineteen	separate
bought	essential	ninety	sergeant
boundary	exaggerate	ninth	similar
brochure	excellent	noticeable	sincerely
brought	executive	objective	strength
budget	existence	occasion	subpoena
bulletin	extraordinary	occasionally	succeed
business	facsimile	occur	successive
calendar	familiar	occurrence	sufficient
campaign	feasible	offered	superintendent
canceled	financial	omission	supersede
cannot	fiscal	opinion	supervisor
cashier	foreign	original	survey
catalog	forfeit	paid	technique
ceiling	forty	pamphlet	technology
column	fourth	parallel	tenant
commission	freight	particularly	thorough
committee	government	permanent	through
competitive	grammar	persistent	transferred
conceive	grateful	persuade	truly
confidential	guarantee	pertinent	usable
conscientious	handicapped	physician	vendor
conscious	harass	possession	volume
continuous	height	precede	yield
convenience	illegal	precedent	
coordinator	immediately	preferred	
correspondence	implement	preliminary	
courteous	importance	privilege	
deceive	initial	procedure	
decision	irrelevant	proceed	
defendant	itinerary	professor	
defense	judgment	programmed	
definite	knowledge	quantity	
dependent	laboratory	questionnaire	
describe	leisure	receipt	
desirable	liability	receiving	
development	library	recipient	
difference	license	recognize	
dilemma	lieutenant	recommend	
disappoint	likelihood	reference	
efficient	maintenance	relevant	
either	manageable	representative	
eligible	material	requirement	
embarrass	mileage	resistance	
emphasize	miscellaneous	responsibility	
employee	mortgage	restaurant	
environment	necessary	resume	

EDITING PRACTICE 1

Use your editing skill to complete this exercise. In each of the following sentences, select the correct spelling of the words shown in parentheses.

1. Will you mail this (questionaire, questionnaire) to all our clients?
2. I haven't had (occasion, ocassion) to observe your leadership abilities.
3. Two employees have (offerred, offered) to work overtime to complete the inventory.
4. The hotel is too small to (accomodate, accommodate) that convention.
5. Please make another appointment at your (convenience, convience).
6. Is there much (likelihood, likelyhood) that you will be transferred to the new branch office?
7. This new design is quite (similar, similiar) to our Model 13A camcorder.
8. We have not yet received a (definate, definite) commitment from the applicant selected for the position.

THREE KEY SPELLING RULES

Many spelling rules can help you improve your spelling. Only three rules are discussed in this unit because they are the ones that can be applied most consistently. These three basic rules do have some exceptions, but they are few, as you will see. Whenever you doubt the spelling of any of these words, be sure to consult a dictionary.

***IE* or *EI*?**   Generally speaking, use the *ie* combination to represent the sound of long *e* (the sound in *meet*).

ch*ie*f	y*ie*ld	p*ie*ce
f*ie*ld	n*ie*ce	gr*ie*f
bel*ie*ve	th*ie*f	p*ie*rce

EXCEPTIONS: either, neither, weird, seize, leisure.

After *c*, however, use the *ei* combination.

rec*ei*ve	conc*ei*t	dec*ei*t
c*ei*ling	rec*ei*pt	dec*ei*ve

EXCEPTION: financier

The *ei* is also used when the combination is sounded like long *a* (the sound in *may*).

w*ei*gh	fr*ei*ght	v*ei*n
n*ei*ghbor	th*ei*r	h*ei*r
v*ei*l	sl*ei*gh	*ei*ght

EDITING PRACTICE 2

Use *ie* or *ei* to complete the correct spelling of the words in the following sentences.

1. Did you get the rec___pt for the repair work?
2. We did not w___gh the package before mailing it.
3. Mr. Jones is our n___ghbor on the left.
4. I cannot bel___ve you are correct.
5. How much did your stock y___ld?
6. N___ther he nor she is correct.
7. What f___ld of work are you in?
8. Do not try to dec___ve the owner of the business.

Double the Final Consonant

When adding an ending to a one-syllable word ending in a consonant, double the final consonant if it is *preceded* and *followed* by a single vowel.

ship + ed	shipped	ban + ed	banned
bag + age	baggage	trim + est	trimmest
plan + ing	planning	wrap + er	wrapper

EXCEPTION: The final consonant of a word ending in *x* or *w* is not doubled.

| tax + ed | taxed | saw + ing | sawing |
| wax + ing | waxing | bow + ed | bowed |

Drop the *E* or Keep the *E*?

Words that end in silent *e* usually drop the *e* before an ending that begins with a vowel (such as *able* or *ing*).

desire + able	desirable	use + ag	usage
decorate + or	decorator	advise + ing	advising
enclose + ure	enclosure		

EXCEPTIONS:

shoe + ing	shoeing	acre + age	acreage
mile + age	mileage	eye + ing	eyeing
dye + ing	dyeing		

When adding an ending that begins with a consonant (such as *ful* or *ment*), retain the silent *e*.

entire + ty	entirety	cease + less	ceaseless
use + ful	useful	bare + ly	barely
state + ment	statement	tire + less	tireless
gentle + ness	gentleness	absolute + ly	absolutely

EXCEPTIONS:

wise + dom	wisdom	acknowledge + ment	acknowledgment
whole + ly	wholly	judge + ment	judgment

EDITING PRACTICE 3

Select the correct spelling of the words shown in parentheses.

1. His (judgement, judgment) is usually correct.
2. Such an investment would not be (adviseable, advisable) now.
3. Is the work (absolutely, absolutly) necessary at this time?
4. Jean was (holely, wholely, wholly) correct in this matter.
5. I will be (adviseing, advising) you regarding your investment.

SPELLINGS OF COMMON SOUNDS

All the words that may cause you spelling difficulties are listed in your dictionary. Even though these words are included in the dictionary, they may not be found easily because many sounds have a variety of spellings. Thus the writer who is not familiar with these spellings will not know where to look in the dictionary.

By learning the various spellings for commonly used word sounds, you can become a better speller. Your dictionary will become a more valuable tool to help you locate the correct spelling of all the words you use. This section focuses on the spellings of commonly used word sounds that appear at the beginning or in the middle of words.

Double Letters   Sometimes certain consonant sounds are expressed with single letters; other times these same sounds are expressed with double letters. In looking up words in your dictionary, remember that a consonant sound may be expressed with either a single letter or a double one. Study the following examples:

SINGLE CONSONANT	DOUBLE CONSONANT
apologize	appoint
inoculate	innocent
imitate	immediate
elate	ellipsis
acoustic	accordion
operation	opposite
melody	mellow
galoshes	gallon
deference	deferred

Vowel Variations   Words are often misspelled because they are mispronounced. Word beginnings that have identical consonant sounds but different vowel sounds fall into this category. When trying to locate such words in the dictionary, keep in mind the possibility that the word may be spelled with a vowel other than the one you have in mind. Notice, for example, the similarity within the following groups.

des	des/cription	mon	mon/ey
dis	dis/tribute	mun	mun/dane
fer	fer/ocious	per	per/suade
for	for/eign	pur	pur/sue
fur	fur/lough	pre	pre/cision
def	def/inite	in	in/sure
dif	dif/ferent	en	en/large
dev	dev/astate	un	un/pleasant
div	div/idend	im	im/prove
men	men/ace	em	em/ploy
min	min/eral		

EDITING PRACTICE 4

Select the correct spelling of the words shown in parentheses. Use your dictionary, if necessary, to locate the correct spelling.

1. We recently established an (indowment, endowment) fund in his name.
2. This site is more (desirable, desireable, disireable) for us.
3. What is your legal (oppinion, opinion) regarding this case?
4. Is your decision based on (realty, reality) or supposition?
5. We intend to (persue, pursue) this matter to its limit.
6. I was (devastated, devestated) by the sad news.
7. I am not allowed to (devulge, divulge) that kind of information.

Common Beginning Sounds

To locate words in the dictionary, you must know the different possible spellings for the common sounds used at the beginning of words—that is, the most common first and second sounds. See the following list of these sounds and their spellings.

SOUND	SPELLINGS	SOUND	SPELLINGS
a	a (about)		
	ai (plaid)	ä	a (father)
	au (laugh)		eau (bureaucracy)
	ea (heart)		o (obligation)
ā	a (able)		
	ai (ailment)	ak	ac (acrobat)
	au (gauge)		acc (acclaim)
	ea (break)		ack (acknowledge)
	ei (neighbor)		acq (acquire)
	eigh (sleigh)		aq (aqueduct)

SOUND	SPELLINGS	SOUND	SPELLINGS	SOUND	SPELLINGS
ār	ar (*area*) aer (*aerial*) air (*air*port)	i	e (*e*nlist) i (*i*diom) ie (s*ie*ve) y (m*y*stery)	o͞o	o (rem*o*ve) oo (f*oo*lish) ou (s*ou*l) ough (thr*ough*) u (r*u*le) ue (bl*ue*) ui (fr*ui*t)
as	as (*as*bestos) asc (*asc*end) ass (*ass*embly)	ī	ai (*ai*sle) eigh (sl*eigh*t) i (*i*dentical) ie (l*ie*) igh (fl*igh*t) y (h*y*peractive)		
aw	aw (*aw*kward) au (*au*dience) augh (t*augh*t) ough (th*ough*t)			ow	ou (pron*ou*nce) ough (b*ough*) ow (br*ow*se)
e	ae (*ae*sthetic) e (*e*stimate) ea (br*ea*kfast) ei (h*ei*fer) eo (l*eo*pard) ie (fr*ie*nd)	j	dg (bu*dg*et) g (de*g*enerate) gg (exa*gg*erate) j (in*j*ure)	r	r (*r*elaxation) rh (*rh*etoric) wr (*wr*inkle)
		k	c (*c*riminal) cc (o*cc*ur) ch (*ch*emistry) k (*k*imono) q (li*q*uidation)	s	c (*c*ivil) ps (*ps*ychology) s (*s*table) sc (*sc*enic) ss (pe*ss*imist)
ē	ae (*ae*on) e (*e*gotist) ee (st*ee*l) ei (perc*ei*ve) eo (p*eo*ple) i (mach*i*ne) ie (rel*ie*ve)	m	lm (ca*lm*) m (*m*edicine)	sh	ch (ma*ch*ine) ci (spe*ci*al) s (*s*ure) sc (con*sc*ious) sch (*sch*illing) se (nau*se*ous) sh (*sh*ampoo) si (ten*si*on) ss (i*ss*ue) ti (par*ti*al)
er	ar (li*ar*) ear (*ear*nest) er (*er*osion) err (*err*oneous) ir (*ir*ksome) or (w*or*thless) our (j*our*nal) ur (*ur*gency)	n	gn (*gn*arled) kn (*kn*itwear) mn (*mn*emonic) n (*n*atural) pn (*pn*eumonic)		
		o	o (*o*rdinary) oa (b*oa*rd)	t	pt (*pt*omaine) t (*t*arnish)
f	f (*f*easible) ff (e*ff*ective) gh (lau*gh*ter) ph (*ph*otograph)	ō	eau (b*eau*) o (n*o*table) oa (thr*oa*t) oe (t*oe*) ou (s*ou*l) ough (th*ough*) ow (kn*ow*)	u	u (*u*pper)
				u	eau (b*eau*tiful) eu (f*eu*d) ew (p*ew*ter) u (*u*seful) ue (c*ue*) yu (*yu*le)
g	g (*g*rievance) gh (*gh*etto) gu (*gu*arantee)	oi, oy	oi (f*oi*l) oy (envo*y*)		
h	h (*h*oliday) wh (*wh*olesale)	o͞o	eu (man*eu*ver) ew (thr*ew*) ieu (ad*ieu*)	w	o (ch*oi*r) u (q*u*artile) w (*w*edding) wh (*wh*arf)

EDITING PRACTICE 5

Use the preceding chart to find the various spellings for the sounds in parentheses. Then find the correct spelling in your dictionary and rewrite each word.

1. Do you enjoy your study of (s)(i)chology?
2. I took the gift in l(oo) of cash.
3. I prefer a natural spray over the (ar)osol can.
4. That was a strange man(oo)ver on his part.
5. I walked up the (i)sle briskly.
6. Helga (ak)(w)ired her accent in Norway.
7. She is a very con(sh)ien(sh)ous employee.
8. I always buy (n)eumatic tires.
9. I asked the butcher to w(a) the ham.
10. There was a great deal of ten(shun) in the office.

WORDS COMMONLY CONFUSED

The spellings or meanings of the following combinations of words are commonly confused. Study these words carefully. Be sure to look up the pronunciation of any word that is unfamiliar.

accede (*v.*) To comply with. "We must *accede* to this customer's request."
exceed (*v.*) To surpass. "Our sales this quarter will *exceed* our projections."

accent (*n.*) A stress in speaking or writing. "Where is the *accent* in the word *profit?*" (*v.*) To stress; emphasize. "The manager's remarks *accented* the need to control expenses."
ascent (*n.*) A rising or climbing. "Her *ascent* in the department was swift because of her qualifications."
assent (*n.*) Agreement. "The customer's written *assent* is necessary before we can charge an account." (*v.*) To agree. "Did Ms. Mendoza *assent* to your request?"

accept (*v.*) To approve; receive with favor. "We *accept* your decision."
except (*prep.*) Other than. "All employees must work this Saturday *except* those with over ten years of service." (*v.*) To exclude. "We can *except* no one from the need to arrive at work on time."
expect (*v.*) To look forward to. "I *expect* our sales to increase soon."

advice (*n.;* rhymes with *ice*) A recommendation regarding a course of conduct. "Mr. Sims' *advice* will help your career."
advise (*v.;* rhymes with *skies*) To counsel. "What do you *advise* me to do about this overdue account?"

affect (*v.*) To influence. "How will the new procedures *affect* our budget?" (*v.*) To pretend. "He *affects* busyness and overwork."
effect (*v.*) To bring about. "We expect this new computerized system to *effect* an upturn in our business." (*n.*) A result. "What *effect* has the new word processing program had upon efficiency?"

all ready (*adj.*) Prepared. "The reports are *all ready* for the meeting."
already (*adv.*) By this time. "I have *already* met my quota."

altar (*n.*) Table used in worship. "The *altar* dominated the cathedral."
alter (*v.*) To change. "If we *alter* the schedule, our customers will be glad."

assistance (*n.*) Support. "Do you need *assistance* with the payroll?"
assistants (*n. pl.*) Those who help. "Our company president has three *assistants.*"

bare (*adj.*) Uncovered. "This report looks *bare* without graphs and charts."
bear (*v.*) Carry. "She *bears* the responsibility for the entire department."
bear (*n.*) Large mammal. "The *bear* wandered freely in a protected part of the park."

billed (*adj.*) Charged. "She *billed* the company $22 an hour."
build (*v.*) To construct. "Mark will *build* near his farm."

board (*n.*) A piece of wood; an organized group; meals. "The *board* meets tomorrow."
bored (*adj.*) Penetrated; weary; uninterested. "The participants seemed *bored.*"

capital (*adj.*) Chief; principal. "Carson City is the *capital* city of Nevada."
(*n.*) The value of accumulated goods. "We used all our *capital* to start this company."
capitol (*n.*) The building in which a legislature meets; capitalized when it refers to the building in which the U.S. Congress meets. "Industry representatives will testify in the *Capitol* on August 4."

chews (*v.*) Masticates. "I noticed that our dog *chews* his food very well."
choose (*v.*) To select; to prefer. "We must *choose* a word processing program that will serve our needs."
chose (*v.; past tense of choose; chōz*) Selected. "You *chose* the best program."

cite (*v.*) To quote; to refer to. "She *cited* our poor delivery record."
site (*n.*) A location. "This is the new *site* for our company headquarters."
sight (*n.*) Vision. "Jane's well-kept ledgers are a *sight* to see." (*v.*) To see. "If all goes well, we will *sight* land tomorrow morning."

close (*v.; klōz*) To shut. "The office will *close* at noon tomorrow." (*n.*) The end. "We balance all accounts at the *close* of the business day."
close (*adj.; klōs*) Stuffy. "The air in this room is *close.*" (*adj.*) Tight. "It will be a *close* fit, but the copy machine will go in that corner." (*adv.*) Near. "The water cooler is too *close* to my office."
clothes (*n.*) Wearing apparel. "Appropriate *clothes* should be worn in an office."
cloths (*n.*) Fabrics. "Are there any more cleaning *cloths* in the supply room?"

commence (*v.*) To begin. "We shall *commence* contract negotiations today."
comments (*n. pl.*) Remarks. "Your *comments* on our marketing problems were very helpful." (*v.*) To mark distinctly. "My supervisor always *comments* on my performance."

complement (*n.*) Something that completes. "Without a full *complement* of workers, we can't handle that contract." (*v.*) To make whole. "The new employees *complement* our staff nicely."

compliment (*n.*) A flattering remark. "A *compliment* for a job well done is always welcome." (*v.*) To express approval. "A wise supervisor always *compliments* good workers."

correspondence (*n.*) Letters. "We answer all *correspondence* immediately."
correspondents (*n. pl.*) Persons conducting correspondence or commercial relations. "Each of our sales *correspondents* works for five representatives."

council (*n.*) An assembly that deliberates. "An advisory *council* sets industry guidelines."
counsel (*n.*) Advice. "The company's legal staff provides management with good *counsel*." (*v.*) To give advice, especially on important matters. "Our personnel department will *counsel* employees on career choices."
consul (*n.*) A government official who represents a nation in a foreign country. "If you need help in negotiating with companies in Germany, notify the American *consul* in Bonn."

defer (*v.*) To postpone. "May I *defer* my payment until next month?" To yield. "When it comes to a knowledge of procedures, I always *defer* to the experienced workers."
differ (*v.*) To disagree; to be unlike. "Successful salespeople often *differ* in their approach to a customer."

dense (*adj.*) Thick. "The *dense* smoke drove us from the building."
dents (*n. pl.*) Depressions in a surface. "This old file cabinet has a lot of *dents*."

dependence (*n.*) Reliance; trust. "The company's *dependence* on a single supplier frightened the purchasing department."
dependents (*n. pl.*) Persons who rely on others for support. "The amount of tax withheld from your check will depend on the number of *dependents*."

desert (*n.;* 'dez-ərt) Arid, barren land. "The new agricultural company hoped to make the *desert* bloom."
desert (*v.;* di-'zərt) To abandon. "This is a good financial plan, and we will not *desert* it." (*n.;* usually plural) Deserved reward or punishment. "He got his just *deserts* for being too greedy."
dessert (*n.*) A sweet course at the end of a meal. "We had chocolate cake for *dessert*."

die (*n.*) A tool for molding or shaping. "We will need new *dies* if we change the product design." One of a pair of dice. "One *die* is red." (*v.*) To cease living. "That tree will *die* unless it is fertilized."
dye (*n.*) A stain or color. "Will this *dye* run when it is washed?" (*v.*) To stain or color. "I *dyed* this coat last month."

formally (*adv.*) In a formal manner. "She has not *formally* accepted."
formerly (*adv.*) Previously. "He *formerly* worked for a competitor."

lead (*n.;* rhymes with *bed*) A heavy metal. "It took three people to lift that large *lead* pipe."
lead (*v.;* past *led*) To guide. "She will *lead* the company into new markets." To guide. "She will *lead* the company into new markets."

loose (*adj.*) Unfastened; not compact. "The *loose* parts will get all mixed up." (*v.*) To set free. "Don't let the dog *loose*."

lose (v.) To mislay; to fail to win. "Please don't *lose* that important report."

patients (n. pl.) Persons under medical care. "The physician examined the *patients* carefully."
patience (n.) The quality of enduring without complaint. "If you have *patience*, you can work with and for anyone."

personal (adj.) Belonging to a particular person. "Never leave your *personal* belongings on the top of your desk."
personnel (n.) Staff of people. "All our *personnel* know how to use a desktop computer.

precede (v.) To go before. "My name should *precede* Ms. Castella's in the company telephone directory."
proceed (v.) To advance. "After the meeting in Denver, we will *proceed* to the conference in Seattle."

precedence (n.) Priority in time or rank. "That rush project takes *precedence* over everything else."
precedents (n. pl.) Established rules; things done that may serve as examples for later actions. "There are several *precedents* to guide us in this kind of sales campaign."

principle (n.) General truth. "The basic *principle* of finance does not change." Rule of conduct. "His company has always been guided by the highest *principles*."
principal (adj.) Chief. "Electronic computers are the company's *principal* product." A chief person or thing. "She is one of the *principals* in the company." (n.) Money on which interest is paid or income received. "We can spend the interest, but we cannot touch the *principal*." One who hires another to act for him or her. "An agent has power to make contracts for a *principal*."

reality (n.) That which is real. "The *reality* is that certain skills are more in demand."
realty (n. and adj.) Real estate. "Our *realty* company is looking for a new office site for us."

residence (n.) A house; dwelling place. "Is your *residence* close to where you work?"
residents (n. pl.) Those living in a place. "The *residents* of the apartment started a bowling league."

right (adj.) Correct. "After weeks of searching, he found the *right* job." (n.) Privilege. "You have the *right* to find a better job."
rite (n.) Ceremony. "We observe the *rite* of opening each meeting with the Pledge of Allegiance."
write (v.) To inscribe. "Please *write* your account number on each check."

stationary (adj.) Fixed in position. "A *stationary* lamp gives better light."
stationery (n.) Writing paper and envelopes. "Our company *stationery* was redesigned last year."

superintendence (n.) Management. "We work directly under the *superintendence* of a district manager."
superintendents (n. pl.) Supervisors. "The *superintendents* of our company's power plants spoke at the energy conference."

COMMUNICATION LABORATORY

APPLICATION EXERCISES

A. On a separate sheet of paper, provide the correct spellings for the sounds shown in parentheses. Then rewrite each word.

1. Your premium notice reg(a)rding my car insurance arrived after the payment due date.
2. When may I expect to rec(e)ve the merchandise?
3. Your savings account will a(k)r(oo) compounded interest at the rate of 6 percent.
4. I am very gr(a)tful for your help in completing this tax form.
5. The X rays showed evidence of (n)umonia in the patient's lungs.
6. I am d(ow)tful that prices for our products will remain at this low level for very long.
7. Our new science fiction release centers around mar(sh)ian life.
8. Be sure to include the fr(a)t charges on the invoice.
9. How large is the mor(g)age on your home?
10. Ms. Cooper is pe(s)imistic about the potential of our new employee.
11. You will be reimbursed for the conference fees and automobile mil(e)ge.
12. How much of this payment has been a(p)lied to the principal of the loan?
13. The grand opening celebration of our Springfield store o(k)u(r)ed last weekend.
14. The bank auditors have held up authorization to proc(e)d with the sale.
15. We have received over ni(n)ty applications for this position.
16. Doing business with your firm has always been a privile(j)e.
17. Please send the a(j)enda of next month's meeting to all the participants.
18. The plaintiff e(gz)a(g)erated the extent of his injuries.
19. Financing for the (e)rban renewal project was approved yesterday.
20. We will begin using the telecommunications features of our new computer installation as soon as the technician installs our mod(u)m.

B. From the words shown in parentheses, select the correct word to complete the sentence. Write your answer on a separate sheet of paper.

1. May I suggest that you seek the (advice, advise) of an attorney.
2. Everyone (accept, except) John was in favor of the new schedule.
3. We have (all ready, already) notified our clients of our new telephone area code.
4. You may reduce your loan (principal, principle) more rapidly by increasing the amount of your monthly payment.
5. This award is a distinct (complement, compliment) to your ability.
6. Our manager has two (assistance, assistants) working in her office.
7. Only three of the walls in this office complex are (stationary, stationery).

CONTINUED

8. The (cite, site) for our new distribution center has not been selected.
9. How many (dependence, dependents) have you claimed on your with-holding tax form?
10. Please let me know which (desert, dessert) you wish to serve at the Tuesday evening banquet.
11. Most of the area (residence, residents) will oppose this tax increase.
12. Unless we (altar, alter) our course of action, we will face substantial losses this year.
13. Our company can no longer afford to (bare, bear) these losses.
14. Your sales for this month will probably (accede, exceed) everyone else's.
15. We hope our new president will (lead, led) the company out of its financial problems.
16. Mr. Lope is in charge of hiring new (personal, personnel).
17. Construction of our new building will (commence, comments) next month.
18. Recent increased costs will certainly (affect, effect) our pricing structure.
19. Our legal (council, counsel) has advised us to obtain more information before investing in the project.
20. Dr. King is highly respected for his (patience, patients) and understanding in working with young adults.

C. Correct all the spelling and word usage errors you find in the following paragraph.

We excepted the offer we recieved from the comittee at the meeting this mourning. We must, however, riquest a larger ammount for our next bujet. This increase is needed because we must perchase sevral new computors, at least two of which must have greater internal storage capacitys.

VOCABULARY AND SPELLING STUDIES

A. Some commonly used words may not be easily located in the dictionary because the spellings of their sounds do not follow usual spelling patterns. Look up in your dictionary the pronunciation and meaning of the following words:

1. quay
2. scenic
3. indictment
4. pneumatic
5. rendezvous
6. rhetoric

B. To each of the following, add the ending pronounced *shun*.

1. frustra___
2. collec___
3. conven___
4. politi___
5. coer___
6. provi___

CHAPTER 4

LANGUAGE SKILLS

More than ever before, people in all areas at all levels today must have effective skills in written communication. Employers are aware that an understanding of language structure provides an excellent basis for good writing, speaking, listening, and reading skills—skills that help businesses succeed.

This chapter will help you choose the correct words and put them together expressively and meaningfully. With these skills you can enhance your ability to communicate well and become an attractive job candidate to employers.

OBJECTIVES

Given a situation that requires polished grammar skills, your mastery of the sections in this chapter will enable you to do the following:

1. Construct complete sentences that will describe your ideas fully.

2. Use verbs correctly to give your writing the proper direction.

3. Use nouns and pronouns precisely, so that who *does* what *is* always clear.

4. Choose the correct verb form to agree with any noun or pronoun so that your sentences are always easy to understand.

5. Select exact descriptive words— adjectives and adverbs that will convey your thoughts.

6. Use conjunctions and prepositions to join words clearly and correctly.

SECTION 4.1

AN OVERVIEW OF GRAMMAR AND THE SENTENCE

If you have not already been exposed to a computer, you may not be familiar with words such as *monitor* or *cursor*. These words are mysterious to those who have not had the opportunity to use a computer. Those who have, however, know that a *monitor* is just another television screen and that a *cursor* is only a blinking light on that television screen.

The concepts behind this jargon are not mysterious or difficult. These words are difficult to understand *only if they are unfamiliar.*

Likewise, the principles of grammar and punctuation are not difficult to understand. Some grammatical terms, however, may be unfamiliar; others you may have heard of but may not fully understand. The best way to understand such jargon is simply to learn what the words mean—which, of course, is the goal of this introductory section.

THE PARTS OF SPEECH

The many thousands of different words that we use can be categorized into just eight groups — the *parts of speech.* The parts of speech are as follows:

1. nouns
2. pronouns
3. verbs
4. adjectives

5. adverbs
6. prepositions
7. conjunctions
8. interjections

Knowing the eight parts of speech will simplify your understanding of the rules of grammar and punctuation. Study the following pages carefully.

Nouns and Pronouns The names of people, places, and things are called **nouns.**

PEOPLE:	friend	Carol Murillo
	neighbor	Alice
	manager	Martin Duffy
PLACES:	city	Dallas
	store	Autoland
	mall	Sherwood Fashion Center

THINGS:	car	Honda
	television	Zenith
	bike	Schwinn

You can easily add hundreds of words to these lists because nouns are *very* commonly used. In fact, almost all sentences contain nouns.

Our *neighbor* bought a *car* at *Autoland*.

Her *friend* borrowed her *bike*.

Carol lives in *Dallas*.

Words that substitute for nouns are called pronouns.

SINGULAR	**PLURAL**	**SINGULAR**	**PLURAL**	**SINGULAR**	**PLURAL**
I	we	me	us	my	our
you	you	you	you	your	your
he		him		his	
she	they	her	them	her	their
it		it		its	

In the following sentences, note how pronouns are used to replace nouns.

Tracy went to the meeting with *Jeff*.

She went to the meeting with *him*.

Don and *Ellen* purchased the *property*.

They purchased *it*.

Mentally note that *pro* means "for," and you will be sure to remember that *pronouns* are substitutes *for nouns*.

Verbs

Verbs are often referred to as *action words* because verbs do, indeed, indicate the motion or the activity of a sentence.

Michelle *signed* the check.

Mr. Murphy *is interviewing* the applicants.

We *will be going* to Chicago next week.

Besides showing action, however, verbs also describe a condition or a state of being.

Wayne *is* tired.

Ms. Brown *has been* away on a business trip.

I *am* the assistant manager.

Verbs can be just a single word, or they can consist of several words.

Our company *has* a warehouse in Toledo.   (*Has* is the verb in this sentence.)

Grace *has been attending* class during her lunch hour.   (The verb is *has been attending*.)

Arthur *should have been* here for this meeting.   (The verb is *should have been*.)

Arthur *should have been asked* to attend this meeting.   (The verb is *should have been asked*.)

Verbs that consist of two or more words are known as **verb phrases.** They consist of a main verb plus one or more helping verbs that function together as one verb within a sentence. The main verb is always the last verb in the verb phrase.

Larry *has been revising* the old procedures manual.   (*Has been revising* is a verb phrase. The main verb in the phrase is *revising*; the helping verbs are *has* and *been*.)

We *should have gone* to the showing on Thursday.   (*Should have gone* is the verb phrase. *Gone* is the main verb, and *should* and *have* are the helping verbs.)

The report *will have been completed* by the time Ms. Simpson returns.   (The verb phrase is *will have been completed*. Which is the main verb? Which are the helping verbs?)

When words interrupt a verb phrase, the complete verb phrase may be confused.

Larry *has* already *been revising* the old procedures manual.   (The adverb *already* interrupts the verb phrase *has been revising*.)

The report *will* certainly *have been completed* by the time Ms. Simpson returns.   (The adverb *certainly* interrupts the verb phrase *will have been completed*.)

CLASS PRACTICE 1

In this section and in all the grammar, punctuation, and style sections, Class Practice and Editing Practice exercises are provided to help reinforce the principles you learn in each section.

To reinforce your skill in identifying nouns, pronouns, and verbs, label the underlined words in the following sentences—*N* for nouns, *P* for pronouns, and *V* for verbs. Use a separate sheet of paper.

1. The <u>representatives</u> at the conference <u>accepted</u> the proposal after <u>they</u> discussed it.
2. My two assistants <u>have been working</u> on an <u>outline</u> for the sales report <u>they</u> must submit next month.

3. As you know, <u>she</u> and <u>I</u> already <u>have sent</u> our applications to the <u>personnel manager</u>.
4. The <u>suggestion</u> <u>you</u> submitted <u>has been approved</u> by the <u>committee</u>.
5. <u>She</u> and <u>Andrew</u> <u>may go</u> to the meeting; if <u>they</u> decide to attend, I will call your <u>office</u>.

Now fill in a word for each blank (marked *a* and *b*) in the sentences below. Identify whether your choices are nouns, pronouns, or verbs.

6. Our __*a*__ obviously __*b*__ more money.
7. Please give __*a*__ a copy of the summary sheet that I __*b*__.
8. Frank __*a*__ extra copies of the __*b*__.
9. __*a*__ rewrote the entire __*b*__.
10. Only __*a*__ has returned the completed __*b*__.

Adjectives   **Adjectives** are words that modify, describe, or define nouns or pronouns. They tell *what kind, which one,* or *how many or much.* Notice how adjectives affect the description of nouns in the following sentences.

The *first* draft was a *wordy, boring* proposal.   (*First* tells which draft; *wordy* and *boring* tell what kind of proposal.)

Your *exciting, dynamic* proposal will surely be accepted by *both* committees. (The adjectives *exciting* and *dynamic* tell what kind of proposal; *both* tells how many committees.)

Note how the italicized adjectives in the following phrases clarify or describe the nouns they modify.

this company	*these* desks
that agency	*those* groups
Mexican food	*Washington* politics
enthusiastic employees	*qualified* applicants
interesting movies	*four* months
three books	*first* client
two-week vacation	*up-to-date* information

Adverbs   As adjectives are to nouns and pronouns, so are adverbs to verbs, adjectives, and other adverbs. **Adverbs** modify and describe these parts of speech by telling *how, when, where,* or *to what degree.*

Joanne draws *beautifully.*   (Draws how? Beautifully.)

Ms. Adams will arrive *shortly.*   (Arrive when? Shortly.)

Put that carton *there.*   (Where? There.)

These pastries are *too* sweet.   (To what degree? Too.)

1. Adverbs modify verbs:

> Jack ran *quickly.* (The adverb *quickly* modifies the verb *ran*.)
>
> The committee *unanimously* agreed to finance the shopping center. (The adverb *unanimously* modifies the verb *agreed*.)

2. Adverbs modify adjectives:

> his *nearly* perfect paper (The adverb *nearly* modifies the adjective *perfect*.)
>
> an *extremely* long speech (The adverb *extremely* modifies the adjective *long*.)
>
> this *obviously* expensive home (The adverb *obviously* modifies the adjective *expensive*.)

3. Adverbs modify other adverbs:

> Jack ran *very* quickly. (The adverb *very* modifies the adverb *quickly*.)
>
> The manager *quite* suddenly decided to sell the team. (The adverb *quite* modifies the adverb *suddenly*.)

Perhaps you noticed that except for *very* and *quite*, all the adverbs above end in *ly*. Indeed, many adverbs are formed by adding *ly* to adjectives:

ADJECTIVE	ADVERB
quiet	quietly
bad	badly
sudden	suddenly
careful	carefully

But there are others that do not end in *ly*, including *very*, *quite*, *almost*, *never*, *here*, *there*, and many, many more.

CLASS PRACTICE 2

A. Identify the underlined words as either adjectives or adverbs.

1. Ms. Hamilton <u>quickly</u> reviewed the <u>four</u> résumés.
2. Leonard decided to open the <u>sealed</u> cartons and <u>carefully</u> check their contents.
3. We need some <u>basic</u> information to complete our analysis; we expect to receive the data <u>soon</u>.
4. Charles <u>obviously</u> objects to raising these <u>high</u> prices even more.
5. The <u>replacement</u> parts will be shipped <u>there</u> before Friday.

B. On a separate sheet of paper, rewrite the following sentences, filling in the blanks with an adjective or adverb as you do so. Identify each of your fill-ins as an adjective or an adverb.

6. My assistant always submits _____ work.
7. My assistant always works _____.
8. Steven generally arrives _____.

9. All of us were _____ happy about Pamela's promotion.
10. We were considering buying a _____ printer.

Prepositions

Prepositions connect groups of words to show relationships among ideas. They include these very commonly used words:

in	to	for	about	except
by	from	with	above	between
of	after	before	behind	into
out	on	over	before	until

Prepositions are always used in prepositional phrases such as the following:

in the morning	*in* April
by the door	*by* Dales Department Store
of the owners	*of* Mrs. Henson
to the company	*to* Collins Chemical Company
from her	*from* Rebecca
for him	*for* Scott
with them	*with* Rebecca and Scott

Now read the following pairs of sentences, and notice the prepositional phrase in the second sentence in each pair.

We plan to meet.
We plan to meet *in the morning.*

Please give me the package.
Please give me the package *by the door.*

He broke the base accidentally.
He broke the base *of the pot* accidentally.

The price was 10 percent higher than we had anticipated.
The price *to the company* was 10 percent higher than we had anticipated.

The letter did not include a purchase order.
The letter *from her* did not include a purchase order.

A gift was delivered early this morning.
A gift *for Mr. Washington* was delivered early this morning.

We went later.
We went *with them* later.

In each case the preposition connects words in the form of a prepositional phrase to the rest of the sentence and serves to add additional meaning.

Conjunctions

Conjunctions, too, are connectors. They connect both single words and groups of words. The most commonly used conjunctions are *and*, *but*, *or*, and *nor*.

> Robert *and* Paula will be promoted.   (The conjunction *and* joins two nouns, *Robert* and *Paula*.)

> Robert, Paula, *and* Daniel are attending the workshop.   (Here the conjunction *and* joins three nouns.)

> We have extra brochures in the storeroom *and* on those shelves.   (The conjunction *and* joins two prepositional phrases, *in the storeroom* and *on those shelves*.)

> The fast, lightweight, *and* compact computer has helped us increase our productivity.   (The conjunction *and* joins three adjectives, *fast, lightweight,* and *compact.)*

> Owen always types quickly *but* accurately.   (The conjunction *but* joins two adverbs, *quickly* and *accurately*.)

In Section 4.8 you will learn about other conjunctions that have special uses.

CLASS PRACTICE 3

On a separate sheet of paper, identify the underlined words as prepositions (P) or conjunctions (C). For each preposition also identify the prepositional phrase.

1. Mr. Reynolds <u>and</u> Ms. McGrath went <u>to</u> the auditorium.
2. Vouchers must be signed <u>by</u> your supervisor.
3. The discount <u>on</u> sale items is valid <u>until</u> June 30.
4. We divided the invoices <u>between</u> Jack <u>and</u> me.
5. <u>For</u> the annual sales meeting, we developed special awards <u>and</u> prizes <u>for</u> the top sales representatives.
6. Sheila sent copies <u>of</u> the report <u>to</u> everyone <u>in</u> the department <u>except</u> Myrna.
7. <u>In</u> March most <u>of</u> the brokers <u>and</u> agents will attend the seminar.
8. Although Amy <u>and</u> Rachel were <u>against</u> the suggestion, the committee voted to increase the budget <u>for</u> promotional brochures.
9. Lewis Annucci was scheduled to be one <u>of</u> the speakers, <u>but</u> he had to cancel.
10. Don <u>or</u> Melanie will be <u>at</u> the convention center <u>in</u> the afternoon.

Interjections

Interjections are words that express strong feeling; they are usually independent of the rest of the sentence.

> *Great!* Joan succeeded in getting the Wilson account.

> *Oh*, so that's what they wanted.

No! We certainly cannot approve the terms of this agreement.

Yes. All our products have a one-year unconditional guarantee on parts and labor.

THE SENTENCE

By themselves, the parts of speech have little meaning. They become powerful only when they are used to construct sentences. When writing, we must make sure that each sentence is complete and that we use sentences to express our thoughts precisely. The first step, of course, is to learn what a sentence is.

You probably have heard a *sentence* defined as "a group of words that expresses a complete thought." Note the word *complete*. If the thought is not complete, then the group of words is not a sentence—it is a fragment.

You should learn to write and speak in sentences; that is, learn to express yourself in complete thoughts, not in fragments. To be able to distinguish between complete thoughts and incomplete thoughts, look at the Quick Trick below.

QUICK TRICK

No Sense, No Sentence

Whenever you must decide whether a group of words is a sentence, consider whether the words make sense. If they do make sense, then the group of words is a sentence. If they do not make sense, the group of words is not a sentence.

We will receive a 10 percent discount for early payment.   (These words make sense; they express a complete thought. Therefore, they make up a sentence.)

If we do not receive the equipment within the next ten days.   (This group of words is not complete; it doesn't express a complete thought. This is not a sentence.)

Use your knowledge of the parts of speech to help you decide whether a word group functions as a complete sentence. A complete sentence contains a noun or pronoun that acts jointly with a verb or verb phrase to produce an idea that makes sense. Notice how each of the following sentences makes sense and contains a noun or a pronoun that works together with a verb or a verb phrase to complete the meaning:

   Noun   Verb
Our *supervisor works* Monday and Friday evenings.   (Makes sense)

   Noun   Pronoun   Verb
Mr. Holloway and *she* often *work* on Sundays and holidays.   (Makes sense)

EDITING PRACTICE 1

Tell which of the following groups of words are sentences and which ones are not. Just say "sense" or "no sense." Then, for additional practice, take each group of "no sense" words and add words as necessary so that the group of words makes sense.

1. The Dallas store will open in June or July.
2. Ms. Purcell has been named vice president of operations.
3. Since the Benefits Department improved the dental coverage.
4. If you need more information.
5. Mr. Bentley sent the bid to the architect.
6. Knowing that the committee had many issues on the agenda.
7. When Donna returns from her trip to the San Diego office.
8. You will need two copies.
9. Because I needed to confirm my reservation for the return flight from Denver.
10. If you decide that you need two copies.

SUBJECTS AND PREDICATES

Each complete sentence may be divided into two parts: the complete subject and the complete predicate. In the following examples, the labeled nouns and pronouns function as the subject of the sentence; they answer *who* or *what* when paired with the verb or verb phrase. The verb or verb phrase is part of the predicate.

<u>   Noun   </u>   <u>Verb</u>
Our district manager / visits the store weekly.   (Ask, *"Who or what visits?"* *Our district manager* stands out clearly as the complete subject.)

<u>Noun</u>   <u>Pronoun</u> <u>Verb Phrase</u>
Sharon and he / have been sharing an office for nearly a year.   (Ask, *"Who or what have been sharing?"* *Sharon and he* is the correct answer—and the complete subject.)

In the examples above and those that follow, the *complete predicate* begins with the verb or verb phrase and ends with the last word in the sentence. The word or word group appearing before the verb or verb phrase is the *complete subject.*

<u>   Complete Subject   </u>   <u>Complete Predicate   </u>
Our new training materials / will be delivered next week.

<u>Complete</u>
<u>Subject   </u>   <u>Complete Predicate   </u>
You / will receive a new payment booklet next month.

CLASS PRACTICE 4

Identify the *complete subject* of each sentence below. (Remember that the rest of the sentence must, of course, be the *predicate*.)

1. The training manual for new employees is being revised.
2. The cartons on the loading platform must be shipped to the warehouse.
3. Betty Russo coordinates all these projects.
4. One of these computers should be moved to the seventh floor.
5. The present discounts for cash purchases may be discontinued.
6. I prefer establishing a committee to analyze the results of these ads.
7. Most of the customers named "courtesy" as the most important trait in sales personnel.
8. One of the main reasons for changing the schedule is to accommodate Ms. O'Brien, who will be out of town next week.

SIMPLE AND COMPOUND SUBJECTS

The complete subject of a sentence includes the *simple subject* or the *compound subject* of the sentence. Now that you are able to identify the complete subject, let's see how to find the simple subject or the compound subject within the complete subject. As you will see later, your skill in finding the simple or the compound subject is very important for correct verb choice.

A *simple subject* is the single most important noun or pronoun in the complete subject.

The *plaintiff* in this suit did not appear in court today.   (The complete subject is *The plaintiff in this suit*. The most important noun in this complete subject is *plaintiff*, which is the simple subject of this sentence.)

A *compound subject* consists of two or more words that are *equally* important. The words are usually joined by *and*, *or*, or *nor*.

The *plaintiff and* her *attorney* did not appear in court today.   (The complete subject is *The plaintiff and her attorney*. In this complete subject the most important nouns are *plaintiff* and *attorney*. The compound subject, therefore, is *plaintiff and attorney*.)

The *plaintiff*, her *attorney, and* the main *witness* did not appear in court today. (The complete subject is *The plaintiff, her attorney, and the main witness*. It has three words that have equal importance—*plaintiff*, *attorney*, and *witness*. Thus the compound subject is *plaintiff, attorney, and witness*.)

WORLD VIEW

Knowing a few words in another language will ease your way in international business. A foreign language phrase book or dictionary will provide such basic expressions as "Good morning," "Nice to meet you," and "Thank you" in the customer's language.

CLASS PRACTICE 5

Identify the simple or the compound subject in each sentence below. (HINT: Identify the complete subject first.)

1. A revised inventory statement and an updated sales report were sent to the executive vice president.

2. James or Laura will probably be assigned to handle this account.
3. Ms. Carole P. Quentin is the senior counselor of our firm.
4. A microcomputer and a fax machine were damaged in the fire.
5. The opinion of each of the attorneys is that we should sue for libel.
6. The issue of copyright infringement was the topic of greatest interest at the convention.
7. A new hotel near the ocean has been selected for the sales representatives' meeting.
8. The folders on her desk contain all the information that you will need.

SENTENCE ORDER

As you examine the principles in the following lessons, you will find that analyzing sentences in *normal order* is an easy way to determine whether a sentence is written correctly. A sentence appears in normal order when the complete subject is followed by the complete predicate, as in all the examples you have seen so far.

None of the customers were aware of the special discount for cash payments. (The complete subject is *None of the customers*; it is followed by the complete predicate, *were aware of the special discount for cash payments*. This sentence is in *normal* order.)

In typical business writing, many sentences appear in *inverted order*; that is, part of the predicate appears before the complete subject. Inverted sentences add interest and variety to one's writing style. Study the following pair to see how they compare:

INVERTED ORDER:
During the third-quarter sales period, two representatives in our division received cash bonuses.   (This sentence is in inverted order because part of the predicate appears before the complete subject.)

NORMAL ORDER:
Two representatives in our division received cash bonuses during the third-quarter sales period.   (In this case the complete subject, *Two representatives in our division*, appears before the complete predicate.)

Because sentences in normal order are easier to analyze, you will often wish to place an inverted sentence in normal order *just to analyze it* and then return it to inverted order. Therefore, you should learn how to place the complete subject first and the complete predicate second. Use the following procedure to change sentences to normal order.

1. Find the verb or verb phrase.
2. Ask "Who?" or "What?" followed by the verb or verb phrase. The answer is the complete subject.
3. Place all the remaining words *after* the complete subject and the verb or verb phrase to complete the predicate.

Apply this procedure to the following sentence:

During the airline strike, we delivered our cargoes by truck.

1. Find the verb or verb phrase: *delivered.*
2. Who or What *delivered? We* delivered.
3. Place the remaining words after the verb or verb phrase to complete the predicate.

*Complete
Subject*   *Complete Predicate*

We / delivered our cargoes by truck during the airline strike.

Have you ever noticed that questions are usually phrased in inverted order? Note these examples:

Will you be going to the convention in Puerto Rico?   (Inverted order)

You will be going to the convention in Puerto Rico?   (Normal order)

Where have all the cartons been placed?   (Inverted order)

All the cartons have been placed where?   (Normal order)

Some sentences will sound odd when you change them to normal order, but do not let this bother you. You are merely using this procedure as a technique to identify subjects of sentences.

EDITING PRACTICE 2

Which of the following sentences are in normal order, and which ones are in inverted order? Identify each; then change the inverted-order sentences to normal order. In addition, identify the complete subject of each sentence.

1. Is this envelope for Mr. Byrd?
2. The file copy of the agreement is on my desk.
3. When she arrives, you should give Sylvia this memo.
4. Were all the proofs corrected and returned?
5. We discussed various ways to solve the temporary backlog of orders.
6. Before the end of the year, our department will test a new computerized billing system.
7. As soon as Lyn calls, we will leave for the airport.
8. Our new supervisor was formerly with the Fitch & Scranton Advertising Agency.
9. Why did the Fargo, North Dakota, office close?
10. The latest addition to the marketing staff transferred from the Midwest Region in January.

COMMUNICATION LABORATORY

APPLICATION EXERCISES

A. Identify the underlined words in the following sentences. On a separate sheet, for each word write the part of speech (*noun, verb, conjunction, preposition, adverb, adjective,* or *pronoun*). Write *VP* for any verb phrases.

1. We <u>sent</u> two of the <u>cartons</u> to St. Louis <u>by</u> airfreight.
2. The proposal is <u>very</u> interesting, <u>but</u> it <u>would be</u> expensive.
3. One <u>of</u> the reasons for changing the <u>policy</u> is that our advisers <u>have recommended</u> tightening our credit.
4. The <u>executive</u> who <u>is</u> in charge of manufacturing is <u>Clara Poole</u>.
5. The <u>discount</u> <u>will be</u> <u>offered</u> <u>until</u> December 31.
6. Of course, we do believe the <u>plan</u> <u>will be</u> effective, <u>but</u> we <u>will need</u> time to prove that it will work.
7. Brenda is <u>obviously</u> happy <u>about</u> her promotion to <u>district manager</u>.
8. One of the <u>best</u> designers <u>on</u> our staff is <u>Caryl</u>.
9. Yes, <u>they</u> <u>finally</u> decided to test <u>these</u> products.
10. The <u>meeting</u> should be over <u>soon</u>; <u>I</u> will call <u>you</u> as soon as Joan leaves the meeting.
11. I am sure that she <u>will want</u> a copy of the <u>new</u> pamphlet; will <u>you</u> please send her a <u>copy</u>?
12. Tom <u>and</u> Ron <u>have been developing</u> the <u>next</u> campaign <u>for</u> this product.
13. All of <u>us</u> want to see Gregory when <u>he</u> returns <u>from</u> England.
14. If you <u>want</u> to share a copy with Mr. Jenkins, I <u>will be</u> glad to bring <u>it</u> to him.
15. Martin has <u>already</u> left for the <u>airport</u> because <u>he</u> had an <u>early</u> flight.

B. On a separate sheet of paper, number from 1 to 15, leaving two blank lines between each number. Then write each sentence or sentence fragment below, adding the words necessary to make any sentence fragment a complete sentence. Change any inverted sentence to normal order on the blank line following the sentence. Underline once the complete subject; circle the simple or compound subject.

1. Gold and silver are subject to price changes, of course.
2. Will Mr. Horne visit our Tennessee office too?
3. One of the most successful franchises.
4. Susan or Bill can probably help you with these programming errors.
5. Leonard said that the Securities and Exchange Commission is now studying the issue.
6. One of the managers at the meeting wants to extend the deadline until April or May.

CONTINUED

7. April or May is usually the best month for television sales, according to these analyses.
8. According to these analyses, April or May is the best month for television sales.
9. Superior Inks is the company that submitted the highest bid.
10. Have you decided whom you will hire as your assistant?
11. You have already interviewed several applicants, haven't you?
12. The manager in charge of the Customer Relations Department.
13. The principal reason for moving the factory to Atlanta is that we lost the lease on the old property.
14. One of the applicants whom I interviewed this morning.
15. Will one of your assistants be able to help me proofread all these advertisements?

VOCABULARY AND SPELLING STUDIES

A. Because the words in the following groups are so similar, they are often confused: *device, devise; precede, proceed, proceeds; mood, mode; command, commend.*

Distinguish between the meaning and the spelling of the words in each group; then write a sample sentence using each word.

B. Which of the following words are misspelled?

1. apologize
2. merchandize
3. realise
4. advertise
5. exercise
6. analyse
7. harmonise
8. authorize
9. antagonyze
10. capitalyse
11. theorize
12. rationalize

C. In the sentences below, choose the correct spelling for the words in parentheses.

1. How many (occurences, occurrences) of tardiness have you had in the last six months?
2. Her supervisor was (dissapointed, disappointed) when she requested a transfer.
3. We all (benefited, benefitted) from the change in vacation policy.
4. Please call the (libary, library) to request a listing of the ten most profitable companies in our state.
5. Send the samples to the (laboratory, labratory) for analysis.
6. I (belief, believe) I have the solution to our problem.
7. (Ether, Either) finish the report this afternoon or work late tonight.
8. If you are ill, report to your (supervisor, superviser) before you go to the nurse.

SECTION 4.2

VERBS

erbs are the core of the sentence. Because they describe what the subject is doing or what is being done to the subject, verbs convey the action or movement that sparks a sentence and brings it to life.

VERBS—THE MOTORS OF SENTENCES

A verb describes a subject's action, condition, or state of being. Therefore, you may find it helpful to think of verbs as the "motors" of sentences. Read the following sentences:

> Denise the changes to the staff.

> Denise angry.

> Denise in the conference room.

Did you notice something wrong with each of these sentences? They are missing verbs—the sentence motors. Therefore, these sentences do not express a complete idea. By adding verbs, we can bring the sentences to life.

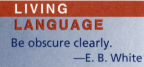

LIVING
LANGUAGE
Be obscure clearly.
—E. B. White

> Denise *announced* the changes to the staff.   (*Announced* is a verb; it describes Denise's action.)

> Denise *looks* angry.   (*Looks* is the verb; it tells Denise's condition.)

> Denise *is* in the conference room.   (*Is* is the verb; it tells Denise's state of being.)

Here are some more sentences without verbs. Note how they are incomplete without their motors.

> Jack and Rosemary the workshop on real estate investments.

> Ross Plastics the contract with the labor unions.

> Mr. Grant someone from the Advertising Department.

Do you understand these messages? Without verbs the above groups of words express no message because they are incomplete. Now watch how these words come to life with the addition of verbs:

> Jack and Rosemary (*teach, enjoyed, attended, will coordinate*) the workshop on real estate investments.

> Ross Plastics (*signed, negotiated, rejected, reviewed, revised*) the contract with the labor unions.

> Mr. Grant (*hired, wants, promoted, accepted, prefers*) someone from the Advertising Department.

CLASS PRACTICE 1

Underline the verb in each of the following sentences. If the sentence has no verb, supply a verb for it.

1. Who presented the certificate to Scott during the luncheon?
2. Ms. Matsui gave each new employee a handbook.
3. My assistant the monthly inventory report.
4. Jerry and Sally the catalog copy for these products.
5. The batteries are in the supply room.
6. Mary the new sales representative for this region.
7. Paul the agenda for next week's training sessions.
8. Helen Munch has the price list and the discount chart.

VERB PHRASES

As you learned in Section 4.1, two or more verbs are sometimes joined in a sentence. Two or more verbs that work together as one verb are called a **verb phrase.** Verb phrases such as *will be going, has been asked,* and *have approved* allow speakers and writers to express their meanings exactly.

In a verb phrase the last verb is the main verb; any other verbs are considered *helping* (or *auxiliary*) verbs.

Frances *should have* a duplicate key to this cabinet.   (Main verb: *have,* the last verb in the phrase. Helping verb: *should.*)

We *should have asked* him for more information.   (Main verb: *asked,* the last verb in the phrase. Helping verbs: *should* and *have.*)

In the examples above, note that *have* is the main verb in the first sentence, but *have* is a helping verb in the second sentence. Remember that the main verb is always the last verb in the phrase, and you will have no difficulty finding the main verb in any verb phrase.

HELPING VERB	MAIN VERB	VERB PHRASE
is	walking	is walking
are	dancing	are dancing
do	deliver	do deliver
will	be	will be
will be	finished	will be finished
has been	accomplished	has been accomplished
did	explain	did explain
should have	insisted	should have insisted
might have	listened	might have listened
had been	returned	had been returned
will have	received	will have received
will have been	budgeted	will have been budgeted

In questions a verb phrase is often interrupted.

Has Jacqueline *returned* from her vacation yet?   (The verb phrase *has returned* is separated by the subject *Jacqueline*. The normal order is *Jacqueline has returned . . . .*)

Will an order blank *be included* in each catalog?   (The verb phrase *will be included* is split by the complete subject *an order blank*.)

Adverbs also split verb phrases, as shown in these examples:

Charles *has* always *been* on time for our morning meetings.   (The verb phrase *has been* is separated by the adverb *always*.)

Sharon and I *have* often *visited* the Museum of Modern Art.   (The verb phrase *have visited* is separated by the adverb *often*.)

CLASS PRACTICE 2

In each of the following sentences, identify the verb phrase and the main verb in the phrase. (HINT: Be on the lookout for split verb phrases!)

1. Charles has already reserved his hotel room for the sales meeting.
2. Tina has often requested to work extra hours on weekends.
3. The class on dog grooming has been canceled.
4. Does Kathy have all the artwork for the brochure?
5. Can Mark assist us with these packages?
6. Her vacation plans have already been made.
7. These errors should have been corrected in the first printing.
8. Will Eric have time to help us with these invoices?

PRINCIPAL PARTS OF REGULAR VERBS

The principal parts of verbs are the forms we use to express the *time of action*, or *tense*, of the verbs. The four parts are the *present*, the *past*, the *past participle*, and the *present participle*. For most verbs these parts are very easily formed, as shown in the table here.

PRINCIPAL PARTS OF SOME REGULAR VERBS			
PRESENT TENSE	**PAST TENSE**	**PAST PARTICIPLE**	**PRESENT PARTICIPLE**
return	returned	returned	returning
answer	answered	answered	answering
prepare	prepared	prepared	preparing
use	used	used	using
reserve	reserved	reserved	reserving

Most verbs form both the past tense and the past participle by adding *ed* to the present form. These same verbs add *ing* to form the present participle.

Other verbs that end in *e* just add *d* to form the past tense and the past participle. Their present participles are usually formed by dropping the *e* and then adding *ing*.

Because most of the verbs in our language form their principal parts in one of the ways described above, such verbs are called **regular verbs.**

Present Tense and Past Tense   Study the present tense and past tense forms of the verb *work*:

PRESENT TENSE		PAST TENSE	
Singular	**Plural**	**Singular**	**Plural**
I work	we work	I worked	we worked
you work	you work	you worked	you worked
he		he	
she } works	they work	she } worked	they worked
it		it	

As you can see, there are only two present tense forms—*work* and *works*. There is only one past tense form—*worked*. This pattern is standard for all regular verbs.

I *work* at the bakery on Tuesday evenings.

He *works* late every night.

Diana *worked* at Facey Medical Clinic for three years.

Past Participle and Present Participle   In verb phrases participles are always the main verbs—the last verbs in the phrases.

Gail *has worked* at the same job for the past fifteen years.

Matthew *has been working* on this project for the past three weeks.

CLASS PRACTICE 3

In the sentences below identify the present tense and past tense forms and the present participles and past participles. (REMEMBER: Past tense and present tense forms never have helping verbs.)

1. Ms. Andrews has accepted our invitation to the luncheon.
2. Yes, Pedro always completes his sales analyses on time.
3. Has Mr. Jacobs mailed his check yet?
4. The final copy has been completed.
5. She has called the office three times this week.
6. Yes, Jean is accepting a transfer to our Mexico City branch.
7. We are now completing our work on the Loomis project.
8. Are you still sending these reports to the branch offices?

PRINCIPAL PARTS OF IRREGULAR VERBS

You have seen that regular verbs form the past tense and past participle forms by adding *d* or *ed* to their present tense forms. A number of other verbs form their principal parts in various ways—often by changing to a different word. Note, for example, the verbs in the table here.

PRINCIPAL PARTS OF SOME IRREGULAR VERBS

PRESENT TENSE	PAST TENSE	PAST PARTICIPLE	PRESENT PARTICIPLE
am	was	been	being
begin	began	begun	beginning
do	did	done	doing
go	went	gone	going
have	had	had	having
write	wrote	written	writing

Obviously, these verbs deserve special attention, as do all the other irregular verbs in the table on pages 84–86. Study these irregular verbs. Memorize them if you don't already know them. Always consult the dictionary for those verbs whose forms you do not know. Most dictionaries list at least the past tense and past participle forms of irregular verbs.

PRINCIPAL PARTS OF IRREGULAR VERBS

PRESENT TENSE	PAST TENSE	PAST PARTICIPLE	PRESENT PARTICIPLE
am	was	been	being
become	became	become	becoming
begin	began	begun	beginning
bid (to offer)	bid	bid	bidding
bite	bit	bitten	biting
blow	blew	blown	blowing
break	broke	broken	breaking
bring	brought	brought	bringing
burst	burst	burst	bursting
buy	bought	bought	buying
catch	caught	caught	catching
choose	chose	chosen	choosing
climb*	climbed	climbed	climbing
come	came	come	coming
do	did	done	doing
drag*	dragged	dragged	dragging
draw	drew	drawn	drawing

PRINCIPAL PARTS OF IRREGULAR VERBS (Continued)

PRESENT TENSE	PAST TENSE	PAST PARTICIPLE	PRESENT PARTICIPLE
drink	drank	drunk	drinking
drive	drove	driven	driving
drown*	drowned	drowned	drowning
eat	ate	eaten	eating
fall	fell	fallen	falling
fight	fought	fought	fighting
find	found	found	finding
flee	fled	fled	fleeing
fly	flew	flown	flying
forget	forgot	forgotten	forgetting
freeze	froze	frozen	freezing
get	got	got	getting
give	gave	given	giving
go	went	gone	going
grow	grew	grown	growing
hang	hung	hung	hanging
hang (to put to death)*	hanged	hanged	hanging
hide	hid	hidden	hiding
hold	held	held	holding
know	knew	known	knowing
lay	laid	laid	laying
leave	left	left	leaving
lend	lent	lent	lending
lie	lay	lain	lying
lose	lost	lost	losing
pay	paid	paid	paying
read†	read‡	read‡	reading
ride	rode	ridden	riding
ring	rang	rung	ringing
rise	rose	risen	rising
run	ran	run	running
see	saw	seen	seeing
set	set	set	setting
shake	shook	shaken	shaking
shine	shone	shone	shining
shine (to polish)*	shined	shined	shining
shrink	shrank	shrunk	shrinking
sing	sang	sung	singing
sit	sat	sat	sitting
speak	spoke	spoken	speaking
spring	sprang	sprung	springing

PRINCIPAL PARTS OF IRREGULAR VERBS (Continued)			
PRESENT TENSE	**PAST TENSE**	**PAST PARTICIPLE**	**PRESENT PARTICIPLE**
stand	stood	stood	standing
steal	stole	stolen	stealing
strike	struck	struck	striking
swear	swore	sworn	swearing
sweep	swept	swept	sweeping
swim	swam	swum	swimming
take	took	taken	taking
teach	taught	taught	teaching
tear	tore	torn	tearing
tell	told	told	telling
think	thought	thought	thinking
throw	threw	thrown	throwing
wear	wore	worn	wearing
win	won	won	winning
write	wrote	written	writing

*These are regular verbs, but their past tense and past participles are often misused.
†Pronounced "reed."
‡Pronounced "red."

As with regular verbs, *always* be sure to use a helping verb with the past participle of irregular verbs. On the other hand, *never* use a helping verb with the past tense. Note, for example, the correct uses of the verbs below.

PAST TENSE	**PAST PARTICIPLE**
She *went*.	She <u>has</u> *gone*.
He *did* a good job.	He <u>has</u> *done* a good job.
We *broke* the vase.	We <u>have</u> *broken* the vase.
I *flew* to Denver.	I <u>had</u> *flown* to Denver.
They *gave* us a discount.	They <u>have</u> *given* us a discount.

In each case note again that the past participle *always* has a helper and that the past tense *never* has a helper. Thus it is always wrong to say or write *she gone, he done,* and so on, because these past participles must have helping verbs.

EDITING PRACTICE 1

In the following sentences, correct all errors in the use of verb forms.

1. Sara has already spoke with Ms. Roosevelt about the new procedures.
2. Apparently the glass had been broke before the package was delivered.

3. We had began to revise the policy manual early last month.
4. Do you know whether Mr. Garabedian has already went to the airport?
5. Yes, I seen both of them at this morning's production meeting.
6. Have you already did your monthly inventory summary?
7. We have wrote only a first draft of our proposal, but we will complete the final draft before the end of the day.
8. After we had ate lunch, we began discussing marketing strategies.

"BEING" VERBS

The "being" verbs are the most commonly used verbs in our language. Unfortunately, they are also among the most misused.

The "being" verbs are all the forms of the verb *to be: am, are, is, was, were, be, been,* and *being.* Now let's see how they are used. To begin, make sure you know the present tense and the past tense forms of the verb *to be:*

PRESENT TENSE		PAST TENSE	
Singular	**Plural**	**Singular**	**Plural**
I am	we are	I was	we were
you are	you are	you were	you were
he she it } is	they are	he she it } was	they were

As you can see, then, the verb *to be* is unique. Its present tense has three forms—*am, are,* and *is.* Its past tense has two forms—*was* and *were.* Memorize these forms because you will certainly use them often.

> I *am* responsible for this project. Steve *is* one of the analysts assigned to the project. We *are* still on schedule.   (Present tense forms.)

> You *were* not at the committee meeting, *were* you? Henry *was* there.   (Past tense forms.)

Past Participle and Present Participle   The past participle *been* can be used as a main verb with a helper, as in *has been, should have been, could have been, might have been,* and so on. In addition, *been* can be used as a helping verb. Note that a verb *phrase* is not considered a "being" verb unless the *main verb* is the "being" verb.

> Joe Paul *should have been* here by noon.   (*Been* is the main verb; *should* and *have* are helping verbs. Therefore, this verb phrase is a "being" verb.)

> He *should have been told* about the change in departure time.   (Now the main verb is *told,* and the helping verbs are *should, have,* and *been.* This verb phrase is not a "being" verb.)

Likewise, the present participle *being* can be used as a main verb, as in *am being, is being, are being, was being,* and *were being.* It can also be used as a helping verb, as in *is being planned, are being reviewed, was being discussed,* and so on. Again, to find out whether *being* is the main verb in a verb phrase, be sure to isolate the entire phrase; then see whether *being* is the *last* word in that phrase.

> We *are being* very careful about storing chemicals at our plants.   (The main verb is *being*; the helping verb is *are.*)

> We *are being trained* to handle chemicals carefully.   (Now the main verb is *trained; are* and *being* are helping verbs.)

> *Are* you *being trained* to handle chemicals carefully?   (In this inverted sentence, the verb phrase *are being trained* is separated by the subject *you.*)

Be   The last form is the word *be* itself. *Be* can also be used as a helper or as a main verb.

> Beatrice *will be* in charge of the newly formed group.   (In the verb phrase *will be, be* is the main verb and *will* is the helping verb.)

> She *will be promoted* soon.   (The main verb is *promoted,* and the helping verbs are *will* and *be.*)

CLASS PRACTICE 4

In each of the following sentences, identify the verb or the verb phrase. Then determine whether that verb or verb phrase is a "being" verb. (HINT: Remember that a verb phrase is a "being" verb only when the *last* verb in the phrase is a "being" verb.)

1. You really should have been at our last panel discussion.
2. The merchandise was shipped to San Francisco on March 30.
3. When are you planning to make the new price list effective?
4. Each of these payments must be acknowledged, of course.
5. In your opinion, is this product worth so much money?
6. Kristen has been selected chairperson of the policy committee.
7. Kristen has been the chairperson of many committees within the past two years.
8. Frankly, we were not expecting this many orders from just one small ad.

USE OF LIE AND LAY

Among the most frequently misused irregular verbs are *lie* and *lay*. To use these verbs correctly, you must first learn the parts for each verb.

PRESENT TENSE	PAST TENSE	PAST PARTICIPLE	PRESENT PARTICIPLE
lie	lay	lain	lying
lay	laid	laid	laying

Although the past part for *lie* and the present part for *lay* are spelled the same (*lay*), do not confuse the use of these parts. Recognize that this spelling can operate as two distinctively different parts, and keep them separate in your mind.

Select the correct part from the correct verb—*lie* or *lay*—depending on how the verb is used in the sentence. If the subject of the verb is doing the reclining (that is, the subject is doing the lying), use a part from the *lie* verb.

SUBJECT IS RECLINING = USE *LIE*

Present part	Outpatients usually *lie* in the recovery room one hour before being discharged. (What is the subject? *outpatients*. Who are reclining or lying? *outpatients*. Therefore, a form of *lie* is correct.)
Past part	I *lay* in bed for nearly a week with the flu. (What is the subject? *I*. Who reclined? *I*. Therefore, a form of *lie* is correct.)
Past participle	This production facility *has lain* idle for nearly three months. (Subject? *facility*. What has been lying or reclining? *facility*. Therefore, a form of *lie* is correct.)
Present participle	The new application form *is lying* on the counter. (Subject? *form*. What is lying or reclining? *form*. Therefore, a form of *lie* is correct.)

When someone or something other than the subject of the verb is reclining or lying, then use a part of the *lay* verb. If the subject itself is not reclining or lying, you may not use a form of *lie*. Use a form of *lay* instead.

SOMEONE/SOMETHING OTHER THAN SUBJECT IS RECLINING = USE LAY

Present part	The accountant always *lays* the payroll checks on my desk for distribution. (What is the subject? *accountant*. Is *the accountant* reclining or lying? No. Therefore, a form of *lay* is correct.)
Past part	I *laid* all the unused file folders on a shelf in the the supply closet. (What is the subject? *I*. Am *I* reclining or lying? No. Therefore, a form of *lay* is correct.)
Past participle	The installers *have* already *laid* the carpeting on the first floor. (Subject? *installers*. Have *the installers* been lying or reclining? No. Therefore, a form of *lay* is correct.)
Present participle	This week crews *are laying* the concrete foundations for the new houses. (Subject? *crews*. Are *crews* lying or reclining? No. Therefore, a form of *lay* is correct.)

In most applications a form of *lie* is used when the subject is the person or thing reclining. There is, however, one exception. When a sentence requires the *past participle* with a "being" verb helper—*was, were, be,* or *been*—always use *laid*.

The concrete foundation for our new warehouse *was laid* yesterday. ("Being" verb helper: *was*. Past participle: *laid*.)

The medical records for tomorrow's patients *have been laid* on your desk. ("Being" verb helper: *been*. Past participle: *laid*.)

USE OF *SIT* AND *SET, RISE* AND *RAISE*

Besides *lie* and *lay*, two other pairs of verbs are similarly confused: *sit* and *set*, and *rise* and *raise*. The parts for each of these verbs follow:

PRESENT TENSE	PAST TENSE	PAST PARTICIPLE	PRESENT PARTICIPLE
sit	sat	sat	sitting
set	set	set	setting
rise	rose	risen	rising
raise	raised	raised	raising
lie	lay	lain	lying
lay	laid	laid	laying

The same rules and exception that govern *lie* and *lay* apply to *sit, set, rise,* and *raise*. If the subject is doing what the verb describes—actually reclining or lying, sitting, or rising—use a form of *lie, sit,* or *rise*. Notice that the second letter of each of these verbs is *i*.

Our customers must *sit* in comfortable chairs.   (Subject? *customers*. Are *our customers* sitting? Yes. Therefore, a form of *sit* is correct.)

You may *set* the package on the counter.   (Subject? *You*. Who or what is on the counter? *package*, not *you*. Therefore, a form of *set* is correct.)

The prices of our raw materials *rise* continually.   (Subject? *prices*. Are *the prices* rising? Yes. Therefore, a form of *rise* is correct.)

Each year we *raise* our prices to cover increased costs.   (Subject? *we*. Who or what is being raised? *prices*, not *we*. Therefore, a form of *raise* is correct.)

CLASS PRACTICE 5

In each of the following sentences, select the correct verb form from the choices shown in parentheses.

1. You may (lie, lay) down in the infirmary until someone arrives to drive you home.
2. Where should I (sit, set) these books?

3. These empty cartons have (lain, laid) here for nearly a week.
4. The tax forms were (lain, laid) here for distribution to the general public.
5. I was (lying, laying) on the sofa when the power failure occurred.
6. You should (rise, raise) this question at the next board meeting.
7. Dana (lay, laid) the contracts on your desk yesterday.
8. Our new condominium project (lies, lays) at the base of the foothills.

COMMUNICATION LABORATORY

APPLICATION EXERCISES

A. Correct any errors in the following sentences. If a sentence is correct, write *OK*.

1. Through her work on the budget committee, Lydia become adept at handling accounting reports.
2. The opening session had began a few minutes before we arrived.
3. If our copier is broke, use the one on the sixth floor.
4. Has Ms. Jefferson wrote her speech?
5. Because of the hot weather, our employees have already drank all the water in the water coolers.
6. I hope that Richard has not forgotten about his 3 o'clock appointment with Dr. Weisel.
7. Although the package had fell off the counter, none of the china was broken.
8. The builder has knowed about these restrictions since the beginning of the contract.
9. With the severe budget cuts, plans for increased services have been temporarily froze.
10. The last time that I seen Ms. Irwin, she was in the conference room.
11. Has Mr. Wong gave you all the signed contracts?
12. Have you flew to Chicago lately?
13. I had driven only a few miles when I noticed a peculiar sound in the motor.
14. Have you took any of the computer courses offered by our Education Division?
15. The manager had already went by the time I arrived.

B. Correct any errors in the following sentences. If a sentence is correct, write *OK*.

1. Several extra brochures are laying on the table in the reception area.
2. For the past three nights, the last person leaving the office has forgot to set the alarm.

3. Because these chemicals have laid in the storeroom too long, we must discard them.
4. Please sit these parcels on the dock for the transport company to pick up.
5. The cost of living has been raising steadily for the last seven months.
6. Dave has already spoke to the staff about the expected increase in work load next month.
7. Do you know when the foundation will be laid?
8. Please do not set on the railings.
9. I really enjoy laying in the sun on summer mornings.
10. We have been instructed to sell the stock when it raises to $75 a share.
11. How long have these sketches lain here in the storeroom?
12. An alarm sounds when the water has raised to a certain level.
13. We have showed this training film to all our sales personnel.
14. I will lie the signed contracts on your desk tomorrow morning.
15. Shannon always sets in the front of the room.

VOCABULARY AND SPELLING STUDIES

A. Distinguish between the meaning and the spelling of the following words, which are often confused: *fineness, finesse; leased, least.* Then write a sample sentence using each word.

B. Some of the following words contain silent letters: *listen, strength, night, island, candidate, doubt.* List the words, and tell which letters (besides *e*) are silent. Use the pronunciation guide in your dictionary.

C. Should *ancy* or *ency* be added to the following to complete the correct spellings?

1. effici _____
2. hesit _____
3. emerg _____
4. flu _____
5. buoy _____
6. occup _____

PLURAL NOUNS

I n Section 4.1 you learned that nouns are words that name something. These words have been traditionally described as naming "persons, places, or things." More precisely, though, nouns name a broader range of categories than this simplistic definition implies:

CATEGORY	EXAMPLES
Person	student, man, Mrs. Greene, manager, baby
Animal	dog, cow, insect, bird, poodle, lobster
Place	country, New York, Asia, park, mall, school, home
Object	computer, desk, Buick, pencil, house, telephone
Thing	company, Christmas, battle, distance, game, flower
Quality	kindness, generosity, sincerity, assertiveness
Concept	grammar, progress, management, democracy
Feeling	love, anger, satisfaction, happiness, grief
Action	running, talking, swimming, golfing, helping
Measure	inch, foot, cupful, mile, liter, milligram, pound
State	health, bankruptcy, illness, complexity, confusion

Nouns are often classified as *common* or *proper*. **Common nouns** are *general* names for persons, places, or things, such as *accountant*, *street*, and *company*. **Proper nouns,** on the other hand, name *specific* persons, places, or things, such as *Linda Rodriquez, Lassen Street*, and *General Motors*.

When speaking or writing, you may use nouns that refer to one or to more than one; for example, you may mention *an employee* (one) or *several employees* (more than one). Here you are called upon to choose either the *singular* or the *plural* form of the noun.

Besides appearing in singular and plural forms, many nouns may show possession by adding an apostrophe and an *s* (*'s*) or just an apostrophe. Thus you may find yourself using *employee's* or *employees'* to express an idea.

The words *employees, employee's*, and *employees'* are all pronounced precisely the same. In speaking, you need not specify which of these three forms you intend to use. The listener must decide which form you mean. In writing, however, errors in using such forms of nouns are obvious, because these three words cannot be used interchangeably. You must show the reader whether the plural form *employees* is what you meant or whether one of the possessive forms, *employee's* or *employees'*, is correct.

In this section you will examine the formation of noun plurals, and in the next section you will examine the formation of noun possessives. Together, these two sections will help you avoid many of the obstacles to correct spelling.

FORMING ROUTINE PLURALS

Most Nouns   Most plural nouns end in *s*. To form these plurals, you simply add *s* or *es* to the singular forms.

ADD *s*

clerk	clerks	Smith	Smiths
building	buildings	Brown	Browns
car	cars	Freid	Freids
attorney	attorneys	Donnelly	Donnellys
machine	machines	John	Johns

ADD *es*

boss	bosses	Adams	Adamses
tax	taxes	Marx	Marxes
bench	benches	Lynch	Lynches
waltz	waltzes	Lopez	Lopezes
wish	wishes	Walsh	Walshes

As you can see, for nouns that end in *s, x, z, ch,* and *sh,* you must add *es* to the singular form. For all other nouns (exceptions are discussed later in this section), just add *s.* Note that the same rule applies both to common nouns and to proper nouns.

Nouns Ending in *y*   As you saw in the list on the previous page, the plural of *attorney* is *attorneys*, and the plural of *Donnelly* is *Donnellys*. But not all nouns that end in *y* form their plurals by adding *s*. Note the following rules:

For Common Nouns   If the final *y* in a common noun is preceded by a vowel (*a, e, i, o,* or *u*), then add *s* to the singular form. If the final *y* is preceded by a consonant (that is, by any letter other than *a, e, i, o,* or *u*), then change the *y* to *i* and add *es*:

ADD *s*		CHANGE *y* TO *i* AND ADD *es*	
day	days	quantity	quantities
valley	valleys	secretary	secretaries
toy	toys	company	companies
ray	rays	facility	facilities
key	keys	territory	territories
relay	relays	factory	factories

For Proper Nouns   For proper nouns ending in *y,* just add *s* to form the plural, regardless of whether the *y* is preceded by a vowel or a consonant.

| Connelly | Connelly*s* | | Haggerty | Haggerty*s* |
| Delaney | Delaney*s* | | Pauly | Pauly*s* |

There are very few exceptions to this rule, but note the following three common ones:

COMPLETE NAME	**SHORTENED NAME**
Allegheny Mountains	the Alleghen*ies*
Rocky Mountains	the Rock*ies*
Smoky Mountains	the Smok*ies*

Both the complete and the shortened names are plural forms, but for the shortened names change the *y* to *i* and add *es.*

EDITING PRACTICE 1

On a separate sheet of paper, write the numbers 1 through 10. Write the plural of the following words beside the matching numbers on your paper.

1. Jones
2. lunch
3. tax
4. Conroy
5. Roosevelt
6. business
7. warehouse
8. factory
9. wrench
10. subsidiary

Now correct any errors in the use of plurals in the following sentences. If a sentence is correct, write *OK.*

1. We asked several companys to send us catalogs.
2. Foreign monies have been used to finance this project.
3. One of the territorys above its quota is our Southern Division.
4. The attornies did not agree on the amount of the settlement.
5. Several of our franchises are located in the Alleghenies.
6. According to the shareholders' report, the Davis own 32 percent of the company.
7. Perhaps the Doughertys will sell both their factories.
8. Of all the propertys that we inspected, only the plot of land on Sunset Street is worth the price.

FORMING SPECIAL PLURALS

In addition to the routine plurals, you will learn how to form the plurals of such special words as *woman, man,* and *child.* You will also learn to form the plurals of compound nouns and of titles used with names. Finally, there are a few plurals that are formed using the apostrophe, and you will also want to master these.

Vowel Changes   Some nouns form the plural by vowel changes.

man	men	woman	women
tooth	teeth	mouse	mice
foot	feet	goose	geese

Note, however, that the plural of *German* is *Germans* (not *Germen*).

Compound Nouns   A compound noun is a noun in which two or more words represent a single idea. When the compound is written as one word (no hyphen), then form the plural at the end of the word.

cupful	cupfuls
toothbrush	toothbrushes
textbook	textbooks
stepchild	stepchildren
courthouse	courthouses
letterhead	letterheads

EXCEPTION:

passerby	passersby

When the compound is written with either a space or a hyphen between the words, make plural the *main word* in the compound. The main word is the *most important* word in the compound.

bulletin board	bulletin boards
general manager	general managers
editor in chief	editors in chief
vice president	vice presidents
daughter-in-law	daughters-in-law
court-martial	courts-martial
notary public	notaries public
attorney-at-law	attorneys-at-law
lieutenant colonel	lieutenant colonels

When there is no main word in the hyphenated compound, form the plural at the end of the noun.

follow-up	follow-ups
write-in	write-ins
hand-me-down	hand-me-downs
tie-up	tie-ups
trade-in	trade-ins

LIVING LANGUAGE

Man does not live by words alone, despite the fact that sometimes he has to eat them.
—Adlai Stevenson

Titles With Names

Sometimes it is necessary to form the plural of a name with a title such as *Miss, Ms., Mrs.,* or *Mr.* In such cases make either the title or the name plural—not both. Note the plurals of these common titles:

SINGULAR	PLURAL
Miss	Misses
Ms.	Mses. or Mss.
Mrs.	Mesdames (*Mesdames* is a French word meaning "more than one *Mrs.*")
Mr.	Messrs. (*Messrs.* is the abbreviation for *messieurs,* the French word for "*misters.*")

Now compare the alternative ways to make a name with a title plural. In each case, only one word, the title *or* the name (not both), is made plural.

SINGULAR (ONE PERSON)	PLURAL (TWO OR MORE PEOPLE WITH THE SAME NAME AND TITLE)
Miss Jensen is the owner of this apartment building.	The *Misses* Jensen are the owners of this apartment building.
	The Miss *Jensens* are the owners of this apartment building.
Inform Ms. Oliver of the price changes.	Inform the *Mses.* Oliver of the price changes.
	Inform the Ms. *Olivers* of the price changes.
Yes, Mrs. Root coordinated the charity drive.	Yes, the *Mesdames* Root coordinated the charity drive.
	Yes, the Mrs. *Roots* coordinated the charity drive.
Please invite Mr. Feinberg to Saturday's event.	Please invite the *Messrs.* Feinberg to Saturday's event.
	Please invite the Mr. *Feinbergs* to Saturday's event.

Plurals With Apostrophes

As you will see in Section 4.4, apostrophes are used in possessive forms of nouns. In rare instances, however, an apostrophe is used in forming special plurals. In these instances the apostrophe prevents possible misreading—for example, plurals of capital or lowercase letters that could be misread if the plurals are formed in the usual way.

NO APOSTROPHE NEEDED	APOSTROPHE PREVENTS MISREADING
several M.D.s	learning your abc's
two CPAs	counting the c.o.d.'s
all Bs	earned three A's

Plurals such as *pros* and *cons, ins* and *outs,* and *dos* and *don'ts* are not likely to be misread.

EDITING PRACTICE 2

Correct any errors in the following sentences. Write *OK* for any sentence that is correct.

1. Does the store have a written policy concerning *trades-in*?
2. This announcement should be posted on all the *bulletins boards*.
3. Please be sure to include the *Messrs. Smiths* on your mailing list.
4. Several of the *woman* in this department are excellent candidates for promotion.
5. All the researchers in our group have earned their Ph.D.s.
6. The *Mesdames Crosbys* have approved the sale of the building and the land.
7. Of course, we consulted two *attorney-at-laws* before we made our final decision.
8. The Medical Department has three full-time *M.D.'s* on staff.

FORMING TRICKY PLURALS

Because there are so many exceptions to the rules for forming plurals of nouns ending in *o* and *f* or *fe*, you should use the dictionary to check the spellings of such plurals. In addition, you will find the dictionary especially helpful for checking nouns that originated in other languages and nouns that have only one form for both the singular and the plural. All these troublesome plurals are covered on the following pages.

Nouns Ending in *o*   When a singular noun ends in *o*, its plural is usually formed by adding *s*. In the examples below, note that all musical terms ending in *o* are included in this category.

dynamo	dynamos	memento	mementos
studio	studios	Eskimo	Eskimos
zero	zeros	ratio	ratios
radio	radios	cello	cellos
piano	pianos	soprano	sopranos
solo	solos	banjo	banjos
trio	trios	alto	altos

However, some nouns ending in *o* preceded by a consonant form the plural by adding *es*.

echo	echoes	motto	mottoes
tomato	tomatoes	veto	vetoes
hero	heroes	cargo	cargoes
embargo	embargoes	potato	potatoes

Nouns Ending in *f* or *fe*

For some singular nouns ending in *f* or *fe*, change the *f* or *fe* to *v* and add *es*. For others simply add *s*.

CHANGE *f* OR *fe* TO *v*; THEN ADD *es*

wife	wives	shelf	shelves
life	lives	loaf	loaves

JUST ADD *s*

plaintiff	plaintiffs	belief	beliefs
proof	proofs	chef	chefs

Foreign Nouns

Nouns that originated in other languages, such as *agenda* and *prospectus*, may form their plurals by adding *s* (*agendas*) or *es* (*prospectuses*). But many foreign nouns have both an "English plural" and a "foreign plural," as shown below.

SINGULAR	PLURAL	ENGLISH PLURAL
addendum	addenda	
alumna	alumnae	
alumnus	alumni	
analysis	analyses	
axis	axes	
bacterium	bacteria	
basis	bases	
crisis	crises	
criterion	criteria	criterions
curriculum	curricula	curriculums
datum	data*	
formula	formulae	formulas
fungus	fungi	
hypothesis	hypotheses	
index	indices	indexes
medium	media	mediums
memorandum	memoranda	memorandums
nucleus	nuclei	nucleuses
oasis	oases	
parenthesis	parentheses	
stadium	stadia	stadiums
stimulus	stimuli	
vertebra	vertebrae	vertebras

Data is now also considered correct in a singular construction, as in "The *data is* summarized on page 121."

In some cases the preferred form is the English plural (for example, *memorandums*); in other cases the preferred form is the foreign plural (for example, *criteria*). Obviously, there is no one rule that will simplify your using these words correctly. Be sure to consult your dictionary whenever you are uncertain about the plural form of a noun of foreign origin. If two different plural forms are given, use the form that appears first, since this is the preferred plural.

Singular or Plural?   Some nouns are always singular; others are always plural. Still others use the same form for both singular and plural. For these and other usage notations, learn to use your dictionary and a comprehensive, up-to-date reference manual.

ALWAYS SINGULAR	ALWAYS PLURAL	ONE FORM FOR BOTH SINGULAR AND PLURAL	
news	thanks	deer	salmon
genetics	trousers	fish	politics
mathematics	proceeds	odds	economics
aeronautics	pants	sheep	statistics
	riches	corps	shrimp
	tidings	Chinese	spaghetti
	credentials	moose	
	belongings	Japanese	
	scissors		

The *news* about the merger *is* certainly encouraging.   (NOT *news are.*)

Lilly's *credentials are* quite impressive.

A Japanese is the inventor of this instrument.

Several Japanese have bought the firm.

Note, too, how words such as *hundred, thousand,* and *dozen* are used in the following sentences.

One *hundred* people are expected.

Three *hundred* customers requested credit cards.   (NOT *Three hundreds.*)

Several *dozen* complaints were received.   (NOT *Several dozens.*)

EDITING PRACTICE 3

Select the correct word in each of the following sentences.

1. Your news about fourth-quarter interest rates (is, are) quite encouraging.
2. According to the reporter, Jim and Darren are the (heros, heroes) of the day.
3. Her (analysis, analyses) of the new financial situation was concise but informative.

4. Blue Star Industries manufactures and distributes (pianos, pianoes) all over the world.
5. The numbers in (parenthesis, parentheses) represent metric equivalents, don't they?
6. All the (datum, data) that we gathered will be compiled in tables at the end of this report.
7. The top and bottom (shelfs, shelves) contain all the file copies that you will need.
8. Bart and Jeff are going to the dinner tonight; their (wifes, wives) are meeting them there.

EDITING PRACTICE 4

Correct any errors in the following sentences. If a sentence is correct, write *OK*.

1. The United States threatened embargoes against both nations.
2. The proceeds from the special drive is expected to top $1 million!
3. Economics have always been a required course for all business students.
4. The company choir is seeking two more altoes for the upcoming holiday show.
5. Increased prices of potatos and tomatos will affect the consumer price index.
6. In both cases the plaintives claimed high damages.
7. The formulas they developed were remarkably similar.
8. To avoid such crisis in the future, our security staff is taking special precautions.

COMMUNICATION LABORATORY

APPLICATION EXERCISES

A. On a separate sheet of paper, write your corrections for any errors in the following sentences. Write *OK* for any sentence that is correct.

1. Most of the radioes that we import are sold through direct-mail advertising.
2. Did you know that the owners of Watts Enterprises are the Franklin's?
3. Nearly 70 percent of the alumnuses of Fitch University live within the tristate area.
4. Needless to say, we gladly reimbursed the Shermans for the defective merchandise.
5. Our interview with two senator-elects should draw a large television audience.

CONTINUED

6. Only one of the countys in the northern part of the state has already put the new system into effect.
7. Mr. and Mrs. Bunch have coordinated this charity drive in the past, but the Bunchs moved to Arizona last month.
8. Before we have this office painted, we must remove all these books from the shelfs.
9. According to the executor, the entire estate will be divided among Mrs. Gordon's four stepchilds.
10. Please be sure to file these letters, reports, and memorandums before we leave for the airport, Leonard.
11. The only important criteria, in our opinion, is the safety of all employees in the plant.
12. We are now waiting to hear from our attornies concerning the validity of the documents.
13. The company is owned by two brothers—the Messrs. Smiths—who have managed to make Smith Enterprises a million-dollar business in a very short time.
14. Because of the various government embargoes, we do not ship computer equipment to certain nations.
15. Only countrys listed on this sheet are permitted to place orders for computers with our firm.

B. Beginning with this exercise and continuing through Section 4.8, each Application Exercise B will contain review sentences to help you reinforce the grammar principles you have studied so far. Correct any errors in the following sentences; write *OK* for any sentence that is correct.

1. Both office's are being moved to the ninth floor.
2. Here are instructions for merging both halfs of the manuscript on to one diskette.
3. If these figures represent thousands, be sure to add three zeroes to each numeral as you enter these columns.
4. Use parenthesis to enclose metric equivalents; for example, 10 yards (9.14 meters).
5. In the past three years, our assets have grew an average of 20 percent a year.
6. Please be careful as you lie these delicate pieces on the countertop.
7. The Hamiltons have owned the firm for three generations.
8. Yes, both my daughter-in-laws are designers for this advertising agency.
9. Two of the bidders are the Mesdames Marxes, who want to build garden apartments on the property.
10. Two sales territorys that are now open are in Rochester, New York, and Boston, Massachusetts.
11. The news about Ms. Peterson confirms the rumors we have heard.

CONTINUED

12. If the Donnellys purchase the land, they will try to resell it quickly for a fast profit.
13. The pipes had froze because the walls were not insulated properly.
14. We have carefully tested all these waxs to ensure that they contain no harmful ingredients.
15. Mr. Claridge been with the law firm since 1986, hasn't he?

VOCABULARY AND SPELLING STUDIES

A. These words are often confused: *adverse, averse; preposition, proposition.* Distinguish between the meaning and the spelling of the words in each pair; then write a sample sentence using each word.

B. What does the suffix *ish* (as in *bookish, bluish,* and *devilish*) mean: (1) "resembling," (2) "full of," or (3) "made of"?

C. What does the suffix *ee* (as in *employee, lessee, mortgagee,* and *nominee*) mean: (1) "native of," (2) "state or quality of," (3) "the recipient of an action," or (4) "having the characteristics of"?

D. How do you spell the following:

1. The verb meaning "to be before"?
2. The number that follows *one*?
3. The adverb formed from *full*?

SECTION 4.4

POSSESSIVE NOUNS AND PRONOUNS

Then pronunciation of both singular and plural possessives is the same for most nouns—*employee's* and *employees', manager's* and *managers',* and so on. Because the simple plurals are also pronounced the same (*employees, managers*), writing these forms often results in misspellings.

You have already learned how to form plurals correctly, and so in this section we will examine identifying and forming possessive nouns. Study this section carefully to make sure that you can avoid errors in using possessive forms.

The first step in using possessive forms correctly is recognizing when a noun shows possession. When does a noun have ownership? What is owned? To show possession, you must answer these two questions. You must clearly identify who or what owns what.

LIVING LANGUAGE

If you don't know where you are going, you will probably end up somewhere else.
—Laurence J. Peter

To verify that ownership does indeed exist, you must be able to test the noun by using it in an ownership phrase. This means using the possessive noun with both a preposition or prepositional phrase such as *belonging to, of,* or *for* and the noun that is owned. Use the following Quick Trick to help you identify ownership nouns and the things owned.

QUICK TRICK

Find the Owner!

Reword the possessive phrase to be sure that you know which word is the "owner" and which word is the "object of ownership":

Ms. Nicholson's check   (the check *belonging to* Ms. Nicholson: object, *check*; owner, *Ms. Nicholson*)

several manufacturers' bids   (the bids *of* several manufacturers: object, *bids*; owner, *manufacturers*)

the boys' gymnasium   (the gymnasium *for* the boys: object, *gymnasium;* owner, *boys*)

With this method, you will be sure to locate the correct object and the correct owner. When you know the owners, of course, you will then know that *Ms. Nicholson, manufacturers,* and *boys* are the words that you must make possessive. The ownership phrase clearly shows you the exact form of the word that must be made to show possession.

POSSESSIVE NOUNS—BASIC USES

When used with a noun, the apostrophe is the symbol of possession: one *woman's* briefcase, several *employees'* records, *Katherine's* promotion. The apostrophe helps you to take a shortcut from the longer possessive expressions *the briefcase belonging to one woman, the records for several employees,* and *the promotion of Katherine.*

Before applying an apostrophe to an ownership word, however, always begin with an ownership phrase to identify the exact form of the noun that must be made to show possession. After isolating the ownership phrase, follow these three rules to place the apostrophe correctly in the possessive noun:

1. Add an apostrophe plus *s* ('s) to a noun that does not end with a pronounced *s*:

One *woman's* suggestion developed into a new product.

Five *women's* handbags were turned in to the police.

Because neither *woman* nor *women* ends in *s*, add an apostrophe plus *s* to form the possessive of these nouns. This rule applies to all nouns, singular and plural, that do not end with a pronounced *s*.

2. Add only the apostrophe to a plural noun that ends with a pronounced *s:*

> The *Smiths'* franchise is in Tampa, Florida.
>
> Several *clients'* contracts expire on December 31 of this year.
>
> We'll need about two *years'* time to renovate this old plant.
>
> A *students'* lounge will be constructed on the first floor.

To form the possessives of *Smiths, clients, years,* and *students,* add only the apostrophe.

3. Add either an apostrophe plus *s* (*'s*) or an apostrophe to a singular noun ending in a pronounced *s.*
   a. Add an apostrophe plus *s* (*'s*) to a singular noun ending in a pronounced *s* if the resulting possessive form is pronounced with an additional syllable.

> His *boss's* solution was to file a lawsuit against the manufacturer.   (*Boss's* is pronounced with an additional syllable—compare *boss's* with *boss.*)
>
> One *actress's* script did not have the revised pages.   (*Actress's* has one more syllable than *actress.*)

   b. Add only the apostrophe to a singular noun ending in *s* if the possessive form is *not* pronounced with an additional syllable. The key to this rule is to determine whether the possessive form would sound awkward if pronounced with the additional syllable.

> Of course, we checked to make sure that it was Ms. *Saunders'* signature. (The pronunciation of *Saunders's* would be awkward.)

NOTE: In official names of certain organizations, banks, or buildings, apostrophes may be omitted from the possessive forms; for example, *the Woman Executives Association, Manufacturers Bank,* and *The Theatrical Agents Building.* In all cases, however, always use the official spelling.

EDITING PRACTICE 1

Once you are confident that you can apply the rules for forming noun possessives, select the correct word in parentheses in the following sentences.

1. Our (employee's, employees') car was not involved in the accident.
2. We received only two (applicant's, applicants') résumés in response to yesterday's ad.
3. If Mr. (Walters', Walters's) bid is accepted, we will sell the Chicago warehouse by the end of the year.
4. Several (representative's, representatives') cars will be affected by the new lease agreement.
5. Is your (boss's, bosses') office still on this floor?

6. A new (woman's, women's) clothing store will open in the Anderson Mall on June 1.
7. You should give the store at least ten (day's, days') notice in such cases.
8. One (agent's, agents') commission check was delayed at our headquarters office.

EDITING PRACTICE 2

Do the following sentences have any errors in the use of apostrophes? Find and correct each error. If a sentence is correct, write *OK*.

1. Jims' car has been parked in the employee lot for three days.
2. Carol Young is handling the estate for the Kellys' children.
3. As you know, the treasurers' signature is required on all checks over $500.
4. Jeanette's new computer will be delivered next week.
5. One store owners' suggestion was to provide added security for the mall.
6. Ask Ms. Jenkins's assistant for an appointment to discuss these problems.
7. As you know, the nations' financial center is Wall Street, which is in New York City.
8. Striker's demands for higher wages will be discussed later this afternoon.

POSSESSIVE NOUNS—SPECIAL USES

Here are some additional rules for using the apostrophe with nouns to show possession. Study them carefully.

Compound Nouns   Form the possessive of a compound noun on the last word of the compound.

my *editor in chief's* budget   (The budget of my *editor in chief*. Because *editor in chief* does not end in *s*, add an apostrophe and *s* to form the possessive.)

both *homeowners'* policies   (The policies of both *homeowners*. Because *homeowners* ends in *s*, add only an apostrophe.)

my *brother-in-law's* new business   (The new business of my *brother-in-law*. Because *law* does not end in *s*, add an apostrophe and *s*.)

Joint Ownership   When two or more "owners" possess something jointly, place the apostrophe (or the apostrophe plus *s*) on the last owner's name.

Jack and Dorothy's original bid was for $25,000.   (One bid, jointly "owned" by both Jack and Dorothy. Place the apostrophe plus *s* only on the second name, *Dorothy's*.)

New York and New Jersey's plan to clean the Hudson River will begin on April 11.   (This is a shared plan, as indicated by placing the *'s* on the second term, *New Jersey's*.)

Separate Ownership   When two or more owners possess things individually or separately, place the apostrophe (or the apostrophe plus *s*) on the name of *each* owner.

> *Jack's* and *Dorothy's* assistants are experienced auditors.   (*Jack's assistant* and *Dorothy's assistant—both* are experienced auditors.)
>
> *New York's* and *New Jersey's* governors were fully supportive of the plan.   (In other words, "*New York's governor* and *New Jersey's governor* . . . ." Separate ownership requires separate possessive forms.)

The key to using possessives correctly to show joint ownership and separate ownership is to analyze the context of each sentence.

EDITING PRACTICE 3

Select the correct word in parentheses for each of the following sentences.

1. (Bliss & Paden's, Bliss's & Paden's) profit for this year is estimated to reach $4.2 million.
2. The annual tax on (Eric and Lisa's, Eric's and Lisa's) property is $3,250.
3. I think we should get (someone's else, someone else's) opinion on this proposal.
4. The projected revenue from (Lord and Wilson's, Lord's and Wilson's) foreign operation is about $5 million.
5. (Ray and Carole's, Ray's and Carole's) joint income tax statement was submitted past the April 15 deadline.
6. I visited (José's and George's, José and George's) homes while I was in Texas.

EDITING PRACTICE 4

Read the following sentences to correct any errors in the use of possessives. Write *OK* if the sentence is correct.

1. Her brother's and sister's shares in the new business are equal.
2. Her brother's and sister's business was recently incorporated.
3. Karen and Anns' new restaurant will open December 1.
4. Andrew's and Fred's new supervisor will arrive on Friday, March 3.
5. Yes, Andrew's and Fred's daughters also work for Burkland Enterprises.
6. Ohio's and West Virginia's shares of the river are different.

POSSESSIVE PERSONAL PRONOUNS

The personal pronouns are *I, we, you, he, she, it,* and *they.* In the chart on page 108, note the possessive forms of these personal pronouns—and note that they do *not* have apostrophes.

PERSONAL PRONOUNS	POSSESSIVE FORMS
I	my, mine
you	your, yours
he	his, his
she	her, hers
it	its, its
we	our, ours
they	their, theirs

The first pronoun in each pair of possessives—*my, your, his, her, its, our,* and *their*—is used as an adjective.

My plane leaves at 2 p.m.

His flight is scheduled to leave at 3 p.m., but *her* flight may be delayed until 4:30.

The pronouns *mine, yours, his, hers, its, ours,* and *theirs* replace possessive phrases such as *my book, your desk, her car,* and so on.

This is *my book.* OR: This is *mine.*

Is this *your pen?* OR: Is this *yours?*

She sent *her check.* OR: She sent *hers.*

As you see, the pronouns *mine, yours, his, hers, its, ours,* and *theirs* may never be used as modifiers; they always stand alone. Using personal pronouns correctly is tricky not because their usage is confusing (the opposite is true) but because some of the possessive forms of personal pronouns sound precisely like other words. Review the following groups, remembering that personal pronouns never have apostrophes. The first word in each heading is the possessive form of the personal pronoun.

Its, It's
The possessive pronoun *its* means "of it" or "belonging to it." *It's* is a contraction—a shortened form of *it is.*

The Willis Corporation is well known for *its* generosity to *its* employees.   (*Its generosity*—the generosity of it. *Its employees*—the employees of it. *Its* is a possessive form of a personal pronoun.)

It's not too late to enroll in a computer class for this semester.   (*It's*—a contraction meaning "it is." *It's* is not a personal pronoun. Note that there is no such word as *its'*.)

Their, They're, There
Their means "of them" or "belonging to them." *They're* is a contraction—a shortened form of *they are. There* may mean "in that place" or be used as an introductory word.

Find out which one of *their* warehouses will be open on Saturday. (Warehouses *belonging to them.*)

They're now in the conference room on the fifth floor.   (*They are* now . . . .)

Please leave the disks *there* when you are finished.   (Leave them *in that place*.)

There are only a few more invoices to process.   (Introductory word.)

Your, You're   *Your* means "belonging to you." *You're* is a contraction—a shortened form of *you are.*

When *you're* traveling, be sure to have *your* Insta-Charge card with you. (When *you are* traveling. The Insta-Charge card *belonging to you*.)

Whose, Who's   *Whose* is a possessive pronoun meaning "belonging to whom." *Who's* is a contraction for *who is* or *who has.*

Whose badge was found in the hallway?   (Badge *belonging to whom*?)

Who's working on the late shift tonight?   (*Who is* working . . . ?)

Who's been named to the committee?   (*Who has* been . . . ?)

Using the following Quick Trick will help you distinguish between contractions and possessive pronouns.

QUICK TRICK

Test the Contraction

To choose between *its/it's, their/they're,* and so on, test the sentence by reading it with the full form of the contraction. If the sentence makes sense, then the contraction is correct. If the sentence does not make sense, then the pronoun is correct.

Do you know when (they're, their) supposed to arrive?   (Read the sentence with the full form of the contraction: Do you know when *they are* supposed to arrive? Does the sentence make sense? Yes, and so *they're* is correct.)

Please give me (they're, their) new address.   (Again, read the sentence with *they are*: Please give me *they are* new address. Does the sentence make sense? No, and so the possessive personal pronoun *their* is correct.)

EDITING PRACTICE 5

In the following sentences, find all the errors in the use of possessive personal pronouns. If a sentence is correct, write *OK.*

1. While you're working at the microcomputer, please make a backup copy of this diskette.
2. Who's voice is that on the loudspeaker?
3. According to the police report, there van was damaged only slightly.
4. As soon as your ready to leave, just call me.

5. Their is one easy way to check this release date: call the West Coast office.
6. One benefit of this equipment is that its easy to operate.
7. Do you know whether this diskette is her's?
8. Alan, who's signature is on this check?
9. No matter whose car that is, it must be moved!

POSSESSIVE BEFORE A GERUND

A **gerund** is a verb form ending in *ing* and functioning as a noun. A noun or a pronoun before a gerund should be in the possessive case.

I heard about *Jack's* winning the monthly sales contest.   (NOT *Jack winning.*)

I heard about *your* winning the monthly sales contest.   (NOT *you winning.*)

We appreciated *Bob's* calling us and *his* sending us the new text on BASIC programming.   (NOT *Bob calling.* NOT *him sending.*)

EDITING PRACTICE 6

Select the correct word in parentheses.
1. She was angry, of course, at (him, his) leaving early on Friday afternoon.
2. Mrs. Meehan appreciated (us, our) volunteering to help her staff with the backlog of orders.
3. (You, Your) informing us of these changes has saved us a lot of time.
4. We are happy to hear about (you, your) accepting a new job offer closer to your home.
5. Thanks to (them, their) helping us with all the invoices, we were able to complete our work on time.
6. Were you bothered by (him, his) being late for the interview, or did you expect his tardiness?
7. (Janine, Janine's) winning the sales contest was assured when Acme Building placed its order.
8. The staff was convinced that (it, its) shipping the order on time depended on (them, their) settling the strike.
9. We are overjoyed at (you, your) receiving the promotion.

COMMUNICATION LABORATORY

APPLICATION EXERCISES

A. Choose the correct word in each of the following sentences.
1. Please inform our customers that there will be a (months, month's) delay in filling all orders for Acme products.

CONTINUED

2. We appreciated (Bob, Bob's, Bobs') helping us plan the sessions for the sales conference.
3. Most of the (executives, executive's, executives') in the training program rated the courses "Excellent."
4. The (Lutzes, Lutz's, Lutzes') have franchise operations in four different states.
5. The (Nelsons, Nelson's, Nelsons') holdings in General Metals Inc. have been drastically reduced during the last two years.
6. With two (weeks, week's, weeks') notice, we can ship and install any of the machines listed in this catalog.
7. Because business has been exceedingly slow, we have cut all our (managers, manager's, managers') expense budgets by 20 percent.
8. (Tim's and Laura's, Tim and Laura's) suggestion was to hire part-time help during the months of July and August.
9. Before we attend this afternoon's meeting, be sure that (your, you're) prepared to answer any questions concerning the manufacturing schedules.
10. The (Consolinos, Consolino's, Consolinos') newest store—their fifth—will be located in the Shadow Ridge Shopping Mall.
11. Please let us know (whose, who's) briefcase was left in the personnel office.
12. Do you know (whose, who's) presently recording in Studio A?
13. One sales (districts, district's, districts') goal is to exceed its last year's revenue by 32 percent.
14. One of our (divisions, division's, divisions') has set very ambitious sales goals for next year.
15. In an effort to help needy people in the area, our company has established a (children's, childrens') fund.

B. On a separate sheet of paper, write your corrections for any errors in the following sentences. Write *OK* if a sentence is correct.

1. The marketing director, according to Margaret, has chose Tampa, Florida, as the site of our annual sales convention.
2. She been asking about transfer opportunities because she enjoys living in the Boston area.
3. Randy said, "If I were you, I would ask one of the manager's to approve these purchase orders."
4. One editor in chief's retirement is scheduled for May; another's, for September.
5. How long have you knew about the potential sale of the property to Rasmussen Homes?
6. The documents that you're looking for have been laying on the reception desk for several days.
7. Paul and Al's wives always join them on their business trips.

CONTINUED

8. Have you heard about the possibility of him helping us with the annual report?
9. Is Gregorys' new office located in the new Host Building?
10. If its necessary to submit a claim to our insurance company also, we will do so.
11. When my assistant's finish this training course, they will begin a special two-week computer-training program in Dallas.
12. You must complete this form if your changing the beneficiary of your life insurance policy.
13. Mr. Langan asked two clerks to work on Saturdays during the summer months.
14. Do you know whether there planning to bring their families with them to this year's convention?
15. Several companies' now participate in and donate to this community drug-awareness program.

C. Write the correct plural or possessive form of each word or phrase in parentheses.

1. Luxor Fashions, Inc., is a well-known manufacturer of (woman) clothing.
2. This request for information was received from the (attorney general) office.
3. Ms. Nugent is the researcher (who) study is now receiving much nationwide publicity.
4. Try to use (someone else) terminal to see whether the same problem occurs.
5. Dr. (Hastings) account is handled by Gordon Moses.
6. We plan to sign a (year) lease for the district office.
7. All (employee) stock options must be exercised before the end of December.
8. Among the (CPA) in our office is Lillian Demarest.
9. All the (Nash) have already returned their response cards.
10. Miriam received all (A) last semester.

VOCABULARY AND SPELLING STUDIES

A. These words are often confused: *finely, finally, finale; expensive, expansive.* Explain the differences.

B. Do you know the difference between the following homonyms: *overdo, overdue; prophet, profit; hear, here*? Define each.

C. The words on page 113 can have either one *l* or two, but most American dictionaries list one spelling as preferred. Write the preferred spelling of each word.

CONTINUED

1. cancellation
2. cancelled
3. traveler
4. skilful
5. marvellous
6. installment

SECTION 4.5

OTHER PRONOUN FORMS

Y ou probably would not say, "Please send this contract to *he*." Nor would you say, "*Her* and *me* attended the meeting." These kinds of errors in pronoun usage are seldom made.

Other kinds of pronoun errors are not always so obvious. How many times have you heard a person say, "Between you and *I*" instead of "Between you and *me*" or "Sue has worked here longer than *me*" instead of "Sue has worked here longer than *I*"? These common errors in case form will be given special emphasis in your study of pronouns.

You have already studied possessive case forms of personal pronouns. Here you will study the other case forms of personal pronouns so that you will be able to avoid *all* the common errors of pronoun use and communicate effectively both in speaking and in writing.

CASE FORMS OF PRONOUNS

Case refers to the form of a noun or pronoun that indicates the relationship of that word to the other words in the sentence. For example, you have already learned that a noun or pronoun in the *possessive* case shows ownership. Other case forms are the *nominative* and the *objective*.

Nouns use the same form for both the nominative and the objective case. Pronouns, however, change their form. Compare these sentence pairs.

NOMINATIVE
Richard wrote this brochure.   (*Richard* is a nominative case noun.)

He wrote this brochure.   (*He* is a nominative case pronoun. *He* substitutes for *Richard* in the sentence above.)

OBJECTIVE
Congratulate *Richard*.   (*Richard* is an objective case noun, object of the verb *give*.)

Congratulate him.   (*Him* is an objective case pronoun, object of the verb *give*.)

POSSESSIVE
This is *Richard's* book.   (*Richard's* is a possessive case noun.)

This is *his* book.   (*His* is a possessive case pronoun.)

These sentences show the basic relationship of the nominative, the objective, and the possessive cases of nouns and pronouns to other words in the sentence. Note how pronouns substitute for nouns—*he* for *Richard* in the first pair of sentences, *him* for *Richard* in the second pair, and *his* for *Richard's* in the third pair.

Here is a list of nominative and objective pronouns. Review them before you continue.

NOMINATIVE PRONOUNS		OBJECTIVE PRONOUNS		EXAMPLES
I	we	me	us	*I* gave; *we* went; for *me*; hired *us*
you	you	you	you	*you* are; with *you*
he she it	they	him her it	them	*he* has; *she* has; *it* will be; *they* know; to *him*; send *her*; on *it*; gave *them*
who	who	whom	whom	*who* has; appointed *whom*

NOMINATIVE CASE

The most common uses of the nominative case pronouns are as subjects of verbs and as complements of "being" verbs.

Subject of a Verb   Pronouns that are the subjects of verbs must be in the nominative case.

I asked Renee and Frank to attend the meeting.   (*I* is the subject of the verb *asked*.)

He was promoted last week.   (*He* is the subject of the verb phrase *was promoted*.)

We will contact you as soon as the shipment arrives.   (*We* is the subject of the verb phrase *will contact*.)

Complement of a "Being" Verb   A noun or a pronoun that completes the meaning of a "being" verb is called a **complement.** As you know, of course, the "being" verbs are *am, are, is, was, were, be, being,* and *been.* A pronoun that follows a "being" verb must be in the nominative case.

The person who recommended changing these procedures was *I*.   (*I* completes the meaning of the "being" verb *was*. As a complement of a "being" verb, the nominative case form *I* must be used.)

The vice president in charge of marketing is *she*.   (*She* completes the meaning of the "being" verb *is*; therefore, the nominative case is required.)

Could the visitors in the auditorium have been *they*?   (*They* completes the meaning of the "being" verb *could have been*; therefore, the nominative case is required.)

Complement of Infinitive *To Be* When *To Be* Has No Subject

Any pronoun that follows and completes the meaning of the infinitive *to be* when *to be* has no subject is in the nominative case. To apply this rule, remember the following:

1. Consider only the infinitive *to be.* Do not try to use the rule in any other situation.
2. The infinitive *to be* has a subject *only when a noun or pronoun immediately precedes it.*

Look at two sentences where the infinitive *to be* does *not* have a subject.

I would not wish to be *he.* (Is there a noun or a pronoun immediately preceding *to be*? No. Then in this situation *to be* has no subject, and the complement *he* is correct because the pronoun must be in the nominative case.)

The owners appear to be *they.* (Since *to be* has no subject immediately preceding it, the complement of the infinitive *to be* must be *they*, not *them*, because *they* is in the nominative case.)

In these sentences the infinitive *to be* does have a subject:

Stanley thought *her* to be me. (*Her* is the subject of *to be.*)

The receptionist mistakenly believed the *visitors* to be us. (*Visitors* is the subject of *to be.*)

The following Quick Trick can help you with the *to be* rule.

QUICK TRICK

No Subject—*Nominative* Case

For a memory hook on which to hang the *to be* rule, make this connection:

NO subject—*NO*minative case.

NO is the word you must remember, and *NO* starts the word *NO*minative. Think this over. You will be amazed to see that the Quick Trick will help you to apply the *to be* rule.

CLASS PRACTICE 1

Choose the correct pronoun in parentheses.

1. Didn't you realize that the person at the front of the room was (I, me)?
2. Yes, she was in the bank this morning, so perhaps the woman you saw was (she, her).
3. No, I would not choose to be (he, him).

4. Frank said that (we, us) would not have the approval of the committee until Monday.
5. As you may have heard, (they, them) are going to reject our offer.
6. Under these circumstances I certainly would not wish to be (she, her).

EDITING PRACTICE 1

Now correct any errors in the use of the nominative case in the following sentences. Write *OK* if the sentence is correct.

1. The instructor thought him to be me.
2. Next November, according to Betty, them will completely revise our procedures manual.
3. Teach your staff members to say "This is he" or "This is she" when a caller asks for them.
4. The executives who voted in favor of expanding the medical and dental benefits were they.
5. The person you saw at the airport could not have been him.
6. Are you sure the assistant who made these excellent suggestions was her?
7. The winners of the quality awards were Leah and him.
8. We trainers knew they would win.
9. Us nominees felt good about the results.
10. It was we who knew the shortest route to the warehouse.

OBJECTIVE CASE

The objective case of personal pronouns is used when a pronoun is the object of a preposition or the object of a verb. The following rules also apply to *whom* and *whomever*, the objective case forms of the pronouns *who* and *whoever*.

Object of a Preposition   A preposition is always used in a *prepositional phrase*. Every prepositional phrase has either a noun or a pronoun as an object.

PREPOSITION	PREPOSITIONAL PHRASE	EXAMPLES
to	to the manager	Give the report *to the manager*. (The noun *manager* is the object of the preposition *to*.)
	to her	Give the report *to her*. (The pronoun *her* is the object of the preposition *to*.)

PREPOSITION	PREPOSITIONAL PHRASE	EXAMPLES
from	from the attorneys	The message *from the attorneys* arrived this morning. (The noun *attorneys* is the object of the preposition *from*.)
	from them	The message *from them* arrived yesterday. (The pronoun *them* is the object of the preposition *from*).
against	against the proposal	The city council was *against the proposal*. (The noun *proposal* is the object of the preposition *against*.)
	against it	The city council voted *against it*. (The pronoun *it* is the object of the preposition *against*.)
for	for David, Anne, and me	Write checks for *David, Anne, and me*. (The object of the preposition *for* is *David, Anne, and me*, which includes the nouns *David* and *Anne* and the pronoun *me*.)
	for us	Sign checks *for us*. (The pronoun *us* is the object of the preposition *for*.)

Object of a Verb   Now notice how objective pronouns are used as objects of verbs.

Michael trained *them*.   (The pronoun *them* is the object of the verb *trained*.)

Janet told John, Chris, and *her* the news about the warehouse sale.   (The pronoun *her* is the object of the verb *told*. The nouns *John* and *Chris* are also the objects of the verb *told*, of course.)

CHOOSING THE CORRECT FORM

Bill and I or *Bill and Me*?   Nouns and pronouns are commonly joined by *and* or *or* in compound subjects and compound objects.

LIVING LANGUAGE
The most valuable of all talents is that of never using two words when one will do.
—Thomas Jefferson (1743–1826)

COMPOUND SUBJECT	**COMPOUND OBJECT**
Bill and *I* will go . . .	. . . to Bill and *me*
Dr. Lopez or *he* is . . .	. . . for Dr. Lopez and *him*
She and *I* wrote . . .	. . . written by her and *me*

To be sure that you always use the correct pronoun in compounds such as these, follow this Quick Trick:

QUICK TRICK

Use the Pronoun by Itself

For compounds that include pronouns, test the pronoun *by itself*, as shown here:

> Kristina and (I, me) may go with Mr. Rosen.   (Omit *Kristina and*, and the answer becomes clear: "*I* may go . . . .")

> Mr. Rosen invited Kristina and (I, me).   (Again, test the pronoun by itself. Omit *Kristina and*: "Mr. Rosen invited . . . *me*.")

Note that pronoun choice in the following constructions can be tested in a similar manner:

> (We, Us) students enjoy reading interesting books.   (Read the sentence omitting the noun *students*, and the answer becomes clear: "(We, Us) . . . enjoy reading interesting books." Obviously, you would say "*We* enjoy," not "*Us* enjoy.

> "They have asked (we, us) students to read another book.   (To decide between *we students* and *us students*, omit the noun *students*: "They have asked *us* . . . to read another book.")

CLASS PRACTICE 2

Choose the correct pronoun in the following sentences.

1. Is Jack or (she, her) among the candidates for district manager?
2. Yes, (we, us) cashiers always double-check one another's receipts.
3. The lab technicians and (they, them) have thoroughly reviewed the new safety procedures.
4. The marketing staff always gives (we, us) sales representatives helpful advice and other support.
5. Early this morning they asked Roberta and (I, me) to substitute for them at tomorrow's budget meeting.
6. Our manager told the president that the booklets were written by Richard and (I, me).

EDITING PRACTICE 2

Correct any errors in the use of pronouns in the following sentences.

1. Please be sure to give we proofreaders enough time to check the galleys carefully.
2. Erica and him will conduct the training program.
3. Only Marsha and her have the authority to sign these documents.
4. Needless to say, we were surprised to learn that Ms. Crawford had appointed Frances and I district managers.
5. Our vice president, Jessica Rosen, informed Larry and I of her decision only this morning.
6. As you requested, I sent additional copies to Mr. Owens, Ms. Cohn, and he.

More Than I or More Than Me?

In the following kinds of sentences, we generally omit the words in brackets because these words are understood in the context of the sentence.

Steve prefers working on microcomputers more than *I* [prefer working on microcomputers.]   (By completing the sentence, you can easily see that *I*, not *me*, is correct. *I* is the subject of the understood verb *prefer*.)

This cough medicine seems to help you more than *me*.   (To choose between *I* and *me*, supply the understood words: "This cough medicine seems to help you more than [*the cough medicine helps*] me." **or** ". . . more than [*it helps*] me." *Me* is the correct form. *Me* is the object of the understood verb *helps*.)

Choosing the correct pronoun in such sentences often requires an understanding of the meaning of the sentence, because sometimes either the nominative or the objective pronoun could be correct.

Jim likes Michelle better than (*I, me*).   (Depending on the meaning, either pronoun could possibly be correct. "Jim likes Michelle better than *I like Michelle*." "Jim likes Michelle better than *he likes me*." The correct pronoun depends on the context, so pay special attention to the meaning of such sentences.)

CLASS PRACTICE 3

Choose the correct pronoun in the following sentences. Be sure to supply the missing words in order to make your choices.

1. Do you think she is as interesting a speaker as (he, him)?
2. Sue and I work together on more projects than (they, them).
3. I usually open as many new accounts each year as (she, her).
4. Andy has been with the company longer than (I, me).
5. This new benefit program has more advantages for you than (I, me).
6. Does Tom have as much experience as (he, him)?

***Self*-Ending Pronouns**   *Myself, yourself, himself, herself, itself, ourselves, yourselves,* and *themselves* are pronouns. They are used (1) to emphasize and (2) to reflect a noun or pronoun already expressed.

To Emphasize   Note how the *self*-ending pronouns add force to the following statements.

Ms. Cooper corrected the debit statements *herself.*   (The sentence reads correctly without *herself,* but do you see how *herself* adds emphasis to the statement?)

I requested those printouts *myself.*   (Again, *myself* can be omitted from the sentence, but without *myself* the sentence is a statement without emphasis.)

Be sure that the placement of the *self*-ending pronoun is correct so that it does not change the meaning of the message.

Bruce *himself* admitted that the results of the study were startling.   (The placement of *himself* is correct, but many may have said or written "Bruce admitted that the results of the study were startling *himself.*" Quite a different meaning!)

To Reflect   The *self*-ending pronouns are also used to refer to nouns or pronouns that have already been identified in sentences.

The sales representatives convinced *themselves* that the new product would not be successful.   (Here, *themselves* refers to *sales representatives,* the subject of the sentence.)

Warren asked *himself* whether he should continue with the project.   (*Himself* refers to the subject, *Warren.*)

Self-ending pronouns are often incorrectly used as replacements for nominative and objective pronouns, as in the following examples.

Larry, Phil, and *myself* would be delighted to assist you.   (The sentence should be "Larry, Phil, and *I* would be . . . .")

Mr. Diaz asked Larry and *myself* for help.   (The sentence should be "Mr. Diaz asked Larry and *me* . . . .")

EDITING PRACTICE 3

Correct any errors in the following sentences. Write *OK* if the sentence is correct.

1. Milton said that he would leave himself at noon.
2. The district manager himself does not want to delay the negotiations.
3. Apparently, Linda Gibson and myself were not on the mailing list.
4. Members of the board were not convinced themselves that they could keep the plant from closing.
5. Our driver education teacher taught me to drive himself.
6. Please be sure to get two tickets for Carla and myself.

Pronouns in Appositives   In writing and speaking, we often use an **appositive,** a word or group of words that explains or gives additional information about a preceding word or phrase.

> Ms. Reilly, *my colleague,* is an acknowledged expert in this area.   (The words *my colleague* give additional information about the subject, *Ms. Reilly. My colleague* is an appositive.)

> The Austin Corporation, *a leader in oil exploration,* is backing the research study.   (The appositive is *a leader in oil exploration;* it gives additional information about the subject, *the Austin Corporation.*)

Errors in the use of appositives frequently occur when an appositive includes a pronoun. Keep in mind that the case of the pronoun is the same as the case of the noun with which the pronoun is in apposition.

> Only two agents, Bruce and *she,* sell thermoplastics.   (*Bruce and she* is in apposition with the subject, *only two agents.* Therefore, *she* is correct.)

> We sell thermoplastics through only two agents, Bruce and *her.*   (*Bruce and her* is in apposition with *only two agents,* which is the object of the preposition *through.* Therefore, *her* is correct.)

Apply the Quick Trick below to these two examples.

QUICK TRICK

Use Only the Appositive

To test whether the pronoun in the appositive should be nominative or objective case, just omit the word or words with which the pronoun is in apposition. The correct answer will then be obvious.

> Our most successful engineers, Susan and (he, him), have been assigned to the Hong Kong project.   (Cross out *Our most successful engineers,* and the sentence then reads: "Susan and (he, him) have been assigned . . . ." Obviously, *he* stands out as the correct pronoun.)

> The Hong Kong project has been assigned to our most successful engineers, Susan and (he, him).   (Again, cross out the words with which the pronoun is in apposition, and the sentence then reads: "The Hong Kong project has been assigned to Susan and (he, him)." The answer is now clear. *Him* is correct; it is the object of the preposition *to.*)

CLASS PRACTICE 4

Select the correct answers to these sentences.

1. Only one of the assistants, Annette or (he, him), will accompany Ms. Carter.
2. Please explain to the auditors, Ronald and (she, her), why we had to change our schedule.

WORLD VIEW

The color *green*—To Americans green suggests freshness and good health, but in countries with dense green jungles, it is associated with disease. Green is a favorite among Arabs but forbidden in portions of Indonesia. In Japan green is a good high-tech color, but Americans would avoid green electronic equipment. (Edward T. Hall, *The Silent Language,* Garden City, New York, Anchor Books, 1973)

   3. Ms. Simmons plans to present a special award to the three supervisors—Leonora, Harold, and (she, her).
   4. The sales brochures written by two of our staff members, Laura and (he, him), have been very effective marketing tools.
   5. Ask either of my assistants, Walter or (she, her), to revise this first draft.
   6. The trainees, Nancy Hardwick and (he, him), will complete their program by the end of this week.

WHO AND *WHOM*, *WHOEVER* AND *WHOMEVER*

The question of whether to use *who* or *whom* arises often, and the same dilemma presents itself with *whoever* and *whomever.*

Selecting the Correct Form   *Who* and *whoever* are nominative forms; *whom* and *whomever* are objective forms. Use the following procedures to help you decide which form is correct.

Example 1

Example sentence: (Who, Whom) is responsible for ordering new equipment?

1. Isolate the word group that *begins* with the pronoun.

   (who, whom) is responsible for ordering new equipment

2. Place the word group in normal order, if it is not already so.

   Word group is in normal order.

3. Substitute *he* for *who* and *him* for *whom.*

   (he, him) is responsible for ordering new equipment

4. If the nominative pronoun *he* is correct, use *who;* if the objective pronoun *him* is correct, use *whom.*

   Who is responsible for ordering new equipment?

Example 2

Example sentence: Lisa Chan is the person (who, whom) our manager selected for the position.

1. Isolate the word group that *begins* with the pronoun.

   (who, whom) our manager selected for the position

2. Place the word group in normal order, if it is not already so.

   our manager selected (who, whom) for the position

3. Substitute *he* for *who* and *him* for *whom*.

> our manager selected (he, him) for the position

4. If the nominative pronoun *he* is correct, use *who;* if the objective pronoun *him* is correct, use *whom*.

> Lisa Chan is the person *whom* our manager selected for the position.

Example 3

Example sentence: The receptionist is not sure (who, whom) the caller could have been.

1. Isolate the word group that *begins* with the pronoun.

> (who, whom) the caller could have been

2. Place the word group in normal order, if it is not already so.

> the caller could have been (who, whom)

3. Substitute *he* for *who* and *him* for *whom*.

> the caller could have been (he, him)

4. If the nominative pronoun *he* is correct, use *who;* if the objective pronoun *him* is correct, use *whom*.

> The receptionist is not sure *who* the caller could have been.   (The pronoun *who* is correct because it completes the "being" verb *could have been.*)

CLASS PRACTICE 5

A. Isolate the *who* or *whom* word group in each of the following sentences.

1. The additional funds should be allocated to (whoever, whomever) will be in charge of the Planning Committee.
2. The additional funds should be allocated to (whoever, whomever) Ms. Guffey appoints to head the Planning Committee.
3. Robert Brereton, (who, whom) established this company in 1978, is still the major stockholder.
4. We intend to give the contract to (whoever, whomever) will provide the best service.
5. Did Mr. Lyons tell anyone (who, whom) he has selected as national sales manager?

B. Using the word groups that you isolated in the exercise above, change to normal order any word group that is not already so.

C. Again using the same word groups, select the correct pronoun for each sentence. Be sure to mentally substitute *he* and *him* before you make your choices.

EDITING PRACTICE 4

Now you should easily be able to find errors in the use of *who, whom, whoever,* and *whomever.* Apply your skill by finding errors in the following sentences. Write *OK* if the sentence is correct.

1. We generally distribute these complimentary consumer guides to whomever asks for one.
2. As you know, Mark, the award will be presented to whoever sells the greatest number of new cars through December 31.
3. I attended college with one of the attorneys who Mrs. Basil hired.
4. Of course, I'd be delighted to work with whoever you assign.
5. I believe I know who will be appointed director of research.
6. Barbara asked, "Does anyone know who Ms. Williams called before she left?"

Interrupter With *Who, Whom* A parenthetical expression such as *I think, we believe,* or *she says* sometimes interrupts a *who, whom* statement clouding the choice of *who* or *whom.* To make the choice correctly every time, just omit the parenthetical expression and follow the usual procedure for selecting *who* or *whom.*

Example 4

Example sentence: Is Sharon the representative (who, whom) he said I should see?

1. Isolate the word group that begins with the pronoun.

(who, whom) he said I should see

2. Omit the interrupting words.

(who, whom) I should see

3. Place the remaining words in normal order, if it is not already so.

I should see (who, whom)

4. Substitute *he* for *who* and *him* for *whom.*

I should see (he, him)

5. If the nominative pronoun *he* is correct, use *who;* if the objective pronoun *him* is correct, use *whom.*

Is Sharon the representative *whom* he said I should see?

CLASS PRACTICE 6

Select the correct pronouns for the following sentences. Omit any parenthetical expressions, and be sure to change the *who, whom* statement to normal order if necessary.

1. The sales representatives in this region selected Elena DeCapo, (who, whom) I suspect they consider their best spokesperson.
2. Is Tyler the trainee (who, whom) you thought I wanted to transfer to the Sales Department?
3. She is a supervisor (who, whom) all of us believe has great executive potential with this company.
4. Janice is the writer (who, whom) most of us think creates the most effective sales brochures and ads.
5. Mike Harrison is one of the engineers (who, whom) I think you should invite to these special planning meetings.
6. Is Mrs. Martino the executive (who, whom) I think you should ask about the new position?
7. Joline is the copywriter (who, whom) we think should be promoted.

COMMUNICATION LABORATORY

APPLICATION EXERCISES

A. Select the correct pronoun for each of the following sentences. Be sure to know the reasons for your choices.

1. Gary Handler, (who, whom) we hired as a consultant, has excellent credentials in the field of electrical engineering.
2. Has Diane been a manager as long as (she, her)?
3. As you know, Ms. Abrams is a person (who, whom) everyone trusts.
4. Frankly, John Lester knows more about this computer than (I, me).
5. Anthony gave the checks directly to the clients, Mr. Dobrian and (she, her).
6. No, Charles and Dennis are not as careful in their work as (we, us).
7. Carole and (I, me, myself) will discuss these benefits with someone in the Department of Human Resources.
8. When will he announce (who, whom) the new manager will be?
9. Among the most successful sales representatives in the company are Cheryl and (he, him).
10. Give these discount coupons to (whoever, whomever) requests them.
11. Do you know (who, whom) Donald asked to complete the analysis?
12. Donna is not sure (who, whom) the caller could have been.
13. Has Ms. Conrad told you (who, whom) she has chosen to attend the convention?
14. Two of our brokers, Daniel and (he, him), will explain the government's rules and regulations.
15. The new dental program benefits full-time workers more than (we, us).

CONTINUED

B. On a separate sheet of paper, correct any errors in the following sentences. Write *OK* for any sentence that is correct.

1. After you revise this report, send a copy to Mr. Rodgers and save one copy for myself.
2. As a result of the budget cuts, each departments' expenses will be reduced by 15 percent.
3. Does anyone know to whom the refund should be sent?
4. Two trainees, Roseanne and he, have been assigned to the Advertising Department.
5. Who should I ask for an explanation of this clause in my automobile insurance policy?
6. Who has Ms. Tavares named as the new representative for the Eastern Region?
7. The movers have already took all the furniture from this floor.
8. Most of those packages have laid there since we moved from our Fifth Street office.
9. As usual, Paul and myself will coordinate the sales meetings.
10. One of the companys that rent space in this building is Granger Plastics.
11. Because he felt faint, we told Evan to lie down for a few minutes.
12. After we had spoken with a tax expert, we understood how to maintain our records.
13. Bill and me are confident that we can complete this study before March 15.
14. If your planning to go to Atlanta, be sure to visit Charles Spivak.
15. We have not yet received Mikes' vacation schedule, have we?

VOCABULARY AND SPELLING STUDIES

A. These words are often confused: *lean, lien; deference, difference.* Explain the distinctions between them.

B. Complete these analogies:

1. *True* is to *false* as *perfect* is to _____.
2. *Familiar* is to *strange* as *major* is to _____.
3. *Abundant* is to *scarce* as *natural* is to _____.
4. *Conservative* is to *liberal* as *valuable* is to _____.

C. Words ending in *-able, -ible, -ance,* and *-ence* often cause writers problems. Which of the following are spelled correctly? Correct the misspelled words.

1. intelligible
2. correspondance
3. incapable
4. collectable
5. intelligence
6. grievence

PREDICATE AGREEMENT WITH SUBJECTS

Nonstandard English is often used in movies, television shows, popular songs, and conversation. In fact, errors such as "he don't" and "it don't" are heard so frequently that many times *they begin to sound correct to listeners*. They are, of course, *not* correct. Standard English requires us to say "he doesn't" and "it doesn't."

In this section you will study subject-verb agreement principles. These agreement principles govern whether a singular or a plural verb should be used with a particular subject or a particular kind of subject.

BASIC AGREEMENT RULE

In Section 4.1 you learned that a sentence can be divided into two parts: the complete subject and the complete predicate. The core of the complete subject is the simple or compound subject. To identify it, you must mentally omit any prepositional phrases from the complete subject:

Our *supply* of machine parts *is stored* in Building C.   (Here the prepositional phrase *of machine parts* must be mentally omitted to identify the simple subject, *supply*.)

The core of the predicate is the verb or verb phrase. In this section you will learn to match the correct verb or verb phrase with the simple or compound subject of the sentence.

The principle of subject-predicate agreement is this: *A predicate must agree with its subject in number and in person*. Specifically, those words in the predicate that must agree with the subject are any verbs and pronouns that refer to the subject. Therefore, you must pay attention to (1) agreement of verbs with the subject and (2) agreement of pronouns with the subject.

Agreement of Verb With Subjects   Notice how the verb agrees with its subject in these sentences:

The vice president *reviews* all salary guidelines.   (The verb *reviews* agrees with the subject *vice president*. Both are singular forms.)

Several executives *review* all salary guidelines.   (Now the subject is *executives*. The verb *review* agrees with the plural subject, *executives*.)

When applying the rules of subject-verb agreement, remember that plural nouns usually end in *s* or *es,* but an *s* ending on a verb indicates that it is a *singular* verb. Thus, in the above examples, "vice president reviews" and "several executive*s* review" both illustrate correct subject-verb agreement. Note the following examples:

SINGULAR NOUN AND VERB	PLURAL NOUN AND VERB
the woman is	the women are
an editor in chief has	both editors in chief have
one person says	two persons say
Mr. Quinn does	Mr. and Mrs. Quinn do
one person writes	two persons write

Agreement of Pronoun With Subject   When the predicate includes any pronouns that refer to the subject, those pronouns must agree with the subject.

Mr. Irwin has signed and returned *his* contract.   (The pronoun *his* refers to and must agree with the subject, *Mr. Irwin.*)

Mrs. Irwin has signed and returned *her* contract.   (Because the subject is now *Mrs. Irwin,* the correct pronoun is *her.*)

Mr. and Mrs. Irwin have signed and returned *their* contract.   (The pronoun *their* agrees with the subject, *Mr. and Mrs. Irwin.*)

I decided to take *my* vacation in August.   (The pronoun *my* refers to and agrees with the subject, *I.*)

Making such pronouns agree with the subject is usually a simple matter, especially when the subject is so easily identified, as in the above sentences.

CLASS PRACTICE 1

Select the correct verbs and pronouns in the following sentences. Assume that the pronoun refers to the subject.

1. The X ray (has, have) been returned in (its, their) original folder.
2. Mary Ellen (wants, want) to change (his, her, their) reservations for tomorrow's flight to Chicago.
3. The technicians still (does, do) claim that (his, her, their) recommendations will ensure greater safety in the plant.
4. One woman from our list of applicants (has, have) been interviewed already: (his, her, their) résumé is on my desk.
5. If Byron (needs, need) another manual for (his, her, their) department, send a copy by messenger.
6. The man who requested a credit (do, does) not know (his, her, their) account number.

EDITING PRACTICE 1

Now correct any agreement errors in the sentences on page 129. Write *OK* if the sentence is correct.

1. Anna prefer answering her own telephone.
2. One manager left their briefcase in the conference room.
3. That client called to say that they want to change the order.
4. He really don't have that information readily available.
5. These apartment buildings has intercoms in its foyers.
6. Customers who have used our credit plan have reported that they find the interest rates reasonable.

COMPOUND SUBJECTS

Compound subjects are those joined by *and* or *or*. Special rules apply to matching verbs with these subjects.

Subjects Joined by *And*   A compound subject in which the parts are joined by *and* is generally matched with a plural verb. Any pronouns appearing in the predicate that refer to the subject must also be written in the plural form.

> One disk drive *and* a color monitor *are* included in this sale price.   (The two parts of the compound subject are *disk drive* and *monitor*. *Are* is the correct verb to agree with this plural compound subject.)

> Yukari *and* Louis *have* been coordinating the seminars.   (Again, two subjects are joined by *and*. The plural verb *have* is correct.)

If the parts of a compound subject joined by *and* represent a single person or thing, use a singular verb. Pronouns referring to the subject also appear in the singular form.

> *Macaroni and cheese is* served in the company cafeteria every Friday. (*Macaroni and cheese* is one meal; therefore, it takes a singular verb.)

> Yesterday my *friend and companion,* Grace Bowshier, *was* injured in an automobile accident.   (Here the subject *friend and companion* represents one person who is both a friend and a companion. The singular verb *was* is correct.)

Compound subjects modified by *each*, *every*, or *many a* take a singular verb. Pronouns referring to the subject are also expressed in singular form.

> *Each* faculty member and administrator *is* expected to take part in the graduation exercises.   (*Is* is correct because *faculty member and administrator* is modified by *each*.)

> *Every* district manager and regional manager *has* been invited to dinner with *his or her* spouse.   (The singular *has* and *his or her* are correct because the compound subject is modified by *every*.)

> *Many a* student and teacher at our school *has* complained about the litter in the eating areas.   (The singular *has* is correct because the compound subject is modified by *many a*.)

CLASS PRACTICE 2

Apply the agreement rules concerning compound subjects to the following sentences.

1. Many a driver and dispatcher in this company (has, have) made a large profit by investing (his or her, their) money in company stock throughout their careers..
2. Every account manager and loan officer (has, have) been carefully selected and trained.
3. Did you know that Emil's agent and adviser (is, are) his sister?
4. No, Jeffrey and Laura (does, do) not agree that these bond funds are safe investments.
5. The computer operators and their supervisor (is, are) developing a training brochure.
6. Every man and woman in our three district offices (needs, need) to receive information about how (he or she, they) can take advantage of the tuition-refund program.

Subjects Joined by *Or* or *Nor* Whenever the parts of a compound subject are joined by *or* or *nor,* make the predicate agree with that part of the subject that is closer to the verb.

Only *Ms. Gaber or* her *assistants have* the authority to sign these vouchers. (Which part of the subject is closer to the verb? Answer: *assistants.* Therefore, the plural verb *have* is correct.)

Neither *you nor I am* responsible for closing the store on Wednesdays. (Since *I* is closer to the verb, the singular verb *am* is correct.)

CLASS PRACTICE 3

The following sentences have compound subjects joined by *or* or *nor.* Choose the words in parentheses that correctly agree with the subjects.

1. According to this manual, an independent auditor or the company treasurer (receives, receive) the official rebate from the government, but (he or she, they) must claim the total amount as income.
2. Of course, the president or the vice presidents (has, have) authority to approve all vouchers and sign checks.
3. Neither Deborah nor Valerie (has, have) discussed this problem with (her, their) supervisor.
4. A branch manager or an executive vice president (is, are) always on the premises during banking hours.
5. Neither Mr. VanNoy nor we (wishes, wish) to cancel the meeting.
6. Generally, Suzanne or Vernon (places, place) all orders for supplies.
7. The new executive director or the members of the administrative staff attend the board meetings. (attend, attends)

EDITING PRACTICE 2

Correct the predicates in the following sentences to make sure that they agree with their compound subjects. Write *OK* for any sentence that is correct.

1. Either platinum or nickel is used in such alloys.
2. Bettejean or her assistants usually does double-check the invoices before they are mailed.
3. I think that Ray, Andrew, and Sara has made his or her reservations.
4. This computer and the attached printer was leased from General Equipment Inc.
5. Either her daughter or her son are coming to the office to pick up this check; please give it to them if I am out.
6. Perhaps the hard drive or the central processing unit were damaged in transit.

SPECIFIC AGREEMENT PRINCIPLES

The agreement principles you have studied so far apply generally to simple and compound subjects. There are, however, a few specific agreement principles that you need to learn to complete your study of this language area.

Each, Either, Every, and Other Indefinite Pronouns

The following words are always singular: *each, every, either, neither, everyone, everybody, someone, somebody, anyone, anybody, nobody,* and *no one.* Note that whether they are used as subjects or as subject modifiers, they are always singular and their predicates must be singular.

Each of the monitors *has its* own antiglare screen.   (Remember to mentally omit the prepositional phrase *of the monitors* to identify the subject, *each. Has* and *its* are singular, to agree with the singular subject, *each.*)

Each monitor *is* now on sale.   (Here *each* modifies the subject, *monitor.* Both *each* and *monitor* are singular, and the singular verb *is* agrees with the subject, *monitor.*)

Neither of the factories *has* had *its* annual inspection yet.   (Mentally omit the prepositional phrase *of the factories. Has* and *its* agree with the singular subject, *neither.*)

Everyone in the Medical Department *has* also been scheduled for *his or her* checkup.   (Mentally omit the prepositional phrase *in the Medical Department. Has* and *his or her* agree with the singular subject, *everyone.*)

Common-Gender Nouns

Whenever the gender of a noun is obviously masculine *(father, brother, man, boy)* or obviously feminine *(mother, sister, woman, girl),* choosing a pronoun to agree with the noun is no problem. **Common-gender nouns** are those that can be either masculine or feminine, such as *instructor, supervisor, customer, president, attorney, secretary, employee,* *nurse, clerk,* and *coworker.* To agree with singular common-gender nouns, pronoun combinations such as *he or she, his or her,* and *him or her* must be used.

> Each supervisor has guidelines that *he or she* must follow.   (*He or she,* singular, to agree with the singular subject, *supervisor,* a common-gender noun)

> Each supervisor has already received *his or her* guidelines.   (*His or her,* to agree with *supervisor*)

> Ask each supervisor to bring the guidelines with *him or her* to tomorrow's meeting.   (*Him or her,* to agree with *supervisor*)

When *he or she* and similar combinations are used too often—especially within the same sentence—the message will be awkward. In such cases the sentences should be revised by changing the subjects and the pronouns that agree with them to plurals.

> The *supervisors* have guidelines that *they* must follow.

> All the *supervisors* have already received *their* guidelines.

> Ask all the *supervisors* to bring the guidelines with *them* to tomorrow's meeting.

CLASS PRACTICE 4

Choose the correct words in the following sentences.

1. An executive must rely on the information that (he, she, he or she, it, they) (receives, receive) from (his, her, his or her, its, their) subordinates.
2. Someone in the Atlanta office (has, have) won the national sales contest.
3. The president (agrees, agree) that one of (his or her, their) most important tasks is to listen carefully to employees and customers.
4. Anyone who (wishes, wish) to increase (his or her, their) life insurance coverage is encouraged to do so.
5. Every employee in the organization (has, have) selected (his or her, their) medical insurance plan from the three offered by the company.
6. Each manager of our district offices (receives, receive) a bonus based on sales in (his or her, their) district.

EDITING PRACTICE 3

Correct any agreement errors in the following sentences. If no corrections are needed, write *OK.*

1. Anyone in these departments who want to discuss these safety procedures further should make an appointment with their supervisor.
2. The manager wants an assistant who knows how to organize and who can manage his or her own time well.
3. No one should invest in these stocks unless they fully understand the risk.

4. Every cost-conscious buyer in the country will benefit from having his own personal subscription to this consumer magazine.
5. No, Brad, neither of the buyers have yet reviewed this agreement.
6. Any customer who is dissatisfied with our products should write to the Customer Service Center nearest their home.

A Number, The Number *A number* is a plural subject, and *the number* is a singular subject. Be sure to make their predicates agree accordingly. Note that any descriptive term immediately before the word *number* (as in *a significant number* or *the large number*) does not affect this rule.

> *The number* of applicants for this position *was* more than we had expected. (*Was* agrees with the singular *the number*.)

> Only *a* small *number* of employees *have* complained about *their* change in work schedules. (*Have* and *their* agree with the plural *a number*.)

Use the following Quick Trick to help you with this agreement rule.

QUICK TRICK

Remember P–A–S–T

Use the word *past* to remember the following:

PLURAL : *a*   SINGULAR: *the*

If you can remember **P–A–S–T,** you can recall the **P**lural term **A** number and the **S**ingular term **T**he number.

EDITING PRACTICE 4

Correct any agreement errors in the following sentences. Write *OK* if the sentence is correct.

1. A number of well-known physicians has agreed to participate in these public information programs.
2. As Phil mentioned, the number of invitations we sent to prospective clients was quite small.
3. The extraordinarily large number of customer complaints have prompted us to review our procedures at the Encino branch office.
4. As you know, the number of parks and other recreational areas have been declining in our city.
5. A number of interested land developers has submitted preliminary bids on the property.

"Part," "Portion," or "Amount" Subject

Words such as *all, any, most, half, some, two-thirds,* and *none* are used in subjects to indicate a part, a portion, or an amount of something. Consider such subjects plural when these words are followed by plural nouns; consider them singular when these words are followed by singular nouns. Study these examples:

Half this room *has* already been painted.   (The singular *has* is correct because *room* is singular.)

Half these rooms *have* already been painted.   (The plural *have* is correct because *rooms* is plural.)

All the money *is* locked in the vault.   (The singular *is* is correct because *money* is singular.)

All the restaurants *are* being redecorated.   (The plural *are* is correct because *restaurants* is plural.)

CLASS PRACTICE 5

Are the following "part," "portion," or "amount" subjects singular, or are they plural? Choose the correct verb for each sentence; be sure to indicate the key word in the complete subject with which each verb agrees.

1. Two-thirds of the payment (is, are) due in advance.
2. Half the supplies (has, have) been stored in this room.
3. None of these buildings (requires, require) repainting.
4. Most of this warehouse (contains, contain) valuable store fixtures.
5. Three-fourths of their payments (has, have) been made in advance.
6. All the property in the estate (has, have) been appraised.

EDITING PRACTICE 5

Identify and correct any agreement errors in the following sentences. Write *OK* for any sentence that is correct.

1. One-third of the storeroom space have been converted to new offices.
2. Half the area that we originally leased are now sublet to a photography studio.
3. All the printing and binding machines in both plants have been reconditioned within the past two years.
4. Unfortunately, most of the toys was damaged during the fire.
5. As we expected, about one-fourth of the forms has been filled out incorrectly.
6. None of the inventory that we checked last week are included in this report.

Collective Nouns

A **collective noun** is a word that is singular in form but refers to a group or a collection of persons or things; for example, *class, faculty, committee, jury, company, audience,* and *herd.* When a sentence with a collective noun indicates that the group is acting *as a whole*, the subject is considered singular and takes a singular verb. On the other hand, when a sentence with a collective noun indicates that the members of the group are acting *as individuals*, the subject is plural and takes a plural verb.

> The jury *are* arguing over several issues concerning this case.   (To argue, more than one person is needed. The plural verb *are* is correct because the jury members are acting *as individuals*.)

> The jury *has* reached *its* decision.   (Here the jury is acting collectively; because the group is acting *as a whole*, the subject is singular and the singular verb *has* is correct. Note, therefore, that the singular pronoun *its* is also correct—to agree with the singular *jury*.)

CLASS PRACTICE 6

Determine whether the collective nouns are singular or plural in the following sentences. Then select the verbs and the pronouns that agree with the collective-noun subjects.

1. The audience (was, were) pleased to participate in the performance, as we could tell by (its, their) reaction.
2. The class (is, are) arguing among (itself, themselves) where the annual class trip should be taken.
3. The softball team (has, have) rescheduled (its, their) game for next Saturday.
4. According to Ms. Simpson, the faculty (wants, want) to ask (its, their) spokesperson to attend the salary negotiations meeting.
5. Mr. Edwards said that a new committee (has, have) been established to develop a code of ethics for all employees.

EDITING PRACTICE 6

Make any necessary corrections in the following sentences. If a sentence is correct, write *OK*.

1. The committee is now working on their individual reports to the treasurer.
2. The city council have been arguing over this ruling since the members met this morning.
3. Our union have filed a grievance against Allied Equipment Inc.
4. Each department must submit their financial statements to the city auditors by June 30.
5. That company have their headquarters in Knoxville, Tennessee.
6. The team selected their leader in a meeting early this morning.
7. The company presented its staff their bonuses based on individual performance this year.

RELATIVE-PRONOUN CLAUSE

The last agreement rule that you will study concerns agreement in clauses that begin with the relative pronouns *who, which,* and *that.* To begin, review these few statements:

1. A clause is a group of words having a subject and a verb.
2. The **relative pronouns** are *who, which,* and *that.* They are called *relative* because they *relate* to another word in the sentence. This other word is called an *antecedent.*
3. The **antecedent** is a noun or a pronoun usually occurring immediately before the relative pronoun.

Study the following examples to make sure that you are able to recognize a relative pronoun and to identify its antecedent. In each sentence the relative pronoun is in italics, and an arrow points to its antecedent.

The inspector *who* checks these machines is Mr. Palmer.   (The relative pronoun *who* begins the clause *who checks these machines.* What is the antecedent of *who?* Answer: *inspector.*)

Send the printouts by Monday, *which* is the deadline.   (The relative pronoun *which* begins the clause *which is the deadline.* What does *which* refer to? Answer: *Monday.*)

Please give me the catalog *that* is on my desk.   (What does *that* refer to? Answer: *catalog.*)

Notice that in each sentence the verb in the relative-pronoun clause agrees with the antecedent. For an easy way to apply this rule, study this Quick Trick.

QUICK TRICK

Omit the Pronoun

By omitting the relative pronoun *who, which,* or *that,* you can quickly match the rest of the clause with the noun or pronoun to which it refers (the antecedent). All you must do is *use the antecedent as the subject of the clause.*

The branch office that (was, were) having (its, their) books audited reopened yesterday.   (Omit the relative pronoun *that,* and use its antecedent, the noun *office,* as the subject of the clause: *office was* having *its* books audited. *Was* and *its* are correct, to agree with *office.*)

Two branch offices that (was, were) having (its, their) books audited reopened yesterday.   (Again, omit *that,* and use its antecedent, the noun *offices,* as the subject of the clause: *offices were* having *their* books audited. *Were* and *their* are correct, to agree with *offices.*)

Any employee who (wishes, wish) to have (his or her, their) vacation schedule changed must see Mr. Helms. (Again, use the antecedent as the subject of the clause: *employee wishes* to have *his or her* vacation schedule changed.)

Employees who (wishes, wish) to have (his or her, their) vacation schedule changed must see Mr. Helms. (Again, use the antecedent as the subject of the clause: *employees wish* to have *their* vacation schedule changed.)

Always Singular Relative-pronoun clauses that are preceded by *the only one* require singular verbs and pronouns.

Did you know that Olga is *the only one* of the agents who *has* exceeded *her* sales budget?

Always Plural Relative-pronoun clauses preceded by phrases such as *one of those employees*, *one of those clients*, *one of those students*, *one of you*, *one of those companies*, and *one of those books* require plural verbs and pronouns.

Robert is *one of those fire fighters* who always *ask* for overtime hours.

No Antecedents *Who*, *which*, and *that* are not always *relative* pronouns. In the following sentences, note that *who*, *which*, and *that* do not relate to anything. They have no antecedents.

Who is the woman talking to Ms. Streebing? (*Who* has no antecedent in this sentence. It is not a relative pronoun.)

Do you know *which* restaurant has been selected? (*Which* has no antecedent.)

Please be sure to handle *that* microprocessor carefully. (*That* has no antecedent.)

CLASS PRACTICE 7

In the following sentences identify the relative pronouns and their antecedents before you make your selections of verbs and pronouns. (Be sure to omit the relative pronoun and use the antecedent as the subject of the clause to make your choice.)

1. Her partner is one of those people who (enjoys, enjoy) (his or her, their) work.
2. Please be sure to complete all these notifications before the deadline, which (is, are) Saturday, December 8.
3. Is this the training course that (has, have) become famous for (its, their) effective selling techniques?
4. Jean is the only one of the product managers who always (completes, complete) (her, his or her, their) marketing plans on schedule.

5. This is one material that (is, are) worth the extra expense because of (its, their) strength and durability.
6. Ms. Anderson is one of those designers who (is, are) very creative despite the pressure of deadlines.

EDITING PRACTICE 7

Now correct any agreement errors in the following sentences. Again, be sure that you are able to identify the relative pronouns and their antecedents.

1. Have you seen all the promotion notices that was posted in the lobby?
2. He is one of those programmers who is working on this difficult project.
3. Do you think that we should order one of those terminals that is on sale?
4. Mr. Sarafian is one of those people who insists that he will not retire.
5. Ms. Fredericks is the only one of the district managers who are permitted to sign company checks.
6. Sheldon Pharmaceutical Company is one of those companies that has relocated to our industrial park.

COMMUNICATION LABORATORY

APPLICATION EXERCISES

A. Select the correct verbs and pronouns in each of the following sentences. Also, identify the subjects with which your choices agree.

1. Mr. Winters or Mr. Rothstein (has, have) an appointment with Ms. Thomas this afternoon, doesn't (he, they)?
2. Many a programmer and instructional designer (has, have) worked on this award-winning educational software package.
3. Mr. Braun is one of those chauffeurs who always (arrives, arrive) promptly.
4. According to the ad, each monitor, disk drive, and printer (is, are) to be sold at a 30 percent discount.
5. Pork and beans (is, are) served annually at the company picnic.
6. Jerry needs one of those language programs that (teaches, teach) conversational Spanish in just a few hours.
7. Norma is one of those CPAs who always (works, work) very carefully.
8. I believe that either Annette or Susan (finances, finance) (her, their) car through the credit union.
9. Neither Jeffrey nor his brothers (owns, own) any interest in the company as of last December.
10. Phil and Marie generally (reads and approves, read and approve) all copy for ads and promotional materials.

CONTINUED

11. Phil or Marie (has, have) the authority to approve expenses over $5000.
12. Perhaps Mr. Erickson or his daughters still (does, do) own part of the company.
13. We need one of those computer programs that (makes, make) electronic bill paying possible.
14. Comp-U-Tab is one of those stores that (is, are) currently offering special discounts to build up (its, their) mail-order business.
15. Timothy or his two assistants (is, are) going to discuss (his, their) recommendations with the committee next Thursday.

B. On a separate sheet of paper, correct any errors in the following sentences. Write *OK* if the sentence is correct.

1. There's only about two dozen more orders for us to process.
2. After she interviews these six applicants, Cheryl will select the one whom she thinks has the best potential.
3. Betty done all she could to complete the order and ship it to Orlando office in time for the sale.
4. If the Grant's send their check before December 1, they are eligible for a 2 percent discount.
5. The Grants' check arrived in this morning's mail.
6. Two or three CPA's on our staff have been assigned to the Gordon account.
7. Do you know whom will be the first speaker at this afternoon's conference?
8. Neither Leo nor the other controllers was sure that Ms. Morris would approve the purchase of this equipment.
9. If you want Larry and myself to help you with this, Ms. Perez, please let us know.
10. No, us cashiers haven't been told of these changes yet.
11. She is one of those branch managers who want to increase the advertising budget.
12. Has Mr. Cooper announced whom he plans to promote to regional manager?
13. Anyone in our Sales Department who wish to work additional hours should notify Mr. Reece.
14. The Harrison's are major stockholders in Pitman Chemicals.
15. Each sales representative is trained to establish goodwill with their clients.

C. Identify whether a singular or a plural verb is required in each of the following phrases.

1. either the manager or her assistants _____
2. one of the people who _____

CONTINUED

3. Cliff and Lorraine _____
4. ham and eggs _____
5. the two clerks or their supervisor _____
6. Colleen or Douglas _____

VOCABULARY AND SPELLING STUDIES

A. These words are often confused: *fair, fare; undo, undue.* Explain the differences.

B. How well can you define the following word processing terms?
1. *Delete* means **(a)** to indent, **(b)** to represent, **(c)** to omit, **(d)** to input copy.
2. *Wraparound* describes the ability of word processing equipment to **(a)** automatically place a word at the beginning of a new line, **(b)** print copy on both the front and the back of a sheet at the same time, **(c)** bind a report in a special wrapper, **(d)** type around the full area of any size sheet.
3. *Hardware* refers to **(a)** the tools that operators must use to adjust or fix equipment, **(b)** the diskettes or disks that are used to store data, **(c)** the mechanical or electronic equipment used in word processing, **(d)** an alternative name for software.

C. Identify the word that is spelled correctly in each of the following groups.
1. wholy, accommodate, symetry
2. specificaly, recolect, Wednesday
3. remembrence, statistical, retreival
4. withold, occasional, aprroximately
5. amateur, expendible, consientious
6. hendrence, necesitate, knowledgeable
7. wraper, baggage, menice
8. neighbor, wiegh, eigth
9. cieling, mileage, greif
10. seperate, calender, deceive
11. likelihood, advising, useage
12. nineth, piece, greatful
13. definate, verify, liesure
14. garantee, cannot, Febuary
15. offerred, convenient, aquire

ADJECTIVES AND ADVERBS

The better you understand the fundamentals that have been presented in the preceding sections, the easier you will find this section on modifiers. This section presents the basic uses of adjectives and adverbs—namely, to make sentences *specific* and *lively*—and ways to avoid their most common *mis*uses.

Let's begin, then, with the first step; let's be sure that you can *identify adjectives* correctly.

IDENTIFYING ADJECTIVES

Remember that any word that modifies a noun or a pronoun is an adjective. An adjective answers the following questions:

What kind?   Which one(s)?   How many or much?

Now look at the following kinds of adjectives to be sure that you can identify them.

KINDS OF ADJECTIVES

Articles—answer *How many?* or *Which one?*
   a, an, the

Descriptive Adjectives—answer *What kind?*
   famous, interesting, intensive, modern, new

Possessive Adjectives—answer *Which one?*
   my, your, his, her, its, our, their
   manager's, John's, company's, employees'

Limiting Adjectives—answer *How many?* or *How much?*
   one, all, several, first, 2.6, four, few, 350

Proper Adjectives—answer *Which one(s)?* or *What kind?*
   New York hotel, *West Coast* travelers
   Italian food, *American* customs, *Victorian* furniture

Compound Adjectives—answer *What kind?*
   an *easy-going* person, a *first-class* trip
   my *data processing* text, a *high school* student

A OR AN?

The words *a* and *an* are called **indefinite articles.** The article *a* is used before a word that begins with a consonant sound, a long *u* sound, or an *h* that is pronounced, as in *a building, a union,* and *a hallway.*

Use the article *an* before a word that begins with a vowel sound (except long *u*) or an *h* that is not pronounced, as in *an airline, an essay, an item, an odor, an umbrella, an honor, an hour.*

CLASS PRACTICE 1

Choose *a* or *an,* whichever is correct, in each of the following sentences.

1. One of the representatives had (a, an) unique idea for spurring holiday sales.
2. Do you know whether (a, an) union delegate has been invited to this meeting?
3. More than (a, an) hour after the first speech had ended, (a, an) question-and-answer session was still in progress.
4. Has she received (a, an) answer to her question?
5. In our opinion, this law gives our competitors (a, an) unfair advantage.

COMPARISON OF ADJECTIVES

Degrees of Comparison of Adjectives   Adjective forms such as *new, newer, newest* represent three different degrees of a certain quality. The three degrees are called *positive, comparative,* and *superlative.*

Positive Degree   This form is used when the person or thing is not compared with anyone or anything else.

a new car   an old car   an expensive stereo

Comparative Degree   This form is used to express a higher or a lower degree than expressed by the positive degree when comparing two items.

a newer car   a more expensive stereo

an older car   a less expensive stereo

Superlative Degree   This form is used to denote the highest or the lowest degree when comparing three or more items.

the newest car   the most expensive stereo

the oldest car   the least expensive stereo

Forms of Adjective Comparison   Adjectives may be compared in one of three ways:

1. By adding *-er* or *-est* to the positive form:

POSITIVE	COMPARATIVE (TWO ITEMS)	SUPERLATIVE (THREE OR MORE ITEMS)
large	larger	largest
friendly	friendlier	friendliest

2. By using *more* or *most* (or *less* or *least*) with the positive form: *3+ syll*

POSITIVE	COMPARATIVE (TWO ITEMS)	SUPERLATIVE (THREE OR MORE ITEMS)
interesting	more interesting less interesting	most interesting least interesting
frequent	more frequent less frequent	most frequent least frequent
successful	more successful less successful	most successful least successful

3. By completely changing the form of the word:

POSITIVE	COMPARATIVE (TWO ITEMS)	SUPERLATIVE (THREE OR MORE ITEMS)
good	better	best
bad	worse	worst
little	less	least
much	more	most
many	more	most

Comparatives and superlatives are formed by using *one* of the three methods just discussed. Do not apply more than one method at a time.

> This package is *larger* than yours.   (NOT *more larger*.)

> In the *simplest* terms possible, Jean explained to all of us how to use the new copier.   (NOT *most simplest*.)

Selection of Correct Forms   Adjectives of one syllable are compared by adding *-er* or *-est;* adjectives of three or more syllables, by adding *more* or *most*.

> Your desk is always *cleaner* than mine.   (Comparative form of one-syllable adjective *clean* is *cleaner*).

> Your desk is always the *cleanest* one in the office.   (Here the superlative form *cleanest* is correct.)

> Arthur is *more ambitious* than Martin.   (You cannot add *-er* to *ambitious*.)

> Iris is one of the *most courteous* agents in the company.   (You cannot add *-est* to *courteous*.)

Adjectives of two syllables, however, may be compared either by adding *-er* or *-est* or by adding *more* or *most*. For those words ending in *y*, change the *y* to *i* and add *-er* or *-est*. Other words add *more* or *most* before the positive form. Remember that all two-syllable adjectives not taking *more* or *most* are irregular comparisons. These irregular comparisons are shown in the dictionary under the positive form of the adjective.

> Your studio is equipped with *more modern* equipment than mine.

> This computer is the *costliest* one on the market.

Choice of Comparative or Superlative Degree The comparative degree (*newer, more enthusiastic, better,* and so on) is used to compare two persons, places, or things.

Dottie is enthusiastic, but Bert appears *more enthusiastic* than she.

Joe's report was good; however, Joan's report was *better.*

The superlative degree (*newest, most enthusiastic, best,* and so on) is used to compare *more than two* persons, places, or things.

Steven appears to be the *most enthusiastic* of all the brokers.

Of all the reports that were submitted, Joan's was the *best.*

CLASS PRACTICE 2

Make the correct choice in each of the following sentences.

1. Mr. Jacobi's suggestion was (good, better, best), but Mr. Torti's idea was (good, better, best).
2. So far, the (logicalest, most logical) method is the one described by Mrs. Meehan.
3. The product managers are discussing among themselves which of the many alternatives is the (most good, more better, most best, best).
4. Try to select from these samples the plastic that is the (clearest, most clear, most clearest).
5. Her flight is (late, more late, later, most late) than mine, but Richard's flight is (early, more early, earlier, most early) than mine.
6. Our San Diego store is (successful, successfuler, more successful, most successful), but our Rochester store is the (successful, successfuler, more successful, most successful) one in the entire chain.

Other and Else in Comparisons When the comparative degree is used to compare a person or a thing with other members of the same group, use the word *other* or *else* as shown in these sentences.

Peter is *more* ambitious than any *other* broker in our company. (Without the word *other*, the sentence would imply that Peter does not work in our company but that he works for another company.)

Peter is *more* ambitious than all the *other* brokers in our company. (Again, the word *other* makes it clear that Peter and the other brokers work for the same company. Without the word *other*, the sentence would imply that Peter works for another company.)

Peter is *more* ambitious than anyone *else* in our company. (Without the word *else*, the sentence would again imply that Peter does not work in our company.)

With the superlative degree, *all* is often substituted for *other* or *else*.

Peter is the *most* ambitious of all the brokers in our company. (Note that *other* or *else* is not used in the sentence because the *of* phrase makes it clear that Peter belongs to the group compared.)

Adjectives That Cannot Be Compared   The positive degree of some adjectives already states a quality that cannot be compared. For example, "a *full* glass" tells it all; you cannot have another glass that is *fuller* or a third glass that is *fullest*. *Full* is the absolute degree, and so this adjective cannot be compared. Other absolute adjectives are as follows:

absolute	final	round
accurate	flat	spotless
circular	immaculate	square
complete	level	straight
correct	perfect	supreme
dead	perpendicular	unanimous
empty	perpetual	unique
even	right	universal

To indicate the degree to which a person or thing approaches the state of being full or complete or correct, use *more nearly* for two items or *most nearly* for three or more items.

Louise's estimate ($4,500) proved to be correct. Except for Louise's, Joe's estimate ($4,350) was *more nearly correct* than any of the others.

Only yesterday's vote was unanimous; however, last week's vote was *more nearly unanimous* than any of the others had been.

CLASS PRACTICE 3

Choose the correct words in the following sentences. How well do you understand when to use *other*, *else*, and *all* in comparisons? How well can you handle adjectives that cannot be compared?

1. Sally is the most experienced of (all the, all the other) nurses in this department.
2. Alex Rivera, one of our programmers, conducts training sessions better than (any, any other) programmer in the company.
3. The West Coast branch has more franchises than (any, any other) branch in the country.
4. All the specifications that were submitted are inaccurate; however, Mr. Brand's specifications are the (most accurate, more accurate, most nearly accurate) of all those which we have reviewed.
5. Gail gives clearer instructions than (anyone, anyone else) in her department.
6. Mario swam faster than (anyone, anyone else) in his division, but Peter was the fastest of (all the, all the other) swimmers in the competition.
7. Of (all the, all the other) citizens in the community, the six of you have been selected to represent the city at the All-American City awards.

ADJECTIVE PITFALLS

Compound Adjectives

A **compound adjective** consists of two or more words that act together as a single thought unit to modify a noun or a pronoun. Certain compound adjectives are hyphenated; others are not. Observe these rules:

1. Do not hyphenate *(a)* compound adjectives that have become familiar from long use and are considered a single unit or *(b)* compound proper nouns used as adjectives.

a high school classroom	social security benefits
charge account customers	real estate contracts
life insurance policies	an East Coast convention
data processing texts	Los Angeles suburbs

2. Hyphenate most other compound adjectives when they precede a noun:

air-conditioned offices	a 10-mile drive
first-class tours	one-hour intervals
up-to-date equipment	well-established business

BUT: a business that is *well established,* an interval of *one hour.*

See the Quick Trick below to help you identify compound adjectives.

QUICK TRICK

Two Adjectives Acting as One

To help you decide whether two words that precede a noun *do* act together as a single unit, try this simple test.

Use *long range plans,* for an example. The noun modified is *plans.* Ask yourself, "What kinds of plans?" *Long* plans? *Range* plans? No, neither one makes sense. The two words work as a single unit: *long-range plans*—plans that are long range.

CLASS PRACTICE 4

Decide whether the compound adjectives in the following sentences should be hyphenated.

1. Mr. Norton, a (well known, well-known) tax expert, will discuss some popular (Wall Street, Wall-Street) investing techniques.
2. There is generally no more than a (10 minute, 10-minute) delay in transmitting data by this method.
3. Gloria Ramsey has been one of our (charge-account, charge account) customers for over five years.

4. Many of the (high interest, high-interest) bonds that she recommends are listed in this (four page, four-page) booklet.
5. A (San Francisco, San-Francisco) corporation has bid on this property, according to Ms. Skinner.
6. We have budgeted several (60 second, 60-second) commercials to introduce this new product.

Those, Them   *Them* is never an adjective and should not be used in place of the adjective *those*.

> Will you be able to help me carry *those* packages to Ms. Lopez?   (NOT *them packages*. The noun following *those* helps you see that the adjective *those* is needed.)

Note that *those* is the plural of *that*; *these* is the plural of *this*. Use *that* and *those* to refer to objects that are at a distance from you; use *this* and *these* for objects that are closer to you.

Kind(s), Sort(s)   *Kind* and *sort* are singular nouns; *kinds* and *sorts*, plural nouns. A singular adjective must be used with the singular nouns *kind* and *sort*. A plural adjective is required for the plural nouns *kinds* and *sorts*.

> The laser printer in our office rejects *this kind* of paper.   (*Kind* is singular and must be modified by the singular adjective *this*.)

> Our broker recommended that we not invest in *these kinds* of bonds.   (The plural noun *kinds* must be modified by the plural adjective *these*.)

Repeated Modifier   Repeating a modifier such as *a, an, the,* or *my* (as in the following example) shows that two different people are referred to:

> The vice president and the general manager are authorized to approve this addendum to the contract.   (Two different people—one, the vice president, the other, the general manager—approved the addendum.)

Omitting the modifier *the* before *general manager* shows that one person is referred to:

> The vice president and general manager is authorized to approve this addendum.   (Here, one person is referred to. This one person simply has two titles, *vice president* and *general manager*.)

WORLD VIEW
Brand names successful in one country may not be so in another. For example, the Japanese once tried to sell a baby soap called Skinababe and a hair product called Blow Up in the United States. In Spanish-speaking countries, Ford's Fiera means "ugly old woman" and General Motors' Nova means, "It doesn't go," if pronounced *no-va*. Esso's difficulties in the Japanese market may have been because phonetically *esso* means "stalled car."

CLASS PRACTICE 5

Select the correct words in the following sentences.

1. Are you sure that Ms. Campbell wants (them, this, these) negatives sent to the studio by messenger?
2. According to the lease agreement, we must return (those, them) training films to the distributor by Friday, March 19.

3. If those (kind, kinds) of monitors are on sale, we will probably buy three or four of them.

4. Please tell Terry to use this (kind, kinds) of font to prepare the executive reports.

5. (Her sister and manager, Her sister and her manager) is always present at business meetings.

6. We looked at several (kind, kinds) of VCRs, but none really met our requirements.

SIMPLE ADVERBS

Like adjectives, *adverbs* are also modifiers. As you study adverbs, you will see that many adverbs are formed simply by adding *-ly* to an adjective—for example, *carefully, quickly,* and *patiently.* In addition, you will note that adverbs, like adjectives, can also be compared.

A **simple adverb** is a word that modifies an adjective, a verb, or another adverb. Simple adverbs answer the following questions:

When? Where? How? To what degree?

Many adverbs are formed by adding *-ly* to adjectives:

ADJECTIVE	ADVERB
random	randomly
quiet	quietly
poor	poorly
sole	solely
simple	simply
lazy	lazily
defensive	defensively
productive	productively

Although many adverbs end in *-ly,* remember that not all adverbs end in *-ly.* Look at the following adverbs:

always	late	often	now	very	up
soon	here	there	then	too	sometimes

Now notice how these adverbs and those ending in *-ly* answer questions such as "When?" "Where?" "How?" and "To what degree?" in the following examples:

arrived *late* (Arrived when? Answer: *late.*)

send *there* (Send where? Answer: *there.*)

selected *randomly* (Selected how? Answer: *randomly.*)

very helpful (Helpful to what degree? Answer: *very.*)

Comparison of Adverbs   The same general rules that apply to the comparison of adjectives (see pages 142–143) also apply to the comparison of adverbs. Adverbs are compared in one of three ways:

1. By adding *-er* or *-est* to an adverb containing one syllable:

POSITIVE	COMPARATIVE	SUPERLATIVE
fast	faster	fastest
late	later	latest
soon	sooner	soonest

2. By using *more* or *most* (or *less* or *least*) with an adverb ending in *-ly* or containing more than one syllable:

POSITIVE	COMPARATIVE	SUPERLATIVE
slowly	more slowly less slowly	most slowly least slowly
quietly	more quietly less quietly	most quietly least quietly
often	more often less often	most often least often

3. By completely changing the form of the adverb:

POSITIVE	COMPARATIVE	SUPERLATIVE
well	better	best
badly	worse	worst
much	more	most

CLASS PRACTICE 6

Identify the adverbs in the following sentences.

1. Barry works productively under pressure.
2. Marian explained the issues clearly, and she summarized the alternatives thoroughly.
3. Frank and Ellen will work together here on the inventory report.
4. Now we must completely revise this procedures manual.
5. Both clients arrived later than we expected.
6. Anthony and Audrey both sing well, but Christine sings best of all.

EDITING PRACTICE 1

Correct any errors in the use of adverbs in the following sentences. Write *OK* for any sentence that is correct.

1. Mr. McMahon speaks well; Ms. Vernon, however, speaks more well.
2. Anne Marie seems to write most legibly than any of the other account executives.
3. Unfortunately, the fire damage was worse than we had thought.

4. These two photocopiers are inexpensive, but they make copies slowlier than the machines we now have.
5. All three candidates performed well on the examination, but Ellen performed better.
6. We must now be sure to check these invoices most carefully.

ADVERB OR ADJECTIVE?

Always use an adjective after verbs that do not show action—linking verbs. Examples of verbs that may be used as linking verbs are *look, seem, appear, sound, feel, taste,* and *smell.* Notice in the following examples how these verbs merely "link" the adjectives to the nouns they modify.

This food *tastes* delicious.   (Here *tastes* is a linking verb—a nonaction verb—linking the adjective *delicious* to the noun it describes, *food.*

The cool water *feels* good.   (Here *feels* is a linking verb because it shows no action. The adjective *good* is correct because it modifies *water.*)

Verbs such as *look, taste,* and *feel* do not always function as linking verbs, however. Review the examples below in which the verbs *do* describe action.

Martha *tastes* hot foods cautiously.   (Here *tastes* is obviously an action verb; it describes something Martha is doing actively—*tasting. Tastes* does not link an adjective to a noun or a pronoun. Tastes how? Answer: *cautiously.* The adverb *cautiously* modifies the verb *tastes.* Only an adverb, not an adjective, can modify a verb.)

You should *feel* the cloth carefully.   (Feel how? Answer: *carefully.* The adverb *carefully* modifies the verb *should feel.* Here, *feel* is obviously an action verb. It does not link an adjective to a noun or a pronoun. Therefore, the adverb *carefully* is correct.)

CLASS PRACTICE 7

Determine whether the verbs in the following sentences are action verbs and therefore require adverbs to modify them. If they are linking verbs, of course, adjectives will follow. Then make your choices.

1. When he realized that he had made a mistake, David seemed (angry, angrily).
2. When the alarm sounded, the security guards appeared (sudden, suddenly).
3. Of course, all of us felt (bad, badly) about the closing of the plant.
4. The auditors checked (immediate, immediately) to find the error.
5. The supervisors seemed rather (worried, worriedly) about possible danger to employees in the factory.
6. As he read the news, Mark's voice sounded (nervous, nervously).

ADVERB PITFALLS

Adverb errors that occur most often are (1) positioning the adverb incorrectly in a sentence, (2) misusing *never* for *not*, and (3) using double negatives. Ways to avoid these errors are discussed here.

Position of Adverbs An adverb should be positioned near the word it modifies. As the following sentences show, misplacing a modifier can change or obscure the meaning of the sentence.

Only my assistant read these computer printouts yesterday.   (My assistant was the only one who read them—I didn't; my boss didn't; my secretary didn't.)

My *only* assistant read these computer printouts yesterday.   (I have only one assistant. Here the word *only* modifies *assistant,* limiting it exclusively to one.)

My assistant *only* read these computer printouts yesterday.   (He didn't do anything else to them. He didn't duplicate them; he didn't mail them; he didn't approve them. He only read them.)

My assistant read *only* these computer printouts yesterday.   (He read no other computer printouts, no reports, no magazines, no letters; only these printouts.)

My assistant read these computer printouts *only* yesterday.   (He read these computer printouts as recently as yesterday: not the day before, not last week, but yesterday.)

My assistant read these computer printouts yesterday *only.*   (He didn't read them on any other day; just yesterday.)

EDITING PRACTICE 2

Are adverbs placed correctly in the following sentences? Correct any misplaced adverbs.

1. As of this morning, we had only invoiced 30 new orders.
2. By the end of the afternoon, they had hardly received any credit applications.
3. The branch manager and her assistant have the combination to the safe only.
4. The costs for renovating the building were not even estimated to be $100,000.
5. We just expect Marisa to call in a few minutes.
6. In just one morning, we nearly received 500 inquiries about our newest product line.

Never and **Not** *Never* means "not ever; at no time; not in any way." Obviously, it is a strong word.

Since Brandon Metals was established in 1948, the company has *never* laid off employees.

The word *not* simply expresses negation. Do not use *never* when a simple *not* will do.

We have *not* received the check that is due from Scotch Plains Printers. (NOT "We *never* received . . . .")

Mr. Durham did *not* deliver the materials to us last week. (NOT "Mr. Durham *never* delivered . . . .")

Double Negatives Do not use two negatives to express a single negative idea. Errors occur most often with the negative statements *scarcely, only, hardly, but, never,* and *not.*

Dr. Hood had but one suggestion for us. (NOT *had not but one* . . . .)

Our manager can hardly believe that we completed all the billing on time. (NOT *cannot hardly believe* . . . .)

CLASS PRACTICE 8

Make the correct selections in the following sentences.

1. Erin (did not say, never said) whether she was changing her vacation schedule.
2. As you know, we can't (help but worry, help worrying) about rising costs and unemployment.
3. The Order Department (has, hasn't) hardly any backlog at this time.
4. Larry (did not say, never said) whether he would attend next Saturday's banquet.
5. These municipal bonds (did not but earn, never earned more than, earned only) 5.75 percent, but all the interest is tax-exempt.
6. Sam and Frank (have, haven't) hardly earned enough money this week to meet their costs.
7. I can't (help but feel, help feeling) sorry for the families who lost their savings in the bank failure.
8. The class (could, couldn't) hardly contain its excitement about the President's visit to the town of Chillicothe.

ADVERB AND ADJECTIVE CONFUSIONS

Certain word pairs (*sure, surely; real, really; good, well; some, somewhat;* and *most, almost*) deserve special attention. As you study them, remember that the first word in each pair is the adjective; the second is the adverb.

Sure, Surely; Real, Really The most common errors in using these word pairs occur when the adjectives *sure* and *real* are used instead of the adverbs *surely* and *really*. Study the Quick Trick on page 153 to choose the right word every time.

QUICK TRICK

Substitute *Very* or *Certainly*

When faced with a choice between *real* and *really* (or between *sure* and *surely*), substitute the adverb *very* (or *certainly*) to test whether an adverb is needed.

> Meg (sure, surely) did a great job in landing the Bullock's account. (Substitute *certainly,* and you will see that *Meg certainly did* makes sense. Therefore, the adverb *surely* is correct because the adverb *certainly* may be substituted.)

> Lawrence did a (real, really) thorough analysis of our competitive products. (Substitute *very:* Lawrence did a *very* thorough analysis . . . . Therefore, the adverb *really* is correct.)

Good, Well   *Good* is the adjective; *well* is the adverb. As an adjective *good* modifies nouns and pronouns. As an adverb *well* should answer the question "How?"

> Margaret really did a *good* job.   (The adjective *good* modifies the noun *job*. It answers the adjective question "What kind?" It does not answer the adverb question "How?")

> Margaret works very *well* under pressure.   (Works how? *Well*. The adverb *well* modifies the verb *works*.)

> *Well* may also be used as an adjective, *but only when referring to health.*

> Scot didn't feel *well,* so he left early.   (Refers to Scot's health.)

Some, Somewhat   To decide when to use the adjective *some* and the adverb *somewhat*, use the following Quick Trick.

QUICK TRICK

Substitute *A Little Bit*

When you can substitute the words *a little bit,* use the adverb *somewhat*.

> Brenda was *somewhat* nervous about the upcoming licensing exam. (She was *a little bit* nervous.)

> They requested *some* help to complete their end-of-month paperwork. (*A little bit* help makes no sense; thus *some* is correct.)

Most, Almost   The adjective *most* is the superlative of *much* or *many*. The adverb *almost* means "not quite" or "very nearly."

Most employees are delighted with the additional coverage this policy provides.   (*Many, more, most* employees)

The draft of the annual report is *almost* finished.   (*Very nearly* finished)

CLASS PRACTICE 9

Select the correct word from the choices given.

1. Dean will (sure, surely) be happy to hear the (good, well) news.
2. Carla has received (some, somewhat) résumés and application letters, but she is (some, somewhat) disappointed in the quality of the candidates.
3. Chatsworth Autoworks treated us (good, well), and its Service Department is certainly (good, well).
4. Harry was (real, really) excited about moving to Boston.
5. We were (sure, surely) disappointed that we did not receive the contract.
6. Tom always does (good, well) work, but today he isn't feeling very (good, well).
7. (Most, Almost) all students ask for help when they need it.

COMMUNICATION LABORATORY

APPLICATION EXERCISES

A. Select the right answer for each of the following sentences.

1. Ms. Werner appeared rather (cautious, cautiously) when she discussed the terms of the union agreement.
2. As you can imagine, Sandra (could, couldn't) hardly wait to travel to Honolulu for the convention.
3. (Most, Almost) of the engineers were (some, somewhat) disappointed to hear that the project had been canceled.
4. Because this report will be sent to all shareholders, we recommend using a (more formal, most formal) tone.
5. When she was asked to substitute for Ms. Martin, Gail (had, hadn't) but two hours to prepare her speech.
6. Please review both columns of figures (careful, carefully) before you send this chart to the Reprographics Department.
7. Donna and her staff always submit (good, well) ad copy because she and her assistants proofread very (good, well).
8. Naturally, we were (real, really) excited to hear that we are tied for first place in the sales contest.
9. Cynthia prefers (only buying, buying only) from Excelsior Computer Equipment.

10. Henry was (sure, surely) delighted to be appointed to the special committee.
11. As Joan proved quite (clear, clearly), the cost of leasing all the computer equipment is prohibitive.
12. After working a double shift, Janice didn't feel (good, well).
13. We knew the food would taste (good, well) because we have often eaten at that restaurant.
14. Mr. Harrison, our supervisor, plans all projects (good, well) and credits his employees for their (good, well) work.
15. Ted was (real, really) surprised to learn that he is a candidate for the open position.

B. Find and correct any errors in the following sentences. If a sentence has no error, write *OK*.

1. Do you know who Louise appointed to head the department during her absence?
2. Jerome enjoys working on technical projects more than I.
3. Both assistants and myself will work overtime to ensure that the analysis is complete and accurate.
4. Mr. Johnsons' suggestion is to hire a consultant with experience in marketing consumer products.
5. In the conference room on the large table is the samples that we reviewed and approved at this morning's meeting.
6. Do not leave all these documents laying on your desk while you go to the meeting.
7. Although the new process sounds rather complicated, it is really more simpler than our old process.
8. Everyone who works with Rose in developing analytical reports comments on how good she writes.
9. Of course, it's very important for an executive to learn to use their time wisely and efficiently.
10. We haven't hardly heard any news about the construction of our new office in Mexico City.
11. The respondents overwhelmingly agreed that the quality of the appliances was real important.
12. Patricia is one of those account executives who always listen carefully to their clients' suggestions.
13. Beth and Gene, both of whom are CPA's, are now working on a presentation to explain the new tax laws to the staff.
14. Us attorneys have been asked to review the federal regulations concerning hiring practices.
15. Most of the sales representative's cars are leased from United Car Leasing.

CONTINUED

C. Select the correct word from the choices in parentheses.

1. Suzanne was obviously (real, really) excited to win the Employee of the Month Award.
2. Read the figures in each column (slow, slowly); as you do so, I will check these charts (careful, carefully).
3. Vera hasn't (any, no) money to invest in these stocks.
4. Nina feels (bad, badly) about the possible closing of the Glendale plant, especially since she has so many friends there.
5. Maxine acted (wise, wisely) in referring the caller to the Legal Department.
6. Mr. Ford advised, "Don't look at the audience so (angry, angrily) while you're speaking."
7. When asked to suggest solutions, Paul rose (immediate, immediately) and cited two good possibilities.
8. Phil always leads the committee meetings very (good, well); he is considered a (good, well) group leader.
9. A benefit of using the new software is that you can draft and revise correspondence more (quick and accurate, quickly and accurately).
10. We became more (confident, confidently) when we were told that we had two months to complete the detailed analysis.

VOCABULARY AND SPELLING STUDIES

A. These words are often confused: *disburse, disperse; equable, equitable.* Explain the differences.

B. Match each word in Column A with the term in Column B that is nearest in meaning.

A	B
1. repetitious	a. with rainbow-like colors
2. iridescent	b. enduring
3. obscure	c. unreal
4. permanent	d. transitory
5. axiomatic	e. monotonous
	f. indistinct
	g. self-evident

C. How are the following words spelled when *ed* is added?

1. admit	6. embarrass	11. fit
2. acquaint	7. appear	12. plan
3. develop	8. worry	13. correspond
4. appall	9. taste	14. address
5. refer	10. respond	15. succeed

PREPOSITIONS AND CONJUNCTIONS

P repositions and conjunctions often go unnoticed as we write and as we speak, but they do important jobs. As you will see, prepositions and conjunctions serve to join words—and joining words helps our writing and speaking make sense! Study carefully how these connectors are used so that you will be able to identify them and to use them correctly in your writing and your speaking.

LIVING LANGUAGE

The best argument is that which seems merely an explanation.
—Dale Carnegie

PREPOSITIONS AND PREPOSITIONAL PHRASES

A preposition is always followed by a noun or a pronoun. In fact, as you look at the word *preposition,* you see the word *position* and the prefix *pre-,* which means "before." Thus a preposition is a word that is *positioned before* a noun or a pronoun and its modifiers.

Of course, not *every* word positioned before a noun or a pronoun is a preposition. A preposition connects a noun or pronoun to another word in the sentence to give this word additional meaning.

The preposition and the following noun or pronoun, together with its modifiers, form a prepositional phrase. Look at the following list of commonly used prepositions and the examples of prepositional phrases:

PREPOSITIONS			PREPOSITIONAL PHRASES
about	between	off	*after* the meeting
above	by	on	*against* the wall
after	down	out	*between* those cars
against	except	over	*by* the building
among	for	through	*except* one manager
at	from	to	*from* her
before	in	under	*in* the summer
behind	into	until	*on* credit
below	like	up	*to* them
beside	of	with	*with* us

Now let's see how prepositions are used in the following sentences.

They plan to return *after the convention.*   (The word *after* connects additional information to the word *return.* Return when? After the convention.)

The man *with her* is the new district manager.   (The prepositional phrase *with her* adds information to the word *man*. Which man? The man with her.)

A representative *from Walden Industries* called you this morning.   (Here again, the preposition *from* connects important additional information to another word, *representative*.)

In the above examples you see that prepositions join words to make phrases. The phrases can then serve to add information to the sentence. The *object of the preposition* is a noun or a pronoun and is the last word in the phrase.

after the convention   (the noun *convention* is the object of the preposition *after*)

with her   (the object of the preposition *with* is the pronoun *her*)

from Walden Industries   (the noun *Walden Industries* is the object of the preposition *from*)

PREPOSITION COMBINATIONS

Certain prepositions must be combined with specific nouns or verbs, as shown below:

abide *by* a decision
abide *with* a person

conform *to* regulations
in conformity *with* regulations

enter *on* the record
enter *into* an agreement

wait *for* someone
wait *on* a customer

Now study the following preposition combinations, which are very commonly used. Whenever you have trouble remembering which preposition is correct in a specific instance, refer to a business writer's manual.

Agree   *Agree* is used as follows: (1) agree *on* or *upon*—reach a mutual understanding, (2) agree *to* (accept) another's plan, (3) agree *with* a person or his or her idea.

They *agreed upon* a solution to the problem.

Our directors *agreed to* the offer from Wilson Associates.

Barry *agreed with* the other programmers.

Angry   Be sure to say "angry *with*" a person, "angry *at*" a thing, or "angry *about*" a condition.

Is Lucy still *angry with* us for delaying the project?

Both of us were *angry at* the copier because we lost so much time.

Everyone was *angry about* the trash the contractors left behind.

Discrepancy   Use (1) *discrepancy in* when referring to *one* item, (2) *discrepancy between* when discussing *two* in number, and (3) *discrepancy among* when mentioning *three or more* things.

> I discovered a *discrepancy in* the accountant's report.
>
> There is a *discrepancy between* the accountant's report and the auditor's report.
>
> There is a *discrepancy among* the three reports submitted by the consultants.

In Regard To   The phrases *in regard to, with regard to,* and *as regards* are all correct and interchangeable, but do not say "in regards to" or "with regards to."

> Ms. Delaney wants to talk with us (in regard to, with regard to, as regards) our policy for reprinting copyrighted materials.   (Which one is correct? All are!)

Miscellaneous Phrases   Memorize the following phrases, because they are very commonly used—and misused.

> different from (NOT *different than*)
>
> identical with (NOT *identical to*)
>
> plan to do something (NOT *plan on* doing something)
>
> retroactive to (NOT *retroactive from*)
>
> try to do something (NOT *try and* do something)

> This model is *different from* the one I ordered.
>
> Your schedule is *identical with* mine.
>
> Does Melanie *plan to* request a transfer to Detroit?
>
> All pay increases are *retroactive to* January 1.
>
> We will *try to* exceed our sales quotas for this quarter.

CLASS PRACTICE 1

Select the appropriate words in the following sentences.

1. The itemized estimate that was originally submitted is identical (with, to) the revised estimate.
2. Please ask Lisa and John whether they are angry (about, at, with) the hotel about the mix-up.
3. Does Wayne want to schedule a meeting with the staff (in regards, in regard) to the proposed changes?
4. She claims that there is a discrepancy (in, between, among) one section of the report.
5. The new specifications for the proposed laboratory are quite different (from, than) the old ones.

6. We hired a staff of experts to ensure that the employment practices manual is in conformity (to, with) government regulations.

7. After they had thoroughly reviewed and discussed the proposal, all the panel members agreed (with, to) the plan.

8. Carol appeared to be angry (at, with, about) us for closing the store too early.

9. These price increases are retroactive (from, to) March 1.

TROUBLESOME PREPOSITIONS

Choosing between certain pairs of prepositions causes writers and speakers some difficulty. Study the following troublesome pairs to make sure that they will cause *you* no difficulty.

Between, Among   Ordinarily, use *between* when referring to *two* persons, places, or things; use *among* when referring to *more than two*.

> *Between* you and me, I am confident that we can finish this assignment at least one week early.

> All commissions will be divided *among* the three agents.

Beside, Besides   Remember that *beside* means "by the side of" and that *besides* means "in addition to" or "except."

> Place these cartons *beside* the bookcase.   ("By the side of" the bookcase.)

> *Besides* pads and pencils, what other supplies will we need for the meeting? ("In addition to" pads and pencils.)

> No one *besides* Gail has the authority to sign checks over $500.   ("No one except" Gail.)

Inside, Outside   Do not use *of* after *inside* or *outside*. When referring to time, use *within*, not *inside of*.

> The drinking fountain is just *inside* that door.   (NOT *inside of*.)

> Trash cans are located directly *outside* each entrance.   (NOT *outside of*.)

> Please send your check *within* 10 days after you receive the shipment.   (NOT *inside of*.)

All, Both   After *all* or *both* use *of* only when *all* or *both* is followed by a *pronoun*. Omit *of* if either word is followed by a *noun*.

> *All of* us will need to work overtime to ready *all* these packages for mailing. (*All of* is followed by the pronoun *us*, but *all* precedes the noun *packages*.)

> *Both of* them will each receive two awards; *both* awards will be given at the banquet.   (*Both of* is followed by the pronoun *them*, but *both* precedes the noun *awards*.)

At, To; In, Into   *At* and *in* indicate position. *To* and *into* signify motion.

> Sarah is *at* the production meeting.   (No action.)
>
> Sarah went *to* the meeting at 9 a.m.   (Action—she *went* to the meeting.)
>
> When I saw the computer *in* the store window, I went *into* the store.   (The computer was *in* position—no action. I went *into* the store—action.)

When either *at* or *in* refers to a place, use *in* for larger places; *at* for smaller places.

> He lives *in* San Francisco and works *at* the University of California.

Behind, In Back Of   Use *behind*, not *in back of.* However, *in front of* is correct.

> I sat *behind* Mr. Simmons while the representative displayed the products *in front of* him.

From, Off   Use *from* when referring to persons or places, *off* when referring to things. Do not use either *of* or *from* with the word *off.*

> Tom received the completed applications *from* Harneet.   (NOT *off, off of,* or *from off.*)
>
> Please take these outdated magazines *off* the end tables in the waiting room. (*Off* things—correct. NOT *off of* or *from.*)

Of, Have   With the helping verb *should*, use the verb *have*—not the preposition *of.*

> You *should have* called the travel agent yesterday.   (NOT *should of called.*)

Help, Help From   The word *from* should not follow *help* in sentences such as this:

> The chairman could not *help* being late to the meeting.   (NOT *help from being.*)

Opposite, Opposite To   Do not use *to* after *opposite;* both words are prepositions.

> A new restaurant will be built *opposite* our office building.   (NOT *opposite to* our office building.)

EDITING PRACTICE 1

Correct any preposition errors in the following sentences. Write *OK* if a sentence is correct.

1. Do you think Nancy and Ed will be able to complete all these invoices inside of two days?

2. Several other agents beside Tyler and Maureen questioned the new marketing strategy.

3. As Ms. Diaz suggested, we should simply divide all the new accounts between Karen, Monty, and Sean.

4. The estimate we received was too high; therefore, we could not help from engaging another contractor.

5. We borrowed some pamphlets off of Mary Lou because the printer was late in delivering ours.

6. All of the children will be taking the field trip to the museum instead of watching the film on construction trades.

7. If you need more blank forms, you will find some in the cabinet opposite to my assistant's desk.

8. Until we move to our new offices, please store these records in back of the file cabinets.

COORDINATING CONJUNCTIONS

A **conjunction** is a word that joins sentences or parts of sentences. The coordinating conjunctions are *and, but, or,* and *nor;* and they are used to connect *similar* grammatical elements—two or more words, phrases, or clauses.

1. Two or more words:

Dan *or* Julie

quickly *but* carefully

books, films, *and* recordings

2. Two or more phrases:

in the morning *or* in the afternoon

in my office, in the conference room, *and* in the hall

3. Two or more clauses:

The producer did not complete the movie on schedule, *nor* did he complete it within the budget.

The director suggested that we revise the questionnaire *and* that we ask a panel to review the questions.

CORRELATIVE CONJUNCTIONS

Correlative conjunctions, too, are used to connect *similar* grammatical elements. They are used in pairs:

both . . . and	neither . . . nor
not only . . . but also	whether . . . or
either . . . or	

Both our manager *and* her production assistant have been out of the office this week.

Neither Ms. Allen *nor* Mr. Sirakides attended the conference.

The board authorized *not only* the purchase of the new site *but also* the payment of $5 million for the property.

CLASS PRACTICE 2

Identify the coordinating and the correlative conjunctions in the following sentences, and label each.

1. Neither Bill Nolan nor Dave Hawkins had been told about the change in schedule.
2. Both the Seattle office and the Denver office have requested more information about this new policy.
3. She asked not only Curt but also Leonard to work on the files for the Anderson account.
4. Write to the manager of human resources in our main office, or discuss the problem with your supervisor.
5. Whether we order 10,000 booklets or we order 110,000, the cost per booklet is the same.
6. Not only has Arnold completely revised the entire operations manual, but also he has keyboarded and printed all the text.
7. The candidate promised many changes during the campaign, but she was able to accomplish only part of her program.

PARALLEL STRUCTURE

As used in the term *parallel structure,* the word *parallel* means "similar" or "equal." Sentences are considered to have parallel structure (or *parallelism*) when matching ideas are expressed in similar ways. For example, in the parallel sentences below, note how the coordinating conjunctions connect similar elements.

POOR: Mr. Morris said to check the value of the property and that our insurance should be increased.   (There are two items after *said,* and both are joined by *and.* The two items are (1) *to check the value of the property* and (2) *that our insurance should be increased.* To be parallel, both should start with *to* or with *that.*)

PARALLEL: Mr. Morris said to check the value of the property *and* to increase our insurance.   (The two elements joined by *and* are parallel.)

PARALLEL: Mr. Morris said that the value of the property should be checked *and* that our insurance should be increased.   (Again, the two elements connected by *and* match.)

POOR: This product is sturdy, lightweight, and costs very little. (The coordinating conjunction *and* connects three elements: (1) the adjective *sturdy,* (2) the adjective *lightweight,* and (3) the phrase *costs very little.* Do the three items match? No.)

PARALLEL: This product is sturdy, lightweight, and inexpensive. (Now that the conjunction joins three *adjectives,* the sentence is parallel.)

Now let's see how parallelism is achieved in sentences with correlative conjunctions.

POOR: You need *both* a completed medical form *and* to get your supervisor's approval. (The elements that follow *both* and *and* should match. As the sentence now reads, a noun, *form,* follows *both,* and a verb, *to get,* follows *and.* Compare this with the next two examples.)

PARALLEL: You need *both* a completed medical form *and* your supervisor's approval. (Now what follows *both* and *and*? Two nouns—*form* and *approval.*)

PARALLEL: You need *both* to complete a medical form *and* to get your supervisor's approval. (Both elements following the two parts of the correlative *both/and* do match.)

CLASS PRACTICE 3

In the following pairs of sentences, one sentence illustrates parallelism; the other does not. Select the parallel sentence, and explain why it is parallel.

1. **a.** She said that you will need both a down payment and an approved loan form.
   b. She said that you will need both a down payment and to have a loan form approved.

2. **a.** Evelyn has neither the dedication nor does she have the management experience for that job.
   b. Evelyn has neither the dedication nor the management experience for that job.

3. **a.** The training director told us to improve our spelling and that our grammar skills needed improvement.
   b. The training director told us to improve our spelling and grammar skills.

4. **a.** Our receptionists not only greet visitors but also handling mail is their responsibility.
   b. Our receptionists not only greet visitors but also handle mail.

5. **a.** Gathering sales information and presenting all the statistics in well-written reports are part of her job.
   b. Gathering sales information and to present all the statistics in well-written reports are part of her job.

6. **a.** Before Tuesday either call Mrs. MacKenzie or meet with her to discuss these stocks.

   b. Before Tuesday either call Mrs. MacKenzie or we should meet with her to discuss these stocks.

7. **a.** The insurance policy neither covers fire nor theft.

   b. The insurance policy covers neither fire nor theft.

8. **a.** The most important part of this job is to analyze consumer trends and reporting such trends to our Sales Department.

   b. The most important part of this job is to analyze consumer trends and to report such trends to our Sales Department.

EDITING PRACTICE 2

Correct any errors in parallelism in the following sentences. Write *OK* for any sentence that has no error.

1. Tell Ida that she should confirm her hotel reservations and to allow an extra half hour for the trip to the airport.
2. Either Marisa will fly to Dallas or drive there.
3. All of us agree that Deanna is efficient, hardworking, and ought to be promoted.
4. Return the enclosed card to get your free subscription, or our toll-free number may be called.
5. Caryl has been not only successful as a photographer but also as a copywriter.
6. Gregory has earned a reputation for being both creative and to be efficient.
7. Irma will tell us when the final report is due, Jack will write the first draft, and Daniel and I will proofread the final copy.
8. We have an all-day meeting both on Wednesday and Friday.
9. Jonathan not only wanted to pass his CPA exam but also to earn his pilot's license.
10. Both writing reports and to prepare presentations are hard for me.

CONJUNCTION PITFALLS

Avoiding the following four pitfalls will help you not only use conjunctions correctly but also improve the quality and style of your writing.

1. Use *but*, not *and*, to join and contrast two elements.

I immediately called Lauren, *but* she was not in her office.

Andy had an ample supply of these brochures, *but* I think that he distributed most of them yesterday.

2. Say "the reason is *that*," not "the reason is *because*." Say "read in the paper *that*," not "read in the paper *where*." Say "pretend *that*," not "pretend *like*."

The reason he called is *that* he needs the latest prices for the catalog.

Yesterday I read in a magazine *that* the average interest rate in money markets is now about 5.9 percent.

Because she works so well under pressure, Nora often pretends *that* every job is a rush job.

3. There is no such conjunction as *being that*. Instead, use *because*.

Because Ms. Marino will be out of town, we need to reschedule her appointment. (NOT *Being that Ms. Marino . . . .*)

I accomplished a great deal today, *since* the office was nearly empty. (NOT *being that the office . . . .*)

4. *Like* is a verb or a preposition, not a conjunction. Yet you will often hear people say, "*Like* I was telling Jim . . . ." Use *as, as though*, or *as if* when a conjunction is needed, not *like*.

We *like* the new design. (Here *like* is a verb.)

Sharon needs a modem *like* mine to transmit data via telephone lines. (The preposition *like* is always followed by a noun or a pronoun.)

This morning Mike looks *as if* he is ill. (NOT *like he is ill.*)

Gregory said that it does not look *as though* our loan will be approved. (NOT *like our loan will be approved.*)

CLASS PRACTICE 4

Review the uses of conjunctions and conjunction pitfalls before you attempt the following exercise. Then select the correct choice for each sentence.

1. (Being that, Because) we had so little time, we decided to airfreight the carton.
2. The policy committee was supposed to have met this afternoon, (and, but) Ms. Takimoto, the chairperson, had to reschedule the meeting.
3. I read on the bulletin board (where, that) employees' travel insurance has been increased.
4. The reason for these training sessions is (because, that) the company intends to expand its marketing staff.
5. When speaking to someone on the phone, pretend (like, that) he or she is standing before you.
6. Be sure to proofread all checks (like, as if) they were written for one million dollars.
7. The applicants were on time, (and, but) the interviewer was late.
8. The explanation for the error is (because, that) the computer malfunctioned.

COMMUNICATION LABORATORY

APPLICATION EXERCISES

A. On a separate sheet of paper, write the correct selections for the following sentences.

1. Briefly describe the discrepancy you found (in, between) the two marketing surveys.
2. The total for each column is not identical (to, with) yours.
3. Do you know whether Ms. Brill plans (on submitting, to submit) the report to the committee at this afternoon's meeting?
4. (Beside, Besides) Jeff McDonald and Jennifer Tran, only one other supervisor was present.
5. Jack, will you please help me stack all these cartons (in back of, behind) the partition?
6. As you suggested, Mr. Baxter, we shared copies of the findings with (all, all of) our field managers.
7. If the price had been lower, we would (have, of) bought two copiers for our offices.
8. Is this sample any different (from, than) the one we received from Princess Fabrics?
9. Following the advice of our attorney, we did not enter (into, upon) the agreement with Central Leasing.
10. When the completed forms are delivered, divide them (between, among) our four clerks for processing.
11. Please tell Judy that we will wait for her if she plans to arrive (inside of, within) an hour.
12. Our attorney clearly communicated our intention to abide (with, by) the panel's ruling.
13. As you can imagine, we were somewhat angry (at, with) our supervisor for not informing us earlier of the mandatory overtime.
14. If you would like a free sample, you may obtain one (off of, from) your local distributor at the Harmony Clothing Center.
15. Our new store location is (opposite, opposite to) the Palace Theater.

B. Choose the words that make the sentences express ideas correctly.

1. Making appointments with sales prospects is sometimes more difficult than (to sell, selling) products to them.
2. (Because, Being that) the construction of the building is two months behind schedule, we will remain in these quarters until November.
3. Allied Office Supplies no longer delivers orders free of charge, (and, but) Allied's shipping charges are very reasonable.
4. According to the illustration in the operating manual, these two keys control the movement of the cursor either to the left or (the right, to the right).

CONTINUED

5. Next fall the Training Department is planning (on offering, to offer) classes in several popular computer software programs.

6. After she returns from an exercise class, Alicia looks (like, as if) she is completely exhausted.

7. In such situations we generally return the merchandise and (a deduction is noted on the invoice, deduct the amount from the invoice).

8. Gathering sales statistics is easier than (to analyze them, analyzing them).

9. If you need more information, either write to our Customer Service Department or (our local sales representative should be asked, ask our local sales representative) for help.

10. Simply insert the diskette into the disk drive (like, as) the diagram illustrates.

11. Next Friday (we must either, either we must) telephone or send a fax to our main office.

12. One adviser suggested buying tax-exempt municipal bonds or (wants us to buy treasury bonds, treasury bonds).

13. She asked one of our attorneys to draw up a standard contract and (explain its terms to her staff, then explaining its terms to her staff).

14. The swatches we received were neither the right fabrics nor (the right colors, of the right colors).

15. As a result of our discussion, we decided neither to move to a new location nor (to expand our office space, expand our office space).

C. Edit the following excerpt from a business memorandum.

A comparison of sales through the first six month's of this year with sales thorough the first six month's of last year show that we are approximately 15 percent ahead of last year. Among the major reasons for this increase are the obvious success of our newest product, Vita-Chews. Parent's are delighted with the high quality and the low price, and children are equal satisfied with the delicious flavor of these chewable vitamins. Indeed, they do taste real well!

As we enter the second half of the year, let us strive for additional improvment. During the months of September, we plan to introduce another new product, ChildSafe. We hope that sales' of this innovative offering—if it's test marketing is accurate—will boost our's second-half sales by at least 8 percent. And if sales of Vita-Chews continues to be strong, our results for the year should be real positive.

VOCABULARY AND SPELLING STUDIES

A. These words are often confused: *fate, fete; census, senses*. Describe the differences.

B. Each of the phrases below can be replaced by a single word that has the same meaning. For each phrase provide such a word.
1. Without meaning to
2. Of his or her own free will
3. With great emphasis
4. Without thinking
5. From time to time
6. Lost consciousness

C. Give at least one synonym for each of the following words:
1. prohibit
2. lucid
3. homogeneous
4. fortitude
5. diminish

CHAPTER 5

Punctuation and Style

Pauses, gestures, body language, volume—these and many other tools we use in speaking are not possible in writing. We can't "write louder" to show how we speak in expressing strong feeling. We don't write something above the base line to show how we raise the pitch of our voices in asking a question.

Instead, as we write, we use marks of punctuation. Punctuation marks provide signals for our readers. Punctuation marks help a reader group words or separate words to organize meaning. Punctuation marks also help readers interpret meaning by indicating questions, exclamations, pauses, interruptions, and stops.

The following sections will teach you how to give your readers clear messages by using the appropriate punctuation marks.

OBJECTIVES

Given a situation that requires polished punctuation skills, you will be able to do the following when you master the sections in this chapter:

1. Use periods, question marks, and exclamation points correctly.

2. Use commas, semicolons, colons, and dashes to provide pauses to guide readers through your message.

3. Identify the exact words of other writers and speakers by using quotation marks.

4. Separate and identify additional information by using parentheses.

5. Form possessives, contractions, and special plurals correctly by using apostrophes.

6. Apply rules for capitalization.

7. Correctly use abbreviations and symbols.

8. Write numbers in words or in figures, whichever is appropriate.

PERIODS, QUESTION MARKS, AND EXCLAMATION POINTS

A famous baseball pitcher, known to be a man of few words, was asked to comment on his last game. He was quoted as replying ".". History records a few other examples of similar replies. For example, one famous author wrote to his publisher to find out how well his book was selling. He simply wrote "?" The book had indeed been selling very well, so his publisher replied "!" (Kay Powell, *Wordwatching,* September 1982).

The period, the question mark, and the exclamation point are marks used to end sentences. Obviously, these punctuation marks are very familiar and easy to learn. This section will review their basic uses and discuss a few problem areas in using these ending marks.

THE PERIOD

The most commonly used mark of punctuation is the period. Use a period after declarative and imperative sentences, indirect questions, and requests phrased as questions.

After Declarative and Imperative Sentences   A *declarative sentence* makes a statement, and an *imperative sentence* is an order or a command. Use a period after each.

Ms. Freeman wants to attend the computer seminar.   (A declarative sentence—it simply makes a statement.)

Send Ms. Freeman the brochure describing our scheduled seminars.   (An imperative sentence—a polite command. In this sentence the subject *you* is understood.)

After Indirect Questions   An *indirect question* is really a statement because it simply rephrases a question in statement form. Use a period after indirect questions. Of course, use a question mark after a direct question.

"Does anyone know," asked Jim, "when the revised procedures manual will be distributed?"   (Jim's actual words are in quotation marks. His actual words constitute a question and require a question mark.)

Jim asked whether anyone knew when the revised procedures manual would be distributed.   (This is not Jim's original question; it is a restatement of his question. This restatement is an indirect question and requires a period.)

After Requests Phrased as Questions Sometimes, as a matter of courtesy, a request is phrased in question form. Use a period when such requests clearly indicate that a specific action is expected. (Requests that end with a period are called *polite requests.*) Use a question mark when such requests are direct requests that require a "yes" or a "no" answer.

> Will you please send us your payment.   (An action is being requested. This is simply a polite way of saying "Send us your payment.")
>
> Will you be able to ship the merchandise in time for our Fourth of July sale? (A genuine question—*can you* ship it in time?)

CLASS PRACTICE 1

Supply the correct ending punctuation mark for each of the following sentences.

1. Will you please send us a copy of your latest catalog
2. Will Mr. Washington be available this afternoon for the marketing meeting
3. May we have your check by March 30
4. A sales representative asked when the new price list will become effective
5. Will you please credit our account for the damaged merchandise we returned
6. Aaron wants to know when the final payment is due

Do not use a closing period after the following items:

1. Numbers or letters in parentheses
2. Headings or titles appearing on separate lines
3. Roman numerals (except when followed by titles, as in outlines)
4. Even dollar amounts
5. Abbreviations ending with a period

> The supervisor cited three reasons for the delay: (1) the recent strike, (2) the backlog in shipments during summer, and (3) the time needed to check customers' credit accounts.   (NOT (1.), (2.), ...)
>
> Summary
> BIBLIOGRAPHY   } (No period after headings that appear on separate lines.)
> Endnotes
>
> Mark Turner III will be the new CEO of Fieldcrest Enterprises.   (NOT *III. will be* . . . .)
>
> Ms. Hauser suggested $20 as a fair list price for our new computer game. (NOT *$20. as a* . . . .)
>
> Store hours are from 9 a.m. until 8 p.m.   (NOT *8 p.m..*)

In addition, do not use a period after items in a list unless the items are complete sentences.

Nancy discussed three problems:

1. The profit margin
2. Increased competition
3. Government regulation

Now notice how the items in the following example *are* complete sentences:

Nancy will discuss the following problems at our next meeting:

1. Profit margins over the past three years have steadily declined.
2. Increased competition has conspicuously eroded our market share.
3. Government regulations have inhibited market expansion.

EDITING PRACTICE 1

Find and correct any errors in the following sentences.

1. By using various commands in this word processing program, you may delete (1.) a single letter, (2.) an entire word, (3.) an entire line of copy, or (4.) an entire paragraph.
2. Tell Andrew to ship this order to Ms. Jackson c.o.d. .
3. Because it exceeds $500., this departmental expense must be approved by Mrs. Chin.
4. Sandra identified the following possible sites for the new warehouse:
   a. Jackson, Mississippi.
   b. Hot Springs, Arkansas.
   c. Mount Hood, Oregon.
5. Is it true that Edward Sloan III. has been appointed to the board of directors?
6. The lowest estimate (only $2500.) was submitted by United Tool Company Inc.
7. We extended our store hours during the holidays; we are now open from 10 a.m. until 10 p.m..

Period Pitfalls   A common error in using periods is to place the closing period *before the end of the sentence,* thereby stranding a group of words and creating a fragment.

Next April we will launch an advertising campaign for our new video recorders. The most expensive and extensive campaign we have ever developed.   (Here the second group of words makes no sense unless it is joined to the first sentence. See the next example.)

Next April we will launch an advertising campaign for our new video recorders, the most expensive and extensive campaign we have ever developed.

A second common error related to period use is to place a comma where a period (or a semicolon) should be used. In other words, a sentence that should end with a period should not be joined to another sentence by a comma.

> Ajax Car Leasing has been offering exceptionally attractive leasing agreements, it's still not too late to apply.   (A period [or a semicolon] should follow agreements. Two sentences have been joined—incorrectly—by a comma.)

EDITING PRACTICE 2

Find the errors in the following sentences, and explain why they are errors.

1. All of us expected the price of computer equipment to drop this year, we deliberately delayed last year's purchases to take advantage of the anticipated price reductions.
2. Our plan calls for increasing our radio advertising extensively. In an effort to reach young adults.
3. Lydia generally conducts the sales training classes, she has been a successful agent in our office for more than fifteen years.
4. These new products are selling better than we had expected, sales are now about 25 percent over our original estimates.
5. Ms. Ella Butler has been placed in charge of the department. While Mr. Edwards is in Dallas to assist with the opening of the new regional office there.
6. Place all these documents in the safe before you leave, they should not be left lying on your desk overnight.
7. We submitted a detailed estimate well before the Friday deadline. In order to qualify for the revised bidding process.

THE QUESTION MARK

The question mark is used after a direct question. It is also used after a short direct question that follows a statement.

> Who has the order from Owens Chemicals?   (Direct question.)
> Have you seen today's closing stock market prices?   (Direct question.)

> This car is too expensive, isn't it?   (The sentence begins as a statement and ends as a question. Use a question mark to conclude the sentence.)

> All these fax machines come with a one-year warranty, don't they?   (Use a question mark because a question is joined to the statement.)

When a series of questions is included in one sentence, use a question mark after each question. Do not capitalize first words in the individual questions.

> Will you be opening branches in England? in Japan? in Germany?

CLASS PRACTICE 2

In the following sentences indicate whether a period or a question mark is needed at the point marked by parentheses.

1. Lynn and Susan have already submitted their petitions to the committee, haven't they( )
2. Will you please send one copy of the discount list to each of the district managers( )
3. Did Mr. Connors advise us to obtain additional bids from Acme Plastics( ) from Reece & Bond Inc.( ) from National Wholesalers( )
4. Yes, Ms. Diaz asked if the discount applies to all orders placed during March( )
5. Eleanor Chu is the head of the Art Department, isn't she ( )
6. Will you have on hand a sufficient number of brochures for all our sales representatives( )

THE EXCLAMATION POINT

To express strong feeling, use an exclamation point after a word, a phrase, or a sentence. Do not, however, overuse the exclamation point—especially in business correspondence.

Congratulations! John and I are delighted to hear that you have been promoted to assistant marketing director.   (Exclamation point after a word. Note that the sentence following the exclamation is punctuated in the usual way.)

Another best-seller! How pleased I was to learn that our second book . . . . (Exclamation point after a phrase.)

Why didn't we think of this sooner!   (Exclamation point after a sentence.)

Note that the need for the exclamation point must often be determined by the writer. For example, the last sentence could also have been written as a simple question:

Why didn't we think of this sooner?   (Now the sentence does not show as strong emotion as with the exclamation point.)

CLASS PRACTICE 3

Indicate the punctuation at the point or points marked with parentheses in the following sentences. Explain your choices.

1. Another promotion( ) All of us congratulate you( )
2. What a surprise( ) I was pleased to learn that you have returned to Chicago( )
3. I certainly appreciate all your help in conducting this survey( ) Thanks so much( )
4. I cannot believe it( ) Did you know that Stephanie and Alan are opening their third store( )

5. What an accomplishment( ) Your sales for July set a new company record, and we congratulate you on this achievement( )
6. Whose idea was this( )

COMMUNICATION LABORATORY

APPLICATION EXERCISES

A. At the point marked by parentheses, indicate the correct punctuation for the following sentences. If no punctuation is needed, write *OK.*

1. Will you please call me as soon as Donald Cook arrives( )
2. Are you aware that Accu-Plus vacuum cleaners—unlike most others—are warranted for a full five years( )
3. Congratulations( ) All of us hope that your new business is a great success( )
4. Do you know when the messenger is scheduled to arrive( )
5. Have you had the opportunity yet to visit our Dallas office( ) our Tampa office( ) our St. Louis warehouse( )
6. Jerry is now seeking another insurance agent( ) the Merrill Agency is relocating to Spokane( )
7. Will you please give my assistant a copy of the minutes of the last sales meeting( )
8. We just heard the good news( )
9. Has Ellen spoken with you yet about the new advertising campaign( )
10. Stephen has already completed the first draft of his presentation, hasn't he( )
11. As you know, Carla is in London( ) her assistant Edward is handling her projects.
12. Our firm is opening a new office in Washington, D.C.( )
13. To understand these concepts clearly, read Chapters III( ) and IV( )of your assigned textbook.
14. Have you registered for the July accounting workshop yet( )
15. The actual price for the computer, the keyboard, the monitor, the printer, the modem, and two disk drives was only $2500( )

B. On a separate sheet, correct the following sentences and explain your reasons for making each correction. If a sentence has no error, write *OK.*

1. Between you and I, I seriously doubt whether this project will ever be approved.
2. You may use the calculator on Tom's desk, he will be out of the office until next Tuesday.
3. Call the messenger before noon, we must ship these cartons to Chicago as soon as possible.
4. What an incredible story.

5. Absolutely not we do not plan to close the Grand Avenue warehouse.
6. Did you know that the Johnson's own only about 4 or 5 percent of the stock in Johnson Industries?
7. We, her assistant and me, quickly discovered the reason for these errors.
8. Betty has been the manager of the Research Department since 1987, she will probably be named an assistant vice president soon.
9. Tell anyone who needs more of them forms to call the Tax Department.
10. Several of the executive's have already commented on the improved service since we installed the new equipment.
11. An additional discount of $10. will be given to anyone who orders this telephone model before December 31!
12. Has he took all the cartons to the Accounting Department yet?
13. May I have your completed application forms by May 1?
14. Three boxes of outdated catalogs have laid in the supply cabinet for over a year.
15. No one knows who the board will select to fill this vacancy.

C. Is the punctuation correct in the following paragraph? Correct any errors as you copy the paragraph on a separate sheet of paper.

Congratulations. Your hard work throughout the last year has certainly paid off. Your total sales for the year were 155 percent of the budget. Everyone here in the headquarters office applauds you for this superb achievement. What do you have planned for *this* year.

VOCABULARY AND SPELLING STUDIES

A. These words are often confused: *expand, expend; interstate, intrastate.* Explain the differences.

B. By adding a prefix to each of these words, change the word to give it a negative meaning.

1. normal	5. literate	9. understood	13. essential
2. engage	6. enchanted	10. achiever	14. popular
3. proper	7. reasonable	11. order	15. convenient
4. noble	8. likely	12. embark	

C. How are the following pairs of words spelled when *-ing* is added to each?

1. hop, hope	4. dote, dot
2. plane, plan	5. bar, bare
3. mop, mope	6. pine, pin

SECTION 5.2

SECTION 5.2
COMMAS—BASIC USES

The comma is certainly a versatile and often-used punctuation mark. Commas may be viewed as leading the reader along a map; errors in comma usage may force the reader to take an unnecessary detour. By learning the uses of the comma in this and the following section, you can guide your reader smoothly—*without* detours.

IN A SERIES

A series consists of a minimum of *three* words or groups of words (phrases or clauses). For clarity always use a comma after each item in the series except the last. Thus the final comma appears immediately before the conjunction (*and* or *or*) that connects the last item to the series.

> Valuable books, periodicals, and directories were destroyed in the fire.   (A series of words. Note the comma before *and.*)

> We spent the entire week on the telephone, in our hotel rooms, or at meetings.   (A series of three prepositional phrases: (1) *on the telephone,* (2) *in our hotel rooms,* and (3) *at meetings.*)

> Jim spent most of the week meeting prospective clients, showing them our products, and describing our services.   (A series of phrases.)

> Jim introduced the program, Jan gave a slide presentation, and Greta made the closing remarks.   (A series of clauses.)

With Repeated Conjunctions   If the conjunction is repeated before each item, then no comma is needed to separate the items.

> Our branch office with the highest sales for this year may be Denver or Houston or Manchester.

When *Etc.* Ends a Series   Whenever the abbreviation *etc.* ends a series, be sure to use a comma before and after it (unless, of course, *etc.* ends the sentence).

> Sales, profits, revenues, *etc.,* were discussed at this morning's session.

> She gave several reasons for increasing the budget estimate—higher costs, overhead, declining market, *etc.*

Always remember that *etc.* (*et cetera*) means "and so forth"; therefore, you must not write *and etc.* (the equivalent of *and and so forth*).

EDITING PRACTICE 1

Where are commas needed in the following sentences? Write *OK* if the sentence is correct.

1. Companies that have shown an interest in purchasing the building are Spectrum Industries Scotchwood Real Estate Corporation and the Lincoln Bank of Commerce.
2. Purchase orders invoice records important contracts etc. will be stored on microfiche.
3. Joyce Steve Terry and Tony conduct all the training sessions.
4. In just two weeks we wrote the script recorded a master tape and duplicated copies for all branch offices.
5. The only one of our stores that is open late on Mondays and Wednesdays and Fridays is located in the Greenbrook Mall.
6. Allen wrote the script Betty edited the copy and Charles narrated all the tapes.

WITH APPOSITIVES AND SIMILAR CONSTRUCTIONS

Appositives   An appositive renames or explains the previous noun. Set off with commas an appositive expression. Since you have already learned how to choose case forms of pronouns in appositives, you may have realized at that time that all the appositives illustrated were separated by commas.

> My supervisors, *Scott McBurney and she,* are in charge of salary administration. (The words *Scott McBurney and she* are an appositive renaming *supervisors;* therefore, a comma is placed before and after the appositive.)

Now note that a one-word appositive that is very closely related to the preceding noun or an appositive expression that answers *which one or ones?* is *not* separated by commas.

> Her brother *Martin* also graduated from Pine Crest Academy.   (No commas are needed to separate *brother* and *Martin,* which are very closely related.)

> The term *user friendly* is used to describe the degree to which automated equipment is easy to use.   (Here *user friendly* identifies which term; therefore, no commas are needed.)

Degrees, Titles, and Similar Terms   Abbreviations such as *R.N., CPA, Ph.D., M.D.,* and *Esq.* following a person's name should be set off by commas.

> Donald P. Phelps, *Ed.D.,* has consented to deliver the commencement address at this year's graduation ceremony.

Terms such as *Jr.* and *Sr.* and *Inc.* and *Ltd.* may appear with or without commas when used after a person's or a company's name. Writers should always follow the style that individuals or companies prefer.

Oscar K. Brereton *Sr.* has been named president of Dallas Research Associates. (Here the individual writes his name without the commas before and after *Sr.*)

The form indicates that James L. Clark, *Jr.,* is the only beneficiary of the policy. (James L. Clark, Jr., uses the commas before and after *Jr.;* at the end of a sentence, of course, the comma after *Jr.* would be omitted.)

The headquarters building for Time *Inc.* is located in Rockefeller Center in New York City.   (The actual company name is *Time Inc.*—no comma.)

Rorden Products*, Ltd.,* has been bought by Giant Brand Toys, *Inc.*   (The actual letterheads of these two companies show commas before *Ltd.* and *Inc.*)

Calendar Dates

Calendar Dates   No comma is needed to separate a month and a year (for example, *May 1999*); but when a day is included, set off the year with commas.

On *May 3, 1999,* the president of our company is scheduled to retire.   (At the end of a sentence, of course, the comma after *1999* would be replaced by a period.)

City and State Names

City and State Names   Whenever a city and state name are written in consecutive order, use commas to set off the state name.

The auditors are now working in our *Seattle, Washington,* office and our *Chicago, Illinois,* warehouse.   (Commas separate the state names.)

Direct Address

Direct Address   When we speak directly to someone, we often use that person's name as we address him or her. Such use is called direct address. Note how commas are used to separate names in direct address in these sentences.

Mr. Rothstein, will you be able to submit your revised specifications to us by March 15?

If you need help, *Wayne,* please let me know.

I will have the final report ready for distribution on Friday, *Mrs. Winbury.*

EDITING PRACTICE 2

Where are commas needed in the following sentences? Write *OK* if the sentence is correct.

1. His sister Virginia is a senior vice president in our Chicago office.
2. Joshua Wooldridge Ph.D. is in charge of the Research Department.
3. We were surprised, of course, to hear that Donald Sampson Sr. voted in favor of the proposal.
4. Although we were awarded the bid on March 10 1994 we did not formally close escrow on the property until January 6 1995.
5. The former president of this company Mary P. Lombardi was recently named to the mayor's special panel.
6. Be sure to specify clearly whether orders are to be sent to Kansas City Kansas or Kansas City Missouri whenever you complete these forms.

7. Pamela Rockwell one of our financial advisers explained the benefits of these government-guaranteed bonds.

8. His wife Marie is a stock analyst with a company in San Antonio Texas.

AFTER AN INTRODUCTORY WORD OR GROUP OF WORDS

To signal the reader to slow down, use a comma after an introductory word or group of words.

Introductory Words   Among the most commonly used introductory words are the following. Use a comma after each.

also	fortunately	moreover	obviously
consequently	furthermore	namely	of course
finally	however	naturally	otherwise
first	in addition	nevertheless	therefore
for example	meanwhile	no	yes

Now notice how these words take the reader from one idea to the next:

First, we must assess recent changes in buying patterns.

Second, we must survey typical customers to determine their basis for product selection. (*Fortunately,* we have an excellent mailing list; *however,* such a survey will be very expensive.) *Finally,* we must choose an advertising agency to represent us.

Be sure that you recognize when these words are introductory and when they are not.

However difficult it may be, Ellen enjoys a challenging project.   (Here, *however* modifies *difficult;* it is not an introductory word.)

Obviously annoyed by the street noises, Rose closed the windows.   (Here, *obviously* modifies *annoyed.*)

Introductory Phrases   A comma is needed after any introductory phrase that contains a verb form. Introductory phrases appear before and introduce the main thought unit.

To qualify, you must be a resident of this state.

To get your copy, just complete and return the enclosed form.

Knowing the exact cost, Karen tried to correct Bill.

Believing he was right, Bill insisted his prices were correct.

Overwhelmed by the project, the director requested more assistance.

Alerted to the problem, the management team assigned additional personnel immediately.

A comma is also used after a long introductory *prepositional* phrase. Most writers omit commas after *short* introductory prepositional phrases to make the transition to the following group of words smoother.

In July we will move to the Dexter Building. (*In July* is a short prepositional phrase. Read this aloud to see how smoothly the thought flows without a comma.)

During the next month she plans to travel to Europe. (This phrase, too, flows smoothly into the following group of words.)

With the additional clerical help now available to us, our department should no longer have such backlogs. (This longer prepositional phrase does require a comma after it.)

Introductory Clauses Clauses contain a subject and a verb. Introductory clauses begin with one of the following words, which signal you to use a comma after the clause.

after	even if	since	whenever
although	if	so that	where
as	in order that	unless	wherever
as soon as	inasmuch as	until	while
because	provided	when	

After Ms. Stephenson arrives, we will discuss the sales promotion campaign.

Whenever you have time to review these proposals, I will share my copies with you.

If your balance is under $5000, you may charge the entire amount to your account.

EDITING PRACTICE 3

Correct any errors in the following sentences. Write *OK* if a sentence is correct.

1. Knowing that the discussion would require at least two hours Robert decided to continue the meeting on Thursday.
2. However do not accept any returns until all the forms have been approved and signed by Mr. Weston or Ms. Corbett.
3. As you probably learned at this morning's meeting there is a chance that the merger may not be approved by the board.
4. To be eligible for the 2 percent discount you must pay the total invoice within ten days.
5. If you need any additional information call us toll free at 800-555-1010.
6. In September we will open two new branch offices in Miami.
7. After you have proofread the catalog copy send your corrections to Dianne Jewel in the Advertising Department.
8. Within the next few days one of our representatives will call on you.

WITH INTERRUPTING ELEMENTS

Words, phrases, and clauses that interrupt the flow of the sentence and do not contribute essential information to the message should be set off by commas. Such *interrupters* are not absolutely necessary to the meaning of the sentence. These elements provide *extra* information, contrast ideas, or connect thoughts so they flow more smoothly.

Words   As you saw in the discussion of introductory words, words such as *moreover, therefore, however, nevertheless,* and *consequently* are used at the beginning of sentences as transitions—that is, as bridges between sentences. Review the list of introductory words on page 182. Such words are also commonly used elsewhere in a sentence—as interrupting words. Place commas before and after such interrupters.

> Shirley Hollingsworth proposed, *therefore,* that we sponsor a course on computer graphic arts.   (The word *therefore* interrupts the sentence.)

> The agent, *of course,* expects to receive her usual commission.   (The words *of course* interrupt the sentence.)

Phrases   In our everyday speech we use many phrases such as the ones that follow:

to say the least	in the meantime
so to speak	on the other hand
after all	in my opinion
for instance	according to
for example	in the first place

Such phrases often add an extra idea, provide a transition, or show a contrast. Since these phrases are not *necessary* to complete the meaning of the sentence, they are separated from the rest of the sentence by commas. Use a comma before and after the phrase when it appears in the middle of a sentence. Use a single comma when the words conclude a sentence.

> The reason for the problem, *in my opinion,* is that the operators have not been thoroughly trained.   (The interrupting words offer extra information.)

> There are several districts that promote new products well; both the Denver and the Seattle district offices, *for example,* consistently exceed their sales budgets for new products.   (The words *for example* help provide a smooth transition.)

> Many of the supervisors, *not just Michael,* prefer the old procedures.   (The interrupting expression provides a contrast.)

> The customer should receive a refund and be reimbursed for his expenses, *to say the least.*   (Extra idea at the end of the sentence.)

Clauses   Among the elements that are commonly used as interrupters are clauses with beginning words such as *as, if, when, although, since,* and *because.* See page 183 for a complete list. When such elements appear in the middle of the sentence, of course, *two* commas are needed to set them off.

> We can*, as soon as the technician completes the installation,* begin using the equipment.

> We will*, if our supervisor approves,* delay the completion date by one week.

Note that like phrases, interrupting clauses can also appear at the end of sentences. When such clauses appear at the end of the sentence, *one* comma is needed to separate the words from the main part of the sentence. The key point is to remember to separate such ending clauses with commas *only* when they add extra information. *Omit* commas when the clauses contain essential information:

> Nancy will send the check by November 15*, when the lease is scheduled to expire.*   (*When the lease is scheduled to expire* does not affect the meaning of the sentence; it merely adds an extra idea. Therefore, a comma is needed to separate this clause from the rest of the sentence.)

> You may charge the entire amount to your account*, if you prefer to do so.* (The clause *if you prefer to do so* is not essential; it does not restrict the first clause in any way. Therefore, a comma is required.)

> Mr. Jefferson has been elected to the board*, as you probably have already heard.*   (The clause *as you probably have already heard* provides additional information at the end of the sentence; therefore, a comma is required.)

> Martha said that she will leave *after she completes her report.*   (The clause provides essential information—she will not leave before she meets the condition stated in the clause. No comma separates the two clauses.)

> We will gladly analyze these statistics *if Clarence is still out of the office tomorrow.*   (Essential information—provides a condition. No comma is required.)

> Send these contracts to the Legal Department *before you leave for lunch.* (Essential information; no comma required.)

EDITING PRACTICE 4

Supply any necessary commas in the following sentences. Look for words, phrases, and clauses that may be transitional words or interrupters. Write *OK* if a sentence is correct.

1. We were able nevertheless to convince Mr. Lopez to get additional estimates.
2. Let's meet on Friday rather than on Thursday to continue this discussion.
3. Eric decided to purchase the less expensive keyboard and monitor as you suggested.
4. The Thousand Oaks Mall has increased steadily in profitability since its opening in 1990.

5. Peggy and Kevin consequently recommended that we hire consultants to locate an ideal site for our warehouse.

6. Since none of the executives were in the office we could not have the check signed.

7. The carpeting that was selected for the reception room is in my opinion too flimsy for this heavily trafficked area.

8. Paul and I must work on July 4 even though it is the Independence Day holiday.

IN A COMPOUND SENTENCE

A **compound sentence** is one that has two or more independent clauses (main clauses, each of which could stand alone as an independent sentence). Use a comma between independent clauses joined by *and, but, or,* or *nor.*

> Carla bought this property in 1992, and she plans to build a home on it in the future.   (Each of these clauses could stand alone as a complete sentence. Therefore, the comma before the conjunction *and* is correct.)

> Our supervisor always approves these purchase orders, but he is out of the office this week.   (Again, note the comma before the conjunction *but* because the two clauses could stand alone as complete sentences.)

Now let us take the above sentences and change the second clause by omitting the subject (*she* in the first sentence; *he* in the second sentence). The result, in each case, is a *simple* sentence. Each sentence has only *one* subject and a *compound predicate.* The two parts of the compound predicate must not be separated by a comma.

> Carla bought this property in 1992 and plans to build a home on it in the future.   (The sentence now has only one subject instead of two independent clauses. Therefore, no comma is required.)

> Our supervisor always approves these purchase orders but is out of the office this week.   (The words following the conjunction *but* are *not* an independent clause because a subject is missing. No comma is required.)

In the above sentences, the rule about using a comma to separate two *independent* clauses does not apply because the words following the conjunction in each sentence do not constitute an independent clause.

EDITING PRACTICE 5

Where are commas needed in the following sentences? Explain your reason for inserting each comma. Write *OK* if the sentence is correct.

1. Brian usually handles the Johnson account but is on jury duty this week.

2. An Italian export firm supplies these products and it offers excellent credit terms.

3. Our supervisor has been promoted to general manager and will be moving to Dallas within the next month.
4. Richard Johnson is eligible for this position but he does not want to leave the Chicago area.
5. Our manager searched the files for the original specifications but was unable to find them.
6. You may obtain a free brochure at your local Rent-All store or you may call our toll-free number to have one sent to you.

COMMUNICATION LABORATORY

APPLICATION EXERCISES

A. On a separate sheet of paper, correct any punctuation errors in the following sentences. Write *OK* for any sentence that is correct.

1. Both contracts were signed by Richard Miles Esq. on June 10 1993.
2. George and Stephanie in the meantime have met with several prospective clients from Brazil.
3. Alice Fuller CPA has been retained as a consultant for Holmes & Tuttle Advertising since 1992.
4. One of the shipping clerks as you know mistakenly sent the cartons to Albany New York instead of Albany Georgia.
5. Mr. Murillo, an experienced interpreter, assists in translating all the proposals we submit to companies in Spanish-speaking South American countries.
6. One of the applicants Lu Ann Keithley will be offered a position in our headquarters office.
7. Castle Productions the European distributor of our films is located in London England.
8. Evelyn suggested that we discuss these marketing strategies with Alex Bentley our Eastern Regional Manager.
9. Place all the extra fliers brochures and catalogs in the cabinet.
10. Naturally we were happy to learn that we would receive a year-end bonus.
11. Donna has completed her audit of the Peterson account and she will present her findings to the committee on Friday.
12. To purchase this equipment we must first obtain Mr. Lee's approval.
13. Martin Duffy owns this property, and has indicated a willingness to sell it.
14. If you wish to change your vacation schedule please obtain your supervisor's approval.
15. Ken and I are unable to attend the meeting scheduled for May 2 but we will be able to attend the next meeting on May 16.

CONTINUED

B. Correct the errors in the following sentences. Write *OK* if a sentence is correct.

1. You may return the merchandise in person if you prefer by visiting any of our convenient stores.
2. Karen will create a survey form send it to the branch managers and analyze the results.
3. Ms. Burrus as you probably already know is the most likely person to replace Mr. Hayworth.
4. The most important factor of course, is the safety of all our employees.
5. Have Mark or Anthony arrived yet?
6. All raises according to Ms. Feinberg will become effective June 1.
7. We should purchase these larger monitors because the screens are more easy to read.
8. If we receive your order by November 30 you will receive an additional 10 percent discount.
9. All of us are concerned as you can well imagine about the practicality of buying this expensive equipment.
10. Please obtain approval from John or myself for refunds or exchanges exceeding $200.
11. Please call me, when Mr. Bradley arrives.
12. One of the reasons for this decision as you know is that we expect prices to rise rapidly within the next year.
13. Consequently we are moving our manufacturing plant and other facilities to Macon, Georgia.
14. A large percentage of our students did very good on their state board examinations.
15. The terms of the service contract are to say the least far below industry standards.

C. You have been promoted! Beginning with this Communication Laboratory, the third set of Application Exercises will require you to edit for all kinds of errors—errors in grammar, spelling, punctuation, and vocabulary. Now that you have this added responsibility, be sure to give your editing special attention. Begin with the following excerpt from a memorandum.

Each customers' opinion of our sales representatives are important to us. Therefore we try to give full attention to the human relations skill, the grooming habits and the speaking ability of our sales representative's. Accordingly we have developed a training program for our sales staff.

CONTINUED

VOCABULARY AND SPELLING STUDIES

A. These words are often confused: *lightening, lightning, lighting; respectively, respectfully.* Explain the differences.

B. Which nouns ending in *-ty* are related to the following adjectives?

1.	rare	**4.**	anxious
2.	real	**5.**	facile
3.	entire	**6.**	notorious

C. How do you spell the "shun" ending for each of the following?

1.	expan _____	**4.**	func _____
2.	connec _____	**5.**	discus _____
3.	comple _____	**6.**	suspi _____

COMMAS—SPECIAL USES

As we speak and write, for various reasons we often alter our basic sentence. We may add other related thoughts, use transitional expressions, or link our main idea to another. In speaking, we make the listener aware of these interruptions and additions through pauses, gestures, and voice changes. In writing, we must use other tools to signal our reader when such interruptions and additions occur. As you learned in the previous section, the basic tool in such cases is the comma.

To complete your study of commas, this section presents the last few important principles and covers some of the most common errors of comma use. Studying this section carefully will help you to write clear, effective messages.

WITH TWO OR MORE ADJECTIVES

When you use two or more adjectives and *each* separately modifies the same noun, use a comma between the adjectives.

Lisa needs a *trustworthy, reliable* assistant to help her manage the Encino branch office.   (An assistant who is both trustworthy *and* reliable.)

This *attractive, sturdy, inexpensive* cabinet is ideal for storing videocassettes. (Each adjective modifies the noun *cabinet:* a cabinet that is attractive *and* sturdy *and* inexpensive. Note that the commas are used *between* adjectives; no comma is used between the last adjective, *inexpensive,* and the noun, *cabinet.*)

Do not use commas after adjectives that are closely connected to the noun or that are considered part of the noun. Adjectives that modify the combination of other adjectives and the noun are also not followed by commas.

Last week one of our agents sold the *old brick* house on Jersey Street.   (Here *brick* may be considered part of the noun *house,* since *brick house* provides a single idea. The adjective *old* modifies *brick house* as a unit.)

In addition to a *large monthly house* payment, the applicants are making payments on several smaller loans.   (Here *house* may be considered part of the noun *payment.* The adjective *monthly* describes *house payment*, and the adjective *large* describes *monthly house payment.*)

If you are not sure whether to use a comma between adjectives, apply the following Quick Trick.

QUICK TRICK

Substitute *and* Reverse the Adjectives

To test whether adjectives separately modify the same noun, place the word *and* between the adjectives and reverse their order in the sentence. If the sentence sounds the same, use a comma between the adjectives.

Lisa needs a trustworthy *and* reliable assistant to help her manage the Encino branch office.   (Trustworthy and reliable; reliable and trustworthy)

This attractive *and* sturdy *and* inexpensive cabinet is ideal for storing videocassettes.   (Attractive and sturdy and inexpensive; sturdy and inexpensive and attractive)

Marian just recently bought a red sports car.   (Here, *red* modifies the compound noun *sports car.* You would not say "a car that is sports *and* red.")

We must renovate our present inefficient, costly storage facilities.   (*Storage* is closely connected to the noun *facilities.* The adjectives *inefficient* and *costly* are separate modifiers [*costly* and *inefficient*]. *Present* modifies all the following adjectives and noun as a unit. You would not say "storage facilities that are *inefficient* and *present* and *costly* " or "facilities that are *costly* and *storage* and *present* and *inefficient.*")

CLASS PRACTICE 1

Use commas as needed to separate adjectives in the following sentences. Write *OK* if the sentence is correct.

1. Bob suggested a lively interesting theme for our next sales campaign.
2. Be sure to store these solutions in small plastic jars.

3. Proofreading these long statistical reports is certainly a difficult tiresome job.
4. We must replace the faded stained carpeting in the reception area as soon as possible.
5. She developed a detailed comprehensive analysis of our sales patterns and customer satisfaction index.
6. There is a large well-defined market for these products.

EDITING PRACTICE 1

Test your editing skill by correcting comma errors in the following sentences. If a sentence is correct, write *OK*.

1. We always receive fast efficient friendly service from Speedy Messengers.
2. Everyone on the staff agrees that Ms. Corrigan's patient, positive, and helpful, attitude is an important factor in maintaining the high morale in this department.
3. Our sales manager considers her an intelligent, hardworking, ambitious representative.
4. Mr. Halby has recommended the purchase of new, inexpensive, computer equipment for each branch office.
5. The panel received several, innovative suggestions for product improvements from the staff.
6. Buy-All is one of the most successful discount stores in this area.

WITH *THAT, WHICH, WHO,* AND *WHOM* CLAUSES

Clauses that begin with *that, which, who,* and *whom* deserve special attention. The following discussion simplifies the use of commas with such clauses.

That and *Which* Clauses
Careful writers use *that* to begin a clause with *essential* information and *which* to begin a clause with *nonessential,* or extra, information. In the following examples, note that *which* clauses are separated by commas because they give extra information.

We sent Ann Freeman a copy of our latest sales report, *which* shows sales by units.   (Because the sales report is clearly identified (the latest one), the *which* clause can obviously give only extra information about it.)

Compare the following example:

We sent Ann Freeman the sales report *that* shows sales by units.   (Assume we have two different sales reports. One shows sales by units; the other shows sales by dollars. Now the *that* clause does not give extra information; it gives essential information. Without the *that* clause we would not know which of the two different sales reports was sent to Ann Freeman.)

Let us look at another set of examples.

I read Dawn Hagel's latest book, *which* was on the best-seller list for six months.   (Dawn Hagel has only one "latest book," so the *which* clause gives extra information about the book.)

Compare the next example:

Dawn Hagel's book *that* was on the best-seller list is her most interesting account of police work against crime.   (She has written several books about police work against crime. The *that* clause identifies one specific book of all the books that she has written.)

Be sure to use *that* when the clause gives essential information and *which* when the clause gives nonessential information. Consequently, because a *which* clause gives extra information, separate it with two commas if it interrupts a sentence and one comma if it ends a sentence.

Dawn Hagel's latest book, *which* was on the best-seller list for six months, is available at our local bookstore.   (Here the *which* clause interrupts the sentence, so two commas are necessary.)

Who or **Whom** **Clauses**   A *who* or *whom* clause should be set apart from the rest of the sentence when it gives extra information, that is, when it is *nonessential*. Use commas to let a reader know when a *who* or *whom* clause gives nonessential information: (1) two commas if the clause interrupts a sentence and (2) one comma if the clause ends a sentence.

Harold Cox, *who* is the vice president in charge of production, can provide you with the information you need.   (The *who* clause simply provides additional information about one person who is clearly identified, Harold Cox.)

The vice president *who is in charge of production* can provide you with the information you need.   (Assume we have two vice presidents. Now the *who* clause gives *essential* information; it identifies one of the two vice presidents— the one in charge of production. Without the *who* clause this sentence would be confusing because the *who* clause provides necessary information.)

Please mail this deposit to Mr. McAlary, *whom* we have contracted to repave the employee parking lot.   (The *whom* clause here provides extra information. It concludes the sentence, so only one comma is required.)

Keep in mind that the pronouns *who* and *whom* refer only to people. The pronouns *that* and *which* refer only to things.

The person *whom* you will interview tomorrow is Rhoda James.   (*Whom* refers to a person.)

Rhoda James, *who* has been hired for the position, will begin work on June 1. (*Who* refers to a person.)

The personal computer *that* I bought has a 4MB memory.   (Here, *that* refers to a thing. Compare this essential *that* clause with the nonessential *which* clause that follows.)

My new personal computer, *which* was on sale for $1695, has 4MB of memory.   (*Which* refers to a thing.)

EDITING PRACTICE 2

Where are commas missing in the following sentences? Find the nonessential clauses, and use commas to separate them from the rest of the sentence. Write *OK* if the sentence is correct.

1. In the November issue of *Business Monthly* which is on my desk Dr. Case's investment tips are discussed in detail.
2. Mr. Erickson who has developed many successful advertising campaigns for Benton Products is coordinating this campaign.
3. The copywriter who generally handles all technical products is on vacation until August 1.
4. You may obtain from Mr. Bagley a copy of the manual that explains these procedures.
5. The new manager of our Publicity Department whom we hired last month teaches business and public relations courses part-time at a nearby community college.
6. The person whom you met with yesterday is one of our most important clients.
7. Please bring me the forms file that includes the latest approved version of our standard contract.

TO INDICATE OMISSIONS

Writers sometimes omit words in order to be brief. Omitting words is appropriate as long as the meaning is still clear. In the following sentences, for example, note how the commas tell the reader where the *understood* words belong.

Lena Kirschner was assigned to the Shields account; John Rohrich, the J&R account; and Patricia Ferreira, the Hanover Funds account.   (Each comma substitutes for the words *was assigned to*.)

TO SEPARATE REPETITIONS

The comma also serves to separate words or phrases that are deliberately repeated for emphasis.

Last week we received *many, many* requests for more information about municipal bonds.

When she discussed her project, Margaret was obviously *enthusiastic, very enthusiastic.*

IN NUMBERS

Commas are generally used to separate thousands, millions, billions, and so on, in numbers of five digits or more.

17,460   43,649 $2,846,094

However, the comma is not used in the following numbers:

four-digit numbers: 3500, 7818 (unless they appear with numbers containing five digits or more)

decimal parts of numbers: 17,460.38427

years: 1993, 1998, 2003

page numbers: pages 1324 and 1343

house numbers: 1301 Rockaway Parkway

telephone numbers: 201-555-6547

ZIP Codes: 91325-1947

serial numbers: Policy 98475

In metric terms a space, not a comma, is used to separate groups of three numbers—*on both sides of the decimal point.*

21 435 kilometers

13 432.875 445 liters

A four-digit metric number, however, is written with no space (for example, *3425 kilograms*) unless it appears in a table column with numbers that have five digits or more.

The comma is not used in weights and measurements that express *one* total unit—for example, *11 pounds 3 ounces, 3 hours 23 minutes,* and *12 feet 7 inches.*

Unrelated figures that appear one after the other should be separated by a comma to avoid misreading.

By 1999, 34 foreign-language editions will be available.   (The comma prevents the possibility of the reader's seeing *199934* or otherwise confusing these two numbers.)

WORLD VIEW

The official language of most South American countries is Spanish. Portuguese, however, is the official language of South America's largest country, Brazil.

IN COMPANY NAMES

Many law firms, stock brokerage houses, accounting firms, and other companies are known by the names of the firm's principal partners. Generally, such company names are written in either of these two styles:

O'Malley, Schwartz, Vernon and Jones

O'Malley, Schwartz, Vernon & Jones

One style places the word *and* before the last partner's name; the other style uses the symbol *&* (called an *ampersand*) before the last partner's name. In either case no comma appears before the symbol *&* or the word *and.*

The "short form" for such company names, generally used only for informal messages, consists of the first two partners' names:

> Let me know as soon as *O'Malley, Schwartz* submits its final report. (Note that no comma follows *Schwartz.*)

In addition, there are other companies that choose to write their official names without commas:

> O'Malley Schwartz Vernon and Jones
>
> O'Malley Schwartz Vernon & Jones

The short form, in both examples, is simply *O'Malley Schwartz.*
In any case, remember that the full, official name is the correct name.

COMMA PITFALLS

Including a comma when it is not needed can slow your reader's progress and cause confusion. Observe these rules:

1. Do not separate a compound element with *one* comma. When a compound subject, compound object, or compound verb is interrupted, use *two* commas to set off the interrupting element.

> The sales representatives and the district managers are very pleased with the new commission schedule. (Do not separate the compound subject with a comma.)
>
> The sales representatives and, *of course,* the district managers are very pleased with the new commission schedule. (*Two* commas are needed to separate the interrupting expression *of course* from the rest of the sentence.)

2. Do not separate a subject from its predicate with one comma.

> The sales representatives and the district managers, *naturally,* are very pleased with the new commission schedule. (Again, *two* commas are needed to separate the interrupting expression—in this case, *naturally*—from the rest of the sentence.)

EDITING PRACTICE 3

Correct any errors in the following sentences.

1. Although the estimated cost was $13500, the actual cost was only $10850.
2. Janet said, "I think that using radio commercials to promote these products is a very very good idea!"
3. Our printing expenses for the months of July and August totaled $1900; travel expenses $3750; entertainment expenses $1155; and miscellaneous expenses $750.
4. The new room is only 22 feet, 8 inches long by 15 feet, 6 inches wide, but it should serve our purposes well.

5. The comprehensive bibliography (see pages 1,180 through 1,192) will be helpful to anyone who wishes to learn more about this topic.

6. One well-respected accounting firm with specific experience in hotel-motel finances is LaCross, Pennyworth, Dixon, & Shapiro.

COMMUNICATION LABORATORY

APPLICATION EXERCISES

A. Practice applying the comma principles presented in this section. On a separate sheet of paper, indicate where you would place or remove commas, and explain why. Write *OK* for any sentence that is correct.

1. Marsha's thorough report which has been distributed to the budget committee will be discussed at Friday's meeting.

2. We are confident, that we can reduce the production costs and make this project profitable.

3. Only Sylvia Cohen who is in charge of the Records Retention Department has the authority to destroy old files.

4. Danielle Woods—a partner in the firm of Simms, Oates, & Godfrey—will speak to our accountants at 4 p.m.

5. We have prepared Room 2,143 for Ms. Woods' presentation, and we will serve refreshments immediately after she has finished.

6. By December 31 144 representatives will have submitted their estimated budgets for the coming year.

7. The total weight of the container and its contents is only 3 pounds, 4 ounces.

8. Paula's idea appears to be feasible and innovative, very innovative.

9. Ms. Whitman's final proposal which we received just last Friday afternoon has not yet been thoroughly reviewed.

10. All the contracts, checks, and other valuable documents were given to Sally Ryan who is a corporate executive.

11. The insurance company's check for $321,754 is incorrect; the correct amount is $231754.

12. We need several large, glass, containers with spillproof lids to store these strong chemicals safely.

13. Payroll deduction is a safe convenient method to save money.

14. In February we received many, many orders to install these machines; in March, only two or three orders.

15. Is the correct address 1,372 Rockaway Parkway, or is it 1,732 Rockaway Parkway?

B. Correct each error in the following sentences. Write *OK* on your paper for each correct sentence.

1. Have you seen the new, executive offices on the ninth floor?

CONTINUED

2. Ruck, Moser, Naldi, Hancher & Torella is one of the foremost consulting firms in the state; we have made an appointment with one of the senior partners from Ruck, Moser to discuss ways to improve our public image.

3. To receive your $5 rebate complete the enclosed card and return it to us before March 19.

4. If you had joined the retirement plan when you began working here you probably would have accumulated several thousand dollars by now.

5. Mr. Winchester do you wish to have the entire order shipped to your warehouse?

6. Francine wants to hire part-time help but David believes that we should ask our own staff members to work overtime.

7. Our manager decided consequently to reassign some of our long-term projects.

8. Ask Claire whether that company is in Springfield Illinois or Springfield Massachusetts.

9. If you wish, of course, you may use the overhead projector which is in the stockroom.

10. Her husband who is also an audio technician works for another radio station.

11. The engine, the transmission, the air conditioner, etc. are covered for five years or 50,000 miles under the terms of this warranty.

12. The model that he ordered is now out of stock but we can probably get it for him within the next week.

13. Century Motors, Inc. provides the vehicles for all our sales representatives and executives.

14. The major features of these products, should be reviewed before the meeting begins.

15. Before the meeting begins, we should review the major features of these products.

C. Make the following message clear by correcting all the errors.

Our experience with Lindeman Motors, has shown that we can expect fair prices and excellent service on all the vehicles it sells or leases. Our experience with Centurion Auto Sales and Rentals on the other hand has been almost entirely negative. Although Centurion has a reputation for very low prices it also has a reputation for poor service and hidden costs. When our current lease agreement with Lindeman expires next month therefore we recommend renewing the lease, for an additional 24 months. The 10 percent increase in our total monthly payment (to $15550) will we believe not be a major disadvantage compared with Centurion's slightly lower price for the same autos ($14995).

CONTINUED

VOCABULARY AND SPELLING STUDIES

A. These words are often confused: *manner, manor; emanate, eminent, imminent.* Explain the differences.

B. For each sentence identify the meaning of the word in italics.

1. Unfortunately, Gerald works with customers in a *perfunctory* way. [*Perfunctory* means (**a**) secretive, (**b**) exhaustive, (**c**) mechanical, (**d**) hasty.]
2. With her knowledge of our procedures, Helen can help you to *expedite* the process. [*Expedite* means (**a**) cancel, (**b**) accelerate, (**c**) understand, (**d**) reverse.]
3. Angela did a *prodigious* amount of work in a very short time. [*Prodigious* means (**a**) sloppy, (**b**) overwhelming, (**c**) formal, (**d**) financial.]

C. Rewrite the following paragraph, correcting spelling and punctuation errors as you do so.

> Our supervisor, Jim Gormly is teaching a short coarse on the basics of word procesing begining next Wendesday. Sponsored by the corporate training program this course will be offerred again in the spring.

SEMICOLONS, COLONS, AND DASHES

Semicolons, colons, and dashes have specific uses within the sentence. Knowing these uses will improve your reading skill, and applying them properly will enhance your writing skills and your ability to communicate effectively.

THE SEMICOLON

The semicolon announces a partial stop significantly stronger than the one indicated by a comma. Thus a semicolon, not a comma, is often required to join the complete thoughts in a compound sentence. In addition, a semicolon is used under certain circumstances before explanatory or enumerating words and in a series of items that already have commas within them.

In Compound Sentences   Before we see how semicolons are used in compound sentences, let's review the definition of a compound sentence: *A compound sentence contains two or more independent clauses.* Remember that an independent clause is a complete thought that can stand alone *and make sense* as a sentence. A compound sentence, therefore, is a sentence with two (or more) such clauses.

The clauses in a compound sentence may be (1) joined by a comma plus a conjunction (*and, but, or, nor*), (2) joined by a semicolon, or (3) written as two separate sentences.

> Janet now works in our headquarters office, but she has also worked in some of our district offices.   (Two independent clauses joined by a comma plus the conjunction *but*.)

> Janet now works in our headquarters office; she has also worked in some of our district offices.   (Two independent clauses joined by a semicolon. A comma is not strong enough to join these two clauses that are complete thoughts.)

> Janet now works in our headquarters office. She has also worked in some of our district offices.   (Two complete thoughts written as two separate sentences.)

Now that you have reviewed the compound sentence, study the three uses of semicolons in compound sentences.

1. *To Join Clauses Without Conjunctions.* A semicolon is strong enough to join two complete thought units that are not joined by a conjunction. A comma cannot do so.

> The committee decided to cut total expenses by 20 percent; the advertising budget was reduced more than others.   (No conjunction joins the two complete thoughts—therefore, a semicolon is required. A comma is not strong enough to join these clauses.)

2. *To Join Clauses With Transitional Expressions.* When the second complete thought in a compound sentence begins with an introductory word or phrase, a comma is not strong enough to join the clauses. They must be joined by a semicolon, with a comma following the introductory word or group of words. Review these commonly used introductory words that serve as transitional expressions:

accordingly	moreover
consequently	nevertheless
however	on the other hand
in addition	therefore

> Robert approves all large purchases for the entire division; however, he is now in Germany on business.   (A semicolon is needed to join these independent clauses. A comma is not strong enough to do so.)

3. *To Prevent Misreading.* If a compound sentence with a conjunction contains commas in either or both clauses *and* a strong break is needed to make the message clear, use a semicolon to separate the clauses—even though a conjunction is used. If no misreading is likely, use a comma.

> The topics in this seminar will include investing in savings accounts, money market accounts, and certificates of deposit; but please keep in mind that these kinds of investments are limited to earning interest only and do not provide opportunities for capital growth.   (The semicolon provides the break needed to ensure that the reader pauses after *deposit*.)

Before Explanatory or Enumerating Words

Words and phrases such as *for example, for instance, namely, that is,* and *that is to say* are joined to an independent clause by a semicolon when they introduce another independent clause or a listing. Such words or phrases should be followed by a comma.

> Ms. Haberman asked the managers to report any personnel changes planned for next year; *namely*, she is interested in projecting staff additions for the budget.   (*Namely* introduces a second independent clause.)

> There are several qualified candidates for the product manager position; for example, Elizabeth Bennett, Mel Moss, Sid Elman, and Anna Marie Torti.   (*For example* introduces a listing.)

In a Series

Series of items that contain internal commas (such as commas in city and state names or in certain company names) should be separated by semicolons instead of commas to prevent misreading. Note that a semicolon, not a comma, precedes the conjunction before the last item in the series.

> Those district offices now participating in the experimental study are in Bloomington, Minnesota; Kansas City, Kansas; Albany, New York; and Seattle, Washington.

CLASS PRACTICE 1

In each of the following sentences, choose the correct punctuation mark within parentheses, and explain each of your choices.

1. One executive in the group questioned the necessity of what she called "extraordinary" merit increases (, ;) all the other executives considered the raises fair and justified.
2. Our warehouse will be closed for inventory during the next two weeks (, ;) consequently (, ;) we are unable to ship any orders until April 20.
3. Any questions concerning the purchase of this property should be addressed to Ms. Lewis, Mr. Jackson, or Mrs. Sanabria (, ;) and Mr. Chu should be given copies of all correspondence pertaining to the sale.
4. Several well-known speakers on tomorrow's program include Marcia Bush (, ;) director of marketing for Panorama Travel (, ;) Andrea Henne (, ;) vice president of Steelcase (, ;) and Jeffrey Frazen (, ;) senior designer for Phelps & Morris Clothing.

5. Sales of this particular model have increased steadily over the past five years (, ;) we sold approximately 25,000 units last year.

6. Mr. Obrandt suggested several ways to test the idea (, ;) for instance, we can survey all our credit card customers.

THE COLON

A colon serves a specific function: It tells the reader "Listen to this," or "Here is something important." Study the following uses of the colon.

Colon Before a List   A colon is used to introduce a list that (1) directly follows its introduction (horizontal listing) or (2) appears on separate lines below its introduction (vertical listing). Even before the colon is used, the reader is often given a hint that a list will follow by such words as *the following, as follows, this,* or *these.*

You may pay for your purchases in any of *these* convenient ways: cash, check, or credit card.

The total price includes *the following* components:

1. A microcomputer with keyboard
2. A hard disk
3. Two disk drives
4. A color monitor
5. The disk operating system (DOS)
6. Four comprehensive system manuals
7. Accounting and word processing software packages

Colon for Emphasis or Explanation   A colon may be used to emphasize or explain a word, phrase, or sentence.

Our manager consistently stresses one aspect of our products: quality.   (Colon to emphasize a word.)

Allen explained the reason for his bonus program: to reward employees for superior efforts.   (Colon to emphasize a phrase.)

Clarence has a good excuse for missing this workshop: he will be on jury duty all week.   (Colon to explain a sentence; the second sentence completes the main thought.)

When a colon introduces a formal rule or words implying a rule, the first word following the colon is capitalized.

The supervisor of the Accounts Payable Department has a well-known rule: Compare each check with the purchase requisition before mailing the check. (Capital letter to indicate a rule.)

At its last meeting the Safety Committee recommended the following policy: Every employee must wear his or her safety helmet before entering the plant. (Capital letter because the words imply a rule.)

Colon Indicating a Significant Remark   Words such as *Note, Caution, Important, Remember,* and *Warning* used to introduce significant information are followed by a colon. The first word following the colon is capitalized.

> *Note: Only* those applications postmarked before or on April 30 will be considered for admission.

CLASS PRACTICE 2

Make the correct choices for each of the following sentences.

1. Only three performances will be given during the summer months (: . ,) July 8, July 20, and August 5.
2. Double-check your guest list to ensure that the following clients are included (: . ,) Wendall Black, Estelle Cory, Sean McBurney, and Laura Beinfest.
3. Sales patterns have been predictable for the past few years (: . ,) Review these sales reports to see for yourself.
4. Caution (: . ,) Use latex gloves to avoid getting the concentrated solution on your skin.
5. Please type this code number in the space below the date on each order form(: . ,) A705-50.
6. You may receive your free catalog by calling the following numbers (: . ,) Of course, if you wish, you may pick up your copy at any one of our stores.

EDITING PRACTICE 1

On a separate sheet of paper, correct any errors in the uses of semicolons and colons in the following sentences. Be sure to look for errors in the use of capitals following colons.

1. Our direct mail campaign was most successful in these areas; Atlanta, Georgia, Memphis, Tennessee, and Louisville, Kentucky.
2. When you return damaged merchandise, be sure to include the following information. The manufacturer's name, the model number, the serial number, and the date of purchase.
3. The warranty expired last December, Mr. Spears: however, the cost of repairing your air purifier will be less than $45.
4. Before sending them to the Shipping Department, be sure to specify where these items are to be shipped: The printer, to our Albany warehouse; the monitor, to our Manhattan district office; and the box of inactive files, to the Records Retention Center.
5. The conference features the following experts. Clay Colbert, Wanda Stitt, Donald Sampson, and Leona Galleon.
6. Important. Be sure to enclose a packing slip with each order before sealing the carton.

THE DASH

The dash is an abrupt, emphatic punctuation mark that has a special impact on a sentence. The dash often replaces a comma, a semicolon, a colon, or parentheses; but the dash has a few of its own unique uses. In any case, it is a strong, forceful mark of punctuation and therefore must be used correctly—and sparingly.

As a Substitute for Other Punctuation
When a dash replaces other punctuation, the emphasis of the words set off by the dash is stronger. For example, compare the following pairs of sentences, noting how much more emphatic the sentences with dashes are.

Commas vs. Dashes

One new steel supplier, Standard Steel Mills, is conveniently located.

One new steel supplier—Standard Steel Mills—is conveniently located.

Semicolons vs. Dashes

The list price of the Electra stereo package is the highest; however, the quality of the Electra is also the best.

The list price of the Electra stereo package is the highest—however, the quality of the Electra is also the best.

Colons vs. Dashes

Buying from Jensen Audio has these advantages: reliable service, low prices, and a wide variety of name brands.

Buying from Jensen Audio has these advantages—reliable service, low prices, and a wide variety of name brands.

Parentheses vs. Dashes

Spectrum Appliances has three convenient stores (on Berkeley Avenue, in the Howard Mall, and on Sunset Road) for your shopping pleasure.

Spectrum Appliances has three convenient stores—on Berkeley Avenue, in the Howard Mall, and on Sunset Road—for your shopping pleasure.

When parenthetical material appears at the end of a sentence, only *one dash* is needed to set off the words—as opposed to *two parentheses*.

For your shopping pleasure, Spectrum Appliances has three convenient stores (on Berkeley Avenue, in the Howard Mall, and on Sunset Road).   (*Two* parentheses.)

For your shopping pleasure, Spectrum Appliances has three convenient stores—on Berkeley Avenue, in the Howard Mall, and on Sunset Road.   (*One* dash to separate parenthetical copy at the end of a sentence.)

After a Listing
Use a dash to separate a listing from a summary statement that follows. A summary statement includes a word such as *these* or *all* to refer to the listing.

Leadership, perception, flexibility, and communication skills—look for *these* qualities as you interview applicants for the manager position in our Springfield store.   (The word *these* refers to the items listed before the dash.)

Safety, high yield, monthly dividends—*all* are available to you as a member of this municipal bond plan.   (The word *all* refers to the list that precedes the dash. The dash provides the necessary pause.)

Before an Appositive With Internal Commas

In Section 5.2 you learned that an appositive renames or explains the previous noun. You also learned to set off appositive expressions with commas. Use a dash before an appositive expression, however, if it contains internal commas. Use a second dash to show the end of the appositive expression if it interrupts the sentence.

At the present time the corporation owns three major department store chains—Bullock's, Bullock's Wilshire, and I. Magnin's.   (Here the appositive with internal commas appears at the end of the sentence.)

Three of our agents—Roy Bridges, Mary Payton, and Pat Freeman—have requested transfers to other offices.   (The appositive with internal commas appears within the sentence, so a dash must be used before and after the appositive.)

With an Interrupting Phrase or Clause Containing an Internal Comma

Use a dash before and after an interrupting phrase or clause that contains an internal comma.

Carol did a superb job—a superb job, indeed—of planning and coordinating the conference.   (The interrupting word *indeed* requires a comma, and so the entire interrupting phrase *a superb job, indeed* must be set off by dashes.)

Total revenue—if you include our foreign offices, London and Frankfurt—reached $5.7 million for the first quarter.   (The appositive *London and Frankfurt* requires a comma; therefore, the interrupting clause *if you include our foreign offices, London and Frankfurt* must be set off by dashes.

With Afterthoughts

Use a dash before a deliberate afterthought to give variety to your writing or to emphasize an idea.

All of us look forward to seeing you at next year's convention—sooner, we hope!   (A planned afterthought.)

Total revenue for all our subsidiaries during the first quarter was $5.5 million—less than our goal of $5.7 million.   (An emphasized afterthought.)

Punctuating Material Set Off by Dashes

Words set off by dashes are punctuated in a variety of ways.

At the End of the Sentence   Whenever "dashed" material ends a sentence, the second dash is omitted, and the sentence then ends with the regular end-of-sentence punctuation.

LIVING LANGUAGE

"The dash says aloud what the parenthesis whispers. The dash is the more useful—since whispering tends to annoy—and will remain useful only if not overused."

—Sheridan Baker, *The Practical Stylist*

LIVING LANGUAGE

When I use a word, it means just what I choose it to mean—neither more nor less.

—Lewis Carroll (Charles Lutwidge Dodgson) (1832–1898)

We buy our supplies from Webster Stationers—*all* our supplies.   (A declarative statement.)

Who is the person standing at the podium—the woman with the briefcase? (A direct question.)

What a tremendous value—a genuine bargain!   (An exclamation.)

Within the Sentence   Words within two dashes may end in a question mark or an exclamation point, when appropriate; a period is used only if the last word is an abbreviation that requires the period.

Her latest book—already a best-seller!—is certain to be made into a movie. (The words within the dashes are an exclamation.)

Analysts predict that Gold Label stock—do you know its present price?—may double by the end of this year.   (The words within the dashes are a question.)

We find that leasing vehicles—we have done so for the past eight years—is less expensive in the long run than buying.   (No period before the second dash.)

We find that leasing vehicles—cars, trucks, vans, etc.—is less expensive in the long run than buying.   (Period before the second dash only because of the abbreviation *etc.*)

Commas within dashes are used in the normal way, as are quotation marks:

Several agents—Carolyn, Frank, Leo, and George, for example—recommended that we review and update the commission plan for all insurance policies.

These executive cars—known in industry jargon as "brass hats"—are being sold at 25 percent below their original list prices.

CLASS PRACTICE 3

Where could dashes be used effectively in the following sentences?

1. Tampa, Seattle, Detroit, Charleston these are the cities in which we are concentrating our advertising.
2. Everyone on the interview committee agreed that Charles is well qualified very well qualified.
3. Take advantage of these discounts from 10 to 25 percent by placing your order before November 15!
4. Are you planning to attend the basic finance workshop the one in Cleveland on February 9?
5. Some of our service departments Customer Service, for instance will be moved to our Grand Avenue building.
6. Springfield, Illinois not Springfield, California is the site of our new distribution facility.
7. All classifications of employees, administrative, sales, clerical, and part-time are eligible to share in the bonus plan.

EDITING PRACTICE 2

Test your ability to use dashes by correcting any errors in the following sentences.

1. The liter, the meter, the gram,—these are the basic units for capacity, length, and mass in the metric system.
2. Hazlett Paper Company and First-Class Paper Products—have you bought supplies from either one of them—submitted the lowest bids.
3. Discount prices, quality merchandise, excellent service,—all are yours when you buy from A-1 Distributors.
4. We selected the 6:30 a.m. flight, not the 2:30 p.m. flight—because our meeting will start at noon.
5. Ms. Wedding has been the top sales representative for the past three consecutive years quite an accomplishment, don't you agree?
6. All of us, of course, are excited about the same thing the upcoming sales meeting in Honolulu.

COMMUNICATION LABORATORY

APPLICATION EXERCISES

A. In the following sentences, parentheses indicate possible missing punctuation. On a separate sheet of paper, indicate the punctuation you would use where the parentheses occur. Write *OK* for any sentence that requires no added punctuation.

1. The latest video produced by our Graphic Arts Department ( ) have you seen it ( ) has been nominated for a special award.
2. Inform the Legal Department of the subpoena ( ) please do so immediately.
3. Only one person in the company ( ) Joe Caruana ( ) has experience in this area.
4. The cancellation was based on one critical factor ( ) the project's total cost was more than 50 percent over its budgeted cost.
5. Among the items that were returned undamaged were these ( ) computer terminals, monitors, printers, and modems.
6. Computer terminals, monitors, printers, and modems ( ) these were among the items that were returned undamaged.
7. The primary focus of the campaign will involve radio and television advertising ( ) however ( ) we will also place full-page ads in major large-city newspapers.
8. Remember ( ) If you feel that you have been treated unfairly, notify the Equal Employment Opportunity officer in the Human Resources Department.
9. Please provide me with a copy of the procedures manual ( ) the one that has illustrations of the newest forms.

10. At the end of the demonstration, you should do the following ( ) summarize the product's major features, repeat the low monthly payment, review our easy credit terms, and close the sale.

11. No, we have not been satisfied with the service we have received from Dallas Central Distribution Company ( ) we have ( ) consequently ( ) begun searching for other potential suppliers.

12. Our survey supported the fact that our clients value highly ( ) our fast service, our cooperative sales representatives, and our low interest rates.

13. Our fast service, our cooperative sales representatives, our low interest rates ( ) these are the features that our clients rated most important in our recent survey.

14. Jim Smyth ( ) not Tim Smith ( ) is the director of sales.

15. Helen Marcus ( ) is she still the senior vice president of marketing ( ) is one of the most respected authors in the area of business management.

B. On a separate sheet of paper, show your corrections for each of the following sentences. (Some sentences may have more than one error.) Write *OK* for any sentence that is correct.

1. Three of our plant managers—Tracy Roland, Michael Fox, and Wayne Coe,—have requested additional funds for plant modernization.

2. As soon as Mr. Ahrens leaves his production meeting. I will ask him about the status of this contract.

3. The survey clearly indicated that customers value one factor more than any other, quality.

4. If you need any additional information just call our Human Resources Department.

5. Mr. Dennison asked us why the printing of the new catalog has been delayed?

6. The managers and their assistants emphasized throughout the meeting, that the production budget must be increased by at least $15,000.

7. Accounts Payable now has a backlog because of employee absences, three of four staff members have been out with the flu for the entire week.

8. Entertaining clients, car repairs, airline fares. These expenses constitute about 60 percent of the budget for travel and entertainment.

9. If Ms. Galloway accepts the position in our main office. She will become the youngest executive in the corporation.

10. Edwin Schwartz, Charles Holt, Anthony Corcio and Nicole Lusk, are permanent members of the Procedures Committee.

11. Needless to say, all of us were pleased to hear that our department had won the cash prize very pleased.

12. Our company has a well-established reputation for manufacturing goods such as: refrigerators, washers, dryers, microwave ovens, and dishwashers.

13. Caution; Smoking is prohibited anywhere in the lab area.

14. Yes, the sale ends on Saturday, we will be open until 9 p.m. each evening until then.

15. Among the products that are especially popular according to our store manager are children's toys, adult board games, mystery books and smoke alarms.

C. Insert the correct punctuation marks in the places with parentheses.

After we review the entire February issue ( ) we should begin laying out our plans for succeeding issues ( ) at least for March and April ( ) How much ad space have we sold for the March and April issues ( ) How many pages will each issue contain ( ) Such questions must be answered immediately ( ) In addition, I do not like the tentative feature story for March ( ) do you ( ) We should meet ( ) Evelyn, Bruce, you, and I ( ) before the end of the week to discuss all these matters.

VOCABULARY AND SPELLING STUDIES

A. These words are often confused: *peace, piece; stationery, stationary.* Explain the differences.

B. On a separate sheet of paper, write the singular forms of the following plural nouns.

1. parentheses
2. teeth
3. CPAs

4. Messrs. Parker
5. notaries public
6. companies

C. Column A lists six words containing prefixes, and Column B lists the meaning of many of the most commonly used prefixes. Match the words with the meanings that refer to their prefixes.

A	B
1. subway	**a.** before
2. contradict	**b.** against
3. postscript	**c.** around
4. inconvenient	**d.** between, among
5. antedate	**e.** one
6. interstate	**f.** beyond
	g. under
	h. above
	i. after
	j. not

QUOTATION MARKS, PARENTHESES, AND APOSTROPHES

As you learned in the previous four sections, punctuation marks are signals that help the reader interpret a message correctly. The same is true for the marks of punctuation you will study in this section. Quotation marks, for example, tell the reader, "These are the exact words spoken or written by a person." Parentheses around an idea indicate its lesser importance, while an apostrophe signifies ownership. These marks also have other related uses, all of which are discussed in this section.

QUOTATION MARKS

Direct Quotations Use quotation marks to record the precise words of a speaker or a writer. As you will see below, a comma helps to separate the quotation from the rest of the sentence.

> Mr. Peters said, "All supervisors and managers are invited to attend an outstanding workshop on interpersonal relations." (Note that the period at the end of the sentence is inside the second quotation mark.)

> "In our opinion, this workshop will help middle-management personnel communicate more effectively with clients and coworkers," Mr. Peters continued. (Note that the comma after *coworkers* is inside the second quotation mark.)

Because quotation marks identify the exact words someone said or wrote, they must be placed around the quoted words only, even when the quotation is interrupted.

> "All supervisors and managers," Mr. Peters said, "are invited to attend an outstanding workshop on interpersonal relations."

> "Will you please tell me," Ms. Shockley asked, "when we can complete the debugging of this software?"

For long quotations (for example, quotations longer than one sentence), use a colon instead of a comma to introduce the quotation.

> During the monthly meeting of our division, Mr. Peters said: "All supervisors and managers are invited to attend an outstanding workshop on interpersonal relations. In our opinion, this workshop will help . . . ."

Terms and Expressions   Writers use quotation marks to give special significance to certain terms and expressions. In the following discussion, note how quotation marks are used for (1) explanations and definitions, (2) unfamiliar terms, (3) slang and humorous expressions, and (4) translations of foreign words.

Explanations and Definitions   Use quotation marks to give special significance to expressions introduced by *marked*, *stamped*, and *signed*.

> Please be sure that each container is clearly marked "Glass: Handle With Care."

> The client's check was returned by the bank stamped "Insufficient Funds."

Definitions of words or phrases are also enclosed in quotation marks. Note that the words defined are printed in italics (or underscored if the italics feature is not available).

> The abbreviation *cps* means "characters per second" and refers to the speed with which a printer prints copy.

> The abbreviation cps means "characters per second" and refers to the speed with which a printer prints copy.   (Note that underscoring may substitute for italics.)

> As used in word processing, the word *wraparound* means "the ability to start a new line of copy automatically."

Unfamiliar Terms   Technical terms and other terms that may be unfamiliar to the reader are generally placed in quotation marks.

> Whichever plan you select, you will enjoy additional savings because all our plans are "no-load funds."   (The technical term *no-load fund*—a mutual fund that charges no commission—may be unfamiliar to readers.)

Slang and Humorous Expressions   When slang and humorous expressions are used in writing, they are enclosed in quotation marks.

> Henry explained that within the next two or three years all these old-fashioned machines would "bite the dust."

> When we asked her for the summary, she told us it "ain't ready yet."
> (Quotation marks show that the deliberate grammatical error is intended to be humorous.)

Translations   Foreign words and phrases are printed in italics (or underscored if the italics feature is not available), and their translations are placed in quotation marks.

> The corporation encourages staff members to work *pro bono publico*—that is, "for the public good"—and gives employees time off for charity work.

EDITING PRACTICE 1

Correct any errors in the following sentences by adding quotation marks. Explain your reason for each correction. Write *OK* for any sentence that needs no correction.

1. We will mail this new brochure to all clients early in September, said Mrs. Estes.
2. Mr. Hayworth specifically said, I want all travel budgets frozen until the first of January.
3. No, I did not know that the French term *par avion* means by airplane.
4. Angela, please take all the folders marked Confidential to Ms. Atkinson before the end of the day.
5. If you prefer, Helene explained to the customer, we can bill you next month.
6. She defined *ad valorem* tax as the tax on the price or the value of a commodity.

Titles   Book, magazine, and newspaper titles (and titles of all other published works that are bound separately) are placed in italics or underscored. Titles of subdivisions—such as chapters, parts, units, sections, articles, or columns—in these works are enclosed in quotation marks.

> Make sure that you read carefully Chapter 4, "Estimating Income Taxes," in *Personal Finance*.   (Quotation marks for the chapter title; italics or underscoring for the book title.)

> Last July she wrote "Stretching Your Personal Income," an article that appeared in The Wall Street Journal.   (Article title in quotation marks; newspaper title italicized or underscored.)

Titles of paintings, sculptures, and television and radio series are italics or underscored. Use quotation marks for the titles of lectures, essays, sermons, mottoes, slogans, and poems.

> The candidate's campaign slogan, "Prepared for Today—Planning for Tomorrow," was certainly effective.

EDITING PRACTICE 2

Correct any errors in the following sentences by adding quotation marks or underscores as needed.

1. Did you read the article European Investment, Boom or Boon? that appeared in last week's Time magazine?
2. Our company sponsors an employee public service group whose motto is Investment in Today's Youth Builds a Better Tomorrow.
3. Mark is planning to give a speech, Your Future in the World of Advertising, to the students at Wilson High School.

4. For an overview of the most popular software programs today, read The Big Ten, which appeared in the April issue of PC Computing.

5. Linda Montgomery, a well-known investment adviser, writes a weekly column entitled The Most for Your Money that appears in major newspapers throughout the country.

6. Correct spellings of major cities throughout the world may be found in the section entitled Geographical Names in Webster's Ninth New Collegiate Dictionary.

7. Did you see the campaign motto, Conserving for the Next Generation, when it appeared in Tuesday's Journal News.

Quotation Within a Quotation

Use single quotation marks (on a computer or typewriter keyboard, the apostrophe key) to set off a quotation within a quotation.

> Vernon's memo specifically stated, "Please request the Shipping Department manager to label all the cartons 'Fragile' and deliver them to the shipping agent by May 4."

> The instructor said, "A wise consumer is not fooled by exaggerations such as 'once-in-a-lifetime offer.'"

Punctuation at the End of Quotations

The positioning of other punctuation marks inside or outside the closing quotation mark sometimes causes confusion. However, the rules governing such cases are few and easy to understand. Study the following three principles:

Commas and periods—always inside the closing quotation mark

Semicolons and colons—always outside the closing quotation mark

Question marks and exclamation points—inside the closing quotation mark if they belong to the quotation; outside the closing quotation mark if they belong to the entire sentence

1. *Commas and Periods.* Always place commas and periods *inside* the closing quotation mark.

> "As you predicted," said Ms. Coleman, "our retail sales have exceeded $1 million this year."   (Note the position of the comma and the period *inside* the second quotation mark.)

2. *Semicolons and Colons.* Always place semicolons and colons *outside* the closing quotation mark.

> For quantity orders the sales agent promises us a "very special deal"; however, we have no room for storing large inventories.   (Semicolon *outside* second quotation mark.)

> Notice these charts in the article "Tomorrow's Interest Rates": Chart 1.4, Chart 1.9, and Chart 2.5   (Colon *outside* second quotation mark.)

3. Question Marks and Exclamation Points. If the words within quotation marks make up a question or an exclamation, then the question mark or exclamation point belongs *with* those words—that is, it belongs *inside* the second quotation mark.

> Larry asked, "What is the current interest rate on Treasury bills?"   (Are the words within quotation marks a question? Yes. Therefore, the question mark belongs *inside* the second quotation mark.)

> As he entered the room, we all shouted, "Congratulations, Bob!"   (Are the words within quotation marks an exclamation? Yes. Therefore, place the exclamation point *inside* the second quotation mark.)

On the other hand, if the quoted words are just *part of a question or an exclamation*, then the question mark or exclamation point belongs to the entire sentence, not just to the quoted words. In such cases place the question mark or exclamation point *outside* the second quotation mark.

> Have you read her column, "The Most for Your Money"?   (Here the words in quotation marks are *part of* the question; thus the question mark is placed *outside* the second quotation mark.)

> According to the agenda this meeting was supposed to be "a short question-and-answer session"!   (The quoted words are not an exclamation; they *belong* to an exclamation. Thus the exclamation point is placed *outside* the second quotation mark.)

If both the quoted words and the entire sentence are questions, use only one question mark to conclude the sentence. Since the question mark for the quoted material appears first, use this one and omit the second. Good writing style does not endorse both the sentence and the quoted material as exclamatory—only one or the other may be so.

> Have you read John Hoover's latest article, "Your Best Investment: Stocks, Bonds, Real Estate—or Education?"

EDITING PRACTICE 3

On a separate sheet of paper, correct any errors in the use of quotation marks in the following sentences. Write *OK* if the sentence is correct.

1. Jim asked, "Who has the most recent information on mortgage rates"?
2. "According to the builders," said Mr. Bender, "we can move into our new offices on Thursday, March 15".
3. Ben exclaimed, "Congratulations on your promotion, Wendy"!
4. "Can you explain," asked Diana, "why these folders are marked 'Confidential'?"
5. Ms. Lopez stated specifically that she wants applicants "with plenty of experience;" therefore, I will share these résumés with her.
6. Did Karen ask, "When can we set up an appointment with Mrs. Dougherty"?

PARENTHESES

Like commas and dashes, parentheses may be used to set off words that give additional information. What, then, are the differences among these three punctuation marks?

Parentheses for Additional Information
While dashes emphasize the information they set off, parentheses *de*emphasize the words they enclose. Commas are generally used to set off additional information that flows smoothly into the sentence—information that does not require the stronger break of dashes or the low-key profile of parentheses. The following examples show typical uses of parentheses, dashes, and commas to set off additional (or parenthetical) information.

> The winner of the sales contest—the prize is a remote-controlled VCR—will be announced on May 10.   (The dashes help provide emphasis for the words *the prize is a remote-controlled VCR.*)

> For the month of June, this Silver Star television and VCR will be on sale for only $795 (plus shipping and tax).   (Parentheses deemphasize the words *plus shipping and tax.*)

> The sale on all Silver Star products, as our store manager explained, will be for the entire month of June.   (The words set off by commas flow smoothly into the sentence and do not require the stronger break or deemphasis that dashes or parentheses would provide.)

Other Uses of Parentheses
Besides their task of setting off additional information, parentheses are also used to enclose (1) references or directions and (2) numbers or letters in enumerations.

> A chart of interest rates (see page 343) is provided to simplify your computations.   (Reference.)

> Since 1989 Addison Appliances has paid its monthly balance promptly (see the annual credit reports attached).   (Direction.)

> For your convenience we have enclosed (1) our latest brochure, (2) a handy order form, and (3) a credit application form.   (Numbers in an enumeration.)

EDITING PRACTICE 4

Insert parentheses where they are needed in the following sentences.

1. Add state sales tax see pages 313 through 363 to the sale price.
2. Call the Personnel Department 555-7000 to discuss these benefits.
3. The main items on the agenda concern 1 the new security system, 2 records retention policies, and 3 merit-increase guidelines.
4. The cost of raw goods usually only 6 percent of total costs is expected to rise dramatically over the next five years.
5. We arrived at the airport on schedule our plane landed precisely at noon but were delayed by local traffic.

Parentheses With Other Marks of Punctuation

Parentheses may be used (1) to enclose words within a sentence or (2) to enclose a sentence that stands alone. The use of other punctuation marks with parentheses differs in each of these two situations.

Parentheses Within a Sentence

Follow these rules when the words enclosed in parentheses are *part of* a sentence.

1. Do not use any mark of punctuation *before* the opening parenthesis; place any punctuation that the sentence would ordinarily require after the closing (or *second*) parenthesis.

> Before we discuss hiring policies (see item 4 on the agenda), we must review these guidelines.   (The normal punctuation after *Before we discuss hiring policies* is a comma. Therefore, place the comma after the second parenthesis.)

> Should we use the same price list (see the attached sample)?   (After *Should we use the same price list,* what punctuation would you use? A question mark, of course. Place the question mark after the second parenthesis.)

> For a true comparison, we used unit sales, not dollar sales (see Column 1); as a result, we noticed the following changes in buying trends.   (The semicolon that would ordinarily be placed after *dollar sales* must be placed after the closing parenthesis.)

2. Place *inside* the closing parenthesis the following marks only:

a. A question mark (if the words within parentheses form a question).

> Bernice said that the standard discount is 25 percent (or did she say 35 percent?).   (Are the words within parentheses a question? Yes. Place the question mark inside the closing parenthesis.)

b. An exclamation point (if the words within parentheses form an exclamation).

> We may be eligible for a substantial discount (perhaps as much as 50 percent!).   (Because the words within parentheses are an exclamation, the exclamation point is placed before the closing parenthesis.)

c. A period (if the period belongs to an abbreviation).

> Mark left early to meet a client at the airport (his client will arrive at 7:45 a.m.).

3. Do not capitalize the first word within parentheses unless that word is a proper noun.

> Yesterday our new front-wheel-drive vehicles arrived (have you seen them yet?), but they will not be displayed until September 23.   (Lowercase for *have.*)

> You will find this reference helpful (Chapter 8 especially).   (Capital for *Chapter* because it is the title of a specific chapter.)

Parentheses to Enclose a Sentence That Stands Alone   When the words enclosed in parentheses are entirely independent and not *part of* another sentence, the first word is capitalized, and the end punctuation is placed *inside* the closing parenthesis.

> It is essential, of course, for every manager to adhere strictly to the corporate guidelines for interviewing and hiring job applicants. (Please read the enclosed booklet, and discuss any questions with someone in the Human Resources Department.)

> Our marketing strategies are based on the plan that the Planning Committee approved last March. (See the minutes of the meeting of the Planning Committee dated March 21, or call Derek Greef for a copy.)

EDITING PRACTICE 5

Apply the punctuation principles you have just learned. Correct punctuation errors in the following sentences.

1. If you wish additional information, (such as daily menus, weather conditions, appropriate attire, and special activities) just call our resort manager at 800-555-3212.
2. Do you agree that the best sites for such stores are malls and major shopping centers (for example, the Thousand Oaks Mall?)
3. She suggested spreading the costs over a three-year period. (I prefer amortizing the costs over a five-year period, don't you)?
4. Ms. Goode will not be able to attend the meeting (she will be attending an engineering conference in Detroit,) but her assistant manager will be available.
5. Will the container that is built into the new refrigerator hold at least 2 liters (about 2 quarts?)
6. One suggestion was to invest in very conservative bonds (for example, Treasury bills;) however, Treasury bills are too short-term for our long-term financial goals.

THE APOSTROPHE

The primary use of the apostrophe is to construct the possessive form of nouns. In addition, the apostrophe is used to show omissions in contractions. Less often, the apostrophe is used to form "special" plurals and to show where numbers have been omitted.

In Possessives of Nouns   As you have already learned, the apostrophe is used to indicate the possessive forms of nouns.

NOUN	POSSESSIVE FORM
attorney	my *attorney's* office
attorneys	our *attorneys'* offices

NOUN	POSSESSIVE FORM
assistant manager	the *assistant manager's* decision
assistant managers	the *assistant managers'* decisions
Mrs. Ford	*Mrs. Ford's* invoice
the Fords	the *Fords'* invoice

In Contractions   Contractions are shortened forms of words or verb phrases, such as *internat'l* for "international," *ack'd* for "acknowledged," *gov't* for "government," *won't* for "will not," *shouldn't* for "should not," *isn't* for "is not," and *weren't* for "were not."

The results of the survey *weren't* what we anticipated.   ("Were not.")

We shouldn't be surprised if the store opens early for the sale.   (Should not.)

In "Special" Plurals   The apostrophe is *not* generally used to form plurals; however, an exception is the plural form of a letter or word that might otherwise be misread without the apostrophe.

Plurals of lowercase letters (*p's* and *d's,* for example) and lowercase abbreviations (*c.o.d.'s*) could easily be confused without apostrophes. Most capital letters do not require the apostrophe for the plural form; only *A, I,* and *U* are exceptions because they could be mistaken for whole words.

This printer seems to be misaligning its *i's* and *a's.*   (Without the apostrophes the plural forms of the letters *i* and *a* might be misread as the words *is* and *as.*)

To Show Omitted Numerals   The apostrophe is used in year numbers such as *'89* and *'93* to show that the first two numbers—*19*—have been omitted.

EDITING PRACTICE 6

Practice what you have just learned by inserting apostrophes as needed in the following sentences.

1. Lets discuss two of our best sales years—91 and 93.
2. Only Eds careful proofreading saved us from a costly error as a result of transposed numbers.
3. Havent you sent these designs to the Marketing Department for review and approval yet?
4. Have you suggested to David that he use fewer *Is* in his correspondence to customers?
5. Did you get your supervisors approval to change your vacation schedule?
6. You shouldnt leave negotiable instruments on your desk overnight.

COMMUNICATION LABORATORY

APPLICATION EXERCISES

A. On a separate sheet of paper, correct any errors in the use of quotation marks, parentheses, apostrophes, and other related punctuation. Write *OK* if the sentence is correct.

1. Because the cost of tin has risen drastically (almost 30 percent over the last two years,) we are now looking for a substitute metal.
2. Did Ms. Atkins say, Deliver each contract by messenger?
3. Yes, Time magazine is published by Time Inc.
4. I can hardly believe that Mr. Simms called this dispute "a slight disagreement over money!"
5. Use the list of authorized dealers it is printed on page 93 to order items shown in this catalog.
6. As you know, 50 percent of our employees arent eligible for this extended medical care coverage.
7. The Class of 84 will have its ten-year reunion on May 25.
8. Her latest article, Taking Advantage of Opportunities During Inflationary Times,' has stirred quite a controversy.
9. By Friday we must 1) submit a budget for travel and product promotion, 2) report all expenses for the first quarter of this year, and 3) update the production schedule for the remainder of the year.
10. The text clearly distinguishes between principle, which means "rule," and principal, which means "chief or primary."
11. Please post these signs saying Thank You for Not Smoking along the corridors.
12. Do you think it's true, asked Fred, that these bonds will soon be selling at a premium?
13. Were the envelopes that contained the contracts marked Confidential?
14. Irene asked, "Do you think that Barbara and Andy would like to attend the ACS Software Products Show next week"?
15. We were pleased to hear Ms. Daruty say that our design shows "energy, vitality, and creativity"!

B. Find and correct any errors in the following sentences. If a sentence is correct, write *OK* on your paper.

1. Has Ms. Fishers agent returned my call?
2. The net operating profit (NOP) for our consumer products division was $1.2 million; our industrial tools division, $2.75 million; and our leasing subsidiary, $2.2 million.
3. Ms. Atkins stated specifically, "Deliver each contract by messenger".
4. Fred will audit the Des Plaines Illinois warehouse before he returns.

5. Checks are accepted the identification requirements are printed on the back of this notice at our main office and all our branch locations.

6. Several items have not yet been delivered, agendas, seating arrangement charts, name tags, handouts, and product brochures.

7. The cost may be slightly over $750 but it should not exceed $900.

8. Dennis, Janice and Mark will be coordinating all the details of the sales conferences.

9. Do you know the meaning of the French expression faux pas?

10. Doesn't that expression mean "a social blunder?"

11. Paula Chin one of the distributors in the Midwest suggested an alternative procedure for setting goals.

12. As soon as she entered the room, we all shouted "Congratulations!"

13. Please contact us as soon as youre available to view the sketches for the new advertising campaign.

14. Each container must be labeled as follows: Poison—Do Not Swallow.

15. Mr. Carney has already posted the salary level for the new position, he listed the salary as $35,000 a year.

C. Edit the following paragraphs.

Please update the attached budget forms and return them to the district office by November 15. As you will see these forms are different than the ones we have been using. For example, one new column (Percent Change) requires you to compute the change for each budget item as compared with last years' budget.

We have enclosed a brief description see page 2 of the instructions of all the changes in the new form to simplify your understanding of the new procedures. Please be sure, to read the entire description before proceeding. If you have any questions just call the district office at 555–8420. Remember, that the enclosed materials are marked Confidential and should be locked in a safe place at the end of each day.

VOCABULARY AND SPELLING STUDIES

A. These words are often confused: *human, humane; forgo, forego.* Explain the differences.

B. In the following sentences, match the letter of the correct term with the definition in italics.

1. *One who is being taught a job* is (**a**) an instructor, (**b**) an understudy, (**c**) a trainee, (**d**) a jobber.

2. *One who has the authority to represent another in a business transaction* is (**a**) a notary public, (**b**) an agent, (**c**) a financier, (**d**) an author.

3. *One to whom a debt is owed* is (**a**) a creditor, (**d**) a cashier, (**c**) an auditor, (**d**) a referee.

SECTION 5.6

SECTION 5.6

CAPITALIZATION

Capital letters make words distinctive. Because they help words to stand out, capitals are used in special cases—for example, to show the reader where a new sentence starts or which words in a title are the most important words. Writers, therefore, must use these special signals correctly. In this section you will review some of the well-known basic uses of capital letters. In addition, you will learn to avoid some of the common errors writers make with capital letters.

FIRST WORDS

One of the routine uses of capital letters is to set off first words. Examples follow.

1. First word in a sentence or a group of words used as a sentence:

In 1986 we sold the warehouse on Elm Street and leased space on Grand Avenue. (*In,* a word that is not ordinarily capitalized, *is* capitalized when it begins a sentence.)

Vera asked us whether we are going to the seminar. *Of course!* (Although *of course* is not a complete sentence, it is treated as a complete sentence and *of* is capitalized. Reason: *Of course* is considered a short way of saying, *Of course we are going to the seminar*—a full sentence.)

2. First word in a direct quotation:

Barry asked, "Shouldn't we send these original photographs by messenger?" (The quotation is part of a sentence, yet the first word of the quotation is capitalized. The first word of a quotation is capitalized *only* if it is a complete sentence or it begins with a proper noun.)

3. First word in a question within a sentence:

All of us are wondering, *Will* this equipment be shipped on schedule? (An independent question is included within the sentence, and the capital letter for the first word of that question helps set it off.)

4. First word of each entry in a list or an outline:

The first mailing will include:

1. *A* cover letter explaining the special offer we are making.
2. *A* brochure illustrating the entire product line.
3. *Our* credit-application form.
4. *An* order form.
5. *A* service contract form.
6. *A* reply envelope.

NAMES OF PERSONS

Names of persons are proper nouns and must be capitalized. The capital letter tells the reader that this is the name of a specific person.

Because there are so many similarities in the spellings of names, be especially careful to follow the exact spelling of a person's name. Note, for example, the following common, similar names:

Steven, Stephen	Kelly, Kelley
Carol, Carroll, Caryl	Smith, Smithe, Smyth
Allen, Alan	Macmillan, MacMillan, McMillan
Clark, Clarke	Van Horne, VanHorne, van Horne

CLASS PRACTICE 1

Provide capitals for the following sentences. Be sure to explain why each of your choices must be capitalized.

1. have jim mcmann and catherine bentley been invited to attend?
2. do you think that you and i can complete all the invoices by friday?
3. perhaps the most important question is, what effect will this have on employee morale?
4. be sure to call mr. carver's office to reschedule our appointment.
5. she distinctly asked, "what is the source of the statistics?"
6. can we process all the invoices by next week? definitely!

NAMES OF PLACES

These few rules will help you to capitalize place names correctly:

1. Capitalize the names of countries and major geographic areas, streets, parks, rivers, shopping centers, buildings, and so on.

United States	Canada
Georgia	Ontario
Augusta	Toronto
Fourth Street	Blake Avenue
Raritan River	Modesto Park
Willowbrook Mall	Sears Tower

2. Capitalize the word *city* only when it is part of the official name of the city: *Kansas City* and *New York City*, but *the city of Provo*.
3. Capitalize the word *state* only when it follows the name of a state: *Pennsylvania State*, but *the state of Pennsylvania*.
4. Capitalize the word *the* only when it is part of the official name: *The Dalles* (a city in Oregon), *The Hague* (capital of the Netherlands).

5. Capitalize *North, South, East,* and *West* when they are used to refer to specific sections of the country.

> Our headquarters office is in the *South.* We plan to open our first district office in the *North* by next September. (Referring to specific sections.)

But do not capitalize such names when they are used simply to indicate directions:

> The warehouse is about 6 miles *east* of Albany and 2 miles *south* of our store.

CLASS PRACTICE 2

Which place names should be capitalized in the following sentences?

1. Our offices in canada—we have one in toronto and one in montreal—submitted the most innovative suggestions.
2. After we attend the conference in st. louis, we will inspect sites in springfield and joplin.
3. Only one store in the pheasant run mall (computer city inc.) has opened so far.
4. A new restaurant in wilkes-barre, pennsylvania, has been selected for our banquet.
5. Do you know where the mayville park section of town is located?
6. Two of our offices in the south—the one in lake city, florida, and the one in new orleans, louisiana—are recording excellent sales.

NAMES OF THINGS

You have already seen how some proper nouns (the names of specific persons and places) are capitalized. To complete your understanding of when to capitalize proper nouns, you will now learn when to capitalize the names of specific *things.*

Organization Names   Capitalize the names of specific companies, associations, societies, commissions, schools, political parties, clubs, religious groups, and government agencies and bureaus.

> Time Inc.
>
> United Van Lines
>
> Warner Communications

Many organization names are equally well known by abbreviations that are written in all-capital letters with no periods.

> Radio Corporation of America (RCA)
>
> Securities and Exchange Commission (SEC)

Society for the Prevention of Cruelty to Animals (SPCA)

University of Southern California (USC)

Names of specific departments or divisions in a company or an organization are also capitalized.

Send these copies to the Payroll Department.   (A specific department.)

Send copies to every manufacturing division in the corporation.   (Not a specific title.)

Product Names

Capitalize the names of commercial products such as *Coca-Cola, Kleenex,* and *Ivory.* But do not capitalize the common nouns that identify the general class of the product.

Ivory soap

Kleenex tissues

Xerox photocopiers

Zenith televisions

Historical Events and Documents

Capitalize the names of historical events or historical periods, specific treaties, bills, acts, and laws.

the Vietnam War

the Bicentennial

the Medicare Act

National Secretaries Week

Holidays, Months, and Days of the Week

Capitalize the names of holidays, months, and days of the week.

Veterans Day	Christmas
Passover	Thanksgiving
Memorial Day	Fourth of July
September	October
Monday	Friday

Do not capitalize the names of the seasons—*winter, spring, summer,* and *fall.*

CLASS PRACTICE 3

Which words in the following sentences should be capitalized? Which words should not be capitalized?

1. Write to the united states government printing office for these free brochures.
2. ms. lee, the owner of hillside fashions, attended elgin high school and emory university.

3. She made a large donation to the museum of modern art.
4. During the intermission we served coke, coffee, and tea.
5. Our next meeting is scheduled for monday, october 9, at the lynchburg supply company.
6. Jack Malone, who also works in the purchasing department, is a member of the rotary club.

PROPER ADJECTIVES

Because proper adjectives are derived from proper nouns, proper adjectives are also capitalized.

Mexican art	Chinese dialects
German food	Italian operas

HEADINGS

In headings and in titles of books and articles, capitalize the first and last words and all major words. Consider as major words all words except:

1. The articles *a, an,* and *the.*

> How to Become *an* Expert in *the* Stock Market   (Book title.)

2. Conjunctions with fewer than four letters, such as *and, but, or, nor, as,* and *if*

> "Stocks and Bonds and You"   (Article title.)

3. Prepositions with fewer than four letters, such as *at, for, out, up,* and *in.*

> Life *in* the Twenty-First Century   (Heading.)

"Investment With Potential for the Future"   (Article. *With* is capitalized because it has four letters.)

> "What Are We Waiting *For*?"   (Article. Note that *for* is capitalized because it is the last word in the title.)

For hyphenated words treat each part of the compound individually.

"An *Up-to-Date* System for Controlling Inventories"

First-Class Travel on a *Second-Class* Checkbook

CLASS PRACTICE 4

Correct any errors in the use of capitals in the following sentences.

1. If you would like to read an interesting article, read "In The Beginning Was The Company."
2. Her first article, "A Day In The Life Of An Ad Writer," described the zany goings-on in the world of advertising.
3. The soon-to-be-available french, italian, and spanish editions are expected to sell well.

4. Ms. Jacorek, a canadian citizen, currently works for an asian exporting company.

5. The 10 percent discount is limited to General Electric Products only.

6. For a good laugh be sure to read "A Woman's View Of The World Of Television."

PERSONAL AND OFFICIAL TITLES

Whenever a person has a title that is written before his or her name, capitalize that title.

Professor Eunice P. Ringenbach

Major Peter Ford MacDonald

Reverend A. J. Loomis

Titles that are written after names are not capitalized unless:

1. The title is that of a high government official.

Among the scheduled speakers is Gerald Weems, a *Senator* who is a leader in environmental protection.   (*Senator* is considered a high official.)

2. The title appears on a displayed line or is being described as part of a displayed line.

Roseanne Ausiello, Treasurer   (The signature line of Ms. Ausiello's letters.)

Ms. Roseanne Ausiello, Treasurer   (The first line of an inside address or an envelope address.)

Send your résumé in confidence to Ms. Roseanne Ausiello, Treasurer, Columbia Productions Inc., 200 Meadowbrook Parkway, Acton, Massachusetts 01720.   (Description of a displayed line.)

In all other cases do not capitalize a title that follows a person's name. In addition, do not capitalize *ex-* and *-elect* and *former* and *late* when they are joined to titles (unless, of course, they begin the sentence).

The story about *ex-*President George Bush will appear in the March issue.

Mayor-*elect* Farley said that she would appoint a special commission to enforce these regulations.

Is *former* Governor Noonan one of the guest speakers?

MISCELLANEOUS RULES

Short Forms   Do not capitalize short forms such as *company*, *corporation*, and *college* when they are used in place of full names.

Edna plans to attend Del Mar College beginning next fall. As you know, the *college* is in Corpus Christi, Texas.

Tom and I work in the Research Department. The *department* is conducting some interesting studies, the results of which should speed the processing of hiring approvals.

However, capitalize short forms that refer to major government bodies, prominent national officials, and well-known places.

Capitol Hill has been Rosemary's beat since she became a reporter. After several years she has earned the respect of everyone on the *Hill.*

Other short forms that are capitalized are the *Bureau* (referring to the Federal Bureau of Investigation), the *House* (for the House of Representatives), and the *Coast* (for the West Coast).

Letter Parts

Capitalize the first word and any title in the salutation of a letter (and any proper names, of course). Capitalize only the first word in a complimentary closing.

Dear Ms. Sinclair:	Sincerely yours,
Dear Margaret:	Cordially yours,

Family Titles

Capitalize words denoting family relationships only when they are used as a part of a person's name or as a substitute for a person's name.

Mother	BUT:	my mother
Aunt Bernice		your aunt

School Subjects

Capitalize the names of languages and of specific numbered courses. Do not capitalize the names of subjects (proper nouns or adjectives are exceptions).

French	Italian
Accounting 101	mathematics
history	business English

COMMUNICATION LABORATORY

APPLICATION EXERCISES

A. On a separate sheet of paper, indicate the correct capitalization of words in the following sentences.

1. Mr. Chesterton, the Comptroller of the Company, must approve all purchases over $5000.
2. We generally begin planning the ads for our Spring styles in september or october.
3. Send a copy of these forms to the Manager of the purchasing department.

CONTINUED

4. Leslie Warner, formerly with our London Office, has joined the executive staff here at our Headquarters.
5. Here is a very informative article: "How To Get The Most From Your IRA."
6. Connie Daniels, the supervisor of the Credit Department, does volunteer work for the democratic party, doesn't she?
7. The store in the oakdale mall offers plenty of space, but the lease agreement is too restrictive.
8. Edna and I enjoy traveling in the south—especially in the Atlanta Area.
9. Can we complete this project by the end of the week? absolutely!
10. When the senator arrives (she's our Keynote Speaker), please seat her at this table.
11. In his latest News Conference, the president announced his plans for increasing employment throughout the Country.
12. Dr. Graham certainly proved to be a superb speaker; he was recommended by the Boston chamber of commerce.
13. Sheila began working for the Company after she was graduated from Iowa central community college, which is in fort Dodge, Iowa.
14. Her speech, "The Secret To A Successful Career On Wall Street," was greeted with loud applause.
15. The site for the annual sales convention is selected on a rotating basis: one year, in the south; the next, in the east; and so on.

B. Correct any errors in the following sentences. Write *OK* for any sentence that has no error.

1. If he had wrote to the client sooner, he would have settled this claim by now.
2. Because Chicago Illinois is the most convenient site for our Sales Representatives, we generally hold our major meetings there.
3. Did you say that Joan Tiller will chair the committee.
4. Wesco Drug Company is one of the leading manufacturers of vitamins, Wesco has been our major supplier of nutritional products since 1973.
5. When he was graduated from Business School in 1985, Howard started working in the security department in our main building.
6. If you would like any more of them booklets for the employees in your Department, Ms. Bentley, please let us know.
7. Yes, the Personnel Department will be able to provide you with part-time help. If you call in advance to discuss your specific needs.
8. Of course, if Marsha wants Annette and myself to coordinate all the workshops, we will be glad to do so.
9. Because Ms. Grayson flight to Amsterdam was canceled, she was able to attend our monthly production meeting.

CONTINUED

10. Since he been in charge of the Graphic Arts Department, Elrod has introduced many timesaving and money-saving procedures.

11. Yes, I am sure that the idea of reorganizing the entire division was her's.

12. Among the successful new franchises on the east coast is the one in Lowell, Massachusetts.

13. John Williams who is considered an expert in this field has reviewed the proposal and has submitted his detailed critique to the Executive Board.

14. The person who is considered an expert in this field is John Williams.

15. Ms. O'Connor has been busy researching materials for an article she is writing, "How To Manage You're Time Effectively."

C. Most of the errors in the following paragraph are capitalization errors— but not all. Find and correct each error.

> The keynote speaker for next saturdays' dinner meeting of the Glenwood civic association will be Dr. Vanessa Gravilek, a Former Professor of Psychology. The title of Dr. Gravileks' speech is "The Need for Improved Productivity among Office Workers." Admission is free to Members.

VOCABULARY AND SPELLING STUDIES

A. These words are often confused: *credible, creditable; metal, medal, meddle.* Explain the differences.

B. Identify the synonyms in the following groups of words.

1. imminent , professional, volatile, approaching

2. genuine, spacious, commodious, infantile

3. superficial, ridiculous, shallow, serious

4. prestige, fairness, renown, panorama

5. disparage, value, discredit, distrust

C. What is the correct plural form for each of the following nouns?

1. runner-up
2. agenda
3. handful
4. bill of sale
5. go-between
6. analysis
7. agency
8. attorney
9. decision-maker
10. layout

ABBREVIATIONS

f you look closely at the way we speak and write, you quickly see that Americans certainly enjoy taking shortcuts! Perhaps the most obvious indicator of our preference for shortcuts is our use of abbreviations. *CRT* (for "cathode-ray tube"), *EFI* (for "electronic fuel injection"), and *WP* (for "word processing") are just a few of the abbreviations that have been coined in the recent past and are already becoming common.

As with all the other tools of writing, abbreviations are indeed helpful, but there are rules for their use. As you study this unit, you will master the correct ways to use abbreviations and symbols in your writing.

PERSONAL TITLES

Because we are so accustomed to using abbreviations such as *Mr., Mrs.,* and *Dr.,* we may be tempted to abbreviate all titles with names. However, as you will see below, not all titles should be abbreviated.

Titles After Names   Always abbreviate the following titles when they are written after a name:

B.S. (for "Bachelor of Science")	Jr. (for "Junior")
Ph.D. (for "Doctor of Philosophy")	Sr. (for "Senior")
D.D. (for "Doctor of Divinity")	

Likewise, abbreviate all other academic titles that follow a name.

Andrew P. Young Jr., D.D.S.

Clarissa Melon-Ross, M.D.

Titles Before Names   Always abbreviate the following titles when they are used before personal names: *Dr., Mr., Messrs.* (the plural of *Mr.*), *Mrs., Ms.,* and *Mses.* or *Mss.* (plural forms of *Ms.*). The titles *Miss, Misses,* and *Mesdames* are complete words and are not followed by periods. Note how the singular and the plural forms of these titles are used before names.

SINGULAR	PLURAL
Miss Clara P. Dubois	the Misses Dubois
Ms. Jane Carlton	the Mses. Carlton
Mrs. Samantha Graye	the Mesdames Graye
Mr. Paul Dunham	the Messrs. Dunham

In general, spell out all other titles used with personal names.

Professor Harris P. Truscott	Mayor DeMaria
Senator Weinberg	Representative Murdock
Governor McKinley	Officer Jenkins

Military Titles   In formal correspondence spell out long military titles. In informal correspondence and when space is limited, abbreviate long military titles.

Brigadier General Clay B. Flagg   (Formal)

Lt. Col. Marilyn C. Hoolihan   (Informal)

Titles of Respect   *Reverend* and *Honorable* are titles of respect used in addressing the clergy and government officials of certain rank. In formal usage spell out these titles and use the word *the* before them. In informal usage omit the word *the* and use the abbreviation *Rev.* or *Hon.* if you wish.

the Reverend James K. Filbert   (Formal)

Rev. James K. Filbert   (Informal)

the Honorable Clarissa J. Fenimore   (Formal)

Hon. Clarissa J. Fenimore   (Informal)

ORGANIZATION NAMES

The name of an organization should follow its *official* spelling, punctuation, and capitalization. Thus, if a company uses an abbreviation such as *Co.* or *Bros.* or a symbol such as & or / in its name, use the abbreviation or symbol when writing the name.

Aetna Life & Casualty

Humphrey Bros. Inc.

R. W. Randall Jr. & Associates

Linda Caldora, Ph.D., P.A.   (*P.A.* means "professional association.")

Larkin/Justin/Brown Advertising

As you saw in Section 5.6, many organizations are as well known by their abbreviations (usually all-capital abbreviations) as by their full names. Except in the most formal writing, using abbreviations such as the following is correct.

AT&T	American Telephone and Telegraph
AMA	American Medical Association
YWCA	Young Women's Christian Association
IRS	Internal Revenue Service
NLRB	National Labor Relations Board

AFL-CIO	American Federation of Labor–Congress of Industrial Organizations
AAA	American Automobile Association
WABC	(Radio station call letters)
CORE	Congress on Racial Equality
NASD	National Association of Securities Dealers

If your reader might not know the meaning of the abbreviation, spell out the full name followed by the abbreviation in parentheses.

Among the bidders was National Cash Register (NCR). In our meetings with representatives of NCR, we discussed all our various requirements for a computerized billing system, and NCR's engineers are now studying our needs.

CLASS PRACTICE 1

Which words should be abbreviated in the following sentences, and which ones should be spelled out? Write *OK* if no changes are needed.

1. Please ask Mister Friedlander to attend this afternoon's meeting, Sara.
2. Does Joanne still work for the IRS?
3. Have you already interviewed Wm. LeBaron for the marketing position?
4. Among the major manufacturers of computers are AT&T, IBM, and NCR.
5. One investment that our analysts favor is stock in Control Data Corporation (CDC). The reasons for recommending CDC stock follow.
6. Yes, Sen. Lloyd is a former partner in this firm.

OTHER ABBREVIATIONS

As you read the following discussions, remember that the "general rule" is to spell out terms and expressions in the body of a business letter or memo. However, when the writing is considered "technical," abbreviations are acceptable because they can often save time without sacrificing clarity. On the other hand, abbreviations are not only acceptable but often necessary on business forms and in charts and tables because of severe space restrictions.

General Terms and Expressions   Spell out most general terms and expressions in business letters and memos.

1. When the days of the week or the months of the year *must* be abbreviated (for example, in charts and tables and on business forms), use the following abbreviations:

Sun.	Thurs.	Jan.	Apr.	Aug.	Nov.
Mon.	Fri.	Feb.	Jun.	Sept.	Dec.
Tues.	Sat.	Mar.	Jul.	Oct.	
Wed.		Do not abbreviate *May.*			

2. Always abbreviate *a.m.* and *p.m.*, but use these abbreviations only when preceded by figures.

> The meeting is scheduled for 10 a.m.   (Note that writing *10:00* is unnecessary.)
>
> Let's begin this project in the morning.   (Not *in the a.m.*)

3. Abbreviate expressions such as the following only on forms and in charts or tables where space is restricted. In all other cases write out the full word or words.

ea.	each
doz.	dozen
acct.	account
chg.	charge
ASAP	as soon as possible

For a complete listing of commonly used abbreviations, refer to a business writer's handbook or a dictionary.

Mailing Addresses

Spell out all parts of street addresses (except numbers, of course). When space is limited, use the following abbreviations:

N.	North	St.	Street
S.	South	Ave.	Avenue
E.	East	Rd.	Road
W.	West	Blvd.	Boulevard
		Pkwy.	Parkway

961 East 96 Street

10 North Willow Avenue

110-75 S. Martin Luther King Jr. Blvd.   (Limited space.)

The words *Post Office* may be spelled out or abbreviated in box numbers.

Post Office Box 789 OR P.O. Box 789

In some areas the use of words such as North, South, Southeast, Northwest, and so on are used following a street name to indicate a section of the city. In such cases abbreviate these words without periods.

1672 Genesee Avenue, SW

444 New York Avenue, NW

On the last line of a mailing address, either spell out the state name or use the appropriate two-letter abbreviation (see the following list). In either case, however, do *not* use a comma before the ZIP Code number.

Bryan, Ohio 43506

Bryan, OH 43506

Do not abbreviate any part of a city name except *St.* in cities such as *St. Louis* and *St. Paul.*

St. Paul, MN 55105

At times it may be useful to abbreviate state names. Use the two-letter abbreviations on the left when abbreviating state names in addresses. In any other situation that calls for abbreviations of state names, use the abbreviations on the right. For a more extensive list—including the provinces and territories of Canada, see the inside back cover.

ABBREVIATIONS OF STATES OF THE UNITED STATES

AL	Alabama	Ala.		NE	Nebraska	Neb.
AK	Alaska	. . .		NV	Nevada	Nev.
AZ	Arizona	Ariz.		NH	New Hampshire	N.H.
AR	Arkansas	Ark.		NJ	New Jersey	N.J.
CA	California	Calif.		NM	New Mexico	N. Mex
CO	Colorado	Colo.		NY	New York	N.Y.
CT	Connecticut	Conn.		NC	North Carolina	N.C.
DE	Delaware	Del.		ND	North Dakota	N. Dak.
DC	District of	D.C.		OH	Ohio	. . .
	Columbia			OK	Oklahoma	Okla.
FL	Florida	Fla.		OR	Oregon	Oreg.
GA	Georgia	Ga.		PA	Pennsylvania	Pa.
HI	Hawaii	. . .		RI	Rhode Island	R.I.
ID	Idaho	. . .		SC	South Carolina	S.C.
IL	Illinois	Ill.		SD	South Dakota	S. Dak.
IN	Indiana	Ind.		TN	Tennessee	Tenn.
IA	Iowa	. . .		TX	Texas	Tex.
KS	Kansas	Kans.		UT	Utah	. . .
KY	Kentucky	Ky.		VT	Vermont	Vt.
LA	Louisiana	La.		VA	Virginia	Va.
ME	Maine	. . .		WA	Washington	Wash.
MD	Maryland	Md.		WV	West Virginia	W. Va.
MA	Massachusetts	Mass.		WI	Wisconsin	Wis.
MI	Michigan	Mich.		WY	Wyoming	Wyo.
MN	Minnesota	Minn.				
MS	Mississippi	Miss.				
MO	Missouri	Mo.				
MT	Montana	Mont.				

Letter and Memo Notations   A few "specialized" abbreviations serve unique functions in letters and memos. One is *cc:* (or *cc*, without the colon), which indicates that a *c*arbon *c*opy or *c*ourtesy *c*opy will be sent to the person or persons listed.

> cc: Myron Schwartz
>   Helen P. Boynton

The abbreviation *PS:* is used to indicate a *p*ost*s*cript—an addition to the body of the letter positioned at the end of the letter.

> PS: Why not use the enclosed coupons to get a 25 percent discount on your next purchase!

The word *Enclosure* is usually spelled out on letters but may be abbreviated *Enc.* The purpose of the enclosure notation, of course, is to indicate that something is included with the letter or memo.

Units of Measurement   In technical writing units of measurement are abbreviated. However, in a letter or memo in which a measurement is given only once or twice, spell out the measurement.

> The desktop model is only 14.1 in long, 15.5 in deep, and 7.4 in high; it weighs 35 lbs; and it handles standard $8^{1}/_{2}$- by 11-in paper.   (Technical copy.)

> The new model handles both $8^{1}/_{2}$- by 11-inch paper and $8^{1}/_{2}$- by 14-inch paper.   (Spell out *inch* in nontechnical copy.)

The abbreviations of some customary and metric measurements are listed below. Note that the same abbreviation is used both in singular and in plural constructions.

CUSTOMARY MEASUREMENTS		METRIC MEASUREMENTS	
in	inch(es)	mm	millimeter(s)
ft	foot, feet	cm	centimeter(s)
yd	yard(s)	m	meter(s)
mi	mile(s)	L	liter(s)
oz	ounce(s)	mg	milligram(s)
pt	pint(s)	g	gram(s)
qt	quart(s)		
gal	gallon(s)		
lb	pound(s)		

For a comprehensive listing use a general or a technical dictionary or a business writer's handbook.

PLURALS OF ABBREVIATIONS

The plurals of abbreviations may be formed in various ways. Read the following general guidelines, but refer to a writer's handbook or a dictionary whenever you are in doubt.

1. For all-capital abbreviations, as well as mixed abbreviations that end in a capital letter, add *s* to form the plural:

   CPA   CPAs   Ph.D.   Ph.D.s

2. For most abbreviations that end in a period, add *s* to form the plural:

   No.   Nos.   dept.   depts.   mo.   mos.

3. However, for abbreviations that consist of individual lowercase letters separated by periods, add *'s* to form the plural:

   f.o.b.   f.o.b.'s   c.o.d.   c.o.d.'s

4. For the plurals of abbreviated personal titles, follow this list:

Mr.	Messrs.	Mrs.	Mesdames
Ms.	Mses. or Mss.	Dr.	Drs.

5. For abbreviations of units of measure, use the same form in both singular and plural constructions:

   1 kg   4 kg   27 kg   1 yd   7 yd   87 yd

6. In references, for the plural of *p.* ("page"), write *pp.;* for the plural of *l.* ("line"), write *ll.*:

   (See pp. 356–357, ll. 120–158.)

As you can see from the number of variations above, it is essential to check a writer's handbook whenever you are in doubt.

CLASS PRACTICE 2

Are abbreviations used correctly in the following sentences? Should any additional words be abbreviated?

1. Because Mister Janusck is now out of town, we are canceling our 3 PM production meeting.
2. We should require about three or four yds of fabric, according to Henry.
3. On Tues. or Wed. of next week, let's review all these accts.
4. Has Doctor Demerest arrived yet? Is she scheduled to be here this a.m.?
5. Do you know the current value of I.B.M. stock, Mister Gregus?
6. Send copies of these price lists to our Tex. office and our Fla. office.
7. A lens of about 135 mms is what we need.
8. When are you leaving for Saint Louis?

COMMUNICATION LABORATORY

APPLICATION EXERCISES

A. On a separate sheet of paper, make any corrections needed in the following sentences. Write *OK* if a sentence has no error.

1. Alicia P. Stephenson, PhD , one of the senior members of the Research Department, has developed this customer survey questionnaire.
2. Ellen suggested that we update the listing of chg. accts., and I fully agree with her.
3. The 20-second commercials on W.Q.X.R. and W.N.C.N. have been the most effective, according to this report.
4. Ron is now working toward his M.B.A., which he expects to complete next June.
5. One of the largest manufacturers of computer components is the Anderson Electronics Corporation in Ft. Washington, PA.
6. The messenger service will not pick up cartons weighing more than 70 lbs.
7. Of course, Mr. Rubin, we will try to replace the damaged equipment ASAP.
8. The I.B.M. technician has already repaired this machine, Mister Kline.
9. Doctor Samuelson has submitted his research study to the A.M.A., hasn't he?
10. Sales for the first three mos. of this year have exceeded estimated budgets by more than 15 percent.
11. In Jan.—certainly no later than Feb.—we will have the new system in operation throughout the comp.
12. We need about a gal of this special glue for photographs.
13. According to this catalog, the price is only $15 ea. when purchased in quantities of a doz. or more.
14. The chairperson said, "We are running late; I suggest that we continue this discussion in the a.m."
15. The directions recommend mixing about an oz or so of the powder in a pt of the liquid.

B. Find and correct all the errors in the following sentences. Write *OK* if a sentence has no error.

1. She asked, "Does Ms. Christenson and Mr. Levesque have any additional information on the status of the union negotiations?"
2. Anne Simpson, who has been heading a committee to study hiring practices throughout the corporation will deliver the speech at this evening's meeting.
3. All the managers agree that we must improve our order-fulfillment services, however, we do not consider a new computer system the answer to all our problems.
4. The new plant is on Kennedy Blvd., not W. Hanson Rd.

CONTINUED

5. Let's take these packages to the P.O. as soon as possible, Carole.

6. Please note that the first package is addressed to Albany, GA, and the second one is addressed to Albany, NY.

7. If you would like to increase your life insurance for just pennies more each month. Complete the enclosed form and return it with your next premium.

8. Because this is a rush project, we will try our best to complete it by Thurs. or Fri.

9. Betty said "Anyone who wants to apply for either of the two supervisory positions that are now open should contact Ira Gregorian in the Personnel Department."

10. Because we were temporarily out of stock on Model X100 microwave ovens. We were instructed to substitute Model X250, which sells for about $50 more.

11. Most of the representatives in this district has already taken the Telephone Techniques workshop.

12. One of the foremost ad agencies in this city is Trent/Hood/Reynolds Associates.

13. Alvin and Yolanda have been assigned to work on the revision of the procedures manual, they have more management experience than anyone else in the company.

14. As a result of the commercials on WRKO, we gained three new accts. in just two days!

15. After you read Chapt. 3, you will better understand how to identify and reach a target audience.

C. Revise the following paragraph.

The personal computer market is growing tremendously each year. I.B.M. , Radio Shack, Apple, and other companies, are predicting increased sales of personal computers for this year and the next. We have decided therefore, to study the potential of a new magazine for owners of personal computers, we have tentatively called this magazine The Home Computer. The Harrison Agency will conduct a feasibility study to determine the potential, of such a magazine. By September 30 we expect to have, all the information necessary to make our decision.

VOCABULARY AND SPELLING STUDIES

A. These words are often confused: *continual, continuous; magnificent, munificent.* Explain the differences.

B. For each of the following words name an *antonym*—a word that is opposite in meaning.

1. different	**3.** sensible	**5.** receive
2. complicated	**4.** objective	**6.** careful

CONTINUED

C. Add *el* or *le* to each of the following words.

1. lab_____   **3.** gigg_____   **5.** pick_____
2. mod_____   **4.** nick_____   **6.** whist_____

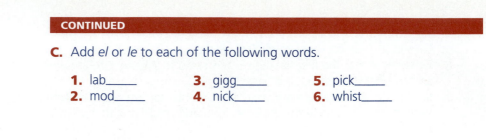

SECTION 5.8
NUMBERS

Numbers provide our communications with specific information—quantities, dollar amounts, percentages, measurements, dates. The importance of numbers and the precision with which they are used are obviously critical to accurate communication. Begin, then, to study when to write numbers in words and when to write them in figures.

NUMBERS WRITTEN AS WORDS

Generally, numbers are expressed in figures in business correspondence. However, there are occasions when numbers are written in words.

Numbers From 1 Through 10   When used in isolated instances, the numbers from 1 through 10 should be written in words.

Each of the *four* speakers has *one* hour to complete his or her presentation.

Of the *nine* proposals that were submitted to the panel, only *five* were accepted.

Numbers That Begin Sentences   Write in words any number that begins a sentence. Rephrase the sentence if the number is too awkward to express in words.

Thirteen districts throughout the country have reported that this new product line is a smashing success.

Two hundred sixty-three sales representatives have attended the Telephone Techniques seminar.   (Awkward.)

The Telephone Techniques seminar has been attended by *263* sales representatives.   (Rephrased sentence is not awkward.)

When spelling out large numbers (numbers over 1000), use the shortest form possible.

Fifteen hundred orders were received in the first week of the sale!   (Not *One thousand five hundred.*)

Twenty-four hundred samples have been distributed to qualified buyers throughout the area.   (Not *Two thousand four hundred.*)

Fractions Standing Alone   Write in words a fraction that stands alone without a whole number.

Approximately *one-half* of the responses commented favorably on the new billing system.

Ages   Ages are spelled out unless they are considered significant statistics or technical measurements.

Caryn Johnson has been appointed director of sales. Caryn began working for Logan Industries at the age of *nineteen,* when she joined our sales staff in Ames, Iowa.   (A general reference to age.)

Only employees who will have reached age *55* by January 1 of next year are eligible for this new policy.   (A significant statistic.)

Periods of Time   General periods of time are usually written in words.

Although these ads were created about *fifteen* years ago, they are still effective among young adults.

CLASS PRACTICE 1

Find and correct any errors in the following sentences. Write *OK* if there are no errors.

1. 19 applicants called for appointments within the past hour.
2. Perhaps we should appoint a panel of 3 or 4 people with production experience to study these issues.
3. The board of directors has voted against the mandatory retirement age of seventy.
4. If you or your staff members need 2 or 3 of these helpful manuals, call Nancy Dobson in the Personnel Department.
5. Mr. Hammond, who has managed our Chicago regional office for the past twelve years, will be appointed to the new position as vice president for sales and marketing.
6. The margin on these products, as Ms. Wilson explained, is about $1/2$ more than the margin on those products.
7. Kay asked whether we will be able to send her 10 or 12 brochures through interoffice mail.
8. One thousand five hundred employees have signed up for the payroll savings plan as of this morning.

NUMBERS WRITTEN AS FIGURES

Writing numbers in figures is generally preferred in business writing because figures are emphatic and specific. Below are the instances in which numbers should be written in figures.

Numbers Higher Than 10
You already saw that numbers from 1 through 10 are written in words. Numbers above 10 are written in figures.

> We requested bids from *16* suppliers that were approved by the committee.

> Sherry estimates that from *200* to *250* employees will opt for the additional coverage.

Sums of Money
Write sums of money in figures.

> According to this estimate, the printing cost for each manual will be $2.43.

> A 4-ounce bottle sells for $6; an 8-ounce bottle, $10.   (Note that the additional zeros in *$6.00* and *$10.00* are not necessary.)

> Amounts smaller than $1 are expressed with the word *cents*.

> Although the estimated savings is only *12 cents* an issue, the total savings at the end of the year is several thousand dollars.

> Amounts in millions and billions are written in figures, with the word *million* or *billion* spelled out.

> The "asking price," according to industry experts, will exceed $3.6 million. (Also acceptable: *3.6 million dollars.*)

Time
Use figures with *a.m.* and *p.m.* Use either words or figures with *o'clock:* words for greater formality; figures for less formality.

> Her estimated time of arrival is *9:45* p.m.

> We will leave for the airport at *9* o'clock.

> We invite you to be our guest at the banquet, which will begin at *nine* o'clock. (More formal than *9 o'clock.*)

House, Street, ZIP Code Numbers
House numbers (except for the number *one*) are always written in figures. Note that the abbreviation *No.* or the sign # should not be used with house or box numbers.

> The new address is *One* Wall Street.

> Mail her correspondence to her home address: *191* Central Avenue, East Peoria, Illinois 61611.

> Send the package under his name to Box *8989*, Indianapolis, Indiana 46227.

> Spell out street names from *1* through *10*. Use figures for numbered street names over *10*. When figures are used, the ending *st*, *d*, or *th* may be omitted if

a word such as *East* or *West* separates the house number from the street number. If there is no such word between the house number and the street number, use the original ending to prevent misreading.

1212 Fourth Street

350 West 67 Avenue

767 23d Street

Use one space before the ZIP Code number; use no punctuation after the ZIP Code in an address block.

Ms. Elana Howard
1125 22d Avenue
Grand Rapids, MI 49502-0000

Decimals   Decimals are always expressed in figures: *5.7, 11.45, 9.6454.* For clarity use a zero before the decimal point when there is no whole number: *0.25.*

Mixed Numbers   Write a mixed number (a whole number plus a fraction) in figures, except at the beginning of a sentence.

The cost of the project was 2$\frac{1}{2}$ times higher than had been estimated.

When spelling out a mixed number (for example, at the beginning of a sentence), use the word *and* to separate the whole number from the fraction.

Three *and* one-half times more orders came in in July than in June.

Numbers in Series; Related Numbers   When one number in a series must be written in figures, write all the numbers in figures.

Our department consists of *one* manager, *two* secretaries, and *six* ad writers.

BUT: Our department consists of *2* managers, *5* secretaries, *12* media buyers, and *13* ad writers.   (Because the numbers *12* and *13* are above *10,* they must be expressed in figures; likewise, all other numbers in the series should be expressed in figures.)

Related numbers are numbers that refer to the same kinds of things. Treat related numbers similarly—write them either in figures or in words.

Kenneth mailed *32* brochures to his special customers and has already received *8* orders in just two weeks! (Ordinarily, *8* would be spelled out; here, however, it is related to the figure *32* and must be expressed similarly—in figures. Note that *two* is not related to the other numbers and is therefore correctly spelled out.)

Percentages   Use figures with the word *percent.*

Last week the interest rate was about *8* percent; this week the rate is fluctuating between *9* and *10* percent.

The symbol % is generally used in technical writing and in tables and invoices, not in general correspondence. Always use figures with the symbol %, with no space between the figure and the symbol: *3.2%, 6.75%,* and so on.

Weights and Measures   Use figures to express numbers in weights, measures, and distances.

> We need several *3*-gallon containers of this lubricant.
>
> Each solution has precisely *4.5* grams of solvent.

Miscellaneous   When a number is considered "significant," it is generally expressed in figures, even when the number is under 10.

> We allow *5* days for a check to clear; for out-of-town checks we allow *6* days. (Here, the numbers *5* and *6* are significant; they deserve the special emphasis that figures provide.)

Consecutive numbers (as in *100 twenty-cent* stamps) deserve special attention. To avoid a statement that may be confusing—*100 20-cent stamps,* write the smaller of two consecutive numbers in words, even if that number would usually be written in figures.

CLASS PRACTICE 2

Check how well you understand the rules for writing numbers in figures. Correct any errors in the following sentences. Write *OK* if there are no errors.

1. Edison Plastics will move to its new offices at 1 Willow Grove Boulevard in September.
2. Predictably, nine of the 12 word processing operators preferred the same equipment.
3. Significantly, the average inventory level last year was nine days; this year, the average has been 12 days.
4. Sales through the month of August have exceeded our estimate for summer sales by five percent.
5. We taped two 14-column sheets to create this chart.
6. This building is now worth one and a half times its value when we purchased it just three years ago.
7. The records of all four hundred and fifty accounts are filed on this diskette.
8. We plan to hire three sales representatives for our New York office; 11 for our Seattle office; and 14 for our San Francisco office.

ORDINAL NUMBERS IN DATES

Numbers such as *1st, 2d, 3d, 4th,* and so on, are called *ordinal numbers.* Follow these rules for using ordinal numbers in dates.

1. Do not use an ordinal ending for the date when the day follows the month: *April 1, September 3, October 13,* and so on.

2. Use an ordinal number when the date precedes the month: *the 1st of April, the 3d of September, the 13th of October,* and so on.

> The report for the sales meeting is due October 1.

> The convention has been rescheduled for the 13th of November.

COMMUNICATION LABORATORY

APPLICATION EXERCISES

A. Can you find all the errors in number expression in the following sentences? On a separate sheet of paper, correct any errors. Write *OK* for any sentence that is correct.

1. 350 of the employees in the Wilkes-Barre factory are enrolled in this special program.
2. Please have a messenger take this envelope to Mr. Kinoy's office—his address is 1,301 Vernon Boulevard.
3. Based on your experience, would you say that $500.00 is a fair price?
4. Let's take advantage of the discount—order 250 5-pound boxes.
5. 10 good reasons for starting an IRA are discussed in this informative booklet.
6. Daily compounding increases the effective rate of interest to as much as 11% annually.
7. The dimensions are five and a half inches long by four inches deep by two inches high.
8. All the screws required (6 3-inch flathead screws and 9 1½-inch roundhead screws) are included in the kit.
9. No more than four and a half grams of fat are included in an average serving.
10. Next year's research budget is the highest ever—$2,500,000.
11. Write the deadline date on your calendar: March 30th.
12. Surprisingly, only ⅓ of the shareholders voted in favor of the merger.
13. The total price (which includes six percent sales tax and all shipping charges) is only $1965.75.
14. Although the quality of this paper is far superior to the paper we used for the last printing, the additional cost is only $.09 an issue.
15. Tomorrow at 10:00 a.m. we will discuss the policy in question: No. 189-876-4301.
16. Angela Whitmore, age 42, was identified as the executive vice president's successor in the newspaper reports.

CONTINUED

17. If you need only 2 or 3 blank forms, you may take these; if you require more, you may pick up blanks at the IRS office nearest you.

18. If we begin now, we can discuss and probably resolve both issues in about 1 hour.

19. Did you know that Mary Clanton won 1st prize in the monthly sales contest?

20. Copy this address and add it to our files for future reference: Ms. Leonora Martin-Ford, 16,075 Halsey Street, Flagstaff, Arizona 86,001.

B. Find all the errors in the following sentences; write your corrections on a separate sheet of paper. Write *OK* for a sentence that has no error.

1. The list price of this modem is $295.00, but the discount price is only $195.00.

2. The directions suggest mixing five grams of powder in one and a half liters of water.

3. Harry been to one of our quarterly regional marketing and sales meetings, hasn't he?

4. Gregory asked whether we had any copies of the affirmative action plan?

5. The increase in the unit cost with the new packaging material is only $.29; however, multiplied over a one-year period, the increase alone totals more than $20,000.

6. The President's goal, as stated in this memorandum to all employees, is to reach ten million dollars in annual sales by the year 1994.

7. 22 of our auditors will be working on this project by the month of July.

8. Please order a supply of 12 14-column accounting pads for marketing assistants, Jim and I.

9. The entire balance is due in thirty days, as stated in the enclosed copy of the original agreement.

10. So far, we have interviewed eight executive assistants, fourteen recruiters, and twenty-five managers.

11. Frances and her assistant, Ken Thompson, is responsible for all the photography.

12. Be sure to send duplicates to Mr. Rose and I.

13. Only Ms. Cranston, Dr. O'Riley and Mrs. Filbin are scheduled to speak at tonight's banquet, according to this program announcement and the newspaper story.

14. One of the primary reasons for appointing a special panel, is to study and improve safety measures in each chemical-producing facility.

15. Karyn is rather eager to start her new job, she will head the Salina, Kansas, district office as of next January 1.

C. Edit the following excerpt from a memorandum.

At Ms. Vernon's request we are scheduling a meeting for the 10 of July. The purpose of the meeting is to discuss sales strategies.

As you know, sales for the first ½ of the year are down about 25%. Among the topics we plan to discuss are, the ways in which we can cut our expense budgets by a total of four hundred thousand dollars. In addition, we will explore some of the reasons we predicted sales so poorly.

VOCABULARY AND SPELLING STUDIES

A. These words are often confused: *deceased, diseased; risky, risqué.* Explain the differences.

B. Among the following words are some of the words most frequently misspelled in the business office. Which words are misspelled?

1. refered
2. sincerly
3. intrest
4. applicible
5. aproximately
6. conveniance
7. comittee
8. reccomend
9. statment
10. aggreement

C. In an effort to save space and at the same time attract attention, vendors often take shortcuts in writing copy for signs. Check the following signs for correct use of numbers. Are there any errors?

1. Special Sale—½ Off!
2. 1 Day Only!
3. All 1-of-a-Kind Bargains!

CHAPTER 6

WRITING STYLE

Even in this era of advanced communication technology, the written word has survived—even flourished. In fact, it is still the basic tool with which ideas, especially in business, are presented. Whether you are writing in longhand or keyboarding on a word processor or working with desktop publishing, you must give life to your ideas. Knowing how to use the principles of effective writing will help you to put your message into a clear, concise but complete, and precise form. Remember: Your goal is to communicate, to have the receiver understand the message you are trying to send.

The techniques mastered by successful business writers apply to all written forms of communication—especially letters, memos, and reports. These techniques include organizing ideas, choosing the right words to express those ideas, writing effective sentences, revising to improve the message, designing the final message, and proofreading to assure error-free final messages.

OBJECTIVES

Given a situation that requires writing in business, you will be able to do the following when you master the units in this chapter:

1. Use words, phrases, and clauses that allow the reader to interpret messages correctly.

2. Use positive, bias-free, standard language on a level that the receiver can understand.

3. Use balanced words, phrases, sentences, and paragraphs.

4. Apply the techniques for effective sentence and paragraph writing to your messages.

5. Develop your written message so that each idea flows smoothly into the next.

SECTION 6.1

USING WORDS EFFECTIVELY

Landing a job in the Customer Service Department for a major ski equipment manufacturer was more than Jennifer Gattis (a genuine ski enthusiast) could have asked for. When the department manager, Ken Ross, assigned her to fill in for Thomas Jenkins, who was on vacation, Jennifer was ready for the challenge: She would answer customers' calls and respond to all customers' inquiries, claims, and complaints.

"Jennifer, you know that words are the foundation of communication," Ken said. "No news here! What many of us tend to overlook, however, is the extent to which *word choice* affects communications. Words that are pompous may turn off prospective customers. Words that are negative may anger them. Words that have double meanings may confuse or mislead."

Although *you* may never consider the words you use as pompous, negative, or confusing—or, for that matter, dull and colorless—your *readers* certainly may! Your readers may not interpret or understand or react to your intended message *as you thought they might.*

Follow Ken's advice: "Choose words that sound 'conversational,' words you'd expect the reader to know. Eliminate needless words, and beware of clichés! Negative words and sexist terms are losers—they can destroy communications. And last, make it a game to find synonyms that your readers will find interesting!"

LIVING LANGUAGE

"There are times when silence has the loudest voice."

—Leroy Brownlow

ADOPT A CONVERSATIONAL TONE

As they keyboard or dictate messages, many businesspeople feel the sudden impulse to impress their readers with an extensive vocabulary. In a telephone or a face-to-face conversation, for example, a person may say:

We need these supplies in our warehouse no later than May 4.

But in a letter that same person may write:

It is imperative that the complete shipment be received at the above-mentioned address by the fourth of May.

Not only are the words *imperative* and *above-mentioned* a bit showy, but the sentence itself would sound self-important even if these words were replaced. Furthermore, the sentence is several words longer than necessary.

Routine business messages are not opportunities to display the richness of your vocabulary. They are business assignments that require writing clear, direct messages—and such messages are best achieved through the use of a *conversational tone.* Of course, your tone will vary depending on how well you know the reader. Writing to a business associate whom you've known very well for several years, you might say:

Dear Marisa:

Thanks for sending me the purchase order for the additional brochures you requested. Because you called me quickly, I was able to change the printing quantity before the job reached the Production Department. Anyway, you will have your brochures—all 25,000 of them!—by Friday, June 6.

By the way, Marissa, ...

On the other hand, if you do not know the client well, you might write:

Dear Ms. Stein:

Thank you for sending us the revised purchase order for 25,000 of your full-color sales brochures. As you originally requested, all the brochures will be delivered to you on Friday, June 6.

Ms. Stein, you may be interested in . . . .

The difference in style is obvious: The very informal, friendly approach of the first example begins with the salutation, *Dear Marisa,* and continues throughout the letter. The second example is more formal. However, both examples use a conversational tone. Despite their differences, neither is stiff or pretentious.

Before you begin writing, then, consider the reader. How well do you know her? What must you tell her? How would you talk with her if she were face-to-face? Consider such questions as you write, and you will develop a conversational tone and a degree of formality that are appropriate for that particular reader.

Whether you know the reader well or not at all, you should avoid the terms listed in the left column below and replace them with other more conversational terms, such as those suggested in the right column.

AVOID SAYING . . .	INSTEAD, SAY . . .
1. *Acknowledge receipt of*	1. *Thank you for* or *I received*
"This is to acknowledge receipt of your letter."	"Thank you for writing me about . . ."
2. *Advise*	2. *Say, tell, let us know*
"Please advise us of your intended delivery date."	"Please let us know when you will deliver the order."
"I cannot advise you as to when the contract will be ready."	"I cannot tell you when the contract will be ready."
3. *Am (Are) in receipt of*	3. *Thank you* or *I have received*
"We are in receipt of your check for $81.20."	"Thank you for your check for $81.20."
	"I have received your check for $81.20 and appreciate . . . ."

LIVING LANGUAGE

"Just as people who don't work out can't do certain things with their bodies, people who don't read can't do certain things with their minds," according to one expert on literacy (Michael Silverblatt, quoted in the *Los Angeles Times Magazine,* September 22, 1991, p. 42).

Writing is one skill that cannot be developed without reading, reading, reading. As the above quotation clearly tells us, reading is the key to mastery of many more skills besides writing.

AVOID SAYING . . .	INSTEAD, SAY . . .
4. *As per* "We are crediting your account as per instructions."	4. *As* or *according to* "As you instructed, we are crediting your account." "We are crediting your account, according to your wishes."
5. *At an early date* "You will hear from us at an early date."	5. *Soon* (Or give a specific date.) "I will write you soon about . . . ." "You will hear from me by August 15 about the new delivery date."
6. *At this time, at present, at the present writing.* "My opinion at this time (or *at present*) is that the meeting will take place."	6. *Now* (Or omit entirely.) "I now think that the meeting will take place." "I believe that the meeting will take place."
7. *Attached hereto* "Attached hereto is the agreement for your signature."	7. *Attached, here, enclosed* "Attached is the agreement for your signature." "Here is the agreement, which I hope you will sign."
8. *Beg* "I beg your indulgence in this matter."	8. *Ask, request, hope,* and so on "I request a 30-day extension." "I hope you will allow me another month in which to pay this bill."
9. *Due to the fact that* "Due to the fact that our factory is on strike, we cannot . . . ." "You have been placed on our preferred list of customers due to the fact that you always pay promptly."	9. *As, because, since* "Because our factory is on strike, we cannot . . . ." "Since you always pay your bills promptly, we are pleased to list you as a preferred customer."
10. *Duly* "I received your February 8 order, which I duly acknowledge."	10. Do not use. Superfluous. "I appreciate your February 8 order."
11. *Enclosed please find* "Enclosed please find your copy of the minutes of our last meeting."	11. *Enclosed* or *here* "Enclosed are the minutes . . . ." "Here are the minutes . . . ."

AVOID SAYING . . .	**INSTEAD, SAY . . .**
12. *Herewith*	12. Do not use.
"I am sending you a duplicate bid herewith."	"Enclosed (or *attached*) is a duplicate bid."
13. *I have before me*	13. Do not use. Superfluous.
"I have before me your reminder of the deadline for my article."	"I am grateful for your reminder of the deadline for my article."
14. *In re*	14. *Regarding, concerning, as to*
"In re the freight charges, I believe they are high."	"Regarding the freight charges, I believe they are high."
15. *In the amount of*	15. *For*
"Our money order in the amount of $6 is enclosed."	"Our money order for $6 is enclosed."
16. *In the event that*	16. *In case* or *if*
"In the event that you cannot arrive on Tuesday evening, I will schedule the conference for Wednesday."	"If you cannot arrive on Tuesday evening, I will schedule the conference for Wednesday."
17. *In this matter*	17. Do not use. Superfluous.
"I will await your action in this matter."	"I will await your action."
18. Kindly	18. *Please*
"If our substitution is not satisfactory, kindly let us know."	"If the substitution we are sending is not satisfactory, please let us know."
19. *Party* (referred to a person)	19. Use a specific name or title.
"According to another party in your firm, your payment . . . ."	"According to our credit supervisor, Ms. Silvero, your payment . . . ."
20. *Same*	20. *It, they, them,* or omit.
"I have received your letter and thank you for same."	"Thank you for your letter."
21. *State*	21. *Say, tell,* or omit.
"In response to your inquiry, I wish to state that we can furnish you with the items you specified."	"We can furnish you with the steel plates you need."
"In your letter you state that you want a ripple finish on the letterheads."	"In your letter you say (or *you mention*) that you want a ripple finish on the letterheads."
22. *Take the liberty of*	22. Omit.
"I am taking the liberty of sending you the beige, rather than the desert tan, drapery material."	"Therefore, I am sending you the beige, rather than the desert tan, drapery material."
"May I take the liberty of telling you we value your business."	"Many thanks for your business."

WORLD VIEW

"The greatest compliment a traveller abroad can pay the local language is not to speak it." This advice (from an international communications expert) is not intended to be taken literally. It is intended as a warning for those of us who (for example) "know a little French" and then use what little we know to exasperate our listeners, when we might have fared better in saving our "French" for reading menus and crossword puzzles.

AVOID SAYING . . .	**INSTEAD, SAY . . .**
23. *Thank you in advance*	23. Do not use. It is presumptuous to thank a person in advance.
"Thank you in advance for any courtesies you can extend to Mr. Phillips."	"I would appreciate any courtesies you can extend to Mr. Phillips."
24. *The writer*	24. *I, me, my*
"The writer wishes to acknowledge receipt of the book."	"Thank you for sending me the book."
"Please send the samples to the attention of the writer."	"Please send me the samples."
25. *Trust*	25. *Hope, know, believe*
"I trust my suggestion will be satisfactory."	"I hope my suggestion will be satisfactory."
"I trust you will agree with the action I have taken."	"I believe you will agree with the action I have taken."
26. *Under date of*	26. Omit.
"I have your letter under date of May 1."	"I have your May 1 letter."
27. *Under separate cover*	27. *Will send, am sending,* and so on
"I am mailing the back issues under separate cover."	"I will send the back issues to you today."
	"The sample you requested was mailed this morning."
28. *Up to this writing*	28. *So far* or omit.
"Up to this writing I have had no word from the Wilson Company."	"So far I have had no word from the Wilson Company."
	"I have not heard from the Wilson Company."
29. *Would ask, would remind, would say*	29. Do not use *would* in this way.
"I would ask that you bear with us on your delayed order."	"I hope you will understand why your order will be delayed."

FOCUS ON THE READER'S VOCABULARY

The importance of written communications often fools businesspeople into using the biggest and rarest words they know. But the importance of a document is not measured by the number of odd words or the number of "big" words it contains!

Therefore, whether you are writing a formal or an informal message, whether you are writing to someone you know or someone you do not know, it is never appropriate to use words that may be outside the reader's vocabulary. Certainly, using such words never contributes to a conversational tone!

Will the reader understand the following?

> A dichotomy in the opinions of the members present was evident: Four members favored increasing our advertising budget, while the remainder sanctioned a diminution of spending in this particular promotional area.

Even if the reader does understand the meaning of *dichotomy, sanctioned,* and *diminution,* do these words contribute to clarity? to a conversational tone? Instead, the writer might have considered saying:

> The members present were split in their opinions: Four preferred increasing our advertising budget; all other members favored reducing our advertising budget.

To communicate effectively, you must use words that are appropriate for your reader or your listener—words that are sure to be part of their vocabulary.

ELIMINATE UNNECESSARY WORDS

"Time is money," according to this most common of clichés. Wasting the reader's time will annoy the reader, much as a 30-minute speech with a 3-minute message annoys a listener.

Economize. Cut sentences. Prune phrases. As we attempt to sound "conversational," we may fall into the trap of using more words than we need. Compare these "before" and "after" examples:

BEFORE	AFTER
check in the amount of $5	$5 check
at this point in time	now
I wish to take this opportunity to thank you for . . .	Thank you for . . .
at all times	always
for the period of a year	annually

Is there a difference in meaning in each pair? No. Is there a difference in directness in each pair? Yes! In each case, the "After" example is more to the point.

USE SPECIFIC NOUNS

Communication always benefits from *specific* words.
Use words that name people as specifically as possible:

One person claimed that these computer tables are difficult to assemble.
(Who is that "one person"?)

A customer claimed that these computer tables are difficult to assemble.
(Better: More specific than "one person.")

LIVING LANGUAGE

"Kind words can be short and easy to speak, but their echoes are truly endless."
—Mother Theresa

Mr. Wilson claimed that these computer tables are difficult to assemble. (Better yet: More specific than "a customer.")

Use words that identify a specific process:

One of the keys to success, we have found, is to conduct regular performance appraisals and to share the results of each appraisal with the employee. *It* has certainly helped improve morale among our employees, as proved by our last survey.   (What does "it" refer to? Not clear.)

Our performance appraisal system has certainly helped improve . . . (Specific. Clear.)

Use words that distinguish one organization among many:

One department is especially concerned that . . .   (Which "department"?)

The Public Relations Department is especially concerned that . . .   (Better: "The Public Relations Department" is specific.)

Use words that pinpoint the heart of the problem or the issue that is under discussion:

We surveyed all our customers to find out their attitudes toward the recent price increases, because *this* is becoming more and more of an issue in our industry.   (What does *this* refer to? It is not clear in the context.)

. . . because *price increases* are becoming more and more of an issue in our industry.   (Specific. Clear.)

AVOID CLICHÉS AND REGIONALISMS

Clichés are overused expressions, such as:

the bottom line	it speaks for itself
a tough road ahead	nothing to sneeze at
it's "no contest"	at a loss for words
as good as gold	as easy as pie
needs no introduction	kill two birds with one stone

The *first* person to use each of these terms showed creativity. The second person was smart enough to copy innovative language. But the tens of millions of us who have copied these expressions since are showing no originality, no creativity, and no imagination. And our readers will quickly realize that we do not care! Avoid clichés.

Whereas clichés have traveled down every street and visited every American home and office, regionalisms have not. Regionalisms are expressions that are limited to specific geographic areas and that, therefore, may not be understood by your reader. For example, in an informal note to his manager, Tyler Edwards wrote:

The sales representatives were as pleased with the suggested changes in the commission schedule as children at a bunking party!

His manager, however, had never heard of a *bunking party,* a regional expression common in Arkansas, Tyler's home state, but commonly called a *slumber party* or *pajama party* elsewhere. While regionalisms are colorful, they may not be understood.

Can you name two regional expressions that are common in your area and their equivalents in other parts of the country?

REPLACE NEGATIVE WORDS

No one enjoys being accused, abused, scolded, berated, censured, or blamed. Yet businesspeople *do* accuse, abuse, and so on, when they use words such as:

blame	delay	fault
careless	dissatisfied	inferior
complaint	error	mistake
defective	failure	negligence

While experienced businesspeople know better, they may unknowingly become overly defensive in clarifying a position. Result: Their negative words make communication impossible, because the reader is now occupied only with the negative words in the message.

Read your drafts carefully to detect—and then to *revise*—wording that may offend your readers, make them angry, or force them to become defensive. Remember: Your goal is to communicate a message, not to right the wrongs of the world. Here are a few examples of negative expressions, along with suggestions for revising them:

BEFORE	AFTER
Your complaint concerning . . .	Your letter concerning . . .
You claim that . . .	In your letter you mentioned that . . .
Your failure to . . .	Because we did not have your check before us, we were not able to . . .
Your criticism of . . .	Your comments regarding . . .
We are sorry that our error . . .	We apologize for delivering your order to your headquarters office instead of your branch office.

USE BIAS-FREE TERMS

America's work force consists of men and women. In all businesses, at all job levels, in all regions of our country, we find both women and men at work, and our language must reflect this reality.

Terms such as *businessman* and *salesman* do not reflect this reality. Worse, such terms completely overlook both the existence of women in the work force and their contributions to government, business, and industry. As a result, businesspeople are careful to avoid biased terms, such as those listed below.

BEFORE	AFTER
fireman	firefighter
mailman	mail carrier
insurance man	insurance agent
foreman	supervisor
stewardess	flight attendant
policeman or policewoman	police officer
businessman	businessperson, business worker
businessmen	businesspeople, business workers
salesman	sales representative, salesperson, salesclerk

Note that even when a bias-free term such as *sales representative* is used, the rest of the sentence may still betray bias:

Every sales representative in the country will improve *his* effectiveness by completing this sales techniques seminar.

Is "Every sales representative in the country" a man? No. Therefore, change the pronoun *his* to *his or her.* Or change the sentence to the plural form.

All sales representatives in the country will improve *their* effectiveness by completing this sales techniques seminar.

ADD EXTRA INTEREST THROUGH SYNONYMS

Word variety contributes to successful writing. Colorless words and overused words are about as interesting as the tenth rerun of a mediocre TV series.

Overused words include the following:

good	awful	little	big	think	fix	fantastic	bad
fine	know	lovely	say	come	go	great	super

Overused does not mean "wrong," of course. But when you want to describe something special, overused words just won't do.

To introduce your new products, Ms. Robertson, we plan to develop a *good* television-advertising campaign. We will begin the campaign with *great* commercials aired during prime time. Our *fine* artists will develop *fantastic* graphics that will do a *really good* job of attracting viewers' attention.

Of course, there is nothing negative about *good, great, fine,* and so on. Quite the contrary! But will Ms. Robertson consider this campaign "special"? Will she willingly spend perhaps millions of dollars of her company's money on this *good* campaign? Will she easily be convinced that your *fine* artists will be successful? All too common and overused, these words no longer convey any special meanings.

Instead, consider these substitutes:

a *unique* or an *extraordinary* campaign

eye-catching, spellbinding, or *viewer-oriented* commercials

Our *talented, creative, and experienced* artists

will develop *startling computer-age* graphics

will do an *especially effective* job

If you were Ms. Robertson, which campaign would you rather pay for?

Here are some additional examples of overused words and suggested substitutes that could be used:

BEFORE	AFTER
a *bad* forecast	an *inaccurate* or a *misleading* forecast
a *good show*	a *compelling performance* or a *dramatic reenactment*
a *nice* supervisor	a *considerate,* a *well-respected,* or a *well-liked* supervisor
an *awful* record	a *deplorable* or an *inconsistent* record
clean offices	*spotless* offices

Develop an awareness of colorless words that you may tend to overuse. Remember that such words are not "wrong," but they are often not very effective either.

COMMUNICATION LABORATORY

APPLICATION EXERCISES

A. Practice your ability to distinguish between the *denotation* and the *connotation* of words. For each of the following words, write the dictionary definition (the word's denotation) on a separate sheet of paper. Then write your personal reaction to each word (its connotation).

1. summer
2. home
3. baseball
4. teapot
5. apple
6. beach
7. chalkboard
8. poodle

CONTINUED

B. Give at least one synonym for each italicized word. Consult a dictionary or a thesaurus if you need help in finding a good word to substitute.

1. This thermometer takes *exact* measurements.
2. The company *commemorates* the anniversary of its founding every year.
3. Every manager must *defend* his or her budget.
4. A salesperson must always *keep* a positive attitude.
5. Andrea offered a new *slant* on our sales problem.
6. *Speed* is to be avoided on some jobs.
7. We must all work together to *shape* a new advertising campaign.
8. Ms. Yamada likes her computer assistants to *test* every program.
9. Is there really a *choice?*
10. The company's decision to cut prices was *brave*.

C. Substitute a more precise adjective for the overworked *little* below.

1. a little town
2. a little locomotive
3. a little mind
4. a little kitten
5. a little matter
6. a little portion
7. a little wire
8. a little build
9. a little computer
10. a little issue

D. Change the following negative statements into positive statements.

1. Do not forget the sales meeting at the end of the month.
2. Don't fail to ship this order by airfreight.
3. You forgot to provide a delivery date.
4. We cannot deliver your order because our plant is closed until July 15.
5. Do not lower the product's quality.
6. Don't anger customers by being late for an appointment.
7. We cannot act on your request at this time.
8. We will not forget your special request.
9. We won't know our prices until April 1.
10. Never forget a customer's preferences.

E. Rewrite the following sentences to eliminate outdated or unpleasant expressions.

1. Kindly favor us with a note if we can help.
2. We are in receipt of your order of May 5, and we thank you for same.
3. Your shipping department's blunder caused us unbelievable trouble.
4. As per our recent discussion, attached hereto is our latest price list.
5. I have your letter under date of August 27.
6. Please be so kind as to find a photocopy of my canceled check.
7. We are forwarding the book you ordered under separate cover.
8. The order will arrive late due to the fact that the railroad is on strike.

CONTINUED

9. This is to acknowledge the receipt of your reservation.
10. We are crediting your account as per your wishes.

VOCABULARY AND SPELLING STUDIES

A. In each of the following groups, three of the four words have similar meanings. Which word is the intruder?

1. impartial, fervent, unbiased, objective
2. offend, entreat, beg, implore
3. blossom, bloom, forbid, flower
4. fabricate, fashion, shape, dodge
5. meddle, invent, interfere, tamper
6. revise, denounce, correct, remedy
7. coarse, gross, refined, crude
8. guarded, wary, watchful, open
9. exception, principle, rule, regulation
10. routine, customary, irregular, uniform
11. speculate, theorize, guess, validate
12. hide, disclose, communicate, tell
13. knowledge, learning, fiction, information
14. significant, meaningful, unimportant, serious
15. complicated, elementary, basic, pure

B. These words are often confused: *morning, mourning; hail, hale.* Explain the differences.

SECTION 6.2

WRITING EFFECTIVE SENTENCES

R ay Carlson has a better-than-average vocabulary. His spelling skills are superb. He has a firm grasp of the rules of grammar and is a good proofreader. Ray applies punctuation rules flawlessly, and he also knows how to format letters, memos, and reports.

Question: Why, then, do Ray's letters and memos sound childish, as if they had been written by a novice? *Answer:* Because his messages do not sound conversational, his sentences lack variety, his expressions are often too long, no thoughts receive any special emphasis, and his ideas are presented without subordination, as if every idea were equally important.

VARY SENTENCE PATTERNS

Ray wrote this letter this morning:

> We received your purchase order this morning. Thank you for ordering from us. We will give you the usual 25 percent discount. We will deliver the merchandise to your store on May 3. We will charge the entire cost to your account . . . .

Boring, isn't it? His message contains no errors in grammar or spelling, and all the facts expressed are correct. The sentences are all approximately the same length, and they use the same kind of sentence construction—the simple sentence. But its pattern of sentences is rigid and inflexible, the way a child might have written it. What gives this message its childish singsong flavor? Its lack of variety.

This monotone of simple sentences could easily be revised to add variety to the writing and to make reading more interesting:

> Thank you for your purchase order, which we received this morning. As usual, you will receive a 25 percent discount, and the total cost will be charged to your account. On May 3 we will deliver the merchandise to your store.

Only a few words are changed, but the *mix* of different sentence structures adds interest and movement to the message. Now it offers some variety and builds some momentum, enough to maintain the reader's interest from start to finish. Gone is the monotone!

Let's analyze the ways in which this revision achieves variety:

1. The first sentence expresses two ideas, one in an independent clause and the other in a dependent clause.

> Thank you for your purchase order,   ← **independent clause**
> which we received this morning.   ← **dependent clause**

2. The next sentence also joins two thoughts, but here the two thoughts are both treated as independent clauses in a compound sentence.

> As usual   ← **introductory phrase**
> you will receive a 25 percent discount,   ← **independent clause**
> and   ← **conjunction**
> the total cost will be charged to your account.   ← **independent clause**

The words *As usual,* which serve to introduce the sentence, add to the variety. The two independent clauses are joined by a conjunction, *and.*

3. The third sentence is a simple sentence (nothing "wrong" with simple sentences!), but it shines extra attention on the words *On May 3.* How? By positioning these key words at the beginning of the sentence. This minor change adds variety *and* emphasis.

As you continue reading this section, you will learn how to employ these and other techniques to help you write a variety of sentence patterns in your business messages.

EMPHASIZE KEY WORDS

When speaking face-to-face with someone, we use gestures, raise or lower our voices, point, and otherwise emphasize what we are saying. In writing, we can use visual devices such as underlining, all-capital letters, and boldface type. In addition to visual emphasis, experienced writers use more advanced, less obvious techniques to provide emphasis within a sentence.

One technique is to control sentence structure to stress the desired words. Depending on their objective, experienced writers can provide emphasis anywhere in the sentence. For example, in an effort to grab the reader's attention immediately and to convince her or him to read on, the writer of this sentence decided to emphasize the first words:

> *A special 45 percent discount*—that's what you will receive, Mr. Stetson, on your next order for Mercury office furniture.

The writer uses several techniques to draw attention to the words *a special 45 percent discount.* Positioning the key words at the beginning of the sentence and separating them from the rest of the sentence forcefully stresses these words. The dash signals a pause, and the pause, in turn, leaves the key words on stage by themselves, getting all the attention.

Did you notice that the sentence is not in normal order? (Normal order is "You will receive a . . . .") By detouring from the normal sentence order, the writer makes the key words stand out all the more. Furthermore, the italics (especially at the beginning of the sentence) have the effect of bright red paint— the italic type draws the reader's eye even before the words are read.

More often, however, the emphasis falls naturally at the end of the sentence.

> The committee members considered the experience of the candidates, evaluated the management potential of each man and woman, analyzed the ability of each to work harmoniously with coworkers, interviewed each candidate twice, and agreed unanimously that the best person for the position is Samantha Edwards.

The sentence is deliberately long. The lengthy sentence mirrors the lengthy process of choosing the right candidate. Also, the length of the sentence helps build suspense and, consequently, gives added emphasis to the final words, the name of the person selected. The reader discovers the "answer" only at the end of the sentence.

> Tomorrow's discussion will focus on the most important reason for accepting Ford Distribution's proposal: a *guaranteed* profit.

> The reason for the change in procedure is a vital one: to eliminate the miscommunication of recent months.

In these examples, once again, the emphasized words are at the end of the sentence. The colon adds to the emphatic effect by deliberately pointing to (and therefore highlighting) the key words.

COORDINATE AND SUBORDINATE IDEAS

A sentence may present one main idea, or it may contain two (or more) ideas. If the ideas are of equal importance, the writer indicates their equality by using a coordinating conjunction (*and, or, but,* or *nor*) to join the ideas.

REMEMBER: A coordinating conjunction joins elements of equal rank.

We must review this proposal, *and* we must complete our inventory analysis.

Harriet is scheduled to speak at the sales meeting in Denver, *but* Martin is scheduled to attend a seminar.

Each example lists two ideas that are equal in strength. The first sentence simply joins the two ideas with the conjunction *and.* The second sentence joins and contrasts two equal-weight ideas with the conjunction *but.*

An alternative way of expressing equal ideas is simply to join the two clauses with a semicolon (and no conjunction), as follows:

We must review this proposal; we must complete our inventory analysis.

Harriet is scheduled to speak at the sales meeting in Denver; Martin is scheduled to attend a seminar.

In some sentences, of course, the two ideas are not of equal weight. In such cases the writer must clearly label the subordinate idea by using a subordinating conjunction such as *because, since, when,* or *although.*

After we left the seminar, we discussed the negotiations with Ms. Halpern.

The subordinating conjunction *after* clearly labels *we left the seminar* as the subordinate clause. The main clause is *we discussed the negotiations with Ms. Halpern.* The conjunction *after* does more than merely *join* the clauses, however; it also specifies a certain *time relation* by telling what happened first.

The opposite time relation could have been indicated by using the conjunction *before.*

Before we left the seminar, we discussed the negotiations with Ms. Halpern.

In either case, with *after* or with *before,* the subordinating conjunction tells the reader "This is the subordinate clause." To understand better how subordinating conjunctions work, let's use the conjunction *and* to join these same clauses.

We left the seminar, and we discussed the negotiations with Ms. Halpern.

The *and* indicates that the two clauses are of equal weight—no time relation is expressed. Let's look at another example:

Because the deadline is March 15, Harold has been working diligently on the inventory report.

The subordinating conjunction *because* shows a cause-and-effect relationship between the subordinate clause, *the deadline is March 15,* and the main clause, *Harold has been working diligently on the inventory report.* In other words, the conjunction *because* tells the reader *the reason why* "Harold has been working diligently on the inventory report." It establishes a cause-and-effect relationship—something that the conjunction *and* cannot do satisfactorily:

> The deadline is March 15, *and* Harold has been working diligently on the inventory report.

Is there any valid *connection*, any special *relationship*, between these two clauses? Apparently not, because the writer merely strings them together with the conjunction *and*.

In the following examples, the subordinating conjunctions are italicized. As you read each sentence, try to determine the specific relationship that the subordinating conjunction indicates. Do you see why the writer did not use *and, or, but,* or *nor* to join these clauses?

> *Since* we bought this high-speed duplicator, we are saving about $250 a month.

> *Although* Marion was attending the shareholders' meeting, her assistant gathered the information for Ms. Haskells.

> *If* I receive another discount coupon, I will share it with you.

ACHIEVE A CONVERSATIONAL TONE

In the previous section you learned that pleasant, conversational words help foster positive business relations. Now you will see that word choice alone cannot guarantee a conversational tone; other factors, too, must be considered.

Prefer Active Voice   Writers generally prefer the active voice to communicate their thoughts directly and forcefully. In the active voice the subject is doing, has done, or will be doing the action. In the passive voice the action is being done to, has been done to, or will be done to the subject.

> Mel is coordinating the distribution of these important materials to the committee members.

The subject *Mel* is doing the action expressed by the verb *is coordinating*. This sentence illustrates the use of the active voice.

> The distribution of the materials to the committee members is being coordinated by Mel.

Now the subject is *distribution*, and the verb is *is being coordinated*. Note that the main verb is a past participle with a "being" verb helper. The sentence is, therefore, in the passive voice.

Read aloud the two sentences above to convince yourself that the first example is much more direct, more straightforward, more natural than the second example. Then, for additional examples, compare the pairs of sentences given on page 264.

Our supervisor prefers getting three estimates for all expenses over $1000. (Active voice)

Getting three estimates for all expenses over $1000 is preferred by our supervisor. (Passive voice)

Ms. Hahn conducted a comprehensive survey of all employees to get their responses on such issues. (Active voice)

A comprehensive survey of all employees was conducted by Ms. Hahn to get employees' responses on such issues. (Passive voice)

Most employees indicated a willingness to pay an additional premium for extended medical and dental coverage. (Active voice)

A willingness to pay an additional premium for extended medical and dental coverage was indicated by most employees. (Passive voice)

In each of the above pairs, the active voice is the better choice. You may wonder, Is the passive voice ever useful? Answer: Yes! For instance, many consumers would react negatively to the following sentence:

We will charge you a $10 fee for late payments.

This sentence stresses a negative idea, almost a threat that "we" will perform. A writer who is aware of the reader's potential reaction would never write such a threatening-sounding statement. And admittedly, the following passive-voice rephrasing is no better:

You will be charged a $10 fee for late payments.

Now, instead of the negative that "we" will do, the sentence emphasizes the negative that will happen to *you*. But there is another, better passive-voice alternative:

A $10 fee will be charged for late payments.

Because it is less personal—no *we*, no *you*—this statement is neither threatening nor negative. It is merely factual. For this reason passive-voice statements are often employed in reports in an effort to strip the reports of any personal bias, as in this sentence:

It was concluded that charge customers who participated in the survey strongly prefer changing the present credit policy.

Thus, as you see, the passive voice *does* serve a useful purpose.

Use Direct Address

In an earlier chapter you were introduced to *direct address*, citing the name of the person you are speaking to. What better way to make sentences sound "conversational" than to include the reader's name!

If you order 100,000 or more imprinted envelopes, *Ms. Johanson,* you will qualify for the quantity discount and for free storage in our warehouse.

Whenever you would like to meet with one of our representatives, *Tyrone,* please let us know.

Of course, *Mr. VanNostrand,* we will be glad to schedule an appointment at your convenience.

It is not surprising that in each case direct address contributes strongly to the conversational tone. Because you are including your reader's name in the sentence, direct address is an almost foolproof method for making sentences conversational. As a general rule, however, be sure to limit the use of the reader's name. Using the reader's name more than once in a paragraph will often appear phony.

CONTROL SENTENCE LENGTH

There is no "correct" or "ideal" length to set as a goal for sentences. A 10-word sentence is too long if it contains unnecessary words. A 50-word sentence is too short if it omits important information. As a result, the careful writer checks every sentence in an effort to cut any repetitive or unneeded words.

All of us here at Quality Crafted Products Inc. sincerely thank you for placing your order with us for an Allied Quality Crafted motor.

This type of sentence may often appear in business letters—that is, in *poor* business letters. To begin, the words *here at Quality Crafted Products Inc.* and *with us* are clearly extra and should be cut. The words *All of us* are not wrong, but they could easily be replaced by a straightforward *We* ("We sincerely thank . . ."). In fact, the writer could simply say, "Thank you for . . ." without seriously affecting the courteous tone or the meaning of the sentence. Also, how about replacing the words *for placing your order . . . for* so that the sentence reads "thank you *for ordering*"?

As you can see, the example sentence could be shortened—without loss of meaning—as follows:

Thank you for ordering an Allied Quality Crafted motor.

Let's look at another example:

When we meet with the managers of our branch offices from the Eastern Region, we must be sure to elicit from them as part of our discussion what they think is the best way to improve productivity.

Compare the above sentence with the revision that follows:

When we meet with the Eastern Region branch managers, we must elicit their suggestions to improve productivity.

The goal is *not* to write the shortest sentences possible. The goal *is* to eliminate unnecessary words, words that add nothing to the meaning and the impact of the sentence. The goal is to control sentence length and offer variety.

The length of a sentence can be deliberately long or deliberately short to create a special effect. For example, a longer sentence helps emphasize key words positioned at the end of the sentence. Another technique is to position a very short sentence after one or more rather long sentences—or vice versa. Examples of both these techniques are discussed in the next section.

BALANCE SENTENCE PARTS

Various elements within a sentence must be treated in parallel fashion—they must be *balanced*. Imagine, for example, writing the numbers *1, 2,* and *III*. A striking imbalance results because two arabic numerals are mixed with a roman numeral. Like elements should be treated in a like manner. To be balanced, all three numbers should be consistent (either all arabic or all roman).

Balance Articles
In a series the article *a* may be expressed only once (before the first item) but "understood" before each subsequent item.

> We need the approval of *a* branch manager, regional manager, or vice president.

It is not necessary to say "*a* regional manager, or *a* vice president." Expressed before the first item, the *a* is understood before the other items in the series.

However, only *a*—not *an*—is "understood."

> We need the approval of *a* branch manager, *a* regional manager, or *an* assistant vice president.

Because *both* articles, *a* and *an,* are required, the correct article must be expressed before *each* item in the series.

Similarly, repeating the article *the* is sometimes essential to the meaning of a sentence:

> She already has the approval of *the* vice president and general manager.

She has the approval of *one person:* that person is "the vice president and general manager." To indicate that *vice president* and *general manager* are *two* different people, repeat the article *the* before *general manager:*

> She already has the approval of *the* vice president and *the* general manager.

Balance Verbs
The verb phrases *will go* and *will attend* share a common element, *will.* In the following sentence, note that *will* is expressed only once, in the first verb phrase, but it is understood in the second verb phrase: "and *will*) attend."

> Ms. Hennessy *will go* to Seattle and *attend* the computer conference.

Now note this common trap:

> We never have, and probably never will, recommend such investments.

The sentence attempts to shorten "We never have recommended, and probably never will recommend, such investments." However, the verb phrases do not share any common elements. The first phrase is "have recommended";

the second is "will recommend." By omitting *recommended,* the writer falls into the trap and forces the first phrase to share an element from the second. The result is "We never have . . . *recommend,*" which is obviously wrong.

Balance Prepositions

You have already learned the need to team certain prepositions with certain words. In Section 4.8, for example, you learned the distinction between "waiting *for* someone" and "waiting *on* a customer."

Two other examples are "respect *for*" and "belief *in*." Watch what happens when the writer tries to share *one* preposition for both purposes:

We have great respect and belief in that organization's policies.

What happened to "respect *for*"? By dropping *for,* the writer forces *in* to substitute so that "great respect *in* . . ." is understood. But *in* is wrong. The sentence, of course, should be:

We have great respect *for* and belief *in* that organization's policies.

Here's another example:

Each executive should strive to listen and work closely *with* his or her staff.

The meaning is "should strive to listen *to* . . . his or her staff." By dropping *to,* the writer incorrectly forces *with* to substitute. Be sure to balance prepositions precisely.

Balance Comparisons

Words are just as frequently omitted in comparisons. As a result, lopsided sentences occur:

Our vice president appreciates your efforts just as much, and maybe more, than I do.

The sentence *should* say "just as much *as* . . . I do." But by dropping *as,* the writer creates "just as much . . . *than* I do," and this, of course, makes no sense.

Whenever you see comparisons using *as* or *than,* be alert for such possible omissions.

The following sentence is correct. Can you identify which word in this sentence is expressed once and is then "understood" later in the sentence?

Her manager attends more sales conventions than my manager.

The verb *attends* is understood at the end of the sentence, after "than my manager (*attends*)." But note that *attends*—and only *attends*—can be "understood."

Her manager attends more sales conventions than the other managers.

Now the sentence reads "than the other managers (*attends*)," and the understood verb is wrong. The plural *managers* now requires *attend.*

Her manager attends more sales conventions than the other managers attend.

The "understood" verb in such sentences must be the *same* verb that is expressed, not a form of that verb.

Balance Clauses

In clauses imbalances may occur either as a result of omissions or as a result of careless positioning of words—sometimes resulting in ludicrous sentences.

> Did Martha lose the check or her supervisor?

> Ask Bill if he can handle this project or his assistant.

The first sentence asks, "Did Martha lose . . . her supervisor?" And the second sentence questions Bill's ability to "handle . . . his assistant." Neither sentence is correct. Possible revisions include:

> Did Martha lose the check, or did her supervisor lose it? *or* Did Martha or her supervisor lose the check?

> Ask Bill if he or his assistant can handle this project.

AVOID COMMON ERRORS

To close this section on effective sentences, let's review some of the most common problems that trap business writers—even *experienced* business writers.

Indefinite Pronouns

As a *writer*, you always know what your pronoun references should refer to, but the *reader* is sometimes puzzled by an *it* or a *they* that appears without a clear prior referent. For example:

> Ms. Blair said to call Personnel and ask *them* for a copy of the report.

The sentence contains no plural word that *them* could correctly refer to. For clarity, say instead:

> Ms. Blair said to ask someone in Personnel for a copy of the report.

Let's look at another example:

> We have been working on the annual inventory report and the product catalog since January, and *it* is very difficult.

What does *it* refer to? The inventory report? The catalog? January? Perhaps the sentence should be:

> We have been working on the annual inventory report and the product catalog since January, and handling both projects at once is very difficult.

In the following example, note how the word *this* betrays fuzzy thinking on the writer's part:

> When our primary supplier is out of stock, we now order from another source. *This* had caused us problems in the past.

What does *this* refer to? Here is one way to avoid the *this* confusion:

> When our primary supplier is out of stock, we now order from another source. In the past, waiting for the primary supplier caused us problems.

A very common error, especially in speaking, is illustrated below:

> *They say* that the market for personal computers will show a remarkable increase next year.

Who is *they?* Such statements bear no weight and have no merit. Instead, cite a specific source, one that will lend credibility to the statement.

> Industry analysts (*or* computer experts *or* salespeople *or* manufacturers) predict that the market for personal computers will show a remarkable increase next year.

That and *Which* Clauses

A *that* clause presents essential information and is therefore *not* separated from the rest of the sentence.

> The district *that* is first in sales this year is the one managed by the team in the Dayton office.

The clause *that is first in sales this year* is critical to the meaning of the sentence. Rather than provide extra information, this clause identifies *one* district out of several possibilities. The clause is essential, therefore, to understanding the sentence. Remember, then, not to separate essential clauses from the rest of the sentence.

Which clauses are *non*essential and *are* separated (by commas) from the rest of the sentence.

> Next Monday my supervisor and I will visit our Dayton office, *which* manages the number-one district in the country, to discuss the new strategy.

Which refers to *Dayton office;* because the *which* clause presents nonessential information, it is separated by commas from the rest of the sentence.

Also, be sure to avoid using a *which* clause to refer to an entire sentence or an entire thought.

> The high estimated retooling cost will be addressed at our meeting on Thursday, *which* is of major concern to all of us.

The position of the *which* clause might mislead the reader into thinking that *Thursday* (or even *our meeting on Thursday*) "is of major concern to all of us." But the "concern" is really for the *cost.* The sentence should be revised to draw a clear relationship between the *which* clause and a specific word in the sentence.

> The high estimated retooling cost, *which* is of major concern to all of us, will be addressed at our meeting on Thursday.

Clear writing reflects clear thinking, and clear thinking is highly valued in the business world. Review the guidelines and techniques in this section to ensure that you can write effective sentences.

COMMUNICATION LABORATORY

APPLICATION EXERCISES

A. Rewrite the following sentences. As you do so, vary your sentence patterns, provide emphasis as needed, and coordinate and subordinate ideas properly. (Add any details needed to make your answers realistic.)

1. The Seattle store now leads all our other stores in total sales. The Seattle store opened only last year.
2. Ms. Breskin joined our staff in April 1991. Ms. Breskin had been a manager for Stearns, Markham & Ulster. Stearns, Markham & Ulster is a well-known accounting firm.
3. The first training session will be held on March 19, and the second training session will be held on August 3. The lecturer for the first session will be Jay Haggerty, and the lecturer for the second session will be Pamela Claye. The first session will be held in Room 2205, and the second session will be held in Room 2360.
4. You placed an order for 50,000 envelopes. We received the purchase order yesterday. You specified that you need the envelopes by April 5. We will ship the entire order to you by truck no later than April 1.
5. We now have more than 300 orders to be processed. Bill and Jane are both on vacation this week. Dan has the flu. He has been out of the office too. That leaves only six order processors handling the entire load. We need temporary help.
6. We must complete this inventory analysis by March 30. Our manager needs the inventory information for her report due April 4.
7. The panel recommended Ellen Simon as a consultant. Ms. Simon is a well-respected attorney. Her office is in Rochester, New York.
8. I want to attend the Chicago sales meeting. Evelyn wants to attend the Denver sales meeting.
9. Frank received an excellent raise. He is responsible for winning the Henderson account.
10. We have planned our project carefully. We are confident that we will finish the project on schedule.

B. Rewrite the following sentences to make them conform to the principles you learned in this section. (Add any details needed to make your answers realistic.)

1. The review of the estimates for accuracy will be handled by me.
2. Per your recent request for an updated new catalog of our products, enclosed please find same.
3. It is suggested by me that we place a classified ad for an experienced consultant, a man who knows about computer training.

CONTINUED

4. They say that this new product will likely be a big success.
5. At the present time, plans for revising the procedures manual have not been formally approved by the company's Policy Committee.
6. One of the sessions at the upcoming conference—time management—is especially interesting to me because it is a really important topic to everyone in business.
7. If you need help with this computer software, ask someone in the Finance Department. They will be glad to help.
8. John never has, and probably never will, learn accurate keyboarding.
9. Emily and Corazan have no appreciation or interest in highly speculative investments.
10. Ask one of the product managers if they can help us complete these product analysis forms.
11. Finally we found the memo that she had written on the floor.
12. Barry and Helen conduct more training sessions than she.
13. Do you know whether Ms. Owens went to Albany or Mr. Barkley?
14. If they are interested in this new service, a customer should call this toll-free number.
15. Due to the fact that the invoice date was entered incorrectly, one of our fellow employees in the Accounts Payable Department rejected the aforementioned invoice and returned it to us for approval.
16. All of us want to improve the efficiency of this department's handling of schedules, which is our goal.
17. It is strongly recommended, Mr. Gibson, that you consider our service contract before the expiration of your warranty, which is certainly a bargain at only $25 a year.
18. An eagerness to begin the challenging project was evident among the employees with whom I work.
19. A reply from you before the ninth of next month as to your ability to accept our invitation will be most appreciated.
20. We are now studying several discount policies that we consider attractive to customers, because it will mean more business for us.

VOCABULARY AND SPELLING STUDIES

A. How are the following words spelled when the suffixes indicated are added?

1. direct- or
2. mile- age
3. prefer- ed
4. perform- ance
5. sunny- er
6. shake- y
7. jealous- y
8. true- ly
9. forget- ing
10. know- ledge

CONTINUED

B. Which words in the following groups are misspelled? Respell the misspelled words correctly.

1. ment, apply, sought, sord
2. ferce, gallon, chanel, panel
3. lawyer, maner, wisper, tennis
4. ballance, relief, secure, acept
5. document, difficult, paralel, citys
6. atractive, storege, reveal, similar
7. grammar, iner, conect, admire
8. suggest, discous, oppose, confus
9. shalow, polish, selfish, sesion
10. decrese, obtain, occupy, ocur

C. Add a suffix pronounced *shun* to each of the following.

1. miss _____
2. men _____
3. mo _____
4. cau _____
5. satisfac _____
6. affec _____
7. instruc _____
8. except _____
9. explor _____

D. Choose *ize, ise,* or *yze* to complete each of the following.

1. notar _____
2. anal _____
3. advert _____
4. adv _____
5. disgu _____
6. rev _____
7. critic _____
8. organ _____
9. exerc _____

E. How are the following spelled when the *uhble*-sounding suffix is added?

1. respons _____
2. cap _____
3. imposs _____
4. vis _____
5. wash _____
6. pass _____
7. sens _____
8. lov _____
9. reli _____

F. Which of the following words ending with the sound of *seed* are misspelled? Spell them correctly.

1. proced
2. succeed
3. exced
4. receed
5. sede (yield or grant)
6. intercede
7. conceed
8. secede
9. superceed
10. acceed

JOINING SENTENCES INTO PARAGRAPHS

I made this copy for you of a recent memo from Jacob Carwright," Fred said as he passed a page over to his manager, Constance Greco. "Fred," she responded, "it's two pages of one endless paragraph, from first page to second, with no breaks! Is it worth reading?" "Believe it or not, Jake has several good ideas, but frankly it is hard to get over the imposing look of the one long solid block of copy."

PARAGRAPH GUIDELINES

Just as words are combined to form a sentence, so, too, are sentences combined to form a paragraph. A **paragraph,** therefore, is a group of related sentences joined for a specific purpose and separated from the rest of the message. The key words, which you will see as we proceed, are *related* and *specific*.

To begin, note that there are no rules concerning paragraph development—only *guidelines*. For most routine business letters, memos, and reports, try to use the following guidelines:

1. Control—and *vary*—paragraph length.
2. Group *related* sentences in each paragraph.
3. Create a logical sequence of sentences.
4. Use transitional devices as necessary to strengthen the link from one sentence to another.

Let's review each of these guidelines.

CONTROL PARAGRAPH LENGTH

There is no "correct" or "ideal" length for an effective paragraph. Successful writers deliberately manipulate paragraph length, just as they manipulate sentence length, in an effort to create certain effects. As a result, a "good" paragraph may be 10, 15, or more lines long, or it may be only 1 line long. More often, of course, a paragraph is neither extremely long nor extremely short. Whenever possible, try to limit the maximum length of a paragraph to about 8 lines.

WORLD VIEW

In a Moscow hotel, this sign greeted English-speaking visitors: "You are welcome to visit the cemetery where famous Russian . . . composers, artists, and writers are buried daily except Thursday."

How *late* do they bury?

Controlling the Number and Length of Paragraphs

Before we discuss the *content* of the paragraph, let's look more closely at the *visual effect* of paragraphs. The length of each paragraph in a letter, memo, or report contributes to the impact of that message on the reader. Compare the three letters shown on pages 274–276. The content of all three letters—both the wording and the sentence sequence—is the same. Only the paragraphing of each letter is different. As a result, the visual impact of each letter differs.

Family Investments, Inc.

1200 Broad Street ■ Santa Monica, CA 93454

310-555-6000   (FAX) 310-555-8329

March 15, 19--

Ms. Thelma P. Mancuso
1200 North Sheridan
Valencia, CA 91355

Dear Ms. Mancuso:

Finding and choosing the "right" investment may be a tough decision for you. After all, you work hard for your money, and you want to invest it wisely. Safety, of course, is an important consideration. A _very_ important consideration! But at the same time, you'd like to get high interest on your investment. You'd also like to take advantage of some of the tax-free investments that you keep hearing about, but how do you go about choosing the municipal bond that is best for you? Do you simply select the highest interest rate? Or do you choose the bond with the highest rating? Should you simply deposit your money in a savings bank, despite the low interest rates? Or should you . . . ?

Yes, there _are_ many options available. Since 1955 nearly 375,000 investors like you have opted to place their savings in the Watson Prime Reserve Bond Fund. The Watson PRB Fund has consistently yielded high interest rates and has met the highest safety standards for preserving investors' principal. In fact, the Watson PRB Fund has set several "records" in the investment community for consistent high yields and safety. In addition, the interest earned from the Watson PRB Fund is completely tax-free. Suddenly, making the "right" investment decision is as simple as calling us (toll-free) for a free information packet: 800-555-6000.

Sincerely,

Janet P. Hare
Vice President

rw

Two solid blocks of copy have a negative effect on the reader. Compare the visual effect of this letter with the appearance of the letter on page 275.

The first letter (page 274) consists of two long paragraphs—two solid blocks of copy that certainly do nothing to encourage the reader to continue. The paragraphs have a forbidding look. For most readers this letter will be as inviting as a *very* long book on a *very* dull subject. Such solid blocks of copy have a negative effect on the reader.

At the other extreme is the message illustrated below. Instead of just two overly long paragraphs, the same sentences are now divided into too many

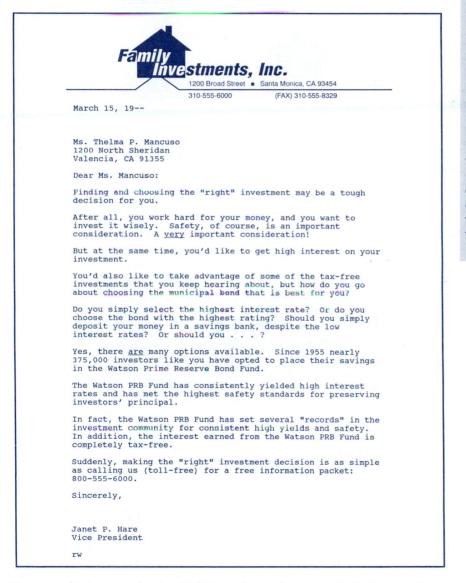

Family Investments, Inc.

1200 Broad Street ▪ Santa Monica, CA 93454
310-555-6000   (FAX) 310-555-8329

March 15, 19--

Ms. Thelma P. Mancuso
1200 North Sheridan
Valencia, CA 91355

Dear Ms. Mancuso:

Finding and choosing the "right" investment may be a tough decision for you.

After all, you work hard for your money, and you want to invest it wisely. Safety, of course, is an important consideration. A very important consideration!

But at the same time, you'd like to get high interest on your investment.

You'd also like to take advantage of some of the tax-free investments that you keep hearing about, but how do you go about choosing the municipal bond that is best for you?

Do you simply select the highest interest rate? Or do you choose the bond with the highest rating? Should you simply deposit your money in a savings bank, despite the low interest rates? Or should you . . . ?

Yes, there are many options available. Since 1955 nearly 375,000 investors like you have opted to place their savings in the Watson Prime Reserve Bond Fund.

The Watson PRB Fund has consistently yielded high interest rates and has met the highest safety standards for preserving investors' principal.

In fact, the Watson PRB Fund has set several "records" in the investment community for consistent high yields and safety. In addition, the interest earned from the Watson PRB Fund is completely tax-free.

Suddenly, making the "right" investment decision is as simple as calling us (toll-free) for a free information packet: 800-555-6000.

Sincerely,

Janet P. Hare
Vice President

rw

Too many short paragraphs give this letter a choppy, fragmented look. Compare the visual effect of this letter with the appearance of the letter on page 276.

short paragraphs. Perhaps the writer, in an effort to avoid scaring the reader with solid blocks of copy, overcompensated.

Whatever the reason, the result of too many short paragraphs is just as disastrous as the result of very long paragraphs. Broken into so many small pieces, the letter has a choppy appearance. It has all the visual appeal of a shopping list. The content, too, suffers: Rather than presenting related ideas logically, the letter challenges the reader to make sense of the message, as if it were a puzzle.

Family Investments, Inc.

1200 Broad Street ■ Santa Monica, CA 93454

310-555-6000   (FAX) 310-555-8329

March 15, 19--

Ms. Thelma P. Mancuso
1200 North Sheridan
Valencia, CA 91355

Dear Ms. Mancuso:

Finding and choosing the "right" investment may be a tough
decision for you. After all, you work hard for your money,
and you want to invest it wisely.

Safety, of course, is an important consideration. A _very_
important consideration! But at the same time, you'd like to
get high interest on your investment. You'd also like to
take advantage of some of the tax-free investments that you
keep hearing about, but how do you go about choosing the
municipal bond that is best for you? Do you simply select
the highest interest rate? Or do you choose the bond with
the highest rating? Should you simply deposit your money in
a savings bank, despite the low interest rates? Or should
you . . . ?

Yes, there _are_ many options available.

Since 1955 nearly 375,000 investors like you have opted to
place their savings in the Watson Prime Reserve Bond Fund.
The Watson PRB Fund has consistently yielded high interest
rates and has met the highest safety standards for preserving
investors' principal. In fact, the Watson PRB Fund has set
several "records" in the investment community for consistent
high yields and safety. In addition, the interest earned
from the Watson PRB Fund is completely tax-free.

Suddenly, making the "right" investment decision is as simple
as calling us (toll-free) for a free information packet:
800-555-6000.

Sincerely,

Janet P. Hare
Vice President
rw

Short opening and closing paragraphs with longer middle paragraphs combine to create an easy-to-read letter.

There is nothing wrong with a short paragraph, even a one-sentence-long paragraph. But several or many consecutive short paragraphs give the message a fragmented appearance.

The paragraphing of the third letter, shown on page 276, is certainly an improvement. It offers no solid block of copy to scare away readers. Instead, the letter is divided into several paragraphs, each presenting one part of the total message.

Note that this letter contains two very short paragraphs, each one sentence long. The writer deliberately uses these short paragraphs to create a special effect. The first, "Yes, there *are* many options available," is positioned between the two longest paragraphs in the letter. Sandwiching this one-sentence paragraph between the two long paragraphs has a double effect: (1) the short sentence enhances the visual impact of the letter and (2) emphasis is placed on the content of this important sentence because the sentence is on center stage.

The last paragraph also consists of only one sentence. It is especially effective because its wording reminds the reader of the first sentence of the letter ("Finding and choosing the `right' investment . . ."). Together, the paragraphs in the third example contribute positively to the visual appeal of the letter.

As you see, then, paragraphing affects the visual impact of your message. For polished writing, control the number and the length of paragraphs in your letters, memos, and reports.

Paragraphing E-Mail Although the preceding guidelines on paragraph length are certainly effective in writing typical business messages, they do *not* apply to electronic mail (*E-mail,* for short)—short notes written on and relayed by a computer. Let's see why.

In today's office, as well as today's home, many businesspeople communicate by computers *networked* (connected) to other computers. Their E-mail messages are exchanged from computer to computer—and therefore to other *people.* The "other people" may be on the same floor as the sender, or (thanks to the use of telephone lines) they may be thousands of miles away. E-mail messages are most often interoffice memos that are read *on screen.* The receiver may print a copy if he or she wishes.

For many reasons E-mail messages are brief:

1. First of all, the purpose of electronic messaging is direct, straightforward communication, and direct communication is best achieved through brevity.

2. E-mail messages are almost always interoffice memos, written from one employee to another. Less formality is required for interoffice communications.

3. Computer time is valuable. Shorter messages require less writing time and less reading time, freeing the computer for other uses and promoting greater office productivity.

4. Screen space is limited to a certain number of characters across the screen and a certain number of lines down the screen. As a result, just as "paper efficiency" in the office requires that routine memos be written on *one* page, "computer efficiency" demands that E-mail messages be written on *one* screen.

5. Many E-mail messages are relayed over telephone lines, and telephone time is costly.

6. E-mail messages usually *stay* "electronic." Although they can be printed and filed, they usually are not. As a result, E-mail messages *very* strongly emphasize the need to communicate specific information very directly.

Family Investments, Inc.

1200 Broad Street ■ Santa Monica, CA 93454

310-555-6000   (FAX) 310-555-8329

```
MEMO TO:   District Managers    FROM:  Georgine Klein
           Regional Managers           Sales Information Department
           Product Managers

SUBJECT:   July Sales Report    DATE:  July 21, 19--


I know that all of you are eager to see the July sales report for
several reasons.  First of all, sales for our two new stores will
be included.  Furthermore, July is always our greatest revenue
month.  Moreover, our Fourth of July sale is our biggest of the
year.

In an effort to provide you with printouts of the July sales
report before the usual date (August 15), we will assemble all
the data, print the report, and distribute copies by August 7.
I know that some of you are busy working on your sales estimates
for next year.  If you must have a hard copy of the July report
before August 7 to finish your estimates, call my assistant,
Abigail Fromme.  Abigail will try to provide you with a hard
copy.  By the way, while the copies are being printed and
distributed, you can call the Sales Information Department for
any specific sales data you may need.

Call me or Abigail if you have any question or problem.  We will
be glad to help.

lem
```

This memorandum was prepared on an electronic typewriter and distributed manually.

For these reasons, then, E-mail is usually one paragraph long—in fact, usually no longer than 50 words. To see the specific differences between paper memos and E-mail messages, read the memo on page 278. It was prepared on an electronic typewriter and distributed manually.

When Georgine wrote and distributed the memo on page 278, her company had not yet installed its sophisticated computer system. Now, when Georgine needs to communicate essential information to people within her company, she uses E-mail to write a *short* message. Today, Georgine would write that same message as follows:

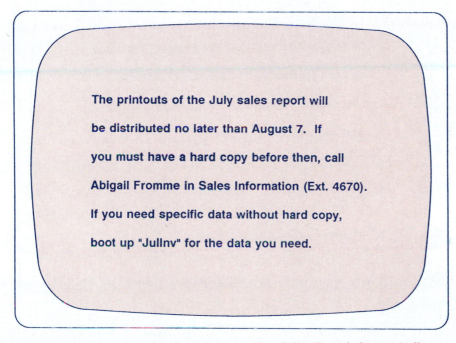

The printouts of the July sales report will

be distributed no later than August 7. If

you must have a hard copy before then, call

Abigail Fromme in Sales Information (Ext. 4670).

If you need specific data without hard copy,

boot up "JulInv" for the data you need.

This memorandum (48 words) was prepared and distributed electronically. Like this message, other electronic transmissions must be brief, direct, and to the point.

Georgine's message is short—under 50 words. She can transmit this message from her computer terminal to the terminals of the 34 other people in her company who need this information. Most of the other people are located in the same building; the rest are located in branch offices throughout the country. The computers that are in the same building are directly wired to Georgine's computer. The computers located in the branch offices use telephone lines to relay and receive messages.

If this sounds "futuristic," it is *not*. Many companies and many individuals are now sending messages by computer, as Georgine now does.

Another example of a typical E-mail message is shown on page 280.

The E-mail message shown below gives information that is both straightforward and brief. Because it is directed to other employees, it does not need to be formal. Further, this message meets the need for "computer efficiency" because it is written on one screen.

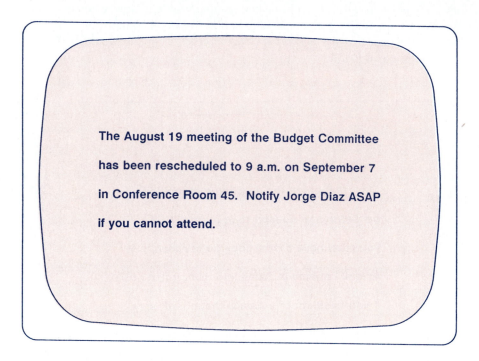

The August 19 meeting of the Budget Committee

has been rescheduled to 9 a.m. on September 7

in Conference Room 45. Notify Jorge Diaz ASAP

if you cannot attend.

REMEMBER: When writing a message that will be transmitted electronically, keep it short!

GROUP RELATED SENTENCES

Earlier we mentioned that a paragraph consists of *related* sentences. Read, for instance, the following letter—a direct, straightforward response to a request. As you do so, note how sentences within each paragraph are related.

Thank you for calling for information on Federal Savings & Loan's new Home Equity Loan Service. We have enclosed the application forms required.

Ms. DePalma, only Federal S&L can boast that it has approved more home-equity loans than any other bank in Greene County. In fact, in the past twelve months Federal S&L has approved more than $23 million in home-equity and home-improvement loans to your neighbors here in Greene County. That's why our motto is "Helping Our Community."

As you complete the application forms, please call me if you should need any information or have any questions. I will be delighted to assist you.

Most straightforward, direct letters such as this one follow a three-paragraph plan: The first paragraph is an introduction. The second paragraph discusses business details. The third paragraph is the close.

Now let's look more closely at the content of each paragraph.

1. In the opening paragraph, the first sentence identifies the purpose of the letter (to respond to the reader's "calling for information"). The second sentence informs the reader that the application forms she wants are enclosed. Thus both sentences are related.

   (Technically, the first paragraph gives the reader all the information she requested. But the writer wants to do more than send the reader her forms. The writer wants to take advantage of this opportunity to sell the reader—to convince her to deal with Federal S&L. The writer devotes the entire second paragraph to this purpose.)

2. The sentences in the second paragraph are also related. Each sentence gently "sells" the reader on the benefits of getting a home-equity loan from this particular bank.

3. In the third paragraph both sentences combine to strengthen the image of Federal S&L as a friendly, helpful bank. Together, these two sentences provide a goodwill statement to end the letter.

What if the reader had called for information on *two* subjects—say, a home-equity loan *and* interest rates on certificates of deposit (CDs)? The writer would then create a separate paragraph (devoted to CDs, of course) positioned *before* the closing paragraph.

CREATE A LOGICAL SEQUENCE OF SENTENCES

A sentence in which the words are jumbled presents the reader with a puzzle:

For Allied Industries I have for ten years worked.

With little effort we can easily assemble the pieces properly to form "I have worked for Allied Industries for ten years." The difficulty of solving such puzzles depends on the number of words and how jumbled they are. This puzzle was rather simple.

Whether the puzzle itself is difficult to solve or not, any sentence with jumbled words is rather easy to *identify* because it always sounds awkward. But when sentences within a paragraph are out of sequence, readers may not realize that they face a puzzle. Consequently, the effect of jumbled sentences is worse because readers may not quickly *identify* the problem.

In other words, writing and assembling related sentences within a paragraph does not guarantee effectiveness. Even if all sentences are related, the sentences must be arranged in a logical sequence—in the order that will best communicate the intended message. For most routine messages, the best arrangement results from the *direct approach*.

The Direct Approach

In a paragraph organized according to the *direct* approach, the first sentence opens immediately with the main idea, and the following sentences then present supporting facts.

> We are seeking authorization to hire (before May 15) at least three additional full-time clerks in the Order Department. As you know, the Order Department now processes an average of about 4000 orders each month—25 percent more than last year. Furthermore, during our busy summer season we receive as many as 5500 orders each month. Moreover, the Order Department now employs fewer full-time clerks (only 14) than were on staff last year (17). To handle both our present high volume and the expected increase in volume, we will surely need additional clerical help.

The approach is obviously straightforward. Using the direct approach, the writer (1) bluntly states the request first and then (2) provides the supporting details, the reasons for the request. Of course, busy executives prefer receiving memos that are direct and factual.

Sometimes there is no "main" sentence. For example, if you were explaining how to assemble a motor, you would follow a direct approach; each sentence in the step-by-step sequence would be equally important. Likewise, in the following chronological arrangement of sentences, there is no main sentence:

> As the enclosed agenda shows, the workshop will begin at 8:45 a.m. Mona Roberts, my assistant, will introduce the speakers, beginning with Claire Reynolds, who will discuss "Time Management" from 9 until 10:30 a.m. After a 30-minute refreshment break, William Cohen will discuss "Project Planning Techniques" from 11 a.m. until 12:30. Then, from 12:30 until 2 p.m., during the luncheon, we will . . . .

Unless you have special objectives, using the direct approach generally results in the most effective organization for routine business letters, memos, and short reports.

The Indirect Approach

For certain sensitive writing assignments (saying "no" to a request, for example), the direct approach will be too tough—harsh enough to lose a customer or annoy a coworker. Beginning the main paragraph with a sentence that says "No, we cannot grant your request" is seldom the best way to gain new and keep old clients!

Using the indirect approach, the writer (1) discusses the relevant facts first and then (2) announces the final decision—the reverse of the direct-approach pattern. By leading up to the sensitive part of the paragraph, the writer softens the blow. Further, by citing the supporting details first, the writer shows that the decision follows logically and naturally from the facts presented.

> The July issue of *Consumers' Monthly* said that B&G Electronics "has the best returns policy in the electronics industry." Indeed, most stores accept returns on merchandise purchased within 30 days, but B&G accepts returns *within 90 days*. Because you purchased your Masters VCR more than ten months ago,

Mr. Hastings, we cannot accept this return. Fortunately, however, since your VCR is still under the manufacturer's warranty, you may send it to the authorized Masters service center nearest you.

If the paragraph opened bluntly with "No, we will not allow you to return the VCR," B&G Electronics might have lost a customer (however unreasonable his request). Instead, the writer develops a reasonable argument, listing first the reasons why and then announcing the decision. Note how the argument gains momentum with each sentence until, finally, the last sentence tells the reader he has only one recourse: send the VCR to a service center.

When faced with sensitive issues (whether the reader is wrong or not), use the indirect approach. Doing so will help you maintain good customer and coworker relations!

USE TRANSITIONAL EXPRESSIONS

A basic goal of paragraph development is to separate a message into manageable parts, each part consisting of related sentences arranged in a logical sequence. But whenever you separate a written message into parts, you must help the reader see how those parts are related.

Certain words and expressions provide bright beams of light to show the reader specifically how parts are related. We call these special tools *transitional words and expressions.*

A **transition** is a word or a phrase that serves as a special connective between two things. Thus a transitional word or phrase is a signal light that shines on the writer's map, leading the reader smoothly from one place to another. Without transitions the reader travels in the dark!

Among the many transitional words and expressions that are popular and effective are the following:

accordingly	first	nevertheless
after all	for example	on the contrary
again	for instance	on the other hand
also	further	otherwise
as a result	furthermore	similarly
at the same time	however	still
besides	in addition	then
consequently	meanwhile	therefore
finally	moreover	yet

As you will see, transitions are indeed important to clear writing. Transitions can be used to show a sequence of steps (*first, then, finally*), to contrast thoughts (*however, on the other hand, nevertheless*), to add emphasis (*again, in addition, moreover*), and so on.

Below you will see how transitions work. Because they carry the reader smoothly from one idea to another, transitions are useful (1) within a sentence, (2) between sentences, and (3) between paragraphs.

Within a Sentence

Read the following sentences—then *re*read them without the italicized transitions. When the transitions are dropped, do the sentences convey the same message?

> The entire staff worked overtime; *nevertheless,* we were unable to process all the back orders.

> She discussed the causes of the problem; *then* she explained the reasons for each.

> The estimated cost was exceptionally high; *therefore,* we decided to scrap the project.

> Ms. Gelden prefers using the same marketing strategy; *on the other hand,* Mr. Forster strongly advocates changing our policy.

> Our supervisor is reviewing our travel-expense budgets; *similarly,* she is checking estimated costs of all major projects.

Without the transition each sentence is still grammatically correct; however, without the transition each sentence seems to be "missing something." The transition serves to bridge the two ideas expressed in each sentence.

Between Sentences

Transitions work the same magic between sentences within a paragraph.

> The committee members carefully analyzed the problem. *First,* we asked all sales representatives for their suggestions. *Then* we scheduled meetings with each branch manager. *Finally,* we developed a questionnaire for our customers.

First, then, finally—these three words provide excellent transitions from one sentence to the next.

Between Paragraphs

Paragraphs are the major subdivisions of the typical letter, memo, or short report. The relation between paragraphs, too, must always be clear to the reader.

> Last July the Research Department conducted a survey of all charge-card customers. One surprising result of that survey was the discovery that nearly 72 percent of our customers labeled our returns policy "unfair."

> *Naturally,* all of us are concerned that so many valuable customers have clearly indicated such a negative response to our long-standing policy against returning any merchandise 30 days or more after the purchase date. *Consequently,* a special committee was appointed to review the problem and submit recommendations for solving customers' dissatisfaction.

> *As a result,* effective next January 1, Smithson Discount Stores' returns policy will be changed as follows: . . . .

The italicized transitions here plainly label the relationship between sentences and paragraphs. Let's look at how each transition accomplishes its task.

1. *Naturally* carries the reader smoothly from the end of the first paragraph to the beginning of the second. Note how *naturally* provides the perfect bridge between these two statements: (1) "our customers labeled our returns policy 'unfair,'" and (2) "all of us are concerned . . . ." (The words *of course* could have done the same job.) In other words, *naturally* helps show a cause-and-effect relationship between the statement at the end of the first paragraph and the statement that begins the second paragraph. It shows that it is *natural* to be "concerned" in such a situation.

2. The transition *consequently* bridges two sentences. Like *naturally*, this transition also shows a cause-and-effect relationship: we were "concerned" about "a negative response"; *as a consequence of this concern*, "a special committee was appointed . . . ."

3. The third paragraph begins with *as a result*, which is really a short way of saying "as a result of the special committee's review." Thus *as a result* includes some understood words. It also tells the reader that "the committee's recommendations will follow."

Did you notice that the above transitions are economical? Each says quite a lot—but does so succinctly.

COMMUNICATION LABORATORY

APPLICATION EXERCISES

A. Select an appropriate transitional word or expression from the choices in parentheses.

(Consequently, As you know, Moreover,) the BSI Salary Administration Committee recently completed a year-long study of industry salaries. (Meanwhile, Naturally, As a result,) last month Benson Services Inc. announced a new salary schedule for all graded employees.

(Therefore, Also, On the other hand,) the Salary Administration Committee recommended that an incentive-compensation plan be established for all employees. (Naturally, However, Furthermore,) company executives were interested in the details of the plan and reviewed it carefully.

(As a result, For example, Besides,) we are pleased to announce that as of next January 1, a new incentive-compensation plan will be in effect. The details of this plan are explained in the enclosed booklet.

(Meanwhile, Of course, Accordingly,) BSI's employees are its most valuable asset. (Therefore, Yet, Still,) we are very pleased to offer this special compensation plan in an effort to reward our employees for their hard work, creativity, and dedication.

CONTINUED

B. Provide acceptable paragraph breaks for the following lengthy block of copy. Also, add transitions as necessary. Use a separate sheet of paper.

Last July we commissioned Fullmer Marketing Consultants to conduct a study of businesses in our area. The specific goals of the study were (1) to determine the number and the size of local businesses that are interested in and have a need for hotel services and (2) to identify the specific hotel services that will best satisfy their needs. Last week FMC submitted its report, which offers valuable information and interesting statistics that will be helpful to us as we plan our future marketing strategies. The report shows that 275 new businesses were established here in Greene County during the past five years. Most (182) of these new companies are firms that have 50 to 125 employees—an ideal market for our hotel services. The report lists the kinds of hotel services that these businesses identified as "most helpful," with "complete conference facilities" heading the list. The report contains very valuable information and must be studied carefully. Because the report is so important to our future marketing objectives, we have invited Leonia Fullmer, who conducted the survey and wrote the report, to meet with us for a full-day session, during which we will review in detail both the findings and their potential impact on our strategies. We are asking you and your staff members to set aside Tuesday, December 3, for this meeting with Ms. Fullmer. We know that all of us will benefit from this session.

C. Read the following memorandum. Then (1) place the sentences in a logical sequence and (2) group the sentences into acceptable paragraphs. Use a separate sheet of paper.

As you know, we have several important decisions to make concerning this year's sales meeting, and we will need ample time to prepare for the meeting, which is scheduled for August 15. First of all, we must begin the site-selection process. Please plan to meet with us on Tuesday, January 9, from 9 a.m. until noon, in Conference Room B, to begin planning this year's meeting. Next, we must develop a theme for the meeting. As you can see, then, we have plenty of work ahead of us! In addition, we must assign the development of the product-information brochures to product managers, and we must select speakers to present each new product. To save time, please review the enclosed materials before we meet on January 9. As you will see, the materials include suggestions for the site for and the theme of this year's meeting, as well as some valuable comments on last year's session.

D. Rewrite the following paragraph so that it flows smoothly.

Last year we closed four branch offices to conserve funds. This decision saved about 8 percent on our operating budget. Sales decreased by 14 percent. A large portion of this decrease can be traced to the closing of the offices. A portion is due to the general decline in the economy. I would suggest that we reopen these offices. Their closings cost us more than we saved.

CONTINUED

VOCABULARY AND SPELLING STUDIES

A. These words are often confused: *threw, through, thorough.* Explain the differences.

B. Three of the four words in each line below are synonyms. The fourth is an antonym. Spot the intruder in each group.

1. frighten, calm, alarm, terrify
2. conform, correspond, deviate, match
3. enthusiasm, eagerness, zeal, indifference
4. happy, miserable, distressed, pitiable
5. forceful, weak, strong, mighty
6. demonstrate, delight, perform, show
7. cover, jacket, erase, coat
8. elite, average, typical, common

C. Complete the following by adding *ar, er,* or *or*—whichever is correct.

1. supervis __
2. lawy __
3. regul __
4. direct __

5. monit __
6. sweep __
7. operat __
8. regulat __

EDITING THE DRAFT COPY

As the director of communications for a large corporation, Dawn Hickerson writes several monthly company newsletters and many ads, brochures, direct mail pieces, news releases, and other documents on a regular basis. "In many ways, I'm essentially a full-time writer," Ms. Hickerson said when she spoke at Clairmont High School's Career Day.

Ms. Hickerson shared this advice with interested students:

I approach writing as a three-step process: draft, edit, proofread. Trying to "do it all" and do it *well* in only one draft is always difficult, usually impossible. I think that the people who spend hours staring at blank paper get "stuck" because they do not know how to edit—they try to do it all *in one step.* They think that extra steps mean more work, but that's simply not true. The additional steps simplify the work. My advice: Always draft, edit, proofread!

EDITING—A KEY STEP IN SUCCESSFUL WRITING

Just what is editing? How does it fit into the writing process? Let's put the three steps of the process (draft, edit, proofread) into perspective before we look at editing in detail.

Drafting Your Message

A draft is more often called a *rough draft*, because in the drafting stage we write quickly, without much fuss over "details." In drafting, your goal is to *get your thoughts down on the page in a logical order.* Do not *agonize* over every word and punctuation mark. You will have time to revise later, during the editing stage. Striving for perfection on the first try is very difficult. Dividing the work into steps (*draft, edit, proofread*) makes the process easier.

HELPFUL HINT: Before you begin to draft your message, jot down key notes that you need, and then write, write, write. In this way you can concentrate on getting all your thoughts down on paper in a logical order. (In later chapters you will learn a number of useful techniques for organizing messages, techniques that will help simplify drafting specific kinds of messages.)

Editing Your Message

According to Ms. Hickerson, "Even the very experienced professional writers I work with make mistakes, and all of them are fully aware that they do. You should see what some of their first drafts look like!"

Professionals have mastered the editing process; they know that this is their opportunity to look for and correct errors. But errors are not the only focus during the editing process. As they look for errors, experienced writers look for ways to improve a sentence, to refine their word choice, to express an idea more clearly, to soften negative news, and so on. As you have just seen, the editing step focuses on two purposes: to make your writing error-free and to refine documents and improve communications.

Much of what you have already learned in this chapter was designed to help you edit your message. As you continue in this section, you will see that effective editing requires you to look for several categories of errors at the same time. At first, you may have difficulty using this "shotgun" approach. With practice, you will soon become adept!

Proofreading Your Message

The last step, proofreading, will be covered in detail in Section 6.5. As you will see, the proofreading process is in some ways similar to the editing process; both are attempts to refine that first draft and to achieve excellence in written communications.

EDIT FOR CONTENT

Errors in the content of a message are the most flagrant. After all, the key purpose in writing a letter or a memo is to convey information to the reader—

dates, discounts, sales units, and so on. If a message is excellent in all other details, it is still a miserable failure if it conveys the wrong information!

While such errors are the most flagrant, however, they are often the most difficult to spot. How can you tell whether *$101.45* is correct? whether *Account No. R104-378-9393* is correct? whether *17.2 percent* is correct? Answer: You cannot (unless, of course, you simply know such statistics from memory).

Double-check all statistics to be sure they are correct in every detail. Refer to a *source document*—a price list, a catalog, a sales sheet, anything that you *know* lists the correct information. Similarly, beware omitting an enclosure notation when you enclose something with your message or including the notation but forgetting the enclosure! These, too, are errors in the content of your message.

EDIT FOR WORD USE, SPELLING, GRAMMAR, AND PUNCTUATION

Any error is a flaw in a document. As you edit, you must look for errors in spelling, word use, grammar, punctuation, capitalization, abbreviation use, and number use:

UNEDITED: Yes, each of our meeting rooms can comfortably *accomodate* 50 guests.   (Beware one of the most commonly misspelled words: *accommodate.*)

UNEDITED: Both Dan Jenkins and Alyssa Robinson recommended the *imminent* Dr. Angela Satterlee as our keynote speaker.   (*Imminent* means "about to happen"; the word intended here is *eminent,* which means "distinguished, illustrious.")

UNEDITED: Only one of the supervisors generally *attend* the weekly budget meetings.   (Grammatically, "Only one . . . attend" is incorrect; it should be "Only one of the supervisors generally *attends* the . . . .")

UNEDITED: Martha Robbins represents our department at the weekly budget *meetings, Martha* is very skilled in budget planning.   (Punctuation error: The comma after *meetings* is incorrect. Use a period or a semicolon instead.)

These and other related errors are addressed, as you know, in Chapters 3, 4, and 5. In this section you will learn to focus on such errors as part of the editing process.

EDIT FOR CONSISTENCY

Editing *consistency* means treating style issues *in the same manner throughout a document.* Many of the principles of capitalization, number use, abbreviation use, and punctuation have more than one "correct" expression. These principles, as well as words and expressions that have more than one correct form, are often subject to inconsistent treatment; that is, the writer incorrectly uses two or more forms. In a report, for example, illustrations may be labeled *Figure 1.1* or *Fig. 1.1;* both styles are acceptable. But *mixing* different styles in the same document is not correct.

Inconsistencies often go unnoticed because occurrences are often pages apart; moreover, most of us have not been trained to look for inconsistencies (we tend to find only what we look for!). Some companies have *style sheets*—lists of preferred ways of writing certain names, titles, references, and so on. You may wish to make your own personal style sheet to help assure consistency in your writing.

Note the following examples of words and expressions that have more than one correct form. Remember, in a real document, the uses may be pages apart, making them more difficult to detect.

1. Use one courtesy title (such as *Ms.* or *Mr.*) or one professional title (*Dr.* or *Professor,* for example) consistently to refer to the same person.

2. Be aware of the spellings of names, because variations abound for both first and last names. Check a source most likely to show the name as the individual spells it. Note these groupings of similar names:

VARIANT FIRST NAMES	VARIANT LAST NAMES
Diana, Diane, Dina	DeVito, deVito
Karen, Karyn, Caren	Johnson, Jonson, Johnston, Johnstone
Miki, Mickie, Mickey	Chan, Chen, Chang, Cheng
Philip, Phillip	McDonald, MacDonald, Macdonald
Jean, Jeane, Jeanne	O'Brian, O'Brien, O'Bryan

3. Treat names in lists consistently. For example, if most names have *courtesy* titles, then be sure to use courtesy titles with all names:

Ms. Pamela Sturdevant

Mr. Henry Pritikin

Jack DeLorenzo

Likewise, if *business* titles are listed for most names, then list business titles for all:

Anne Divine, Director of Advertising

Bart DiGiralamo, Comptroller

Leslie Anne Edwards

4. Use one consistent style for expressing numbers:

$1 million $1,000,000

5. Capitalize headings consistently throughout a document. Inconsistent headings such as these, separated by several pages, may be difficult to

detect. Note how these two headings, both primary headings, are treated differently:

ON PAGE 3:

LIFE INSURANCE BENEFITS

ON PAGE 14:

Health Insurance Benefits

With experience, you can easily develop an eye for detecting inconsistencies—correcting them is easy!

EDIT FOR CLARITY

Okay, your message is correct and consistent in every detail. But is it clear?

Because Ms. Hanson will be out of the office on Thursday and Friday, we canceled our morning meeting for *that day.*   (Which day? The words *that day* might refer to either Thursday or Friday. How will the reader know which?)

Many different issues affect clarity. As the writer, of course, you always know what you intend to say. But do not assume that the reader will know! Only by carefully editing your draft will you be sure to uncover vague or misleading phrases. A well-known writer once suggested writing not just so that you can be understood but so that you cannot be misunderstood.

EDIT FOR COMPLETENESS

Equally unclear are messages that omit key information, such as:

Please be sure to note on your calendar that all managers must attend the corporate planning meeting on Wednesday, November 11, at 9 o'clock in Conference Room B.   (Despite all the facts this sentence *does* offer, it fails to say how long the meeting is expected to last. Will it likely be all day? one hour? three hours?)

The "key information" can be almost anything, depending on the situation. Often you will find it useful (both for you and your reader) to provide key information in list form. Then review the list to make sure you haven't omitted anything!

EDIT FOR COURTESY AND FRIENDLINESS

How are courtesy and friendliness reflected in a message? Saying *please* and *thank-you* helps, but do not overwork these two words in an effort to make your message effective. Instead, follow these suggestions:

1. Adopt a courteous and friendly tone:

We sincerely appreciate your sending us . . . .

Sheila and I are grateful to you for . . . .

Ms. Ames, you were very kind to . . . .

How thoughtful of you, Patricia, to . . . .

2. Do not talk down to the reader:

UNEDITED: As you will see in Step 14 on the directions sheet, ...

EDITED: I can understand, John, why the directions were less than clear.

3. Avoid accusations:

UNEDITED: If you would have read all the steps before proceeding, perhaps you . . . .

EDITED: In the future we will be sure to correct our directions sheet. Step 12 should have clearly explained that . . . .

UNEDITED: If you had looked in the bottom of the box, you would have found . . .

EDITED: We are sorry that our packaging materials allowed the instructions manual to slip to the bottom of the box.

4. Take responsibility for errors that you or someone else in your company made:

We can hardly believe that we did not ship the samples we promised you in time for your sale, and we sincerely apologize for our error.

5. Make an extra effort to help your reader:

Although we do not carry the designer models that you are looking for, we can recommend an excellent, reliable source: Premier Showcase, which is located in . . . ."

To implement these suggestions, always try to *demonstrate an understanding of the reader's point of view.* REMEMBER: Your courtesy and friendliness reflect on you as a professional (as well as a person) and on your company as a business. Your skill at building goodwill through your communications may not be measurable, but it *will* help your career!

EDIT FOR SUCCESS!

Perhaps these editing techniques make sense now, as you are reading this book. But on the job, when you are caught in the rush of the business day, you may sometimes be tempted to skip the editing step to save time. You may convince yourself that you have time for only one draft. You may try to make your *first* draft the *final* draft.

Developing the final message on the first try is always difficult, sometimes impossible. Rather than skip a step, you can often save time if you *draft quickly and edit slowly.* This section tackles some of the ways in which you can review your draft critically, for the purpose of revising it. Toward this end, this section focuses on the broader methods of editing your draft. Then the next section focuses on proofreading the final draft, that last step "just to make sure."

COMMUNICATION LABORATORY

APPLICATION EXERCISES

A. Rewrite each sentence below from the reader's point of view.

1. I would like to work for your company because of your fine benefit plans.
2. Your immediate order would allow us to reduce inventories.
3. We need your proposal by the middle of the month to avoid problems with our authorization procedure.
4. Your early confirmation will make it easier for us to hold your room.
5. Your prompt arrival will allow us to maintain our interview.
6. If you don't return our calls, we can't help you.

B. The following sentences do nothing to build goodwill. Rewrite them.

1. Please submit your order again; we can't seem to locate the original.
2. You made an error in not advising us of your room preference.
3. A careful customer would have brought this complaint to our attention much earlier.
4. You should have completed a credit application.
5. It is far too late for you to receive our special discount.
6. Because so many people fail to pay promptly, we do not ship merchandise until we receive the customer's check.
7. Your order will be delayed because the size of the order is so unusual.
8. All our other watch purchasers are completely satisfied.
9. It can't possibly be that we sent you the wrong batteries.
10. Our careful order clerks never make that kind of mistake.

C. Each of the following messages lacks some important information. Rewrite each message, providing the information that will make it clear and complete.

1. We would like to introduce our new line of sweaters to you at the Colony Hotel.
2. I would like to receive a copy of your schedule of upcoming events.
3. Please send six of your best white shirts to me at 81 Exeter Drive, Sunderland, MO 63042.
4. Would you like to attend our meeting at 10 a.m. tomorrow morning?
5. When does the plane leave?
6. Please reserve a room for Friday, April 23.
7. I need to rent a car this weekend.
8. I'm calling to cancel my appointment for Wednesday.

CONTINUED

D. Rewrite the following message. Paragraph it correctly by applying the principles you learned in Section 6.3. Add connecting words as necessary.

> We received your order today for three dozen Holt portable AM/FM radios. We welcome this opportunity to serve you. There has been such a great demand for Holt radios. We are temporarily out of stock. This fine product will again be available in eight days. Our plant is working overtime. Your order will be shipped very soon. Once again, we very much appreciate your order. We are convinced that the quality of Holt products will make up for the slight delay.

VOCABULARY AND SPELLING STUDIES

A. These words are often confused: *deprecate, depreciate; bow, beau, bough.* Explain the differences.

B. Many of our most frequently used words are derived from Latin or Greek roots. Using the root in the first column, add two or more words containing this root to each word in the third column.

ROOT	MEANING	WORDS BUILT FROM ROOT
1. *dict-*	*say*	*predict*
2. *fer-*	*carry*	*transfer*
3. *scrib-*	*write*	*describe*
4. *geo-*	*earth*	*geography*
5. *voc-*	*call*	*vocal*

C. Change the present-tense forms of the verbs within parentheses to the past-tense forms.

1. The clerk (tear) the invoice by mistake.
2. We (see) the new word processing system last week.
3. She (begin) the meeting on time.
4. The rest of our group (catch) the last plane for Chicago.
5. Our general manager (send) invitations to all our loyal customers.
6. Clarissa (write) a letter that explained the delay.

PROOFREADING THE FINAL COPY

I'm going to be a manager—my assistant will be responsible for proofreading.' That's what I thought before I *became* a manager," said Amy Chang. "Now I realize that my assistant *is*, of course, responsible, but so am I. I share responsibility for every document that bears my name." While Amy's assistant answers to Amy for any document errors he makes, Amy in turn answers to *her* management for those errors!

Conclusion: Proofreading skill is worthwhile for anyone who develops business documents, regardless of level. And because it is a *skill*, proofreading improves the more you use it.

PROOFREADING—ONE LAST CHANCE

Proofreading is a critical part of the writing process. Because it's the last step, many people call it the most important, and it may be. But the success of the writing process, as well its simplicity, depends on your ability to apply all three distinct steps.

Let's see where proofreading fits into the process:

- In *drafting*, you jot down all your thoughts in a rough, unpolished way. You write a draft quickly, knowing that the next two steps permit you to polish that draft. In your draft you should focus on completeness and on the accuracy of your facts and statistics.

- In *editing*, you focus narrowly on the details in your draft: Is this date correct? this percentage? this dollar amount? Should this word be capitalized? Is a comma correct here? Are these words spelled correctly? You also focus broadly on ways to polish your draft: Can my word choice here be improved? Is the phrasing of this sentence clear? Do the transitions work as I want them to? Should I join these two paragraphs? Are these headings treated consistently?

- In *proofreading*, you double-check the details—that is, you make sure that no errors in the original draft were overlooked, that all changes noted during the editing stage were made, and that no errors were accidentally introduced during the revision process.

As you learned in Section 6.4, you *edit a first draft*, and you *proofread a final draft*. The rougher the first draft, the more you will need to rewrite and rephrase and reword. Careful editing should—*should!*—erase all the flaws in a document. But in real life, we do make errors, even during or after editing.

That's why a document always needs one final check, and we provide that final check by *proofreading*.

USE PROOFREADERS' MARKS

Proofreaders' marks provide a standard method for noting corrections. Because they *are* standard, proofreaders' marks are widely used. Because they are symbols, these marks save time. And because they are widely known, proofreaders' marks help eliminate errors and miscommunications.

Get to know the following proofreaders' marks, and use them whenever appropriate on drafts, manuscripts, and so on. Until you become expert in using them, keep a chart of proofreaders' marks handy (your desk dictionary may also have a list):

REVISION	MARKED DRAFT	FINAL COPY
Transpose letters	thier	their
Transpose words	to directly call you	to call you directly
Insert letter or letters	convient	convenient
Insert word or words	a customer	a charge account customer
Delete stroke	reduces or reduces	reduce
Delete stroke and close up space	electronic	electronic
Delete punctuation mark	On May 5/we	On May 5 we . . . .
Change stroke	correspondance	correspondence
Omit word or word group	a charge account customer	a customer
Change word or word group	. . . book which we sent you.	. . . book that we sent you.
Capitalize letter	bushnell corporation	Bushnell Corporation
Use all capitals	stop sign	STOP sign
Use lowercase letter	the Company	the company
Use a series of lowercase letters	FDI CORPORATION	FDI Corporation
Insert semicolon, comma, or colon	. . . today,there-fore please send us the following	. . . today; there-fore, please send us the following:
Insert period, question mark, or exclamation point	⊙ ? !	Yes. Yes? Yes!
Insert apostrophe or quotation marks	. . . the company's innovative policies.	. . . the company's "innovative policies."

REVISION	MARKED DRAFT	FINAL COPY
Spell out	③ . . . 20% . . . 4 doz.	three . . . 20 per- cent . . . 4 dozen
Close up space	sales person	salesperson
Insert a space	inaddition	in addition
Hyphenate	up-to-date files	up-to-date files
Underscore	The word <u>receive</u> is often	The word <u>receive</u> is often . . . .
Restore word or words deleted	stock and bond certificates	stock and bond certificates
Start new paragraph	¶ May we have your	May we have your . . . .
Do not start new paragraph	no¶ This information is	This information is . . . .
Indent 5 spaces	5 In the future . . .	In the future . . .
Single-space	ss ⎡When we receive your report, we will ⎣submit it to	When we receive your report, we will submit it to . . . .
Double-space	ds ⎡One of our sales representatives will ⎣call on you	One of our sales representatives will call on you . . . .
Move as indicated	only bought it yesterday	bought it only yesterday
Move to the left	Send in your report.	Send in your report.
Move to the right	Send in your report.	Send in your report.
Center	January 25, 1995	January 25, 1995

DEVELOP THE PROOFREADING HABIT

Amy and her assistant Ron have been working on a long report, a project that has taught Ron a lot about proofreading. On page 298 is an edited page from the draft of that report with Amy's corrections noted. On page 299 is the revised copy, after Ron entered all of Amy's corrections.

But did Ron make *all* the corrections Amy indicated? Did Amy overlook any error in the original draft copy? If the answer to both questions is yes, the final copy *should match* Amy's revised draft. In other words, the purpose of proofreading is to ensure that the final copy contains no errors.

12

RECOMENDATIONS

From analyses of the data gathered in the study, the following conclusions are drawn:

1.   Current dictation and transcription practices wastes time.

2.   Almost half the letters that are individually written could be form letters or could make use of form paragraphs.

3.   Little use is made of available dictation equipments.

4.   Most of them who dictate do not know how to dictate effiæciently.

5.   Secretaries are rarely permitted to compose letters.

6.   Only half of the secretarys have word processing or computer equipment at their work stations.

7.   A variety of letter styles are used, depending upon each writer's preference.

With these conclusions in mind, the following action are recommended.

1.   Expend the information processing network, so that word processing as well as data processing can be done on the network.   from all workstations

2.   Make dictation equipment or computer terminals available to appropriate staff members (those who originate memos, letters, and reports).

3.   Provide each of them staff members with appropriate training to use the equipment.

4.   Adopt the block-style letter format as the standerd letter style to be used through out the company.

5.   ~~Keep~~ Track comparative communication costs as a bases for determining wheather the network should be expanded to include branch offices of the company.

SUMMARY

This study recommends that a word procesing center be established at the home office of Renovators' Resources Inc. and shows that such a center would improve correspondence practices and decrease correspondence costs. The specific datas

Errors in and additions to the first draft of the report are marked for correction.

Look again at the proofread "final" copy on page 299. When Amy received this "final" copy, she compared it by matching it, word for word, punctuation mark by punctuation mark, line by line, against that edited first draft. As you see, she discovered a few errors, and she marked those errors using proofreaders' marks. But not all her corrections concern "errors"; in one case she made a change that she thinks will improve clarity. Sometimes, the "final" copy is nothing more than a second draft.

12

RECOMMENDATIONS

From analysis of the data gathered in the study, the following conclusions are drawn:

1.   Current dictation and transcription practices waste time.

2.   Almost half the letters that are individually written could be form letters or could make use of form paragraphs.

3.   Little use is made of available dictation equipment.

4.   Most of those who dictate do not know how to dictate efficiently.

5.   Secretaries are rarely permitted to compose letters.

6.   Only half of the secretaries have word processing or computer equipment at their workstations.

7.   A variety of letter styles is used, depending upon each writer's preference.

With these conclusions in mind, the following actions are recommended:

1.   Expand the information processing network, so that word processing as well as data processing can be done from all workstations on the network.

2.   Make dictation equipment or computer terminals available to appropriate staff members (those who originate memos, letters, and reports).

3.   Provide each of those staff members with appropriate training to use the equipment.

4.   Adopt the block-style letter format as the standard letter style to be used throughout the company.

5.   Keep comparative communication costs as a basis for determining whether the network should be expanded to include branch offices of the company.

6.   Train and encourage secretaries to compose letters.

SUMMARY

This study recommends that a word processing center be established at the home office of Renovators' Resources Inc. and shows that such a center would improve correspondence practices and decrease correspondence costs. The specific data

Check carefully to make sure that all corrections are made. If additional corrections or additions are needed, make those changes and then proofread the new copy.

APPLY PROOFREADING TECHNIQUES

Ron had read the final copy before he submitted it to Amy, yet she found a few errors that Ron—despite his genuine care—missed. New at his job, Ron optimistically believed that he could find all errors in one reading. Ron will soon learn the lesson that experienced business writers know so well: Proofreading is a multistep process!

To proofread a document, apply these distinct steps:

1. *Review the format and the parts. Without reading,* skim the document, focusing only on its format.

   • Are paragraphs all flush left—or all indented? Are line spaces between paragraphs correct? Are margins correct?

   • If the letter style is modified block, are both the date line and the complimentary closing indented?

   • If you are checking a memo that was not prepared on a printed form, are all the guide words (*MEMO TO, FROM, DATE,* and *SUBJECT*) included?

   • If the memo continues onto another page, does page 2 have a continuation-page heading?

   With practice, this step will take just a few seconds—no more—but it will ensure that your documents are formatted correctly and consistently.

2. *Scan the document.* The next step, too, is completed quickly. Scan each page of the document. *Scanning* means "*selective* reading"; it means looking over each page and spot-checking the document parts that most often contain errors.

   • In letters, *read separately* (a) the date, (b) each line of the inside address, (c) the salutation, and (d) all the closing information. Why? Because most of us overlook all these parts and, instead, start proofreading with the body.

   • In all enumerations, check the sequence of numbers. Often you will find a jump from, say, 5 to 7 in the final copy because item 6 was deleted in the draft.

   • In a report, scan headings. Are all treated consistently (all caps or initial capitals and lowercase? bold, underscored, or italicized? and so on).

   • In a multipage document, check the pagination. Pages are often misnumbered, even when word processing software is used!

   Because scanning uncovers the kinds of errors we often miss in even a careful reading, it is a very important step in the proofreading process.

3. *Double-check all numbers and statistics.* The *words* in sentences must make sense; when they do not, we detect the error as we read. But numbers usually make no sense. Therefore, most numbers can be accidentally changed without destroying or changing the meaning at all! That's why you must double-check all numbers and statistics. Compare the numbers in your document with a source you know to be accurate.

4. *Read slowly and carefully.* Question: Why do intelligent people with expert spelling skills often overlook the most obvious errors as they proofread? Answer: Because accurate proofreading is not dependent exclusively on intelligence or on spelling skill.

There are a number of reasons why we must work deliberately to acquire proofreading skill:

- Most of us have years of experience in reading for content but no experience in reading for the specific purpose of finding errors. Without knowing specific techniques, we easily overlook typographical errors and errors in numbers and statistics.

- As we read, we have a tendency to mentally fill in omitted words. In fact, some speed-reading programs use fill-in exercises to help people learn to read faster; for example:

  All emplo— who belong to the exec— commit— reques—

- When reading quickly, as we usually try to do, we naturally pay no attention to the details of spelling, grammar, punctuation, and so on.

- In reading quickly, we may not notice a repeated word, especially if the first occurrence is at the end of one line and the second at the beginning of the next line, for example:

  the number of usable PCs with hard drives *in*
  in our department, therefore, must be

- Most of us make an intense effort to focus on spelling errors, and in the process we may not even notice punctuation, much less *errors* in punctuation use.

- Inexperienced business writers naively believe they can simultaneously read for content *and* for typographical errors *and* for format errors *and* for inconsistencies *and* for . . .

- Most of us are unaware that inconsistencies are errors; how, then, can we be expected to uncover and correct inconsistencies?

The solution: Read slowly and carefully—and practice, practice, practice!

READ FOR SPECIFIC TYPES OF ERRORS

Pay close attention to the following discussion on proofreading for specific types of errors.

Typographical Errors Typographical errors are common keyboarding errors such as transposed (reversed in order) letters, omitted letters, extra letters, and incorrect letters. Transpositions of individual letters are marked as follows:

Please answer the following questions:

The symbol may also be used to transpose words, phrases, or clauses.

Note how these typographical errors are corrected:

tran**sp**osed letters

omit**t**ed letter

e**x**tra letter

in**c**orrect letter   *or in**c**orrect*

To insert, use a caret ($\wedge$) to indicate where the additional letter, word, or phrase should be placed. To delete, use a forward-slanting diagonal line (/) through the unwanted letter; close up the extra space with loops above and below ($\bigcirc$). Incorrect letters can be changed easily by running the forward-slanting diagonal line through the incorrect letter and then writing the correct letter directly above the diagonal.

Typographical errors often blend in with the text. Read the following sentences carefully:

Your last three bank statement have shown an incorrect balance.

As soon as we hear form you, we will ship your order.

Only by reading for meaning can you locate the errors in the above examples.

Your last three bank statement **s** have shown an incorrect balance.

As soon as we hear f**or**m you, we will ship your order.

The accurate proofreader not only must look at the words but also must read for content.

If you use word processing software, you probably are familiar with spell-check features. Although these features can be a time-saver, they can't replace proofreading. Spell-checkers can tell you only if a word is misspelled, not if you've used the wrong word (but spelled it correctly). Use spell-checkers to help you, but don't rely on them to replace proofreading.

PROOFREADING PRACTICE 1

On a separate sheet of paper, write the numbers from 1 to 8. Read the following sentences for typographical errors; write the incorrect word as it is shown in the sentence. Then use the appropriate proofreaders' mark to show the needed change. If a sentence is correct as shown, write OK on your paper.

1. Please sign adn date the application before returning it.
2. Do you stilll wish us to reinvest your dividends?
3. We are pleased to establish an acount for you at Nash's Department Store.
4. If you will return the enclosed bussiness reply card, one of our experienced salespeople will call you.
5. You should receive our signed contract within the next few days.
6. Do you wish to resckedule your son's appointment time from 9:30 a.m. to 2:30 p.m.?

7. May we have you reply by October 1.

8. Have all our customers been sent copies of thier monthly statement showing interest paid for the year?

Omitted Words and Lines   As you read for content, be alert for omitted words:

> For further information please your local sales representative.

This sentence does not make sense without the missing word. Should the reader write, phone, see, contact, or ask the local representative?

> For further information please your local sales representative.

(*phone* inserted with caret mark after "please")

Sometimes you must compare the copy with the rough draft. Can you locate the error in the following sentence?

> The balance in your account will earn interest at the rate of 7 percent compounded daily.

Probably not! You see, the omission of a word does not obviously cloud the meaning. The sentence was supposed to read, "The balance in your *checking* account will earn interest at the rate of 7 percent compounded daily." The word *checking* is necessary because it clarifies which account, but this error might not have been discovered unless the proofreader checked the final copy against the rough draft. As you proofread, check the revised copy against the original copy for omissions. Do not limit this check to single-word omissions, but look for omissions of word groups, a complete line of type, and sentences as well.

Repeated Words and Lines   Delete repeated words and lines by drawing a straight horizontal line through them. Be sure to check for a word or part of a hyphenated word at the end of one line that is repeated at the beginning of the next:

> Next week we will meet with you to select word processing, spreadsheet, and and data base programs for our new microcomputers.

> Next week we will meet with you to select word processing, spreadsheet, desk-desktop publishing and data base programs for our new microcomputers.

When a keyboarder's eyes "jump" to identical words on another line, words will be omitted or repeated, as in this example:

> Line repetition errors usually occur when vocabulary in a document is repeated. The typist often shifts focus and returns to the inappropriate spot. The document is repeated. The typist often shifts focus and returns to the inappropriate spot. The document is then typed with an extra line, one repeated from an earlier copy.

PROOFREADING PRACTICE 2

On a separate sheet of paper, copy the following sentences. Use the proper proofreaders' marks to show your corrections.

1. For further details please your instruction booklet.
2. Who will be manufacturing the movable parts for our new line of exer-exercise equipment?
3. Your computer desk and printer table are both scheduled for delivery on on June 28.
4. Please the contract and mail it to us in the enclosed envelope.
5. As soon we receive approval from our central office, we will notify you.
6. Two of our older stores and our new warehouse need to have more up-up-to-date security systems installed.

Number Errors   All figures should be checked for accuracy. First, ask yourself, "Does the number make sense?" If you saw the weight of a newborn infant stated as 70 pounds, you might suspect that this was an error for 7 pounds. Likewise, a ZIP Code with six digits, 911135, instead of five or nine digits is an obvious error.

Other numbers must be checked against the original copy. To make sure the numbers in the rough draft and final copy coincide, follow these procedures. For a long number, count the digits in the original copy and make sure the same number of digits appears in the copy being checked. Then compare in groups of three the digits in the original with the digits in the copy.

In some cases you may need to verify computations and recalculate totals. Be sure to think through each calculation!

PROOFREADING PRACTICE 3

On a separate sheet of paper, write the numbers from 1 to 12. Compare the figures in Column A with those in Column B; use proofreaders' marks to make any necessary corrections in the figures appearing in Column B. If no corrections are needed, write *OK* on your paper.

A	**B**
1. 3624 West 59 Place	1. 3626 West 59 Place
2. 212-873-5669	2. 213-873-5669
3. San Diego, CA 92143-1896	3. San Diego, CA 921143-1896
4. 567-44-7478	4. 567-44-7748
5. December 13, 1973	5. December 31, 1973
6. XT 954782643	6. XT 954782543
7. 818-365-3827	7. 818-365-3837
8. $17,923.81	8. $17,932.81
9. KRT647934648	9. KRT84793648
10. Serial No. 965468325679	10. Serial No. 965468325679
11. 7463901743	11. 746390173
12. 432-82-8987	12. 423-882-8987

Spelling Errors Keep an up-to-date dictionary or wordbook handy as you proofread, and look up any word whose spelling you doubt. Use the appropriate proofreaders' marks to make any corrections.

Use your MAGNA-CHARGE to send flowers for this special occasion.

Punctuation Errors Internal punctuation marks may be added to copy by using the insertion mark; just place the comma, semicolon, or colon inside the caret at the point of insertion. Closing punctuation marks (periods, question marks, and exclamation points) may be added to copy without insertion marks; periods are circled to make them more visible.

Vans campers and trucks are prohibited from parking in Lot A.

Three packages of crystal arrived today when may we expect the remaining four?

Extra or incorrect punctuation marks may be deleted by using the forward-slanting diagonal (/). If another punctuation mark must be substituted, just delete or change the incorrect mark and follow the procedure for inserting the correct one.

ORIGINAL: This apartment complex will be converted to condominiums, therefore we must notify all tenants by October 1?

REVISION: This apartment complex will be converted to condominiums/ therefore we must notify all tenants by October 1.

ORIGINAL: Would you be able to assume responsibility for the following duties; locating a restaurant, selecting a menu, and coordinating the arrangements.

REVISION: Would you be able to assume responsibility for the following duties locating a restaurant, selecting a menu, and coordinating the arrangements?

Grammar Errors Pay close attention to the grammatical construction of sentences in the copy you are proofreading. Watch for errors in subject-verb agreement, noun plurals and possessives, compound adjectives, and other principles of grammar (presented in Chapter 4). Use the proofreaders' marks to make any necessary changes.

PROOFREADING PRACTICE 4

Copy the following sentences on a separate sheet of paper. Then make any necessary corrections using the proofreaders' marks presented in this section.

1. We do not want to loose this opportunity to thank you for your patronage during the past year.
2. July 11, will mark our twenty-fifth anniversary serving the residents of Springfield.
3. We was disappointed to learn that you will be moving your offices.

4. Did you notify your insurance company of your address change.
5. Unfortunately, we cannot accommodate you on February 14.
6. Please provide us with the name address and telephone number of your family physician.
7. Both switchs on this computer monitor are defective.
8. Did you recieve the information I sent you?

Capitalization Errors   While proofreading, look for capitalization errors. To show that a letter should be capitalized, place three short lines under it; to capitalize entire words, underline the word or word group three times.

You may buy copies of *The Lundberg Letters* at Dalton's bookstore.

Ms. Deschiff will be transferred to our east coast office next month.

Use a forward-slanting diagonal through a capital letter that should appear in lowercase form. Words appearing in all-capital letters that should be written in a combination of capital and lowercase letters may be changed by using the forward-slanting diagonal in conjunction with a straight horizontal line.

Your Century Living Room Suite will be delivered by Z-EXPRESS AIRFREIGHT SERVICES the week of December 17.

Number-Usage Errors   When proofreading copy, check to see that each number is expressed properly (review Section 5.8). If a figure should be spelled out, circle it. If a number in word form should be expressed in figures, draw a horizontal line through the word(s), and above it write the figures as they should be written.

Last week ⑤ of our sales personnel each sold over ~~thirty thousand dollars~~ $30,000 in video recording accessories.

PROOFREADING PRACTICE 5

Proofread the following sentences. On a separate sheet of paper, write the error or errors as they are shown in each sentence. Use proofreaders' marks to make the necessary corrections.

1. These prices will be in effect 1 day only, October 25.
2. How many english classes have been scheduled for next semester?
3. Our division sells Copiers, COMPUTERS, and Electronic Typewriters.
4. Because Marisa's new job requires a security clearance, the fbi is interviewing her references.
5. Only one hundred twenty-seven of the five hundred questionnaires were returned.
6. Please send your claim directly to amalgamated life insurance company.

Inconsistencies   Proofread for inconsistencies, using the same techniques you learned in *editing* for inconsistencies. Review the discussion of inconsistencies in Section 6.4.

COMMUNICATION LABORATORY

A. On a separate sheet of paper, write the numbers from 1 to 20. Proofread the following sentences. If a sentence contains an error, write the error on your paper. Then use the appropriate proofreaders' mark to make the necessary correction. If a sentence does not contain an error, write *OK* on your paper.

1. Please send us this information by December seventh.
2. Have all the tenants their rent for this month?
3. When may we expect delivery of this order.
4. Your apointment with Dr. Eckles has been changed to May 3.
5. Copies of your transcript and test scores have been sent to michigan state university.
6. Be sure to save your signed reciept for this payment.
7. We do not except coupons from any other markets.
8. Checks will be honored for the ammount of the purchase only.
9. You may submit the report to John Ellen or Chris.
10. Our local High School is sponsoring a number of fund-raisers to help finance the new auditorium.
11. Only three of our salespersonnel have met their quotas for this month.
12. Obtain three copies of these forms from the CALIFORNIA FRANCHISE TAX BOARD.
13. Please specify the amt. of your payment on the enclosed stub.
14. If you can not attend this meeting, please let us know by March 10.
15. Only 1 office in our building, is available for lease.
16. How many of your staff members have completed the questionnaire?
17. Two irs officials will audit the company books next week.
18. In response to you advertisement, I am requesting a copy of your free booklet on lawn care.
19. You are one of our valued customers, and we appreciate the the business you have given us in the past.
20. Please include with your reservation a deposit for the first night

CONTINUED

B. Reading carelessly when checking amounts of money and other figures often leads to problems. Compare the following two lists. On a separate sheet of paper, indicate which pairs of figures do not agree by writing *X* next to the appropriate numbers. Write *OK* if a pair is correct.

List A	List B	Do *Not* Agree
0. 7654321	7653421	**0.** __X__
1. $846,783	$846,873	**1.** _____
2. 8734972390	8724972390	**2.** _____
3. $382,479.23	$382,479.23	**3.** _____
4. 1DSE479-6843	1DSE479-6843	**4.** _____
5. 437-81-9823	437-881-9823	**5.** _____
6. R6243778109TT	R642377810TT	**6.** _____

C. Test your proofreading skill by comparing the following letter with the copy that appears directly below it. On a separate sheet of paper, number and list the errors that appear. Then use proofreaders' marks to show the needed corrections.

Copy to Be Proofread

Dear Msr. Andrews:

We welcome you as a charge acount customer of field's department store. Enclosed is your charge card and a broshure discribing our charge plan. We hope that you will take advantage of our many bargins and use you card often.

This month we are featuring a sale on famous-brand stainless-steel cookware. The prices of all pots and frying pans inthis line have been by 25 to 50 persent. If you need to replace your cookware now is the time to do so. Also, if your need a wedding gift for the June bride, consider giving this fine cookware.

What ever your needs in the department store line maybe, be sure to visit field's first. We are eager to to serve you with our complete line of high quality merchandize.

Sincerly,

Correct Copy

Dear Mrs. Andrews:

We welcome you as a charge account customer of Field's Department Store. Enclosed are your charge card and a brochure describing our charge plan. We hope that you will take advantage of our many bargains and use your card often.

This month we are featuring a sale on famous-brand stainless-steel cookware. The prices of all pots and frying pans in this line have been reduced by 25 to 50 percent. If you need to replace your cookware, now is the time to do so. Also, if you need a wedding gift for the June bride, consider giving this fine cookware.

Whatever your needs in the department store line may be, be sure to visit Field's first. We are eager to serve you with our complete line of high-quality merchandise.

Sincerely,

D. Proofread the following excerpt from a business letter, and on a separate sheet of paper, make a list of the errors. Then rewrite the excerpt, correcting the errors.

We received you letter of Febuary 14 and the check for $182 enclosed. Every store appreciate the patronage of it's customers. We have credit your account for $182 and hope that their will be many more opportunity to serve you.

VOCABULARY AND SPELLING STUDIES

A. Without consulting your dictionary, indicate which of the two spellings shown for the following words is preferable. Then check your selections in the dictionary.

1. judgement, judgment
2. realize, realise
3. usable, useable
4. labelled, labeled
5. accidently, accidentally
6. acknowledgment, acknowledgement
7. instalment, installment
8. quartet, quartette

B. The following brief definitions indicate frequently used words that contain silent letters. Spell the words. To help you, the number of letters in each word is given.

1. The opposite of right (5 letters).
2. A visitor (5 letters).
3. A twenty-fourth part of a day (4 letters).
4. A body of land surrounded by water (6 letters).
5. The opposite of day (5 letters).
6. Unruffled; still (4 letters).
7. The branch of medicine that deals with mental disorders (10 letters).
8. To strike or rap on a door (5 letters).
9. A religious song (4 letters).
10. A lien on property by which the property is made security for a loan (8 letters).

CHAPTER 7

BUSINESS LETTERS

July 13, 1993

Walter R. Frump
Acme Widget Company
1122 East Elm Street
Midtown, WA 98121

Dear Mr. Frump:

Thank you for your letter dated July 1 of thi[...]
duction department has calculated that [...]
proximately 300 more widgets th[...]
to purchase from your compa[...] need ap-
vised purchase order reflect[...] contracted
[...]ed a re-

Your prompt attention to [...]

Sincere[...]

John D[...]

    Enc.

No matter what career path you follow, what industry you work in, what area of the country (or the world!) you choose to work in, or what position you hold in a firm, you will very likely write business letters, perhaps lots of them.

The reason is simple: A business letter is a universal tool. People at every level within a firm write letters, not only managers and top executives. Not only are letters common, but they are also important. They are important *because* they are tools that people use to conduct their business. *They are important because* they relay key messages *among* business associates, clients, vendors, manufacturers, distributors, and others. *They are important because* they represent your company. *And they are important because* they reflect on you and on your skill as a businessperson—*not only as a "business writer."*

What will your business letters tell your readers about you and your business skills?

If you learn and use the basic guidelines for planning and writing business letters, your letters can indeed represent you to your best advantage. These guidelines are simple and easy to follow, and they are logical and easy to remember. In fact, after a short while, you will probably implement the guidelines automatically.

OBJECTIVES

When you complete the sections in this chapter, you will be able to do the following:

1. Select the most appropriate of three letter-writing plans to help you organize your ideas.

2. Position letter parts according to standard arrangements, classify different kinds of business letters, and plan your letters before you begin the writing process.

3. Plan and write routine letters that request, transmit, acknowledge, or respond, and prepare envelopes according to a standard format.

4. Plan and write letters that persuade the reader to follow a certain course of action or approve a request.

5. Plan and write letters that refuse or that convey bad news yet still maintain goodwill.

6. Plan and write attention-getting sales and public relations letters.

7. Plan and write thoughtful social-business letters.

FORMATTING BUSINESS LETTERS

Christa Beck is studying fashion design. For Christa, *style* means clothing style. Frank Carson owns a beauty salon. For Frank, *style* means hairstyle. While Elaine Danneman is working nights toward her A.A. degree, she is working days as a computer operator for an architect. Before this job, Elaine never thought of *style* in terms of building design and bridge construction. Now she does.

What does *style* mean to you? For most of us, the word *style* refers to general appearance, look, mode, or manner. To distinguish one specific style from another, you usually add a descriptive term. For example, you might describe a certain jacket as "sporty," a dress as "formal," a shirt as "businesslike," and a pair of slacks as "casual." Each of these terms helps us to picture a specific style of clothing, because each style has its own flavor, its own uniqueness, its own look.

LETTER STYLE

You may never have considered "letter style," but letters also have different appearances, or looks. We are talking not about writing style here but about the visual appearance of letters.

Just as a jacket, a hat, shoes, and other articles of dress combine to create a clothing style, a letter style is also determined by a number of visual factors, such as:

- Paper quality, weight, and color
- Letterhead and logo design
- Ink colors used in printing
- Style and size of type used for the body of the letter
- Format

Here we are concerned with *format*, which refers to *how the letter parts are arranged on the page.* Unless you've completed keyboarding or word processing courses, you may not realize that business letters have standard parts—parts common to all business letters—and optional parts. Knowing these letter parts is important because their arrangement determines format.

Three standard formats dominate business letter style:

- Block format
- Modified-block format
- Modified-block format with indented paragraphs

As you continue, you will learn about two special types of business letters that use variations of these three business formats:

- Social-business format   (used for social-business letters)
- Personal-business format   (used for personal-business letters)

Perhaps you're wondering, Why does format matter? Think of dressing for an interview. You may dress any way you want, of course, but if your clothing style doesn't fit the expected business standards, you may be penalized—you may not get the job. Business does have standards in many areas, including letter format. Take the time to learn these standards now so that on the job you can apply the format that your company prefers.

The easiest way to master letter format is to review the *parts* of business letters, which is the next topic.

LETTER PARTS

The key to distinguishing one letter format from another lies in knowing the *parts* of a letter. Reason: It is the *placement* of letter parts that determines format.

The illustration on page 314 labels all letter parts clearly. Take the time now to review those labels. As you do so, note that an asterisk (*) identifies optional parts, those parts that you may need in some letters. All the other parts are standard—they appear in all business letters.

Usually a letter is divided into four sections:

1. The heading
2. The opening
3. The body
4. The closing

The Heading   Envelopes are not usually filed in business offices. Therefore, the information that the reader needs to answer a letter must be included in a *letterhead* and *date line*.

The Letterhead   Almost every company uses high-quality stationery with its name, address, and telephone number printed on it. These identifying items, and often such additional data as the names of the company's top executives and its slogan, are referred to collectively as the "letterhead." Some examples are shown on page 319.

The content and design of the letterhead help to project the company's image. Although the reader is primarily interested in the message, the letterhead is almost sure to be glanced at first. An opinion of the company may be formed

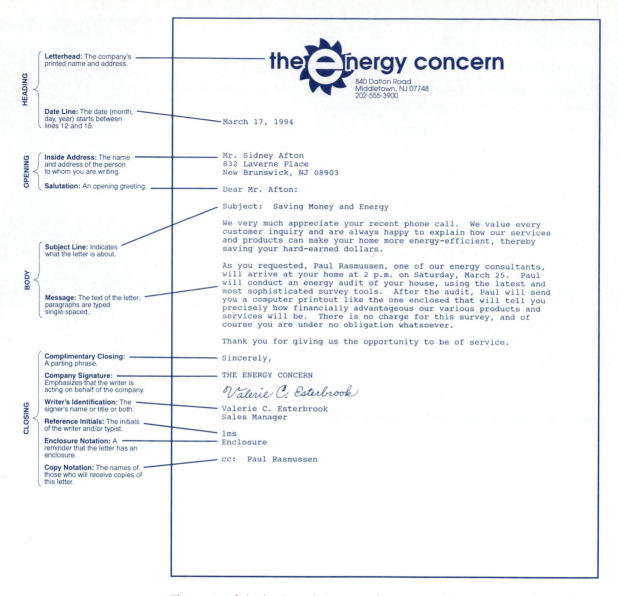

Letterhead: The company's printed name and address.

HEADING

Date Line: The date (month, day, year) starts between lines 12 and 15.

OPENING

Inside Address: The name and address of the person to whom you are writing.

Salutation: An opening greeting.

Subject Line: Indicates what the letter is about.

BODY

Message: The text of the letter; paragraphs are typed single-spaced.

Complimentary Closing: A parting phrase.

Company Signature: Emphasizes that the writer is acting on behalf of the company.

Writer's Identification: The signer's name or title or both.

Reference Initials: The initials of the writer and/or typist.

CLOSING

Enclosure Notation: A reminder that the letter has an enclosure.

Copy Notation: The names of those who will receive copies of this letter.

the energy concern

840 Dalton Road
Middletown, NJ 07748
202-555-3900

March 17, 1994

Mr. Sidney Afton
832 Laverne Place
New Brunswick, NJ 08903

Dear Mr. Afton:

Subject: Saving Money and Energy

We very much appreciate your recent phone call. We value every customer inquiry and are always happy to explain how our services and products can make your home more energy-efficient, thereby saving your hard-earned dollars.

As you requested, Paul Rasmussen, one of our energy consultants, will arrive at your home at 2 p.m. on Saturday, March 25. Paul will conduct an energy audit of your house, using the latest and most sophisticated survey tools. After the audit, Paul will send you a computer printout like the one enclosed that will tell you precisely how financially advantageous our various products and services will be. There is no charge for this survey, and of course you are under no obligation whatsoever.

Thank you for giving us the opportunity to be of service.

Sincerely,

THE ENERGY CONCERN

Valerie C. Esterbrook

Valerie C. Esterbrook
Sales Manager

lms
Enclosure

cc: Paul Rasmussen

The parts of the business letter must be arranged in a sequence that will make the parts meaningful. An asterisk (*) labels optional parts.

(perhaps subconsciously) because of its letterhead: It's old-fashioned or it's modern; it's futuristic or it's ultraconservative; it's middle-of-the-road or it's progressive; and so on.

The Date Line Knowing when a letter was written is often *very* important—important to both the reader and the writer. REMEMBER: The file copy provides a *record* for the writer. Every letter should therefore carry a date line consisting of the month, day, and year. Position the date somewhere between lines 12 and 15 on the letter.

There are two widely used date line styles—one for general business correspondence and one for military and international correspondence. In either style, do not use *st, nd, rd, th,* or *d* after the day of the month.

BUSINESS	**MILITARY**
April 15, 1993	15 April 1993
September 7, 1993	7 September 1993

NOTE: Do not use number abbreviations such as *4/15/93*.

Personal or Confidential Notation (Optional) A personal or confidential notation is typed on the second line below the date at the left margin to indicate that a letter is private. The notation may be typed in all-capital letters or in initial capital and lowercase letters that are underscored.

PERSONAL OR <u>Personal</u>   CONFIDENTIAL OR <u>Confidential</u>

The Opening
The functions of the opening are to direct the letter to a specific individual, company, or department, or to some other destination, and to greet the reader. The *inside address* directs the letter, as does an *attention line,* if used; and the *salutation* greets the reader.

The Inside Address The name of the addressee, which should always be preceded by a courtesy title (except when followed by *M.D.* or another abbreviation), is usually the first line of the inside address. Common courtesy requires including the person's job title when it is known—either on the same line as the name or on the line following the name. The name of the addressee's company; the street address; and the city, state, and ZIP Code are also included. The following are examples of accepted inside-address styles:

Mr. Melvin T. Moss	Ms. Linda R. Schur, Chairperson
Chairman of the Board	Business Education Department
Continental Insurance Company	Laguna Hills High School
1300 Laurel Canyon Avenue	400 West Haskell Avenue
Ogden, UT 84401	Milwaukee, WI 53203
Sarah R. Granados, M.D.	Mrs. Elizabeth Wong
(OR Dr. Sarah R. Granados)	46 Breighton Heights Way
8750 Griswoll Street	San Francisco, CA 94111
Albuquerque, NM 87101	

The Attention Line (Optional) When a letter is addressed to a company or to a department within a company rather than to a specific person, an attention line may be used to speed up handling of the letter. This line is typed below the inside address and above the salutation. The following are various styles of attention lines:

ATTENTION: MS. JOYCE T. ARNTSON	<u>Attention: Ms. J. T. Arntson</u>
ATTENTION: GENERAL MANAGER	<u>Attention: General Manager</u>

Notice that they are typed in all-capital letters *or* in underlined upper- and lowercase letters. Remember to use one of the following salutations with an attention line: *Ladies:* or *Gentlemen:* or *Ladies and Gentlemen:*

The Salutation   Your salutation reflects the tone of the letter. Note how the following salutations progress from informal to formal.

SINGULAR FORM	PLURAL FORM	USED FOR
Dear Steve:		Informal business
Dear Angelica:		letters—implies a personal friendship.
Dear Mr. Dixon:	Dear Messrs. Dixon	Routine business corre-
Dear Mr. Brauman:	and Brauman:	spondence addressed
Dear Ms. Stresino:	Dear Ms. Stresino	to one or several indi-
Dear Mrs. Crosby:	and Mrs. Crosby:	viduals—formal but cordial.
	Ladies and Gentlemen:	Correspondence ad-
	Ladies or Gentlemen:	dressed to a company or to a group.
Dear Madam:	Dear Mesdames:	*Very formal* correspon-
Dear Sir:	Dear Sirs:	dence.
Dear Madam or Sir:	Dear Mesdames or Sirs:	
Madam:	Mesdames:	
Sir:	Sirs:	
Madam or Sir:	Mesdames or Sirs:	

If you know the name of the person to whom you are writing, then use the name in the salutation. This approach shows more consideration and meets the receiver's ego needs, since we all like to see our name in print (spelled correctly, of course). If you don't know the person's name, use an attention line with the person's job title (*ATTENTION: PERSONNEL MANAGER*). Then use a salutation such as *Ladies and Gentlemen:*.

The Body

The body of the letter is the *message,* the most important section of the letter—from both the writer's and the reader's points of view. Here the writer makes every effort to get his or her thoughts effectively across to the reader. The body of the letter may optionally include a *subject line.*

The Subject Line (Optional)   The writer can give the reader advance notice of what the letter is about by including a subject line immediately *below* the salutation (just before the message). The subject line is typed in all-capital letters or in underlined upper- and lowercase letters. The word *Subject* may be omitted, but when it is used, it is followed by a colon:

SUBJECT: ANNUAL STOCKHOLDERS' MEETING
Subject: Annual Stockholders' Meeting

In legal correspondence or when referring to policy or project numbers, the term *In re:* or *Re:* may be used in place of *Subject:*

The Message   The message is the "body and soul" of the whole letter—all the other parts are appendages, arms and legs, that support the message and help make the message work. By using the principles of writing style discussed in Sections 6.1 through 6.5, the writer gives the message a purpose that is meaningful to both the writer and the reader.

The message of every business letter usually consists of at least two paragraphs—even if the second paragraph is nothing more than "Best wishes to you" or something along that line.

The Closing

Just as a person usually says "Good-bye" at the end of a conversation, so a writer usually uses a *complimentary closing* at the end of a business letter.

The Complimentary Closing   Complimentary closings, like salutations, vary in form and tone. The important thing to remember is to match the tone of the complimentary closing with that of the salutation as closely as possible. *Dear Bob* and *Very truly yours,* for example, obviously would make a rather absurd combination in a letter. Here are some forms that are commonly used:

FORMAL	INFORMAL
Yours very truly,	Sincerely,
Very truly yours,	Cordially,
Very sincerely yours,	Sincerely yours,
Very cordially yours,	Cordially yours,
Respectfully yours,	Best regards,

The Company Signature (Optional)   The company signature is the *typed* name of the company. Some companies prefer this optional part on the theory that the letter is legally from the company, not the writer. Most companies do not use a company signature in their letters.

Type a company signature in all-capital letters on the second line below the complimentary closing, as in this example:

Sincerely yours,

NORTH ATLANTIC SHIPPERS INC.

Follow a company signature with the usual spacing (that is, 3 blank lines) for the writer's signature.

The Writer's Signature   This is simply the *handwritten* signature of the person who has written the letter.

The Writer's Identification   In most instances the writer's name and job title (and/or department) are typed below the signature. Sometimes only the writer's title and department are used. Several examples are shown below.

Ellen R. Reynolds, General Manager　　William C. Carlton
　　　　　　　　　　　　　　　　　　　　Executive Vice President

S. W. Whitcomb, Manager
Accounting Section　　　　　　　　　　Assistant Manager
Agency Management Department　　　　Service Department

Reference Initials　　Because it is sometimes valuable to know who pre-pared a letter, the administrative assistant's reference initials have become a standard part of the business letter. Pat A. Jaworski keys her initials in lowercase letters:

Martina J. Poole
Executive Director

paj

Some assistants prefer using all-capital letters, which are also acceptable. An older style also includes the writer's initials, but this style is used less and less frequently:

MJP:PAJ

Enclosure Notation (Optional)　　When something is included with the letter in the same envelope or package, indicate this fact with an *enclosure nota-tion.* Such a notation helps writers, recipients, and secretaries confirm that all the enclosures are included when the letter is sent and received. The following are widely used enclosure notations:

Enclosure	Enclosure: Contract	Enclosures:
Enc.	2 Enclosures	1. Contract
		2. Check
Enclosures (2)	1 Enc.	3. Envelope
Enc. 2	2 Enc.	

Delivery Notation (Optional)　　When you use a special service such as Express Mail, add a note indicating that service on the original copy and on all other copies of the letter. Key the notation below the reference initials (or below any enclosure notation). See, for example, the delivery notation in the letter illustrated on page 322.

Copy Notation (Optional)　　When you plan to send a copy of the letter to someone, key the copy notation *c* or *cc* (or, if you prefer, the more traditional *cc:* or *c:*) on the original and on all copies. The copy notation goes on the line below the delivery notation, the enclosure notation, or the reference initials, whichever comes last.

cc John D'Amato　　　　　　　　　　　c Glenda Abdul
　　　　　　　　　　　　　　　　　　　　A. J. Whittier

cc: Advertising & Promotion Department　　c: Elisa Greenspan

When you list more than one person's name with the notation, align the names as shown above.

The content and design of a company's letterhead identify the company and project the company's image.

Blind Copy Notation (Optional) The copy notation, discussed above, appears on the original letter, informing the reader who received copies. At times, you may not want to inform the reader that copies are being sent to others. For example, if you solve a customer's problem, you may want to send a copy of your reply to your manager, Sara Davis.

Instead of a copy notation, in such cases use a *blind copy notation*. "Blind" here means that the notation does not appear on the original. On the seventh line from the top, at the left margin, key *bc Sara Davis* or *bcc Sara Davis*—but only on copies!

Postscript Before word processors, it was not possible to "squeeze in" a new paragraph in a handwritten or a typewritten letter. You had to rewrite or rekey the entire letter. Or you could simply add a *postscript*, an additional paragraph tacked on to the *end* of a letter.

Today word processors make it very easy to insert an additional paragraph and print out a fresh copy of the letter. But writers use postscripts anyway—deliberately, in fact, because a postscript is sure to get the reader's attention.

Begin a postscript a double space after the last line in the letter (which line is "last" depends on whether your letter has an enclosure notation, a delivery notation, or a copy notation). Key *PS:* or *PS.*, leave 2 spaces, and then key the body of the postscript in paragraph format, following the letter style you are using. The letters *PS* are optional; if you prefer, simply key the paragraph without this label.

BUSINESS LETTER FORMATS

Earlier we said that three formats dominate business letter style. Now we will discuss each:

- Block format
- Modified-block format
- Modified-block format with indented paragraphs

As you review these three popular formats, note that the *sequence* of letter parts is the same in all formats! What, then, is "different"?

The only differences among these styles lie in:

1. Where you start keying certain letter parts—at the left margin or at the center.
2. Whether you indent the first line of each paragraph 5 spaces or begin keying it at the left margin.

Now let's take a closer look at these business letter formats.

Block Format   Letters in which *all* the parts begin at the left margin are written in block style. This style, which is illustrated on page 321, saves keying time, since it requires no tabbing.

Modified-Block Format   In the modified-block format, the date line, the complimentary closing, and the writer's identification start at the horizontal center of the page. See page 322.

Modified-Block Format With Indented Paragraphs
The letters in this format look exactly the same as letters in the modified-block format except that the first line of each paragraph is indented 5 spaces. See page 323.

SOCIAL-BUSINESS AND PERSONAL-BUSINESS FORMATS

Two specialized letter formats are used for special purposes. Both of these formats are discussed in the sections that follow.

OFFICE TECHNOLOGY NETWORKS, INC.
4833 Gateway Boulevard East
El Paso, Texas 79905
713-555-1348

February 6, 1994 ↓6

Ms. Geneva Clauson
Investment Properties Company
708 Talton Avenue
San Antonio, TX 78285 ↓2

Dear Ms. Clauson: ↓2

Subject: Form of a Block Letter ↓2

This letter style is fast becoming the most popular style in use today. Efficiency is the main reason for its popularity. The keyboard specialist can save time and eliminate the necessity of working out placement. Some organizations are even designing letterheads to accommodate this style. A few years ago some people felt the block style looked odd. That complaint is seldom heard today, however. ↓2

This letter also illustrates the subject line and the enclosure. A subject line may be typed with initial caps or all in caps. It should start at the left margin. It always appears after the salutation and before the body of the letter. An enclosure notation starts at the left margin and always appears on the line after the reference initials. ↓2

Sincerely, ↓4

Annette G. Fuentes

Annette G. Fuentes
Manager, Customer Services ↓2

nkm
Enclosure

The block letter is the fastest to key because each line begins at the left margin.

Social-Business Format

Think of *social-business format* as the format for "social" letters written to "business" associates. In Section 7.7 you will learn the who, what, why of these critical pieces of correspondence. Here, we are concerned only with the unique features of the social-business format:

1. Place the inside address at the bottom of the letter, on the sixth line below the writer's name or title (whichever comes last).

OFFICE TECHNOLOGY NETWORKS, INC.
4833 Gateway Boulevard East
El Paso, Texas 79905
713-555-1348

February 6, 1994 ↓6

Ms. Carla Furman
Steffins and Wasserman Ltd.
1382 Victoria Street
Toronto, Ontario
CANADA M5C 2N8 ↓2

Dear Ms. Furman: ↓2

This modified-block letter style is still very popular for two
reasons: ↓2

    1. Many people feel comfortable with the traditional
        appearance. ↓2

    2. The blocked paragraphs make it slightly more efficient
        to type than a letter with indented paragraphs. ↓2

Lists, quotations, and addresses may be indented on either side
for a clearer display. If it is necessary to use more than one
paragraph for a quotation, a standard single blank line is left
between paragraphs. ↓2

Special mail or delivery services (such as certified mail,
priority overnight air service, or messenger service) is shown on
the line below the reference initials. We do so only to record
this information for our files. ↓2

When the letter is being sent to a foreign address, the country
is typed in all-capital letters on a separate line, as CANADA is
shown above. ↓2

        Sincerely, ↓4

        Annette G. Fuentes

        Annette G. Fuentes
        Manager, Customer Services ↓2

nkm
Registered ↓2

PS: We treat postscripts in the same way that we treat other
paragraphs, except that we precede each postscript by PS: or PS.

The modified-block letter is very popular. Note that the mailing notation is
below the reference initials and that all-capital letters are used for *CANADA*
in the inside address.

2. Use a comma (not the "traditional" colon) in the salutation to make it less
formal.

3. Use an informal complimentary closing, such as *Cordially, Regards, Sincerely,* or *Best wishes.*

4. Omit all notations.

An example of social-business format is illustrated on page 324.

OFFICE TECHNOLOGY NETWORKS, INC.

4833 Gateway Boulevard East
El Paso, Texas 79905
713-555-1348

February 6, 1994↓6

Banton, Turchon, and Vick, Inc.
9004 18th Street NW
Washington, DC 20009↓2

Attention: Training Director↓2

Ladies and Gentlemen:↓2

The modified-block letter with indented paragraphs is still popular because of its traditional appearance. The indented paragraphs give this style a distinctive look.↓2

This modified-block letter also shows an attention line. Like the subject line, the attention line is positioned at the left margin, but above the salutation. The attention line is usually keyed in initial caps but may also be all in caps.↓2

Cordially,↓4

Annette G. Fuentes

Annette G. Fuentes
Manager, Customer Services↓2

nkm↓2

cc: Ms. T. Spock
    Dr. F. Mantel

In the modified-block letter with indented paragraphs, the first line of each paragraph is indented—usually five spaces.

Personal-Business Format

Nowadays many people have word processing equipment at home that permits them to develop nicely designed "letterheads" for their personal stationery. Those who do not have such equipment, as well as those who still use typewriters, use the personal-business format whenever they write business letters of a personal nature—that is, when they write on behalf of themselves, not their companies.

FREDERICO, KLINE & DILLMAN

Three Peachtree Plaza • Atlanta, Georgia 30303
404-555-2371   FAX 404-555-7777

September 13, 1994

Dear Nancy,

How delighted I am to hear that you've opened your own ad agency! Congratulations!

In the few years that I've been in advertising, I've been very fortunate to meet, work with, and learn from some of the best creative directors in the business. And you, Nancy, are at the top of that list. I enjoyed working for you at Reynolds & Bishopp. You really "sold" me on advertising as a career, and I thank you for that.

By the way, you were right about Federico, Kline & Dillman. The people are great (just as you told me they'd be), and I am learning, learning, learning. I enjoy my work more than ever.

Carl and I haven't forgotten your offer. He may have a trip to Chicago in October. If he does, I'm going to join him so that we can both see you. I'm looking forward to that.

Again, my best wishes for success.

Sincerely,

Yvonne

Yvonne Gilroy

Ms. Nancy Costa
President
The Costa Advertising Group
121 Michigan Avenue
Chicago, Illinois 60202

The social-business letter uses a comma (not a colon) in the salutation, and it positions the inside address 5 lines below the signature line. In all other respects, it follows a block or a modified-block format (as this letter does).

For a personal-business letter, key a three-line heading with (1) your street address, (2) your city, state, and ZIP Code, and (3) the date, as follows:

center
↓
1301 Rockaway Parkway
Palmyra, PA 17078
February 9, 1994

Then follow formatting guidelines for modified block letters.

FORMATTING WRAP-UP

Now let's tackle a few miscellaneous concerns related to letter format. One is setting margins for letters. Another is envelope format, which is simple and straightforward. And a third is continuation pages—how do you handle letters that are longer than one page?

Margins   Most word processing software packages have preset 1-inch left and right margins for letters prepared on standard $8^1/_2$- by 11-inch stationery. With these margins, letters will be $6^1/_2$ inches wide, and this standard is perfectly acceptable.

If you are using a word processor, find out what its preset (or default) margins are. Also, learn how to change the margins for other paper sizes. Note the following recommended margins for three popular letter sizes (all figures are in inches):

IF YOU ARE USING . . .	USE A LINE LENGTH OF . . .	FOR LEFT AND RIGHT MARGINS OF . . .
Standard ($8^1/_2 \times 11$)	$6^1/_2$	1
Monarch ($7^1/_4 \times 10^1/_2$)	$5^1/_4$	1
Baronial ($5^1/_2 \times 8^1/_2$)	4	$^3/_4$

Envelopes   Envelopes should be of the same quality and color as the letterhead paper, as illustrated on page 326. Here are some points to remember when addressing envelopes.

1. On a small (No. 7, $6^3/_4$, or $5^3/_8$) envelope, start the address on line 13 about $2^1/_2$ inches from the left edge; on a large (No. 10) envelope, start the address on line 14 about 4 inches from the left edge.
2. Single-space all addresses, and use block style.
3. Always type the city, state, and ZIP Code on the last line.
4. Leave 1 or 2 spaces between the state and ZIP Code.
5. Type the attention line or any notation below the return address. Begin on line 9 or on the third line below the return address, whichever is lower. Capitalize each main word, and underscore the entire notation.
6. If a special mailing service is required, type the service in all-capital letters on line 9 in the upper right corner of the envelope. It should end a half inch from the right margin.
7. If the envelope does not contain a printed return address, be sure to type a return address in the upper left corner—*not* on the back of the envelope. Begin on line 3 about a half inch from the left edge.

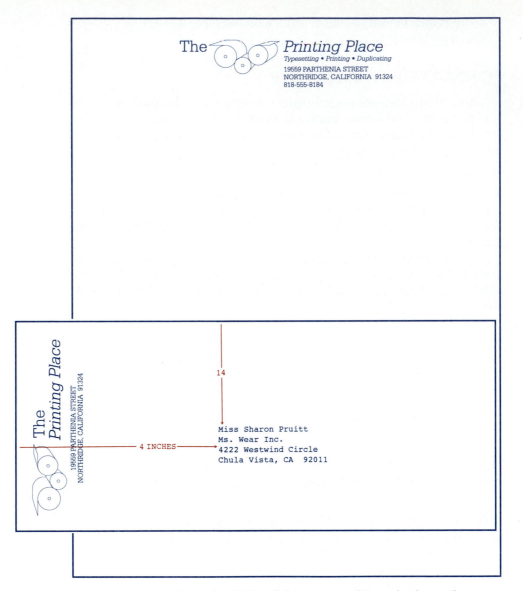

A company's envelopes should be of the same quality and color as the letterhead.

Continuation Pages   Use plain (not printed letterhead) paper of the same size and quality as the letterhead sheet for *continuation pages*:

1. *Side margins.* Use the same side margins that were used on the first page.
2. *Top and bottom margins.* Leave 1-inch top and bottom margins.
3. *Continuation-page heading.* Add a heading consisting of the name of the addressee, the page number, and the date at the top of each continuation page. Two of the commonly used arrangements for such headings are illus-

trated below. Remember that 2 blank lines should be left between the last line of the heading and the first line of the continued message.

Ms. R. D. Norland   2   February 3, 1995

OR:

Ms. R. D. Norland
Page 2
February 3, 1995

4. *Division of paragraphs.* When dividing a paragraph at the bottom of any page, leave at least the first two lines on the page, and carry at least two lines to the continuation page. If this isn't possible, carry the whole paragraph over to the continuation page. Do *not* divide the last word on any page.

COMMUNICATION LABORATORY

APPLICATION EXERCISES

A. Can you find the errors in the following letter parts? Rewrite each, correcting the errors.

1. Dear Ms. Montgomery,
2. Walter Drury
429 Zelzah Avenue
Columbia, MD 21045
3. 9/3/1993
4. lrc:PKW
5. Mr. William Schaefer
9320 Independence Avenue
Jericho, NY
6. A-1 Plumbing Supplies, Inc.
1450 McClay Street
San Fernando, CA 91340

SUBJECT: YOUR ORDER NO. 123788

Gentlemen:

B. Write the salutation and complimentary closing for each of the following.

1. A letter to a competitor, Ms. Lisa Stanfield, who has just received a promotion in her firm.
2. A letter to a state senator, Thomas Griswell, inviting him to speak at a monthly meeting of a trade association.
3. A letter to your state's Department of Economic Development inquiring about plant sites.
4. A letter to a good customer, Mr. Kenneth Killion, that includes an invitation to a formal dinner party.

C. Bring to class some business letters that you or a member of your family has received. Be prepared to discuss the appropriateness of the format, style, and letterhead for each letter.

VOCABULARY AND SPELLING STUDIES

A. These words are often confused: *pursue, peruse; populous, populace.* Explain the differences.

B. Which of the words that follow each of these sentences is nearest in meaning to the italicized word in the sentence?

   1. We *partitioned* the office to give each worker some privacy. (**a**) restored (**b**) divided (**c**) examined (**d**) scattered

   2. We developed a *calculated* plan for expanding our share of the furniture market. (**a**) secret (**b**) unusual (**c**) reckless (**d**) deliberate

   3. I remained *composed* as the customer enumerated ways in which our product was inferior. (**a**) distressed (**b**) intense (**c**) calm (**d**) defiant

SECTION 7.2

PLANNING YOUR CONTENT

 hen Clarkson High School invited Theresa Marino to speak on Career Day, Theresa knew exactly what she wanted to share with the student body.

"As a counselor for a personnel agency, I review many, many job letters and résumés. The letters and résumés I see have a very professional look. Most are prepared on computers. They use fancy display type. All are printed on fairly expensive paper, often with matching envelopes. Some are printed in color! Today's graduates certainly know the value of presenting attractive correspondence.

"My positive reaction to the appearance of some letters is, unfortunately, blunted when I start reading. If only the writers spent as much time planning what they wanted to *say* as they spent planning how the letter should *look!*"

THE NEED FOR A PLAN

Knowing the standard letter formats presented in Section 7.1 ensures that you can indeed prepare attractive, modern-looking letters. Applying these standards will be relatively easy, especially after you've had some practice.

By itself, however, developing letters that look inviting does not guarantee success. To be effective, your letters *must* be well organized, and well-organized letters are not accidental: They are the result of careful planning.

In this section you will master a simple approach to planning business letters, a technique that relies on a well-established principle of business letter writing: *Write so that you demonstrate an understanding of the reader's point of view.* To better understand what you are asking the reader, let's take a look at the reasons for writing business letters and the kinds of business letters you will most likely write on the job.

REASONS FOR WRITING BUSINESS LETTERS

Businesspeople at all levels—executives, managers, supervisors, assistants—write letters for a wide variety of reasons. During the business day, for example, people write letters:

To request information.
To send information.
To correct and to apologize for an error.
To refuse a request.
To explain a procedure or present a problem.
To sell products and services.

Businesspeople also write a host of *personal-business letters,* letters written not on behalf of their companies but for themselves. For example, people write:

To correct or clarify their personal (not their business) bank or credit accounts.
To establish personal credit.
To present claims to manufacturers for defective products.

In addition, people write a number of *social-business letters,* letters written:

To express thanks to a vendor for a special favor.
To congratulate a colleague who has been promoted.
To express sympathy to a colleague who has experienced a loss.

And yet, the list is not complete. There are additional letters that you will very likely write. To make the planning process as easy as possible, we can group most of the letters you will write into just a few general categories.

THREE SIMPLE PLANS

If every type of letter had its own unique plan, you'd have many, many different plans to memorize! Luckily, that is not the case.

An exceptionally simple, yet very effective, method for planning letters relies on *considering the letter's effect on the reader.* Using this approach, we can classify virtually all letters into three basic categories *based on the reader's anticipated reaction to the letter:*

1. *Everyday letters* include all the common letters that businesspeople write. These letters are routine; they deal with nothing out of the ordinary. Therefore, they are easy to handle.
2. *Persuasive letters* are those intended to convince readers to change their minds, do something extra, take a risk, approve a special request. They are not routine.
3. *Bad-news letters* are those which say "No" to requests or convey some sort of disappointing news. They, too, are not routine.

Let's take a closer look at each of these categories.

EVERYDAY LETTERS

For most professionals, the following letter-writing situations are strictly *routine:*

A well-established customer asks you to send a copy of your company's new catalog "as soon as it's available."

A vendor wants to know the procedure for submitting cost estimates.

A customer sends in his or her payment.

A client suggests a date and time for a meeting.

A consultant submits her bill for a project she has satisfactorily completed for you.

You decide to send a good customer some advance information on a new product line.

Each of these is a routine situation, and each requires you to write a routine letter. You do not need to convince or persuade. You have no worry about hurting your reader's feelings. You have no reason to struggle over the right thing to say.

In such situations, you will simply present the information in a matter-of-fact, straightforward way. You should use the **everyday letter plan.**

Organize your everyday letters as follows:

1. Begin with a **direct opening statement** indicating the purpose of your letter.
2. Provide the **necessary details** (if any) concerning the subject matter.
3. Close with a **goodwill ending.**

As an example of this *direct opening/details/goodwill ending* approach, let's look at a rough organization for the first situation above (*A well-established customer asks you to send a copy of your company's new catalog "as soon as it's available"*):

1. *Direct opening statement:* Send her one of our advance copies as soon as we receive our shipment from the printer.
2. *Necessary details:* Point out that our new catalog presents all our product lines—we no longer print a separate catalog for each line.
3. *Goodwill ending:* Look forward to seeing you at the ABC Convention next month.

Everyday letters take a *direct approach* and are simple to write. In the next section, you will practice applying the direct approach to everyday letters.

PERSUASIVE LETTERS

Not every letter you write will be routine, of course. The direct approach will not work in all instances. Imagine, for example, how readers will react to these opening paragraphs:

> My Convex dehumidifier does not work properly, and although the warranty expired only two days ago, I demand that you repair it at no charge to me.

> SofStuf leather products are the most beautiful, handsomely crafted, artistically designed items available. Fill out the enclosed order form to indicate which products you want to buy.

Clearly, neither letter will be successful. Neither provides any reasons why the reader should act as requested. Neither tries to *persuade* the reader to act, to convince the reader to do what the writer wants him or her to do. In many instances, you will need to convince readers to accept your decision not to grant their request, persuade them to take a risk and try your services, show them why your products are worth the extra cost, or lead them to see how they will benefit by following your suggestion.

To get readers to act positively, you cannot open persuasive letters directly. Instead, to show the reader *why* he or she should buy, order, try, or approve your suggestion, you must use an **indirect approach.**

What makes *you* act positively in response to someone's suggestion or recommendation? Your basic human needs often play a strong role here—your needs for health, security, family, financial gain, status, leisure time, and comfort and convenience. These needs often provide the most effective "hooks" to persuade people, either in business or in personal situations.

Note how the indirect approach leads the reader to grasp your logic through its step-by-step organization and appeals to the *reader's* human needs:

1. Use an **attention-getting opening statement** to encourage the *reader* to continue reading.
2. List **factual statements** targeted at meeting the *reader's* needs.
3. Present your **request** in terms of how it will benefit the *reader*—not you!
4. Specify the **action** the *reader* must take to receive the benefits you've listed.

A reader will more likely accept this *attention/facts/request/action* approach because it leads the reader to see why, to understand why, he or she *should* take the action indicated. Thus a letter to the Convex Corporation requesting service after a warranty has expired might get better results if it follows an indirect organization:

1. *Attention-getting opening:* Praise Convex for its reputation for quality and dependability.
2. *Facts:* Humidifier broke 2 days after warranty expired. This is the third Convex product I've bought, and I've always been very pleased in the past.

3. *Request:* Approval to bring the humidifier in to the authorized Convex service center in my area and have it repaired under the terms of the warranty.
4. *Action:* To notify you and the service center that the repair will be covered under the terms of the warranty.

Of course, an indirect approach does not guarantee success, but it greatly improves the odds that your letter will get and keep the reader's attention and will present your argument in the most forceful way.

BAD-NEWS LETTERS

Saying no to requests isn't easy for most people, and saying no in writing can often present additional problems. Added to the difficulty is the fact that most "bad-news" situations involve risks such as losing customers, decreasing goodwill, tarnishing reputations (both yours and your firm's), and even incurring legal battles in some cases.

But at times you simply must say no. At times you simply must present bad news. You may need to announce a price increase, deny a discount, refuse a credit application, reject an offer, inform bidders that their proposals are unacceptable, or turn down a customer's demand. You will face bad-news situations from time to time.

To make the best of a bad-news situation, use the indirect approach. The indirect approach will help you salvage goodwill and help you avoid losing a customer, if possible. Organize your bad-news letters using this indirect outline:

1. Begin with a **neutral opening statement**—a comment that both you and your reader will find agreeable.
2. List the **reasons** for the bad news (but not the news itself) in the most positive, tactful, and courteous terms.
3. State the **refusal** (or whatever the bad news is).
4. Suggest **alternatives,** if any.
5. End with a **goodwill closing.**

If you follow this outline carefully, you will be able to handle many sensitive situations with the tact and diplomacy that will mark you as a professional businessperson. Even the undesirable task of informing one of your bank's customers that his request for a $7500 loan cannot be approved can be handled rather smoothly using the outline for bad-news letters:

1. *Neutral opening:* Thank customer for his credit request.
2. *Reasons* leading up to the yet-unstated refusal: Discuss the need for collateral. Discuss income requirements for loans without collateral.
3. *Refusal:* Mention politely and courteously that the customer's qualifications do not meet these requirements and that therefore the loan cannot be granted.
4. *Alternatives:* Bank can lend $4000 on the basis of the customer's collateral. Or if the customer wishes, he can provide additional collateral and resubmit his application.

5. *Goodwill closing:* Look forward to hearing whether either alternative is acceptable. Am sending information on new banking services available.

Remember that these three outlines—for everyday, persuasive, and bad-news letters—are tools. On the job, you can use these tools over and over again. Each time you use these tools, you will find that your planning and your outlining will get easier. And as planning becomes easier, writing, too, becomes easier!

PLANNING FOR BETTER RESULTS

A blueprint helps the carpenter build a house; a pattern helps the dressmaker make a dress. Without the blueprint and the pattern, the carpenter and the dressmaker would be lost. When you write a letter, your "blueprint" can be of great help to you, for an effective letter does not just happen—it combines knowledge, experience, and careful planning.

How to Plan   The first step in any planning process is to gather all the materials you will need to do the job. In writing a letter, these materials may include the letter to which you are replying, a good dictionary, and pertinent information, such as prices and delivery dates. Only when you have all the necessary tools and information at hand can you plan an effective letter.

Using this information, you may wish to make brief notes—either on a scratch pad or on the letter to which you are replying. From these notes you can prepare a rough draft of your letter.

First, however, you should prepare an outline of what you wish to say, for an outline will help you organize your thoughts. This practice will save you time and money, and it should prevent the necessity for writing follow-up letters to add information or explain something that was not previously stated clearly.

Using your outline, you should next prepare a rough draft of the letter. Then check this draft for correct spelling and grammar and for completeness and accuracy of details. You may wish to improve the wording or change the order of some sentences so that your meaning is clear, your words are vivid, and your ideas flow. This is the process of editing, as described in Section 6.4.

Probably you will want to prepare another draft, and perhaps still another, before you arrive at a final draft. In each you will incorporate the changes made in the preceding draft. This procedure is time-consuming, but it results in a better letter.

As you gain experience in letter writing, you will find that you need to spend less and less time in detailed planning; in time many facets of the letter-writing process will become almost automatic.

A Successful Example   An outline for a letter quoting the wholesale prices of personal computers to a retail store might look like the one given on page 334. Notice how this outline follows the organizational plan for everyday letters.

1. Send catalog of complete line of Computab computer products.
2. Appreciate interest in the Computab line.
3. Recommend economical Basic 4 model for Laramie Electronics' special anniversary sale.
4. Quote price of $539.95 each in lots fewer than 25 and $489.95 each in lots of 25 or more.
5. Promise delivery one week after order is received.
6. Reassure retailer that Computab products are good sellers because of their low prices and fine values.

Eventually, when you have had more experience in planning and writing business letters, you will need only brief notations to direct you. Your condensed outline then might look like this:

1. *Send catalog; acknowledge inquiry.*
2. *Basic 4 model $539.95 each in lots fewer than 25 and $489.95 each in lots of 25 or more.*
3. *Delivery in a week.*
4. *Goodwill closing.*

Here is the letter written from this outline:

Dear Mr. Meyer:

As you requested, here is the current Computab catalog that describes our complete line of personal computers and accessories. We appreciate the opportunity to acquaint you with our products.

For Laramie Electronics' special anniversary sale, we recommend the economical Basic 4 model, which is described on page 7 of the catalog. The Basic 4 wholesales at $539.95 each in lots fewer than 25 and at $489.95 each in lots of 25 or more. You can expect delivery one week after you place an order.

We predict that the Basic 4 will be a big seller for you. Because its retail price is under $1000, the Basic 4 represents a superior value and meets the growing demand for this kind of equipment. Like many other retailers throughout the country, you will have great success with this fine product.

Sincerely yours,

COMMUNICATION LABORATORY

APPLICATION EXERCISES

A. List all the types of letters that you have received or written.

CONTINUED

B. List and describe the purposes of most business letters that the following people might write in a typical month:

1. Electronics store owner
2. Police chief
3. High school or college teacher
4. Automobile dealer
5. Librarian
6. Physician or dentist

C. Bring to class at least four examples of different types of letters that you collected at home or from people in business. Be prepared to discuss:

1. The kind of plan used for letter.
2. The reason the letter was written.
3. The way the receiver probably would react to the letter.

D. For each situation, tell which business letter plan you would use.

1. To send a customer a requested price list.
2. To order 3000 pens imprinted with the company's name.
3. To request payment on a long overdue account.
4. To interest a potential vacationer in a resort.
5. To thank the Richmond Corporation for an interview.
6. To sell a lawn maintenance service.
7. To congratulate a competitor on a promotion.
8. To invite potential customers to a plant tour.
9. To complain about a long overdue shipment.
10. To reject someone who has applied for a job.

VOCABULARY AND SPELLING STUDIES

A. These words are often confused: *intense, intents; insoluble, insolvable, insolvent.* Explain the differences.

B. Use either *raise* or *rise* to complete each of the following sentences. (Some sentences require the past tense or past participle form.)

1. You can be sure that those two members of the staff will always _____ objections to any new ideas.
2. If stock prices continue to _____, we may wish to reinvest these funds.
3. Because your rates have _____ so sharply, we must find another method for shipping our products.
4. How many students _____ their hands to answer the question?
5. Last year the cost of living _____ 3 percent.

C. Which of these words are misspelled? Spell each correctly.

1. application
2. apointment
3. akward
4. necessary
5. lisence
6. posess
7. sincerely
8. unconscious
9. privlege
10. anual

EVERYDAY LETTERS

Since Sheila Warren graduated from high school last June, she has been working as a marketing assistant for Sun View Products while she attends a community college in the evenings. "I want to be an actress, not a marketing assistant, but I treat my job seriously, even though it's not exactly what I want. After all, I'm a professional!"

At first, Sheila says, she "felt a bit pressured, especially in handling the mail, because my manager travels often. We receive two mail drops a day, and I handle almost every piece of mail without any input from my manager. Now that I have experience and know company policies, I know that 95 percent of my letters are everyday letters. *No problem!*"

WHAT ARE "EVERYDAY" LETTERS?

Let's use the term *everyday letters* to group all the routine correspondence that most people prepare or receive in the course of a typical workday. Sheila, for example, typically writes or receives:

- Letters requesting information or materials. ("Is your packaging recyclable?" "May I please have a copy of your catalog?" "Will you please send me a copy of the brochure mentioned in last week's newspaper?")

- Letters transmitting (that is, *sending*) information or materials. ("I have enclosed an order form and a check . . . ." "The revised auto maintenance agreement for your sales representatives is enclosed." "Two copies of our signed contract are enclosed for your countersignature.")

- Letters requesting or confirming appointments. ("I'd like to confirm our appointment for . . . .")

- Letters making routine claims. ("After only two weeks, my new Sonic-Jet printer is malfunctioning.")

- Letters acknowledging receipt of money, key documents, and orders. ("Today I received your signed lease agreement, and . . . ." "This afternoon we received your order for 2 dozen canoe paddles.")

- Letters inviting her manager to speak. ("On behalf of the local Business Opportunities for Youth Committee, I am pleased to invite you to give a presentation on Monday, September 9, at the . . . ." "I understand that you will be in Cincinnati on May 9. Is it possible that you might visit our school . . . ?")

What do these letters have in common? All concern average, routine business situations, situations that are easy to handle effectively. They are not unimportant situations; they are simply common situations.

ORGANIZATION OF EVERYDAY LETTERS

The reader's reactions to everyday letters will be positive or neutral—that's one reason why these letters are "routine." As a result, everyday letters get directly to the point. No elaborate explanation is required.

The key word here is *direct.* Organizing everyday letters is easy because you can use a direct, straightforward approach, as shown in this outline:

1. Begin with a **direct opening statement** indicating the purpose of your letter.
2. Provide the **necessary details** (if any) concerning the subject matter.
3. Close with a **goodwill ending.**

Using this *direct opening/details/goodwill ending* approach, let's look at a sample outline for a reply to a request from a well-established customer for a copy of your company's new catalog "as soon as it's available":

1. Direct opening statement: Send her one of our advance copies as soon as we receive our shipment from the printer.
2. Necessary details: Point out that our new catalog presents all our product lines—we no longer print a separate catalog for each line.
3. Goodwill ending: Look forward to seeing you at the ABC Convention.

With practice, you will develop shorter outlines than this one. Then, once you have your outline, you can draft your letter. As you continue, note how the sample letters in this section follow this basic outline.

REQUEST LETTERS

Companies welcome requests that may help increase business. In fact, through their advertising they actively encourage such requests for free samples, trial subscriptions, special discounts, catalogs, or brochures—all you need to do is call, complete a coupon, or send a request letter. Thus many request letters ask for something that the reader is very willing to give!

These are, indeed, routine requests, and the everyday letter plan works very effectively in such cases.

Requesting Information, Literature, or Free Service

Most letters requesting information, literature, or free service are short. They should give only the information needed by the reader to fulfill the request.

Dear Mr. Halbert:

Please send me a schedule of ExecPro training programs for the July–December period. Specifically, I would like listings of program schedules for Texas, Oregon, and Illinois for this period.

In addition, Mr. Halbert, I recently heard that ExecPro now offers audio cassettes for some of its popular training programs. I would appreciate receiving information on which programs are available and the cost of each.

Sincerely yours,

With practice using this outline, you will be able to develop letters that are simple, clear, complete, and effective.

Requesting Appointments

In business the usual practice is to make an appointment by telephone or letter when you wish to call on an individual at his or her office. Of course, if you are requesting an appointment with someone nearby, the use of the telephone is quicker and less expensive. Out-of-town appointments are often made by letter.

Dear Mr. Koltai:

I am planning to spend December 9 in Oklahoma City and would like very much to talk with you or one of your associates while I am there. We are setting up a profit-sharing program in our organization, and I have been told that you have a very effective plan at Walton Industries.

Would you find 10 a.m. on the 9th a convenient time to see me? An hour of your time should be sufficient and would mean a great deal to me.

Sincerely yours,

Making Reservations

While hotel reservations may be made by telephone, many persons prefer writing letters so that they are assured all the information has been conveyed correctly. What kinds of information need to be included? Of course, the dates of arrival and departure are paramount, but other kinds of information are important too. The hotel needs to know the name of the person who is to occupy the room. If there are other persons in the party, their names should be given too. Does the guest want a single room or a double room? What will be the arrival time? (A room is usually not held after 6 p.m. unless the person making the reservation asks that it be held for late arrival.) Is payment for the first night included to guarantee that the room will be held? Other information that might be given—although it is not always essential—is the guest's preference for a room location, the expected price, and any special required services.

Ladies and Gentlemen:

Please reserve a single room for Mrs. Frances Cates, National Sales Manager of Data Products Inc., for March 23 and 24. Mrs. Cates will arrive at approximately 7:30 p.m. on March 23, so please hold the reservation for late arrival. If possible, Mrs. Cates would like to have a room facing Lake Michigan.

Please confirm this reservation, and let me know if a deposit or credit card number is required.

Sincerely yours,

Ordering a Product or a Service

Most business firms of medium and large size use a purchase order form when ordering goods. Such a form centralizes in one department the responsibility for ordering merchandise and helps to eliminate the possibility of employees' ordering goods on their own initiative. Also, a purchase order form is quicker to prepare than a letter.

Orders may also be placed on an order blank supplied by the company from which goods are being bought. Some companies supply such order forms.

A third way of ordering merchandise, used widely in small companies and by individuals, is through letters and postcards.

Accuracy is extremely important in preparing order letters. Figures and items must be checked and rechecked. To make an order letter easier to read and to check, the competent writer places each order item on a separate line in tabular form.

Ladies and Gentlemen:

Please send us the following daisy wheels for our Model 4050 International printers:

Quantity	Item	Price	Amount
2	No. 732 (Courier, 10 pitch)	$7.80	$15.60
4	No. 737 (Letter Gothic, 12 pitch)	7.80	31.20
1	No. 734 (Orator, 10 pitch)	8.30	8.30
1	No. 739 (Courier, 12 pitch)	7.80	7.80
Subtotal			$62.90
6% Sales Tax			3.77
TOTAL			$66.67

Our check for $66.67 is enclosed. Please let us know when we may expect delivery of this order.

Sincerely yours,

Enclosure

Every order letter must contain all the information needed to process the order. Besides giving the quantity, price, and amount, the order letter should pay careful attention to additional specifications. If applicable, is color and size information included? Has the method of payment been discussed? Is a specific date of shipment important? Are both the customer and the supplier in agreement on the method of shipment and on who will pay the freight charges? All these items need to be considered in composing the order letter.

LIVING LANGUAGE

Commenting on the great variety of synonyms available in English, one writer said, "In the family of words, there are no twins, only cousins."

TRANSMITTAL LETTERS

A check, a money order, or an important business paper sent by mail should always be accompanied by a letter. A letter helps to identify what is being sent so that the recipient knows exactly what you *intended* to send. The letter also provides a valuable record for future reference because of the enclosure notation on your file copy.

Good transmittal letters should be able to accomplish the following:

1. Identify *what* is being sent and *how many* (if money, the *amount*).
2. Specify any action necessary on the part of the recipient.

3. If you are transmitting money, identify the purpose for which the money is to be used—to be applied to the account, in payment for a certain invoice number, for services rendered, or for purchases made.

ACKNOWLEDGMENT LETTERS

A usual business practice—always a very good one—is to acknowledge by letter receipt of any money, business papers, orders, favors, appointments, and oral agreements. Letters are important in acknowledging such business matters to avoid misunderstandings, to provide a record, and to show courtesy.

Letters of acknowledgment help avoid misunderstandings or mistakes. If you have received an order and will make shipment as soon as possible, the customer will want to know. If you do not acknowledge the order, the customer may assume that you did not receive it or wonder what you are doing about it if you did. A written acknowledgment should state that you have the merchandise in the requested quantity and tell the customer when you are going to fill the order. In this way misunderstandings and mistakes can be avoided.

Acknowledgment letters provide a record, and records provide the internal control and memory of a business. You would not want to trust your own memory as to the date on which you promised delivery of an order, especially if you are responsible for hundreds of orders. The copy of your acknowledgment, therefore, provides the information. A written record may also be needed for legal proof.

Courtesy builds goodwill for a business organization, and writing acknowledgment letters is one way to show courtesy. By reassuring the reader that you have received the order and are doing something about it, you show courtesy and build goodwill.

Acknowledgment letters, because they are routine letters, generally follow the everyday letter plan. After you have expressed appreciation for the reader's action, you may then supply the necessary details before giving your goodwill closing.

Acknowledging Receipt of Money When money is received on a regular basis, such as in the monthly payment of an account, usual business practice calls for acknowledging the current month's payment on the next month's statement. Isolated payments or payments received on an irregular basis, however, require individual attention and should be acknowledged through a form or letter. Remember these special considerations when writing letters that acknowledge the receipt of money:

1. Express thanks for the money, even though payment may be long overdue.
2. Be sure to mention the amount that is received. This letter provides a valuable record for the future. Rather than just saying, "Thank you for your check," say, "Thank you for your check for $123.50."
3. When appropriate, mention how the money is to be used—for example, to be applied to the account or to be used as full payment for merchandise.

4. If you can think of something pleasant to say to the sender, say it. "We appreciate your prompt payment" or "Doing business with you is always a pleasure" or "I hope you will enjoy your new Cranston hardwood floors."

Following is a typical example of a letter acknowledging the receipt of money.

Dear Ms. Baca:

Thank you for your check for $87.50. This amount has been applied to your account, leaving a balance of $93.

We appreciate your promptness in making this payment, Ms. Baca, and we are always pleased to serve you.

Sincerely yours,

Acknowledging Receipt of Business Papers

The receipt of important business papers—such as contracts, securities (stocks and bonds), notes, insurance policies, and bids—should always be acknowledged promptly, since they are often just as important as money. In writing such letters, be specific as to just what was received and any identifying numbers. If any action is required, your acknowledgment should state clearly that you have taken such action.

Dear Mr. Hedge:

Your life insurance policy, No. BFLS1003468, arrived today. As you requested, we will cancel the policy and send you the cash surrender value, $4312. You will receive a check within 30 days.

May we recommend, Mr. Hedge, that you consider the possibility of maintaining your current protection through the purchase of term insurance. Considerably less expensive than ordinary life, this kind of insurance would enable you to retain the same amount of protection with up to 70 percent less in premium payments.

If you are interested in looking into this program, or if we can be of further service, please call Sylvia Padilla at 555-9875.

Sincerely yours,

Acknowledging Orders

Some business firms acknowledge all orders they receive for goods or services. Automation makes possible the easy use of form letters or postcards for this purpose. However, to welcome a new customer, to acknowledge an unusually large order, or to remind longtime customers how much you appreciate their business, individually written letters are much more effective. Customers, especially, appreciate the "extra touch" of a personal letter.

Letters acknowledging orders follow the same plan as other acknowledgment letters. Because the customer is primarily interested in when the merchandise will arrive, this information is supplied in the opening sentence. Once you have expressed the main idea, you may then follow up with a statement of appreciation and other necessary details pertaining to the order.

CLAIM LETTERS

A claim letter states a problem with a product or service and requests a solution. Essentially, then, a claim letter is really a *complaint letter,* and many complaint or claim letters are not routine, everyday letters. Answering them often requires excellent persuasive abilities! Letters that persuade are covered in Section 7.4.

Here we will address only routine claims, those problems that are obvious and minor and that should require only a straightforward presentation of the facts. Companies expect routine claim letters; they do not need to be persuaded to correct obvious problems.

Ladies and Gentlemen:

This morning I received the two SonicTone answering machines I ordered recently. Both machines are black, as I requested, but on one machine the handset cord is white.

Will you please replace the enclosed white cord with a black cord? The model number is listed on the enclosed copy of my shipping form. I'd appreciate your shipping the new cord to me at the above address as soon as possible.

Sincerely yours,

Enclosure

Clearly, this is a routine claim. If you are dealing with an honest company, presenting the facts accurately, and making a reasonable claim, a direct approach will work very effectively.

EDITING OF EVERYDAY LETTERS

In Chapter 6 you learned a number of techniques that will improve your writing and ensure professional results. In all letters, including your everyday letters, your ability to write concisely, completely, correctly, and courteously will determine your success, so be sure to review the principles presented in Chapter 6.

Remember that your goal is to *write letters that you would like to receive.*

COMMUNICATION LABORATORY

APPLICATION EXERCISES

A. In a magazine or a newspaper, find an advertisement offering a free pamphlet or booklet that you might like to have. Clip the advertisement. Then write a letter requesting the booklet or pamphlet, and attach the advertisement to your letter. After your teacher returns your letter to you, you may want to send for the booklet or pamphlet.

B. You have been offered a summer job with Dalton Community College, which you will attend in the fall. You will work in the student records office processing applications from entering freshmen. To get the job, you need three letters of reference. Your business English teacher, Dolores Wysocki, has moved to this address: 9432 Sunglow Street, Homestead Park, PA 15120. Write Ms. Wysocki, asking her if she would send a letter of recommendation to Mr. Angelo Amato, Personnel Director, Dalton Community College, P.O. Box 749, San Diego, CA 92109.

C. Assume that you are employed by a small legal firm and have been asked to investigate the possibility of computerizing its billing system. The firm presently owns an IBM personal computer that is used for word processing. While reading *PC News,* a national computer magazine, you notice an advertisement for a variety of software packages designed for the legal office—among which is a billing program. Write Legal Beagle Software Inc., 3854 Centinella Avenue, Topeka, KS 66604, to request information describing specifically the functions, contents, and features of its billing program. Inquire also whether the company has a booklet describing its other programs for the legal office. If it does, request this additional information in your letter.

D. Write a letter to the Del Coronado Hotel, Coronado, CA 92118, to make a reservation for your five-day vacation. Request a room in the Ocean Towers at the lowest possible rate. You will need a room with two double beds. Because this hotel is in a resort area, a deposit is required; include with your letter a $100 check. Supply dates and other details.

E. You receive a signed contract from a client, Agnes Ride, Health Crest Industries, 9300 Washington Boulevard, Detroit, MI 48233. The contract is to provide leased automobiles for all Health Crest's sales representatives for the next two years, which makes Ms. Ride a major client. Acknowledge receipt of this contract, and use this opportunity to generate continued goodwill for your company.

F. A regular customer, George Muhlhauser, writes to renew a contract with your company. Your supervisor, Alice Haberman, who is in charge of such contracts, will be out of town until October 5, and you have no authorization to renew contracts. Ms. Haberman has asked you to acknowledge receipt of all correspondence in her absence. Write a letter acknowledging receipt of this customer's letter, but avoid making any commitment for your company that is beyond your area of responsibility.

G. Donald Sampson, an industrial client whom your company represents, called to request a Tuesday, May 5, appointment at 9 a.m. He inquired as to whether you have a carousel slide projector available, since he wishes to show the sales staff some slides illustrating the features of his new product line. Write a letter acknowledging the appointment and confirming the

CONTINUED

availability of the equipment. Mr. Sampson's address is 8750 Arminta Street, SE, Portland, OR 97213.

H. Last week Mrs. Agnes Streebing, a counselor from nearby Los Altos Hills College, visited your school. Just as she was leaving, you managed to ask her for an appointment to see about enrolling at Los Altos Hills College. You will graduate from Kennedy High School in June and would like to continue your education in some field of business, possibly computers. Mrs. Streebing suggested that you drop by her office after school a week from Thursday to discuss Los Altos Hills' business curriculum and the possibility of your attending this college. Write the letter you would send to Mrs. Streebing confirming your appointment. Los Altos Hills College is located at 5600 Woodlake Street, Raleigh, NC 27611.

I. Assume that you work in the Visitors' Bureau of the Rocky Point National Wildlife Preserve, Rocky Point, NC 28457. You receive a letter from Ms. Sally Abramowitz, Sarames & Abramowitz Travel Agency, 3575 Osborne Street, Huntsville, AL 35801. Ms. Abramowitz asks for literature and any other information needed to plan a trip through the preserve. Send her several pamphlets. The best time to visit the preserve is during the spring and fall. Food facilities are available, but she may also bring her own box lunch and take advantage of the picnic grounds or indoor dining facilities.

J. Assume that you work in the offices of the Miami Chamber of Commerce. Kym Freeman, a student at Washington High School, has written a letter requesting information about Miami for her term report. She would like to have up-to-date information about population, industrial growth, housing, and recreational facilities. Answer Ms. Freeman's inquiry. Include various pamphlets published by the Chamber of Commerce and other civic groups. In your letter point out one or two interesting facts about Miami. Address the letter to Ms. Freeman at 1350 Shawnee Avenue, Des Moines, IA 50313.

VOCABULARY AND SPELLING STUDIES

A. These words are often confused: *elicit, illicit; key, quay.* Write each in a sentence that illustrates its meaning.

B. Are these statements correct?

1. Two adjectives that precede a noun are always connected by a hyphen.
2. In typewritten material, words referred to as words are either underscored or enclosed in quotation marks.
3. Words that interrupt a direct quotation are also enclosed in quotation marks.
4. Slang is capitalized for emphasis.
5. Commas and periods are always placed inside, never outside, quotation marks.

CONTINUED

C. In which of the following words should an e appear in the blank space?

1. d__scriminate
2. d__scribe
3. d__sease
4. exist__nce
5. restaur__nt
6. bull__tin
7. calend__r
8. materi__l
9. correspond__nce
10. __nquired
11. p__rsuade
12. memor__ndum
13. s__parate
14. listen__rs
15. d__stinctly

SECTION 7.4

LETTERS THAT PERSUADE

Since childhood, Barbara Benson has worked in the family business, Benson's Grain Supply Company, where she is now president.

"One day stands out. It was Saturday, and I remember spending the whole day stuffing fliers into envelopes. I thought, 'What a waste!' We were inviting people to ask us for *free* catalogs! Fliers, envelopes, and catalogs are all costly. I asked my father, 'How do we *make* money?' He said, Barbara, '*You must spend money to make money.*' I learned a very basic business lesson."

THE NEED TO BE PERSUASIVE

Benson's Grain Supply *wants* to send catalogs to potential customers. If you're a potential customer, all you need to do is ask.

But if you write to Barbara Howard asking her to give a speech at your annual convention, you will need to persuade her. If you want her to make a donation to your organization, you will need to convince her. And if you want to sell her your merchandise or services, you will need to present the advantages and benefits of the merchandise or services clearly, forcefully, logically, and concisely.

THE PERSUASIVE APPROACH

When you know that the reader must be persuaded or convinced, you should approach your writing *indirectly*. You build up reasons, present facts, and show benefits before you make the actual request.

What will persuade readers to buy a product? subscribe to a service? say yes to a request? make a donation? approve a loan? Will they compare your product with others solely on the basis of quality? Will they evaluate your service exclusively on the basis of cost? Will they be more likely to make a donation to a local rather than a national organization?

Whenever you plan a persuasive letter, consider how the reader will react. Why will the reader approve my request? What are the "pluses" that will motivate the reader to react positively to my recommendation? When you can answer these questions, then ask yourself, How can I arrange the information so that it is really convincing, forceful, and effective?

ELEMENTS OF PERSUASION

The reasons why businesspeople approve some requests and reject others vary, of course, because each situation is unique. Targeting your product's superior quality may persuade one reader, but another reader may react positively only to costs. Each persuasive letter requires analysis and insight, because the elements of persuasion vary from situation to situation, and from person to person, and, therefore, from letter to letter.

Apply the "Basics"   While it is difficult to generalize, there are, however, some qualities that all readers want, expect, or perhaps demand if they are to agree with your request. Readers are more likely to react positively to letters that are *concise, complete, clear,* and *courteous* (these "basics" have already been discussed in detail in Chapter 6).

Be Reasonable   All the writing skills in the world cannot convert an *un*reasonable request into a reasonable one!

Consider carefully what you are asking the reader. Does the reader have the authority to grant your request? Are you asking him or her to spend hours and hours to provide you with information? Is the information you are asking for confidential company business?

In your rush to get your job done, don't fall into the trap of asking others to do too much or to provide something inappropriate.

Make the Reader Feel "Special"   All of us enjoy feeling honored and special, and the language of a letter contributes positively or negatively to that feeling on the part of the reader.

> With your help, Ms. Mendoza, we know that our customer survey will provide the information we need to continue serving your business needs.

> We hope we can depend on you, Mr. Shapiro, to share your unique business insights with our students. Just one hour for you, but a lifetime of invaluable advice for aspiring entrepreneurs in your own community.

Share that feeling with your reader!

Make It Easy for the Reader to Say Yes   When you ask someone for a favor, common courtesy and common sense both demand that you make it as easy as possible for the other person to do the favor.

Imagine calling a friend and asking her to lend you money until next week. Would you also ask her to *deliver* the money to you, or would your common sense dictate that *you* should go to her?

How can you make it easy for your reader to give a positive response? That depends. You could include a stamped, addressed envelope or suggest that the reader call you collect, if either of these options is appropriate.

Another option is to enclose a courtesy copy on which the reader can simply check off his or her response and quickly make note of any other information needed to complete the response. Remember that the purpose is to make the reader's response more convenient.

With the growing popularity of facsimile (fax) communications, you may offer the reader the alternative of a toll-free fax number using your letter to note his or her response. Of course, to use that choice, both you and the reader must have access to fax equipment.

Of course, all these techniques have the goal of persuading the reader to act as you want him or her to act—to buy a product or service, to accept an idea, to send for a catalog.

Use an Indirect Approach   Readers are also apt to react favorably to letters that are logical and forceful—letters that are arranged *indirectly*.

The section below presents an organizational plan for persuasive letters.

ORGANIZATION OF PERSUASIVE LETTERS

Developing an outline for a persuasive letter is simple. But before you can outline a letter, you must:

- Focus on your specific target: What specifically do you want from your reader? Focusing on the target requires you to analyze your goals. What do you want from the reader—*specifically*?

- Map out a path for hitting the target: What will convince the reader to agree? What facts or statistics or information will make the reader react favorably? Mapping a path requires you to switch places with the reader in an effort to identify what motivates him or her.

Focusing on the Target   Only by knowing specifically what *you* want will you know what to ask for!

- Asking for a "donation" is too vague. Effective fund-raising letters show the reader what his or her $100 or $500 or $1000 donation will do.

- Inviting someone to speak is too general. Suggest a topic or a title. Specify how many people will be in the audience, and tell who they are. Suggest a specific length (30 minutes? 45 minutes? 60 minutes?) for the presentation. And be sure to state the day, date, time, and place of the presentation.

THE SKYWAY CORPORATION
REAL ESTATE DEVELOPERS

One Skyway Plaza • Philadelphia, Pennsylvania 19106 • 215-555-7000

April 1, 1994

Ms. Andrea DelSarto
DelSarto & Minsk, Electrical Contractors
Glendale Building
987 West Taylor Square
White Plains, NY 10604

Dear Ms. DelSarto:

Enclosed are two copies of your new lease agreement for your office suite in the Glendale Building.

As you know from our recent conversation, Ms. DelSarto, the lease agreement, when approved by you, will expire on June 30, 1998. According to the terms we discussed, the new monthly rental for your corporate suite, $2,750, will take effect next July 1.

As a long-term tenant, you will find the rest of the lease terms "standard," I am sure. Nonetheless, we always recommend that tenants call us or consult an attorney, if necessary, to discuss any terms or conditions that appear questionable or that are not clearly worded in the agreement.

If you agree to the terms of this lease, please sign both copies and return both signed to us in the enclosed addressed envelope. We will then sign both copies and return your copy to you within one week.

We appreciate having you as one of our valued tenants.

Sincerely,

Thomas J. Haggerty

Thomas J. Haggerty Jr.
General Manager

Enclosures

This transmittal letter identifies specifically what is being sent (a lease) and how many copies (two). Further, it specifies what the reader should do with the lease agreements.

Mapping a Path to the Target
Now put yourself in the reader's place, and brainstorm reasons why the reader will agree. "If I were Ms. Brandon, what would motivate me to agree to give this presentation?"

Financial reasons? ("We will, of course, gladly reimburse you for expenses for travel to and from the convention center, as well as for your hotel expenses for both nights.")

Need for personal recognition? ("In the past, our speakers have included such distinguished people as . . . .")

Desire to help others? ("More than my personal gratitude, Ms. Brandon, will be the appreciation of all the ABC members who look to this convention for leadership.")

Professional pride? ("Your experience in the world of computers combines with your well-known entrepreneurial spirit to make you the ideal keynote speaker for this event.")

You will not always be sure of the answer, of course. Writing persuasive letters requires you to apply your knowledge of communication psychology.

Outlining the Letter   Once you know what *you* want and have carefully considered what the *reader* wants, you are ready to develop your outline.

Note how this indirect approach leads the reader to grasp your logic through its step-by-step organization and appeals to the reader's human needs:

1. Use an **attention-getting opening statement** to encourage the reader to continue reading.

2. List **factual statements** targeted at meeting the *reader's* needs.

3. Present your **request** in terms of how it will benefit the reader—not you!

4 Specify the **action** the reader must take to receive the benefits you've listed.

This *attention/facts/request/action* approach leads the reader step by step to understand why he or she *should* take the action indicated. The letter on page 350 uses this indirect approach in a most persuasive way.

- The *opening* certainly does command attention because the readers are physicians. As an extra attention-getter, a real X-ray was enclosed with the letter!

- Here, the *statements targeted at meeting the reader's needs* are strong reminders of what the reader felt when he or she applied to medical school—feelings no doctor will ever forget. (The word *felt* is even underscored at one point.) Additional reasons are also provided, underscoring the need for the reader's help.

- The *request* is presented in terms of how it will benefit someone just like the reader! A very strong human-interest appeal. Note, too, that the request is specific. It doesn't merely say "a donation"—it specifies amounts.

- The *action* the writer wants is clear and definite; even a time is specified: "Your gift, *today,* . . . ."

Clearly, this is an exceptionally persuasive letter. The writer focused on a specific target (by identifying a specific goal), mapped out a path to hit that target (by switching places with the reader), and outlined an effective letter (by using the indirect approach).

You, too, can apply these steps to develop persuasive letters.

University of Illinois at the Medical Center, Chicago

UNIVERSITY OF ILLINOIS COLLEGE OF MEDICINE

Office of the Executive Dean
1853 West Polk Street, Chicago, Illinois 60612
(312) 663-3500

You're a physician . . .

can you look at this X ray and

tell what's wrong with this young man's heart?

You can't. Even if you could examine every detail of John Williams' heart with an X ray . . . you still couldn't <u>see</u> the problem. Why? Because John's heart condition is much like the one <u>you</u> experienced when you first realized you had to become a physician. And that type of heart condition must be <u>felt</u> to be diagnosed.

It's an ache. A longing. And while you fulfilled your ambition at the University of Illinois College of Medicine . . . John's chances are slim. John, like hundreds of other qualified applicants, is being held back because of our limited instructional space--limited equipment and teaching aids-- limited number of faculty.

Right now, we're actively seeking funding for the basic instructional necessities from the Legislature. But to maintain <u>high-quality</u> standards in the face of expansion calls for support in areas not covered by state financing. We also need funds to provide flexibility of program planning, adaptation of technological advances to education, and scholarships.

You can help us fulfill, with unequaled excellence, the heart's desire of hundreds of young people by making a gift of $50, $100, $500, or $1000 to the unrestricted <u>Granville A. Bennett Dean's Fund</u>.

Your gift, today, will give someone else the opportunity to earn the title you proudly possess . . . Doctor.

Sincerely yours,

W. J. Grove

William J. Grove, M.D.
Dean, College of Medicine

This persuasive request letter uses a human-interest appeal to encourage the reader to respond.

KINDS OF PERSUASIVE LETTERS

Requests for Donations   Donations of money, products, and time for worthy causes are often solicited through business letters. These letters generally use the persuasive letter plan, since their purpose is to motivate the reader to take an unselfish action. See how the following letter attempts to secure a food donation for a function to benefit senior citizens.

Just as your commercials advertise, "All family members—from toddler to grandpa—love the smooth, zesty flavor of Coria's spaghetti with meat sauce." And Coria's is easy to prepare too, either for lunch or for dinner.

Many of us in the Chicago Area Youth Association (CAYA) are big eaters of your pasta platters, and that is why we thought of Coria's in connection with our forthcoming Senior Citizens Festival on September 9. CAYA, a nonprofit community youth group, is sponsoring a festival for 50 less fortunate senior citizens who reside in convalescent homes in our city. We plan to transport the senior citizens to our center, serve them lunch, and then provide a show with old-fashioned "big band" music and entertainment.

CAYA is financed solely through contributions from community members; therefore, our budget is quite limited. To provide a delicious and nutritious lunch for the senior citizens, we are asking manufacturers like you to donate sufficient quantities of their food products. Would you be able to send us 12 spaghetti with meat sauce platters to help highlight an afternoon in the lives of these individuals?

Of course, your contribution is tax-deductible. Special thanks will also be given to Coria's in our monthly newsletter, which is distributed to over 1000 families in the Chicago area.

May we count on you to help brighten the day for 50 less fortunate senior citizens? I would appreciate receiving your answer by August 6 so that we can confirm our menu plans.

Sincerely yours,

Letters Asking Favors   Another type of persuasive letter that sometimes must be written is one requesting a special favor. Of course, these letters should have the same characteristics as any other persuasive letter, and they are organized according to the same letter plan.

Your very interesting article in the November issue of The Administrative Assistant magazine prompted me to write you.

The Denver chapter of Professional Secretaries Inc. (PSI) is having its annual Administrator-Secretary Night on Thursday, January 18. Our members and their administrators (we expect about 80 people in all) have expressed a particular interest in hearing a lively talk on letters secretaries can send in their administrators' absence. We are especially interested in having our administrators hear something about what the secretary can do to help the employer with communication problems. Our program calls for a 30-minute presentation from the speaker.

Would you be able to address our group on January 18? You can build your speech along the same lines as your article, if you wish. As you know, this night is the highlight of our year's meetings, and we would be pleased to have you as our guest speaker.

I hope you can accept this invitation, Ms. Sarver. If you can, I will write you again to give you all the details—time, place, and complete program plans.

Sincerely yours,

Responses to Inquiries With Sales Potential

One of the main purposes of advertising is to get readers and listeners so interested in a product that they will make a trip to a dealer for a closer look or they will write a letter asking for more information. Inquiries received as a direct result of advertising have a great deal of sales potential. Therefore, when a writer shows interest, some companies respond with a polished sales promotion letter instead of a simple response to an inquiry.

Letters of response to inquiries with direct sales potential need to show the reader *why* the desired action should be taken—that is, why the product should be purchased. Persuasive letters written from the reader's point of view stimulate action—to purchase the new car, the aluminum siding, the air conditioner, or the stereo. Therefore, the persuasive letter plan is used in responding to inquiries with sales potential.

Notice how the first two paragraphs of the following letter get the reader's attention and develop interest. The presentation of the request and the request for action are carried out in the concluding paragraph.

> Naturally, we are delighted that you are interested in the Sphinx. Thank you for giving us a chance to tell you more about this captivating new model that has just received Sports Car International's sweepstakes award.
>
> The enclosed booklet, <u>Continental Sports Cars</u>, was prepared especially for you and others like you whose taste runs to the bold, the daring, the unusual— <u>the discriminating</u>. Only in the Sphinx does the true sports car lover find the ideal ride. You will be thrilled with its sleek lines, its handling, its economy.
>
> May I suggest that you visit your local dealer, Andre's Sports Car Village, to test-drive the new Sphinx. Only when you get behind the wheel of the Sphinx can you fully appreciate the sensational advantages of this little masterpiece.

Here is another example of how a response to an inquiry can be used to bring a potential customer closer to the sale.

> We are so pleased that you thought of the Fireside Lodge for the annual awards dinner of the Dallas chapter of the National Management Association.
>
> We have two excellent private dining rooms—the Regency Room and the Garden Court—ideal for a group the size of yours. Each banquet room seats 100 to 125 people and is equipped with a loudspeaker system, a piano, and a movie projector and screen. The Regency Room also has a raised dais where the speaker's table may be placed. Both rooms are still available for May 18.
>
> The decor of both the Regency Room and the Garden Court will give you a delightful, absolutely private dining atmosphere. Each room is air-conditioned and sound-conditioned. As you know, the Fireside Lodge has an excellent reputation for the finest meals and service. I am enclosing our banquet menu, featuring full-course dinners ranging from $15.25 to $24.95.
>
> May I show you these two lovely dining rooms, Miss Jacobs, when it is convenient for you to visit the Fireside Lodge? Would it be possible for you to have lunch here with me one day next week? Just telephone me at 555-2491.

WORLD
VIEW

"How embarrassing! I didn't know we were supposed to remove our shoes when we entered their home!"

In today's business world, women and men born in Peoria, Brooklyn, Houston, and Phoenix are dealing with associates living in Japan, Russia, Singapore, and Istanbul. In the process, all are introduced to new social customs. And in the process, many fall into the plentiful social traps.

Need help in learning the right customs and courtesies? Look for *Culturgrams*, brief, informative overviews of other cultures published by Brigham Young University David M. Kennedy Center for International Studies, Publication Services, 280 HRCB, Provo, UT 84602 (telephone: 801-378-6528).

As you can see from the examples in this section, you must be able to see things from the reader's point of view to write letters that persuade. If you can help the reader obtain or achieve something *he or she wants,* you will have little trouble achieving *your* goal.

COMMUNICATION LABORATORY

APPLICATION EXERCISE

A. You have just accepted a position as an administrative assistant at the American Institute for Cancer Research in Washington, D.C. One of your first tasks is to critique the following letter and make suggestions for improving its effectiveness in raising funds for cancer research. This letter will be sent out nationally by direct-mail advertisers to potential contributors.

Make a list of suggestions that your administrator may give to the person responsible for writing the letter.

Dear Friend,

The American Institute for Cancer Research (AICR) is now conducting its Annual Fund Drive.

During this time tens of thousands of Americans will make their annual contribution to fight cancer through AICR.

In the next several weeks I will be meeting with several members of the AICR Board of Directors to plan our coming year's budget. During these meetings it would be a big help to know what programs we will be able to afford next year.

So if you could please use the enclosed postage-paid envelope to make your contribution to fight cancer, it would be greatly appreciated.

I want you to know that we look forward to counting you among our friends and supporters in the coming year.

Sincerely,

J. Richard Nicklin, M.D.
President

pr
Enclosure

PS. If you make only one contribution to fight cancer every year, please use the enclosed postage-paid envelope to make your gift now during our Annual Fund Drive.

CONTINUED

B. Your immediate supervisor, Louise Peebles, is the chairperson for the National Information Management Association convention to be held in Madison, Wisconsin, from April 4 through April 7 at the Remington Arms Hotel. You expect nearly 1200 people—word and information processing managers and supervisors—from throughout the country to attend this convention. For many of these people, this will be their first visit to Wisconsin.

At the April 5 banquet Ms. Peebles would like to provide as favors samples of various Wisconsin cheeses. A small (perhaps 1-ounce) individually wrapped packet to be placed at each seat would suffice. Write the Wisconsin Cheese Manufacturers Association to request a donation of 1200 packages of cheese. One of your members in Madison would be able to pick up the cheese several days before the convention. Of course, you would publicize that the cheeses were donated by the Wisconsin Cheese Manufacturers Association. Address your letter to Mr. James Reikl, Director of Public Relations, Wisconsin Cheese Manufacturers Association, 780 Adams Boulevard, Madison, WI 53701.

C. You are employed by the American LifeTime Trainer Co., Inc. The company has developed a questionnaire it wishes to send to those people who have purchased a new LifeTime Trainer within the last five years. You wish to learn how well that exercise equipment met the buyer's needs.

Your company is committed to satisfying its customers—and improving its products and service. That is why you need to hear from experienced owners. Write the cover letter to accompany the questionnaire, persuading the reader to fill out and return the questionnaire.

D. Answer the following letter of inquiry. Use this letter as an opportunity to persuade the reader to purchase and install Carson authentic oak kitchen cabinets, which are made by your company. Address the letter to Mr. Edward Young, 3129 Miller Road, Flint, MI 48507.

Gentlemen:

Please send me a copy of your pamphlet Modern Kitchenware, which was advertised in Decorator's World magazine. I am interested in replacing my present kitchen cabinets with Carson authentic oak cabinets.

While I am at it, I am also thinking of having my kitchen floor recovered. Do you have any suggestions for colors that would blend with authentic oak?

Sincerely yours,

E. You are employed by Crickton Realty, 1732 Henway Drive, Des Moines, IA 50318. You receive a letter from Henry T. Bonner, 2231 Treadway Street, Los Angeles, CA 90069, requesting information about available housing in Des Moines for a family of six. Respond to his letter, referring to an enclosed list of suitable dwellings. You would very much like to sell Mr. Bonner a house, so make your letter as friendly and persuasive as possible.

VOCABULARY AND SPELLING STUDIES

A. These words are often confused: *raise, raze, rays, costume, custom.* Write each in a sentence that illustrates its meaning.

B. Indicate the prepositions that should be used in these sentences.

1. The contract states that our salary increases are retroactive _____ January 1.

2. The office is adjacent _____ the elevator.

3. This computer table is identical _____ those I ordered.

4. Did Mr. Rodriguez give his approval _____ the new sales campaign?

5. Ms. Otabe was not satisfied _____ the last shipment.

6. *Rug* is synonymous _____ *carpet.*

C. Add an *e* to the end of the following:

A Word Meaning:	To Result in a Word Meaning:
1. Pertaining to or characteristic of people	Kind, merciful, tender
2. Relating to a choir or chorus	A simple tune sung in unison
3. Ethical	A confident state of mind
4. Melodious, harmonious	A social entertainment featuring music
5. Characteristic of cities	Smoothly polite

SECTION 7.5

LETTERS THAT REFUSE REQUESTS OR BRING BAD NEWS

Would you prefer (a) telling your assistant that he has earned a raise and a promotion or (b) telling him that his promotion was not approved that and he will receive no salary increase? Would you prefer (a) granting your assistant time off to attend a workshop he wants to attend or (b) denying his request to attend that workshop?

The expected answer is (a) in both cases. After all, handling positive situations is easy. Communicating good news is simple. These are the situations that bring us enjoyment, satisfaction, and fulfillment, often on both a personal and a business level.

But the bald fact is that in the real world, you must sometimes say "no raise," "no promotion," "no time off"—and saying no is difficult, especially in writing. The word *no* can cause more ill will than any other word in the English language. Your success will often depend on your skill in saying no so smoothly that you do not offend others, whether you are writing or speaking.

With your knowledge of human behavior and a little practice in applying it, you can write a "no" that gives your reader the feeling of "yes." Or at least you'll be able to keep the reader's goodwill as you communicate your "no" message.

QUALITIES OF THE REFUSAL LETTER

All the principles of good business writing are essential in writing letters that say no. The following four guidelines, however, are of particular importance to bad-news and refusal letters.

Be Prompt   Most firms consider answering letters of inquiry within 48 hours good business practice. Delayed negative responses can only offend the reader even more and lessen your chance of retaining goodwill. Of course, to avoid writing the refusal letter by handling more pleasant duties instead is tempting. But the longer the letter is delayed, the more difficult it will be to write and the more likely you are to compound the problem.

Be Positive   Avoid using negative words such as *fault, refuse, unfair,* and *unreasonable.* Maintain a positive tone in your writing, and use words that convey pleasant images. Always try to phrase your refusal in a positive way by emphasizing what you *can* do for your readers instead of what you *cannot* do. Notice how much more positive it is to say "Your order will be shipped in two weeks" rather than "Your order will be delayed for two weeks." "We sell only through authorized dealers" is more friendly than "We refuse to sell directly to the public."

Be Helpful   In writing a refusal or bad-news letter, you can occasionally provide an alternative solution. Although you cannot comply with the original request, you may be able to suggest some other plan that may help the reader. For example, if you cannot accept an invitation to speak at a certain meeting, you may recommend someone who can. Or if you cannot accept an appointment for June 17, you may suggest that the reader see you on June 19. When possible, you should try to help the reader by providing a substitute plan.

Be Tactful   While the inquirer's request may be unreasonable or the tone insistent, you should always respond with a tactful letter. Do not insult the reader or indicate that the request is unreasonable. Avoid accusations and other discourtesies in writing your letter. Be careful to explain the circumstances fully and in such a way that the reader accepts the refusal or bad news as being necessary. Study these pairs of tactless and tactful responses.

ABRUPT: We cannot send you the personnel information breakdown requested in your April 3 letter. The time and money involved in preparing such a pamphlet would be prohibitive, a fact that you, as a manager, should have taken into consideration before making your request.

TACTFUL: We wish we could send you the personnel information breakdown requested in your April 3 letter, but we do not have the data readily available. As a manager, you can see that the time and money involved in preparing such a pamphlet would be prohibitive.

SARCASTIC: Surely you cannot seriously expect us to accept a return of the clothing you purchased from us on January 4 of last year. We are sending the items back to you today and will notify you whenever we decide to go into the used-clothing business.

TACTFUL: We would like very much to accommodate you by accepting the return of the clothing purchased from us on January 4 of last year, but we are unable to do so. To protect all our customers who may purchase returned merchandise, we place a two-week limit on the return of all wearing apparel.

ORGANIZATION OF THE REFUSAL LETTER

A refusal letter can alienate the reader and thereby lessen the chance of retaining goodwill. If readers can be shown *why* you must refuse the request, delay the order, or refuse the invitation *before* they are told no, they may be more tolerant and understanding. Their self-images may not be as threatened, since they have been taken step-by-step through the reasoning process that led to the refusal or bad news. As you read in Section 7.2, the indirect plan holds the negative statement until later in the message. Consequently, the *indirect* organizational plan should be used for refusal letters and letters conveying bad news:

1. Neutral opening statement on which both the reader and the writer can agree.
2. Reasons for the refusal stated in positive, tactful, and courteous terms.
3. Statement of refusal.
4. Suggested alternatives, if any.
5 Statement to retain goodwill of reader.

As you read the sample letters in this section, note how each follows or adapts this indirect organizational plan.

REFUSING UNREASONABLE REQUESTS

Businesses sometimes receive requests for information that must be refused. A request may be unreasonable, or the requested information may be confidential. For example, a physician or a hospital employee cannot divulge medical information about a patient; a bank will not give information regarding a depositor except to those authorized by the depositor to receive such information. Letters refusing to give information follow the bad-news plan. Study the following example:

Dear Mr. Wexler:

I appreciate your letter in which you ask for information concerning markup rates on drug products sold in our store. Because markup rates vary considerably, Mr. Wexler, a figure that would apply to all drug products does not exist. Putting together detailed information would require more time than we can afford just now.

May I refer you to Service Bulletin 16, Markups in the Drug Industry, issued by the State Bureau of Commerce and Industry. This 50-cent booklet contains markup rates for the drug industry as a whole, and I am sure it will be helpful to you. You can obtain a copy by writing to the State Bureau of Commerce and Industry, 3001 Central Avenue, Hartford, CT 06103.

Sincerely yours,

REFUSING INVITATIONS

A business organization and its employees receive numerous invitations to participate in exhibits, to speak before groups, to take part in various kinds of community activities, and so on. Most business executives feel that to participate in these affairs is wise—they help to build goodwill for the business. However, not all such invitations can be accepted because of time or financial limitations. In writing a letter refusing an invitation, you may adapt the bad-news plan to include the following three points:

1. Express appreciation for the invitation.
2. Give a logical reason for having to refuse.
3. Keep open the possibility of accepting a similar invitation in the future (if desirable).

Note the following example of a letter refusing an invitation to speak:

Dear Ms. Ridley:

I was pleased and complimented by your invitation to speak at the February meeting of the Philadelphia Rotary Club.

Because I plan to be out of town during the last week in February, I am unable to accept your invitation. An important company business trip is scheduled for that time, and it cannot be postponed. I am genuinely sorry that I cannot be with you.

If you wish, I would be pleased to address the Philadelphia Rotary Club on the topic "S-t-r-etching Your Investment Dollar" at a later date. Just let me know at least a month in advance.

Sincerely,

EXPLAINING DELAYS IN FILLING ORDERS

Delays generally occur because the customer has not given you enough information to fill the order or because the goods ordered are temporarily out of stock. In either case, be sure to open your letter with a statement of appreciation for the customer's order.

When writing letters concerning delays because you are temporarily out of stock, explain why the merchandise is not being shipped immediately, and tell the reader when the order will be delivered. For both the incomplete order and the out-of-stock acknowledgment, conclude with a statement designed to reinforce confidence in your company and its products. The writer may wish to add information about a new or special service that will improve customer goodwill.

In the following example, notice how the bad-news plan is used to tell a customer about a shipping delay.

Dear Mr. Yamato:

We appreciate receiving your order for Tax Pro software, which was featured in the April issue of Computerworld. Apparently, a good many others saw the article also, for we have been swamped with orders for this new software sensation.

I am sending you today two units; the remaining four will be shipped on Monday, June 14. I regret, Mr. Yamato, that you have been inconvenienced on your very first order, but I hope you will understand that we were not prepared for the large quantity of orders received. You may be sure that our factory is now geared for round-the-clock production of Tax Pro to keep all our dealers supplied.

I hope you find keeping Tax Pro in stock just as hard as we do—it is becoming increasingly popular! We look forward to doing business with you on a regular basis and promise our usual prompt service on your next order. For even faster service you may wish to fax your next order. Our toll-free fax service number (orders only) is 800-555-7272.

Sincerely yours,

In writing letters of this type, observe the following rules of tact, courtesy, and goodwill:

1. Always tell the customer first what you *can* do; then tell what you *can't* do. ("We are sending two of the units now; the rest will have to be sent later.")
2. Keep the tone positive. Even though you must apologize for the delay, don't overdo it. Assume that the customer understands. ("This rush of business naturally caught us unprepared.")
3. Reestablish customers' confidence in your firm by encouraging them to place additional orders. ("We look forward to future business. We will give you our usual prompt service.")

STUDY TIP

"What concerns me," remarked the philosopher Epictetus, "is not the way things are, but rather the way people think things are." If you think you're creative, you'll act that way—and vice versa. It's a self-fulfilling prophecy. Are you creative?

—Roger von Oech, *Creative Whack Pack* (©1989 Roger von Oech)

COMMUNICATION LABORATORY

APPLICATION EXERCISES

A. The Nashville Center for Handicapped Children, 5900 Jackson Highway, Nashville, TN 37205, requests a donation from your company for a minibus to transport wheelchair-bound children. Your company, Customline Vans, makes a large donation each year to the Nashville Community Fund for distribution. You cannot possibly make donations for all the requests you receive. Write a tactful refusal letter. Suggest that the Nashville Center for Handicapped Children contact the Nashville Community Fund. Write the letter so that the Nashville Center for Handicapped Children will not be offended; the center is highly respected in the community.

B. What is wrong with the following letter? Note specific errors; then rewrite the letter.

Dear Ms. Atkinson:

We are returning your check for $119.90. We stopped carrying Neato lawn trimmers when the manufacturer went out of business last year.

Yours truly,

C. You are employed in the Denver supply center of MBI, a major manufacturer of computers and other office machines. Your company's latest computer printer, the SilentWriter, has been such a best-seller that you are now completely out of stock on ribbons for this printer. You expect to be able to replenish your stock by March 10 (three weeks from today). Write a form letter to be sent in response to the many orders you are receiving for SilentWriter ribbons.

D. You are a public relations associate at Dimension Electronics. You receive a request from Ms. Sara Davis, a career counselor at Chatsworth Hills High School, 430 East Mountain Avenue, Kansas City, MO 64141, for a plant tour. Your plant is not set up to give tours, mainly because of safety regulations. However, you do provide speakers—together with a slide presentation and free literature—for young people's groups; the speakers discuss the topic of careers in electronics. Your company will even provide refreshments after the presentation. Write a letter refusing the request for a plant tour but retaining Ms. Davis's goodwill.

E. You work for Lake Discount Appliances, 845 Lindley Avenue, Columbia, SC 29208. You receive an order from Jamal Parker, 1821 Aldea Street, Greenville, SC 29611, for the compact-size Minisnack Model 6 office refrigerator. This model had a lock. The manufacturer found there was not enough demand for this model and discontinued it. You now carry the Model 8, which has no lock but is 15 percent larger than the Model 6 and sells for the same price ($135). You also have the Safe-Guard Model 21A refrigerator, which has a lock. Although this refrigerator is the same size as

CONTINUED

the former Model 6, it sells for $155. Recommend the Minisnack Model 8 if he doesn't need a lock, the Safe-Guard 21A if he requires a lock.

F. You are employed by LTU Precision Valves. You receive an order from Vandock Oil Tools, 1200 Elmer Street, Missoula, MT 59801, for 125 No. 81A7 valves. You welcome the business; but unfortunately, because of a recent steel strike, you are out of stock on these valves. About ten days will be needed to fill this order. Write the kind of letter you would like to receive if you worked for the company that placed the order.

G. You are the purchasing supervisor at The Gourmet Pantry, 1115 Parkway Plaza, Minneapolis, MN 55455. Ms. Anna May Brock, 540 Clearbrook Road, Rochester, MN 55901, sends you an order for a Culinary Art food processor. You carry several models with different-sized feeder tubes, blades, and container capacities. The accessories that accompany each model differ also. Send her a pamphlet that illustrates the models of Culinary Art food processors you have available. Provide her with an easy way to reply.

VOCABULARY AND SPELLING STUDIES

A. These words are often confused: *appraise, apprise; pretend, portend.* Write each in a sentence that illustrates its meaning.

B. Correct the capitalization in these sentences:
1. The president left the white house on Wednesday.
2. The Bordens will celebrate their Tenth Wedding Anniversary at Rick's steak house.
3. She is qualified to take accounting II next Semester.
4. He enjoyed his Tour of the west.
5. Have you read *Better Health through exercise*?
6. I plan to study Business English during my junior year.
7. the company Vice President is touring the Country to introduce the new stock-option plan.
8. My new article, "To Tell The Truth Is The Best Policy," won rave reviews from the critics.
9. Drive South until you come to the bridge, and then turn East.
10. The name of her new business is Cathy's captivating cookie company.

C. What are the plurals of the following?
1. business
2. century
3. 1980
4. deer
5. a
6. handful

SALES LETTERS AND PUBLIC RELATIONS LETTERS

N ot all salespeople work in the Sales Department.

An actor "sells" his or her skills and abilities at every casting call and every rehearsal.

A doctor "sells" each patient on the accuracy of the diagnosis.

A minister "sells" a point of view.

A firefighter "sells" safety.

A receptionist "sells" the company's image.

Similarly, all letters—not only sales letters—"sell" the company's image, reputation, dependability, service, and so on. Your letter-writing ability, therefore, strongly depends on your skill in "selling" in writing.

SALES VS. "PR"

Sales letters is the term for those messages designed to sell specific products or services. In today's business world, most sales letters are written by professionals, often specialists hired by companies to develop effective letters to promote their products or services. Depending on your position and your company, you may never actually develop a sales letter. Although you may never sell merchandise or services, all your letters must "sell" an idea, a point of view, a proposal, or a recommendation, and your employment letters must "sell" *you*!

Public relations letters are more subtle forms of sales letters—that is, they do not directly or obviously promote a product or service, nor do they request an order or stress a particular action. Instead, public relations ("PR" for short) is designed to create goodwill. The specific purpose of PR letters is to show the company (and its products and services and employees) in the most favorable way. If the reader thinks well of the company, respects the firm, believes it is a better company, he or she will be more likely to buy its products or services.

Whenever you write a business letter of any kind, you represent your company. Whenever you represent your company, you have an opportunity to improve its image—that's where public relations comes in!

Learning and applying the principles of writing sales and public relations letters will be especially valuable to you, no matter what kind of career path you follow. Reason: You can apply the same underlying principles to selling ideas, images, goodwill, or points of view, both in writing and in speaking. So, listen up!

SALES LETTERS

A sales letter is effective if it achieves its purpose. The purpose may be to get prospects to come to your place of business, to think of your firm when they are in the market for your firm's product, or to place an order by return mail. In any event, the effective sales letter requires careful planning. In planning a sales letter, you should:

1. Determine your market—the people to whom you are writing. Who are your readers?
2. Set your goal. What do you want the readers to do?
3. Select the appeals that are appropriate for your readers. Why would people want to buy your product? What will it do for them?
4. Organize the facts according to a logical, effective, clear, and easy-to-follow plan.

Determine Your Market   For whom is the sales message intended? Do you want to appeal to a mass audience—*all* the people in a particular area, regardless of occupation, income, and educational background—or a selected audience whose tastes and interests are known to be similar? The kind of person who will receive and read the sales letter should determine to a large extent the kind of letter you will write. If you are selling air conditioners, are you selling them to *consumers* who want the comfort and convenience of air conditioners, to *retailers* who want to make a profit in reselling the air conditioners, or to *industrial users* ? The same sales letter could not be used very effectively for all three groups, even though the product is the same. Therefore, the first step in the sales process is to identify the people to whom the letter is to be sent.

Set Your Goal   Why are sales letters written? Sales letters are written because face-to-face selling is not always necessary or possible. A sales letter may be written to accomplish any one of four purposes:

1. To get new customers to buy your product now.
2. To develop an interest in your product that will induce customers to buy later.
3. To get customers to visit your place of business.
4. To get customers to try your product or to ask questions about it.

Once you have determined the market for your letter, you must decide which of these purposes you would like your sales letter to accomplish—and build your letter around this one purpose. A letter that tries to accomplish too many things at the same time usually winds up accomplishing nothing. If the goal is to get a customer to buy now, you will build your letter around the idea of getting the customer to take *immediate* action.

Select Appropriate Appeals   Once the writer has determined the market to *be reached* and the purpose of the letter, he or she must then determine the *appeals* the product will have for the reader. Although the air conditioner discussed in the following letter will do the same thing for everyone who uses it, different people will buy it for different reasons. The home consumer probably is concerned primarily with comfort and relaxation; the office or industrial user, with increased employee efficiency. Some appeals, however, are effective for every kind of audience. Most people like to save money, so the thrift of operation of the air conditioner may appeal to both the home consumer and the office or industrial user.

A sales letter for air conditioners sent to home consumers might read like the following letter. Notice that several appeals—pleasure, comfort, health, and thrift—are used in this letter. The central, or main, appeal, though, is the comfort of the prospective buyer.

Dear Mr. Ramirez:

Do you remember the prolonged heat and humidity of last summer? For five nights in a row, the temperature did not go below 87 degrees!

Another "long, hot summer" is coming, bringing with it many uncomfortable days and nights. But this year you don't have to let the hot weather get you down. Relax and enjoy life this summer!

The new Comfort-Zone air conditioner has just arrived at our store. It is not only beautiful—but also beautifully cool! The 2-ton model will comfortably cool the average five-room home, providing 24 hours of relaxing comfort and permitting restful sleep. In addition, you breathe pure air, free of the dust and pollen to which so many of us are allergic. Its quiet operation and low-wattage consumption make the Comfort-Zone a pleasure to own.

Why sacrifice comfort when for a few cents a day you can own and operate the Comfort-Zone? Come in today. You'll want to see and try the Comfort-Zone, the ultimate in modern air conditioning.

Sincerely yours,

From the appeals used to sell a product, *buying points* must be developed. Notice how in the previous letter an appeal was used to develop a buying point.

APPEAL	BUYING POINT DEVELOPED
Comfort	Helps you to get a restful night's sleep
Pleasure	Helps you to relax and enjoy your home
Health	Purifies your air; especially helps people with allergies
Thrift	Costs you little to own and to operate

A letter attempting to sell air conditioners for office use might read this way:

Dear Ms. Dykstra:

How would you like to increase the efficiency of your office staff by 8 percent this summer?

Tests in over 150 business offices using Comfort-Zone air conditioners have proved that worker efficiency increased 8 percent after the Comfort-Zone was installed. Since increased worker efficiency means greater profits for your organization, the Comfort-Zone will pay for itself in just a few short years. And if you would like to spread the cost, you have 36 months in which to pay.

Improvements in the new model make your operating costs even lower. A 3-ton unit consumes only $9.80 worth of electricity each workday. Isn't that a small sum to pay for the comfort and increased working efficiency of your employees?

Won't you call and ask us to send our engineer to determine the air-conditioning needs of your office? Each day's delay costs you money.

Very sincerely yours,

Notice that the emphasis here is on increased worker efficiency, low initial cost, and low operating cost. Since one primary purpose of a business is to make a profit, increasing worker efficiency and keeping costs low contribute to this profit motive. The following buying points are developed by these appeals:

APPEAL	BUYING POINT DEVELOPED
Thrift	Low initial cost
Thrift	Low operating cost
Profit	Increased worker efficiency

The writer of sales letters has a choice of many different appeals. Those used depend on the goal of the letter, the nature of the product, and the market—the people who will receive the letter. People usually spend their money for these reasons:

- For comfort (air conditioner)
- To make money (real estate investments)
- To save money (home insulation)
- To save time (microwave oven)
- To imitate others (designer clothes)
- To be different (unique hat)
- For health (toothpaste)
- For enjoyment (videocassette recorder)
- For cleanliness (soap)
- To avoid effort (power lawn salon)
- To safeguard possessions (home security system)
- To satisfy appetite (candy)
- To be attractive (jewelry)
- To be adventurous (travel)
- To attract the opposite sex (cologne or perfume)
- To escape physical pain (aspirin)
- To be entertained (electronic game)
- To protect family (smoke detector)
- To be in style (new shirt or dress)
- To avoid trouble (casualty insurance)
- To take advantage of opportunities (clearance sales)
- To be popular (health and fitness mower)
- To enhance reputation (charitable contribution)
- For beautiful possessions (crystal stemware)

Of course, some products may be used to satisfy a number of desires. A down coat has several appeals—to keep warm, to appear attractive, to be in style, and to impress others. Health insurance may be sold to satisfy the multiple needs for financial security, good health, and peace of mind, as in the letter on page 366.

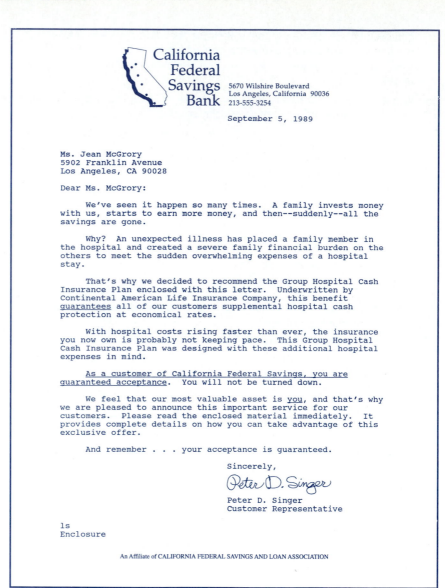

California
Federal
Savings
Bank

5670 Wilshire Boulevard
Los Angeles, California 90036
213-555-3254

September 5, 1989

Ms. Jean McGrory
5902 Franklin Avenue
Los Angeles, CA 90028

Dear Ms. McGrory:

We've seen it happen so many times. A family invests money
with us, starts to earn more money, and then--suddenly--all the
savings are gone.

Why? An unexpected illness has placed a family member in
the hospital and created a severe family financial burden on the
others to meet the sudden overwhelming expenses of a hospital
stay.

That's why we decided to recommend the Group Hospital Cash
Insurance Plan enclosed with this letter. Underwritten by
Continental American Life Insurance Company, this benefit
guarantees all of our customers supplemental hospital cash
protection at economical rates.

With hospital costs rising faster than ever, the insurance
you now own is probably not keeping pace. This Group Hospital
Cash Insurance Plan was designed with these additional hospital
expenses in mind.

As a customer of California Federal Savings, you are
guaranteed acceptance. You will not be turned down.

We feel that our most valuable asset is you, and that's why
we are pleased to announce this important service for our
customers. Please read the enclosed material immediately. It
provides complete details on how you can take advantage of this
exclusive offer.

And remember . . . your acceptance is guaranteed.

Sincerely,

Peter D. Singer

Peter D. Singer
Customer Representative

ls
Enclosure

An Affiliate of CALIFORNIA FEDERAL SAVINGS AND LOAN ASSOCIATION

The writer of a sales letter has a choice of many appeals, depending on the aim of the letter, the nature of the product, and the people who will receive the letter.

Organize the Facts   You are now ready to begin composing your sales letter. You must, therefore, gather all the facts about your product and the various appeals that may be used and organize them according to the persuasive letter plan. This plan, as adapted to the sales message, calls for four steps, the ABCDs of sales letters:

Attracting attention
Building interest and desire
Convincing the reader
Directing favorable action

Let's take a look at what is involved in each of these steps.

Attracting Attention   A sales letter can attract the reader's attention even before it has been removed from the envelope. The envelope may be a color instead of the traditional white. It may have a thought-provoking question or statement printed on the outside. Or it may contain a logo or a picture, as does the one shown below.

When the letter has been removed from the envelope, it can continue to attract attention through these devices:

1. Tinted stationery.
2. An unusual or clever letterhead design.
3. A colored typewriter ribbon or print.
4. An unusual style of type, such as a script type.
5. A gimmick to step into the letter.
6. All-capital letters for certain words or sentences.
7. Underscores, boldface, or italics for key words or phrases.
8. Dashes or exclamation points for emphasis, as in "Call us today—tomorrow may be too late!"
9. An elaborate, graphics-filled descriptive brochure included with the letter.
10. Relevant and interesting graphics, perhaps in the margins or in the body of the letter.

All these devices are aimed at attracting attention. However, be sure not to "gimmick" the letter to the extent that these eye-catchers get in the way of the message.

A sales letter can attract attention even before it is opened if the envelope containing it is creative and colorful.

The opening paragraph of the letter—in fact, *the very first sentence*—should excite curiosity, start a train of thought, attract attention in some way that will make the reader continue reading the letter. These opening sentences may be either questions or statements, and they should be original and concise. Questions should not be phrased so that they can be answered with a mere yes or no. Statements should contain a startlingly new, interesting, or different fact that leads the reader to the major buying point. Here are some examples of opening sentences that have proved effective in sales letters.

PERTINENT QUESTIONS

"How can you become the most fashionably dressed individual in Pittsfield?"

"Where can you save 8 cents on each gallon of fuel oil you buy for your home?"

"How much is your family's health worth to you?"

"If you lost your job today, how would you pay your bills?"

STARTLING OR SIGNIFICANT STATEMENTS

"They said it couldn't be done, but *we* did it!"

"Word processing equipment can increase production by up to *40 percent!*"

"You can*not* afford to be without one!"

"Three out of four families use hospital services at least once each year."

To decide which device would best attract attention, the writer should consider one or more of these factors:

1. The kind of firm sending the letter. (Is it a conservative bank? a store selling gardening supplies?)
2. The nature of the product. (Is it a religious book? a lawn mower?)
3. The kind of audience to receive the letter. (Are they nurses? electricians?)

Building Interest and Desire   When you have succeeded in getting the reader's attention, you must hold that attention. The best way to hold it is to build interest—by vividly describing your product so that the reader can virtually experience it. With colorful, descriptive words and expressions like those listed below, you can make readers feel, taste, or smell your product as well as see it—and you can also make readers see themselves using your brand and getting satisfaction from it. To stimulate readers to buy your product, you must use descriptions that will activate your readers' emotions.

OBJECTIVES	SUGGESTED DESCRIPTIONS
To sell no-wax flooring	"It's a bright shine. A tough shine. An easy-to-wipe-up shine."
To sell laundry detergent	"Softness—you can feel it in the *powder* . . . feel it in the *clothes!*"
To convince readers to send for a catalog from a plant nursery	"Lifelike illustrations you can almost smell and touch!"

OBJECTIVES	**SUGGESTED DESCRIPTIONS**
To sell hardwood paneling	"The soft beauty and warmth of fine hardwoods."
To sell small cars	"The driver who is fed up with bigger, thirstier cars switches to ___."
To sell air travel	"For travel elegance, fly with ___."
To sell a station wagon	"From a frisky, sturdy little workhorse to the jauntiest little sedan of them all!"
To sell a soft drink	"You'll really welcome the cold, crisp taste that so deeply satisfies . . . the cheerful lift that's bright and lively."
To sell a deodorant	"New spray-on deodorant with staying power."
To sell an air deodorant	"Makes air smell flower-fresh."
To sell mustard	"A mustard that is shy and retiring is no mustard at all; a great mustard should be a delightful contradiction of emphatically hot and delicately mild."
To sell fruit punch	"The circus-red color, the candy-and-ice-cream taste."
To sell shampoo	"Hair so satin-bright—airy-light!"

Suppose that you are writing a letter to sell compact disc decks. You attract the reader's attention in the first paragraph by asking, "How would you like to bring the concert hall into your living room?" You hope that the reader is interested in—or at least curious about—finding out how this can be done. So you vividly describe your product, appealing to the desire for relaxation. You continue your letter as shown:

> You have just come home after an exhausting day. Your body sinks into the comfort of your favorite chair, but your mind is still racing. Then you touch the power button on your Sound Giant compact disc player. Suddenly you are surrounded by your favorite music. Or you can be carried away to the shore by sounds of a rolling surf. The sounds can fill the room through your Sound-a-Round speaker system or take you to your own private world with Listen-Ease headphones. Every sound is as lifelike as the concert hall—in the comfort of your living room.

Notice how the paragraph builds interest by emphasizing the desire for relaxation.

Convincing the Reader   If you have done your work well to this point, the reader is already strongly interested and partially convinced. The readers who really want to buy can certainly find reasons for doing so. Nevertheless, you must still convince readers that Sound Giant ownership is an advantage. In fact, you must be able to convince them that they really cannot afford *not* to buy a Sound Giant. Therefore, you are ready now to bring out other features of the product that will convince them.

You have attempted to sell readers on the beautiful performance they can expect from the Sound Giant and the effect that performance will have on their pleasure and relaxation. Now, what other features might appeal to them? Size may be a factor in your customers' decision. A compact system with the quality and power of larger systems may be the added feature that can make the sale, so you tell the readers:

> Guests, too, will enjoy the concertlike quality of the sound and the compact size of your state-of-the-art system. You will own the finest compact system available today at a remarkably low price.

Now some readers may think, "Well, this Sound Giant is going to cost more than I can afford." You must convince them that this is not so. Therefore, your letter might continue:

> The magnificent Sound Giant can be yours for only $50 down and $50 a month for 24 months, and your monthly payments will not begin until August.

Directing Favorable Action If each of the preceding steps has accomplished its purpose, you must now move the reader to act. To spur the reader to action, you might:

1. Enclose a return envelope or postcard.
2. Imply that the reader should "act now before it is too late."
3. Offer special inducements for prompt action.
4. Briefly repeat the advantages to the reader.
5. Mention that many others have taken advantage of the offer.

The letter to sell the Sound Giant compact disc player, therefore, might conclude as follows:

> If you act before May 15, you may select $50 worth of CDs from those we have in stock as a FREE addition to your music library. Won't you come in today and listen to the Sound Giant?

PUBLIC RELATIONS LETTERS

A public relations letter is a special type of sales letter that sells *indirectly.* In fact, the chief difference between public relations and sales letters is that public relations letters *seem* to be selling nothing at all. Instead, they are written with an eye to the future—that is, with the thought that if you treat your customers well today, they will perhaps buy from you tomorrow.

Public relations letters are generally written to accomplish one of the following purposes:

1. To express appreciation to customers for their business. ("Thank you for your business during the past year.")
2. To capitalize on some special occasion—a holiday or a birthday, for example. ("We wish you and your family a joyous holiday season.")
3. To offer service to the customer. ("We have opened a branch bank in your neighborhood, and you will find that banking with us will be even more convenient.")
4. To show concern not only for customers but also for other people everywhere. ("We have invested over $50,000 in new antipollution equipment this year.")

Expressing Appreciation

You may not feel that you are accomplishing much when you write to thank a customer for business. However, a courteous "thank you" serves as a gesture of goodwill and paves the way for future business with the customer. Don't you like to feel appreciated? When someone thanks you for something you have done, don't you feel an inner glow of satisfaction? So it is when a firm takes the time to thank you for your patronage; you certainly feel more kindly toward that firm. The next time you need its type of product or service, you will be more likely to think of dealing with that firm rather than with any other.

How do you think the recipient of the following letter might react to it?

Dear Mrs. Robles:

As another year draws to a close, Essex House feels very grateful for having customers like you.

Thank you for the business you have given us during the past year. We certainly appreciate your friendship and hope that you have derived much satisfaction from your purchases.

Please remember that we are here to be of service to you. During the coming year we hope that you will continue to give us the opportunity to serve you.

Sincerely yours,

A letter such as this will not sell a specific item, but it will certainly cement good relations. Notice that the letter is written in a friendly style and does not push the reader in any way. The letter illustrated on page 372 is written in the same spirit and looks to possible future sales.

Capitalizing on Special Occasions

A holiday, the beginning of a new season, a birthday or an anniversary, the arrival of new merchandise, a new type of product, a new service, or some other special event—any of these may prompt writing a letter to customers. Of course, in letters of this type you do not attempt to sell a specific item. However, by making customers aware of the new service or product—or by calling attention to some special event—you may be indirectly stimulating their desire to buy. In these letters you are attempting to give customers the impression of doing them a favor rather than of trying to sell them something.

HEALTHY FOODS FOR A HEALTHY WORLD

NIGHT & DAY 145 Wantagh Parkway
Danville, Illinois 61832
217-555-1515

September 6, 1994

Mr. Thomas Angelino
1301 Rockaway Parkway
Brooklyn, NY 11236

Dear Mr. Angelino:

Thank you for calling us to ask about our product packaging. We
are glad to have an opportunity to discuss such an important
environmental issue with you. We wish everyone shared your
interest in recycling!

Mr. Angelino, perhaps the enclosed booklet, "Recycling for the
Future," will provide you with more technical information than I
was able to share with you. And if it does not, then I invite
you to call us collect at your convenience whenever you need
additional information.

By the way, Citizens for Recycling, a nonprofit group of concerned Americans, can also provide you with valuable information
that you may find helpful in your research project.

Sincerely yours,

Jack DeLorenzo
Jack DeLorenzo
Consumer Affairs Division

Enclosure

Public relations letters do not "push" the reader into buying the company's products. Instead, PR letters use a friendly pitch that sells the company indirectly and therefore promotes future sales.

Note, for example, the following letter announcing a sale especially for charge customers.

Dear Mr. Lombardi:

Tropic Isle is now preparing for its annual summer clearance sale. As you can see in the enclosed brochure, all our summer merchandise—women's dresses, men's sportswear, children's play clothes, patio tables and chairs, and a host of other items—will be drastically reduced.

Before we offer these bargains to the general public, however, Tropic Isle wishes to say "Thank you" to our charge account customers by giving them an exclusive opportunity to take advantage of these savings. On Monday, August 30, our store hours will be extended from 6 p.m. to 10 p.m. This extra time will give you and our other special customers an opportunity to shop before the general sale begins on August 31.

Just give the enclosed ticket to our representative at the door, who will admit you to Tropic Isle's special preview. If you wish to take advantage of these bargains, do plan to come early, as many sizes, styles, and colors are limited.

Sincerely yours,

Offering to Be of Service

Offering to be of service to the customer is another important function of the public relations letter. Whereas the sales letter says "Buy," this letter says "Let us be of service to you."

When a new family moves into the community, some businesses send a welcome to the new residents and offer to be of service. If the service is not a costly one, an invitation to try the service at no charge or at a reduced cost is not an uncommon gesture. For example, here is a letter written by a dry cleaning establishment to new residents who move into the community it serves:

Welcome to the Robinson family . . .

It is a pleasure to have you as residents of St. Louis, and we hope you enjoy the community as much as we do.

Will you give us an opportunity to show you the excellent dry cleaning, pressing, and laundering services we make available to St. Louis residents? And at low cost too! Our courteous drivers will pick up and deliver your clothing, or you may prefer to bring it to any one of our twenty stores in your area. All twenty have convenient drive-in windows, so you don't need to get out of your car—and you save 10 percent by using our cash-and-carry service.

We are enclosing an introductory card that entitles you to a 50 percent discount on your first order—no matter how large or how small. Won't you come in to see us and let us give you a personal welcome to St. Louis.

Sincerely yours,

Enclosure

Showing Concern for People

All businesses must make a profit in order to survive. Besides their profit goals, however, most organizations also establish "people goals"—to provide equal employment opportunities for all, meet employees' needs, treat customers honestly, provide safe products and services, support projects that improve the quality of life in their communities, and so on. They know that their concern for people not only will help their employees and their customers but also will improve their productivity and profitability. Thus organizations use a variety of means to let the public know about their people-oriented activities. One of the most commonly used—and most effective—means is the public relations letter.

The following public relations letter offers to be of service. At the same time, it might attract good future employees and more customers because it shows concern for people.

Dear Mrs. Columbo:

As the principal of Polytechnic High School, you have a great responsibility for the education of our youth. Sound Studio Electronics thanks you for your efforts.

We hope the following invitation will help you give students more insight into how products are manufactured, packaged, and distributed to dealers. You are invited to send your senior class to spend the day with us. We will plan a full schedule of activities for the seniors, and they will be our guests for lunch in our cafeteria. You may choose a date that is most convenient for you.

Please call Ginger Campbell, our Public Relations Director, at 555-3434 to make arrangements.

Sincerely yours,

COMMUNICATION LABORATORY

APPLICATION EXERCISES

A. For each reason for buying given on pages 368–369, name at least one other product or service that might be bought.

B. Bring to class ten different sales letters or magazine advertisements. Identify the sales appeal used in each letter or advertisement, and evaluate the effectiveness of the appeal.

C. You have been asked to work on the school football program committee and have been placed in charge of getting advertisements from local businesses. Half-page ads sell for $25; full-page ads, $50. Proceeds from ads are to be used partially for financing the cost of the program and partially for student transportation to out-of-town games. The ads will be read by all the high school students, as well as by many of their parents. Since the community really turns out for games, the ads will be seen by many people. Write a shell letter that can be sent to the businesses in your community, requesting that they purchase an ad in your school football program. The letter should say that if they agree to purchase an ad, a student will call to arrange a visit to obtain information regarding ad content and layout. Be sure to make it easy for a business to give a "yes" response.

D. You work part-time for a photographer in your community. Marcy Studios, your employer, specializes in wedding photographs. For storage in the

CONTINUED

firm's computer, write a shell letter that is to be personalized and sent to women who have announced their engagements in the local newspaper. Sell them on having Marcy Studios take their wedding pictures.

E. Choose a product (such as a clock radio, a camera, a video game, a set of cookware, a video recorder, a home computer, or an electronic calculator), and gather sufficient information to write a sales letter. Define the group to whom you will write, set a goal for your letter, select an appeal for the group, and write the appropriate letter.

F. You work for Bouquet Florists. At the end of each year, you mail a calendar to all customers who have ordered flowers from you that year. Write a transmittal letter to accompany the calendars. Use this opportunity to build goodwill for Bouquet Florists by making this transmittal letter a public relations letter.

G. You work for Gelson's Country Store, which will open a specialty and gourmet foods department next month. This department will offer such items as imported teas, fresh pastries, and exotic fruits. Write an appropriate letter telling Gelson's customers about the enlarging of the store and the new department.

H. As an employee of your county library, write a letter to welcome new people who move into your growing community. Enclose a card that lists library hours, information services, and activities for children.

VOCABULARY AND SPELLING STUDIES

A. These words are often confused: *detract, distract; carton, cartoon.* Write each in a sentence that illustrates its meaning.

B. Should *a* or *an* precede these words?

1. opposite	**6.** harvest
2. half	**7.** entry
3. appetite	**8.** highway
4. egg	**9.** underdog
5. ulcer	**10.** indication

C. Which of the following commonly used words are misspelled?

1. canidate	**6.** seperate
2. omitted	**7.** bullitin
3. liesure	**8.** accommodate
4. anilize	**9.** calander
5. occasionally	**10.** attornies

SOCIAL-BUSINESS LETTERS

Business is conducted by people, among people, with people, and for people. Business is a very social activity.

In today's business world, women and men are as likely to explore a business deal, negotiate financing, and approve a contract on a golf course, across a dinner table, on a tennis court, and at the opera as they are at a business meeting or on the telephone. In the process, friendships develop.

Even if you conduct all your business in your office, you will still develop relationships, perhaps friendships, not only with coworkers but also with clients, vendors, and suppliers. Business relationships often involve families as well.

Good social-business relationships contribute to the success of a business by fostering a warm friendship and developing goodwill and trust among business associates. Writing effective social-business correspondence plays a key role in developing—and nurturing—this success.

PURPOSE OF SOCIAL-BUSINESS LETTERS

Social customs are well established over a long period of time:

- When a relative sends you a birthday present, you write a thank-you note.
- When a friend's parent dies, you send a sympathy card or write your own condolence note.
- When a close, long-time neighbor is promoted, you send a congratulatory letter.
- When a schoolmate is hospitalized because of a sports injury, you send a personal note expressing your "get-well" wishes.

These are accepted (and expected!) practices. How you fulfill your social obligations determines how well you are accepted by others within a particular circle of family, friends, and associates. In general, fulfilling a social obligation makes us feel good. It also makes others feel good about us.

Social-business customs strongly reflect *non*business conventions and practices and are just as well established. Receiving a present from coworkers also requires a thank-you note. The death of someone in your supervisor's family also deserves a sympathy note. An illness or an injury suffered by your assistant also demands a written message. And the promotion of a colleague in another department, too, warrants a written acknowledgment on your part.

Your colleagues will be sure to notice that you care enough, know enough, and are thoughtful enough to fulfill your social-business obligations—and they won't forget. Unselfishly doing for others has its own rewards.

SOCIAL-BUSINESS LETTER FORMAT

The format for social-business letters is special. It uses a particular arrangement of letter parts, omits certain parts, and adopts an alternative to the "standard" colon in business letter salutations. Refer to the illustration on page 324 as you review the following discussion.

To format a social-business letter:

1. Place the inside address at the bottom of the page.
2. Use a comma (not a colon) in the salutation (*Dear Martha,* for example).
3. Use an informal complimentary closing, such as *Cordially, Regards, Sincerely,* or *Best wishes.*
4. Omit all notations.
5. Follow standard letter format for all other details.

Use this format for all types of social-business correspondence, including letters expressing thanks, letters of congratulation, formal invitations and replies, announcements, and letters of condolence. All are presented below in more detail.

LETTERS EXPRESSING THANKS

People in business who receive gifts or are granted special favors should acknowledge the gifts or favors and express their appreciation. The following are examples of the kinds of thank-you letters frequently written by business executives and other employees. Note the direct approach used in each of these examples, as well as the brevity of the letters.

FOR A GIFT

Dear Karen,

I was pleased to receive the World Peace prints you so generously sent me. As you may know, I have several other pieces, both drawings and prints, by the same artist. The new pieces are going to be framed for my office and will look very handsome with the new oak paneling.

Thank you for your generosity. The next time you visit us, you can see the good use to which I am putting your gift.

Cordially,

Ms. Karen Freeman
Continental Portrait Company
7400 Lassen Court, Suite 280
Muskegon, MI 49445

FOR A FAVOR

Dear Bill,

I appreciate very much your thoughtfulness in getting tickets for Catherine and me to The Jazz Kid. We enjoyed this musical enormously—and the seats were just perfect.

Thank you for helping to make our visit to New York this Christmas an enjoyable one.

Cordially,

Mr. William Paige
41 White Oak Road
Somers, CT 06071

FOR A BUSINESS REFERRAL

Dear Ann,

Thanks for telling Hank Wu of United Savings and Loan Association how pleased you are with the computer system we installed for your company. He called me last week, and we met today to discuss the possibility of installing a similar system at United.

I certainly appreciate your referring a new business prospect our way. If at any time we can help you in a similar way, we will do so.

Sincerely,

Ms. Ann Brower, Manager
Accounting Department
Lincoln Thrift and Loan
2800 Canoga Avenue
Dallas, TX 75225

LETTERS OF CONGRATULATION

Like all the other social-business letters you write, your letters of congratulation should be warm and personal, as is the one shown on page 379. The following are also examples of letters of congratulation:

TO A BUSINESS ACQUAINTANCE

Dear Joanne,

I was pleased to hear that you have been promoted to national sales manager of Harris & Braun Enterprises. Congratulations! Harris & Braun is certainly fortunate to have such a dynamic and hardworking person in charge of its marketing operations.

If ever I can be of assistance to you in making contacts on the West Coast, please let me know.

Sincerely,

Business executives take the time to recognize a milestone in the career of one of their employees, and their thoughtfulness is certainly appreciated. How do you think Ted reacted to the following letter from his employer?

THE DAILY POST

SERVING NORTHERN MINNESOTA FOR 100 YEARS

230 West Superior Road • Duluth, Minnesota 55802
Advertising: 612-555-2100 • Editorial: 612-555-2135

May 3, 1994

Dear Louise,

Congratulations on being named State Journalist of the Year by
the State Association of News Journalists. All of us at The
Daily Post agree that your superb coverage in our weekend
magazine section of the construction of the new State Center
deserved the Association's top honors. We know that this is just
the first of many awards that you will receive for your
outstanding creative work.

To celebrate your winning this award, we'd like very much to have
you as our guest for dinner on June 5. Will you be free?

Cordially,

Dick O'Hara

Dick O'Hara
Managing Editor

Ms. Louise Flores
2160 Trinity Road
Duluth, Minnesota 55811

nw

As with all other social-business letters, a letter of congratulations should be warm and personal.

TO AN EMPLOYEE

Dear Ted,

During the ten years you have been with Martell's, you have seen our company grow from a small local factory to a nationwide organization. Responsible for this remarkable growth are highly productive and loyal employees like you. I am pleased to write this congratulatory letter on your tenth anniversary, for it gives me an opportunity to thank you for your contribution to our success.

As the supervisor of our data processing staff, you have set up a highly flexible and effective system for handling the increasing volume of documents. I am sure you have heard this often-repeated statement around the office: "If you don't know, ask Ted." This statement is indeed a tribute to your efficiency.

I look forward to working with you in the years ahead. When I think of the slogan "Martell's is people," I can't help calling to mind a picture of you and all those like you who help to make our firm the congenial, effective group it is today.

Sincerely yours,

FORMAL INVITATIONS AND REPLIES

Occasionally businesspeople receive formal invitations—to an open house, to a special party honoring a distinguished person, to a special anniversary celebration, or to a formal social gathering. These invitations, such as those shown on page 381, are usually engraved or printed and are written in the third person. When these invitations are handwritten, however, they are placed on plain white notepaper.

Replies to formal invitations are often requested by stating *Please reply* or *R.S.V.P.* (an abbreviation of the French *Répondez, s'il vous plaît,* which means "Please answer"). Even if such a notation is not placed on the invitation, there is an unwritten obligation to respond. If the invitation is written in the third person, the reply is also written in the third person and follows the wording and arrangement of the invitation, as shown in the replies on page 381. If the invitation includes a formal reply card and return envelope, the reply card may simply require a check (✓) to indicate whether the receiver will attend.

ANNOUNCEMENTS

Many companies send printed announcements to business associates to publicize the affiliation of a new partner or executive. Companies also use these notices to inform customers or potential customers of new sales representatives. Formal announcements also publicize new services, new branch offices, new locations, and company mergers. A typical announcement is shown on page 382.

LETTERS OF CONDOLENCE

Letters of condolence are among the most difficult letters to write. Such letters should be brief, dignified, and sincere. Obviously, the writer should not be depressing or recall too vividly the grief recently suffered. These letters should be written by the person signing them—not by a secretary or an assistant. Following is an example of a letter of condolence:

The Local Bank Tellers Club
requests the pleasure of your company
at a tea
in honor of
Nancy Fitzgerald
on Saturday, May the sixth
at four o'clock
Suite 13 of the Howard Building
Please reply

Formal invitations

Mr. and Mrs. John Shensa
request the pleasure of the company of
Mr. and Mrs. Barry Greenberg
at dinner
on Monday, the fourth of April
at eight o'clock
8106 Keats Road

R.S.V.P.

Mr. William Gregory
accepts with pleasure
the kind invitation of
The Local Bank Tellers Club
to attend a tea on
Saturday, May the sixth
at four o'clock
Suite 13 of the Howard Building

Formal acceptance

Formal refusal

Mr. and Mrs. Barry Greenberg
regret that a previous engagement
prevents their accepting
the kind invitation to dinner
at the home of
Mr. and Mrs. John Shensa
on Monday, the fourth of April

Formal invitations and replies may be handwritten, printed, or typed.

Dear Cheryl,

Please accept my sincere sympathy on the passing of your mother last week. I understand the difficult time you are going through, since I lost my mother last year.

My thoughts are with you and your family at this time of grief.

Sincerely,

For a more personal touch, the letter should be handwritten rather than typewritten. However, except in the case of a close personal friend, a typewritten message is acceptable.

Global Travel Services
is pleased to announce the opening of our new
computerized business / vacation travel department.
Ms. Vi Brown, a travel industry veteran, will assist
you or your company with personal, professional travel
planning. Stop by our Raintree Center offices
or give Vi a call.
Global Travel Services, Inc.
5855 Raintree Circle
Suite 540
Woodland Hills, California 91367

213-555-7033

Monday - Friday
9:00 a.m. - 5:00 p.m.

Many companies send printed announcements to publicize new services.

COMMUNICATION LABORATORY

APPLICATION EXERCISES

A. While driving to work one day, you see a good customer, Lynn Merrick, having car trouble. You take Ms. Merrick to a nearby service station for help. Three days later you receive a letter thanking you and saying that arrangements have been made for you and a guest to have dinner at a very fine restaurant. You have a delicious meal and a delightful evening at the restaurant. Write a thank-you letter to Ms. Merrick, Merrick's Personnel Agency, 12 Hunter Avenue, Memphis, TN 38122.

B. Police Sergeant Marie Hannah spoke to your Employees' Service Club on the topic "Making Your Home Burglarproof." Write Sergeant Hannah a thank-you letter. Two employees have mentioned to you that Sergeant Hannah's advice may already have saved their homes from being robbed.

C. You read in the paper that a friend of yours, Chris Adams, is being given a three-month leave of absence from work to help with the summer job program for underprivileged youths. Write a letter congratulating your friend and offering your help.

CONTINUED

D. You read in your association newsletter that your friend Tyrone Pernell has been promoted and is now a word processing supervisor in the Los Angeles offices of Atlantic-Ridgefield Company (ARCO). Write Tyrone a congratulatory letter.

E. Carl Irwin's father passed away yesterday. Carl works in your department. Write him a letter of condolence.

F. You are employed by Reed, Barton & Howe, an insurance and investment counseling firm. Prepare a formal announcement about Michele Allen's joining your firm. The announcement will be sent to Ms. Allen's prospective clients and to her friends.

G. Prepare a formal invitation to attend a reception honoring the new president of Los Angeles Pierce College. The reception is being sponsored by the Pierce College Foundation. Invitations are to be sent to all community service organization members.

H. You have received a formal dinner invitation for the Saturday after next. Either accept or reject it. Supply all the necessary details.

VOCABULARY AND SPELLING STUDIES

A. These words are often confused: *liable, libel; ingenious, ingenuous.* Write each in a sentence that illustrates its meaning.

B. Which of the three words following each of these phrases is closest in meaning to the italicized word in the phrase?

1. *Provincial* attitude. Positive, elevated, narrow.
2. *Minute* detail. Tiny, simple, unnecessary.
3. *Volatile* temper. Violent, changeable, stable.
4. *Unobtrusive* lighting. Precise, regular, unnoticed.
5. *Articulate* speaker. Distinct, humorous, controversial.

C. Where are apostrophes needed in the following sentences? Write *OK* for any sentence that is correct.

1. Whose pen is this?
2. Theres a three-week trial period before the warranty goes into effect.
3. Theyre all taking their books. Where are yours?
4. Our photocopier has been broken since last week, but its scheduled to be repaired tomorrow.
5. Theres no way we can believe that the estate is completely theirs.

CHAPTER 8

MEMORANDUMS

People within an organization conduct much of their business by talking with one another face-to-face and on the telephone, in formal meetings and at conferences, during lunches, in the hallways, on elevators—in every possible situation.

Of course, they also conduct business in writing. The primary form of written communication within an organization is the **memorandum.**

Memorandums (or memos) are considered "in-house letters." Just like letters, memos also cover a wide variety of subjects, address routine matters as well as critical issues, and severely impact business operations and success. Clearly, memos are important to a business. But memos are also important to you for very personal reasons: Executives and coworkers will use your memos to evaluate your business know-how, your ability to get things done, your potential, your human relations skills, your persuasiveness, and more.

You can ensure that your memos are, indeed, working for you, not against you. After all, the business world is tough enough; is it reasonable to expect to succeed if you cannot skillfully use one of the most basic business tools, memos?

OBJECTIVES

When you complete the sections in this chapter, you will be able to do the following:

1. Explain the specific ways in which letters and memos are different.

2. Identify the parts of memo forms.

3. Format memos according to standard styles, whether using printed memo forms or plain paper.

4. Plan memorandums, using either the direct or the indirect approach.

5. Plan and write routine memorandums.

6. Plan and write informational memorandums.

7. Plan and write analytical memorandums.

8. Plan and write recommendation memorandums.

9. Plan and write progress report memorandums.

10. Use visual techniques to improve the effectiveness of memorandums.

PLANNING ROUTINE MEMOS

Brenda Jordan has good reason to be excited: Today she starts her new job—for a major-league basketball team—her favorite sport!

After only a few hours on the job, Brenda realized that *the size of an organization and its level of formality contribute markedly to the way its employees communicate.* In the insurance agency where she had worked, she seldom had the need to write memorandums. Because there were only four employees (three agents and Brenda), they communicated informally, and memorandums were rare. On the other hand, because the team had a much larger organization, with many different departments (some in other cities), preparing memos was as commonplace as making telephone calls. It didn't take Brenda long to understand why memos were so important!

Brenda will soon learn that even dream jobs require effective communication skills. In the operation of a basketball team, the coaching staff and the players must communicate. Likewise, all members of the team organization—just like any business—must send and receive information.

WHY ARE MEMORANDUMS NEEDED?

Memorandums serve the same general purposes that letters serve. Like letters, memos are also used to:

- Request information.
- Request and confirm appointments.
- Reply to someone else's request.
- Transmit materials.
- Acknowledge receipt of materials.
- Report information on sales, progress, schedules, assignments, and so on.
- Clarify a procedure, solve a problem, make a suggestion, and so on.

Brenda soon realized that it's just as important to keep a file record of a *memo* transmitting a contract as it is of a *letter* transmitting a contract. It's just as important to confirm in writing the day, date, time, and place of a meeting, the purpose of the meeting, and who will attend when the meeting is among *coworkers* as it is when the meeting is with *clients*. And it's just as important to clarify procedures or correct errors in writing with *assistants and coworkers* as it is with *suppliers*.

Memos are just as important as letters; both are key business tools.

HOW ARE MEMOS DIFFERENT FROM LETTERS?

Memos, as you see, perform the same functions as letters—but they are directed to a different audience. This difference and two other key differences between memos and letters are important to note:

1. *Reader or audience.* Memos are specifically intended for people *within the same organization.* Letters are written to people *outside the organization.*
2. *Format.* Memo format, as you will see, is very different from letter format. Memos are simpler, more direct, more personal—and their format reflects these differences.
3. *Tone and language.* Because the audience for memos is composed of coworkers, memo tone and language tend to be less formal and more friendly than letter tone and language.

If you work for a very small, very informal firm, you may write few memos. But the few that you do write will still be important.

Memos are tools that people use in day-to-day business operations. By providing a simple, standard way to communicate in writing, they support the inner operations of a business and provide a record of those operations, a record that serves an important historical function.

MEMORANDUM PARTS

Memorandums may have three parts: *letterhead, heading,* and *message.* The letterhead is optional, as you will see in the following discussion.

Letterhead   Many companies have memo forms commercially printed with the company name in a special letterhead just for memos. The letterhead generally consists of only the company name and logo—no address, phone number, and so on. See, for example, the memo on page 388.

Other companies do not have a letterhead printed on their memo forms. Because everyone in the company knows the company name, many firms consider it unnecessary to print a memo letterhead. The letterhead is optional.

Yet other businesses use a standard memo heading stored as a computer file to be called up when needed, just as a writer might insert a sheet of letterhead into a typewriter.

Heading   All memos have a section for heading information. The heading usually begins with a title such as *MEMORANDUM* or *INTEROFFICE MEMORANDUM,* which labels the message as a memo.

Below the title are *guide words,* such as:

TO:
FROM:
DATE:
SUBJECT:

Company Logo {

Spectrum Paints & Supplies Inc.

MEMORANDUM

Heading {

Guidewords
TO: Theresa Pembroke ↓2

FROM: Martha Kiosko *MK* ↓2

DATE: March 19, 1994 ↓2
        2 spaces
SUBJECT: ↓Demo for Henson Paints (Kansas City, Kansas) ↓2

Message {

Theresa, will you please schedule an "advance" demo of the new MixMaster 500 equipment for Tom Henson of Henson Paints (account number K1301). ↓2

When Tom called this morning to order a replacement for his old MixMaster 300 machine, we informed him that our newest model, the 500, would be available at the end of April. Understandably, he wants to see the equipment in action so that he can decide which options to select. ↓2

By the way, Tom will be leaving for vacation on March 30, so please be sure to set up an appointment before he leaves. ↓2

hls

Spectrum Paints uses printed letterheads for its memo forms. Employees fill in the information after the guidewords and key in the body of the message.

Let's see the purpose of these guide words:

1. The *TO:* line immediately identifies the receiver (or receivers) of the memo. Usually, no courtesy title is needed before the receiver's name, but as always there are exceptions. To show greater deference to a top executive, you may include *Ms., Mr., Dr.,* or whatever else is appropriate.

2. *FROM:* identifies the writer. Do not include a courtesy title before the writer's name.

3. The *DATE:* line is *always* important, even for the most routine memos. Spell out the full date, using the same style you use for letters: *May 12, 1994,* for example. Do not write *5/12/94;* memos are not *that* informal!

4. The *SUBJECT:* line briefly identifies the topic in a concise, specific phrase. Examples:

> SUBJECT: Correction in Catalog Copy

> SUBJECT: Quarterly Budget Meeting

Companies with lots of departments and offices in many cities often include additional guide words intended to help make the heading information more specific—for example, *DIVISION:* or *DEPT.:* or *LOCATION:* or *EXTENSION:*. In any case, *all memos have guide words.* These fill-in reminders help you prepare memos that are complete, and they allow you to do so quickly, without a fuss. Note the guide words in the memo illustrated on page 388.

Message   The message is the body of the memorandum, the paragraphs that make up the memo. The message of a memo fills the same function as the body of a letter. The message is the reason for preparing the memo!

MEMORANDUM FORMAT

Formatting memos is a very easy process, but any "standard rules" depend on whether you are using printed forms or plain paper. When you are using a printed form, the format of the already-printed guide words affects *your* format, of course. When you are using plain paper, you can develop your format more freely.

Plain Paper   To prepare a memo on plain paper in "standard" format, as shown on page 390, follow these steps:

1. Set 1-inch left and right margins, or use your word processor's default margins (usually 1 inch).

2. Set two tab stops, one 10 spaces in from the left margin and another 4 inches in from the left margin.

3. On line 7, center the word *MEMORANDUM* (or, if you prefer, *M E M O R A N- D U M* or *INTEROFFICE MEMORANDUM*). (Optional)

4. Space down 4 lines, key *TO:* at the left margin, tab, and key the name of the person receiving the memo. If you are addressing the memo to more than one person, space down to the next line, tab, and key the name of the next person. Repeat this process for each person you are addressing the memo to. An alternative for memos addressed to a number of people is to use the word *Distribution* in the *TO:* line and then to display a list of recipients below the message. (Note: If you choose to omit the centered word *MEMORANDUM,* the *TO:* line should read *MEMO TO:.*)

M E M O R A N D U M

TO: Paul Iverson

FROM: Danielle Kiluty *DK*

DATE: February 10, 1994

SUBJECT: Customer Service and Punctuality

<u>CONFIDENTIAL</u>

Customer service (not interest rates) is the number-one factor in
choosing a bank, according to the latest independent surveys.
What do customers identify as the main indicator of "service"?
How long they wait on line.

Every morning we find customers waiting for us to open. Because
opening is a very critical time for all banks, we stress the
importance that all tellers arrive on time. Only with their
cooperation can we ensure a high level of customer service.

During the past few weeks, Paul, your late arrivals have forced
more customers to wait on line for longer periods shortly after
opening our doors for business. On the surface, a "few minutes"
really does not sound as if it matters. But it does matter,
especially to customers' perceptions of us. And while your
willingness to work later, after closing hours, is appreciated,
it does nothing to help our early-morning crunch.

When one teller is late, the other tellers are forced to try to
make up for that absence. But they cannot. It's tough enough to
meet our full potential when <u>all</u> tellers are present, are at
their windows, and are trying hard. It's impossible when even
one is not.

You are an exceptionally talented and skilled employee, and we
(like you) want you to maximize your potential. If there is some
hardship, some reason for your lateness, or some factors we
should know about, we will certainly appreciate the opportunity
to help you work out any temporary problem. Please meet with me
at 4:30 this afternoon so that we can discuss this, Paul.

                                        DK

btr

bc: Rene Levesque

Use the margins and the alignment in this standard format to prepare a
memo on blank paper. Note the *Confidential* notation. Note too that the *bc*
notation appears only because this is a copy of the memo.

5. Space down 2 lines after the last name *TO:*, key *FROM:*, tab, and key your
   name (or the name of the person you are keying the memo for).
6. Space down 2 lines, key *DATE:*, tab, and key today's date (*May 13, 1994*, for
   example).
7. Space down 2 lines, key *SUBJECT:*, tab, and key a brief phrase that identifies the topic.

8. Space down 3 lines, and at the left margin begin keying the message in block format:
   a. Single-space paragraphs.
   b. Double-space after each paragraph, including the last paragraph.
9. Tab to the *second* tab stop, and then key the writer's initials in all-capital letters (with no periods and no spaces).

   Now note these options:

10. When you prepare a memo for someone else, double-space after the person's initials, and key your initials at the left margin, as you do when preparing letters for someone else. (When you prepare a memo for yourself, skip this step; your initials as writer are sufficient.)
11. When you are including an item (or items) with the memo, space down 1 line after the reference initials, and key *Enclosure* (or *Enclosures* and the number of items), beginning at the left margin.
12. When you are sending a copy to someone, space down 1 line after the enclosure notation, if used, or the reference initials, and then key *c:, c,* or *cc:* (or *bc:,* if appropriate), leave 2 spaces, and key the person's name. If there are two or more people, position each name on a separate line, and align the names as shown in the memo on page 390, which indicates that Rene Levesque will receive a blind copy. (See Section 7.1 for a discussion of blind copies.)

This standard format is particularly effective for preparing memos on plain paper. Reason: The block style makes it easy to prepare memos, whether you are using sophisticated word processing equipment or an unsophisticated typewriter. See "Electronic Equipment" below.

Printed Forms   If your company has commercially printed memo forms, you may need to adapt your format to "fit" those forms.

Look at the two memo forms shown on page 392. One form positions the guide words in one "column," allowing users to align the fill-in lines with the message below. The second memo form arranges the guide words in two columns.

Indeed, there are other variations. One of the printed forms on page 392 positions the *DATE:* line first, then *TO:, FROM:,* and *SUBJECT:*. The two-column formats arrange *TO:* and *SUBJECT:* in the left column, *FROM:* and *DATE:* in the right column.

In all cases, however, the guide words are the key to memorandum format; they provide a standard (no matter how they are arranged) for preparing complete memos and preparing them quickly.

ELECTRONIC EQUIPMENT

If you have a word processor or an electronic typewriter, you may want to create a "shell" of your memo format—a computer file that you can retrieve

RIVER VALLEY ADVERTISERS, INC.

INTEROFFICE MEMORANDUM

DATE: November 28, 1994

TO: John Werner III

FROM: Cynthia Lewis CL

SUBJECT: Earned Vacation Time for 1994

This year my staff and I have been involved in a number of crucial advertising contracts that simply did not allow us to take all my earned vacation time. I had hoped to squeeze in the two weeks owed to me this month, but filming delays in the Zip-a-Cola account have made that impossible. Several other members of my staff are in the same situation. We are now running three weeks behind! If we ever hope to catch up, we will simple have to stay with it.

I am aware of the company's policy that vacation time be taken between January 1 and December 31 of the year in which the time is accrued. Because of the intense work load in this department and the promotion of two creative team leaders, members of my staff and I have not been able to schedule vacation breaks and still manage to meet deadlines. For these reasons I request permission to carry over this year's vacation time for the following people, with the stipulation that the time be used by the end of the first quarter next year.

Allied Insurance and Affiliated Companies

INTEROFFICE MEMORANDUM

TO: Thomas Pearson   FROM: Elizabeth Genet

SUBJECT: Loss From December Storm   DATE: February 9, 1994

The analysis of the company's losses as a result of the storm that hit the northeast states on December 11 and 12 of last year is now complete. This is the study that you requested in your memo of January 19.

As you are aware, most of the losses were suffered as a result of high winds and water damage along the shore from New Jersey north to Maine. Although the damage done to residential property was significant, the greater damage occurred to retail businesses in damage not only to buildings but also to inventory and to time lost for repairs.

EG

The arrangement of guidewords on printed memo forms varies, as these two forms illustrate.

again and again, for you are always saving the original file for future use. Thus you can design a memo form once and then reuse it as needed.

Each time you retrieve the original file, you:
- Fill in the information required for the new memo.
- Save the new file under its new name (always keeping the original).
- Print out a copy of your new memo.

Refer to a word processing manual for specific techniques for creating and using shell documents.

MEMORANDUM TONE AND LANGUAGE

Do you use the same language when playing tennis with a friend that you would use when talking to an interviewer? Do you use the same tone when giving a friend career advice that you would use when recommending a good movie? Of course not. One of the keys to effective communication is your ability to analyze, or "size up," situations and then adapt your language and tone appropriately. *This ability applies not only to face-to-face conversations but also to memo writing!*

How do you "size up" situations? One good technique is to ask yourself questions such as the ones in this checklist:

What is the topic?
How much formality does it (or the organization) demand?
How serious is it?

The language and tone of a routine transmittal memo should be friendly, informal, and businesslike. Writers who do not size up situations accurately may tend to be overserious, as in this example:

Please find enclosed the price quotations pertaining to the printing of sales manuals for your division. The specific quotations, submitted by the three printers our firm employs most frequently (Acme, Supreme, and Allied), are all itemized, and all assume a print run of 1000 manuals.

Does sending a coworker price quotations require this degree of stuffiness? Hardly. Here is a friendlier (but still businesslike) alternative:

Marianne, I've enclosed the price quotes you requested for printing 1000 sales manuals. These quotes are from the three printers we use most often—Acme, Supreme, and Allied. Please note that the quote from . . . .

On the other hand, sending a new bank teller a memo pointing out that he has consistently been arriving late to work *does* require a less friendly, more formal, more serious tone. Read the memo on page 390, noting how most of the memo is deliberately impersonal and more formal throughout.

The topic greatly influences your decision on tone and language.

Who is the reader?
What is your relationship to him or her?

Are you writing to the senior vice president, who works in the headquarters office in another state? Are you making a routine suggestion to your assistant?

To the senior vice president, you might write:

Ms. Valdez, in an effort to speed up order processing during the heavy months of June and July, we recommend . . . .

To your assistant, you might write:

Helen, I think we can speed up order processing during the heavy months of June and July if we . . . .

Your relationship to the reader also influences the tone and language of your memos.

ORGANIZATION OF MEMOS

Earlier you learned two general plans for organizing letters, the direct plan and the indirect plan. Both also apply to memo writing!

The Direct Plan for Routine Memos

Most memos use the *direct* plan; directness is especially important and more appropriate in most coworker-coworker situations. In Section 7.3, you learned the direct plan for letters, which uses a *direct opening/details/goodwill ending* approach. (Review Section 7.3 before you continue.) You can use this same plan for memos, but because memos are addressed to coworkers, the goodwill ending often has a different flavor—or it may be omitted altogether.

Let's see how the memo on page 388 adapts the direct plan:

1. Begin with a direct opening: "Theresa, will you please schedule . . . ."
2. Provide details: ". . . Tom called this morning . . . . He wants to see . . . ."
3. Close by restating: "Please be sure to . . . ."

What's different? The ending here is not really a "goodwill ending"; this ending restates the request in the opening paragraph. Other endings for direct-plan memos may summarize, provide a conclusion, or ask a question—it all depends on the specific purpose of the memo.

Let's say, therefore, that the direct approach for memos is *direct opening/details/ending*.

The Indirect Plan for Persuasive Memos

Like letters that persuade, memos that persuade are more effective when they use an *indirect* approach. Review the indirect plan used for persuasive letters in Section 7.4:

1. Use an attention-getting opening.
2. Make factual statements.
3. Present your request.
4. Specify the action.

For memos, "attention-getting" has a slightly different meaning than it does for letters. REMEMBER: Coworkers read memos—they have an obligation to read memos that are addressed to them! Still, the opening does attract attention.

> In the past four years, our budget for computer equipment has grown at half the rate of our budget for office furniture.   (This attention-getting opening is appropriate because this memo attempts to persuade an executive to increase the budget to purchase new computer equipment.)

> This year more than most, meeting our sales revenue goals is truly critical. (Addressed to the sales manager, for whom sales revenue is life itself, this opening is sure to attract attention. Then the writer goes on to make her point: "I need your approval to hire a part-time word processing operator in order to *exceed* my sales goals." She stands a good chance of persuading!)

Use the same general plan *(attention/facts/request/action)* for your persuasive memos that you use for persuasive letters.

The Indirect Plan for Bad-News Memos

Review the plan for bad-news letters in Section 7.5:

1. Use a neutral opening statement.
2. State the reasons for the bad news (but not the bad news itself) positively, tactfully, and courteously.
3. State the bad news.
4. Suggest alternatives, if any.
5. Close with a goodwill statement.

Use this same plan for memos that bring bad news. For example, note how the memo illustrated on page 390 adapts this plan as a bank supervisor warns a teller about his repeated lateness.

1. The first two paragraphs are neutral.
2. The third paragraph begins with the reasons for the news: "your late arrivals have forced . . . ."
3. The fourth paragraph explains how the bad news affects the other tellers.
4. "Alternatives" does not apply here.
5. The last paragraph does all that it can to retain the employee's goodwill:
    It does not accuse or scold.
    It leaves the door open for the possibility that Paul has some serious problems and therefore justifiable reasons for his lateness.
    It compliments him on several of his positive characteristics as an employee.
    It shows every desire to be reasonable.

Master the indirect plan so that you can apply it effectively to both letters and memos.

COMMUNICATION LABORATORY

APPLICATION EXERCISES

A. You are the secretary of your school club, Future Business Leaders. Gloria McKimmey, a partner in a local accounting firm, has accepted an invitation to speak to your club about job opportunities in the accounting field. She is a knowledgeable and effective speaker and has a genuine interest in informing others about her field. Prepare a memo that will be posted in each classroom announcing Ms. McKimmey's speech, "Accounting—A Field of Opportunity." The program is scheduled for 3:15 p.m. on March 19 in Room 101.

B. A friend who works for another firm has shown you a copy of a new monthly magazine called *Office Automation Update.* Since the publication features the latest advances in office products and procedures, you believe it would be useful to several people in your office. Write a memo asking your supervisor for permission to subscribe to the magazine in your company's name. It is issued monthly and costs $28 for 12 issues.

C. Write a memo to Adela Garcia, your supervisor, asking for funds to attend a weekend communication conference in a city 150 miles away from your own. The conference, which will be held on October 18 and 19, will focus on ways of improving employee efficiency through better internal communication. The conference leaders are people of established reputation in the field. Your estimate of the cost is about $330, an amount that includes mileage allowance, a hotel room for one night, meals, and a $150 registration fee for the conference.

D. Employees have been using the office postage meter as well as prestamped envelopes for personal correspondence. Write a memo to employees explaining that postage and stationery costs have risen greatly and that personal correspondence simply cannot be paid for by the company.

E. John Franz, one of your sales representatives, has been with a customer all morning. Two recent orders from this customer were poorly handled and arrived very late. John has spent the morning soothing the customer and promising that service will improve dramatically. John is not the only one of your salespeople who has had problems with slow deliveries from the warehouse. Write a memo to Bob Lyons, manager of the warehouse, explaining the situation and inquiring whether any steps can be taken to speed up deliveries.

F. A long-time employee, Evan Maas, from a nearby branch office has requested information about early retirement. He would like to know what his monthly combined pension and social security payments would be if he retired at age 62 instead of age 65. He would also like to know how much notice the company needs if he plans to take an early retirement. As assis-

CONTINUED

tant personnel manager, respond to Mr. Maas with a memo that includes a booklet on retirement benefits. The company requests that employees provide three months' notice before retirement. Your department also has a retirement counselor who works individually with employees who are considering retirement. By making an appointment with Robyn Hatcher, Mr. Maas can obtain firsthand information specific to his circumstances in terms of monthly income, medical benefits, and life insurance.

VOCABULARY AND SPELLING STUDIES

A. These words are often confused: *marital, martial, marshal; charted, chartered.* Use each word in a sentence that illustrates its meaning.

B. Match each definition in the left-hand column with a word in the right-hand column.

1. a travel schedule
2. showing great abundance
3. sturdy
4. to remove
5. to overthrow
6. not authentic
7. bright or colorful
8. exact

a. delete
b. profuse
c. subvert
d. itinerary
e. stalwart
f. vivid
g. derive

h. precise
i. fraudulent
j. pandemonium

C. What are the superlative forms of the following adjectives and adverbs?

1. clear
2. complicated
3. good
4. less
5. carefully
6. few

D. Select the correct word from the words in parentheses to complete each sentence.

1. Just (among, between) the two of us, I hope Jericho Construction wins the contract.
2. No one (beside, besides) Ms. Jeremiah is going to the regional meeting in Bangor, Maine.
3. How did the extraordinary amount of rain (affect, effect) the start of construction on our new building?
4. You (may be, maybe) able to transfer to the Denver office to work in product development.
5. Please (bring, take) the Jorgensen file to my office for the 2 p.m. meeting.
6. Who (raised, rose) the issue of drug testing?
7. We finished all parts of the report (accept, except) the charts and graphs.
8. The letters (sat, set) on your desk all day waiting to be signed.

PREPARING SPECIAL MEMOS

Tyrone Pernell's plans had changed quite a bit since high school. Originally, Tyrone had planned to go into the family restaurant business, but his plans changed when economic conditions forced the family to sell the restaurant. He had never planned to work as a clerk in an insurance company, which is where he found himself, three years after high school.

But Tyrone works hard and learns fast. Last week he was promoted to department supervisor! He enjoys managing his small staff. He likes having additional responsibilities. And he's not complaining about the additional money. In fact, Tyrone is discovering that he has excellent management skills and interpersonal skills. He *knows* that he will be successful; he also knows that his success will depend to a great extent on how well he prepares special memos. He spends most of his day writing such memos!

WHAT ARE "SPECIAL" MEMOS?

Routine memos concern everyday transmittals, ordinary acknowledgments, and common requests. *Special memos* are not routine, ordinary, or common. As a supervisor, Tyrone must now write **informational memorandums, analytical memorandums, recommendation memorandums,** and **report** (or **progress report**) **memorandums.** All these types of special memos are covered in this section.

Compared with routine memos, these special memos:

- Tend to be longer.
- Deal with more complex and more important issues.
- Deserve a higher degree of formality.
- Receive more executive attention.
- Are subject to greater scrutiny and criticism because of their importance.

On your first job, you may prepare special memos only rarely, or perhaps not at all. But after your first promotion, all that may change, and you may spend most of your workday preparing special memos.

INFORMATIONAL MEMORANDUMS

The *informational memorandum* presents facts or data on a single topic. This special-purpose memorandum differs from the routine memorandum only in complexity and length.

Consider, for example, the plant manager who wishes to inform all the staff about new safety requirements. He or she may need to discuss hazardous zones, various kinds of safety equipment, issuance of safety equipment, care of safety equipment, safety procedures, and emergency procedures. All this information needs to be spelled out carefully in detail for present reference and future referral. Informational memorandums such as these set policy and govern action.

Informational memorandums use a direct approach. Begin by telling your readers what your topic is. Then organize your ideas logically, and provide your readers with the necessary details under each idea. Be careful to take your readers smoothly through each concept and, more important, from one concept to the next. An example of an informational memorandum appears on pages 400 to 402.

ANALYTICAL MEMORANDUMS

The *analytical memorandum* defines the problem for the reader, indicates the means by which the writer gathered and analyzed the data, shows the reader how the writer arrived at conclusions, and presents recommendations based on the conclusions drawn.

Suppose your supervisor asked you to investigate a series of group medical insurance plans. The purpose of your investigation is to select several options from which employees in your company may elect plans to suit their needs. You would need to respond to your supervisor's request by writing an analytical memorandum, but first you would need to plan your study.

After gathering information about available medical insurance plans, you would need to establish a set of criteria by which you would be able to *evaluate* each option. For example, you might wish to consider, among other things, the following: illnesses or injuries covered, specific exclusions, dollar allowances for coverages, selection of doctors and hospitals, annual cost per employee, and maximum benefits. Your goal would be to select options that provide the greatest insurance value for the dollar amount invested and at the same time furnish employees with broad coverage.

Your memorandum not only would present the results of this analysis but also would show *how you arrived at your conclusions.* Your organizational plan might be to:

1. Describe the problem analyzed or the task assigned.
2. Explain the procedures used for gathering the data.
3. State your conclusion and give *full* supporting details.
4. Include relevant issues if any.

RECOMMENDATION MEMORANDUMS

Recommendation memorandums are used to suggest new ideas designed to streamline procedures, institute new products, lower operating costs, increase efficiency, or improve the company operations in some other way.

LIVING LANGUAGE

"Jargon and in-house clichés resemble tonsils—organs that have outlived their usefulness. Chop them out."

—Jonathan Price, *Put That in Writing*

Central Bank

INTEROFFICE MEMORANDUM

DATE: March 14, 1994

TO: Estate Planning Staff

FROM: Steven P. Drengson *SPD*

SUBJECT: Guide for Advising Clients on Estate Planning

A number of staff members have inquired about guidelines for advising clients in the development of their estate plans. Many clients request information about the kinds of people who should be selected as guardians for minor children. Should the same people have guardianship over the resources? What is the difference between a guardian, a trustee, and an executor? The following information may prove helpful to you in educating clients on these matters.

Guardians

Clients who have minor children are concerned about trying to select guardians for them. You may wish to provide them with the following guidelines in making their selection.

First of all, advise them to think of other couples most nearly like themselves. Often such couples are found among brothers and sisters, but not always. Good friends may be the best choice. The ideal couple will have most of the following characteristics:

1.   Their financial situation will be similar to the clients'. The clients should make sure that their children, through life insurance and other means, wouldn't become a financial burden.

2.   They will be experienced parents with children of their own, preferably a little older than the clients'. The clients' children and their children should know and like one another.

3.   They will profess the same religious faith as the clients, if the clients want their children raised in that faith.

4.   They will live in the community where the clients live so that the clients' children would be able to keep their old friends and wouldn't have to change schools.

The informational memorandum presents facts or data on a single topic. It differs from the routine memo only in complexity and in length. This informational memorandum is three pages. It begins above and continues on the next two pages.

These memorandums take a direct approach by telling the reader what the idea will do for the company and then following this disclosure with the necessary details.

Suppose you work in the offices of a large metropolitan insurance company. Everyone crowds into the elevators to arrive at his or her desk by 8 a.m., and

Estate Planning Staff   2   March 14, 1994

5. Their educational level is the same as the clients'; they
    will share the clients' views about higher education.

6. They will have room to house <u>all</u> the clients' children.
    Separation can be very hard on children, especially in time
    of loss.

7. They will be willing, even honored, to have the job.

As the last point implies, clients should never name people as
guardians without talking to the prospective guardians about it
first. There is no place for surprise in this area. In many
states minors aged 14 or older have the right to pick their own
guardians, so children should be included in the selection of
their guardians.

Advise the clients not to select either of their parents to be
guardians. Although they did a good job in raising the clients,
there's an old saying about grandparents: The joy of having the
grandchildren come to visit is exceeded only by the joy of having
them leave. Child-rearing is a young person's business; the
fifty-year-old grandmother will be in her late sixties when
Johnny is in high school.

Usually the same person serves as "guardian of the person" and
"guardian of the property." However, if the child has a large
estate not protected by a trust, it may be wise to appoint a
trust company to serve as guardian of the property. Thus the
personal guardian won't have responsibility for managing the
estate and can concentrate on raising the child.

<u>Trustees</u>

Trustees, either persons or organizations, hold title to property
for the benefit of someone else. A trustee's duties fall into
two categories: disposition and administration. The former
identifies the beneficiaries and specifies when and if income and
principal are to be distributed and when the trust terminates.
Administration pertains to investment, accounting, and tax
decisions.

The skills needed to handle dispositions are quite different from
those needed for administration. Some trustees can do both--but
some can't. Provide clients with the following examples:

1. A trustee's discretionary right to spend trust income for
    children's education and living requirements takes detailed
    knowledge of the children and their needs. Perhaps such a
    trustee should be the same person who is acting as guardian.

The informational memorandum (page 2).

people are often late because they have to wait 10 or 15 minutes for an empty
elevator. The company cafeteria, too, is almost unbearable because everyone
breaks for lunch between 12 noon and 1 p.m. Unless you are first in line, you
can count on spending almost the whole hour getting through the serving line.
A repeat performance of the morning rush at the elevators occurs each afternoon at 5 p.m. as people leave the building for home. In fact, some people have
been known to leave early to avoid the rush.

Estate Planning Staff   3   March 14, 1994

2. A trustee's management of trust property requires investment
    skills and, if the property consists of an operating
    business, a thorough knowledge of the business. This may
    call for use of a trust company, perhaps with the guidance
    of managers of the business.

In some cases it is better to have two trustees rather than just
one. In this respect picking trustees is something like picking
guardians: one for the person and one for the property.

Clients sometimes have difficulty deciding whether to use an
individual or a trust company as a trustee. Both have advantages
and disadvantages:

1. An individual may take a more personal interest in the
    beneficiary's welfare--but individuals die, get sick, take
    vacations, and so on. Trust companies don't and can always
    be reached when needed.

2. Individuals are sometimes thought to be more imaginative
    investors than trust companies and therefore able to get
    better results. Remind clients that imagination is a two-
    edged sword, and many trust companies have excellent
    investment track records.

3. Fees and expenses are likely to be the same. An individual
    may charge a lower fee but may incur accounting expenses
    built into a trust company's fee.

Executors

An executor's basic tasks are very much the same as the
trustee's: to administer a decedent's property and dispose of it
according to the decedent's will. For that reason there is
rarely any reason for the client not to name the same person or
institution as executor and as trustee.

In considering an estate plan, clients should first consider
naming a trustee and _then_ naming the same individual or
organization as executor. The tail shouldn't wag the dog. The
trustee's job is likely to be long-lasting, perhaps for the
lifetime of the trust beneficiary. The executor's work, which
ends with the distribution of the estate assets to the heirs or
to trusts for their benefit, normally lasts only 12 to 24 months.

                                    SPD

des

The informational memorandum (page 3).

You believe that efficiency could be increased if employees worked in staggered shifts. By having half the staff work from 7:30 a.m. until 4:30 p.m. and the other half work from 8 a.m. until 5 p.m., the company could cut down on time lost because of tardiness and early departures. Likewise, if there were two staggered lunch shifts—11:30 to 12:30 and 12 to 1—congestion problems in the cafeteria could be reduced. Your coworkers encourage you to share your idea with management, so you decide to write a recommendation memorandum.

Your first step would be to summarize your recommendation in the opening paragraph. Indicate that because of the crowded conditions prevailing in the morning, at the noon hour, and in the afternoon, you recommend a staggered work schedule for employees in your company. Follow the recommendation with specific details:

1. Explain in detail the circumstances that prompted your recommendation.
2. Outline specifically all aspects of your recommendation. Be sure to include suggestions for implementing your ideas and any costs that may be incurred.
3. Show how the company will benefit from adopting your recommendation.
4. Offer to answer any questions or supply additional information, if necessary.

PROGRESS REPORT MEMORANDUMS

Progress report memorandums provide an update on projects presently under way. They furnish management with information regarding the status of a long-term activity.

Suppose your company was converting its manual accounting procedures to a computerized system over a three-month period. Management would certainly want to know whether the conversion procedures were being implemented according to the projected timetable. If your company was building a new branch office that was scheduled to open on August 1, management would assuredly wish to know whether the building plans were progressing as scheduled. If your consulting firm had promised a procedures manual to a client by the end of January, management would undoubtedly want to keep tabs on its progress to ensure that the manual was delivered by the date promised. All these situations present good cases for writing progress report memorandums. Those people charged with the development of projects find themselves in the position of having to write such memorandums.

Progress report memorandums cover the developments and advancements made on a particular project for a specified period. Let us examine more closely the company that is converting its accounting from manual procedures to computerized procedures over a three-month period. The first progress memorandum may have been written after the project was under way thirty days; the second, after sixty days. These memorandums report in detail the advances made for a definite time period.

Begin the progress report memorandum by identifying the project and briefly describing the expected outcome. Summarize the progress reported previously before providing a detailed presentation of the activities, accomplishments, and setbacks for the specific period under consideration. Organize the information for the current period by topic or in chronological order, depending on the complexity of the project. Conclude your progress report memorandum with a projection for future developments and a timeline for completion. An outline for this organizational plan follows:

1. Identify the project by name, and briefly describe its objectives.
2. Summarize the progress reported in previous memorandums.

3. Provide a detailed presentation of activities, accomplishments, and setbacks for the specific period covered by the progress report memorandum. Use one of two presentation methods:
  a. Presentation by topic
  b. Chronological presentation
4. Project future progress in terms of a completion timeline.

VISUAL TECHNIQUES FOR SPECIAL MEMOS

The memo formats you learned in Section 8.1 are also used for special memos. Because special memos tend to be longer and more complex, experienced writers use a number of visual techniques to present the information in the clearest possible way, to arrange the material attractively, and to display particularly important data, trends, or ideas for emphasis. Some key techniques are offered below.

Display Lists   Lists help to *display* information, ideas, or statistics. The format of a list draws attention to the list because the items in a list stand out from the surrounding blocks of text.

Lists are usually:

- Numbered or bulleted.
- Treated as individual lines or individual paragraphs.
- Indented from the left margin (and sometimes from the right margin too).
- Separated by extra line space.

Because lists stand out, they are very useful for:

- Enumerating steps, as in a process or procedure.
- Sequencing information, as in an alphabetic column of names or a list of annual revenues.
- Identifying (and therefore stressing) key points, as in a summary or a list of objectives.
- Separating information from text, as in an address.

As a writer, you will find lists especially helpful for presenting your ideas clearly. As a reader, you will find that they help you understand the information more quickly and more easily.

Tables, Charts, and Graphs   Tables, charts, and graphs are also tools of simplification. They make it easy for the writer to present statistical data, and they make it easy for the reader to grasp the general picture and find specific statistics. See, for example, the table in the memo on page 405.

TRICOUNTY AIRLINES

MEMORANDUM

TO: Benjamin Spitzer   FROM: T. A. Arthur *TAA*

SUBJECT: Monthly Boardings for Last   DATE: January 9, 1994
         Year: Cranston-Titusboro

Following are the monthly boarding tables for last year on
all our flights operating between Cranston and Titusboro. As
you will recall, we began this service on January 1. The
seat-occupancy rate, which is based on the total of 1000
seats that are available monthly between these two points is
also included.

Month	Number	Occupancy Rate
January	362	36%
February	427	43%
March	512	51%
April	598	60%
May	673	67%
June	718	72%
July	640	64%
August	639	64%
September	729	73%
October	810	81%
November	830	83%
December	710	71%
TOTAL	7648	AVERAGE 64%

As you can see, this service has grown steadily since we
began it, largely as a result of our effective promotion in
the area. Since the break-even point for our aircraft is 42
percent, it has been a profitable service as well. The only
decrease in growth came in July and August, when many of our
business passengers were on vacation. The December decrease
was due to the storm at the beginning of the month.

These figures do not report on the increase in our service
between Titusboro and Wheeling, which is obviously affected
by the Cranston-Titusboro route. I am gathering this
information, and you shall receive it within ten days.

                    TAA

wp

When a memorandum contains statistical material, the writer should display
this material in tabular form for easier reading.

When your table is much longer, separate it from the rest of the memo. Prepare the table on a page by itself (or on several pages), and then provide a
cross-reference in your memo, such as "See the table on page 4" or "Table 1.3
shows the average cost of . . . ."

Charts and graphs are commonplace in memos, thanks to the computer

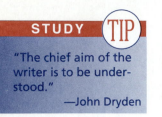

software that makes it possible to develop fancy illustrations with a minimum of effort. The old cliché "A picture is worth a thousand words" applies here. Charts and graphs provide an impact that several paragraphs without a visual simply cannot match.

Whether you create tables, charts, or graphs, be sure that you write clear, complete, and accurate (1) titles, (2) headings, and (3) source notes.

1. Write concise titles, using clipped phrases that "tell the story." Be sure to identify what you are providing, for which company or division or product or region, for which time period, and so on.

Note these three examples of titles:

ESTIMATED FIVE-YEAR SALES REVENUE

CONSUMER PRODUCTS DIVISION

1994–1998

ANNUAL TURNOVER

EASTERN AND WESTERN REGIONS

1993 and 1994

AVERAGE MONTHLY COMMISSIONS

INDUSTRIAL GROUP SALES REPRESENTATIVES

JANUARY THROUGH DECEMBER, 1994

If your memo has several tables or charts, number them, using one consistent style. Here are two examples:

Table 1

SALES REVENUE, CONSUMER PRODUCTS DIVISION

1993 AND 1994 COMPARED

Table 1. SALES REVENUE, CONSUMER PRODUCTS

DIVISION, 1993 AND 1994 COMPARED

Consult a company style manual or a business handbook for additional information or guidance, when necessary.

2. In tables, write column headings that are accurate, complete, and clear, as in this partial example:

District	1993 Sales ($)	1994 Sales ($)	Increase/Decrease (%)
Central	145,000	159,500	10.0

Similarly, for charts and graphs, make sure that your legends (the explanatory lists that tell the meaning of the symbols used in the charts and graphs or that explain the sections in pie charts) are clear; for example:

------- 1993 Sales

_____ 1994 Sales

3. Write source notes that will help readers find the information (if they should want to) and that will add credibility to your memo. Here is an example:

Source: _1990 U.S. Population and Housing Report,_ U.S. Department of Commerce, Bureau of the Census, May 1991.

Using these specialized formats can help you provide complicated information in an easy-to-read form. Use them to help you make special memos clear and concise.

COMMUNICATION LABORATORY

APPLICATION EXERCISES

A. You are the administrative assistant to William Norlund, manager of the Mail Services Department at Transcontinental-America, a major insurance company. Mr. Norlund is concerned that many employees seem to be unfamiliar with how to use the mail services of the U.S. Postal Service. Domestic letters are often marked "Airmail" or "Priority Mail"; packages are marked "Second Class"; or items that should be sent "Certified" are marked "Registered."

Prepare an informational memorandum for Mr. Norlund's signature that describes the various classes of mail and the special services offered by the U.S. Postal Service. Direct the memorandum to _All Department Heads_, and request the heads to distribute copies to members of their departments who use mailing services. Include in your memorandum information about the following classes of mail: first class, second class, third class, and fourth class (parcel post). Also, provide the readers with information about priority mail, certified mail, registered mail, insured mail, and special delivery. For assistance in preparing this memorandum, consult your local post office for up-to-date booklets and brochures describing mail classes and services.

CONTINUED

B. As the sales manager for Rathbourne Pharmaceutical Company, you have been requested by the vice president for marketing, Joshua Ravetch, to select a car to be issued to all salespersons. Your salespeople require a medium-sized vehicle that is sturdy and dependable. The trunk must be large enough to accommodate catalogs, samples, literature, and, in some cases, customer orders. You are to base your recommendation on initial price, cost of operation, and estimated maintenance expenses.

Consult recent issues of *Consumer Reports* to begin your research. Select several cars to research further on the basis of the facts contained in *Consumer Reports*. Obtain additional information about these cars from dealerships and brochures, and prepare an analytical memorandum to send to Joshua Ravetch upholding your choice.

C. You are employed in a legal office. Your office prepares many repetitive documents that require only minor changes in wording and documents that use many of the same kinds of paragraphs—for example, wills, contracts, leases, adoption papers, and divorce agreements. You feel that the computerized preparation of these documents would reduce costs, save time, and improve quality. Write a recommendation memorandum in which you suggest that a computer, printer, and word processing program be purchased for your office. Address your memorandum to Rosalyn Kalmar, the senior partner of the firm. Gather any additional information you may need to justify your recommendation.

VOCABULARY AND SPELLING STUDIES

A. These words are often confused: *ensure, insure; continual, continuous.* Define each word; then write each one in a sentence that illustrates its meaning.

B. Select from the words in parentheses the correct plural form of each noun.
1. What (criteria, criterions) were used to select the new plant site?
2. (Cargoes, Cargos) from both ships were seized by the port authorities.
3. Neither of the (attornies, attorneys) has indicated a willingness to compromise.
4. Last year Mr. Fry turned over the business operations to his (son-in-laws, sons-in-law).
5. None of the (companies, companys) on this list have received our new sales catalog.

CONTINUED

C. Here are 12 words that you are likely to encounter frequently. If you prepare documents with either a typewriter or a computer, you must know the correct points at which to divide these words in order to make line-ending decisions. Although many computer programs offer automatic hyphenation features, as the originator you must proofread word division as you check the rest of the message. Words may be divided only between syllables. Without consulting your dictionary, indicate the syllable divisions. Then, using the dictionary, check the accuracy of your choices.

1. congratulate
2. accumulate
3. inadequate
4. repetition
5. privilege
6. obstacle
7. surprising
8. acquaintance
9. conscious
10. visible
11. utilize
12. similar

CHAPTER 9

BUSINESS REPORTS AND OTHER WRITTEN MESSAGES

From your reading of Chapters 7 and 8 you should know that different job situations call for different records and different kinds of communication. Sometimes you will have to write a response letter or a routine memo. Other times you may be called on to write a longer, more formal document called a report.

Many forms have been standardized to save time and yet assure the completeness of a message. Most job situations call for at least occasional use of message forms, routing slips, fax cover sheets, and electronic mail. Even business writers who do not have full-time public relations responsibilities may now and then write news releases.

Effective business writers must be ready to write a wide variety of documents as part of the job, documents as simple as a telephone message form or as complex as an analytical report..

OBJECTIVES

Given a situation that requires writing business records, you will be able to do the following when you master the sections in this chapter.

1. Write informational and analytical reports.

2. Write records of meetings.

3. Use message forms, routing slips, and fax cover sheets accurately and effectively.

4. Write electronic mail messages.

5. Write news releases.

INFORMATIONAL AND ANALYTICAL REPORTS

When Angela Malcolm was named assistant supervisor in the shipping department at Wilcox Nutritional Products, she did not know what her new job would be like. On the production line, where she had worked a few years, the employees often joked about the "office people." What did they *do* all day long? As assistant supervisor, she soon learned.

As assistant supervisor, Angela never touches products. Instead, she spends her entire workday:

Assembling employee productivity statistics and then organizing the statistics in a report for management.

Gathering data on the number of orders shipped each day and then putting the data into a report for management.

Reviewing shipping costs and then summarizing costs in daily and weekly reports for management.

Compiling spoilage statistics (that is, how many products are broken or ruined or lost during the shipping process) and then reporting on spoilage losses to management.

Measuring employee performance (by determining the average number of orders shipped per employee each day) and then reporting on performance to management.

As her manager, Stephanie Lewis, pointed out, "We spend about *20 percent* of our time actually 'supervising' and working with our staff. We spend *80 percent* of our time *reporting*—providing Wilcox executives with information and analyses on a daily, a weekly, and a monthly basis."

THE NEED FOR INFORMATION

"You see, Angela," Stephanie continued, "executives need *information*—facts and statistics such as dollar volume, averages, costs, estimates, percent increases, and percent decreases—so that they can measure productivity, monitor sales, project costs, and determine profits. Without such information, they cannot possibly know what's going on and cannot possibly operate efficiently—not for long, anyway."

Executives also need *analyses* of those facts and statistics; they need to hear potential trends, projections, and forecasts based on those hard facts. Information and analyses—these are the two forms of input that business managers and executives need, and they get both in the form of *reports*.

Business executives thrive on reports—or, more accurately, on the information and analyses that reports provide. The president and vice presidents in an organization rely on information and analyses as much as the supervisors and middle-level managers do. While the information and the analyses may vary greatly in complexity, importance, length, scope, formality, distribution, reliability, and accuracy, business managers cannot make wise, effective decisions without such input.

In the business world, much of this input is *spoken* (during phone conversations, meetings, lunches, conferences, project reviews, and so on). But key information and important analyses are always in writing, that is, in the form of written reports.

Written reports may be classified as *analytical* or *informational:*

- *Analytical reports* are generally longer and more formal (both in language style and in format). They may require in-depth research and investigation. Often they include conclusions and recommendations to management.

- *Informational reports,* on the other hand, are generally simpler, more straightforward, and more direct. Often informational reports are prepared on standard memo letterheads or on specially designed printed forms.

Both categories are discussed below.

INFORMATIONAL REPORTS

Generally, informational reports are developed on memo forms (as you learned in Section 8.2) or on other specially printed forms.

Memorandum Reports   Angela and her manager submit different kinds of informational reports to executives:

- At the end of every week, Angela and her department manager submit an Order Backlog report, which tells management precisely how many orders are "sitting" in the shipping department waiting to be filled and presents related information. Angela prepares this daily report in standard memo format, as shown on page 414.

- At the end of every week, Angela and her manager also submit an Employee Performance report, which lists the names of all employees who worked on the order-fulfillment line that week, their total hours, their average hours, and related information.

- Once a month, Angela and her manager develop an Employee Time Report, which tells how many part-time employees were hired during the past month, the total cost of hiring these part-timers, and related information.

In addition to these regular informational reports, Angela also develops a number of reports on specific topics as needed, such as the report shown on page 415.

Informational reports are also frequently prepared on *printed forms.*

M E M O R A N D U M

DATE: February 9, 19--

TO: Edward R. Compton

FROM: Angela Malcolm *AM*

SUBJECT: Order Backlog for Week Ending February 9

Despite the fact that several staff members were on vacation this past week, we were able to hold down the number of unfilled orders to a satisfactory level:

Orders Pending	Total Value ($)	Unfilled +2 Days	Unfilled +3 Days*
22	21,876	4	1

*As of 6 p.m. today the only unfilled order is for out-of-stock merchandise (#R40-455), which is scheduled for delivery to us on February 12 (shipment to the customer on February 13).

The standard memo format or a company's individualized memo format is a popular base for use in submitting informational reports.

Printed-Form Reports   To save time and ensure uniformity, most companies use preprinted forms for regularly submitted reports, especially reports that require little narrative copy and are completed by a number of employees; see the monthly Expense Summary Report illustrated on page 416.

WILCOX CORPORATION

Interoffice Memorandum

TO: Edward R. Compton *EC*   FROM: Angela Malcolm

SUBJECT: Maintenance Estimates   DATE: September 27, 19--

At your request, I asked the Purchasing Department to secure estimates from outside suppliers to provide janitorial and maintenance services for our new warehouse. The estimates are based upon the service specifications that were drawn up by our purchasing staff. They match in all essential respects the specifications established for our home office facility.

Supplier	Monthly Cost	Yearly Cost
Aspen Cleaning	$10,632	$127,584
Rogers Associates	11,812	141,744
Republic Services	9,112	109,344
Wheelwright Company	12,005	144,060

In spite of the fact that the Wheelwright Company's bid is the highest, the Purchasing Department is recommending that we contract with that firm. Sources in the area that are known to us are enthusiastic about their services, which are reported to be superior. The firm is well established and very reliable.

Please let me know if you agree with the Purchasing Department's assessment. If you do, I will advise Purchasing to enter into an agreement with the Wheelwright Company.

EC

rd

An informational report must be accurate and complete, but also direct and to the point. It is usually prepared in an interoffice memorandum format.

Printed forms may be professionally designed, but often a form is created by one employee to fill a specific need; then the form is duplicated for all employees to use. The sales representatives in one small company, for example, use the Weekly Sales Call Report shown on page 417.

Expense Report Summary

Name _____ Sara Cohen _____

Division _____

Department _____

Location _____

Period Ending ____ December 30 _____ 19 _ _

THIS REPORT IS DUE **15 DAYS** FOLLOWING PERIOD ENDING.
Advance privileges will be suspended, if Report is not submitted **WITHIN 45 DAYS** following Period Ending.

	DUE CO.	DUE ME
Last Month's Closing Balance		4695
Error Corrections: Use this line only when notified		
Cash Advances or Travel Orders Date 12/2/ – –	50 00	
"		
"		
"		
Transportation Advances Date		
"		
"		
"		
"		
Travel Refund		
Month's Expenses		16271
Amount Surrendered to Cashier		
Amount of Remittance Enclosed		
Total Each Column	50 00	20966
Insert Difference Between Totals Above into Proper Box	DUE CO.	DUE ME
CLOSING BALANCE ▶		15966

I certify this report
to be correct: _____
                              (Date)

Dept. Head Appr. _____
                              (Date)

Add'l Appr. _____
                              (Date)

Add'l Appr. _____
                              (Date)

ENTERTAINMENT and MISCELLANEOUS EXPENSE RECORD

Date	Place	Misc.—Explain Expense Entertainment—List Guests & Affiliation	Business Purpose & Business Discussion	Total Expended
12/2	Pierre's	Luncheon with Graff of advertising department.	Annual budget for advertising and promotion.	39 60
12/10	Hungry Lion	Dinner meeting with Mr. and Mrs. Jason Cukor, clients.	Discussion of marketing program for Cukor Department Stores.	81 15
12/15	Hotel Ashe	Cocktails with Morton Giles and Martin Tor.	Discussion of plans for next local community affairs meeting.	41 96

If this space is insufficient, use a plain sheet of paper and staple to this form.

TOTAL FOR PERIOD ▶ | 162 71

Periodic reports such as this expense summary are usually prepared at regular intervals. They are usually completed on printed forms.

ANALYTICAL REPORTS

Analytical reports go beyond providing straightforward information. Analytical reports:

1. Identify or define a specific topic or problem area.
2. Offer data specifically related to the topic or problem.
3. Interpret the meaning of the data—that is, indicate the trends or significant facts supported by the data.
4. Draw conclusions based on the data, the trends, and the significant facts.
5. Make recommendations based on the conclusions.

WEEKLY SALES CALL REPORT

DATE: _____

DISTRICT: _____

TERRITORY: _____

SALES REP: _____

FOR THE WEEK ENDING: _____

DATE	STORE NUMBER	CONTACT PERSON	COMMENTS

cc: National Sales Manager

This form for reporting weekly sales calls was created by an employee and then duplicated or stored as a computer file for use by appropriate employees.

As you can see, analytical reports are not routine, straightforward, or simple. They are thorough and extensive and may require months of detailed research and in-depth investigation. They may require a team of contributors. But analytical reports are worth all the effort because they deal with important issues and affect major company decisions.

Complicated Topics, Critical Subjects, Important Decisions

Complicated topics are usually addressed in analytical reports. For example, the executives in a large manufacturing company are considering building a new plant, an investment of millions of dollars. They will need lots of related information about possible sites, construction costs, the local community, transportation facilities, the nearest airport, the local labor supply, future trends for the general area, and much, much more. To help the decision-making process, the executives may commission several analytical reports, one on each major part of the subject.

Critical subjects usually deserve special investigation, the kind of treatment that analytical reports deliver. For example, when employees complained that A&L Industries was following unsafe practices in both its plants, the company immediately authorized a full-scale investigation by an independent consultant. After three months of intensive scrutiny, the consulting firm submitted an analytical report, more than 200 pages long, that described present practices, compared them with accepted industry practices, evaluated equipment, reviewed plant safety procedures, examined accident reports, and made several recommendations. Results: The company accepted and implemented all the recommendations, to the satisfaction of all employees.

Important decisions warrant the close attention of analytical reports. Elaine Hill, vice president of a medium-size executive recruiting agency, needed to identify her company's computer-system needs for the next five years and make recommendations to her firm's executive committee. With the help of her staff and some outside consultants whom she hired, Ms. Hill submitted a detailed analytical report with specific recommendations.

Parts of the Analytical Report

Most analytical reports are long—long enough that they need to be separated into distinct parts. While format models vary from one organization to another, one well-established standard, accepted by many organizations, breaks reports into these parts:

1. Letter of transmittal (or memo of transmittal)
2. Summary
3. Body
4. Conclusions and recommendations
5. Appendix

NOTE: There are several other parts that may be used in some analytical reports. These include cover, title page, and bibliography.

Let's take a closer look at each of these parts.

Letter of Transmittal   Since analytical reports are longer and more formal than informational reports, a memorandum or letter of transmittal usually accompanies an analytical report. The letter of transmittal is used to serve several purposes:

1. It tells why the report is being submitted. The report may be the result of a project that was assigned several months earlier. Therefore, readers should be reminded of the reason for the report.

2. It identifies the report. Since executives receive many reports, it is important to identify each one so that it is easily recognizable.

3. It acknowledges sources of information and help. The people who helped gather and analyze data for the report should be acknowledged, of course.

Summary   Reports are presented to busy executives who will make decisions based on them. Many executives will not read an entire report. Since they are interested in getting directly to the heart of the material, they will be favorably impressed by the writer who provides a well-done summary. A report that does not contain a summary is not a welcome sight to a busy executive!

The summary includes (1) the purpose for writing the report, (2) the methods for collecting data, (3) the conclusions based on the data, and (4) the recommendations based on the conclusions. Some executives prefer a summary that begins with the recommendations. As a general rule of thumb, the summary is about one-tenth the length of the body of the report.

Body   The body begins with a brief introductory paragraph stating why the topic is of interest. Then the main sections of the body (in order of appearance) are labeled as follows:

1. Purpose—explains what the writer hopes to accomplish.

2. Scope—tells what the report does include and what topic areas are to be covered.

3. Limitations—tells what the report does *not* include; usually specifies geographic locations and dates on information that is included.

4. Justification—lists those who will benefit from the report and explains why.

5. Related Publications—lists any articles the writer may have studied as background before gathering the data.

6. The Present Study—presents the pertinent facts that have been gathered for this particular report.

In the "Related Publications" section, the writer will probably summarize the most relevant points of published articles on the subject. By showing what experts have said on the subject, this section adds credibility to the entire report. More important, these readings often provide direction for the writer in gathering and analyzing data. Report writers generally find appropriate articles in trade magazines, professional journals, newspapers, and other periodicals. A complete bibliography of the articles should appear at the end of the report for those who are interested in reading more on the subject.

The facts offered in "The Present Study" section must be carefully assembled and clearly presented. Since there is no excuse for carelessness in a written report, the writer must be sure of the accuracy of the data presented. Careless errors will damage the writer's reputation for accuracy.

STUDY TIP

The longer the report, the more critical are its headings, for the headings guide the reader through the materials, presenting your thoughts in an orderly fashion.

Many writers overlook the value of their headings; often, in draft after draft, writers critique the sentences and the paragraphs and the order of the topics, but not the headings themselves.

Reevaluate your headings critically.

Conclusions and Recommendations Up to this point the writer has explained why the report was written and what was discovered. Sometimes this is all that is required, and the writer's conclusions and recommendations may not be necessary. In some cases, however, the report may be incomplete without conclusions—especially if the report writer has been asked to include them. By asking for the writer's conclusions and recommendations, the executive is showing (1) faith in the writer's judgment and (2) interest in what the writer will say. The writer's conclusions and recommendations should be based strictly on the "Related Publications" and "The Present Study" sections of the report. Writing the "Conclusions and Recommendations" section gives the writer a prime opportunity to show his or her ability to think. In fact, good writing ability combined with the skills to prepare a successful report have in many cases brought the writer favorable attention and promotions.

Appendix The appendix may include working papers that show statistical computations; graphics and visual aids (tables, pie charts, trend lines, maps, graphs) that were too numerous to include in the body; and computer printouts—in other words, any kind of material that supports the report. A report may have a relatively short body with a long appendix. If the appendix is very long, it may be divided into sections, each with its own title page. The appendix material should be fully identified in the table of contents for the report. A good appendix can lend much credibility to a report.

HEADINGS AND SUBHEADINGS

Like signs on freeways, headings and subheadings help readers proceed smoothly to their destination. Headings and subheadings are important communication tools—especially in reports. They (1) form an outline for your report, (2) improve your organization, (3) prepare your readers for the next topic, and (4) help readers to keep on track. Within a report the wording of headings should be balanced; the wording of the subheadings below each heading should be balanced; and so on.

CHOICE OF AN APPROPRIATE TONE

Just as "appropriate" clothing varies according to the occasion, so, too, does the "appropriate" *tone* for a report vary according to the specific circumstances. Is the report a routine informational report? If so, a direct, straightforward, conversational style is appropriate:

> As you requested, Tom, I've investigated all the delays caused by Acme Shipping during the months of June and July. Below is a summary of all late shipments, which . . . .

Here, addressing the reader by his first name ("Tom") and using contractions ("I've") contribute to the informality of the writing style.

Is the report an analytical report? If so, a more formal style will usually serve best. For example, an excerpt from an analytical report might read as follows:

> At the request of the Executive Committee, an investigation was conducted to determine the cause of each shipping delay during the months of June and July 1993. First, Shipping Department records were analyzed for the purpose of . . . .

No use of the reader's first name here. No contractions. In fact, no use of the personal pronoun "I" at all! Instead of the informal "I investigated" (which uses an active-voice verb), the more formal example prefers the passive voice: "an investigation was conducted . . . ." The passive voice serves a purpose in such cases: "I feel," "I reviewed," "I studied," "I analyzed"—all sound like personal opinions, and personal opinions are more likely to be in error.

Note, however, that formal style does not mean stiff, old-fashioned, cumbersome, or vague! It is impersonal and objective, not artificial and archaic. As a general rule, increased formality is appropriate when a larger number of people will read the report *and* when the report addresses a complicated topic, discusses a critical subject, or will serve as the basis for an important decision.

USE OF GRAPHICS

Statistical information should be presented as visual aids such as tables, charts, graphs, and trend lines. The elements are called *graphics*. See the table below. Statistical data is much easier for the reader to comprehend when in visual rather than paragraph form. Since graphics are usually grouped in the appendix, they should be mentioned in the report body. However, do *not* repeat all the data in the body; emphasize only the most significant points.

1993 ANNUAL ABSENCE RECORD OF BRANCH OFFICES

MONTHS OF SERVICE PER EMPLOYEE

LOCATION	TOTAL EMPLOYEES	OVER 240	OVER 180	OVER 120	OVER 60	FEWER THAN 60
Boston	40	15	18	24	16	30
Detroit	20	8	10	12	11	12
Fort Worth	25	9	12	14	15	16
Las Vegas	10	4	5	6	8	10
Los Angeles	50	16	18	21	21	30
Totals	145	52 days	63 days	77 days	71 days	98 days

When developing graphics, be sure to:

1. Label each graphic. Use a title that is clear and complete, and be sure to add dates. The graphic should be able to stand alone—away from the report— and still be understandable. See, for example, the table shown above.

2. Identify the original source of the data. Give the full source for each graphic. List whatever information would help the reader identify and find the graphic: author's name, publisher's name, place of publication, date of publication, volume number, and page numbers for books and periodicals; dates, locations, and names for interviews; and so on.

3. Explain the meanings of any typographic or artistic devices such as colors, shaded areas, and symbols. For example, in a graph projecting sales for three different years, three different lines may be used to identify the years. The reader must therefore be told that the dotted line represents 1997, the solid line represents 1998, and the wavy line represents 1999. If a graphic device has a specific purpose, be sure to let the reader know that purpose.

FORMAT FOR ANALYTICAL REPORTS

Expert keying and setting up of a report will increase the forcefulness of the communication by helping the reader to absorb the main points quickly. The long analytical report usually consists of the following parts:

1. Cover
2. Title page
3. Letter of transmittal
4. Table of contents
5. Summary
6. Body
7. Conclusions and recommendations
8. Bibliography
9. Supplementary material or appendix

Reports should be keyed on plain white bond paper, 8½ by 11 inches. Keying should be done on only one side of each sheet. All reports should be double-spaced, and each page in the body after the first should be numbered. (The first page should be considered page 1, but the number should not appear on the page.) A left margin of approximately 1½ inches should be allowed for the binding. The top, bottom, and right margins of all pages except the first should be 1 inch.

Most analytical reports require a title page. The illustration on page 423 shows the title and contents pages for a report on advertising needs.

Creating Headings and Subheadings   In creating headings and subheadings, observe the following points:

1. Use the same format for each level of headings.
2. Main headings are usually (*a*) displayed in all-capital letters, (*b*) centered, and (*c*) keyed on separate lines. Two blank lines are used above main headings and one blank line below them.

A title page (left) and a table of contents (right) are standard parts of any analytical report.

3. Subheadings, a secondary level of headings, are aligned at the left margin and keyed in capital and small letters. They are underscored. Two blank lines are used above these headings and one blank line below them. However, if a main heading directly precedes a subheading, then only one blank line is used above the subheading. If you use boldface type, do not underscore the headings.

4. If a third heading level is needed, the headings are usually run in with the text. They are (*a*) indented (like the first line of paragraphs) 5 spaces from the left margin, (*b*) keyed in capital and small letters, (*c*) underscored, and (*d*) followed by a period (or a question mark or an exclamation point, if appropriate). Two spaces are used after the period. One blank line precedes these headings.

If all three levels of headings are required in a report, the headings are structured as follows:

MAIN HEADING

<u>Second-Level Heading</u>

<u>Third-Level Heading</u>. Text copy follows this run-in heading.

NOTE: Some writers prefer keying both the main heading and the second-level heading in capital and small letters. The main heading would still be centered (but not underscored), and the second-level heading would still be aligned at the left margin.

Binding the Report   When the report is completed, it may be bound at the side with staples (usually three vertical staples close to the left edge) or fastened at the top with a paper clip. Some reports are placed inside a special folder made for the purpose; others are bound by special backing paper of a heavy stock.

COMMUNICATION LABORATORY

APPLICATION EXERCISES

A. You have been asked by your supervisor, Carol Crumley, to prepare a report on the types of telephone calls placed by your firm. She would like to know the weekly number of local calls placed and the weekly number of long-distance calls placed (station-to-station and person-to-person calls, collect calls, conference calls, and international calls). Ms. Crumley would like to know the number of directly dialed calls versus those requiring operator assistance. She would also like suggestions for cutting the cost of telephone calls.

1. Prepare an outline for the proposed report, even though you will not actually gather the information.
2. Describe the procedures you would use in gathering the information and preparing the report.
3. List the sources of information that you would use.

B. Your supervisor has asked you to investigate the methods used to conserve energy in five firms in your area. Assume that you have interviewed five employees of different firms. Prepare a report of your findings.

C. Survey your class or a group of 25 students to determine the students' after-graduation plans. If students plan to attend college, determine which colleges and what major fields they expect to pursue. If students expect to apply for a job, determine the types of jobs for which they plan to apply. Prepare a graphic—a table, a chart, a graph, or a trend line—that displays your data most effectively. Discuss the information revealed by the visual aid.

CONTINUED

VOCABULARY AND SPELLING STUDIES

A. How would you edit the following phrases to eliminate the redundancies?

1. at about
2. up above
3. add up
4. and etc.
5. pay out

6. repeat again
7. both alike
8. new beginning
9. same identical
10. connect up

B. On a separate sheet of paper, write the corrections you would make in the following sentences.

1. We chartered each salesperson's sales for the week.
2. The computer has all ready prepared the printout.
3. This typewriter has required a great deal of maintainance.
4. The work will be divided between Robert and I.
5. Its a great pleasure to have you as a customer.
6. I can not understand two aspects of your report.
7. Will you interduce me to your employer?
8. I spent many hours in the liberry yesterday.
9. The goverment changed its policy.
10. 10 of the employees were absent today.

SECTION 9.2

MINUTES, NEWS RELEASES, AND OTHER FORM MESSAGES

When he began working as an assistant in the publicity department of one of the country's largest unions, Jack DeLorenzo encountered some forms of communication he did not know existed. "I thought that memos, letters, and reports covered it all! I had never heard of 'minutes,' for example. (Now I prepare formal minutes twice a week.) I would have guessed that 'press releases' are intended for newspapers, and they are. (But I really didn't understand the what, who, why, when, and how of press releases.) I've certainly learned a lot of valuable information in this position."

MINUTES OF MEETINGS AND RESOLUTIONS

The larger the organization and the wider its range of activities, the greater the "stage" on which it performs, the more far-reaching its policies, and the more attention it receives from news media and government regulatory agencies. One method that organizations use to monitor change, evaluate policies, study problem issues, and make recommendations is to *create task forces and committees.*

The Role of Task Forces and Committees

When D&G Industries realized that it had a severe problem with employee morale, it established an Employee Relations Task Force for the specific purpose of studying the problem, developing potential solutions, and recommending an action plan to the executive vice president. This task force had eight members (four mid-level managers and four nonmanagement employees) and was chaired by a senior vice president. After six months of investigation and analysis, the task force reported its findings and made its recommendations, after which it was disbanded; it had effectively completed its mission.

A **task force** *is a group of people who are appointed to solve a specific problem—their "task."*

D&G has a Budget Committee, which meets on the first Monday of every month to review any budget-related issues. The committee:

Monitors each department's actual expenses and compares them with estimated expenses month after month so that it can uncover any major problem before the problem gets out of hand.

Recommends increasing or decreasing budgets for the remainder of the year, depending on changes in needs, availability of company funds, sales, and other key factors.

This Budget Committee is a *standing committee.* It operates monthly, year after year. Unlike a task force, it is not disbanded, for its mission is ongoing. Members may serve for, say, a year and then leave (other members are then appointed, but the controller always heads this committee).

A **standing committee** *is a committee that operates permanently, year after year.*

Records of Task Force or Committee Meetings

The written record of the proceedings of a task force meeting or a committee meeting is called the **minutes** of the meeting. Usually, the minutes of a meeting:

- Record the date, time, and place of the meeting.
- Identify the presiding officer.
- List the names of the members who attended and, separately, the names of members who were absent.
- Summarize the discussions, suggestions, recommendations, and so on, that were carried on and made during the meeting.
- Are signed by the person who took the minutes (and sometimes by the presiding officer as well).
- Are duplicated and then distributed to all task force or committee members and to other key people in the organization.

As you can see, then, minutes provide key records of the proceedings of every task force or committee meeting. The minutes of an investment club's meeting are shown on page 428.

Formality of Minutes   How formal the minutes are depends on the company. The minutes shown on page 428 are informal and differ somewhat from formal minutes, which follow the rules of parliamentary procedure. For an example of formal minutes, see the illustration on page 429.

In comparing the informal and the formal minutes illustrated on pages 428 and 429, note that the formal minutes:

- Do not include discussions—only resolutions, committee assignments and reports, and other specific accomplishments are included.
- Include topical headings for easy reference.
- Include summaries of each speaker's remarks.
- Use specific wording for motions ("It was moved, seconded, and unanimously approved that . . .") and follow each motion with the name of the person who made the motion and the name of the seconder, both in parentheses.

Resolutions   Resolutions to express sympathy, appreciation, congratulations, and the like are often passed at formal meetings. The form of resolutions follows a rather definite pattern, as illustrated below.

Notice that the paragraphs giving the reasons for the resolution are introduced by the word *WHEREAS* (followed by a comma) and that the paragraphs stating the action to be taken are introduced by the word *RESOLVED* (also followed by a comma).

NEWS RELEASES

All businesses are eager to get as much favorable publicity as possible in newspapers and magazines, on radio or television—wherever there is a reading or listening or viewing audience. Larger businesses—even schools or school

The Market Focus Investment Group

MINUTES OF MONTHLY MEETING

May 15, 19--

Presiding: Herman Samuels

Present: Andrew Bolivero   John Levering
            Sara Dorman   Barbara Oliverio
            Mark Habib   Jane Masters
            Joseph Hernando   Frederick Noonan

Absent: Lily Fields   Helen Tiller
            Irene Isaacs   Donald Westin

After calling the May 15 meeting to order at 4 p.m., the
president requested the treasurer's report. The treasurer
distributed to each member a statement in the club's holdings.
The treasurer noted that a single share is currently worth $24.50
and that this month's contribution plus accumulated dividends
amount to a total of $450 that the club may invest.

The president asked Joseph Hernando, chairperson of the
investment committee, for the committee's recommendation. Mr.
Hernando said that the committee has recently studied the stocks
of computer manufacturers. He reported that the committee
believed that the present depressed market would improve in the
next two years, which would result in improvement in the stock.

Mr. Hernando said that his committee had located two companies
whose shares were presently quite low and would probably benefit
from a rebound: the Thibault Computer Manufacturing Company and
Compuset, Inc.

The president asked Mark Habib of Bennett, Duffy & Rooney, the
club's broker, to comment. Mr. Habib agreed with the committee's
analysis and suggested Thibault as the best buy. He noted that
the firm had assets that were undervalued and that the 6.4
percent dividend is quite secure. Ms. Dorman then moved that
Thibault be purchased. Mr. Noonan seconded. The motion was
approved, with one member abstaining.

Mr. Samuels announced that the club's annual picnic is scheduled
for Saturday, July 3, at Walker Park in Afton. Each member may
bring one guest. More details will be mailed to each member next
week. The meeting was adjourned at 5:05 p.m.

Respectfully submitted,

Barbara Oliverio

Barbara Oliverio, Secretary

The minutes of an informal meeting include the following information:
summaries of discussions, the date, the opening and closing times, the names
of presiding officers, and the names of present and absent members.

systems—employ publicity directors whose job is to attract favorable public attention to the organization. A movie star once said, "I don't care what you say about me as long as you spell my name correctly," showing how valuable publicity is to some people. Businesses, however, want only stories that show them in a favorable light, for public confidence is at stake. Unfavorable publicity can lose customers and lower stock values.

The Historical Society of Kansas City

MINUTES OF THE MONTHLY MEETING

April 17, 1994

TIME AND PLACE
The regular monthly meeting of the Historical Society of Kansas City was called to order by the president, Walter Accaro, on April 17, 1994, at 7 p.m. in the Truman Room of the Hartley Hotel.

MINUTES
The minutes of the last meeting were read and approved.

TREASURER'S REPORT
The treasurer, Victoria Angelini, gave the following report:

Balance on hand, March 15, 1994	$2,500.00
Cash received March 15-April 15	750.00
Total	$3,250.00
Paid Out March 15-April 15	475.00
Balance on hand, April 15, 1994	$2,775.00

The treasurer's report was accepted.

OLD BUSINESS
It was moved, seconded, approved unanimously that a leaflet be printed to solicit new membership. This leaflet would be distributed to local chambers of commerce and PTAs (Thomas Rooney, Lloyd Ulery).

NEW BUSINESS
After some discussion about improving communication between the club and the local media, the chairperson appointed a committee to report on this topic at the next meeting. The committee will be Sandra Peebles, chair; Ronald Wallen; and Gladys Robbins.

PROGRAM
Walter Accaro introduced Marvin Esterman, an archaeologist at the University of Kansas. Dr. Esterman's topic for this evening was "Improving Historical Site Selection in Kansas City." His remarks are briefly summarized here: "It is necessary to establish a list of criteria for site selection, based upon investigation and research. Such criteria might be based upon what other historical societies are doing, as well as recommendations from the national society." These recommendations were discussed in detail by the speaker and by several members of the audience.

ADJOURNMENT
The meeting was adjourned at 9:05 p.m.

Respectfully submitted,

Lawrence Chrisman

Lawrence Chrisman, Secretary

The minutes of a formal meeting do not include summaries of discussions leading up to votes.

The physical form in which the planned news or publicity is given to news outlets is called a **news release,** illustrated on page 431. Any subject that the business executive thinks may be of public interest or may bring the company name before the public may be the basis for a news release. It may be an announcement of a new product or service, the promotion of a major executive, a retirement, a death, an honor for an employee, the election of employees to

RESOLUTION

WHEREAS, our beloved colleague Carl Schultz passed away on June 6, 1993, and was one of the most sympathetic and hardest-working members of the Toledo Lions Club; and

WHEREAS, his wise counsel and unselfish services will be missed not only by the members of the Toledo Lions Club but also by the community at large; therefore be it

RESOLVED, that we, his fellow Toledo Lions Club members, take this means of expressing our deep appreciation for his untiring and unselfish service to the organization and to the community, be it

RESOLVED, further, that we extend our sincerest sympathies to his widow, Mrs. Anna Strong Schultz; to his son, Mr. Victor Schultz, of Dayton, Ohio; and to his sister, Mrs. Maria S. Kraft, of Portland, Oregon; and be it

RESOLVED, further, that a copy of this resolution be included in the minutes of the Executive Committee of the Toledo Lions Club; that a copy be sent to the members of the immediate family, and that a copy be supplied to both the local press and the area television station.

ADOPTED, unanimously, by the Board of Directors of the Toledo Lions Club, this twelfth day of June, 1993.

Marvin Bradley
Marvin Bradley
Chairman

Ralph Farnsworth
Ralph Farnsworth
Secretary

The form of a resolution follows a definite pattern, including the use of the words *WHEREAS* and *RESOLVED*.

civic posts, company anniversary celebrations, and so on. News releases are usually written, or at least approved, by one executive in an organization. In larger firms a public relations department or publicity department handles such releases. In smaller firms releases may be written by various executives. To prevent inaccurate or conflicting information from leaking out, however, these releases are usually channeled through one executive.

```
                              Blessings Hospital
                              Indianapolis, Indiana 46026

     N E W S   R E L E A S E     Release:  Immediate

                              From:  Annjean Conway
                                     Public Relations Director
                                     317-555-6397

        HIDEHIRO NAKAMA NAMED CHIEF ADMINISTRATOR OF BLESSING HOSPITAL

            INDIANAPOLIS, May 1--Hidehiro Nakama has been appointed chief

       administrator of Blessings Hospital of Indianapolis, according to the

       announcement made yesterday by Frances Howe, president of the

       Hospital Association of Indiana.

            Dr. Nakama succeeds Hector Bowman, who retired April 10 after 26

       years of service.

            The new hospital administrator joined the hospital staff in 1990

       as second assistant administrator of the children's wing.  In 1992 he

       was appointed as first assistant administrator of the hospital.

            Dr. Nakama lives in the Cheshire Apartments with his wife,

       Uchii, professor of pediatrics at the University Medical College in

       Indianapolis.  The Nakamas have two children, both of them enrolled

       at University Medical College.

            In commenting on his new post, Dr. Nakama paid tribute to the

       fine work done by his predecessor.  "I shall try to continue the fine

       program established by Dr. Bowman and to develop the fine reputation

       for quality care and service that has been built over the last thirty

       years."

                              - END -
```

Any subject that a business thinks may be of public interest or may bring the company name before the public may be the subject of a news release.

The purpose of the news release is to get a story into print or on the air. Newspaper, magazine, radio, and television editors receive hundreds of news releases every day from all types of businesses and individuals. Each editor appraises these releases by one basic rule: "Is this item of current, specific interest to our readers (or listeners or viewers)?"

A news release shares many features with other kinds of business writing. Two of the most important characteristics for news releases are completeness and accuracy. Make sure that (1) all important information is included and (2) all information (including names, dates, figures, and so on) is checked for accuracy.

Form of the News Release   The style in which releases are written is highly important. Since news editors cannot accept for publication every news release they receive, everything else being equal, they will usually choose those that require the least amount of additional checking and editing. Therefore, a release should give complete information and follow as closely as possible the newspaper style of writing, as does the one on page 431.

News releases must be formatted and then reproduced (usually by photo-offset or photocopying). Releases should be kept as brief as possible—rarely should they be more than a page and a half. The shorter and more interesting the news release, the better its chance of getting into print.

Companies that issue a great many news releases have special forms on which to write them. Reporting a story on a special news release form is much more effective than writing a letter. Editors like to be able to read quickly; they cannot waste time going through the formalities of a letter. Like a letterhead, a news release form usually contains the name, address, and telephone number of the company. This information, however, may be placed at the bottom of the form. In addition, the name of the person who issued the release is included so that the editor can call for more information.

When writing or issuing news releases, be sure to observe all the points outlined here:

1. Always double-space the news release. Double spacing is a must for all news releases so that the editor has room to make changes in the copy.
2. Use generous side margins, and leave plenty of space at both the top and the bottom. This permits room for the editor to add typesetting or computer coding and filing instructions.
3. At the beginning of the story, give a brief headline so that the editor may learn quickly what the release is about; for example, "New Plastic Office Accessories Announced" or "New President Appointed" or "Printing Press Handles Sheets 110 Inches Wide." (Editors will nearly always write their own headlines; nonetheless, news release writers should include a suggested headline.)
4. At the top of the form indicate when the news release may be made public. "For Release Upon Receipt" means that the story may be printed immediately upon receipt. Sometimes a news release may be issued several days in advance of the time it is to be used, in which case it will be marked "To Be Released on July 1" or "Not to Be Released Before July 1."
5. Indicate the end of the release by keying the word *END* in parentheses or by keying three *x*'s:—*xxx*—. (The three *x*'s stand for "30," the signal telegraphers once used to signify "the end.")
6. If there is more than one page, add the word *more* in parentheses at the end of each page except the last page.

7. If the news release is long, insert subheads between paragraphs of the text to help break the monotony of type.

NOTE: Some news outlets accept faxed news releases. Before faxing the release, the sender should make a personal contact to determine the need for quick transmission.

Text of the News Release   Whether your story heads for the wastebasket or the news channel may depend on the words you use in your first paragraph. The first paragraph should summarize the basic idea of the story. It should be able to stand by itself if necessary, giving the *who, what, why, when,* and *where,* as stories appearing in newspapers generally do. Here is an example:

> Edith Wilson has been named comptroller of Austin, Lavalle, and Gentry, a legal corporation in Bergen, New Jersey. Her appointment effective immediately, Ms. Wilson replaces Jefferson Evans, who was recently named head of the West Coast operation.

The news angle of the story is Ms. Wilson's appointment rather than Mr. Austin's participation. Put the accent on Wilson; don't write as follows:

> Mr. Garrett Austin, president of Austin, Lavalle, and Gentry, a legal corporation in Bergen, New Jersey, has announced the appointment of Edith Wilson as comptroller.

After the lead paragraph is written, move on to the background facts:

> She succeeds E. Arnold Rooney, who retired July 1.

Additional background worth noting may then be given:

> The new comptroller joined the firm in 1991 as an auditor. In 1992 she was made accounting supervisor and in 1993 was appointed assistant comptroller.

A well-written news release follows all the guidelines on the previous pages.

MESSAGE FORMS

Message forms allow people to take complete, accurate messages for others quickly. Thus they help us and our coworkers to build goodwill with customers and to work more efficiently with one another.

Since the forms usually include printed guide words (*To, Phone No., Date,* and so on) and easy-to-check boxes, the person who takes a message writes very few words. In the example on page 434, note that the check-off boxes make this form useful both for telephone messages and for messages from visitors.

To: *Harvey Lentz*

Here is a Message for You

Helen Sturgis

of *Sturgis + Wells*

Phone No. *555-7229*   Ext _____

- ☑ Telephoned
- ☐ Returned Your Call
- ☑ Please Phone
- ☐ Will Call Again
- ☐ Came To See You
- ☐ Wants To See You

She wants to inform you of the progress made on the Fuller case.

Taken By *Andy*   Date *10/28*   Time *3:40 p.m.*

Message forms help people take complete, accurate messages.

COMMUNICATION LABORATORY

APPLICATION EXERCISES

A. Prepare a set of minutes for either a class session or a meeting of a club that you belong to. Use the informal form discussed in this section.

B. Prepare a formal set of minutes for an actual meeting that you have attended. The minutes might come from a club meeting or from the meeting of a local government agency. If you have not attended such a meeting, you may make up the necessary information.

C. Prepare a news release for your school or for a club or group that you belong to. If the release is for your school, it might announce a graduation, an athletic schedule, special student awards, or an annual play. If the release is for a club or group, it might announce an important upcoming meeting, a special activity or speaker, or a fund or membership drive.

D. A long-time employee from a branch office has called for information about early retirement. He would like to know what his monthly combined pension and social security payments would be if he retired at age 62 instead of age 65. He would also like to know how much notice the company

CONTINUED

needs if he plans to take early retirement. Leave a telephone message for the personnel director.

VOCABULARY AND SPELLING STUDIES

A. These words are often confused: *suit, suite, sweet; bearing, baring, barring.* Explain the differences.

B. Substitute a modern word or phrase for each of the following trite expressions:

1. At an early date
2. Kindly advise us
3. We trust
4. We beg to remain
5. Under separate cover

C. Three of the four words in each of the following groups are synonyms. The fourth word is an antonym. Underline this intruder.

1. attach, add, append, detach
2. start, begin, commence, terminate
3. conscious, asleep, awake, alive
4. invalidate, verify, authenticate, confirm
5. unskilled, expert, efficient, able
6. lively, dull, animated, alert
7. instantly, immediately, now, later
8. factual, true, correct, wrong
9. virtually, almost, every, nearly
10. objective, biased, just, fair

CHAPTER 10

ORAL COMMUNICATION

Just as written communication needs both a writer and a reader, oral communication is also a two-way process. For oral communication to be possible, there must be both a listener and a speaker.

Your oral communication skills, listening and speaking, are always in use. Whether you are at home, at school, at social activities, or at work, what you hear, what you say, and how you say it are equally important. When you speak, communicate verbally and nonverbally in such a way that your receiver understands your messages without the benefit of a written record. When you listen, use facial expressions and gestures to give the speaker clues that you are understanding or that you need more information to understand the message.

It is easy to see how effective listening and speaking skills influence business situations. Giving and taking messages, conducting and participating in meetings, making and listening to formal presentations, giving and taking spoken directions—all these important business situations involve oral communication.

OBJECTIVES

Given a situation that requires listening and speaking skills, you will be able to do the following when you master the sections in this chapter:

1. Take brief—but complete—written notes at meetings, demonstrations, and lectures and of telephone instructions.

2. Remember more of what you hear and the names of people to whom you are introduced.

3. Eliminate common misunderstandings that can result from the spoken word.

4. Improve your ability to follow instructions on the job.

5. Address an audience confidently.

6. Learn to use the telephone efficiently.

7. Plan and conduct successful meetings.

DEVELOPING EFFECTIVE LISTENING SKILLS

Listening occupies more time than any other communication activity: we spend more time listening than we spend talking, reading, or writing. Obviously, then, improving our listening skills can improve our ability to receive communications.

The rewards of listening include (1) increased knowledge, (2) broadened experience, (3) more and deeper friendships, (4) increased job opportunities and promotions, (5) facility in using language, and (6) an increased appreciation of the spoken word.

On the other hand, ineffective listening may have a disastrous effect on any of these rewards, resulting in disappointments and failure. Frequently, potential school dropouts fail in their studies not because they can't learn but because they don't know how to listen. Employees may be fired not because they can't perform their jobs well but because they don't know how to listen to instructions.

Tests have shown that immediately after most people have listened to someone talk, they remember only about half of what they heard. Two months later, they remember only about a fourth of what was said. In other words, the average person is only 25 percent efficient in listening skills.

WHY IMPROVE LISTENING EFFICIENCY?

What does all this mean to you? Well, suppose through instruction and practice, you are able to double your listening efficiency. You become 50 percent efficient in listening rather than just 25 percent. Consider what this improvement will mean in relation to your social life, your learning, and your job.

Listening and Your Social Life   We find it easy to listen attentively to a good conversationalist, but courtesy demands that we *always* be good listeners. We should listen to others not only out of courtesy but also so that we can understand *what* they are saying and *why*. In this way good listeners gain new friends and enrich and deepen their existing friendships.

Listening and Your Education   In high school today, many class hours are devoted to lectures and discussions, so doubling your listening effectiveness would increase your learning productivity. Efficient listening—resulting in improved learning and remembering—also would give you more time for other subjects and for extracurricular activities.

Listening and Your Job   The rewards of improved listening are more tangible when you have a job, for often the rewards are in money. Beginning employees must listen to instructions and directions from their supervisors and coworkers. They must listen to suggestions and criticisms in order to improve their job performance. To advance in a job, they must be aware of what's going on in their department and in the company. This awareness comes in part from intelligent listening.

LISTENING AND JOB SUCCESS

Efficient listening contributes to success in all areas of life, but particularly in business and industry. So important are good listening habits that many large corporations—American Telephone and Telegraph, General Electric, and General Motors among them—provide listening training for many of their executives and supervisory personnel.

Supervisors Must Know How to Listen   Businesses know that to be effective, management must be able to listen. Successful supervisors and managers don't just give orders; they also do a lot of listening. They listen to their employees so that they can establish good employee relationships. They also listen to their employees because they know that employees often contribute timesaving and money-saving ideas.

All Employees Must Know How To Listen   Listening is important at all levels of employment. Many employees in business and industry rely on listening skills to help them carry out their daily assignments. The telephone operator must listen carefully in order to handle the requests of hundreds of callers. The salesperson must listen just as carefully to understand the requests of customers.

One large retailing organization found that two out of every three former customers had taken their business elsewhere because its sales personnel were indifferent to customers' needs. Additionally, the organization found that much of the indifference was expressed through poor listening.

No one in business and industry is immune to the need for effective listening. All employees who provide service of any kind—and that includes most workers—are dependent on their listening ability to do their jobs. Every worker—every secretary, accountant, shipping clerk, machine operator, maintenance worker—receives information and instructions orally from coworkers, from supervisors, and from customers. Failure to listen can result in errors and misunderstandings that can be costly in time, money, and goodwill.

Because effective listening is so important in every aspect of your life—social, school, and work—you should be eager to begin the listening improvement program suggested in this chapter.

STUDY TIP

"A large part of communicating is listening well. Listen closely to others instead of concentrating on what you're going to say next; then what you do say will make more sense."
—Phyllis Martin, *A Word Watcher's Handbook*

PREPARATION FOR LISTENING

We *hear* many sounds, but we don't *listen* to all of them. We can't; we would be overrun by sound if we did. In self-defense we block off many sounds from our consciousness—we "tune out" unwanted sounds.

Blocking off sounds can be useful, as it often aids concentration. But too often we also block off sounds to which we *should* be listening. Most of us have acquired bad habits of nonlistening, even with our best friends, and these habits are very hard to break.

Fortunately, bad listening habits can be unlearned and replaced by good listening habits. The first step is to become *aware* of your deficiencies in listening and of your need for good listening habits. When you have made this awareness a habit, you will be well on your way to becoming a good listener.

In order to prepare yourself for listening, try to follow these guidelines:

1. Determine your purpose for listening.
2. Get ready to listen.
3. Accept your share of responsibility for communication.

Determine Your Purpose   The chief difference between hearing and listening is that listening involves both the mind and the ears. Another way of expressing this difference is that *listening has a purpose.* Different *purposes* in listening imply different *kinds* of listening.

Your purpose may be (1) to act friendly and sociable (a party conversation), (2) to obtain information (a lecture), or (3) to analyze critically (a political debate).

Listening to a pep talk at a football rally is not the same as listening to a formal speech. Listening to a friend introduce you to someone is not the same as overhearing a conversation on a bus. In an introduction you would listen carefully for the person's name and note any specific details that you could use in conversation. When listening to a speech, you would listen for main ideas and supporting facts. In a pep talk you would listen for the general tone of the meeting, and with the bus conversation you might want to tune out after a few minutes.

In each situation listening calls for different skills and for different degrees of attentiveness. The demands are different because the purpose is different, so you must determine your purpose for listening in every listening situation. You will be a better listener as a result of knowing *why* you are listening.

Get Ready to Listen   Good listening implies a *readiness* to listen. Prepare yourself for listening—physically, mentally, and emotionally. Literally turn your back on distracting sights and sounds, and give yourself maximum opportunity for listening by sitting close enough to the speaker to see and hear easily. If possible, read about the topic in advance; the more you know about a topic, the more interested you will be in what the speaker has to say about it. Mental preparation automatically leads to emotional involvement because it supplies you with a purpose for listening.

Accept Your Share of Responsibility   Too often listeners approach speakers with an "I dare you to interest me" attitude. Such an attitude is tough on the speaker and is obviously discourteous. Remember that as a listener you share the responsibility for communicating with the speaker; therefore, you must be courteous to the speaker.

The quality of your listening can affect the speaker's talking—it may even control it! The reason is simple: we all crave good listeners, and we react according to the listeners' actions. Imagine that you are in the midst of telling an interesting story. One of your "listeners" is flipping the pages of a magazine; two others are whispering to each other; another is openly yawning. How would you react? Would you go on with your story? As you can see, then, an audience can influence the delivery, and even the length, of a speech.

BASIC RULES FOR LISTENING

Just as there are guidelines for preparing to listen, there are some basic rules for listening:

1. Listen with understanding.
2. Listen with an open mind.
3. Listen actively.
4. Listen with empathy.

Listen With Understanding   Be sure you understand the speaker's ideas fully and completely; don't jump to conclusions about a false or half-true idea. To understand the speaker's ideas, you must listen *carefully*. If necessary, ask questions to clarify anything that is vague.

Listen With an Open Mind   Keep your mind open when you listen. Forget your biases and prejudices for the moment, and be ready to receive new ideas. Don't refuse to listen to new ideas just because they may *conflict with* those you believe. Hear everything the speaker has to say; don't tune in only what you want to hear. Of course, it is possible that your point of view may be changed somewhat as a result, but you should be courageous enough to take that chance. After all, the change may be for the better.

Listen Actively   Active listening implies work on your part. Primarily, it means three things: (1) concentrating, (2) relating what you hear to what you already know, (3) and reading between the lines.

To concentrate, you must be selective about the sounds you hear. Focus your attention on what a speaker is saying, and disregard any noises and distractions. Being an active process, concentration takes both willpower and energy.

Relating ideas and facts just heard to your existing store of knowledge means that change will take place. No change, no learning. And naturally, learning takes concentrated effort.

Reading between the lines—or sensing the implications of a speaker's message—is another rule of good listening. The good listener analyzes the speaker's word choice and observes closely the speaker's posture, facial expressions, tone of voice, manner, general appearance, and so on.

Listen With Empathy   Listening with empathy means putting yourself in the speaker's place—making an extra effort to understand the speaker's point of view. Naturally, such listening requires imagination. However, because it results in attentiveness that is very flattering to most speakers, listening with empathy draws them out and helps eliminate any shyness, suspicion, or hostility they may have. Thus listening with empathy aids communication and usually results in many rewards for the listener.

CRITICAL LISTENING

Critical listening is a special kind of listening—listening with a view toward analyzing and evaluating both what speakers say and how they say it. It involves all the basic rules of listening, plus a few others:

Listening for main ideas and supporting details
Reviewing points already made and anticipating what is coming next
Analyzing the evidence
Accepting or rejecting the speaker's conclusions based on the evidence

To listen critically may seem to be a large order, given that you are expected to listen intently at the same time. However, good listeners do both all the time. They use their *spare listening time* to reflect on the words they have just heard.

All of us have some spare listening time because we think much faster than most speakers talk. The rate of speech for most Americans is around 125 words a minute, but we think at a rate four or five times that fast.

The half-listener or nonlistener generally uses this time to daydream or to turn his or her attention elsewhere. Using spare listening time to daydream will not work out well. Daydreamers usually find their attention focused more on distractions than on the words of the speaker. The listener becomes less interested in the topic and more interested in the distractions. Finally, the listener gives up completely and tunes out the speaker.

Good listeners use their spare listening time to think about what the speaker says; in other words, they listen *actively*. Active listening results in increased understanding and longer remembering. Following are some rules for using your spare listening time:

1. Note major points.
2. Recognize details.
3. Rephrase and review.
4. Detect bias and determine motives.
5. Take notes.
6. Practice.

Note Major Points   A well-prepared speech usually consists of a few major points. Often a good speaker may indicate these points near the beginning of the talk.

Suppose the speaker says the following:

> In the world of word processing in the past ten years, there has been a major revolution in both equipment and business practices that makes many traditional practices obsolete. Today we shall deal with the effects of word processing in the business classroom. We shall discuss this technological upheaval as it relates to the preparation of young men and women to work in the automated world of work. In our discussion of desirable changes in this preparation, let us consider three principal topics. First, the power of computerized word processing in changing the way the work is performed. Second, the changing purposes for preparing people for work in the computerized world. And third, the changes in classroom methods required to teach young people to learn.

Thus the speaker actually reveals an outline in the presentation, and you should grasp this outline by noting these three principal points:

1. The changing methods of working
2. The changing purposes of education and training
3. The changing methods of teaching

Recognize Details   As soon as you grasp the speaker's major ideas, you should recognize that everything else is designed to support these main ideas. The details will help fill in the structure of the speech and lead you to a better understanding of the speech. Details will also tell you a lot about the way a speaker thinks.

In the following excerpt from a speech, note that while the sidelights add color and interest to the main idea, they are not separate ideas in themselves; the main idea is only the italicized words.

> *One of the major factors in locating manufacturing sites today is the availability of trained personnel.* For example, Beverly Township, in the eastern part of the state, would be a suitable site for our new computer manufacturing facility except for one factor: lack of educational facilities. There is no university in the area producing engineering and administrative personnel. There are no technical institutes or training schools. The high schools in the vicinity lack both comprehensive vocational training programs and developed business courses. Although transportation facilities are ideal, taxes are low, land is inexpensive, and the climate is outstanding, it would be extremely difficult to staff such a facility in this location. Our only choice would be to institute our own training programs, and to do so would be extremely expensive.

In the preceding paragraph, note the words *for example*. Speakers often provide the listener with cues to indicate whether an idea is a new one or whether it merely supports an idea already presented.

Rephrase and Review   Effective listeners work to retain the speaker's message in two ways: by *rephrasing* silently the speaker's words and by *reviewing* the major points of the speech from time to time. Using both methods will reinforce your understanding of the speech and help you remember the principal ideas.

Rephrasing is similar to taking notes, except that you rephrase mentally: you concentrate on main ideas and summarize them as briefly as possible. You must practice the rephrasing process again and again to master this listening skill. Note in the following illustration how you can mentally rephrase a speaker's words:

WHAT THE SPEAKER IS SAYING

An ideal salesperson tries to ascertain a customer's real needs and then attempts to meet those needs. A successful salesperson usually tries to figure out what the customer really desires—a factor that often escapes the customer. Yet the good salesperson is able to bring these desires out into the open. For example, a person looking for a computer might very well put price above everything else, because we are all conditioned to be careful about money. However, the skillful salesperson soon determines that the customer really wants those options that add "something" to the computer. For example, the customer may say, "It would be nice to have color, but I don't think it is worth an extra $1000." Realizing what the customer *really* wants, the skillful salesperson says, "You know, in the final analysis, it really costs very little, since it will add to the value of your computer should you want to sell it or trade it in for another model. It will add about $600 to the value of your computer and, therefore, really cost you only $400. If you keep the computer for only two years, that's about $200 a year, or only about 60 cents a day." The salesperson is not being dishonest; the salesperson is merely helping the customer get what he or she really wants.

WHAT YOU ARE SAYING TO YOURSELF

The ideal salesperson meets the customer's real needs. Once a customer lets it be known that he or she would really like something, the salesperson does everything possible to make it appealing. The good salesperson fulfills the customer's needs and desires.

Detect Bias and Determine Motives   A biased viewpoint is a partial, or prejudiced, viewpoint. In business, bias and preconceived opinions are natural because a company wants to sell its product or service; this desire then becomes its primary motive. But the critical listener must learn to recognize this bias and this motive.

For example, people who sell automobiles may focus all their attention on the favorable features of a particular make of car. But as a good listener you must recognize this bias and realize that what you hear from the seller may not be the whole truth. Automobile salespeople would be foolish to let you know all the weaknesses of their cars, since their motive is to sell them.

The customary warning *caveat emptor* ("let the buyer beware") applies to listeners as well: let the listener beware of the words of biased or emotional speakers.

Take Notes   Note-taking can be an aid to remembering, not a substitute for listening. When listeners spend too much time taking notes, they miss the heart of the message. Therefore, notes should be made with caution. Here are specific suggestions for note-taking.

1. Have plenty of notepaper, a good pen, and an extra pencil or two.
2. Use an uncluttered writing surface that provides backing for the paper.
3. Label your notes for easy identification later.
4. Listen for such speaker's cues as "first," "second," and "third"; "another important consideration"; "finally"; "the most significant thing"; "on the other hand"; "in summary"; and questions posed by the speaker, pauses, changes of emphasis in voice, and gestures.
5. Flag important parts of your notes with brackets, underscores, arrows, indentions, or other signals.
6. Listen for special instructions.
7. Go over your notes promptly after the speech to fix the major points more firmly in your mind.

Practice, Practice, Practice   Efficient listening, like other communication skills, requires practice. To become a good listener, take every opportunity to put the techniques presented in this section into practice. In other words—practice, practice, practice!

THE EFFECT OF LISTENING ON OTHER COMMUNICATION SKILLS

Each of the communication skills can reinforce the others to produce a higher degree of learning and remembering. For example, listening can be reinforced with reading, with speaking, and with writing to produce understanding and longer remembering.

Listening and Reading   Like reading, listening is a message-receiving skill. But listening is more difficult than reading because, generally, you cannot *relisten* to a spoken message as you can reread a written one. You must get the message right the first time, or else you'll lose it.

Reading about a topic in advance will enable you to listen more effectively to the speaker's message because you'll bring more knowledge to the topic and thus derive greater benefit from it. When planning to attend an important committee meeting, if you examine the agenda and reread the minutes of previous meetings beforehand, you will be able to listen much more effectively during the meeting.

Listening and Speaking

Speaking reinforces listening in various ways. Good listeners repeat to themselves the speaker's important points, and they mentally rephrase these points in their own words; this process adds to the listeners' understanding. In addition, good listeners ask questions to clarify what a speaker is saying.

Speaking is often an aid to memory; it helps the listener to remember. When you are introduced to people, for example, you will be more likely to remember their names if you repeat each name orally and use the name as much as you can in talking with the person or in talking with others about the person.

Listening and Writing

Writing, perhaps more than any other communication skill, contributes to effective listening. Often, the listener must take written notes in order to retain for future reference the information that has been transmitted. The student attending a lecture, the secretary taking a telephone message, and the accountant receiving oral instructions from a supervisor are but a few examples of note-takers who write notes to *reinforce* their listening. Helpful suggestions for effective note-taking are presented on page 445.

COMMUNICATION LABORATORY

APPLICATION EXERCISES

A. On a separate sheet of paper, answer each of the following numbered questions by writing *yes, sometimes,* or *no.* The questions are designed to help you evaluate your own listening habits.

1. For a class on a given topic, do you read and think about the topic before the class meets?
2. When your teacher or others are speaking, do you pay close and considerate attention to what they say?
3. When in class, do you alertly listen to and accurately follow all the instructions and directions of the teacher?
4. When you enter an auditorium to listen to a speech, do you deliberately seat yourself where you can easily see and hear the speaker?
5. When listening, do you carefully take note of the speaker's facial expressions?

CONTINUED

6. When you receive instructions or directions that must be carefully followed, do you write them on a piece of paper?
7. When another person is introduced to you, do you mentally practice saying and spelling the name to fix it in your memory?
8. Do you take notes during all class presentations and discussions?
9. As soon as possible after an introduction, do you use the new name when speaking to the person you just met to help fix it in your memory?
10. When listening in class, do you mentally rephrase in your own words what you have heard?
11. Do you suspect that you have a hearing or vision problem that a physician should check?
12. When you do not understand what a teacher or another student has said in class, do you ask questions to make the message clear?
13. When speaking on the telephone, do you try to picture the other person's facial expressions in order to participate more fully in the conversation?
14. In listening to a speech or lecture, do you mentally repeat to yourself important points that the speaker makes?
15. Do you deliberately make a mental note of oral messages you need to remember?

B. Certain words have an emotional effect on the listener, creating either a positive or a negative effect. For example, the word *happiness* might have a positive effect, while the word *poverty* might have a negative effect. Can you think of five words that might have a positive effect and five words that might have a negative effect? List these words under appropriate headings on a separate sheet of paper.

C. Good listeners are able to distinguish facts from opinions. On a separate sheet of paper, indicate which of the following are facts and which are opinions.

1. I own an IBM computer.
2. Rentals in this city are high.
3. This car is the best one on the market.
4. The play I saw tonight is very funny.
5. He enjoyed his vacation in Europe.
6. Jack's motorcycle is worth about $750.
7. Jack paid $2000 for his motorcycle.
8. I think the play I saw tonight is funny.
9. Neckties are uncomfortable.
10. I think your motorcycle is worth more than $750.

CONTINUED

VOCABULARY AND SPELLING STUDIES

A. In each of the following sentences, choose the word in parentheses that correctly expresses the meaning.

1. The program enacted today will (affect, effect) us.
2. In which (edition, addition) did your article appear?
3. There is no logic in that (inane, insane) remark.
4. We have seats for the match on the upper (tier, tear).
5. I have just signed a (partition, petition) against the tax.
6. The (trial, trail) was scheduled in Judge Greenberg's court.
7. (Immortal, Immoral) books should be in all libraries.
8. When the lunch hour was increased, the (moral, morale) improved.
9. The judge asked two (disinterested, uninterested) parties to settle the dispute.
10. A large (amount, number) of customers bought the new product.

B. The following words appear in this section. Read through the section, locate each word, and guess its meaning from the way in which it is used in its sentence. Check the meaning of the word in a dictionary. Then use each word in a sentence of your own.

1. device
2. interpret
3. quizzical
4. disastrous
5. dividends
6. attentively
7. reinforce
8. indifferent
9. immune
10. aspect

C. Use each of the following nouns in the sentence that it best completes: *adjacent, bias, deterrent, discretion, empathy, frequency, involvement, noxious, retention, transformation.*

1. Mr. Adams has a _____ against lazy workers.
2. We had much _____ for the earthquake victims.
3. The ambassador was criticized for his _____ in foreign affairs.
4. The _____ of workers makes additional training programs unnecessary.
5. At your _____, we may get a holiday next week.
6. The _____ of our business trips has decreased since the company sold the West Coast division.
7. The high cost of recycling tires has been a _____ to our plans for installing the shredder.
8. The _____ of the building from a warehouse to luxury condominiums was remarkable.
9. The city's annexation of the _____ property angered the nearby village.
10. The release of _____ gases into the atmosphere was reported to the EPA.

SECTION 10.2

DEVELOPING EFFECTIVE SPEAKING SKILLS

W e all use each of the four communicating skills—reading, writing, listening, and speaking. However, we spend most of our time communicating with our voices. For example, in school we ask and answer questions, we contribute to discussions, we participate in debates, and we give oral presentations. Those who are most successful in extracurricular activities often depend on their ability to express ideas orally. In your relationships with your friends and family, you talk about events of the day and plans for the future. Whether you work in an office, a store, or a gasoline station, you certainly spend much time talking—giving instructions or explanations, asking questions or answering them, promoting good business relations, selling ideas, or selling your personal qualities.

To many people your speech is *you.* Since most of us talk much more than we write, we are judged more by our speech than by our writing. Speech is an important part of your personality—it is individually and particularly yours. The words you use, the way you put them together, the sound of your voice (tone, pitch, volume, and rate), and your enunciation and pronunciation all add up to the *you* that others hear. You can't separate your voice from your personality.

CREATE A FAVORABLE IMPRESSION: DRESS, POSTURE, EXPRESSION, MANNERS, AND MANNERISMS

Effective speech depends on factors other than the words spoken. The setting, or atmosphere, in which words are spoken often determines how they are received by the listener. Just as a successful play or film needs the proper setting, musical background, and costumes, so must successful speaking have the appropriate atmosphere. The speaker must make a favorable impression on the listener.

An impression is the result of many factors. Each of these factors needs to be studied and mastered. They must be practiced. Among the elements that help a speaker make a favorable impression are the following:

1. Appropriate dress and grooming
2. Good posture and carriage
3. Pleasant facial expressions
4. Good manners
5. Lack of distracting mannerisms

Appropriate Dress and Grooming

No single set of dress standards will apply to every business situation today. The best advice is to suggest that you first determine who will judge your dress and grooming in a particular situation and how important this judgment is to you. If the judgment is important to you, then determine what is acceptable in terms of dress and grooming to that individual or group. Then dress accordingly.

Although business dress standards tend to be somewhat conservative, many offices have relaxed these standards slightly. However, extremes in clothing, hairstyles, or makeup are not likely to be acceptable to those businesses that wish to convey a feeling of conservatism to their customers. To determine what will be acceptable, observe other employees in your company, and read employee manuals that describe dress and grooming codes.

Regardless of dress standards, two aspects of grooming that are always important are cleanliness and neatness. Your overall appearance makes a strong impression. If you are well-groomed and neatly dressed, your appearance will inspire a basic confidence in your work habits.

Good Posture and Carriage

The positive effect you wish to create by wearing carefully chosen clothing and practicing good grooming can be completely destroyed if you do not sit, stand, and walk correctly. The fit and the hang of an article of clothing are best when posture and carriage are good. Therefore, if you take pride in your appearance, you should analyze your sitting, standing, and walking habits and make any necessary improvements.

Your Posture Tells The way you carry yourself seems to reveal traits of personality and character. Do you sprawl when you sit? Then you are lazy. When you stand, do you always rest all your weight on one leg and hip? Then you tire or lose interest quickly and have no drive.

"Not so," you say? Well, perhaps the tales told by your posture and carriage are false. But such is the impression you give, and erasing the impression of laziness will be very difficult.

When you get ready to sit, bend your joints and sit. Do not fall into a chair as a rag doll would. Once in the chair, sit up straight—do not be rigid, but do not slump either. For correct sitting posture, the best practice is to be sure that the end of your spine touches the back of the chair. A little practice in taking a seat and in sitting correctly will pay dividends. And if you like to sit with your legs crossed, make sure that you do not look awkward.

Stand Tall, but Not Stiff People who stand correctly stand tall and hold their heads up. Their shoulders are in line with the rest of their body—not far back, not caved in toward the chest. They hold themselves erect, but not stiff. They stand with their weight distributed evenly on both feet. Standing tall will make you look self-confident and will give others a good impression of you.

There are as many variations in the manner of walking as there are people. You will find that it is impossible to change completely your own distinctive style of walking. You can, however, learn just one thing that will help. Walk as though you have somewhere to go and you intend to get there without stopping at way stations! Walking purposefully, you will give an impression of being ambitious, industrious, and self-directing.

Pleasant Facial Expressions

The education of an aspiring actor or actress includes practicing facial expressions that reflect various emotions— joy, fear, pleasure, sorrow, and so on. Through intelligent practice, you, too, can change your facial expressions. First, of course, you need to know what kind of expression creates a favorable impression. You need some pointers on how to assume such an expression. You need, too, to know where your own shortcomings are. And you need to practice before a mirror.

Look Interested A pleasant, interested, alive-looking expression is a winning expression. Even a hasty glance at such an expression generates a feeling of warmth, of liking. In an interview, a meeting, a conference, or any other working situation, pleasant facial expressions promote pleasant relationships. Fortunate, indeed, are those of you who naturally and habitually have this type of facial expression.

Too many persons tell a story of indifference, boredom, or discontent with their expressions. Some very intelligent people are afflicted with shyness, which they try to hide behind a "deadpan" face or a bored facial expression. These are the ones who will profit from studying the following discussion.

The eyes are the focal point of a facial expression, as you can prove by doing this: stand in front of a mirror, and think of something very pleasant that has happened to you recently. See how your eyes light up your whole face? With practice you will find that it is not necessary to smile or grin in order to look pleasant but that it *is* necessary to *feel* pleasant. However, if you have a warm, attractive smile, use it whenever you can.

Really Look at People Suppose that you do not look at those who are talking to you. Since they cannot see your eyes, they are unable to form a favorable opinion of your personality and disposition, and you run the risk of being misjudged. For instance, there are interviewers who will not hire an applicant who looks everywhere but at the interviewer. They think that this habit indicates that the applicant is shy and shifty. So after you have worked to acquire a facial expression that will contribute to your advancement, be sure to look at people. Otherwise, your efforts will have been wasted.

Learning to look pleasant, interested, and alert is purely an individual problem. Only you can study your own expression, and only you can put in the practice time necessary to achieve the results you wish. You are the one who must consciously assume the facial expression that produces a favorable impression. You must remember to look at people when you talk to them. The rewards, also, are yours alone. One of the rewards is that in a relatively short time, your improved facial expression will become your habitual expression.

Good Manners

Another factor in creating a favorable impression is good manners. The atmosphere of polish created by those who do and say the correct thing at the correct time earns the respect and admiration of all.

WORLD VIEW

Among all the intercultural differences affecting international communication, one nonverbal message appears to mean the same across all cultures—a smile.

The Basis Is Courtesy The basis of good manners is courtesy, and the basis of courtesy is consideration for others. Without courtesy, good manners are only a false front.

However, natural courtesy is not enough for correct behavior. Do not minimize the importance of knowing and observing the rules of etiquette. You must know such things as how to make and acknowledge introductions properly. You should, in short, be familiar with all the rules that govern correct social and business relationships. This means that you need to know and to review periodically the contents of an etiquette book. There are some slight differences between social and office etiquette, and you can learn them by studying a book on business etiquette.

Introductions The aspects of social correctness that are frequently important in business usage are introductions and handshakes. Although there are numerous rules for making introductions, they may all be simplified by determining quickly which of the two or more people being introduced you wish to honor or which has the more important position. Then say that person's name *first.* For instance, if you were introducing someone to your mother, you would say, "Mother, may I present . . . ," "Mother, I'd like you to know . . . ," or "Mother, this is . . . ." If you wished to introduce your manager, Mr. Alda, and a young man who is with you, you would say, "Mr. Alda, this is . . . ." You might call this technique a Quick Trick that will prevent those first embarrassing moments of silence that occur while you are trying to remember the various methods of presentation.

The second suggestion is that you learn to shake hands in a manner that will give an impression of decision and determination, that will indicate that you have a mind of your own. Clasp hands firmly, and shake hands once, without overdoing the up-and-down motion. Firmly does not mean "bone crushing." You should use just enough hand pressure to show some strength.

WORLD VIEW

If you're doing business with other countries, you should be aware of differences in etiquette and nonverbal communication. For example, most Europeans shake hands before and after social and business occasions. The Japanese, on the other hand, usually bow instead of shaking hands.

Lack of Distracting Mannerisms

The person who sits at the desk next to yours may be first-rate in grooming, posture, manners, and pleasant facial expressions. But what about that annoying habit of knuckle cracking? And what about the person who comes to tell you something, stands behind you, and breathes down your neck? or chews gum? Often, ambitious young people may work very hard to improve themselves but are still defeated because they have overlooked some mannerism that will annoy others.

As a finishing touch to your study of how to create a favorable impression, examine your own mannerisms. To appear favorably to others, you must let nothing detract from the impression you have worked so hard to produce. It is difficult to study yourself because you may not realize that you have distracting or annoying habits. For best results first study the people around you. Watch to see whether they have any behavior quirks. Whenever you observe a mannerism that you think is objectionable, say to yourself, "Do I do that?" After you have had practice in looking for these faults in others, you will be more likely to see your own faults.

VOICE QUALITY

How you say something can be as important as what you say and how you look while saying it. Your voice quality plays an important role in determining how your words affect the listener. Your voice can soothe people or make them angry, thus helping or hindering a situation. The first time people hear you, they are likely to classify you as cheerful or solemn, interesting or dull, lively or lazy. Since most people in business communicate more frequently by speaking than by writing, voice quality can work for or against you and your company.

Voice quality is determined by four principal factors: volume, pitch, tone, and tempo. The effectiveness of your voice depends also on enunciation and pronunciation, as well as on breath control.

In order to improve your voice, you must be able to control your breathing. Breath control depends both on correct posture and on deep breathing. Good posture enables a person to breathe into the lungs the maximum amount of air and also to control the amount of air expended. Deep breathing adds resonance to your tones because you have more air with which to vibrate the vocal chords. Be sure to breathe from the diaphragm, the muscle partition that separates the chest from the abdominal cavity.

Volume *Intensity, force,* and *volume* are all similar words that describe the quality in your voice that enables people to hear you. Speakers must be heard, or else they will lose their audience. Since good breath control is so important in providing volume, you should practice correct breathing so that you will not have trouble being heard.

Pitch *Pitch* refers to the degree of highness or lowness of a sound. A shrill voice is much too high. A moderately low voice is usually the most pleasing. If your voice is unpleasantly high, you can lower it by making a conscious effort to do so over a long period of time.

If possible, tape-record your voice, and listen to it several times. Try to hear your voice as others hear it, and ask your friends or classmates to criticize it. Practice lowering your voice, and then record the same material a second time to see whether there has been any improvement.

Tone It is your tone that reveals your attitudes and feelings to your listeners. In business relations, as well as in social life, try to use a pleasant and cheerful tone whenever possible. However, variations in tone, as well as in volume and pitch, will add interest to your speech. Think about what you are saying when you are talking or reading orally; then adapting your tone to your meaning will not be difficult.

Tempo The rate of speed at which you talk is the tempo of your voice. Since tempo often determines whether your speech is understandable, you should speak at an appropriate rate of speed. Use pauses to stress major points, for they add variety to a speech besides emphasizing the points you want the listener to remember. By speaking important words slowly and less important

WORLD VIEW

The tone of voice is significant when one is communicating orally. Russians speak in flat, level tones, which Americans might consider indicative of boredom. Speaking in loud tones, a trait of Middle Easterners, could be construed as emotional. The Japanese habit of speaking in soft tones exhibits humility or courage. Voice usage can cause misunderstanding unless the communicators understand the differences.

words or phrases more rapidly, you contribute both variety and clarity to your speaking.

SAY WORDS CORRECTLY AND DISTINCTLY

A person applying for a position may be carefully groomed and may give the outward appearance of being a promising employee. But faulty pronunciation and poor enunciation may cost the applicant the position, particularly if the job calls for frequent oral communication with the public, either in person or over the telephone.

Pronunciation means "saying words *correctly*," while *enunciation* means "saying words *distinctly*." Both are necessary if you are to be understood and to make a good impression on others.

To some of us English is a second language, for we were raised in an area where some other language was spoken primarily. Some of us were brought up in parts of the United States where the language pattern is different from that where we are now living. We should not be ashamed if we speak with an accent. An accent may add character to one's speech and make the voice more colorful and interesting to the listener. Remember that the principal purpose of communication—in whatever form—is to be understood by the person or persons with whom you are communicating. As long as the listener understands you, you are achieving this goal.

Even those brought up in an English-speaking environment make mistakes in enunciation and pronunciation, usually because of carelessness. So regardless of background, everyone needs to make every effort to improve the speaking voice, particularly in the enunciation and pronunciation of words.

ENUNCIATION

Listen to yourself. Do you run words together, leaving out some sounds? Do you say "jeet" for *did you eat?* "hatta" for *had to?* "gonna go" for *going to go?* Poor enunciation results from running words together, from leaving out letters or syllables, or from adding letters or syllables. Let us look first at a group of useful and common words that are sadly mistreated when letters or even whole syllables are dropped.

Lost Consonants   The final consonants most often dropped are *t, d,* and *g* when they are in combination with some other consonant. Thus *tact* becomes "tac," *field* becomes "feel," and *being* becomes "been." The *wh* sound, too, frequently is carelessly pronounced; for example, "wat" for *what*. Practice saying the following phrases aloud until you are sure you do not slight the sounds of the underlined consonants.

arrangin**g** pic**t**ures   attemp**t**ed bankrup**t**cy

assistin**g** an**d** managing   beyon**d** an**d** beyon**d**

collect payment

competent party

consigning a consignment

current asset

demand payment

doing typing and working

earned a discount

factual matter

first of February

kept a strict accounting

length and width

library list

lingering longingly

next payment

outstanding debt

recognized candidacy

seemingly strict

test of strength

thirty-three

threat and threatening

three hundred

through thick and thin

tourist list

trust fund

while whistling and thinking

why white wheels

Lost Vowels   When two vowels occur together in a word, the sound of one often tends to be slighted. Thus *li-on* becomes an indistinct "line." A single vowel used as a syllable is frequently overlooked and not sounded. A careless person will say "captal," completely ignoring the single-vowel syllable *i*. Pronounce the word correctly: "cap-i-tal." In the list below be sure to notice each vowel, and be sure you do not lose any vowel sounds when you practice these phrases:

accurate and regular

alphabetic list of liabilities

cruel lion

eleven manufacturers

especially positive

excellent family

family history

federal cabinet

generally separately

indirect and indefinite

indirectly responsible

ivory tower

metropolitan area

municipal regulation

original company

particularly quiet

popular battery

positive verification

ridiculous habit

separate poem

singular sophomore

temporarily separated

terrible and trite

usually interesting

variable capital

variable regulation

veteran general

Lost Syllables   People who drop consonant and vowel sounds often drop syllables from words too. Such a person "c'lecs stamps" instead of "collects." It is as though the speaker wishes to make a contraction (shortened form like *it's*) out of every word spoken. Try to avoid losing syllables as you practice saying these phrases:

perhaps (not *praps*)

little people (not *lil*)

laboratory technician (not *labatory*)

just *obligation* (not *obgation*)

five-year *guarantee* (not *garntee*)

detailed *itinerary* (not *itinree*)

generally acceptable (not *genrally*)

occasionally wrong (not *occasionly*)

Addition of Letters or Syllables The frequent mistake of adding sounds is another enunciation fault. As you say aloud the following italicized words, listen carefully to see whether you ordinarily add incorrect sounds to them.

a fine *athlete* (not *athalete*)

the *height* of fashion (not *heighth*)

across the street (not *acrost*)

broken *umbrella* (not *umberella*)

one roll of *film* (not *filum*)

drowned duck (not *drownded*)

grievous fault (not *grievious*)

rhythm for dancing (not *rhythum*)

pop *singer* (not *sing-ger*)

fourth *finger* (not *fing-ger*)

disastrous results (not *disasterous*)

entrance examination (not *enterance*)

a *hindrance* to progress (not *hinderance*)

a *mischievous* child (not *mischievious*)

a good *preventive* (not *preventative*)

a *burglar* alarm (not *burgular*)

One remedy for these types of enunciation errors is giving attention to spelling. If you spell these words correctly, you will be more likely to pronounce them correctly and enunciate them distinctly. If you misspell them, you may also mispronounce them.

Some Troublemakers Some words are more difficult to enunciate than others. They require an even slower rate of speech to allow maximum use of the jaw, lips, and tongue. You will be surprised to know that most of these words are short three- to five-letter words. They usually include one or more sounds that are difficult to distinguish. Thus, *ache* requires both the long *a* sound and a definite hard *k* sound.

Most of your practice so far has been with phrases. Now practice saying the following words out of context so that each one of them is clear.

ache	corn	fine	kit	nap	peat	tang
at	darn	gas	kite	nick	race	tent
balk	earn	grow	lay	oils	scab	very
big	else	heed	map	our	sign	wag
climb	fill	jam	nab	path	tan	wield

PRONUNCIATION

All of us learned to talk by imitating the speech of those around us: first, of members of the family; then, of neighbors and friends; later, of schoolmates, teachers, coworkers, and others with whom we came in contact. Of course, many of us have moved from one part of the country to another and have changed our original pronunciation and other speech habits to conform to the characteristics of the region in which we now live. Thus our present speech patterns reflect the wide variety of social, cultural, regional, and other influences to which we have been exposed.

Variations in Pronunciation   The dictionary usually decides whether a particular pronunciation is correct. However, this statement is a bit misleading.

As indicated in the preface of explanatory notes of the dictionary, it is impractical and unnecessary for a dictionary to show all the pronunciations that are in use for a particular word. Most dictionaries show only the one or two pronunciations that occur with the greatest frequency among educated speakers.

PRONUNCIATION DIFFICULTIES

In addition to regional and other differences in speech, certain types of incorrect pronunciations are quite common. They may be grouped according to the following categories.

Incorrect Vowel Sounds   Many words are not pronounced correctly because certain vowels are sounded wrong. Pronunciation information in your dictionary can help with any words you are uncertain of.

***The Sound of Long* U**   The use of the $\overline{oo}$ sound instead of the correct long *u* sound (heard in *human*) is a common error. It makes a decidedly unpleasant impression on listeners who are speech-conscious.

***Troubles With* A**   In another group of words the sound of long *a* (the sound in *hate*) is incorrectly replaced by the sound of short *a* (the sound in *hat*).

The following words are typical of this group. Read the list aloud, pronouncing the long *a* as indicated.

āviator	gāla	stātus
blātant	ignorāmus	tenācious
dāta	lātent	ultimātum
flāgrant	rādiator	verbātim

In the following words, the short *a* should be used instead of the long *a*.

Ărab	măltreat	păgination
deprăvity	păgeant	Spokăne

Troubles With I In some words the sound of long *i,* as heard in *wide,* is incorrectly replaced by the short *i* sound, as heard in *hit.*

alumnī   grīmy   stīpend

On the other hand, in the following words, the short *i* rather than the long *i* should be used.

Ĭtalian   respĭte

Substitution of One Vowel for Another In another type of mispronunciation, an entirely different vowel is substituted for the correct one. In the following words, the underscored letters are often replaced. Read the list aloud, clearly enunciating the underlined letters. If in doubt about any pronunciation, consult your dictionary. Mispronunciations of these and other words are often closely linked with misspellings.

accurate	just	preparation
description	mathematics	privilege
despair	optimistic	restaurant
divide	particular	sacrilegious
escalator	percolator	separate
existence	permanent	

Incorrect Accent Many pronunciation errors are caused by placing the stress, or accent, on the wrong syllable of a word. The pronunciation shown for each dictionary entry will also show which syllable or syllables should be stressed.

In the following words, the accent should be on the *first* syllable.

'ad-mirable	'dic-tionary	'in-teresting
'am-icable	'for-midable	'pref-erable
'ap-plicable	'in-famous	'the-ater
'com-parable		

In these words the accent should be on the *second* syllable.

con-'do-lence	ir-'rev-ocable	om-'nip-otence
de-'mon-strative	ob-'lig-atory	su-'per-fluous
ex-'traor-dinary		

In these words the accent should be on the *final* syllable.

automo-'bile	di-'rect	rou-'tine (*n.*)
bou-'quet	po-'lice	

Some words have more than one accented syllable. In those words one syllable will have primary stress; another, secondary stress.

Silent Letters A chief stumbling block to correct spelling is silent letters, which occur in many of our most frequently used words. Because we do not hear these letters, they are not usually a problem in pronunciation. However, there are a few important words in which letters that should be silent are often sounded. As you read aloud the following words, make a special effort *not* to sound the letters that are underscored.

corps	posthumous	salve
indict	often	sword
mortgage	salmon	vehement

Just Plain Tricky Many words often mispronounced cannot be classified under any of the above headings. There is only one way of mastering the correct pronunciations of these tricky words. Concentrate on each one, first looking up the word in your dictionary and then repeating the word many times. Here are sample words of this type.

absorb	deaf	once
absurd	denunciation	partner
apron	err	peremptory
associate	gist	perhaps
association	homogenous	perspiration
attorney	hundred	possess
bona fide	library	prerogative
censure	luxurious	quay
clothes	luxury	reservoir
codicil	martial	soot
column	medieval	strength
congratulations	mercantile	suppose
coupon	Nebraska	tremendous

SOME TIPS TO HELP YOU

These suggestions will help you in your battle against mispronunciation and poor enunciation.

1. Be careful in pronouncing personal names. People resent having their names mispronounced just as they resent having them misspelled. Make an effort to learn the correct pronunciation of a person's name and to follow that preference. Don't be afraid to ask people for the correct pronunciations of their names. Don't assume that because you've heard a name pronounced one way, it was pronounced correctly.

2. Likewise, be careful in pronouncing geographic names. Often the spelling is no guide to pronunciation. If you are uncertain, check the gazetteer in your dictionary. Following are a few geographic names that bear watching. You may be surprised when you verify their pronunciations. Some names are pronounced differently in different areas.

Abilene	Haverhill	Marseilles	Valparaiso
Cannes	Houston	Norfolk	Versailles
Cherbourg	Illinois	Salina	Worcester
Edinburgh	Lima (Peru)	Southampton	Ypsilanti

3. Be careful with foreign words and phrases. Some very amusing (and embarrassing) mistakes can be made by pronouncing them, especially French words, as they are spelled. The dictionary gives the closest approximation possible to the English sounds.
4. Guard against running words together, making such sounds as "wotcha doon?" (what are you doing?), "shoulda" (should have), "willyuh?" (will you?), or "jeet?" (did you eat?). Nothing more quickly brands a person as careless, if not illiterate, as does sloppy enunciation.
5. When you learn a new word, check its correct pronunciation at once. In other words, when you look up the spelling and meaning of a word, notice also its pronunciation, and practice saying it correctly.
6. When you speak to a group of people, speak more slowly than you do in ordinary conversation, and enunciate carefully.

If you faithfully carry out the suggestions outlined in this chapter you will soon find that your improved speaking qualities will improve your relations with people.

GIVE A TALK

You will probably have to talk before an audience sometime, if you have not already done so. Does this idea bother you? Many people have a fear of getting up before a group of people to give a talk. Instead, they should feel complimented by any invitation to speak. The very fact that you are asked to make a presentation indicates that someone believes in your ideas or experience; someone believes that they will be of interest and value to others and that you will do a good job.

The length and nature of talks vary. You may be asked to introduce another speaker, or you may be asked to be a member of a panel discussion group. On the other hand, you may be invited to give a five- or ten-minute talk or even to present a longer speech at a meeting.

Your success in any one of these roles will depend on how carefully you plan your presentation. Only with careful planning will you be able to develop the feeling of confidence that will enable you to communicate your ideas to others, for an effective talk is the result of more than just knowing your subject. Not only do good speakers know what they are talking about, but also they know how to prepare and deliver the speech. You will learn the best techniques for preparing and giving a talk in this section.

EFFECTIVE PREPARATION

Every good talk requires careful preparation. The speaker-to-be must be ready to cover the subject thoroughly and must carefully organize the presentation. Use the following guidelines whenever you prepare a talk.

1. Determine your purpose and topic.
2. Adapt your talk to the audience.
3. Limit your subject.
4. Collect and organize your materials.
5. Prepare your outline.
6. Arouse and hold interest.
7. Talk; don't read or recite.
8. Practice, practice, practice.

Follow Grooming Guidelines

Special advice to female speakers:

Choose jewelry that is tasteful and that will not distract the audience from what you are saying. Above all, avoid jewelry that makes a jangling noise.

Choose makeup suitable to your appearance, and apply it skillfully.

Although a touch of bright color is appropriate—even desirable—be careful not to overwhelm your listeners with bizarre color combinations or dazzling prints or stripes. You want your listeners' attention on what you are saying.

Special advice to male speakers:

Wear a dress shirt and appropriate tie. Make sure that the style and color are currently acceptable. However, don't be too conservative with the necktie you choose—some experts recommend bright flecks of color.

In all but the most informal situations, leave at least one button of your jacket fastened, whether or not you wear a vest.

Because you may be seated while you are talking, wear long socks that cover your shins. Make sure that your socks harmonize with your suit and tie.

Determine Your Purpose and Topic

First of all, you must know the purpose of your talk. Are you going to inform, explain, convince, entertain, or combine two or more of these purposes? Only when you know *why* you are going to talk can you select your subject. Ask yourself these questions.

1. Why was I asked to speak to this audience?
2. What is the reason for this meeting?
3. How long am I expected to talk?
4. What does the group expect to gain from listening to me?
5. Am I personally in harmony with the interests and background of this group?
6. How can I capture the audience's interest?

The answers to these questions will guide you in selecting a topic that will be timely and interesting.

Adapt Your Talk to the Audience   Who is your audience? What is the age range, sex, educational and social background, economic status, experience? What are their interests? A talk presented before one group may have little appeal for another group. For example, a discussion of modern office design that would be exciting to office workers might cause a group of musicians, athletes, or truck drivers to go to sleep. Failure to know and to consider the audience can destroy the effectiveness of the talk.

Limit Your Subject   Don't select a two-hour subject for a ten-minute speech! It is better to make two or three specific points in a talk—and do the job well—than to ramble on about too broad a topic. The secretary who talked about "The Computer in Today's Office" would have presented a more interesting talk on a more limited topic, such as "How I Use Word Processing." Limit your subject so that you can emphasize two or three important points in the time allotted to you.

Collect and Organize Your Materials   Collect much more information about your subject than you will use. Use 3-by-5 cards to jot down ideas. Use your own personal experiences; talk with people who can help you; read newspapers, magazines, and books. Take good notes from as many sources as possible. As you organize the material you have collected, you will be able to select the most important ideas to include in your outline.

If the use of visual materials (transparencies, for example) or handouts (duplicated materials) will make your presentation more effective, carefully prepare these materials, and determine at what point they may best be used.

Prepare Your Outline   A good outline is a "must" in preparing a talk. Prepare notes on cards first. Then arrange and rearrange them according to major ideas and order of importance. In the following example, note that only important ideas are included in the outline.

DETERMINING CAREER AVENUES

I. Introduction
   A. Thank chairperson for complimentary introduction.
   B. Explain personal interest in topic.
   C. Explain importance of topic to all young people.
   D. Preview the major points to be made:
      1. Take an inventory of interests and abilities.
      2. Learn about jobs that are of interest.
      3. Observe people doing these jobs.
II. Take an inventory of interests and abilities:
   A. Indoor person or outdoor person?
   B. Working with people or alone?
   C. Concentration or action?

III. Learn about jobs that are of interest:
  A. Read about the jobs.
  B. Talk with people who do such jobs.
IV. Observe people doing these jobs:
  A. Ask to be an observer.
  B. Observe a typical day.
  C. Ask questions.
  D. Honestly judge your reactions to what you saw.
V. Conclusion of presentation:
  A. Summarize principal points.
  B. Express appreciation for audience attention.

Arouse and Hold Interest   The success of your talk will depend on how well you are able to arouse and hold the interest of your audience. Make sure that you have variety and pep in your talk. Insert an amusing story here and there. Emphasize new ideas. You can hold interest by using personal experiences and examples. Your talk should have a certain element of suspense as the plot unfolds. Complicated ideas, such as figures or statistics, should be omitted, simplified, or supplemented by charts and graphs. As you prepare your talk, consider carefully how you will arouse and hold the group's interest.

Talk; Don't Read or Recite   How should you prepare your talk? Should you write your speech word for word? use only your outline? use notes on 3-by-5 cards? plan to talk without notes? These methods are all used by speakers to prepare their talks. Some people prefer not to speak from a written manuscript because they feel that their talk will sound stilted. Whatever method you select, be sure that your talk will sound natural—not like an oral reading or a class recitation.

A written talk will be of value as you practice your presentation. It will enable you to fix each idea in your memory and to time your delivery. Having memorized the *what* and *how* of your talk, you can then use brief notes when you deliver it.

Practice, Practice, Practice   As you practice, try to anticipate the conditions of the actual talk. Imagine your audience in front of you. Stand tall and look at the audience. Talk loud enough for the person in the farthest corner of the auditorium to hear you. Make slow and deliberate movements. Use hand gestures sparingly, and then only if they seem natural to you. If a mirror is available, practice your talk in front of it. The person you see there should be the severest critic of your facial expressions and your platform appearance. Perhaps you can ask family members and friends to listen and offer suggestions. If you have access to video equipment, make a videotape of your practice. Then evaluate your performance as if you were watching someone else. Don't be satisfied with your practice until the talk flows along from idea to idea without the aid of a written script.

LIVING LANGUAGE

"To keep an audience's attention, make sure your speech is full of visual images. Examples are an excellent means of creating pictures."
—Phyllis Martin, *A Word Watcher's Handbook*

EFFECTIVE DELIVERY

Now that you have planned and practiced your talk, are you ready to deliver it to the audience? Study the following tips carefully. These pointers will help you present most effectively the thoughts and ideas that you have so carefully prepared.

Hide Your Nervousness　Face the fact that you will be nervous as you wait for your introduction. But remain confident, knowing that you have carefully prepared your talk. If you have stage fright, take a deep breath before opening your mouth. The deep breath will help relax your vocal cords. Speakers who are not at all anxious are either those who give talks often or those who do not know enough to be nervous. Controlled nervous anticipation is good for you. It will key you up and give your delivery some sparkle and liveliness.

Check Your Volume　You know how annoyed, disinterested, and bored listeners become if they can't hear the speaker. Don't create this problem for your audience. If possible before the meeting, check your volume in the room where you are to speak. Have someone stand in the back of the room to tell you whether you can be heard perfectly. If you cannot make this test or if you sense that the audience cannot hear you, ask at the beginning of your talk whether everyone can hear; then adjust your volume accordingly. If you will use a microphone, test it—even rehearse with it—before the time for your presentation.

Keep Your Head Up　Good speakers hold their heads high. This position gives an appearance of authority and helps the speaker project the voice better. Your words are more likely to reach your listeners instead of getting lost as they fall to the floor.

Use a Conversational Tone　Remember that you are talking to an audience, not giving an oration. Your voice should reflect the warm, easy, conversational tone that you would use if you were talking to a group of your very good friends.

Look at Your Audience　An audience responds favorably to a speaker who seems to be talking directly to each person in the audience. One way of making your listeners feel that you are talking to each one individually is to look directly at the assembled people. Look at those in the middle section, then those to the right, and then those to the left. As you look, you may see nothing but a blur, a mass of faces. Let your eyes rest on different sections of the blur, and the audience will feel that you are giving a person-to-person talk. With experience, you will begin to see the faces and expressions of individual listeners. Find a focus point and use it.

Stand at Ease   How you stand and what you do with your hands will help or hinder your presentation. If possible, stand behind a lectern (a speaker's stand). The lectern will provide a place for you to put your notes. Avoid holding them, for nervousness may cause the papers to rattle like leaves in a storm. To keep your hands from getting in the way, grasp the lectern on each side, or occasionally hold your hands behind your back. If you shift your weight from one hip to the other when you are nervous, train yourself to stand with your weight evenly distributed on both feet.

Avoid Mannerisms   Mannerisms such as playing with objects, clearing the throat or wetting the lips, repeating "uh" or "and" frequently, and overusing slang expressions are objectionable to audiences. If you do not know whether you have such mannerisms, ask some of your friends to watch and listen and report any they observe. A speaker with even one annoying habit cannot give the best possible talk, for mannerisms distract the audience and obstruct communication.

Use Only the Time Allotted   If you are asked to talk for five minutes, don't talk for six minutes. A program with several speakers is usually timed to the last minute; anyone who goes over the time limit forces other speakers to shorten their talks. Not only are long-winded talkers thought inconsiderate; they are also marked as egotistical. They think that what they have to say is so important that the other speakers can be disregarded. To avoid going over the time limit, you might ask the presiding officer of the meeting to give you a warning when you have only one minute left.

Observe Audience Reaction   You can and should train yourself to watch the audience as you speak and to be sensitive to its changing moods. If, as you talk, you see blankness or boredom on the faces before you, this signal tells you that your listeners need perking up. You might then tell one of the amusing stories you keep in reserve. Remember, however, that jokes are only effective if used intelligently.

If your audience seems tired, if the hour is late, or if the previous talks have been overlong, you have two choices: accept the situation as a challenge and give such an interesting and sparkling performance that everyone perks right up, or have pity on your audience and cut your talk to the bare essentials. Sometimes it is better to omit part of a speech rather than give the whole speech before a weary audience.

Carefully Select the Closing Words   Inexperienced talkers often give themselves away by lowering their voices as they say the last few words or by dashing off the ending in a hurried rattle. Of course, a beginner is happy to see the end in sight and is eager to get the ordeal over. What a pity, though, to spoil the effect of an otherwise fine talk with a poor ending! Remember to maintain a pleasing pitch and to observe good timing to the very end.

COMMUNICATION LABORATORY

APPLICATION EXERCISES

A. Ask yourself the following questions to determine how you set your stage for speaking. Answer each question with *usually, sometimes,* or *rarely.* Compare your answers with those of other members of the class to see whether they agree with yours. Then make a list of the items needing improvement.

MY PERSONALITY

1. Do I like to be with other people and make the first move to gain other acquaintances?
2. Do I look for ways to say complimentary things about people both to them and to others?
3. Am I understanding of the ways other people act or think, and do I avoid direct criticism and argument?
4. Am I positive and optimistic instead of gloomy and pessimistic when presented with a new problem or situation?
5. Do other people like to be in my company because I am likable and friendly?

FIRST IMPRESSIONS

1. Do I try to find ways of being helpful to other people and sympathetic to their problems?
2. Do I steer clear of controversial topics when I enter into a conversation with a new acquaintance?
3. Do I consciously think about other people's interests and their comforts when I converse with them?
4. Do I take the first step to meet, greet, and introduce strangers?
5. Do I avoid talking about personal problems, strong personal likes or dislikes, rumors, and personal prejudices when I first meet someone?

MY PERSONAL APPEARANCE

1. Do I know what appropriate dress is?
2. Am I careful about cleanliness and good grooming?
3. Do I usually feel well dressed?
4. Are my clothes clean, pressed, and in good repair?
5. Do my personal health habits contribute to my appearance?

MY FACIAL EXPRESSIONS

1. Do I avoid showing nervousness or indifference toward others in my facial expressions?
2. Do I refrain from allowing my facial expression to reflect my personal problems or sad feelings?
3. When I meet people, does my facial expression show genuine interest?
4. Do my facial expressions reveal the way I want to be understood?

CONTINUED

5. Am I willing to allow my facial expression to reflect how I think instead of remaining deadpan and noncommittal?

MY MANNERISMS

1. Does the way I move about suggest alertness or lack of interest?
2. Is my posture straight without being stiff?
3. When I walk, is my weight well distributed on both legs?
4. Do I control meaningless gestures when I talk?
5. Do my movements suggest control rather than uncertainty, fright, and nervousness?

B. Conduct an informal survey of persons you know who are employed in business offices. In your survey you would like to determine:

1. Whether there are dress and grooming rules enforced in their offices.
2. What rules there are for men.
3. What rules there are for women.
4. How strictly these rules are enforced.
5. What happens if someone does not abide by the rules.

Be prepared to contribute your findings in a class discussion and to indicate your feelings regarding these regulations.

C. Your supervisor, upon his return from a three-day business trip, requests a list of the people who have telephoned the office during his absence. As you read the following names and telephone numbers, remember to make maximum use of your jaw, lips, and tongue in pronouncing each name. You may want to spell difficult names. For example: "Agawam Shoe Company (Agawam A-g-a-w-a-m) of Springfield, Massachusetts. Ms. Lillian Bohack (B-o-h-a-c-k), the sales manager, would like you to telephone her at 617-555-9765."

COMPANY AND CITY	PERSON CALLING	TELEPHONE NUMBER
Raul and Siegfried Haverhill, Massachusetts	Nestor Raul	617-555-7312
Peebles & Byron P.C. Elko, Nevada	Taylor Peebles, *Auditor*	702-555-6453
Computer Assistance Co. Oswego, New York	Joseph Wilton	315-555-7815
McNeer Corporation Severna Park, Maryland	Barton Brandt	301-555-2777
Excello, Inc. Olympia, Washington	Judson Sims	206-555-3004

CONTINUED

D. From the following job titles, select one in which you are particularly interested. Collect information about the job, particularly the duties performed by someone in that job and the skills that the job demands. Prepare an outline for a 5-minute talk. Prepare your talk and present it in class. (If none of these titles appeal to you, select your own job title.)

Accountant or auditor	Administrative assistant	Paralegal
Sales representative	Computer programmer	Bookkeeper
Teacher	Word processing operator	Receptionist

VOCABULARY AND SPELLING STUDIES

A. These words are often confused: *censor, censure; read, reed, red.* Explain the differences.

B. Use either *sometime, some time,* or *sometimes* to complete each of the following sentences.

1. _____ next week I will complete the project I started.
2. I have already spent _____ working on the audit.
3. _____ he is late arriving at the plant.
4. Do you have _____ to devote to helping me?
5. All workers need _____ for relaxation.

C. Correct the error in the use of the underscored word in each of the following sentences.

1. Victor Simmons is the <u>soul</u> owner of this business.
2. You have no <u>rite</u> to question my integrity.
3. The payment on your note will soon be <u>overdo</u>.
4. How will the new policy <u>effect</u> your salary?
5. All your efforts to change his thinking were in <u>vein</u>.

D. A letter or syllable has been either added to or dropped from each of the following words. Spell each word correctly.

1. libary
2. strenth
3. brillant
4. probly
5. temperture
6. Febuary
7. canidate
8. suprise

USING SPEAKING SKILLS ON THE JOB

BASIC RULES FOR MEETING THE PUBLIC

The rules for meeting the public—in person or by telephone—are based on courtesy, consideration, and friendliness. These are the same qualities that make a visitor in your home feel welcome, comfortable, and at ease. Applied to business callers, the rules include those discussed below:

1. Give prompt attention to callers.
2. Greet callers pleasantly.
3. Treat all callers as honored guests.
4. Obtain needed information.
5. Save the caller's time.
6. Be discreet.
7. Keep within your authority.
8. Say "no" gracefully.
9. Show a genuine desire to serve.

Give Prompt Attention to Callers

Telephones should be answered promptly, before the second ring if possible. Have you ever waited and waited for a telephone call to be answered? Have you ever had to stand and wait for someone to assist you in a store and felt completely ignored? If so, you know that you became increasingly uncomfortable, even angry, as you waited. You hung up the telephone, or you turned on your heel and walked out of the store. In a well-run business this inattention does not happen. Salespeople, for example, are trained to recognize a caller immediately. Then callers know that they are not being overlooked. As you meet the public, you must follow the same procedure for all callers and give them prompt attention.

Greet Callers Pleasantly

The tone of voice you use to greet people should be cheerful and friendly. Even an angry caller will feel better hearing your pleasant greeting: "Good morning, Mr. Kenney. How nice of you to call." Of course, if you don't mean what you say, it is best not to say it; your tone of voice and your facial expressions will often reveal that you are not sincere.

If possible, vary your greeting to fit the visitor. Treat all visitors as though they are special in some way—as they are! Try also to make the greeting fit the occasion. One of the following greetings may fit many situations: "Good morning." "What may I show you?" "Whom do you wish to see?" "How may I help you?" "What a pleasant surprise!" "We were expecting you." "How nice of you to call." "How are you today?" Adding the name of the person, if you know it, will tailor the greeting for each caller. Often, too, the same words may be varied by a change in emphasis or in the way they are said.

Treat All Callers As Honored Guests

Be friendly and courteous to everyone. Never let a caller's voice or appearance influence what you say. Some very important people do not dress expensively, and not everyone has had the advantage of voice training. All callers deserve the same courteous and considerate treatment.

Prepare yourself for an occasional irritable or even rude caller. Treat such people with an understanding smile, and gloss over their discourtesies. You represent the firm, and these people are your guests. If you must make some response, express sympathy: "I'm sorry you feel that way." Your own graciousness will often soften the caller's anger and might even make the caller friendly again toward you and your company.

Obtain Needed Information

Before you can refer a caller to someone else, you must find out the caller's name and the reason for the call. You can then relay this information to your boss, who will determine specifically who will handle the call.

Because people sometimes resent being asked about their business, you may need a lot of tact to get the needed information without harming pleasant relations. To a telephone caller you might say, "May I tell Miss Chin who is calling, please?" When greeting a caller in person, you might point a pen over a pad and say pleasantly, "Your name is . . . ?" And as you write the name on the pad, you will probably repeat it: "Oh, yes, Ms. Olga Komorov." Next you would ask, "And you would like to see Mrs. Nevsky about . . . ?" and also write her answer on your pad. Completing a leading question is a natural thing to do, and so your caller usually will freely and willingly supply the information you need.

Save the Caller's Time

Let callers know if they have to wait. On the telephone, if the wait is to be longer than two or three minutes, it is usually better to take the number and call back. You can say, "I'll have to get the information from the files, Mr. Foster. It will take about five minutes to do so. May I have your number and call you back?"

Let callers know how long they must wait, even if it is a relatively short time. You might say, "I'm sorry, but Mr. Stavas will not be available for at least another hour. Would you like to make an appointment for later?" or "Mr. Stavas is in a meeting but should be free in about five minutes." Callers will appreciate this courtesy.

Be Discreet

Protect your employer by watching what you say—and what you don't say. If your manager is late in arriving at the office, for example, don't say, "Mr. Rosen has not come in yet this morning." The tactful thing to say is: "Mr. Rosen is not in the office just now. I expect him in a few minutes." Make certain that your remarks reflect favorably on your employer.

Protect your employer's business, also. Certain business information is confidential, and you must keep it so. Imagine what a visitor would think of your company (and you) if you were indiscreet enough to say, "Business is so poor that Mr. Rosen had to let some workers go last week." A prospective customer would not be favorably impressed! So be discreet in what you say on the telephone and in person.

Keep Within Your Authority   Know the limits of your authority, and don't exceed them. If you think your company will replace a defective part, for example, but it is not your responsibility to make adjustments, don't say: "Certainly we'll replace this for you. Just take it to the service manager." Both you and your company will be embarrassed if for some reason the service manager is unable to make the adjustment. Keep within your authority by saying, "Why don't you talk with Ms. Curtis, the service manager?" Be sure you know the names of the people in your company who are authorized to make various kinds of decisions. You can then help callers by referring them to the appropriate person, and you will be keeping within your authority.

Say "No" Gracefully   Some of the decisions you must convey to callers will be unfavorable to them. Be pleasant but firm. Your knowledge of how to say "no" in a letter will help you. Review Chapter 7 so that when you must refuse a caller, you can do so without losing goodwill.

Show a Genuine Desire to Serve   An extra courtesy or some thoughtful touch should be extended to guests to make their visit memorable. In business, too, you should be on the lookout for the little extra that makes the difference. Think, for example, how much an out-of-town visitor might appreciate your offer to reconfirm a returning flight. "While you're talking with Mr. Lugo, I'll call the airline to reconfirm your reservation." This kind of added service helps a business to get new customers and also to keep current customers coming back.

With these basic rules in mind, you are ready to receive the public—in person or by telephone. When greeting callers on the telephone, however, you need to know certain additional techniques.

TELEPHONE TECHNIQUES

Telephone techniques differ somewhat from techniques for greeting callers in person because of the nature of telephone conversations and the technical equipment used.

A telephone caller is unable to see the other person's facial expressions or surroundings and must depend entirely on the voice at the other end of the line. In voice-to-voice meetings, therefore, you should remember the following guidelines:

1. Identify yourself immediately.
2. Keep the caller informed.
3. Be ready to write information.
4. Use the telephone efficiently.

Identify Yourself Immediately   Callers cannot see you. They need to know whether they have the right number, company, or person. A switchboard operator usually identifies only the firm's name: "Ashe and Levin" or "This is Trend Office Supply Company." In answering an office or department telephone, identify both the office and yourself. You might say: "Dr. Gold's office; Joan O'Loughlin speaking"; "Personnel, Arthur Oliver"; or "Good morning. This is the Advertising Department; Morton Damson speaking." "Accounting, Bromberg" is technically correct, but the abruptness of the identification might confuse some people, and the purpose of this identification is to indicate who you are. Whatever greeting you use, remember that on the telephone you must identify yourself at once.

Keep the Caller Informed   Telephone callers can't see what is happening, so you must tell them. If you must leave the line to get some information, excuse yourself, saying, "I can find that information in just a few moments, if you wish to hold the line." Of course, all delays must be explained, and the best business practice requires that you report to the caller every minute. You can make an appropriate remark, such as "We're still trying to locate Mrs. Leland" or "I'm sorry, Mrs. Leland is still talking on the other line. Do you wish to wait, or shall I have her call you?"

You must also let your callers know that you are following what they are saying. In person you might nod your head; on the telephone your voice must do the notifying. You can show that you are listening attentively by simple responses such as "yes" or "I see."

Be Ready to Write Information   Have pencils, paper, and message forms ready for use near the telephone. Then you won't delay the caller with, "Will you wait while I get a pencil?" Be sure, too, to verify the message. For example, after taking the message "Wants refrigerator serviced free under CS contract—wants service *today*," you would verify the information by saying: "You would like Mr. Rivera to call you regarding free servicing of your refrigerator under our company's service contract, Mrs. Spanswick—and you want service today. Let's see, you spell your name S-P-A-N-S-W-I-C-K? And your number is 555-6212? Thank you. Good-bye."

Use the Telephone Efficiently   The telephone is a sensitive instrument. Knowing how to use it correctly will enable you to greet telephone callers courteously and efficiently. Follow these suggestions:

1. Hold your lips about an inch from the mouthpiece. Don't let the mouthpiece slip down under your chin, and don't cut off your voice by holding your hand over the mouthpiece.

2. Adjust your voice to the equipment. Remember, you don't have to shout over the telephone. Use your natural voice. But enunciate clearly so that you will be understood.

3. Transfer calls efficiently and quickly. To transfer a call from the outside to another extension within the company, say to the caller, "If you will hold for just a moment, I'll have your call transferred." How you get the attention of the operator depends on the phone system in your company. Usually, you should simply depress the cradle button once—firmly. When the operator answers, say, "Please transfer this call to Ms. Hepburn at Extension 4893."

4. Avoid irritating mechanical noises. If you must leave the line, place the receiver on a book or magazine. The noise made when the receiver is bumped or dropped on a desk is magnified over the wire and will not be appreciated by the caller. At the completion of a call, place the receiver gently in the cradle. Of course, the courteous person will allow the caller to replace the receiver first.

WORLD VIEW

A knowledge of geography can be useful in international communication. For example, 2 p.m. Central Standard Time is 10 p.m. in Egypt—a bit late for a business call. Many almanacs and appointment books have information about time zones that will enable you to determine what time it is around the world.

INPUT FOR ELECTRONIC DEVICES

Today's office technology frequently includes dictating and transcribing equipment and computers linked into networks or connected by modems.

Writers of letters and reports can dictate their materials at any time or in any place instead of waiting for a secretary or stenographer to find time to take the dictation. Even at home, after regular working hours at the office, or "on the road," the preparation of letters and reports need not be delayed because there is no opportunity for face-to-face dictation. Business writers can even key in drafts and transmit them for editing and formatting into final documents.

Computers and Voice Input   In today's office computers are frequently used for communicating information. Computers can be linked in networks (groups of computers within one business organization), or they can be connected with remote data banks (computerized sources of all types of information at other locations). In addition, one business's computers can be linked to computers in another business.

Until recently the information to be communicated by means of computers had to be keyboarded. However, today computers may be activated by the human voice (called "voice input") and material inserted into the computer with oral commands. The voice input is able to tell the computer what to do and how to do it. Furthermore, the voice input can provide the information that

WORLD VIEW

If you or your boss will be traveling abroad, find out how to use public telephones in the respective countries. In England and France, for example, you can buy phone cards with a certain number of units. These can be used instead of coins.

is to be transcribed into a written document—such as a letter, a memorandum, or a report—or that is to become some form of telecommunication. In other words, with voice-activation computer software, you will be able to dictate a letter to the computer and tell it what style to use, how many copies to make, and how the letter is to be sent. It may even do the actual transmitting. As voice activation for computers is further developed, effective oral communication will become more and more important.

VOICE INPUT GUIDELINES

Whether the voice is to be used for face-to-face dictation, for dictation into a machine, or for activation of a computer, certain guidelines must be adhered to if the finished product is to be acceptable.

1. Plan in advance what you want to say—how the job is to be performed, what you want to include in the document to be prepared, and the general details regarding its preparation.
2. Practice using the equipment—the telephone, the dictating equipment, the computer—correctly and efficiently. The instructional manual that accompanies the equipment is one important source that should be consulted.
3. Give the individual or machine the necessary instructions for performing the job to be done.
4. Speak clearly and slowly and at a pitch that will not distort the voice. This action involves enunciating each syllable and correctly accenting and pronouncing each word.
5. Give the spelling of any names, unusual words, and words that may be confused, such as homonyms.
6. Indicate the beginning of each new paragraph and the placement of any tables or lists that are to be inserted.
7. Include proper punctuation marks, since machines do not know how to punctuate, and individuals do not always agree on necessary punctuation.
8. List any special instructions regarding the number of copies required and the method of transmitting, as well as any enclosures to be included.

MEETINGS AND CONFERENCES

Participating in group activities is good training for the person who hopes someday to be successful in business or industry. Therefore, you should make an effort to become active in one or more social, civic, religious, or school organizations.

More and more, in all walks of life, decisions happen as a result of group thinking. Many business groups and committees are organized to make the best use of the talents and ideas of employees. Often the work of each of the people in a group—the participating members as well as the leader—is carefully evaluated by the people who help determine who should be promoted. Why? How well a person works in a group and how well that person communicates with others are important considerations for advancement into leadership positions. Therefore, every person who plans to enter business should know how to participate effectively in a group.

THE GROUP MEMBER

For every leader in a group there are many more working members. You, therefore, will probably serve more often as a member than as a leader. Every person who is invited to join a group discussion has an obligation to contribute his or her best. Time and money are wasted when employees take meetings for granted and do not contribute their maximum efforts to the discussion.

Principles to Follow   Some rules for participating effectively in a group are discussed below. Knowing and practicing these rules will help you to be a valuable group member.

Respect the Opinions of Others   It is easy to respect the opinions of people whom you like and whose ideas agree with yours. Good group members, however, respect the opinions of all others in their group and are courteous to everyone, even though they may not agree with some people's ideas.

Because good group members are open-minded, they listen attentively to each of the other members of the group and respond with appropriate comments. Discourteous behavior—fidgeting, gazing into space, or trying to start an unrelated private conversation—marks the group member as a poor risk for promotion. The courteous person, on the other hand, is considerate of everyone at all times. You may have strong convictions, but you do not close your mind to a different point of view. You know that by considering the ideas and beliefs of others, you will grow and learn, you will gain a new respect for the thinking of others, and you will become a more effective employee.

Use Only Your Share of Talking Time   Every member has a contribution to make to the group. Some people, however, exaggerate the value of their ideas and attempt to monopolize a meeting. Good group members know that everyone has an equal right and responsibility to talk. By limiting their own talking, they make sure that others are not robbed of their fair share of talking time.

Help to Harmonize Differences of Opinion   Good group members try to see the value of each opposing view and to balance opposing views to keep peace in the group. They recognize good ideas and encourage others in the group to make compromises that will help get results. Such a member might say, for example: "That's a good idea, and I can see how it would work under some conditions; but the other plan is good too. Shall we take the best from each?" Thus by emphasizing the good aspects of all ideas, the effective group member is able to harmonize differences of opinion.

Help to Keep the Discussion Relevant Some members in a group easily let their talking wander from the discussion at hand. However, good group members stick to the subject and also help direct the ideas of others to the topic at hand. They may do so by reminding the group of its goal or purpose: "As I understand it, our purpose is to. . . ." Or when the discussion begins to wander, "Let's see now, what is it we hope to accomplish in this meeting?" Summarizing the progress made or pointing out stumbling blocks to reaching the goal may also help to keep group thinking on track. Thus the good group member takes action to let the group know whether it is reaching its goal.

Attitudes to Avoid

Of course, you probably realize that positive principles make you a good group member, but it is just as important for you to understand the attitudes and practices that *prevent* effective group work. An understanding of these attitudes and practices will help you avoid pitfalls and make you better able to harmonize differences of opinion and keep a discussion on the main track. The attitudes and practices of the following types of people hinder the smooth progress of a group.

The Selfish-Interest Pleader "I don't care what the rest of you think— what I want to see is . . . ," says the selfish-interest pleader. Marvin has decided what *he* wants. Everything he says and does is intended to help him get his way despite the good ideas of others.

The Blocker The blocker is opposed to every new idea. "That isn't the way to do it. Here's what we've been doing for years . . ." or "That's an idiotic idea. It won't work." Whatever the idea is, Ellen is against it. She often displays a negative, stubborn resistance. She opposes in a disagreeable manner and frequently without reason.

The Aggressor The aggressor is usually unaware of the feelings of others. Dimitri may try to build his own importance by deflating the ego of others: "That's a silly thing to do. If I were doing the work, here is how I'd go about it." But, alas, Dimitri usually avoids doing much! He may attack the group, its purposes, or the importance of the topic. He usually attempts to assert his superiority by trying to manage the group. As the name implies, the aggressor wants to take command.

The Sympathy Seeker Alan, the sympathy seeker, may accept responsibility to do something for the group, but then he doesn't carry it through. He says: "I thought Fred was supposed to do that" or "I was just so busy that I couldn't get that done." Alibis, confessions of shortcomings, and exaggeration of personal problems are all used to gain the sympathy of the group. Such a person would like the group to compliment him or her for personal weaknesses!

The Disinterested Bystander   Ursula, the disinterested bystander, may make a display of her lack of involvement. Through childish tactics, she may attempt to disrupt. Or she may patronize the group with a frozen smile that permits her to escape mentally from the boring proceedings.

Success as a Group Member   Study your role in a group. Make sure that you practice the principles that contribute to group success and eliminate all actions that might prevent you from being a good group member. REMEMBER: A leader is usually selected from among the good group members.

THE GROUP LEADER

People who consistently block group action will not need to know how to lead a group. They won't be given the opportunity. However, people who know and practice the positive principles that help the members of a group work together will soon be selected for a leadership post—an honor, but also a serious obligation. Before you take on the responsibility of chairing a group, therefore, make sure that you know the duties involved in planning and conducting a meeting.

Planning a Meeting   When you chair a group, you will usually plan all meetings—whether they are programs or business meetings. If the group does not have a constitution or bylaws to define your responsibilities, you can usually assume that you are responsible for all aspects of planning—place and time, publicity, pattern of the program, and speakers and other participants.

The Program   The first step is to write a plan for the program. This plan should answer the following questions:

1. What is the purpose of the meeting?
2. What theme or topic is to be considered?
3. Where and when will the meeting be held? Should reservations for a room or hall be made now?
4. Who will attend?
5. How many will attend?
6. What publicity will be needed?
7. How much money is available for speakers, arrangements, decorations, and so on?
8. What persons or committees should be appointed to make arrangements, sell tickets, publicize, act as hosts?
9. What form or pattern should the program take—speaker or symposium of speakers? demonstration? panel discussion? mock television or radio program? panel, with audience questions and answers? debate? small-group discussions? brainstorming? other?

Delegation of Authority   At this point in planning you may feel overwhelmed by the size of the job ahead of you. Don't be, however, for an important characteristic of the leader is an ability to delegate authority. Specific tasks are assigned, usually in writing, to other people. Delegate as many details as you can, but be sure to follow up on each assignment. Copies of letters announcing committee appointments or of letters written to the speakers can be used as a tickler (reminder) file. To avoid any last-minute slipup, send reminders to all committees and speakers at least two weeks before the meeting. If you have carefully planned and effectively delegated responsibility, you can go before the group feeling confident that the meeting you conduct will be a good one.

The Agenda　In an agenda for a business meeting, like the one shown on page 479, the discussion items should be listed in the order of increasing controversy. For instance, the first item will be the one most likely to meet with almost total agreement. Next will come the item on which the leader expects less agreement, and so on. A sound psychological principle is behind this practice. If a group starts by agreeing, the members will be in a friendly and positive frame of mind that will carry over to succeeding discussion topics. Untrained leaders who start their meetings with the "big question"—the topic likely to provoke the widest difference of opinion—should not wonder why nothing is accomplished at their meetings.

Conducting a Meeting　You, the leader, set the tone for the meeting as you follow the agenda or program. If you are stiff and formal, the other people on the program are likely to be stiff and formal too. If you are natural and informal (but in good taste, of course), the others on your program will probably be natural and informal too. Most audiences today prefer a moderator who conducts an informal kind of meeting, whether or not parliamentary procedure is followed.

Using Parliamentary Procedure　The bylaws of most clubs state that business will be conducted according to Robert's *Rules of Order*. As the presiding officer, you will need to know some of the basic principles of Robert's *Rules* and how to apply them. For example, you should know how to call a meeting to order and how to determine whether a quorum is present; how to make and follow an agenda; how to recognize members who wish to make a motion; what an appropriate motion is and how it is seconded, amended, and voted on; and how to adjourn a meeting. Most organizations will appoint a parliamentarian to help the group leader, but the leader who possesses a working knowledge of the rules is that much ahead.

Introducing a Speaker　An introduction should be short and simple and should include (1) some gracious remark that will make the speaker feel warmly welcome, (2) a statement of the speaker's topic, (3) a brief summary of the speaker's background or special interests, and (4) the presentation of the speaker by name. The announcement of the name of the speaker is usually made last so that it serves as a signal for the speaker to come forward and begin the talk.

LIVING LANGUAGE
Silence can be an effective form of communication—one often ignored in the United States. Someone has said that Americans will agree to almost anything if the opposite negotiating party is silent long enough.

```
                    WRIGHT AUTOMOBILE COMPANY

           Meeting of the Employee Welfare Committee

                  October 5, 1995, 4:30-5 p.m.

                  Executive Conference Room


                            AGENDA

      1.  Call to order by Chairperson O'Brien.

      2.  Approval of the minutes of the September meeting.

      3.  Approval of today's agenda.

      4.  Announcements.

      5.  Old Business:

          A.   Report of the subcommittee on employee rights
               and duties.

          B.   Discussion of revision of awards criteria
               and procedures.

      6.  New Business:

          A.   Plans for the annual holiday dance.

          B.   Discussion of the employee incentive plan.

          C.   Nominations for officers for 1996.

          D.   Other items.

      7.  Adjournment.
```

In an agenda for a business meeting, the discussion items should be listed in the order of increasing controversy.

Responding to a Speech   The leader, of course, wishes the meeting to end on a high note. After an effective talk there is little to say. Even after a poor speech the leader shouldn't say too much. One or two comments about the importance of the talk or a short anecdote to leave the audience in good spirits is all that is needed. You should thank the speaker, express appreciation to those who helped plan the meeting, and adjourn.

COMMUNICATION LABORATORY

APPLICATION EXERCISES

A. Your supervisor asks you to write a one-page memo that summarizes the correct procedures to be followed by all office workers who receive telephone calls. As you plan your memorandum, give special attention to the following points:

1. Be prompt in answering calls.
2. Get and give proper identification.
3. Treat callers as honored guests.
4. Establish ways to handle delays.
5. Obtain needed information from callers.

B. Mrs. Dvorak has told her staff that she must complete a very important report and is not to be disturbed by anyone under any circumstances. But in the middle of the morning, Mr. Walter Keys telephones and insists, "I must talk with Mrs. Dvorak immediately about an important contract, the bids for which are closing at five o'clock this afternoon." What would you say to Mr. Keys? Would you use any of the following responses? Why or why not? Indicate your response, and defend it in a paragraph.

1. "I'm sorry. I simply cannot disturb Mrs. Dvorak."
2. "Mrs. Dvorak is not in the office today."
3. "Please give me a telephone number where I can reach you within an hour. I will get your message to Mrs. Dvorak."
4. "If it's important, I'll connect you right away."

C. Which of the following statements were made by people who practice principles for being a good group member? Do any of the statements represent attitudes that are likely to hinder group progress? If you were a chairperson, how would you respond to these negative statements?

1. "I don't think that this foolish scheme will work."
2. "I think there is a way to combine both of the ideas we have been discussing into one workable plan."
3. "My ten years at the Goodman Institute taught me that there is only one way to accomplish our goal."
4. "As far as I can tell, our purpose is simply to make a proposal, not to test its feasibility."

D. Write a plan for an important meeting of a group to which you belong. Include a speaker in the meeting plan. Use the questions on page 477 to guide your plan. Finally, write the introduction that you will use to present the speaker.

VOCABULARY AND SPELLING STUDIES

A. The following words related to computer technology are used in this section. Show that you understand the meaning of each of these words by constructing a sentence in which the word is used.

1. network
2. data bank
3. voice activation
4. software
5. telecommunication

Using your dictionary or another source, define the following computer terms:

6. ergonomics
7. desktop publishing
8. byte
9. RAM
10. ROM

B. These words are often confused: *rout, route, root; incite, insight.* Explain the differences.

C. From each pair of words in parentheses, select the word that correctly completes the sentence.

1. I use (those, that) kind of disk in my computer.
2. Of the four printers available, I prefer the (smaller, smallest) one.
3. Jeremy was (real, really) happy to hear that you were elected.
4. In order to get there on time, we must hurry (some, somewhat).
5. Mark is (sure, surely) acceptable as a candidate.

D. Choose the item that answers each of the following questions correctly.

1. Which one of the following expressions *should not* be hyphenated? first-rate opportunity, equipment that is up-to-date, high-quality merchandise
2. Which one of the following compound nouns *should be* hyphenated? notary public, vice president, trade in
3. Which one of the following words with prefixes *should not* be hyphenated? co-owner, non-neutral, ex-president, semi-independent
4. Which one of the following compound nouns *should not* be hyphenated? building-contractor, tie-up, follow-up

CHAPTER 11

EMPLOYMENT
COMMUNICATION

Effective communication skills will influence all aspects of your life, but never more so than when you enter the world of employment. From the day you begin your job search to your final day of employment, your skills in reading, writing, speaking, and listening will have an impact on your success. Even the most basic business situations involve speaking, listening, reading, and writing.

Your command of communication skills will benefit you not only in a job situation but also in the job search itself.

OBJECTIVES

Given a situation that requires communicating on the job, you will be able to do the following when you master the sections in this chapter:

1. *State your qualifications for employment in a complete, attractive résumé.*

2. *Complete employment application forms accurately and thoroughly.*

3. *Organize and write effective letters of application.*

4. *Prepare letters requesting others to serve as your references.*

5. *Write letters accepting or refusing positions offered to you.*

6. *Prepare yourself for a successful interview.*

7. *Write letters resigning from a position.*

RÉSUMÉS AND JOB APPLICATIONS

Finding the job you want is in some ways like taking a final examination. You must bring together all you have learned and all you can do. Then you must present yourself and your skills to employers in such a way that at least one of them will want to hire you for a position in his or her organization.

Throughout this text you have worked on developing your communication skills—listening, speaking, reading, and writing. The job search will likely give you an opportunity to use not only your writing and speaking skills but your reading and listening skills as well.

Reading skills: Search advertisements and job postings, proofread your résumé and application letters, and understand the information requested on application forms.

Writing skills: Develop your résumé, write letters of application, and complete employment applications.

Speaking skills: Schedule appointments, and make a favorable impression during interviews.

Listening skills: Make yourself look good during interviews—listen carefully so that you can understand and answer questions asked by the prospective employer.

Remember that in your job search you must put together all you have learned and then make it work for you. Whether you want a part-time job for now or a career for a lifetime, your communication skills will help you prepare for and succeed in your job search.

ANALYZING YOUR ABILITIES

You will be hired because you have skills that an employer needs. Your first step is to analyze yourself, your knowledge, and your skills. On the basis of your personal and educational background, you begin by listing specific skills and knowledge that would benefit an employer. Then you decide which jobs need the skills and knowledge you possess.

Which of the positions you have listed interest you most? Which ones interest you least? Direct your job-seeking efforts to the most interesting positions for which you are qualified.

For example, suppose that in high school your major is a general clerical program. Courses in the program may include keyboarding, accounting, general business, business law, business English and communication, filing and data-

LIVING LANGUAGE

"We must open the doors of opportunity. But we must also equip our people to walk through those doors."
—Lyndon B. Johnson

base systems, business mathematics, and office practices. At the end of your high school training, you will probably be able to key at least 50 words a minute, perform basic recordkeeping functions, operate various calculating and copying machines, and compose business letters.

In addition to analyzing yourself, your knowledge, and your abilities, you should look at the kinds of activities that interest you. What kind of work do you want to do? Do you enjoy working with numbers? Do you like interacting with people? Would you prefer to work at a desk, or would you like a job that involves traveling? Are you more comfortable doing repetitive tasks, or do you like variety? Do you need a predictable schedule, or would you accept a position that frequently requires overtime?

Once you have analyzed your skills and your needs and determined the jobs for which you are qualified, you must select the job that interests you most. How can you locate such a position?

SEEKING GOOD JOB SOURCES

How do you find the job you want? Where do you look for the job for which you are qualified? Several employment sources are available to you.

School Placement Offices   Your school placement office may be a good place to begin. If your school has established a reputation for providing training in occupational areas, then you may be able to obtain a job through your school placement office. In addition, your teachers may be able to supply specific names of employers who are looking for graduates in your particular field of interest. If your school has internship programs, businesses sponsoring interns may be possible employers.

Newspaper Advertisements   Newspaper advertisements are a good source of employment opportunities. These ads may ask you to apply in person for the positions listed, or they may ask you to submit an application letter and a résumé.

Sometimes local professional journals or newspapers contain job listings. For example, the *Los Angeles Daily Journal,* a publication for the legal profession, is a good source of legal secretarial positions in the Los Angeles area.

Employment Agencies   Both state employment agencies and private employment agencies list job openings. Your local state agency places applicants in positions that have been referred to its office. This service is performed without cost to either the employee or the employer.

Private employment agencies charge either the employer or the applicant a fee for filling an opening that has been referred to them by the employer. Some companies prefer to refer all openings to private employment agencies to save the time and expense of screening applicants.

Starting with an agency that provides temporary personnel may be a way to find a permanent position. Sometimes temporary workers learn of available positions or receive offers of permanent employment during their temporary assignments.

Federal, State, County, and City Offices

Opportunities in civil service employment should not be overlooked. Local federal, state, county, and city employment offices regularly publish announcements of job opportunities. Persons interested in working in civil service should consult local government employment offices to learn about available jobs and to inquire about taking the civil service examinations for the jobs in which they are interested. Officials from various government offices will visit high schools to recruit qualified applicants and to administer civil service examinations right on campus.

College and University Offices

All institutions of higher education have business offices that employ many clerks, secretaries, managers, and administrators. Colleges and universities offer their employees some major advantages. Some institutions, for example, permit their employees to take a course during working hours. In addition, employees have the advantage of working in a different environment—the college campus.

Individual Companies

Many companies do not actively recruit prospective employees through newspaper advertisements or employment agencies. Sufficient numbers of applicants present themselves to the companies and directly request employment. While companies may not always have immediate openings in every area, a qualified applicant's résumé is usually filed for future reference.

Large companies with hundreds or thousands of employees are constantly busy recruiting and placing personnel. Therefore, contacting these companies directly may lead to employment.

DEVELOPING YOUR RÉSUMÉ

Once you have decided what you have to offer an employer, you should prepare a written summary of your qualifications. This summary—your *résumé*—is a description of your qualifications. It usually includes a statement of your education, your employment record (experience), a list of references, and other data that will help you obtain the job you wish.

A résumé may be sent with a letter of application, be presented to an employer at the interview, or be used to assist you in filling out an employment application form.

Since résumés are sales instruments, they must be prepared just as carefully as sales letters. In your résumé you are marketing yourself. Therefore, your résumé should present the best possible impression of you.

The act of preparing the résumé is just as valuable as the résumé itself, for it forces you to think about yourself—what you have to offer an employer, what you want in a job, and why you should be hired. Everyone brings unique talents to a position, but perhaps only after you prepare a résumé do you realize your true worth.

The Look of Your Résumé

Remember that your résumé is an important sales tool in your job search. Your résumé may afford the first chance (sometimes the only chance) you have to make a good impression on the person you want to work for.

You may think that writing a résumé is easy. It's not a difficult task, but it's definitely worth the time and effort you will put in to do it well. A sloppy, poorly written, or incomplete résumé is likely to be tossed aside by an employer. Here are some guidelines to help you prepare your résumé.

1. Your résumé, unless you have extensive job-related experience, should be only one page long. This one page should be filled with useful information about you.
2. Choose a format that is easy to read. Use headings, underlining, columns, and capital letters to make your qualifications easily identifiable. Place your résumé attractively on the page.
3. Select a good-quality paper with matching envelopes. White stationery is used most often, but you can select a professional-looking color such as cream, gray, or light blue.
4. Use brief statements rather than complete sentences. Say "President, Accounting Club" rather than "I was president of the Accounting Club."
5. Choose a typewriter or word processor that has clear, crisp print. After preparing one good copy, you can photostat additional copies. Use a good-quality copier and stationery so that each copy looks as good as the original. You might consider having a typesetter or professional résumé service complete your résumé. Charges for this work vary, but if the employment market is tight, the extra cost may be justified because a professionally prepared résumé may give you a competitive edge.

As you prepare your résumé, remember that the care with which it is prepared and the information that it supplies often determine whether you will be invited for a personal interview. The résumé is your personal introduction to an employer. You must edit and proofread it carefully to make sure that the spelling, grammar, and facts are correct and that the wording is clear. These two steps are essential in creating a résumé that will make the all-important first impression a favorable one.

The Main Categories of a Résumé

The format of the résumé varies according to your individual taste and, more importantly, according to the job for which you are applying. If the job is at a bank or an accounting firm, you should probably use white paper and a conservative format. But if the job is at an advertising agency, you may want to exhibit creativity by using a tinted paper and a more original format.

The résumé shown on page 489 is an example of an effective résumé. Notice that it contains four main headings: "Objective," "Experience," "Education," and "References." The information at the top includes the name, address, and telephone number of the applicant. This is all the personal data needed here; you will supply other personal details on the application form.

Objective   The employer wants to know the job you are seeking. It is best to find out in advance whether there is a vacancy in the company and, if there is, to specify that position by its correct title, such as "secretary to the assistant credit manager." If you don't know the specific job title, it is satisfactory to write "payroll clerk," "sales trainee," "receptionist," and so on.

Experience   If you are a recent high school graduate, the employer will not expect you to have had a lot of experience. Employers understand that you have been in school and have used most of your summers for vacation. Nevertheless, any paid work experience, regardless of its nature, will impress an employer and will help your prospective employee to evaluate basic qualifications such as reliability, promptness, attitude and so on. Therefore, be sure to mention such experience as temporary, part-time, after-school, Saturday, or vacation work—mowing lawns, baby-sitting, delivering newspapers, and so on. Even volunteer typing or clerical work for a teacher or a community agency should be listed.

Include the following facts about your experience:

1. Name and address of your employer (including the telephone number is always very helpful).
2. Type of work you performed (the title of the position and a brief description of the work).
3. Dates of employment. Employers usually prefer that you start listing your work experience with your *last* job and work back to your first job. When listing full-time experience by dates, it is important to leave no obvious unaccounted-for time gaps:

January 1990–September 1990	Did not work during this period; I cared for my mother, who was recovering from surgery.
	OR:
August 1991–July 1992	During this period I was a part-time student at the Martin Business College. I was not employed.

If you have held one or more full-time positions prior to making the application, you may wish to state why you left each position. For example: "I left this position because I was needed at home."

Education   For most high school students, the education section of the résumé will be the most important, since work experience will at this point be limited. Therefore, give specific details about your training that qualify you for the position. Study the information presented in the résumé illustrated on page 489. Note that the courses emphasized are those that have particular bearing on the position being applied for. Note also that special skills and interests are described. On your résumé be sure to list any honors you have received in school,

```
                          COLIN WESTIN
                        7638 Rockrose Drive
                     La Jolla, California 92126
                       Telephone:  603-555-9876


   POSITION
   APPLYING FOR:        Accounting Assistant


   EXPERIENCE:

   June 1994-present    San Diego Tire Manufacturers, 252 Harbor
                        Drive, San Diego, California
                        Position:  Assistant to receptionist
                        Supervisor:  Ms. Marguerite Antony
                        Duties included preparing weekly phone and
                        visitation log, assisting with switchboard
                        during high-traffic times, filing, inventory
                        of office supplies, and some proofreading.

   June-September of    Martin Dairy, La Jolla, California
   1992 and 1993        Position:  Counter server (Summers only)
                        Supervisor:  Mr. Rico Vittori
                        Duties included serving customers at retail
                        counter (carryout and 18-seat counter),
                        refilling supplies, maintaining clean food
                        service area, and occasionally closing for
                        the day.

   EDUCATION:

   September 1991-      La Jolla High School, La Jolla, California.
   present              Will graduate in June 1995 with honors in
                        accounting and communication.  Served as
                        treasurer of the Bookkeeping Club and
                        president of junior class.  Currently
                        treasurer of student council.

                        Have been accepted to Occidental College, Los
                        Angeles, California, with goal of accounting
                        major and CPA certificate.

   REFERENCES:          Miss Risa Gomez, instructor, San Diego
                        Business College, 983 Kester Drive, Point
                        Loma, California 92126.

                        Dr. Albert Syres, Veteran's Hospital,
                        Victory, California 92128.

                        Ms. Ellen Puckett, Principal, La Jolla High
                        School, La Jolla, California 92126.
```

A résumé should give specific details about the applicant's experience and education.

even though they may not appear to be of great significance to you. Employers *are* interested.

Some people who take part in out-of-school activities mention their hobbies as indications of their broad interests. Mentioning outside interests is a good idea, especially if these hobbies give the prospective employer a clue to your personality and talents. For example, the hobby of working on cars will impress the manager of an automobile agency or an auto parts store. The hobby of reading will be of interest to a publisher. If art is your main hobby, this talent will appeal to a large number of employers.

References   At the end of your résumé, list the names of people whom the employer can contact for information about you. Common courtesy requires that you obtain permission before using a person's name for reference. (The letter requesting such permission is discussed in Section 11.2.) Ordinarily, only three or four names need be listed, but others should be available if additional references are required to attest to your experience, education, and character. If possible, select your references according to the job for which you are applying. And let your references know what kind of position you are applying for so that they will be guided in their replies. If you are applying for a position as an accounting clerk, for example, a reference from someone in that type of work would be more appropriate than one from your family doctor. When you ask someone to write a letter of recommendation for you, include a stamped envelope addressed to the prospective employer.

The following information should be given about each reference you include on your résumé:

1. Full name (check spelling) with appropriate or preferred title (such as *Ms., Mr., Miss, Mrs., Professor,* or *Dr.*).
2. Business title (such as *president, director,* or *data processing manager*).
3. Name of company or organization and complete address.
4. Telephone number (with area code).

FILLING OUT EMPLOYMENT APPLICATIONS

Most business firms like to have a standardized record for each employee. You will probably be asked to fill out the company's application form either before or after you have been hired. Frequently, personnel interviewers use the application form as they interview you. Since interviewers are familiar with this form, they can quickly select from it items to talk about. The application form also provides a great deal of information about the applicant other than the answers to the questions asked—legibility of handwriting, accuracy and thoroughness, neatness, and ability to follow written directions. A sample application form appears on pages 491–492.

Here are some helpful suggestions to follow when you must fill out application forms:

1. Bring with you:
   a. A reliable pen. Many pens provided for public use are not dependable. An ink-blotched or unevenly written application form will reflect unfavorably on your neatness.
   b. Two or more copies of your résumé, one or more for the interviewer and one for you to use in filling out details on the application form.
   c. Your social security card.

ALLIED INSURANCE COMPANY, INC.

an equal opportunity employer

APPLICATION FOR EMPLOYMENT

(Please Print)

<table>
<tr><td rowspan="4">COMPANY USE ONLY</td><td colspan="3">DATE APPOINTED
Month   Day   Year</td><td colspan="2">REAPPOINTMENT:
☐ With continuous service
☐ Without continuous service</td><td colspan="2">DIVISION</td><td>SALARY</td><td>INITIALS</td></tr>
<tr><td colspan="2">☐ HO
☐ HO Fld.
☐ Corp.
☐ Service</td><td>☐ Reg.
☐ Temp.

_____ Hours Per Week</td><td>☐ Day
☐ Night</td><td colspan="2">TITLE OR DESIGNATION</td><td>JOB NO.</td><td>JOB LEVEL

HOURS PER DAY:</td><td>VACANCY</td><td>TITLE CODE</td></tr>
</table>

DO NOT WRITE ABOVE THIS LINE

NAME	(First)	(Middle)	(Last)	DO YOU			DATE OF APPLICATION (Month) (Day) (Year)
	Celia	Elise	Jackson	☒ Live with parents ☐ Live with other relatives	☐ Board ☐ Own your home ☐ Rent		9 4 9–

RESIDENCE ADDRESS	(Street)	(City or Town)	(State)	(Zip Code)	DATE OF RESIDENCE
173	Auburn Avenue,	Cincinnati,	OH	45201	FROM / TO

PREVIOUS RESIDENCE	(Street)	(City or Town)	(State)	(Zip Code)	MO.	YR.	MO.	YR.
N/A					2	71	Present	

PREVIOUS RESIDENCE   (Street)   (City or Town)   (State)   (Zip Code)

TELEPHONE NUMBER	SOCIAL SECURITY NUMBER	ARE YOU A CITIZEN OF THE U.S.A.?
(419) 555-9845	723-52-9076	☒ YES ☐ NO

ACCOUNT COMPLETELY FOR YOUR TIME FROM THE FIRST YEAR OF HIGH SCHOOL TO THE PRESENT IN THE BOXES BELOW.

NAMES OF SCHOOLS ATTENDED	CITY & STATE	NO. OF YRS Day Eve.	MAJOR SUBJECTS	GRAD. Mo. Yr.	GRADE AVERAGE	DEGREE
Millard High School	Cincinnati, Ohio	4 Yrs.	General Business	6 ––	B–	
			Business Law			

EXTRACURRICULAR ACTIVITIES (ATHLETICS, CLUBS, FRATERNITIES, ETC.)

ACTIVITY HIGH SCHOOL	OFFICES HELD	ACTIVITY COLLEGE	OFFICES HELD
Senior Class	Treasurer		
Future Business			
Leaders of America	Vice President		

SCHOLASTIC HONORS (SOCIETIES, AWARDS, SCHOLARSHIPS, ETC.)

Having a résumé on hand makes filling out an application form easier.

ACTIVE SERVICE WITH UNITED STATES ARMED FORCES

BRANCH OF SERVICE	SERIAL NO.	RANK OR RATE AT DISCHARGE
N/A	N/A	N/A

DATE (Mo.) (Day) (Yr.) OF ENTRY	DATE (Mo.) (Day) (Yr.) OF SEPARATION	TYPE OF SEPARATION (i.e., Expiration of Enlistment, Medical, etc.)
N/A	N/A	N/A

PREVIOUS WORK EXPERIENCE—PART TIME AND FULL TIME (List in order, last employer first)

NAME OF COMPANY	CITY & STATE	TITLE	PERIOD OF EMPLOYMENT FROM Mo.	Yr.	TO Mo.	Yr.
Clayton's (Department Store)	Cincinnati, Ohio	Accounting Clerk		--	present	
		Sales Clerk	6	--	7	--

FOR WHAT SPECIAL KIND OF WORK HAVE YOU A PREFERENCE?	ARE YOU WILLING TO BE TRANSFERRED TO ANOTHER LOCATION
Claim Adjuster	☐ Yes [X] No

WERE YOU REFERRED BY AN EMPLOYEE? ☐ YES [X] NO	IF YES, STATE NAME	DEPARTMENT

HAVE YOU ANY RELATIVES, FRIENDS OR ACQUAINTANCES NOW EMPLOYED BY US? [X] YES ☐ NO	IF YES, STATE NAME	RELATIONSHIP	DEPARTMENT
	Peter Martinez	Friend	Sales

CHARACTER REFERENCES (Do not use the names of relatives or former employers).

NAMES	ADDRESSES
Dr. John Kniss, Principal	Millard High School, 50 Delta St., Cincinnati, OH 45201
Mrs. Ruth Sanchez, Credit Manager	

I authorize investigation of all statements contained in this application blank if I am considered for employment and hereby authorize previous employers, personal references named, or any other person or persons to whom the Company may refer to give any and all information regarding my employment or scholastic standing together with any other information, personal or otherwise, than may or may not be on their records.

I understand that misrepresentation or omission of any fact called for hereon, or on any other statements made in connection with my request for employment, or receipt by the Company of unsatisfactory references, will be sufficient cause for dismissal from the Company's service if I shall have been employed.

Applicant's Signature *Celia* *Elise* *Jackson*
                       (First)   (Middle)   (Last)

NOT TO BE COMPLETED BY APPLICANT	TO BE COMPLETED AFTER EMPLOYMENT
	I have seen _____
DATE OF INTERVIEW / COMMENTS	and am satisfied that
	_____ Month Day Yr.
	is employee's correct date of birth.
	INITIALS

Make sure that all information you put on an employment application form is accurate.

2. Write legibly. Your handwriting does not need to be fancy, but it must be legible. You should take particular care that any figures you write are clear. If the interviewer has difficulty reading your writing, you will start your interview with one strike against you—that is, if you get as far as an interview!

3. Be accurate and careful. Double-check all the information you have included. Have you given your year of birth where it is asked for, not this year's date? Are your area code and telephone number correct? Be careful to avoid any obvious carelessness.

4. Don't leave any blanks. If the information asked for does not apply to you, draw a line through that space or write "N/A" (not applicable) or "Does not apply."

5. Follow directions exactly. Since you have the opportunity to reread the directions to make sure you are completing the form correctly, reread them. If you ask unnecessary questions, you show that you cannot follow simple written instructions. The interviewer will then wonder how you would follow complicated oral instructions once you were on the job! If the directions say to print, then do not write. If the instructions call for your last name first, then do not give your first name first. If you are asked to list your work experience with your last job first, then be sure you do not list your first job first.

COMMUNICATION LABORATORY

APPLICATION EXERCISES

A. Investigate the kinds of jobs that are available in your community by studying the advertisements published in your local newspaper. List specific jobs that are of interest to you. Then list the kinds of jobs for which there are many ads.

B. Prepare a résumé that fits your qualifications. Assume that you will complete your high school training within the next few months.

C. Obtain application forms from two local business firms. Complete them just as you would if you were going to apply for a position. Be prepared to discuss in class the kinds of information that the forms required you to supply.

D. Exchange each of your application forms with other students in the class. Write a critique of each of the forms you receive.

VOCABULARY AND SPELLING STUDIES

A. These words are often confused: *born, borne; coarse, course, lesson, lessen.* Explain the differences.

B. What are the adjective forms of these verbs?

1. despair	**3.** spend	**5.** harm
2. investigate	**4.** predict	**6.** supplement

C. Add either *-ant* or *-ent* to each of the following to form a correctly spelled word.

1. quoti ___   **3.** ten ___   **5.** defend ___
2. eleg ___   **4.** solv ___   **6.** independ ___

D. Write the present participle form (ending in *-ing*) of each of the following verbs:

1. sit   **3.** believe   **5.** plan
2. occur   **4.** develop   **6.** duplicate

SECTION 11.2

EMPLOYMENT LETTERS

Your ability to write an effective employment letter will help you compete successfully with others applying for the same job. At some point in your career, you will surely have occasion to write one or more of the following types of employment letters:

1. A letter of application. This letter may be written *(a)* in response to a newspaper advertisement; *(b)* at the suggestion of a relative, friend, teacher, or business acquaintance; or *(c)* on your own initiative, even though you do not know of a specific job opening in the business to which you write.
2. Letters to various persons requesting permission to give their names as references.
3. A follow-up letter to thank an employment interviewer for the time given you and to reemphasize some of your qualifications that make you particularly suited for the job.
4. A letter accepting a position.
5. A letter refusing a position.
6. A thank-you letter to each person who helped you in your job-seeking campaign.
7. A letter resigning from a position.

LETTERS OF APPLICATION

Employers sometimes receive hundreds of applications for one job, and they cannot possibly interview each person who applies. Therefore, the personnel recruiter uses the letter of application and other written documents to select candidates for a personal interview. An effective application letter can open doors to a bright future; a poor one can quickly close those doors. However, an application letter alone will rarely get you a job. An employer needs more than your letter to decide whether to hire you, but your letter can make you stand out from other applicants. It can give you a chance to make an impression in person—its main purpose.

The Appearance of the Letter   The appearance of your application letter gives the employer a first clue to your personality and work habits. A sloppy letter suggests that you may not be careful about your own appearance or about your work habits—not the kind of impression you want to make.

Appearances *do* matter. Imagine, for example, getting caught in the rain before you are to meet an important person for the first time. Even though you explain that you have been caught in the rain, your bedraggled appearance will create a negative first impression. Likewise, a sloppy letter will give a prospective employer a negative first impression of you, one you may not have the chance to correct.

Thus, in writing your application letter, you want to impress favorably the prospective employer and to earn the chance for an interview. The physical appearance of your letter can help create a favorable impression. Follow these instructions, therefore, in preparing your letter:

1. Use a good grade of $8\frac{1}{2}$- by 11-inch bond paper (white). Be certain that your letter is clean and free from smudges and finger marks. Avoid paper that is specially treated so that the print erases easily. A good grade of bond paper is usually a better choice.
2. Use either a word processing system or a typewriter with correction capability. Either one offers you both easy correction and lack of smudging.

Here are some suggestions to follow when writing your application letter:

1. Address your letter to a specific person in the organization, if possible.
2. Don't expect to get your letter exactly right the first time. Use your editing and proofreading skills to create a well-written, error-free letter. Be willing to rewrite it until it represents you in the best possible light.
3. Never copy an application letter out of a book. Let your letter express your own personality.
4. Choose a typewriter or word processor that has clear, crisp print. Use good-quality $8\frac{1}{2}$- by 11-inch stationery with matching envelopes.

The Beginning of the Letter   An application letter is usually accompanied by a résumé, such as the one illustrated on page 498. It is neither necessary nor desirable to describe fully your education and experience in the letter. Such is the job of the résumé. The letter's main purpose is to transmit the résumé and to supplement it with a personal sales message:

> Does your word processing staff produce errorless copy hour after hour, documents that pass all tests for accuracy? I can—and I can verify this ability.
>
> Is there a place in your organization for an accountant whose work is accurate and meticulous and who accepts a demanding atmosphere as a challenge?

Another good beginning for an application letter is a summary statement of your special qualifications. This type of beginning gives the prospective employer an immediate indication of your ability and training. If these are the qualifications for the job, the employer will want to read further. Here are some examples:

> A solid background in secretarial science at Rugby High School, combined with more than two years of experience in the Trust Department of the Federal Savings Bank, has given me both the knowledge and the experience to qualify me for the secretarial position advertised in the June 23 edition of the *News Register.*

> My four years as a receptionist for the Muller Marketing Corporation has provided me with the experience of working with people that your customer service position requires.

When you have been told about a vacancy by another person—an employee of the organization, or a friend of the person to whom you are writing, or a teacher or guidance counselor—it is often effective to use that person's name (with permission) in your opening paragraph.

> My accounting teacher, Dr. Alice Geary, has told me that you are looking for someone you do not have to train. I believe my qualifications would be of interest to you.

> Mr. Alex Foster, a family friend, has told me that you need a reliable secretary. I have been an executive secretary for more than five years, and I believe that I have the qualifications you want.

> Mr. Raymond Gerson, who is an order fulfillment supervisor, has informed me that you are looking for someone who is used to working with details. Would over one year of experience as a statistical clerk in the U.S. Securities and Exchange Commission in Washington be of interest to you?

Development of the Body of the Letter

In the body of the letter, you should support the statements in the opening paragraph. Emphasize the highlights of your educational background and work experience that are specifically related to the job. You may also indicate why you would like to be employed by the firm to which you are applying. To impress the company favorably, get some of its literature and learn about its locations and activities. *Predicasts F & S Directory* lists newspaper and magazine articles that have appeared about companies. Read some, and then you may be able to give specific reasons for being interested in a particular company. Following this suggested plan, the second paragraph of your application letter might read like one of the following:

> I routinely take dictation at 140 words a minute. I can also operate a switchboard without becoming flustered during even the busiest hours of the day. I type accurately and rapidly and am able to compose routine letters. I also have a solid background in tax recordkeeping procedures. Furthermore, I have practiced and sharpened all these skills for the last eighteen months in the offices of the law firm of Brown and Litton, Inc.

LIVING LANGUAGE

Alternatives to sexist terms:
chairman—chair, moderator, head, presiding officer, chairperson
craftsman—artisan, craftsworker, skilled worker
girl friday— assistant, office assistant, aide
manmade—artificial, hand-made machine-made, synthetic, manufactured
manpower—staff, personnel, labor supply, available workers, work force, employees, human resources
—from Rosalie Maggio, *The Nonsexist Word Finder*

My enclosed résumé sets forth both the training and the experience that I have had during my first two years in business. I believe that you will agree that my training and experience qualify me for the position of administrative assistant with your firm.

The Conclusion of the Letter   A good conclusion in any letter tells the reader what you wish him or her to do. In a letter of application you would like the reader to grant a personal interview. Therefore, ask for an interview, and make your request easy to grant. Here are some suggested ways to accomplish this:

May I explain further during a personal interview my qualifications for the position? I can be reached at 555-1357.

I believe that I can tell you, in just a few minutes, why I am a likely candidate for the position you have available. May I have an interview with you? Just indicate a convenient date and time on the enclosed postcard.

To a prospective employer some distance away, the applicant may write:

I will be in the Baltimore area from July 1 to July 6. May I talk with you on any of these dates? My phone number is 203-555-9876.

Sample Letters   Application letters written by students seeking employment are shown on pages 498 (application for a specific position) and 499 (response to a blind newspaper ad).

LETTERS REQUESTING REFERENCES

Almost every prospective employer likes to have information regarding the character, training, experience, and work habits of job applicants. You may need to supply only the names, titles, and addresses of references, leaving to the interested prospective employer the task of obtaining the desired information. Under some circumstances you may request that the person speaking on your behalf write a letter of reference directly to the prospective employer. (In most cases a letter of reference that you carry with you is not too effective.)

Before using a person's name as a reference, you should request permission to do so. This permission may be obtained in person, by telephone, or by a letter such as the following:

Dear Mr. Lee:

I am applying for the position of order clerk currently available at the Grafton Mining Corporation in Alton.

As a student in your clerical practices class two years ago, I received the background that is needed for this position. I would like very much to use your name as a reference.

I have enclosed a return postcard for your reply.

Sincerely yours,

Enclosure

830 East State Street
Pompano Beach, Florida 33062
June 28, 1994

Mr. Carl Rush
Director of Personnel
Carlton Electronics Company
876 Colina Parkway
Fort Lauderdale, Florida 33322

Dear Mr. Rush:

Ms. Sarah Bowman, a business education counselor at Union High School, has told me that your organization has an opening for an entry-level administrative assistant. I would very much appreciate your permitting me to explain why I believe that I have the necessary qualifications for this position.

As the enclosed résumé points out, I have had two years of word processing training (beginning and advanced) including applications in desktop publishing. My experience includes training in WordPerfect and Microsoft Word word processing programs and PageMaker desktop publishing software. I have had the opportunity to improve these skills as a full-time summer replacement at the main office of the Broward County Bank. This experience also served to acquaint me with the daily routine of a busy office. I have enjoyed both my training and my work experience and believe that I can satisfactorily fill the position you have available.

I can begin work at any time after July 10.

You can reach me at 555-4116 any day after 5 p.m. May I have a personal interview at your convenience?

Sincerely yours,

Josefina Torres

Josefina Torres

Enclosure

This letter of application briefly summarizes the writer's interest, education, and experience.

A courtesy copy of your letter and stamped return envelope might be used instead of the postcard.

If you are writing to request that a reference be sent directly to a prospective employer, you may say:

I am applying for the position of assistant payroll clerk at King's Department Store in Lincoln.

876 Lowell Place
Abbotsville, Minnesota 56321
June 1, 1994

The Valley Record
Box No. 8798
Dales, Minnesota 56324

Ladies and Gentlemen:

Two years of high school accounting, supplemented by summer work
at an accounting firm and strengthened by an evening program in
accounting at the Lakes Business College, have equipped me to
handle the general demands of accounting work. I would therefore
appreciate it if you would consider me for an accounting position
in your firm.

I am presently employed as a tax clerk with the Broad Furniture
Corporation. But I am looking for a position that would make
greater use of my broad training. I would also value the opportunity to get into a more advanced phase of accounting. I plan
to continue my accounting education in a night school program at
our local community college.

The enclosed résumé summarizes my education and experience. It
also includes the names of three people from whom you may obtain
information about my character and ability.

I would very much like to talk with you in person. I may be
reached by phone at 555-4200, Ext. 160, from 8:30 a.m. to 5 p.m.
or at 555-1072 after 5:30 p.m.

Sincerely,

Craig Jorgensen
Craig Jorgensen

Enclosure

The applicant who wrote this letter included information about future educational and career goals.

Since I worked under your supervision for two years in the Claims Department of the Waterman Insurance Company, I believe that you are in a position to evaluate both my character and my ability. Would you be willing to send a letter of reference for me to Mrs. Ivy Rojos, the personnel director at King's Department Store in Lincoln? I am enclosing a stamped, addressed envelope for your convenience.

FOLLOW-UP LETTERS

Application letters and letters requesting references are written before the interview with a prospective employer. After the interview there are several types of follow-up letters you may write. Here are some examples.

The Interview Follow-Up

If your application letter and your résumé have succeeded in obtaining a personal interview for you, the next letter you should write will follow the personal interview. This letter may have one or more of the following purposes:

1. To thank the interviewer for the time and courtesy extended to you.
2. To let the interviewer know you are still interested in the position.
3. To remind the interviewer of your qualifications for the position.
4. To provide any additional data requested by the interviewer that you may not have had available at the time of the interview.

Notice how the interview follow-up uses the everyday letter plan by directly thanking the reader for the interview and then following up with details related to the interview.

> Dear Mr. Lester:
>
> Thank you for discussing with me yesterday afternoon the position that you have available in your accounts payable office. You told me exactly what would be demanded of me in that position.
>
> I am more interested than ever in this job. I believe that the position I have held for the last two years at Coy Recycling Corporation has given me the background I would need to perform the work required.
>
> I have asked my references to write to you directly. I hope that you will look positively upon my application. Please let me know if I can supply you with any additional information.
>
> Sincerely yours,

Letters of Acceptance

If you are notified by mail that you are being offered the position for which you applied, you should write a letter of acceptance. This letter does the following:

1. Notifies your employer-to-be of your acceptance.
2. Reassures the employer that she or he has chosen the right person.
3. Tells the employer when you can report for work.

The letter of acceptance, which follows the everyday letter plan, may read as follows:

> Dear Ms. Greene:
>
> It is a pleasure to accept your offer of a secretarial position at Abbott Clothing Company, Inc. You can be sure that I will do everything possible to justify the confidence you have expressed in me.

Since June 30 is my graduation day, Monday, July 2, will certainly be a convenient starting date for me. I will report to your office ready to work at 9 a.m.

Thank you for the opportunity that you have given me.

Sincerely yours,

Letters of Refusal

Letters of Refusal Perhaps you have been offered a position for which you applied, but you have also received another offer that you believe is better. You should return the courtesy extended to you by writing a tactful, friendly letter of refusal. You may want to reapply to this same company in the future. Structure your letter according to the bad-news plan. Refuse the position only after you have expressed appreciation for being offered the job.

Dear Mr. Sawyer:

Thank you for offering me the position of inventory clerk at the Pacific Seas Company's warehouse.

It would have been a pleasure working with you and the other fine people at Pacific Seas. However, just two days before receiving your offer, I accepted a similar position at another company.

I very much appreciate the time that you gave me.

Sincerely yours,

Thank-You Letters When you have obtained a position, remember that the people who wrote reference letters for you undoubtedly helped you. You should be courteous enough to let them know that you have accepted the position. You might write a letter such as the following:

Dear Mrs. Torrington:

Thank you for the letter of reference that you sent on my behalf to the Porter Bank. You will be pleased to know that I have accepted the position of assistant treasurer of that bank.

I want you to know how very much I appreciate your support.

Sincerely yours,

RESIGNATION LETTERS

Occasionally you may need to write a letter resigning from a position. (Of course, you should discuss your resignation with your supervisor before writing a letter.) Regardless of your reason for resigning, your letter should be friendly in tone and tactful. Someday you may want this employer as a reference, and you want the employer to remember you favorably. The following letter, which uses the bad-news plan, is a good example of a letter of resignation.

Dear Mr. O'Conner:

I want you to know how much I have enjoyed my last three years at the Baylor Tool and Die Company. I have learned a great deal here and have made many permanent friends as well.

Because I would like to make greater use of my sales background, I have accepted a position at the brokerage firm of Smythe and Dale. I would therefore appreciate it if you would accept my resignation effective August 15.

Thank you for all that you have done to make my work here both interesting and enjoyable.

Sincerely yours,

COMMUNICATION LABORATORY

APPLICATION EXERCISES

A. The following advertisements appeared in a recent edition of your local newspaper. Write a letter of application answering one of these advertisements.

> SECRETARY: Small office needs talented self-starter. Good position for the right person. Apply to Mr. Colby Adams, 162 Reede Avenue.
> ACCOUNTANT: Entry-level position for person with good training. Salary open. Apply to Box 82, *Daily Mail*.
> TRAVEL COORDINATOR: Entry-level position. Work for a busy manufacturing firm with people who frequently must travel. Will teach the use of Official Airline Guide and routing maps. Much telephone work. No typing. Personnel Director, Lester Company, Oaks Mall.

B. Write a letter to a teacher or an acquaintance requesting permission to use his or her name as a reference.

C. You have had a personal interview for one of the jobs in Exercise A. Write a follow-up letter to the person who interviewed you.

D. You have received a letter notifying you that you have been selected to fill the opening for which you have applied. Write a letter accepting the position.

E. Suppose that you have decided not to accept the position offered to you in Exercise D. Write a letter of refusal.

F. Write a letter to the person who wrote a letter of reference for you, notifying him or her that you have accepted a position.

G. You have been employed by Internat Travel Agency for four years. A friend who works for Pacific World Travel has told you about an opening in that firm. You have applied for and been offered that position. It pays much more than your current salary; the opportunities for learning and advancing appear to be better; there are many more fringe benefits, including a college tuition plan and a dental plan; and the office is much closer to your home. You decide to leave your current position. Assume that you

CONTINUED

have already discussed this new job with your supervisor. You must now put your resignation in written form. Write the appropriate letter.

VOCABULARY AND SPELLING STUDIES

A. These words are often confused: *breath, breathe, breadth; decent, descent, dissent.* Explain the differences.

B. From each pair of words within parentheses, select the one that correctly completes the sentence.

1. The usher kept the (isles, aisles) of the theater open.
2. The (lone, loan) reason for not going to the picnic is my mother's illness.
3. Webster has no (allusions, illusions) about the job.
4. A city (ordnance, ordinance) prohibits parking here.
5. You should (canvass, canvas) the class to see how the members will vote in the election.

C. Remove the extra letter from each of the following words.

1. referred
2. judgement
3. potatoe
4. picknic
5. choosen
6. acknowledgement
7. accommoddate
8. possitions
9. callendar
10. votting
11. envellope
12. corresppondence
13. offerring
14. writting
15. handicapp

SECTION 11.3

EMPLOYMENT INTERVIEWS

For any job opening, one or more applicants have a personal interview. The most important use you make of oral communication may be at this interview, for your future may depend on how well you sell yourself during the interview. It is in the interview that job applicants reveal whether they possess the communication skills required for the position they are seeking. Does the applicant *speak* well, *listen* attentively, *read* and follow instructions carefully, *write* an effective résumé? A "yes" answer to all of these questions demonstrated in the interview may bring a job offer.

GETTING READY FOR THE INTERVIEW

In addition to developing your résumé and writing letters of application, you have other preparation to do. When offered a personal interview, there are several steps you should take to get ready.

Do Your Homework
Do some research about your prospective employer. The interviewer may ask you some questions about your interest in the company. Also, your research can help you make sure the company is a place where you would like to work.

You may find help from several easy-to-locate resources. If you know someone who works at the company, that person may provide some helpful information. The Chamber of Commerce in a community can give you information on both small and large companies in that city or town. Finally, the public library may have published data, especially for national or international companies.

Know Your Qualifications
Make sure you review your résumé and letter of application before you go for an interview. Interviewers generally will have on their desk your letter or application form and your résumé. You need to be sure of the information so that you can answer the questions completely, honestly, and confidently.

You may also wish to take with you extra copies of your résumé and application letter, your school transcript, and any other materials that support your qualifications for the position.

Know the Job
Many employers advertise for experienced people to fill a position because they believe an experienced person is more likely to know the job—what is expected and how to perform. But the requirement of experience is not the handicap it may at first seem to be. An inexperienced applicant may be able to make up for a lack of experience by learning everything possible about that job. Thus prepared, the applicant can show the interviewer that a realistic understanding of what the job involves may make up for the lack of experience.

To learn about a job, you can talk with employees in that field. Before you leave school, you might ask a recent graduate who is now working in the company of your choice to talk about the job. If you have an opportunity to do so, take a field trip through the offices or plant. Read about the products manufactured or about the services or goods sold. Through friends, you may even be able to learn something about the people who own or operate the company and about the particular person who will interview you. The more you know about the job, the company, and the people you will meet, the better able you will be to relate your abilities to the specific job.

Match Your Qualifications to the Job
Well-intentioned, well-qualified applicants have been known to enter a personnel office with a general statement such as "I want to apply for a job." This shows lack of wisdom

and immaturity. Such people might as well say that they have not considered what job they wish to apply for, what qualifications are needed, or how their own qualifications are related to the needs of the job. These applicants usually do not get past the receptionist. To avoid such a disappointment, you must prepare for the employment interview by considering how your abilities qualify you for the specific job for which you are applying.

CONDUCTING YOURSELF DURING THE INTERVIEW

If you have prepared carefully for the interview, you should make a favorable first impression. Your dress and behavior will be correct for the situation, and you will appear self-confident and poised.

Your Appearance and Posture   Care in grooming, in the selection of clothing, and in the way you carry yourself, as discussed in Section 10.2, is of major importance to every applicant. The clothing you wear to the interview should be neat, clean, comfortable, and, of course, appropriate. As interviewers talk with you, they will notice such details as your nails, teeth, and hair. A full night's sleep will contribute to a fresh, alert appearance. Any detail of appearance and dress that attracts unfavorable attention may count against you.

The ways that you walk and sit are clues to your personality and mental attitude. Walk with purpose and confidence; sit with composure and ease. Trained interviewers know that there is a direct relationship between personal habits and work habits—sloppy appearance, sloppy work; neat appearance, neat work. Therefore, make your appearance speak favorably for you at the interview session.

Your Manner and Manners   Good manners are often taken for granted, but any lack of good manners is noticed immediately. Follow these tips on common courtesy and etiquette during job interviews.

Arrive on Time or Early   It is rude to be late for any appointment. If you are late for a job interview, you may make the interviewer wonder how often you will be late if you are hired. The interviewer might also conclude that you do not really want the job, since you are late. Rushing to arrive on time will leave you breathless, however; so start early enough to allow for any possible delays.

Meet the Unexpected With Poise, Tact, and Humor   If the interviewer is not ready to see you, take a seat and occupy yourself while you're waiting. Imagine the childish impression made by a person who says, "But Mr. Balducci told me that he would see me at eleven o'clock."

Follow the Interviewer's Lead   Remember that you are a guest. Shake hands if the interviewer offers to do so, and give a firm handshake. A limp handshake indicates weakness. Wait for an invitation before seating yourself, and let the interviewer tell you where to be seated. You are being a good guest if you follow the lead of the interviewer.

Be Tactful and Gracious in Conversation Listen carefully. Don't interrupt, even if the interviewer is long-winded and you think of something to say right away. Follow the interviewer's conversation leads, and show that you understand the importance of what has been said. Don't bore the interviewer with long, overdetailed answers; but do reply with more than a meek yes or no to questions. Never contradict the interviewer or imply that an error has been made, under any circumstances. Such lack of tact is rude and will do nothing to help you in the interview.

Show Appreciation for the Interviewer's Time and Interest At the close of the interview remember to express appreciation, just as you would thank any host as you take your leave. Don't let the excitement and tension of the interview make you forget this courtesy. Failing to show appreciation could spoil an otherwise effective interview.

Your Speech and Conversation

The speech principles you have studied will aid you in demonstrating your oral communication skills. Have you worked to improve your voice? How are your enunciation, vocabulary, and pronunciation? Do you still say "yeah" when you mean "yes"? If you have worked hard and applied all you have learned, your voice and speech will be a credit to you. You can concentrate on what you say.

What you say reflects your attitudes and tells what kind of person you are. During the interview, for example, if you show an intense interest in salary, your lunch hour, vacation, sick leave, or short working hours, you may reveal that you are more interested in loafing than in working. Interviewers have a responsibility to employ people who want to work!

Typical Interview Questions

Understanding the intent of the interviewer's questions will help you answer more intelligently. Here are some typical interview questions, with the reasons behind them and suggestions as to what you might say in reply.

Why Have You Selected This Kind of Work? The interviewer wishes to know how interested you are in the work and what your goals are. An answer like "Oh, I just need a job" shows lack of purpose. Isn't the following a better answer? "I've wanted to be a secretary ever since I started school. That was my reason for taking the stenographic course. I believe I'll like this type of job too." This type of answer tells the interviewer that you know what you want from a job, that you have interest, and that you have a purpose.

If You Had Your Choice of Job and Company, What Would You Most Like to Be Doing and Where? Watch your answer to this question. The interviewer is trying to gauge just how satisfied you will be working in this job and in this company. The best answer, if you can truthfully say so, is: "Ms. Andersen, the job I want is the one for which I am now applying. The company?

Yours. Before too long I hope to have proved myself and to have been promoted to greater responsibility."

What Are Your Hobbies?   The interviewer is not interested in detailed information about your stamp collection. What the interviewer really wants to know is whether you have broad interests, for a person who has few outside interests is likely to become restless. Be ready to list briefly your major interests in hobbies and sports.

In What Extracurricular Activities Have You Participated?   To what clubs do you belong? What offices have you held? What honors have you received? These and similar questions are asked to determine the scope of your interest in people—whether you are able to work with people and whether you have leadership qualities. These are the characteristics of a well-rounded, well-adjusted individual. In preparing for the interview, review your extracurricular activities so that you can give the facts without hesitation.

Would You Be Willing to Work Overtime?   Employers like to see a willingness, even an eagerness, to perform well in a job. Overtime may seldom be required, but if it is, employers want to have people who will accept this responsibility. You would be entering a job with the wrong attitude if you were not willing to work overtime when necessary.

COMMUNICATION LABORATORY

APPLICATION EXERCISES

A. Make a list of your personal and educational qualifications for one of the following positions: receptionist, accounting clerk, secretary, word processing operator, clerk-typist, retail salesclerk. From the standpoint of an interviewer, make a list of qualifications for the job, including some that you may not currently have.

B. Make a list of your leisure-time activities. Include all extracurricular activities, clubs, offices held, and awards received. The completed list will include things that you might mention in an employment interview.

C. Make a list of grooming and dress standards that you might consult before going to an employment interview.

D. Assume that you are the personnel manager for one of the largest employers in your community. You have an opening for a general clerical worker. Make a list of questions that you might ask an applicant. Explain what each answer would tell you about the potential employee. In class use your questions to enact the interview in the form of a skit.

CONTINUED

VOCABULARY AND SPELLING STUDIES

A. These words are often confused: *indignant, indigent, indigenous; imitate, intimate.* Use each word in a sentence that illustrates its meaning.

B. Select the word or phrase in parentheses that best completes each of the following sentences.

1. The suffix *-ist* in *pianist, journalist, economist,* and *specialist* gives these words the meaning of (one who, the study of, the science of, the act of).
2. The prefix *mis-* in *misguide, misstep, misuse,* and *misdirect* gives these words the meaning of (before, partly, wrongly, throughout).
3. The prefix *re-* in *reconsider, reunite, remit,* and *return* gives these words the meaning of (under, again, after, beyond).
4. The suffix *-ician* in *technician, electrician,* and *magician* gives these words the meaning of (the service of, the state of, the quality of, specialist in).

C. Replace the italicized words with correctly formed contractions.

1. You *would not* believe how many applied for the job.
2. Margaret *did not* carefully proofread the copy.
3. *It is* difficult to determine the cost of the work.
4. I can't be certain *who is* going to be assigned to that job.
5. *Let us* hear from you when you make your decision.

MODEL LETTER FORMATS

The following pages are a handy reference section on business-letter style. This material has been covered in the textbook, but it is organized here for easy use. Included on the inside back cover of this textbook are such useful items as proofreader's marks for rough drafts and revisions and abbreviations of states, territories, and possessions of the United States.

OFFICE TECHNOLOGY NETWORKS, INC.
4833 Gateway Boulevard East
El Paso, Texas 79905
713-555-1348

February 6, 1994 ↓6

Ms. Geneva Clauson
Investment Properties Company
708 Talton Avenue
San Antonio, TX 78285 ↓2

Dear Ms. Clauson: ↓2

Subject: Form of a Block Letter ↓2

This letter style is fast becoming the most popular style in use today. Efficiency is the main reason for its popularity. The keyboard specialist can save time and eliminate the necessity of working out placement. Some organizations are even designing letterheads to accommodate this style. A few years ago some people felt the block style looked odd. That complaint is seldom heard today, however. ↓2

This letter also illustrates the subject line and the enclosure. A subject line may be typed with initial caps or all in caps. It should start at the left margin. It always appears after the salutation and before the body of the letter. An enclosure notation starts at the left margin and always appears on the line after the reference initials. ↓2

Sincerely, ↓4

Annette G. Fuentes

Annette G. Fuentes
Manager, Customer Services ↓2

nkm
Enclosure

The block letter is the fastest one to type because each line begins at the left margin. (See page 320 for more information about business letter formats.)

ON INC OFFICE TECHNOLOGY NETWORKS, INC.
4833 Gateway Boulevard East
El Paso, Texas 79905
713-555-1348

February 6, 1994 ↓6

Ms. Carla Furman
Steffins and Wasserman Ltd.
1382 Victoria Street
Toronto, Ontario
CANADA M5C 2N8 ↓2

Dear Ms. Furman: ↓2

This modified-block letter style is still very popular for two
reasons: ↓2

    1. Many people feel comfortable with the traditional
        appearance. ↓2

    2. The blocked paragraphs make it slightly more efficient
        to type than a letter with indented paragraphs. ↓2

Lists, quotations, and addresses may be indented on either side
for a clearer display. If it is necessary to use more than one
paragraph for a quotation, a standard single blank line is left
between paragraphs. ↓2

Special mail or delivery services (such as certified mail,
priority overnight air service, or messenger service) is shown on
the line below the reference initials. We do so only to record
this information for our files. ↓2

When the letter is being sent to a foreign address, the country
is typed in all-capital letters on a separate line, as CANADA is
shown above. ↓2

                Sincerely, ↓4

                Annette G. Fuentes

                Annette G. Fuentes
                Manager, Customer Services ↓2

nkm
Registered ↓2

PS: We treat postscripts in the same way that we treat other
paragraphs, except that we precede each postscript by PS: or PS.

The modified-block letter is very popular. Note that the mailing notation is
below the reference initials and that all-capital letters are used for *CANA-
DA* in the inside address. (See page 320 for more information about business
letter formats.)

OFFICE TECHNOLOGY NETWORKS, INC.

4833 Gateway Boulevard East
El Paso, Texas 79905
713-555-1348

February 6, 1994 ↓6

Banton, Turchon, and Vick, Inc.
9004 18th Street NW
Washington, DC 20009 ↓2

Attention: Training Director ↓2

Ladies and Gentlemen: ↓2

    The modified-block letter with indented paragraphs is still popular because of its traditional appearance. The indented paragraphs give this style a distinctive look. ↓2

    This modified-block letter also shows an attention line. Like the subject line, the attention line is positioned at the left margin, but above the salutation. The attention line is usually keyed in initial caps but may also be all in caps. ↓2

Cordially, ↓4

Annette G. Fuentes

Annette G. Fuentes
Manager, Customer Services ↓2

nkm ↓2

cc: Ms. T. Spock
    Dr. F. Mantel

In the modified-block letter with indented paragraphs, the first line of each paragraph is indented—usually five spaces. (See page 320 for more information about business letter formats.)

FREDERICO, KLINE & DILLMAN

Three Peachtree Plaza • Atlanta, Georgia 30303
404-555-2371   FAX 404-555-7777

September 13, 1994

Dear Nancy,

How delighted I am to hear that you've opened your own ad agency!
Congratulations!

In the few years that I've been in advertising, I've been very
fortunate to meet, work with, and learn from some of the best
creative directors in the business. And you, Nancy, are at the
top of that list. I enjoyed working for you at Reynolds &
Bishopp. You really "sold" me on advertising as a career, and I
thank you for that.

By the way, you were right about Federico, Kline & Dillman. The
people are great (just as you told me they'd be), and I am
learning, learning, learning. I enjoy my work more than ever.

Carl and I haven't forgotten your offer. He may have a trip to
Chicago in October. If he does, I'm going to join him so that we
can both see you. I'm looking forward to that.

Again, my best wishes for success.

                              Sincerely,

                              Yvonne

                              Yvonne Gilroy

Ms. Nancy Costa
President
The Costa Advertising Group
121 Michigan Avenue
Chicago, Illinois 60202

The social-business letter is a social letter—an informal letter—
written to a business associate. (See pages 321–324 for more information
about social-business letters.)

FORMS OF ADDRESS

Refer to the following list whenever you need the correct forms of address for government, military, religious, or education officials. In addition to forms of address, the list includes appropriate salutations, listed in order of decreasing formality.

The forms of address and salutations given include (for the sake of simplicity) only the masculine forms. Of course, change *Mr.* to *Miss, Mrs.,* or *Ms.,* change *Sir* to *Madam,* and change *His* to *Her* as appropriate.

Government Officials

PRESIDENT OF THE UNITED STATES
The President
The White House
Washington, DC 20500

Mr. President:
Dear Mr. President:

VICE PRESIDENT OF THE UNITED STATES
The Vice President
United States Senate
Washington, DC. 20510

Or: The Honorable . . . (full name)
Vice President of the United States
Washington, DC 20501

Sir:
Dear Mr. Vice President:

CHIEF JUSTICE OF THE UNITED STATES
The Chief Justice of the United States
Washington, DC 20543

Or: The Chief Justice
The Supreme Court
Washington, DC 20543

Sir:
Dear Mr. Chief Justice:

CABINET MEMBER
The Honorable . . . (*full name*)
Secretary . . . (*department*)
Washington, DC   ZIP Code

Or: The Secretary of . . .
(*department*)
Washington, DC ZIP Code

Sir:
Dear Mr. Secretary:

UNITED STATES SENATOR
The Honorable . . . (*full name*)
United States Senator
Washington, DC 20510

Or: The Honorable . . . (*full name*)
United States Senator
(*local address and ZIP Code*)

Sir:
Dear Senator . . . :

UNITED STATES REPRESENTATIVE
The Honorable . . . (*full name*)
House of Representatives
Washington, DC 20515

Or: The Honorable . . . (*full name*)
Representative in Congress
(*local address and ZIP Code*)

Sir:
Dear Mr. . . . :

GOVERNOR
In Massachusetts, New Hampshire, and by courtesy in some other states:

His Excellency the Governor of . . .
State Capital, State   ZIP Code

In other states:
The Honorable . . . (*full name*)
Governor of . . .
State Capital, State   ZIP Code

Sir:
Dear Governor . . . :

STATE SENATOR
The Honorable . . . (*full name*)
The State Senate . . .
State Capital, State   ZIP Code

Sir:
Dear Senator . . :

STATE REPRESENTATIVE OR ASSEMBLY MEMBER
The Honorable . . . (*full name*)
House of Representatives
   (**or** The State Assembly)
State Capital, State   ZIP Code

Sir:
Dear Mr. . . . :

MAYOR
The Honorable . . . (*full name*)
Mayor of . . . (*city*)
City, State   ZIP Code

Or: The Mayor of the City of . . .
City, State   ZIP Code

Sir:
Dear Mr. Mayor:
Dear Mayor . . . :

Members of the Armed Services

The addresses of both officers and enlisted persons in the armed services should include title of rank and full name followed by a comma and the initials *USA, USN, USAF, USMC,* or *USCG.* Following are some specific examples together with the appropriate salutations.

ARMY, AIR FORCE, AND MARINE CORPS OFFICERS
Lieutenant General . . . (*full name*), USA
Address

Sir:
Dear General . . . :
   (***not:*** Dear Lieutenant General . . . :)

For first and second lieutenants, use:

Dear Lieutenant . . . :

NAVY AND COAST GUARD OFFICERS
Rear Admiral . . . (*full name*)
   USN
Address

Sir:
Dear Admiral . . . :

For officers below the rank of Commander, use:

Dear Mr. . . . :

ENLISTED PERSONS
Sergeant . . . (*full name*), USA
Address

Seaman . . . (*full name*), USN
Address

Dear Sergeant (**or** Seaman) . . . :

Roman Catholic Dignitaries

CARDINAL
His Eminence . . . (*given name*)
   Cardinal . . . (*surname*)
Archbishop of . . . (*place*)
Address

Your Eminence:
Dear Cardinal:

ARCHBISHOP AND BISHOP
The Most Reverend . . . (*full name*)

Archbishop (**or** Bishop) of . . .
(place)
Address

Your Excellency:
Dear Archbishop (**or** Bishop)
. . .:

MONSIGNOR
The Right Reverend Monsignor
. . . *(full name)*
Address

Right Reverend Monsignor:
Dear Monsignor . . . :

PRIEST
The Reverend . . . *(full name,*
followed by comma and
initials of order)
Address

Reverend Father:
Dear Father . . .:

MOTHER SUPERIOR
The Reverend Mother Superior
Address

Or: Reverend Mother . . .
(name, followed by comma
and initials of order)
Address

Reverend Mother:
Dear Reverend Mother:
Dear Mother . . . :

SISTER
Sister . . . *(name, followed by*
comma and initials of order)
Address

Dear Sister:
Dear Sister . . . :

Protestant Dignitaries

PROTESTANT EPISCOPAL BISHOP
The Right Reverend . . . *(full*
name)

Bishop of . . . *(place)*
Address

Right Reverend Sir:
Dear Bishop . . . :

PROTESTANT EPISCOPAL DEAN
The Very Reverend . . . *(full*
name)
Dean of . . .
Address

Very Reverend Sir:
Dear Dean . . . :

METHODIST BISHOP
The Reverend . . . *(full name)*
Bishop of . . .
Address

Reverend Sir:
Dear Bishop . . . :

MEMBER OF THE CLERGY WITH
DOCTOR'S DEGREE
The Reverend Dr. . . . *(full*
name)
Address

Or: The Reverend . . . *(full*
name), D. D.
Address

Reverend Sir:
Dear Dr. . . . :

MEMBER OF THE CLERGY WITHOUT
DOCTOR'S DEGREE
The Reverend . . . *(full name)*
Address

Reverend Sir:
Dear Mr. . . . :

Jewish Dignitaries

RABBI WITH DOCTOR'S
DEGREE
Rabbi . . . *(full name)*, D. D.
Address

Or: Dr. . . . *(full name),*
Address

Dear Rabbi (*or* Dr.) . . . :

RABBI WITHOUT DOCTOR'S
DEGREE
Rabbi . . . *(full name),*
Address

Dear Rabbi . . . :

Education Officials

PRESIDENT OF A COLLEGE OR
UNIVERSITY
. . . *(full name, followed by
comma and highest degree)*
President, . . . *(name of
college)*
Address

Or: Dr. . . . *(full name),* President, . . . *(name of college)*
Address

Dear President . . . :
Dear Dr. . . . :

PROFESSOR
Professor . . . *(full name)*
Department of . . .
. . . *(name of college)*
Address

Or: . . . *(full name, followed by
comma and highest degree)*
Department of . . .
. . . *(name of college)*
Address

Or: Dr. . . . *(full name)*
Professor of . . . *(subject)*
. . . *(name of college)*
Address

Dear Professor (*or* Dr.) . . . :
Dear Mr. . . . :

SUPERINTENDENT OF
SCHOOLS
Mr. (*or* Dr.) . . . . *(full name)*
Superintendent of . . . Schools
Address

Dear Mr. (*or* Dr.) . . . :

MEMBER OF BOARD OF
EDUCATION
Ms. . . . *(full name)*
Member, . . . *(name of city)*
Board of Education
Address

Dear Ms. . . . :

PRINCIPAL
Mr. (*or* Dr.) . . . *(full name)*
Principal, . . . *(name of school)*
Address

Dear Mr. (*or* Dr.) . . . :

TEACHER
Ms. (*or* Dr.) . . . *(full name)*
. . . *(name of school)*
Address

Dear Ms. (*or* Dr.) . . . :

PROOFREADERS' MARKS FOR ROUGH DRAFTS AND REVISIONS

Proofreaders' Mark	Draft	Final Copy
Transpose letters	thier	their
Transpose words	to directly call you	to call you directly
Insert letter or letters	convient en	convenient
Insert word or words	a customer charge account	a charge account customer
Delete stroke	reduces	reduce
Delete stroke and close up space	electronic	electronic
Delete punctuation mark	On May 5, we . . .	On May 5 we . . .
Change stroke	correspondance	correspondence
Omit word or word group	a charge account customer	a customer
Change word or word group	. . . book which we sent. that	. . . book that we sent.
Capitalize letter	bushnell corporation	Bushnell Corporation
Use all capital letters	stop sign	STOP sign
Use lowercase letter	the Company	the company
Use a series of lowercase letters	FDI CORPORATION	FDI Corporation
Insert comma, semicolon, or colon	. . . today, therefore please send us the following.	. . . today; therefore, please send us the following:
Insert period, question mark, or exclamation point	⊙ ? !	. ? !
Insert apostrophe or quotation marks	. . . the companys latest revolutionary product	. . . the company's latest "revolutionary product"
Spell out	3 . . . 20% . . . 4 doz.	three . . . 20 percent . . . 4 dozen
Close up space	sales person	salesperson
Insert a space	inaddition	in addition
Hyphenate	up to date files	up-to-date files
Underscore or italic type	The word receive is . . .	The word receive is . . . OR The word receive is . . .
Restore word or words deleted	stock and bond certificates	stock and bond certificates
Start new paragraph	¶ May we have your . . .	May we have your . . .
Do not start new paragraph	no¶ The issue is . . .	The issue is . . .
Indent five spaces	▣ In the future . . .	In the future . . .
Single-space	ss ⌈ At next week's meeting, we will review your . . .	At next week's meeting, we will review your . . .
Double-space	ds ⌈ One of our members will call you before . . .	One of our members will call you before . . .
Move as indicated	. . . only follow my lead.	. . . follow only my lead.
Move to the left	⌐ Send in your report.	Send in your report.
Move to the right	⌐ Send in your report.	Send in your report.
Center	⌐ January 25, 1994 ⌐	January 25, 1994